STRANGERS
TO THESE SHORES

VINCENT N. PARRILLO

The William Paterson College of New Jersey

STRANGERS TO THESE SHORES

Race and Ethnic Relations
in the United States

FOURTH EDITION

MACMILLAN PUBLISHING COMPANY
NEW YORK

Editor: Susan Rabinowitz
Production Supervisor: Katherine Evancie
Production Manager: Muriel Underwood
Text Designer: Robert Freese
Cover Designer: Cathleen Norz
Cover Illustration: International Stock Photography/Michael Kingsford
Photo Researcher: Diane Kraut
Illustrations by ECL Art Studio

This book was set in Palatino and Zapf International by Carlisle Graphics and printed and bound by Book Press. The cover was printed by Phoenix Color Corp.

Macmillan Publishing Company
866 Third Avenue, New York, New York 10022

Macmillan Publishing Company is part of the Maxwell Communication Group of Companies.

Maxwell Macmillan Canada, Inc.
1200 Eglinton Avenue East   Suite 200
Don Mills, Ontario M3C 3N1

LIBRARY OF CONGRESS CATALOGING-IN-PUBLICATION DATA

Parrillo, Vincent N.
    Strangers to these shores : race and ethnic relations in the
United States / Vincent N. Parrillo.—4th ed.
        p.   cm.
    Includes bibliographical references and index.
    ISBN 0-02-391752-0
    1. United States—Race relations.   2. United States—Ethnic
relations.   I. Title.
E184.A1P33   1994
305.8'00973—dc20   93-12047
                                                                     CIP

Printing   2 3 4 5 6 7   Year: 4 5 6 7 8 9 0

To my Italian American father
And my Irish American mother

Foreword

> "Keep, ancient lands, your storied pomp!" cries she
>   With silent lips. "Give me your tired, your poor,
>   Your huddled masses yearning to breathe free,
>   The wretched refuse of your teeming shore.
>   Sent these, the homeless, tempest-tost to me,
>   I lift my lamp beside the golden door!"

These words by Emma Lazarus, written as if spoken by "the mighty woman with a torch," the Statue of Liberty, are well known to American children schooled in the romantic notion of the United States as a haven, an island in a stormy sea, a free and open society that extends "world-wide welcome" to the downtrodden as well as adventurous. From its title to its content, *Strangers to These Shores* is about that poem. However, as the reader soon learns, while clearly suffused with the spirit of the most famous of our national icons (Lazarus called her the "Mother of Exiles"), Vincent Parrillo's *Strangers to These Shores* is tempered by the reality of the true history of this democracy, a history marked by progress in many spheres of social and political life but also marred by the legacy of colonization, slavery, nativism, class conflict, and too many broken dreams.

He tells about these things and details their consequences. But *Strangers to These Shores* is not a history book. It is a sociological examination of the structure and character of the United States, which is today one of the most racially and ethnically diverse, promising, and troubled nations in the modern world, and surely one of the most interesting.

As a textbook for courses on race and ethnic relations in the United States, *Strangers to These Shores* is a comprehensive examination of the sharpest edges and more nuanced quality of American pluralism. Its 14 chapters provide students and readers—even those for whom it is not assigned!—a well conceived, carefully constructed, and highly readable introduction to a very complex subject. It also offers a point of view. The entire volume is linked to the author's notion of the dynamic relationship between insiders and outsiders (or "strangers") and his contention—sometimes made explicitly, but more often implied—that the degree of integration that exists at any given time is determined by a variety of cultural, socioeconomic, and situational factors.

In Part I of the book, we are provided with a framework for studying dominant–minority relations. Professor Parrillo introduces, defines, explicates, and imaginatively illustrates key sociological concepts and social processes useful to any critical analysis of the subject. Among the former are culture, diffusion, ethnocentrism, social distance, marginality, minority status, prejudice, discrimination, and the stranger, too—all, including the last, treated as social constructs. Among the processes described and discussed are modes of differentiation, patterns of adaptation, and reactions to discrimination. The author also provides an overview of three of the most widely adopted theoretical frameworks, two of them macrosociological. The first, structural–functionalism, is seen by many as a conservative approach that encourages reform through expanding tolerance limits of acceptable behavior; the second, conflict theory, emphasizes institutionalized exploitative inequities in power relationships and the need for radical change. The third theoretical framework is microsociogical. Known as symbolic interaction, it focuses attention on rules, roles, and the meaning of social acts.

Although Professor Parrillo is not wedded to any of the grand theory approaches (and could not be called a Parsonian or a Marxist or anything else that is associated with particular perspectives or theorists), he does see the utility in having readers recognize the importance of viewing society from different angles, from the top and from the bottom and at the intersections (as each of these tend to do). He demonstrates this in subsequent sections of the book.

Grand theory is not the only framework sociologists use to assess the character of the social order. There are many middle range theories that focus on particular issues. The fourth chapter, "Dominant–Minority Relations," gives quick takes on three such explanatory models relating to interethnic affairs: Power-Differential Theory, the theory of Internal Colonialism, and the Split Labor Market Theory. Further, and most welcome, Vincent Parrillo offers his own views of the advantages and limitations of each of these.

In each chapter in Parts II and III, the author applies what the reader has learned in the beginning of the text to the detailed treatment of a variety of American racial and ethnic cohorts, beginning with Northern and Western Europeans and Southern and Eastern ones and then discussing people of color, in particular, Native-, East Central and West Asian-, African- and Hispanic- Americans, among others. Each case is treated as something apart from and yet linked to the others, a skillful heuristic device that helps the reader gain knowledge of and insight into the complex character of American social history, the mixture of motives for coming to our shores (or of forcing reluctant leavers to cross the forbidding oceans), the varied responses of newcomers to those in the dominant group and to each other, and the move on the part of so many from being immigrants or refugees (or in the case of the descendants of Africa, slaves, captives) to becoming minorities and, eventually, American-style ethnics.

While the principal focus of *Strangers to These Shores* is on newcomers (and, to a limited degree, on natives—both Indians and those who laid claim to being the "Founders"), the author also considers the plights of religious minorities and women of all backgrounds, using some of the concepts introduced early on to examine what he implies are subcultural variants on the theme of ethnicity. This device of spiraling back and forth is especially useful in maintaining the continuity of the volume. So, too, is the practice of ending every case study with the three now-familiar sociological perspectives— "Functionalism," "Conflict," and "Interactionism"—introduced and explained in Part I.

Much of this fourth edition is already well-established text that has been rewritten and updated. Most noteworthy is Part V, which deals with the "Present and Future Status of Minority Groups." Here Professor Parrillo offers particularly insightful examinations of several old debates including "Hansen's Law" (what the son wishes to forget, the grandson wishes to remember), "symbolic" versus real ethnicity, and ethnic bases of "achievement motivation." He also considers such timely matters as the current fears of increased immigration, the thorny issues of illegal aliens, the question of the efficacy—and political ramifications—of "English Only," and the lively and often polarizing controversy over "multiculturalism," often played out ethnosyncratically as the latest rendition of an attempt to answer that an old query, "What is America to me?" posed some 50 years ago in a ballad by Lewis Allen and Earl Robinson.

It is noteworthy that Allen and Robinson—and those like the young Frank Sinatra who sang their song in the early 1940s—answer the question with words that still resonate, especially in the minds and souls of liberal pluralists like this writer—and Vincent Parrillo.

"What is America to me?" the songsters ask. And then, answering their own question, they spell it out in a series of stanzas, including this one:

> The house I live in.
>   My neighbors white and black.
>   The people who just came here.
>   Or from generations back.
>
> The townhall and the soapbox.
>   The torch of Liberty.
>   A home for all God's children . . .
>   That's America to me.

The question remains a challenging one—as Vincent Parrillo repeatedly shows.

Peter I. Rose
Smith College

Preface

Race and ethnic relations is an exciting, challenging, and dynamic field of study. It touches all of us, both directly and indirectly in many ways, and it does so on personal, regional, national, even global levels. Each generation thinks it lives through a unique situation, as shaped by the times or the "peculiarities" of a group's characteristics. In truth each generation is part of a larger process that includes behavioral patterns from past generations who also thought their situation unique.

In March 1993 I spent almost two weeks in Germany and Sweden either lecturing or conferring with educators, students, political leaders, officials and other immigration experts as part of a bilateral dialogue arranged through the U.S. Information Agency, an independent foreign affairs agency within the executive branch of the U.S. government. This rewarding experience reaffirmed for me how universal these patterns are, regardless of time or place.

Intergroup relations change continually, through alternating periods of quiet and turmoil, of entry of new groups of immigrants or refugees, or of problems sporadically arising between different, native-born racial or ethnic groups within the country. These changes can be understood within the context of discernible, recurring patterns influenced by economic, political, psychological, and sociological factors.

To understand both the dynamics and the larger context of changing inter-group relations, particularly the reality of historical repetitions of behavior, we must utilize social science theory, research, and analysis. Moreover, we can only truly appreciate a diverse society like the United States, as well as the broader applications of social science by examining many groups, rather than by the more limited scope of competing books that focus only on a few groups.

I have been gratified by the widespread adoptions of *Strangers to These Shores* and the favorable response from colleagues and students throughout the United States and Europe. Their helpful comments and suggestions have been incorporated into this fourth edition to make an even better book. New sections in this edition include Afrocentrism, multiculturalism, political correctness, a Mexican–Puerto Rican comparison, Dominicans, Salvadorans, other Central and South American immigrants, and U.S. minority population projections for 2050. Another new feature is the inclusion in each chapter of an international situation, illustrating a cross-cultural application of that chapter's content. All other sections have been updated in their demographics. Where appropriate, new research findings or analysis of recent events have also been included.

The first four chapters present a conceptual and theoretical overview of the subject area, providing students with a basis from which they can examine the experiences of the different minority groups discussed in subsequent chapters. Major sociological perspectives—functionalist, conflict, interactionist—as well as some middle-range theories are applied throughout the book, though overall it remains eclectic in treatment of topics. Instructors can similarly follow this approach or emphasize their own theoretical viewpoint because the book's structure allows for varying applications.

After some introductory concepts in the first chapter, particularly that of the stranger as a social phenomenon, we examine differences in culture, reality perceptions, social class, and power as reasons for intergroup conflict. In addition, we look at the dominant group's varying expectations about how minorities should "fit" into its society. Chapters 1 and 2 include some middle-range interactionist theories also. Chapter 3 explores the dimensions and interrelationships of prejudice and discrimination, and Chapter 4 covers the dominant–minority response patterns regardless of a specific group or time period. Included in this chapter are middle-range conflict theories about economic exploitation.

Chapters 5 through 13 offer the reader some insights into the experiences of a wide array of minority groups. In-depth studies of the cultural orientations and assimilation/nonassimilation of each group are not possible, because the intent is to provide a broad scope rather than extensive coverage of only a few groups. Not every racial and ethnic group is discussed, though almost fifty have been included to illustrate the diversity among North Americans. For a more comprehensive examination of any subject or group discussed in this book, the reader should consult the sources listed in the chapter notes or suggested readings.

Chapter 14 provides insights into the mosaic of American society through demographic analysis and intergroup comparisons from various field investigations. Specifically, we look at ethnic consciousness and ethnic stratification. Present concerns about legal and illegal immigration and bilingual education follow. A discussion of multiculturalism, political correctness, and the future of ethnicity completes our study of minorities.

Included in the book are several features to enhance student understanding. A sociohistorical perspective opens each chapter to the study of specific groups. Preceding a retrospective summary at the end of each chapter is a sociological analysis of the group experiences utilizing the functionalist, conflict, and interactionist perspectives. Within each chapter are boxed firsthand immigrant accounts and text summary highlights, as well as extensive photo, map, and line art illustrations. Use of key terms, review questions, and an annotated bibliography appear at the end of each chapter. An easily understandable glossary and appendix of 1820 through 1991 immigration statistics appear at the end of the book.

Many people helped in the writing of this book. My appreciation goes to Christine Moore, Arraceli Serrano, Sherri Tucker, and Ina Willis for their able librarian assistance in retrieving articles. The following students completed exceptional immigrant tape projects, whose excerpts appear in Chapters 5 through 12: Bruce Bisciotti, Doris Brown, Hermione Cox, Milly Gottlieb, Daniel Kazan, David Lenox, Sarah Martinez, Chairath Phaladiganon, Terrence Royful, Michelle Schwartz, Geri Squire, Luba Tkatchov, Leo Uebelein, and Yu-Jie Zeng. Their contributions bring a very human touch to the study of minority peoples.

I would like to thank the following reviewers for their helpful comments: Margaret Brooks-Terry, Baldwin-Wallace College; Racine Butler, East Los Angeles College; Anthony J. Cortese, Colorado State University; Bernardo M. Ferdman, State University of New York at Albany; Juan L. Gonzalez, Jr., California State University at Hayward; Kathleen M. Hardy, Louisiana State University at Shreveport; Maurice Jackson, University of California at Riverside; Garfield A. Jackson, Columbus State Community College; Christopher Jay Johnson, Northeast Louisiana University; Terry Jones, California State University at Hayward; Michael C. LeMay, Frostburg State College; R. Paul Maiden, University of Maryland; John P. Myers, Glassboro State College; Cynthia Rolling, Edgewood College; Earl Smith, Washington State University; Marios Stephanides, Spalding University; W. Austin VanPelt, Arapahoe Community College; Bruce B. Williams, Vanderbilt University

I have also had the good fortune to work with a team at Macmillan whose competence, cooperation, and dedication have made the production of this edition a most satisfying work encounter. My special thanks go to Susan Rabinowitz, sociology editor, and D. Anthony English, executive editor. Katherine Evancie, production supervisor, meticulously brought the book into print, with John Sollami overseeing its production. Diane Kraut researched excellent photo illustrations, and Robert Freese created a book design that is visually appealing.

I am especially grateful to my friend and colleague Peter I. Rose of Smith College for writing the Foreword to this edition. My thanks also go to Stanford M. Lyman of Florida Atlantic University for his contributions to previous editions: the Foreward in the second and third editions as well as his guidance in the development of the first edition.

Finally, I want to acknowledge my gratitude to my wife, Beth, and my children, Chrysti, Cara, Beverley, and Elizabeth, for the joy they bring to my life.

V.N.P.

Contents

6 Southern, Central, and Eastern Europeans   **167**

PART III
PEOPLE OF COLOR _____ 217

7 The Native Americans   219

10   African Americans   351

STRANGERS
TO THESE SHORES

PART I

SOCIOLOGICAL FRAMEWORK

"As long as minorities suffer from discrimination and the denial of civil liberties, the dominant group also is not free."

— *Louis Wirth, 1945*

1

Robert Fox/Impact Visuals

The Study of Minorities

We pride ourselves on being a nation of immigrants. Many still call the United States a great melting pot where people of all races, religions, and nationalities come to be free and improve their lives. Certainly a great number of immigrants offer living testimony to that ideal, their enthusiasm for their adopted country evident in countless interviews, some of which you will read in this book. Most of you, as college students, regardless of how long ago your family emigrated to the United States, also give evidence to the American Dream of freedom of choice, economic opportunity, and upward mobility.

Yet beneath the Fourth of July speeches, the nation's absorption of diverse peoples over the years, and the numerous success stories lies a disquieting truth. Native-born Americans have not always welcomed the newcomers with open arms; indeed they have often responded with overt acts of discrimination ranging from avoidance to violence and murder. The dominant group's treatment of native-born blacks and American Indians (Native Americans) is a disturbing illustration of subjugation and entrenched inequality. Today we still face serious problems in attitudes toward and treatment of reservation Indians, poor blacks in urban ghettos, and large concentrations of recent Asian and Hispanic immigrants. For some, the American Dream becomes a reality; for others, blocked opportunities create an American nightmare.

Interethnic tensions and hostilities within a nation's borders are a worldwide phenomenon dating from thousands of years ago to the present. In 1992–93, for example, Serbs and Croats killed many Muslims in Bosnia-Herzegovina, simultaneously destroying Sarajevo, the centuries-old beautiful city that had escaped destruction through two world wars. In another part of the former Soviet Union, Azerbaijan Muslims and Armenian Christians clashed. Religious factions in Lebanon and Northern Ireland continue to kill each other. Animosity remains among the Hausa, Ibo, and Yoruba tribes in Nigeria, where a bloody war raged among them in the 1980s. A few years earlier, appalling bloodbaths among Kampucheans (Cambodians), Chinese, Laotians, and Vietnamese horrified the world. Iraq killed hundreds of Kurds with poison gas in 1988, including infants and children. Elsewhere, other minorities, such as West Indians in Britain, Algerians in France, Turks in West Germany, Cypriots and Filipinos in Saudi Arabia, and Palestinians in Israel, have encountered prejudice, discrimination, and occasional violence. Within any society the groupings of people by race, religion, tribe, culture, or lifestyle can generate prejudices, tensions, and sporadic outbursts of violence.

Although individuals of the dominant group usually absolve themselves of blame and see specific flaws within a minority group as causes for its low status and problems (for example, slowness in learning the main language of the country or supposed lack of the work ethic), sociologists note among different groups distinct patterns of interaction that transcend national boundaries, specific periods, or idiosyncrasies of particular groups. Opinions may vary as to the causes for these patterns of behavior, but a consensus does exist about their presence.

THE STRANGER AS A SOCIAL PHENOMENON ____

To understand intergroup relations, we must recognize that differences among various peoples cause each group to look on other groups as strangers. Among isolated peoples, the arrival of a stranger has always been a momentous occasion, often eliciting strong emotional responses. Reactions might range from warm hospitality to conciliatory or protective ceremonies to hostile acts. In an urbanized and mobile society, the stranger still evokes similar responses. From the Tiwi of northern Australia, who consistently killed intruders, to the nativists of any country or time, who continually strive to keep out "undesirable elements," the underlying premise is the same: The outsiders are not good enough to share the land and resources with the "chosen people" already there.

Similarity and Attraction

Since Aristotle observed, "We like those who resemble us, and are engaged in the same pursuits," social observers have been aware of the similarity–attraction relationship.[1] Numerous studies have examined the extent to which a person likes others because of similar attitudes, values, beliefs, social status, or physical appearance. Examining the development of attraction among people initially strangers to one another, an impressive number of these studies have found a positive relationship between the similarity of one person and that person's liking for the other. Most significantly, the findings show that people's perception of the similarity between themselves is a more powerful determinant than actual similarity.[2] Cross-cultural studies also support this conclusion.[3] Considerable evidence exists showing greater human receptivity to strangers perceived as similar than to those perceived as different.

Social Distance

One excellent technique for evaluating how perceptions of similarity attract closer interaction patterns is the ranking of **social distance.** First devised by Emory Bogardus in 1926, this measurement device has been used repeatedly since then.[4] In five comparable studies spanning 50 years, researchers obtained responses from a fairly evenly divided group of undergraduate and graduate students aged 18 to 35, about 10 percent of them black. The students selected the degree of social closeness or distance personally acceptable to

TABLE 1.1

CHANGES IN SOCIAL DISTANCE IN THE UNITED STATES, 1926–1977

I 1926		II 1946		III 1956		IV 1966		V 1977	
1. English	1.06	1. Americans (U.S. white)	1.04	1. Americans (U.S. white)	1.08	1. Americans (U.S. white)	1.07	1. Americans (U.S. white)	1.25
2. Americans (U.S. white)	1.10	2. Canadians	1.11	2. Canadians	1.16	2. English	1.14	2. English	1.39
3. Canadians	1.13	3. English	1.13	3. English	1.23	3. Canadians	1.15	3. Canadians	1.42
4. Scots	1.13	4. Irish	1.24	4. French	1.47	4. French	1.36	4. French	1.58
5. Irish	1.30	5. Scots	1.26	5. Irish	1.56	5. Irish	1.40	5. Italians	1.65
6. French	1.32	6. French	1.31	6. Swedish	1.57	6. Swedish	1.42	6. Swedish	1.68
7. Germans	1.46	7. Norwegians	1.35	7. Scots	1.60	7. Norwegians	1.50	7. Irish	1.69
8. Swedish	1.54	8. Hollanders	1.37	8. Germans	1.61	8. Italians	1.51	8. Hollanders	1.83
9. Hollanders	1.56	9. Swedish	1.40	9. Hollanders	1.63	9. Scots	1.53	9. Scots	1.83
10. Norwegians	1.59	10. Germans	1.59	10. Norwegians	1.66	10. Germans	1.54	10. American Indians	1.84
11. Spanish	1.72	11. Finns	1.63	11. Finns	1.80	11. Hollanders	1.54	11. Germans	1.87
12. Finns	1.83	12. Czechs	1.76	12. Italians	1.89	12. Finns	1.67	12. Norwegians	1.93
13. Russians	1.88	13. Russians	1.83	13. Poles	2.07	13. Greeks	1.82	13. Spanish	1.98
14. Italians	1.94	14. Poles	1.84	14. Spanish	2.08	14. Spanish	1.93	14. Finns	2.00
15. Poles	2.01	15. Spanish	1.94	15. Greeks	2.09	15. Jews	1.97	15. Jews	2.01
16. Armenians	2.06	16. Italians	2.28	16. Jews	2.15	16. Poles	1.98	16. Greeks	2.02
17. Czechs	2.08	17. Armenians	2.29	17. Czechs	2.22	17. Czechs	2.02	17. Negroes	2.03
18. Indians (American)	2.38	18. Greeks	2.29	18. Armenians	2.33	18. Indians (American)	2.12	18. Poles	2.11
19. Jews	2.39	19. Jews	2.32	19. Japanese Americans	2.34	19. Japanese Americans	2.14	19. Mexican Americans	2.17
20. Greeks	2.47	20. Indians (American)	2.45	20. Indians (American)	2.35	20. Armenians	2.18	20. Japanese Americans	2.18
21. Mexicans	2.69	21. Chinese	2.50	21. Filipinos	2.46	21. Filipinos	2.31	21. Armenians	2.20
22. Mexican Americans	—	22. Mexican Americans	2.52	22. Mexican Americans	2.51	22. Chinese	2.34	22. Czechs	2.23
23. Japanese	2.80	23. Filipinos	2.76	23. Turks	2.52	23. Mexican Americans	2.37	23. Chinese	2.29
24. Japanese Americans	—	24. Mexicans	2.89	24. Russians	2.56	24. Russians	2.38	24. Filipinos	2.31
25. Filipinos	3.00	25. Turks	2.89	25. Chinese	2.68	25. Japanese	2.41	25. Japanese	2.38
26. Negroes	3.28	26. Japanese Americans	2.90	26. Japanese	2.70	26. Turks	2.48	26. Mexicans	2.40
27. Turks	3.30	27. Koreans	3.05	27. Negroes	2.74	27. Koreans	2.51	27. Turks	2.55
28. Chinese	3.36	28. Indians (from India)	3.43	28. Mexicans	2.79	28. Mexicans	2.56	28. Indians (of India)	2.55
29. Koreans	3.60	29. Negroes	3.60	29. Indians (from India)	2.80	29. Negroes	2.56	29. Russians	2.57
30. Indians (from India)	3.91	30. Japanese	3.61	30. Koreans	2.83	30. Indians (from India)	2.62	30. Koreans	2.63
Arithmetic mean of 48,300 racial reactions	2.14	Arithmetic mean of 58,500 racial reactions	2.12	Arithmetic mean of 61,590 racial reactions	2.08	Arithmetic mean of 78,150 racial reactions	1.92	Arithmetic mean of 44,640 racial reactions	1.93
Spread in distance	2.85	Spread in distance	2.57	Spread in distance	1.75	Spread in distance	1.56	Spread in distance	1.38

SOURCES: From Emory S. Bogardus, "Comparing Racial Distance in Ethiopia, South Africa, and the United States," *Sociology and Social Research* 52 (January 1968), 152; and Carolyn A. Owen, Howard C. Eisner, and Thomas R. McFaul, "A Half-Century of Social Distance Research: National Replication of the Bogardus Studies," *Sociology and Social Research* 66 (October 1981), 89. Reprinted by permission.

— 708/920-0571 —

I 57 N   TO 5 94 N

Exit - @ Ogden Ave
W/B.
2 Stop Lights
2nd stop is York Rd
Turn Right go 1
Block
Across From
McDonalds -

In September 1992 these two Bosnian Moslem girls and their grandmother were released during a prisoner exchange. They were among 450 Hadzici villagers seized as part of a Serbian Christian "ethnic cleansing" operation to expel the nationally or religiously different in order to create homogeneous areas. (*Corinne Dufka/Reuters/Bettmann*)

members of a particular group. The available choices were in the following categories:

1. To close kinship by marriage (1 point)
2. To my club as personal chums (2 points)
3. To my street as neighbors (3 points)
4. To employment in my occupation (4 points)
5. To citizenship in my country (5 points)
6. As visitors only to my country (6 points)
7. Would exclude from my country (7 points)

Researchers then totaled, averaged, and ranked the responses, creating social-distance indices. The scale ranges from 1.00 to 7.00 —the higher the number, the greater the social distance (see Table 1.1). Responses of minority-group members remain very similar to those of dominant-group members, except that their own group moves to the top of the scale. The range of social-distance indices has declined over the years both in absolute level of expressed prejudice (from 2.14 in 1926 to 1.93 in 1977) and in range of distance between top and bottom groups (from 2.85 in 1926 to 1.38 in 1977). With a few exceptions, the relatively consistent positioning of response patterns illustrates the similarity–attraction relationship. Italians have moved up steadily, becoming the first group not from northwest Europe to break into the top 10. The lead upward in 1977 by blacks is even more dramatic. International politics or war usually causes groups to drop (Germans, Italians, and Japanese in 1946) and Russians since 1946 (Cold War, McCarthyism, Vietnam).[5] With the major political changes in Russia, we may expect a lessening of their social-distance indexes the next time they are measured.

Sometimes the social distance kept between minority groups is greater than that kept between each minority and the dominant group. For example, one study of 708 Anglos, 249 blacks, and 256 Mexican Americans in Texas found blacks and Mexican Americans more accepting of Anglos than they are of each other. However, higher-status members of all three groups (those having more education and higher incomes) and youth were generally more accepting of contact with the outgroup minority than were lower-status group members.[6]

Another interesting aspect of social distance appears to be its relationship to immigrants becoming citizens. A 1990 study found that immigrants belonging to ethnic groups less accepted by Americans were five times more likely to become American citizens than immigrants of low social distance who were otherwise similarly situated.[7] Perhaps lacking much social acceptance impels these immigrants to seek citizenship to gain at least a legal acknowledgment that they belong.

Perceptions

By definition the stranger is not only an outsider but also someone different and personally unknown. People perceive strangers primarily through **categoric knowing,** the classification of others based on limited information obtained visually and perhaps verbally.[8] People make judgments and generalizations on the basis of scanty information, confusing an individual's characteristics with typical group-member characteristics. For instance, if a visiting Swede asks for tea rather than coffee, the host may incorrectly conclude that all Swedes dislike coffee.

Native-born Americans have perceived immigrants, first-generation Americans of different racial and ethnic groups, to be a particular kind of stranger: one who intends to stay. As the presence of immigrants became less of a novelty, then fear, suspicion, and distrust often replaced the natives' initial curiosity. The strangers remained strangers as each group sought its own kind for personal interaction.

The role of a stranger can be analyzed regardless of the particular period in history. Georg Simmel (1858–1918) theorized that strangers represent both *nearness*, because they are physically close, and *remoteness*, because they react differently to the immediate situation and have different values and ways of doing things.[9] The stranger is both inside and outside: physically present and participating but also outside the situation, being from another place.

The native perceives the stranger in an abstract, typified way. That is, the individual becomes the *totality*, or stereotype, of the group. The stranger, however, perceives the natives in concrete, individual terms. Simmel suggests that strangers have a higher degree of objectivity about the natives because the strangers' geographical mobility reflects mobility in their minds as well. The stranger is free from indigenous habit, piety, and precedent. Furthermore, because strangers do not participate fully in society, they have a certain mental detachment, causing them to see things more objectively.

Interactions

Simmel approaches the role of the stranger through an analysis of the formal structures of life. In contrast Alfred Schutz—himself an immigrant to the United States—analyzes the stranger as lacking "intersubjective understanding."[10] By this he means that those from the same social world mutually "know" the language (including slang), customs, beliefs, symbols, and everyday behavior patterns that the stranger usually does not.

For the native, then, every social situation is a coming together not only of roles and identities but also of shared realities—the intersubjective structure of consciousness. What is taken for granted by the native is problematic to the stranger. In a familiar world people live through the day by responding to daily routine without questioning or reflection. To strangers, however, every situation is new and is therefore experienced as a crisis.

Strangers experience a "lack of historicity"—a lack of the shared memory of those with whom they live. Human beings who interact together over a period of time "grow old together"; strangers, however, are "young," being newcomers, and they experience at least an approximation of the freshness of childhood. They are aware of things that go unnoticed by the natives, such as their customs, social institutions, appearance, and life-style.

Sometimes the stranger may be the comical butt of jokes because of unfamiliarity with the everyday routine of life in this new setting. In time, however, strangers take on the natives' perspective; the strangers' consciousness is lowered because the freshness of their perceptions is lost. Also, the natives' **abstract typifications** about the strangers become more concrete through social interaction. As Schutz says, "The vacant frames become occupied by vivid experiences." As acculturation takes place, the native begins to view the stranger more concretely and the stranger becomes less questioning about daily activities. Use of the term *naturalized citizen* takes on a curious connotation when examined from this perspective, because it implies that people are in some way odd or unnatural until they have taken on the characteristics of the natives.

As its title suggests, this book is about the many strangers who came—and are still coming—to the United States in search of a better life. Through an examination of sociological theory and the experiences of many racial and ethnic groups, the story of how the stranger perceives the society and is received by it will be continually retold. The adjustment from stranger to neighbor may be viewed as movement along a continuum, but this continuum is not cyclical and assimilation is not inevitable. Rather, it is the process of social interaction among different groups of people.

ETHNOCENTRISM

An understanding of the concept of the stranger is important in order to understand **ethnocentrism**, a term meaning the "view of things in which one's own group is the center of everything, and all others are scaled and rated with reference to it."[11] Ethnocentrism thus refers to people's tendency to identify with their own ethnic or national group as a means of fulfilling their needs for group belongingness and security. (The word is derived from two Greek words: *ethnos,* meaning nation, and *kentron,* meaning center.) As a result of ethnocentrism, people usually view their own cultural values as somehow more real and thus superior to those of other groups, and they prefer their own way of doing things. Unfortunately for human relations, such ethnocentric thought is often extended until it negatively affects attitudes and emotions toward those who are perceived as different.

Sociologists define an **ingroup** as one to which individuals belong and feel loyalty; thus everyone—whether a member of a majority group or a minority group—is part of an ingroup. **Outgroups** are defined, in relation to ingroups, as groups consisting of all people who are not members of one's ingroup. Studying majority groups as ingroups helps us to understand their reactions to strangers of another race or culture entering their society. Similarly, considering minority groups as ingroups enables us to understand their efforts to maintain their ethnic identity and solidarity in the midst of the dominant culture.

From European social psychologists comes one of the more promising explanations for ingroup favoritism. **Social identity theory** holds that ingroup members almost automatically think of their group as better than outgroups as a means of enhancing their own social status or social identity and thus raising the value of their personal identity or self-image.[12]

There is ample evidence about people from past civilizations who have regarded other cultures as inferior, incorrect, or immoral. This assumption that *we* are better than *they* are generally results in outgroups becoming objects of ridicule, contempt, or hatred. Such attitudes may lead to stereotyping, prejudice, discrimination, and even violence. What actually does occur depends on many factors, including structural and economic conditions, which will be discussed in subsequent chapters.

Despite its ethnocentric beliefs, the ingroup does not always view the outgroup as inferior. There are numerous documented cases of groups who have retained their values and standards while recognizing the superiority of another group in some specific areas.[13] Also, countless people reject their own ingroup by being "voluntary exiles, expatriates, outgroup emulators, social climbers, renegades, and traitors."[14] An outgroup may become a positive **reference group**—that is, it may serve as an exemplary model—if members of the ingroup perceive it as having a conspicuous advantage over them in terms of survival or adaptation to the environment, success in warfare, a stronger political structure, greater wealth, or a higher occupational status.[15]

Ethnocentrism is an important factor in determining minority-group status in society, but because of many variations in intergroup relations, it alone cannot explain the causes of prejudice. For example, majority-group members may view minority groups with suspicion, but not all minority groups become the targets of extreme prejudice and discrimination.

Some social-conflict theorists argue that when the ingroup perceives the outgroup as a real threat competing for scarce resources, the ingroup reacts

"Free Trade Lunch"

The immigrant laborer often was seen as an economic threat. Here English, Italian, Mexican, Russian, and German immigrants are shown devouring meat—symbolizing American workingmen's wages—and bread—symbolizing prosperity. In the background immigrants are shown preventing the American laborer from entering the restaurant to get his share of the free lunch. This cartoon appeared in *Judge* on July 28, 1888. (*The Distorted Image, courtesy Anti-Defamation League of B'nai B'rith, John and Selma Appel Collection*)

with increased solidarity, ethnocentrism, and hostility toward the outgroup.[16] According to this view, ethnocentrism can lead to prejudice, discrimination, and hostility, the degree of which depends on several economic and geographic considerations. It would thus appear that ethnocentrism leads to negative consequences when the ingroup feels threatened. One counterargument to this view would be that ethnocentric attitudes—thinking that because others are different, they are thus a threat—initially caused the problem. However, the major difficulty with this approach is that it does not explain variations in the frequency, type, or intensity of intergroup conflict from one society to the next or between different immigrant groups and the ingroup.

In the United States

An ethnocentric attitude often is not deliberate but instead is an outgrowth of growing up and living within a familiar environment. However, if recognized for the bias it is, it can be overcome. Consider, for example, that Americans have labeled their major-league baseball championship games a *World Series,* although until recently not even Canadian teams were included in an otherwise exclusively U.S. professional sports program. *American* is another word we use—even in this book—to identify ourselves to the exclusion of people in other parts of North and South America. The Organization of American States (OAS), which consists of countries in both North and South America, should remind us that others are equally entitled to call themselves Americans.

At one point in this country's history, many state and national leaders identified their expansionist goals as Manifest Destiny, as if Divine Providence had ordained specific boundaries for the United States. Indeed, many a member of the clergy has preached a fiery sermon over the years regarding God's special plans for this country, and all presidents have invoked the Deity in their inaugural addresses for special assistance to this country.

In Other Times and Lands

Throughout history people of many cultures have demonstrated an ethnocentric view of the world. For example, the British once believed they were obliged to carry the "white man's burden" in colonizing and "civilizing" the nonwestern world. Yet 2,000 years earlier, the Romans thought natives of Britain were an inferior people, as indicated in this excerpt from a letter written by the orator Cicero to his friend Atticus:

> Do not obtain your slaves from Britain because they are so stupid and so utterly incapable of being taught that they are not fit to form a part of the household of Athens.

The Greeks, whose civilization predated the Roman Empire, considered all those around them—Persians, Egyptians, Macedonians, and others—distinctly inferior and called them barbarians. (*Barbarikos,* a Greek word, described those who did not speak Greek as making noises that sounded like *bar-bar.*)

Religious chauvinism blended with ethnocentrism in the Middle Ages when the Crusaders, spurred on by their beliefs, considered it their duty to free the Holy Land from the control of the "infidels." They traveled a great distance by land and sea, taking with them horses, armor, and armaments, to wrest control from the native inhabitants because the "infidels" had the audacity to follow the teachings of Mohammed rather than Jesus. On their journey across Europe, the Crusaders slaughtered Jews (whom they incorrectly labeled "Christ-killers"), regardless of whether they were men, women, or children, all in the name of the Prince of Peace. The Crusaders looked on both Moslems and Jews as inferior peoples as well as enemies.

In the following passage Brewton Berry offers several other examples of ethnocentric thinking in past times:

> Some writers have attributed the superiority of their people to favorable geographical influences, but others incline to a biological explanation. The Roman, Vitruvius, maintained that those who live in southern climates have the keener intelligence, due to the rarity of the atmosphere, whereas "northern nations, being enveloped in a dense atmosphere, and chilled by moisture from the obstructing air, have a sluggish intelligence." A certain Ibn Khaldun argued that the Arabians were the superior people, because their country, although in a warm zone, was surrounded by water, which exerted a cooling effect. Bodin, in the sixteenth century, found an astrological explanation for ethnic group differences. The planets, he thought, exerted their combined and best influence upon that section of the globe occupied by France, and the French, accordingly, were destined by nature to be the masters of the world. Needless to say, Ibn Khaldun was an Arab, and Bodin a Frenchman. The Italian, Sergi, regarded the Mediterranean peoples as the true bearers of civilization and insisted that Germans and Asiatics only destroy what the Mediterraneans create. In like manner, the superiority of Nordics, Alpines, Teutons, Aryans, and others has been asserted by those who were members of each of these groups, or thought they were.[17]

Anthropologists, when examining the cultures of other peoples, have identified countless instances of ethnocentric attitudes. One frequent practice has been in geographic reference and mapmaking. There have, for example, been commercially prepared Australian world maps that depicted that continent in the center in relation to the rest of the world.

> There is nothing unusual about this type of thinking: the Chinese, who called their country the Middle Kingdom, were convinced that China was the center of the world, and similar beliefs were held by other nations—and are still held. The British drew the Prime Meridian of longitude to run through Greenwich, near London. Europeans drew maps of the world with Europe at the center, Americans with the New World at the center.[18]

Ethnocentrism is more than just a group-centered approach to living. It also is of utmost significance in understanding motivation, attitudes, and behavior when members of racially or ethnically distinct groups interact, for it often serves as a basis for misunderstandings, prejudice, and discrimination.

Eurocentrism and Afrocentrism

In recent years many scholars and minority leaders have criticized the underrepresentation of non-European curriculum materials in the schools and colleges, calling this approach Eurocentric. **Eurocentrism** is a variation of ethnocentrism in which the content, emphasis, or both in history, literature, and other humanities primarily, if not exclusively, concern Western culture. Critics argue that this focus, ranging from the ancient civilizations of Greece and Rome to the writings of Shakespeare, Dickens, and other English poets and authors, ignores the accomplishments and importance of other peoples.

One counterforce to Eurocentrism is **Afrocentrism,** a viewpoint emphasizing African culture and its influence on Western civilization and the behavior of American blacks. In its moderate form, Afrocentrism is an effort to counterbalance Eurocentrism and the suppression of the African influence by teaching African heritage as well.[19] In its bolder form, Afrocentrism becomes another variation of ethnocentrism. For example, a New York professor of Afro-American Studies, Leon Jeffries, became enmeshed in controversy when he asserted the superiority of African "sun people" over European "ice people." Others who argue that Western civilization is merely a derivative of the black African influence on Egyptian civilization find critics who charge them with an excessive distortion of history.[20]

For most pluralist advocates, however, ethnocentrism in any form is erroneous. What is needed is the balanced approach that is inclusive, not exclusive, of the cultures, civilizations, and contributions of all peoples, both in our curriculum and in our thinking (see Box 1.1 for an international example).

OBJECTIVITY _____

When discussing people, usually those who are different from ourselves, it is not unusual for us to offer our own assumptions and opinions more readily than in some other area, such as statistics or biology. But if we are to undertake a sociological study of ethnicity, we must question our assumptions and opinions—everything we have always believed without question. How can we scientifically investigate a problem if we have already reached a conclusion?

Sociologists attempt to examine group relationships objectively, but it is impossible to exclude their own subjectivity altogether. All human beings have **values,** socially shared conceptions of what is good, desirable, and proper or bad, undesirable, and improper. Because we are human we cannot be completely objective, since these values influence our orientations, actions, reactions, and interpretations. For example, selecting intergroup relations as an area of interest and concern, emphasizing the sociological per-

Professor Leonard Jeffries is an advocate of Afrocentrist teaching, emphasizing African cultural influence on Western culture and American black behavior. His views sparked considerable controversy, leading to his removal as chair of the Black Studies Department at CUNY and his subsequent court victory over that decision. (*F.M. Kearney/Impact Visuals*)

spective of this subject, and the thematic organization of the material in this book all represent value judgments regarding priorities.

Although **value neutrality** may be impossible to attain (and many would even argue that it is undesirable), it is nevertheless most important to exercise a conscientious effort to maintain an open mind in order to examine this subject as objectively as is humanly possible. You must be aware of your own strong feelings about these matters and be willing to examine new concepts, even if they challenge previously held beliefs. To study this subject properly, you should try to be a stranger in your familiar world. Look at everything as if you were seeing it for the first time, trying to understand how and why it is rather than just taking it for granted. Also, you should recognize that all of

BOX 1.1   **THE INTERNATIONAL SCENE**

In 1991 CDS International, an organization that runs exchange programs, distributed a pamphlet, "An Information Guide for Germans on American Culture," to Germans working as interns in American companies. Based on the German interns' own experiences and interviews with other colleagues, the pamphlet's intent is to provide insights into American culture and to overcome ethnocentric reactions.

• Americans say "Hello" or "How are you?" when they see each other. "How are you?" is like "Hello." A long answer is not expected; just answer "Thank you, fine. How are you?"
• Using deodorant is a must.
• American women usually shave their legs and under their arms. Women who don't like to do this should consider wearing clothes that cover these areas.
• Expect to be treated like all other Americans. You won't receive special treatment because you are a German. Try not to talk with other Germans in German if Americans are around; this could make them feel uncomfortable.
• Please consider the differences in verbal communication styles between Americans and Germans. The typical German speaking style sounds abrupt and rude to Americans. Keep this in mind when talking to Americans.
• Be polite. Use words like "please" and "thank you." It is better to use these too often than not enough. Also, be conscious of your voice and the expression on your face. Your voice should be friendly, and you should wear a smile. Don't be confused by the friendliness and easygoing, non-excitable nature of the people. They are deliberate, think independently, and do things their own way. Americans are proud of their independence.
• Keep yourself out of any discussions at work about race, sex, religion, or politics. Be open-minded; don't make judgments based on past experiences in Germany.
• Be aware that there are a lot of different cultures in the United States. There are also many different churches, which mean a great deal to their members. Don't be quick to judge these cultures; this could hurt people's feelings.
• Do it the American way and try to intermingle with the Americans. Think positive.

us are members of groups, and therefore the debate about and study of intergroup relations is itself part of what we are studying. As part of an ingroup, we find all other outgroup members unlike our reference group, and thus our judgments about these "outsiders" will not be as fully informed as those we make about known "insiders."

Trying to be *objective* about race and ethnic relations presents a strong challenge. People tend to use selective perception, accepting only information that agrees with their values or interpreting information so that it remains consistent with their attitudes about other groups. Many variables in life influence people's subjectivity about minority relations. Some views may be based on personal or emotional considerations or even on false premises. However, sometimes quite reasonable and responsible people disagree on the matter in an unemotional way. Whatever the situation, the study of minority-group relations poses a challenge for objective examination.

The subject of race and ethnic relations is a very complex one, and it touches our lives in many ways. All who are reading this book must face the realization that they are in fact coming to this subject with preconceived notions as members of the groups we are studying. Because many individuals have a strong tendency to "tune out" disagreeable information, you must make a continual, conscientious effort to remain open-minded and receptive to new data.

BEHAVIOR

Contrary to popular belief, most forms of social behavior are not "natural." We learn how to do things through the socialization process, which propagates cultural values, attitudes, customs, and beliefs. We even satisfy our hunger and sexual needs in culturally determined ways.

Certain Native American tribes consider dog stew a fine delicacy to serve honored guests, although someone from a different culture may not find the prospect of such a meal very appetizing. Many Americans eat beef, much to the chagrin of Hindus or pork much to the chagrin of Moslems, and Orthodox Jews. Westerners may find distasteful the Chinese fondness for aged, foul-smelling eggs, but the Chinese may find equally repugnant the Westerners' fondness for aged, foul-smelling milk, better known as cheese. Others enjoy eating raw fish, cooked squid, eel, snake, or insects, to the clear disgust of still others.

Incest has not been an acceptable practice in most societies, but certain cultures have considered it critically important, as, for example, did the pharaohs of ancient Egypt. During the Eighteenth Dynasty the daughter inherited the throne, and the son acquired title to the throne by marrying his sister.[21] Many Americans do not condone extramarital affairs, although they occur in our society, and many resent women being treated as sex objects. However, among the central Eskimo peoples of Alaska and the Bahimas of East Africa, a man would be branded a poor host if he did not share his wife (or wives) with his overnight guest.

Therefore what we consider "proper" behavior, or "pleasurable," or "right," or "wrong," does not necessarily correspond to what others believe. What we consider to be "natural" is more likely to be culturally prescribed. Yet our ethnocentric judgment of behavior different from our own, including such basic areas as eating and sex, often results in our branding the behavior with such labels as "strange," "inferior," "disgusting," and "immoral." Although some of the behavior one would regard as most exotic is practiced by peoples who are rather isolated from the rest of the world, the United States itself, as the greatest receiving nation of immigrants, has always been comprised of many diverse types of people who have had varying orientations to living.

The diversity of culturally learned behavior patterns is interesting in itself, but what happens when different groups interact? Sociologists are interested in why prejudicial attitudes and discriminatory actions may or may not arise when groups whose actions or appearances differ come into contact with one another. What factors influence attitudes, expectations, and behavior toward the other group? Numerous theories and findings about such matters exist, and these will be examined in this book.

A SOCIOLOGICAL PERSPECTIVE

Sociology is the study of human relationships and patterns of behavior. Through scientific investigation sociologists seek to determine the social forces that influence behavior as well as the recurring patterns through which they can better understand that behavior.

When two different groups of people come into contact with one another, many possible forms of interaction can occur, ranging from open conflict to close cooperation. The initial relationship, whatever it is, may later change or become even more solidly entrenched. For instance, the two groups may adopt some of each other's culture and intermarry. In contrast, they may live separately in the same area, with one group dominant over the other and with continuing prejudice and hostility toward one another. These examples do not exhaust the possibilities, of course, but they do illustrate various behavior patterns and indicate that behavior may change over time.

Using historical documents, reports, surveys, ethnographies, journalistic materials, and direct observation, the sociologist systematically gathers empirical evidence about such intergroup relations. The sociologist then analyzes these data in an effort to discover and describe the causes, functions, relationships, meanings, and consequences of intergroup harmony or tension. Ascertaining reasons for the beginning, continuance, intensification, or alleviation of readily observable patterns of behavior among different peoples is a complex and difficult matter, and not all sociologists concur when interpreting the data. Different theories, ideas, concepts, and even ideologies and prejudices also may influence a sociologist's conclusions.

Disagreement among sociologists is no more unusual than in other areas of scientific investigation, where such matters as the way in which the universe was created, what constitutes a mental disorder, or whether heredity or environment is more important in shaping behavior are discussed. However, these differing sociological theories have had an important role in influencing the pattern of relations and are grounded in the social scientists' values regarding those relations. In sociological investigation, three major perspectives shape analysis of the study of minorities. Each has a contribution to make and should be considered as a different lens providing a separate focus on the subject. Each will thus serve as a basis for sociological analysis at the end of subsequent chapters.

Functional Theory

Proponents of the **functional theory** perspective, such as Talcott Parsons and Robert Merton, believe that a stable, cooperative social system is the basis of society. All the elements of a society function together to maintain order and stability. Under ideal conditions a society would be in a state of balance, with all its parts working in harmony with each other. When problems arise, it is because some parts of the system have become dysfunctional, upsetting the social equilibrium. This system disorganization can occur for many reasons, but the most frequent cause is rapid social change. Changes in any one part of the system require compensating adjustments elsewhere, but these usually do not occur fast enough, thereby creating tensions and conflict.

Functionalists view dysfunctions as temporary maladjustments to an otherwise interdependent, relatively harmonious society. Because this perspective focuses on societal stability, the key factor in this analysis of social disorganization is whether to restore the equilibrium as it was or to seek a new and different equilibrium. For example, how do we overcome the problem of illegal aliens? Do we expel them to eliminate their exploitation, alleged depression of regional wage scales, and high costs to taxpayers for health, education, and welfare benefits? Or do we grant them amnesty, help them enter the economic mainstream, and seal our borders against further illegal entries? Whatever the solution, and these two do not exhaust the possibilities, functionalists emphasize that all problems regarding minorities can be resolved through adjustments to the social system, returning it to a state of equilibrium. Instead of major changes in the society, they prefer smaller corrections in the already functioning society.

Conflict Theory

Conflict theorists, influenced by Karl Marx's view of an elite exploiting the masses, see society as being continually involved in a series of disagreements, tensions, and clashes as different groups compete for limited resources. Rejecting the concept of societal parts usually working harmoniously, they see disequilibrium and change as the norm. Their focus is on the inequalities generating racial and ethnic antagonisms between groups. To understand why discrimination persists, conflict theorists ask the question, "Who benefits?" Those already in power, the employers and holders of wealth and property, exploit the powerless, seeking even greater profits at the expense of unassimilated minorities. Because lower wages allow higher profits, ethnic discrimination serves investors and owners by weakening workers' bargaining power.

According to this view, one major technique of maintaining power and control of resources is **false consciousness,** getting workers to adopt attitudes not accurately reflecting the objective facts of the situation. If workers believe the economic gains of other groups would adversely affect their own living standards, they will not be supportive of actions to end discriminatory practices. If workers struggling to improve their situation believe other groups entrenched in better job positions are holding them back, they will view their own gains as possible only at the expense of the other ethnic groups. In both cases the wealthy and powerful benefit by pitting racial and ethnic groups against each other, causing each to have strong negative feelings about the other. This distorted view foments conflict and occasional outbursts of violence between groups, preventing workers' realization of their common bond of joint oppression.[22]

Interactionist Theory

A third theoretical approach, **interactionist theory,** examines the microsocial world of personal interaction patterns in everyday life (e.g., social distance when talking, commonly understood terms) rather than the macrosocial aspects of social institutions and their harmony or conflict. **Symbolic interaction,** the shared symbols and definitions people use when communicating with one another, provides the focus for understanding how individuals create and interpret the life situations they experience. Symbols are what constitute our social worlds: our spoken language, expressions, body language, tone of voice, appearance, and images of television and other mass media.[23] By means of these symbols we communicate, create impressions, and develop understandings of the world about us.

Essential to this perspective, suggest Peter L. Berger and Thomas Luckmann, is how people define their reality through a process they called the **social construction of reality.**[24] Individuals create a background against which to understand their separate actions and interactions with others. When a social situation is a continuing one, the participants' interactions create a shared history resulting in **reciprocal typifications,** or mutual categorizations, of each other. Taken-for-granted routines emerge, based on shared expectations. Participants see this socially constructed world as legitimate by virtue of its "objective" existence. When problems arise, specific "universe-maintenance" procedures become necessary to preserve stability; such conceptual machineries as mythology, theology, philosophy, and science may be used. In short, people create cultural products: material artifacts, social institutions, ideologies, and so on (externalization); they lose awareness of having created their own social and cultural environment (objectification); and then they learn these supposedly objective facts of reality through the socialization process (internalization).

| BOX 1.2 | SOCIOLOGICAL PERSPECTIVES |

Functional Theory

- A stable, cooperative social system in which everything has a function is the basis of a harmonious society.
- Societal elements function together to maintain order and stability, a state of balance.
- Social problems, or dysfunctions, result from temporary disorganization or maladjustment.
- Rapid social change is the most frequent cause of loss of societal equilibrium.
- Necessary adjustments will restore the social system to a state of equilibrium.

Conflict Theory

- Society is continually involved in a series of disagreements, tensions, and clashes.
- Disequilibrium and change are the norm because of societal inequalities.
- If we know who benefits from exploitation, we understand why discrimination persists.
- False consciousness is a technique of maintaining power and control of resources.
- Group cohesiveness and struggle against oppression are necessary to effect social change.

Interactionist Theory

- This theory focuses on the microsocial world of personal interaction patterns in everyday life.
- Shared symbols and definitions provide the basis for interpretation of life experiences.
- A social construction of reality becomes internalized, making it seem like supposedly objective facts.
- Shared expectations and understandings, or lack of same, explain intergroup relations.
- Better communication and intercultural awareness improve majority–minority interaction patterns.

MINORITY GROUPS

Although the term *group* is commonly used to refer collectively to a racial or ethnic people, it is a very problematic word. **Group,** in its sociological usage, usually connotes a small, closely interacting set of persons. The term *minorities* sometimes refers to aggregates of millions of persons, clearly a size even larger than a **secondary group,** people who interact on an impersonal or limited emotional basis for some practical or specific purpose. Nonetheless, *group* is a familiar term to most readers, and with the above caveat in mind, I shall use that term throughout this book when referring to racial and ethnic groupings.

Development of a Definition

Sociologists use the term *minority* to designate not a group's numerical representation but rather its relative power and status in a society. The term was first used in the World War I peace treaties to protect approximately 22 million out of 110 million people in East Central Europe, but it was most frequently used as a description of biological features or national traits. Donald Young in 1932 thus observed that Americans make distinctions among people according to race and national origin.[25]

Louis Wirth expanded Young's original conception of minority groups to include the consequences of those distinctions: group consciousness and differential treatment.[26] The significance of Wirth's contribution was that it marked two important turning points in sociological inquiry. First, by broadening the definition to include any physical or cultural trait instead of just race or national origin, he enlarged the range of variables to include also the aged, the handicapped, members of various religions or sects, and groups with unconventional life-styles. Second, his emphasis on the social consequences of minority status leads to a focus on prejudice, discrimination, and oppression. Not everyone agrees with this approach. Richard Schermerhorn, for example, notes that this "victimological" approach does not adequately explain the similarities and differences among groups or analyze relationships between majority and minority groups.[27]

A third attempt to define minority groups rests on examining relationships between groups in terms of each group's position in the social hierarchy.[28] This approach stresses a group's social power, which may vary from one country to another, as, for example, does that of the Jews in Russia and in Israel. The emphasis on stratification instead of population size explains situations in which a small-sized group subjugates a larger number of people (for example, the European colonization of African and Asian populations). A variation on this viewpoint is represented by Schermerhorn. He also viewed social power as an important variable in the determination of a group's position in the hierarchy, but he believed that other factors were equally important. Size (a minority group must be less than one half the population), ethnicity (as defined by Wirth's physical and cultural traits), and group consciousness also help to define a minority group.[29]

Minority-Group Characteristics

As social scientists reached some consensus on a definition of minority groups, anthropologists Charles Wagley and Marvin Harris identified five characteristics shared by minorities worldwide:

1. The group receives unequal treatment compared to other groups.
2. The group is easily identifiable because of distinguishing physical or cultural characteristics that are held in low esteem.
3. The group feels a sense of peoplehood, that each of them shares something in common with others like themselves.
4. Membership in the minority group is **ascribed;** one is born into it.
5. Group members practice **endogamy;** they tend to marry within their group, either by choice or by necessity because of their social isolation.[30]

In our discussion of racial and ethnic minorities, these five features will serve as helpful guidelines. However, we should also understand that the last two characteristics do not apply to certain other types of minority groups: Women obviously do not fit the last category (causing some controversy over whether or not they are a minority group), nor necessarily do the aged or handicapped. One is not born old, and handicapped people are not always born that way.

Because our discussion of various minority groups rests on their subordination by a more powerful, although not necessarily larger group, we shall use the term **dominant group** when referring to a minority group's relationships with the rest of society. Another consideration is that dominant- and minority-group memberships are not mutually exclusive categories. For example, an American Roman Catholic who is white belongs to a prominent religious minority group but also is a member of the racially dominant group.

RACIAL AND ETHNIC GROUPS _____

Race may seem at first glance an easy way to group people, but it is not. Among the more than 5 billion humans inhabiting this planet, we find a wide range of physical differences in body build, hair texture, facial features, and skin color. Centuries of migration, conquest, intermarriage, and evolutionary physical adaptation to the environment have caused these varieties. Anthropologists have attempted racial categorizations, ranging from three to more than a hundred. Some, such as Ashley Montagu, even argue that only one race exists, the human race.[31] Just as anthropologists apply different interpretations to biological groupings, so do most people. It is in these social interpretations that sociologists attempt to analyze and explain racial prejudice.

Racial classification is a sociopolitical construct, not a biological absolute. In Latin America various gradations of race exist, reflecting the multiracial heritage of the people. Well over a million people of mixed racial parentage live in the United States, but here a more rigid racial categorization exists. Some social scientists have recently called for the "deconstruction of race," arguing against the artificial boundaries that promote racial prejudice.[32]

Racism may be defined as linking the biological conditions of a human organism with alleged sociocultural capabilities and behavior to assert the superiority of one race. When people believe one race is superior to another because of economic advantages or specific achievements, racist thinking prevails. The subordinate group will experience prejudice and discrimination, which the dominant group justifies by means of such perceptions. In this book we shall discuss how not only blacks but also Native Americans, Asians, Hispanics, and even white southern Europeans have encountered hostility because of social categorizations of their abilities based simply on their physical appearance.

Members of an ethnic group (which may or may not be racially different from the dominant group in a society) have a common cultural heritage. As Max Weber observed, they share a sense of belonging based on national origin, language, religion, and other cultural attributes.

The word *race* often is incorrectly used as a social rather than a biological concept. Thus the British and Japanese often are classified as races, as are Hindus, Latins, Aryans, Gypsies, Arabs, Native Americans, Basques, and Jews.[33] Many people, even sociologists, anthropologists, and psychologists, use *race* as the general rubric to include both racial and ethnic groups, thereby giving the term both a biological and a social meaning. Recently, *ethnic group* has been used more frequently as the general rubric to include the three elements of race, religion, and national origin.[34] Such varied use of these terms results in endless confusion, for racial distinctions are socially defined categories based on physical distinctions. Some groups, such as African Americans, were once defined on racial grounds but emerged as ethnocultural groups. Various ethnic groups often get lumped together in racial categories, such as Asians and Native Americans.

In this book the word *race* will refer to the common social distinctions made on physical appearance. The term *ethnic group* will refer only to social groupings that the dominant group considers unique because of religious, linguistic, or cultural characteristics. Both terms will be used when discussing groups with an overlapping of racial and ethnic characteristics.

THE DYNAMICS OF INTERGROUP RELATIONS

The study of intergroup relations is both fascinating and challenging because they are continually changing. The patterns of relating may change for many reasons: industrialization, urbanization, shifts in migration patterns, social movements, upward or downward economic trends, and so on. However, sometimes the changing relationships also reflect changing attitudes, as, for example, in the interaction between whites and Native Americans. Whites continually changed the emphasis: exploitation; extermination; isolation; segregation; paternalism; forced assimilation; and, more recently, tolerance for pluralism and restoration of certain, but not all, Native American ways. Similarly, blacks, Asians, Jews, Catholics, and other minority groups have all had varying relations with the host society.

Some recent world events also illustrate changing dominant group orientations toward minority groups. In 1982 economic difficulties prompted Nigerian leaders to expel once-welcomed immigrants from other African countries. A few years earlier Ugandan leader Idi Amin had expelled all Asians, who had formerly enjoyed harmonious relations in that country. After experiencing economic problems and numerous racial incidents, Britain severely curtailed its liberal immigration policy for the people of all its former colonies. When Iranians seized American hostages at the U.S. embassy in November 1979, hostile attitudes and actions against Iranian Americans in this country suddenly manifested themselves. Similarly, blacks and whites in South Africa, Hindus and Moslems in India, Moslems and Christians in Lebanon, Arabs and Jews in the Middle East, Catholics and Protestants in Northern Ireland, and many other groups too numerous to mention all go through varying periods of stability and instability in their dealings with one another.

The field of race and ethnic relations is alive with theoreticians and investigators examining changing events and migration patterns. Each year a vast outpouring of information from papers presented at meetings and from articles, books, and other sources adds to our knowledge. New insights, new concepts, and new interpretations of old knowledge inundate the interested observer. What both the sociologist and the student must attempt to understand, therefore, is not a fixed and static phenomenon but rather a dynamic, ever-changing one about which more is still being learned.

Retrospect

Human beings follow certain patterns when responding to strangers. Their perceptions of newcomers are a result of categoric knowing; if the perception is that the newcomers are similar, people are more receptive to their presence. What makes interaction with strangers difficult is the varying perceptions of each to the other, occasioned by a lack of shared understandings and perceptions of reality.

Ethnocentrism, the tendency to identify with one's own group, is a universal human condition contributing to potential problems in relating to outgroups. Examples of ethnocentric thinking and actions can be found in all countries throughout history. Eurocentrism and Afrocentrism are views emphasizing one culture or civilization over others.

The study of minorities presents a difficult challenge because our value orientations and life experiences can impair our objectivity. Sociologists, being human, also encounter difficulty in maintaining value neutrality. Some people argue that sociologists should take sides and not attempt a sterile approach to the subject.

Functional theory stresses the orderly interdependence of a society and the adjustments needed to restore equilibrium when dysfunctions occur. Conflict theorists emphasize the tensions and conflicts that result from exploitation and competition for limited resources. Interactionists concentrate on everyday interaction patterns operating within a socially constructed reality perception.

Minority groups, regardless of size, receive unequal treatment; possess identifying physical or cultural characteristics held in low esteem; have a self-consciousness about their shared ascribed status; and tend to practice endogamy. Racial groups are biologically similar groups, and ethnic groups are ones sharing a learned cultural heritage.

Key Terms

Afrocentrism	Interactionist Theory
Abstract Typifications	Minority Group
Ascribed Status	Outgroup
Categoric Knowing	Racial Group
Conflict Theory	Racism
Dominant Group	Reciprocal Typifications
Endogamy	Reference Group
Ethnocentrism	Social Construction of Reality
Eurocentrism	Social Distance
False Consciousness	Social Identity Theory
Functional Theory	Symbolic Interaction
Ingroup	Values

Review Questions

1. What is the difference between a race and an ethnic group? Between a minority group and an ethnic group?
2. What is ethnocentrism? Why is it important in relations between dominant and minority groups?
3. Why is the objective study of racial and ethnic minorities a difficult matter?
4. What are the focal points of the functional, conflict, and interactionist theories?

Suggested Readings

ALBA, RICHARD D. (ed.). *Ethnicity and Race in the U.S.A.* New York: Routledge, 1985.
    Anthology of articles analyzing the mainstreaming gains of various minority groups and goals yet to be achieved.

ASANTE, MOLEFI K. *The Afrocentric Idea*. Philadelphia: Temple University Press, 1987.
    Presents the provocative thesis that African culture permeates Western civilization and American black behavior.

BERGER, PETER L., AND THOMAS LUCKMANN. *The Social Construction of Reality.* Garden City, NY: Doubleday, 1963.
A highly influential work discussing how people define their reality and interact on the basis of shared expectations.

DOOB, CHRISTOPHER B. *Racism: An American Caldron.* New York: HarperCollins, 1993.
Examines the economic, political, and social forces that create racism, and their functions and consequences today.

LEVINE, ROBERT A., AND DONALD T. CAMPBELL. *Ethnocentrism: Theories of Conflict, Ethnic Attitudes, and Group Behavior.* New York: Wiley, 1972.
A detailed, analytical, and quantitative study of the interplay of ethnic attitudes and outgroup interactions.

SIMMEL, GEORG. "The Stranger," in *The Sociology of Georg Simmel,* Kurt H. Wolff (ed.). New York: Free Press, 1950.
A classic analysis of the role of the stranger made through an analysis of the formal structures of life.

SCHUTZ, ALFRED. "The Stranger," *American Sociological Review* 69 (May) 1944, 449–507.
An early, influential essay, still highly pertinent today, explaining the interaction problems of a stranger.

2

Culture and
Social Structure

Understanding what makes people receptive to certain strangers and not to others requires knowledge about the role of culture and social structure in affecting perceptions and response patterns. Culture provides the guidelines for people's interpretations of situations they encounter and the actions they should take. **Social structure,** the organized patterns of behavior among the basic components of a social system, establishes relatively predictable social relationships among the different peoples in a society. The distinctions and interplay between culture and social structure are important to the assimilation process as well. For example, cultural orientations of both minority and dominant groups shape expectations about how a minority group should fit into the society.

In this chapter we shall first examine the various aspects of culture impacting on dominant–minority relations. Following that will be a discussion of the significance of social class within the social structure. Both cultural and structural differentiation as a basis for conflict then comes under study, followed by varying cultural expectations about minority integration.

THE CONCEPT OF CULTURE _____

Human beings create their own social worlds. Adapting to environment, new knowledge, and technology, we learn a way of life within our society. We invent and share rules and patterns of behavior that shape our lives and the way we experience the world about us. Whether the actual material aspects of our society (cars, VCRs, Reeboks, and so on) or the nonmaterial components of our beliefs, values, and social institutions, these shared products of society that we call culture make social life possible and provide meaning to our lives. **Culture,** then, consists of the values, attitudes, customs, beliefs, habits, and physical or material objects that are shared by members of a society and transmitted to the next generation.

These cultural attributes provide a sense of peoplehood and common bonds through which societal members can relate (see Box 2.1). Most sociologists, therefore, emphasize the impact of culture in shaping behavior.[1]

| BOX 2.1 | **BASIC AMERICAN VALUES** |

Within this diverse American society of many different racial, ethnic, and religious groups with their distinctive sets of values exists a common core of Anglo-American values. Sociologist Robin Williams, after decades of study, has identified 15 value orientations, the foundation of our beliefs, behaviors, definitions of social goals, and life expectations. Some are contradictory—freedom, individualism, and external conformity; equality and group superiority; nationalism and freedom—and thus spark divisions among people. Still widely held by powerful groups, these values continue to have enormous impact in shaping our society.

1. **Achievement and Success.** Competition-oriented, our society places much value on gaining power, prestige, and wealth.
2. **Activity and Work.** We firmly believe in everyone working, and we condemn as lazy those who do not work.
3. **Moral Orientation.** We tend to moralize, seeing the world in absolutes of right and wrong.
4. **Humanitarian Mores.** Through charitable and crisis aid, we lean toward helping the less fortunate and the underdog.
5. **Efficiency and Practicality.** We seek problem solutions through the quickest and least costly means.
6. **Progress.** We think technology can solve all problems, and we hold an optimistic future outlook.
7. **Material Comfort.** We share the American Dream of a high standard of living and owning many material goods.
8. **Equality.** We believe in this abstract ideal, relating to each other informally, as equals.
9. **Freedom.** Individual freedom from domination of others is a highly cherished value.
10. **External Conformity.** Despite our professed belief in individualism, we join, conform, or go along, suspicious of those who do not.
11. **Science and Rationality.** We believe through science we can gain mastery over our environment and secure a better life-style.
12. **Nationalism.** We think the American way of life is the best and distrust "un-American" behavior.
13. **Democracy.** We believe everyone has the right of political participation, that our government is highly democratic.
14. **Individualism.** We emphasize personal rights and responsibilities, giving the individual priority over the group.
15. **Racism and Group Superiority Themes.** We place higher value on some racial, religious, or ethnic groups than on others through our attitudes and actions.

SOURCE: Robin M. Williams, Jr., *American Society: A Sociological Interpretation,* 3d ed. (New York: Knopf, 1970).

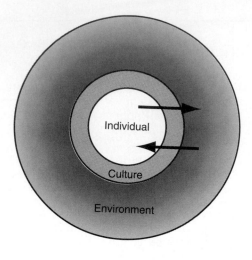

FIGURE 2.1
Cultural Reality
INDIVIDUAL observes the world
through SENSE PERCEPTIONS, which
are evaluated in terms of CULTURE:
values, attitudes, customs, and beliefs.

Through language and other forms of symbolic interaction, the members of a
society learn the thought and behavior patterns that constitute their commonality as a people.[2] In this sense culture is the social cement that binds a society
together.

Shared cultural norms encourage solidarity and orient the behavior of
members of the ingroup. **Norms** are a culture's rules of conduct—internalized
by the members—embodying the fundamental expectations of society.
Through norms ingroup members (majority or minority) know how to react
toward the acts of outgroup members that surprise, shock, or annoy them or
in any way go against their shared expectations. Anything contrary to this
"normal" state is seen as negative or deviant. When minority-group members
"act uppity" or "don't know their place," majority-group members often get
upset and sometimes act out their anger. Violations of norms usually result in
strong reactions because they appear to threaten the social fabric of a community or society. Eventually, most minority groups adapt their distinctive
cultural traits to those of the host society; this process is called **acculturation.**
Intragroup variations remain, though, because ethnic group members have
different reference groups they use as role models.

The Reality Construct

Our perception of reality is related to our culture; that is to say, through our
culture we learn how to perceive the world about us. Cultural definitions help
us to interpret the sensory stimuli from our environment and tell us how to
respond to them. Thus "culture is something that intervenes between the
human organism and its environment to produce actions."[3] It is the screen
through which we "see," and we cannot get rid of it (Figure 2.1).

Language and Other Symbols

Culture is learned behavior, acquired chiefly through verbal communication or language. A word is nothing more than a symbol—something that stands for something else. Whether it be tangible (*chair*) or intangible (*honesty*), the word represents a mental concept that is based on empirical reality. However, words reflect the culture, and one word may have different meanings in different cultures. If you have a *flat* in England, you have an apartment, not a deflated tire; if you could use a *lift,* you want an elevator, not a ride or a boost to your spirits. Because words symbolically interpret the world to us, the **linguistic relativity** of language may connote both intended and unintended prejudicial meanings. For example, the word *black* sometimes suggests dirty, or evil, and white sometimes suggests clean, or good, and these meanings may be subtly transferred to black and white people.

Walter Lippmann, a prominent political columnist, once remarked, "First we look, then we name, and only then do we see." What he meant was that until we learn the symbols of our world, we cannot understand the world. A popular pastime in the early 1950s called "Droodles" illustrates Lippmann's point. The object was to interpret drawings such as those in Figure 2.2. Many people were unable to see the meaning of the drawings until it was explained. They looked but did not see until they knew the "names."[4] Can you guess what these drawings are? (See "Notes" section for answers.)

Interpreting symbols not only is an amusing game but also is extremely significant in real life. Human beings do not respond to stimuli but to their definitions of those stimuli as mediated by their culture.[5] The definition of beauty is one example. Beyond the realm of personal taste, definitions of beauty have cultural variations. For instance, in different times and places a woman's beauty has been based on her having distended lips, scar markings, tattoos, or beauty marks, or on how plump or thin she was.

Nonverbal communication, or body language, is highly important, too. Body movements, gestures, physical proximity, facial expressions (there are between 100 and 136 facial expressions, each of which conveys a distinct meaning![6]), and **paralinguistic signals** (sounds but not words, such as a sigh, a kiss-puckering sound, or the *m-m-m* sound of tasting something good) all convey information to the observer-listener. Body language is important in

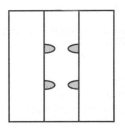 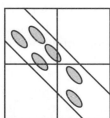 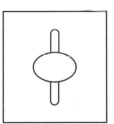 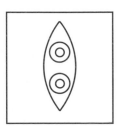

FIGURE 2.2
"Droodles"

intergroup relations, whether in conversation, interaction, or perception. Body language may support or belie one's words; it may suggest friendliness, aloofness, or deference.

Although some body language is fairly universal (for example, most facial expressions), many cultural variations exist in body language itself and in the interpretation of its meanings. Body movements such as posture, bearing, and gait vary from culture to culture. The degree of formality in a person's environment (both past and present) and other cultural factors have an influence on such forms of nonverbal communication. Consider the different meanings one could attach to a student's being unwilling to look directly into the eyes of a teacher. The Anglo teacher may consider this behavior to reflect embarrassment, guilt, shyness, inattention, or even disrespect. Yet if the student were Hispanic, such an action would be a mark of respect. The symbol's definition, in this case the teacher's interpretation of what the student's action means, determines the response.

A person who is foreign to a culture must learn both its language and the rest of its symbol system, as did the members of the culture through socialization. Certain gestures may be signs of friendliness in one culture but obscene or vengeful symbols in another. For example, in America, placing thumb and forefinger in a circle with the other fingers upraised indicates that everything is fine, but in Japan this sign refers to money, and in Greece it is an insulting anal expression.[7] Kisses, tears, dances, emblems, silence, open display of emotions, and thousands of other symbols can, and often do, have very different meanings in different cultures. Symbols, including language, help construct a reality for an ingroup that may be unknown to or altogether different for an outgroup. Members of one group may then select, reject, ignore, or distort their sensory input regarding the other group because of cultural definitions.

The Thomas Theorem

Many years ago William I. Thomas made an oft-repeated observation that if people define situations as real, those situations become real in their consequences.[8] His statement is further testimony to the truth of reality constructs: Human beings respond to their definitions of stimuli rather than to the stimuli themselves. People often associate images ("Yellow Peril," "Indian menace," for example) with specific minority groups. They then behave according to the meaning they assign to the situation, and the consequences of their behavior serve to reaffirm the meaning; the definition becomes a self-fulfilling prophecy. For example, when whites define blacks as inferior and then offer them fewer opportunities because of that alleged inferiority, the result is that blacks are disadvantaged, which in turn supports the initial definition.

Several variables determine the initial definition, but culture is a very important one. Culture establishes the framework through which an individual perceives others, classifies them into groups, and assigns them certain general characteristics. Because ethnocentrism leads people to consider their way of life as the best and most natural, their culturally defined perceptions of others often lead to suspicion and differential treatment of other groups. In effect, each group constructs myths about other groups and supports those myths through ingroup solidarity and outgroup hostility. As each group's attitudes and actions toward other groups continue, the **vicious-circle phenomenon** is at work.[9] In such instances people create a culturally determined world of reality, and their actions reinforce their beliefs. Social interaction or social change may counteract such situations, leading to their redefinition.

Gregory Razran conducted a study illustrating how cultural definitions can influence perception.[10] Twice within a 2-month interval, he showed the same set of 30 pictures of unknown young women to the same group of 100 male college students and 50 noncollege men. Using a five-point scale, the subjects rated each woman's beauty, character, intelligence, ambition, and general likableness. At the first presentation, the pictures had no ethnic identification, but at the second presentation, they had Irish, Italian, Jewish, and old American (English) surnames. All women were rated equally on the first presentation, but when the names were given, the ratings changed. The "Jewish" women received higher ratings in ambition and intelligence. Both "Jewish" and "Italian" women suffered a large decline in general likableness and a slight decline in beauty and character evaluations. This study is one of many illustrating how cultural definitions affect judgments about others.

Through **cultural transmission** each generation passes on its culture to the next generation, which learns those cultural definitions at an early age. This fact is dramatically expressed in the Rodgers and Hammerstein musical *South Pacific*. The tragic subplot is the touching romance between Lieutenant Cable and Liat. Although he and the Tonkinese girl are sincerely in love, his friends remind him that the couple's life would not be the same in America. Their differences in race and culture would work against a happy marriage for them, as would his own acceptance in Philadelphia high society. Miserable because of the choice his cultural values force him to make, he sings "Carefully Taught," a poignant song about how prejudice is taught to children:

> You've got to be taught to hate and fear,
>   You've got to be taught from year to year.
>   It's got to be drummed in your dear little ear,
>   You've got to be carefully taught.
>
> You've got to be taught to be afraid,
>   Of people whose eyes are oddly made,
>   Of people whose skin is a different shade.
>   You've got to be carefully taught.
>
> You've got to be taught before it's too late,
>   Before you are six or seven or eight,
>   To hate all the people your relatives hate.
>   You've got to be carefully taught.
>   You've got to be carefully taught.[11]

These lyrics help reinforce our understanding of the reality construct discussed earlier and illustrated in Figure 2.1. From family, friends, school, mass media, and all other sources of informational input, we learn our values, attitudes, and beliefs. Some of our learning reflects the prejudices of others, which we may incorporate in our own attitudes and actions.

CULTURAL CHANGE

Culture is continually changing. Discoveries, inventions, technological advances, innovations, or natural disasters can all alter the customs, values, attitudes, and beliefs of a society.

Cultural Diffusion

A striking paradox is that although the members of a dominant culture wish to keep their society untainted by the influence of foreign elements, all cultures are inevitably influenced by other cultures. Ideas, inventions, and practices spread from one culture to another, though the rate of diffusion varies considerably. Negative attitudes and a large distance between groups can be effective barriers, and sometimes cultural diffusion occurs only under the right conditions. Also, sometimes ideas are modified or reinterpreted before being accepted, such as when some Latin American Indian tribes of the early twentieth century showed a fondness for automobile tires: They used them to make sandals, for they neither owned nor drove cars.[12]

American anthropologist Ralph Linton calculated that any given culture contains about 90 percent borrowed elements. To demonstrate both the enormity and the subtlety of cultural diffusion, he offered a classic portrait of the "100 percent American" male.

> Our solid American citizen awakens in a bed built on a pattern which originated in the Near East but which was modified in Northern Europe before it was transmitted to America. He throws back covers made from cotton, domesticated in India, or linen, domesticated in the Near East, or wool, from sheep, also domesticated in the Near East, or silk, the use of which was discovered in China. All of these materials have been spun or woven by processes invented in the Near East. He slips into his moccasins, invented by the Indians of the Eastern woodlands, and goes to the bathroom, whose fixtures are a mixture of European and American inventions, both of recent date. He takes off his pajamas, a garment invented in India, and washes with soap, invented by the ancient Gauls. He then shaves, a masochistic rite which seems to have been derived from either Sumer or ancient Egypt.
>
> Returning to the bedroom, he removes his clothes from a chair of southern European type and proceeds to dress. He puts on garments whose form originally derived from the skin clothing of the nomads of the Asiatic steppes, puts on shoes made from skins tanned by a process invented in ancient Egypt and cut to a pattern derived from the classical civilizations of the Mediterranean, and ties around his neck a strip of bright-colored cloth which is a vestigial survival of the shoulder shawls worn by the seventeenth-century Croatians. Before going out for breakfast he glances through the window, made of glass invented in Egypt,

and if it is raining puts on overshoes made of rubber discovered by the Central American Indians and takes an umbrella, invented in southeastern Asia. Upon his head he puts a hat made of felt, a material invented in the Asiatic steppes.

On his way to breakfast he stops to buy a paper, paying for it with coins, an ancient Lydian invention. At the restaurant a whole new series of borrowed elements confronts him. His plate is made of a form of pottery invented in China. His knife is of steel, an alloy first made in southern India, his fork a medieval Italian invention, and his spoon a derivative of a Roman original. He begins breakfast with an orange, from the eastern Mediterranean, a cantaloupe from Persia, or perhaps a piece of African watermelon. With this he has coffee, an Abyssinian plant, with cream and sugar. Both the domestication of cows and the idea of milking them originated in the Near East, while sugar was first made in India. After his fruit and first coffee, he goes on to waffles, cakes made by a Scandinavian technique from wheat domesticated in Asia Minor. Over these he pours maple syrup, invented by the Indians of the Eastern woodlands. As a side dish he may have the egg of a species of bird domesticated in Indo-China, or thin strips of the flesh of an animal domesticated in Eastern Asia which have been salted and smoked by a process developed in northern Europe.

When our friend has finished eating he settles back to smoke, an American Indian habit, consuming a plant domesticated in Brazil in either a pipe, derived from the Indians of Virginia, or a cigarette, derived from Mexico. If he is hardy enough he may even attempt a cigar, transmitted to us from the Antilles by way of Spain. While smoking he reads the news of the day, imprinted in characters invented by the ancient Semites upon a material invented in China by a process invented in Germany. As he absorbs the accounts of foreign troubles he will, if he is a good conservative citizen, thank a Hebrew deity in an Indo-European language that he is 100 per cent American.*

Cultural diffusion is also an important element in ethnic relations within our pluralistic society. It can take many forms, including widened food preferences such as tacos or burritos, or use within American corporations of Japanese management techniques such as employee participation in setting work goals. Whatever the form, cultural diffusion is an ongoing process, influencing various aspects of our culture and sometimes our views of those of other peoples.

Culture Contact

Another way in which culture can undergo change is through people of different cultures coming into contact with one another. Because people tend to take their own culture for granted, it operates at a subconscious level in forming their expectations. When people's assumptions are jolted through contact with another culture with different expectations, they often experience **culture shock,** which is characterized by feelings of disorientation and anxiety and a sense of being threatened.

Culture shock does not always occur. When people of two different cultures interact, many possible patterns can emerge. The two groups may live in

*Ralph Linton, *The Study of Man* (1936), 326–327. Reprinted by permission of Prentice-Hall, Inc., Englewood Cliffs, N.J.

peaceful coexistence with a gradual cultural diffusion occurring. History offers some excellent examples of connections between migrations and innovations, wherein geographical conditions and native attitudes have determined the extent to which a group has resisted cultural innovations, despite invasions, settlements, or missionary work. The persistent pastoralism of Bedouin tribes and the long-sustained resistance to industrialization of the Native Americans are but two examples.[13] Stanley Lieberson, however, suggests that power alone determines the outcome, causing one group to become dominant and the other subservient.[14] If the subordinate group was not the migratory group, the changes to their social organization can be particularly devastating. No longer possessing the flexibility and autonomy they once enjoyed, they may suffer material deprivation and find their institutions undermined.

If the migratory group finds itself in the subordinate position, it must adapt to its new environment to survive. Most commonly the minority group draws from its familiar world as it attempts to cope with the different conditions. Group members form a subculture in which their behavior and interests are unique to themselves, not shared with others in the larger society. In doing so they create a modified version of the culture of the old country that also reflects the influence of the new country. For example, both Catholicism and Judaism have undergone changes in form and expression since taking root in America. Each of the ethnic subcultures has represented a blend of native and American cultures as group members have acclimated to their new environment.

Subcultures

Most large societies—especially complex, industrial ones—contain various subgroupings of people. Quite commonly people share some characteristics of the society at large, but they have other characteristics unique to their own group. Such groups are called subcultures, which can be regional, age-related, occupational, racial, ethnic, and so on.

Usually immigrants follow a **chain migration** pattern, settling in an area already containing family, friends, or compatriots who had located there earlier. An ethnic community evolves, providing an emotional support system to these strangers in a strange land striving to forge a better life for themselves. Part of this process of cultural insulation among others like themselves is the re-creation in miniature of the world they left behind. Appearing are **parallel social institutions**—their own clubs, organizations, newspapers, stores, churches, and schools duplicating those of the host society—which create cohesiveness within the minority subculture, whether an immigrant or native-born grouping.

As ethnic subcultures among immigrants in the United States evolved in response to conditions within the host society, the immigrants sometimes developed a group consciousness unknown in their old countries. Many first-generation Americans possessed a village orientation toward their homeland rather than a national identity. They spoke different dialects, feuded with other regions, and had different values. However, their common experience in the United States caused them to coalesce into a national grouping. One example is Italian Americans, who at first identified with their cities of origin: Calabria, Palermo, Naples, Genoa, Salerno, and so on. Within a generation many came to view themselves as Italians, partly because the host society classified them as such.

Yet even as a newly arrived group forges its community and subculture, a process called **ethnogenesis** occurs.[15] Shaped partly by the core culture in selectively absorbing some elements and modifying others, the group also retains, modifies, or drops elements from its cultural heritage in adapting to its new country. The result is a distinctive new ethnic group unlike others in the host country, dominant or minority, but also somewhat different from their countrymen still living in their homeland. Thus German Americans, for example, differed from other ethnic groups and native-born Americans, but also possessed cultural traits and values that distinguished them from non-migrating Germans.

Convergent Subcultures

Most white ethnic subcultures are *convergent;* that is, they tend toward assimilation with the dominant society. Although recognizable by residential clustering and adherence to the language, dress, and cultural norms of their native land, these ethnic groups are nonetheless becoming assimilated. As the years pass—possibly several generations—the distinctions between the dominant culture and the convergent subculture gradually lessen. Eventually this form of subculture becomes completely integrated into the dominant culture.

Because this subculture is undergoing change, its members may experience the problems of **marginality,** living under stress in two cultures simultaneously. The older generation may seek to preserve its traditions and heritage, but the younger generation may be impatient to be fully accepted within the dominant society. Because the impetus is to assimilate, time obviously favors the younger generation. Dutch, Germans, and Irish are some examples of once-prevalent ethnic subcultures barely visible today, and Italians, Poles, and Slovaks have also begun to converge more fully. These nationality groups still exhibit ethnic pride in many ways, but for the most part they are no longer set apart by place of residence or subcultural behavior. Based on their multigenerational length of residence, these nationality groups are less likely to live in clustered housing arrangements or to display particular behavior patterns, such as conflict, deviance, or endogamy, to any greater degree than the rest of the majority group.

Persistent Subcultures

Not all subcultures assimilate, some do not even desire to do so, and others, particularly nonwhite groups, have not been allowed to assimilate. Some steadfastly adhere to their own way of life as much as possible, resisting absorption into the dominant culture. Two relatively isolated religious groups, the Amish and the Hutterites, have long insisted on maintaining a way of life

Immigrant groups commonly attempt to preserve their special identity and cultural heritage within the minds of their children. As the assimilation process among the young takes its usual course, the adults seek to instill in them an awareness and appreciation of who and what they are, fearful that otherwise they will lose their sense of peoplehood and simply be absorbed into the dominant society. (*Katrina Thomas*)

different from that of the "ungodly" majority and may represent the purest form of a persistent subculture in American society. Other ethnic groups adopt a few aspects of the dominant culture but remain adamant about preserving their own way of life; examples are most Native Americans who live on reservations and many Spanish Americans in the Southwest. Chinatowns also manifest in many ways the preservation of the Chinese way of life.

A minority group's insistence on the right to be different has not usually been very well received among dominant-group members. This clash of wills has the potential for conflict; at the very least it is the breeding ground for stereotyping and prejudice on both sides (see Box 2.2 for an international example).

Just as convergent subcultures illustrate assimilation, persistent subcultures illustrate pluralism. We shall discuss these two forms of minority integration shortly.

STRUCTURAL CONDITIONS _____

Relationships between dominant and minority groups are influenced as much by structural conditions as by differences in culture. The nature of the

THE INTERNATIONAL SCENE

The 20 million Kurds are an ethnic group with their own language mostly living in the bordering lands of Iran, Iraq, and Turkey—a region known as Kurdistan, or "Land of the Kurds." After World War I this territory was partitioned among Turkey, Syria, and Iraq. Once a nomadic people who followed the seasonal migrations of their sheep and goat herds, the Kurds were thus compelled to abandon their traditional ways for village life and settled farming.

In the Kurdistan region the Kurds have remained a persistent subculture, whereas those living in urban areas are at least nominally assimilated. Marriages are typically endogamous, with a strong extended family network. The Kurds were once a tribal people under the firm leadership of a sheikh or an aga; however, that aspect of societal life is now felt in a much lesser degree only in the villages.

In 1924 the Turkish government engaged in cultural repression by renaming Kurds "Mountain Turks," outlawing their language, and forbidding their wearing the distinctive Kurdish costume in or near major cities. The government also encouraged many to migrate to the urbanized portion of western Turkey to dilute their population concentration. Uprisings in 1925, 1927–30, and 1937–38 were crushed with hundreds of thousands killed or expelled from the area.

Saddam Hussein's killing of thousands of Iraqi Kurds in 1988 with chemical weapons brought these relatively unknown people to the attention of Western cultures. Then came the Kurds dramatic flight from Hussein's military forces in the spring of 1991 across snowclad mountains. Encouraged by the coalition Gulf War victory, the Kurds had risen against the repressive Baghdad regime only to have Hussein's remaining forces drive them out. Iran let 1 million refugees cross its border to safety, but Turkey closed its border to about 500,000, trapping the Kurds in the mountains under harsh weather conditions. After 2 months the coalition enticed the Kurds back into Iraq into a designated "safe haven."

Today Kurds remain divided between assimilationist and nationalist goals. Facing varying degrees of government repression in all three countries, their future remains uncertain.

social structure influences not only the distribution of power resources (economic, political, and social) but also the accessibility of those resources to groups who are seeking upward mobility. An expanding economy and an open social system allow for increased opportunities for minority-group members, thereby reducing the possibility of tensions arising. A stagnant or contracting economy thwarts many efforts to improve status and antagonizes those who feel most threatened by another group's competition for scarce resources. Such a situation may breed conflicts among minority groups even more than between majority and minority groups, because the group next highest on the socioeconomic ladder may perceive a threat more quickly and react negatively.

The state of the economy is just one of the important structural factors influencing the opportunities for upward mobility. Another factor is the degree of change between a minority group's old society and the new one. A traditional or agrarian society will have a much more stable social structure than a society undergoing a transformation through industrialization. The latter society will offer dramatic changes in opportunities and life-styles, not all of them for the better. For a minority group migrating to another country, its compatibility with the social structure of the new land will be contingent on the degree of similarity with structural conditions in its homeland. A person who leaves an agrarian society for an industrial one is poorly prepared to do anything but enter the lowest stratum in a low-paying position. Opportunities for upward mobility, however, may exist if the economy is growing rapidly. In this sense the structural conditions of 1880 to 1920 were better for the unskilled immigrant than are conditions today. Low-skill jobs are not as plentiful today as they once were, and an unskilled worker's desire to support a family through hard work and sweat may not be matched by the opportunity to do so.

Another consideration is the advances made in technology that create a smaller world. Rapid transportation and communications (radio, television, telephone, telegraph, satellites, and airmail) make it possible for ties to other parts of the world to remain stronger than in the past.[16] Accessibility to one's homeland, friends, or relatives may make one less interested in becoming fully assimilated in a new land. Befriending strangers in the new country becomes less necessary. Additionally, people's greater knowledge of the world, the rising social consciousness of a society, and structural opportunities for mobility all help to create a more hospitable environment for minority-group members.

STRATIFICATION

Social stratification is the hierarchical classification of the members of society based on the unequal distribution of resources, power, and prestige. The word *resources* refers to such factors as income, property, and borrowing capacity. *Power,* usually reflected by the stratified layers, concerns the ability to influence or control others. *Prestige* relates to status, either *ascribed*—based on age, sex, race, or family background—or *achieved*—based on individual accomplishments.

The process of stratification may serve to moderate or exacerbate any strains or conflicts between groups, depending on the form that the stratification takes. The form can range from rigid to flexible and subtle; from the rigidity of slavery, caste, and forced labor to class distinctions and discrimination based on race or ethnic group. Whether racial and ethnic groups face insurmountable barriers or minor obstacles in achieving upward mobility is determined by the form of stratification. The more rigid the stratification, the more likely racial, religious, or other ideologies justifying the existing arrangements are to arise.

The form of stratification affects how groups within the various strata of society view one another. Some people confuse structural differentiation with cultural differentiation. For example, they may believe a group's low socioeconomic status is the result of its values and attitudes rather than the result of such structural conditions as racism, economic stagnation, and high urban unemployment. The form of stratification is an important determinant of the potential for intergroup conflict. In the United States both the possibility of upward mobility and structural obstacles to that possibility have existed. When the disparity between the perception of the American Dream and the reality of the difficulty of achieving it grows too great, the possibility of conflict increases.

SOCIAL CLASS

Social class is one categorization by which sociologists designate people's place in the stratification hierarchy; people in a particular social class have similar income, amount of property, degree of power, status, and life-style. Many factors help to determine a person's social class, including that individual's membership in particular racial, religious, and status groups. Although no clearly defined boundaries exist between class groupings in the United States, people have a tendency to cluster together according to certain socioeconomic similarities. The concept or image of social class reality results from sociopsychological distinctions people make about one another based, for example, on where they live and what they own as well as on the types of interactions that occur because of those distinctions.

In the 1930s W. Lloyd Warner headed a classic study of social-class differentiation.[17] Using the **reputational method**—asking people how others compared to them—Warner found a well-formulated class system existing. In Newburyport, Massachusetts, a small town of about 17,000 that he called "Yankee City," Warner identified six classes: upper-upper, lower-upper, upper-middle, lower-middle, upper-lower, and lower-lower. When he and his associates examined the distribution of ethnic groups among the various classes, certain factors emerged. First, a significant relationship existed between an ethnic group's length of residence and class status; the more recent arrivals tended to be in the lower classes. Other factors also were found to have an important influence on class status. An ethnic group tended to be less assimilated and less upwardly mobile if its population in the community was relatively large, if its homeland was close (such as in the case of the French Canadians), if its members had a sojourner rather than a permanent-settler orientation, and if limited opportunities for advancement existed in the community.[18]

Social class becomes important in intergroup relations because it serves as a basis for expectations. As Alan Kerckhoff states, social class provides a particular setting for the interplay between the formative experiences of a child, others' expectations of the child, and what kind of adult the child becomes.[19] Beyond this significant aspect, social class also serves as a point of reference in others' responses and in one's view of oneself. As a result, social class helps to shape an individual's world of reality and influences group interactions. Attitudes and behavior thus formed within a social-class framework are not immutable; they can change if circumstances change.

Class Consciousness

Just how important are the ethnic factors that Warner and others have reported in shaping an awareness of social class? The answer is that the significance of ethnic factors depends on a great many variables; some of these variables are economic conditions, mobility patterns, and prevailing attitudes. John Leggett found that class consciousness depends on the ethnic factor: The lower a group's ethnic status in the society, the higher the level of class consciousness.[20] Other studies have shown that working-class ethnic groups tend to view their class as hostile to, and under the political control of, the higher classes.[21]

Because ethnic minorities are disproportionately represented among the lower classes and because middle-class values dominate in the United States, a reasonable assumption is that at least some of the attitudes of each group result from people's value judgments about social class. That is to say, the dominant group's criticism and stereotyping of the minority group probably rests in part on class distinctions.

Ethnicity and Social Class

Social-class status plays an important role in determining a minority group's adjustment to and acceptance by society. For example, because the first waves of Cuban (1960s) and Vietnamese (1970s) refugees arrived possessing the education and occupational experience of the middle class, they succeeded in overcoming early native concerns and did not encounter the same degree of negativism as had earlier groups. On the other hand, when unskilled and often illiterate peasants have entered the lower-class positions in American society, many Americans have belittled, avoided, and discriminated against them because of their supposedly inferior ways. Frequently these attitudes and actions have represented an awareness of class differences as well as cultural differences. Because the dominant group usually represents a higher stratum in the social-class hierarchy, the differing social-class values and life-styles provide a source of friction in addition to the ethnic cultural differences.

Social class and ethnic group membership are closely intertwined, but, according to Colin Greer, many social observers have placed too much emphasis on ethnic-centered analyses and ignored the larger question of class:

This kind of ethnic reductionism forces us to accept as predetermined what society defines as truth. Only through ethnicity can identity be securely achieved. The result is that ethnic questions which could, in fact, further our understanding of the relationship of individuals to social structures are always raised in a way that serves to reconcile us to a common heritage of miserable inequities. Instead of realizing that the lack of a well-defined stratification structure, linked to a legitimated aristocratic tradition, led Americans to employ the language of ethnic pluralism in exchange for direct divisions by social class, we continue to ignore the real factors of class in our society. . . . What we must ultimately talk about is class. The cues of felt ethnicity turn out to be the recognizable characteristics of class position in this society: to feel black, Irish, Italian, Jewish has meant to learn to live in accommodation with that part of your heritage that is compatible with the needs and opportunities in America upon arrival and soon thereafter.[22]

In 1964, 10 years before Greer's observations, Milton Gordon first suggested that dominant-minority relations be examined within the larger context of the social structure.[23] This proposition marked an important turning point in racial and ethnic studies.[24] Although he believed that all groups would eventually become assimilated, Gordon offered an explanation of the present pluralistic society. His central thesis was that four factors or social categories play a part in forming subsocieties within the nation: ethnicity (by which Gordon also meant race), social class, rural or urban residence, and regionalism.[25] These factors unite in various combinations to create a number of **ethclasses.** These subsocieties result from the intersection of the stratifications of race and ethnic group with the stratifications of social class. Additional determinants are the rural or urban setting and the particular region of the country in which a group lives. Examples of ethclasses are lower-middle-class white Catholics in a northeastern city, lower-class black Baptists in the rural South, and upper-class white Jews in a western urban area.

Numerous studies have supported the concept that race and ethnicity, together with social class, are important in social structures and intergroup conflicts.[26] For example, social scientists such as Thomas Pettigrew and Charles Willie have argued that the intersection of race and class is a key element in understanding the continued existence of black poverty.[27] Not only do ethclass groupings exist, but also people tend to interact mostly within them for their intimate primary relationships. To the extent that this is true, multiple allegiances and conflicts will occur. According to this view, both cultural and structural pluralism currently exist; numerous groups presently coexist in separate subsocieties based on social class and cultural distinctions. Even those whose families have been here for several generations are affiliated with, and participate in, subsocieties. Gordon does, however, view assimilation as a linear process in which eventual assimilation, including structural, will occur.

Blaming the Poor or Society?

Beginning in 1932 with E. Franklin Frazier's conception of a disorganized and pathological lower-class culture, a controversial school of thought has existed that has become known as the **culture-of-poverty** theory.[28] The culmination of this idea came in 1965 with the release of a U.S. Department of Labor document known as the "Moynihan Report."[29] The report actually contained nothing new, relying heavily on Frazier's observations. However, this time it came from a federal government agency at a time when the civil rights movement was at its height. The report angered a great many people, including blacks, civil rights workers, and social workers.

Family Disintegration

In examining the problems of high unemployment, welfare dependency, illegitimacy, low achievement, juvenile delinquency, and adult crime, Moynihan argued that family deterioration was a major factor:

> At the heart of the deterioration of the fabric of Negro society is the deterioration of the Negro family. It is the fundamental source of weakness of the Negro community at the present time. . . . The white family has achieved a high degree of stability and is maintaining that stability. By contrast, the family structure of the lower class Negroes is highly unstable, and in many urban centers is approaching complete breakdown.[30]

Moynihan described black males as occupying an unstable place in the economy, which prevents their being strong fathers and husbands. This environment serves as a breeding ground for a continuing vicious cycle: The women often not only raise the children but also earn the family income. Consequently the children grow up in a poorly supervised, unstable environment; they often do not do well or stay in school; they can secure only low-paying jobs—and so the cycle begins anew.[31]

> At the center of the tangle of pathology is the weakness of the family structure. Once or twice removed, it will be found to be the principal source of most of the aberrant, inadequate, or anti-social behavior that did not establish but now serves to perpetuate the cycle of poverty and deprivation. . . .
>   What then is the problem? We feel that the answer is clear enough. Three centuries of injustice have brought about deep-seated structural distortions in the life of the Negro American. At this point, the present tangle of pathology is capable of perpetuating itself without assistance from the white world. The cycle can be broken only if these distortions are set right.[32]

Moynihan recently reaffirmed his position, citing the social deterioration since the 1960s, particularly the startling rise in out-of-wedlock births. "In 1963, 3 percent of white births in the nation were illegitimate, but 24 percent of black births were out of wedlock. By 1987, these ratios had increased to 16 percent for whites and 63 percent for blacks."[33] Moynihan also repeated a 1965 statement:

> From the wild Irish slums of the nineteenth-century Eastern seaboard, to the riot-torn suburbs of Los Angeles, there is one unmistakable lesson in American history: a community that allows a large number of young men to grow up in

broken families, dominated by women, never acquiring a stable relationship to male authority, never acquiring any set of rational expectations about the future—that community asks for and gets chaos. Crime, violence, unrest, disorder—most particularly the furious, unrestrained lashing out at the whole social structure—that is not only to be expected; it is very near to inevitable.[34]

In a highly discussed television documentary in 1986, Bill Moyers echoed Moynihan's message of a link between cultural value deficiencies and deteriorating conditions in black family life.[35]

Perpetuation of Poverty

The crux of the culture-of-poverty thesis, and its most controversial point, was the contention that distinctive lower-class values were transmitted from one generation to the next. Oscar Lewis gave perhaps the most persuasive commentary for the culture-of-poverty school in his introduction to his classic case study of a Puerto Rican family:[36]

> The culture of poverty, however, is not only an adaptation to a set of objective conditions of the larger society. Once it comes into existence it tends to perpetuate itself from generation to generation because of its effect on the children. By the time slum children are age six or seven they have usually absorbed the basic values and attitudes of their subculture and are not psychologically geared to take full advantage of changing conditions or increased opportunities which may occur in their lifetime.[37]

This proposition—that poverty continues because of subcultural patterns—has had important implications. Those who hold this view often believe that federal efforts to eliminate poverty would be more successful if they turned to a more direct, sociopsychological approach. Edward Banfield, for example, felt that this was the best solution to the poverty problem. He argued that good jobs, good housing, tripled welfare payments, new schools, quality education, and armies of police officers would not stop the problem. He continued:

> If, however, the lower classes were to disappear—if, say, its members were overnight to acquire the attitudes, motivations, and habits of the working class—the most serious and intractable problems of the city would all disappear with it. . . . The lower-class forms of all problems are at bottom a single problem: the existence of an outlook and style of life which is radically present-oriented and which therefore attaches no value to work, sacrifice, self-improvement, or service to family, friends, or community.[38]

Public opinion once supported the culture-of-poverty hypothesis. Although many social scientists decry the view, pre-1972 survey polls indicated the majority of Americans thought the poor were responsible for their own poverty. For example, in one national cross section of adults, 53 percent said that the poor were at fault for their dilemma and 22 percent felt that the social structure was at fault. In contrast, a 1988 *Newsweek* poll found that 42 percent of whites and 44 percent of blacks faulted society compared to 29 percent of the whites and 30 percent of the blacks who blamed the poor for staying poor.[39]

Other Explanations

Critics of the culture-of-poverty school have argued that fatalism, apathy, low aspiration, and other similar orientations are situational responses within each generation and are not passed down. In 1963 Michael Harrington's *The Other America* helped spark the federal government's "War on Poverty" program. He maintained that society was to blame for poverty:

> The real explanation of why the poor are where they are is that they made the mistake of being born to the wrong parents, in the wrong section of the country, in the wrong industry, or in the wrong racial or ethnic group.[40]

Critics such as William Ryan and Charles Valentine contend that poverty can be eliminated only by first recognizing that the problem is caused by society and that lower-income people are the victims, not the offenders. The blocked life opportunities may result from discrimination, structural conditions, or stratification rigidity, for example.

To Ryan, blaming the victim results in misdirected social programs. By rationalizing away the socially acquired stigma of poverty as the result of a genetic character defect, we ignore the continuing effect of current victimizing social forces. As a result we attempt to help the "disorganized" black family instead of overcoming racism, or we strive to develop "better" attitudes and skills in low-income children rather than revamping the poor-quality schools they attend.[41]

Valentine argues that many of Lewis's "class distinctive traits" of the poor are either "externally imposed conditions" (unemployment, crowded and deteriorated housing, and lack of education) or "unavoidable matters of situational expediency" (hostility toward social institutions and low expectations and self-image).[42] The poor, suggests Valentine, possess many positive values and behavior patterns similar to the middle class, but their life situation has obliged them to develop some distinctive subcultural traits in order to cope and survive. Only changes in the total social structure and in the resources made available to the poor will bring about changes in any subcultural traits of survival.

Similarly, others have argued that all people would desire the same things and cherish the same values if they were in an economic position to do so. Because they are not, they adopt an alternative set of values in order to survive.[43] Eliot Liebow, in a participant-observer study of lower-class black males, concluded that they try to achieve many of the goals of the larger society but fail for many of the same reasons as their fathers did: discrimination, unpreparedness, lack of job skills, and self-doubt.[44] The similarities between generations are due not to cultural transmission but to the sons'

This youth at an L.A. tent city for the homeless is one of more than 12 million children under age 18 living in poverty. Struggling to survive, they can easily fall victim to poor education, street violence, and blocked life opportunities as adults. Unless a change occurs, many are on a life's journey to nowhere. (*Gene Richards/Magnum*)

independent experience of the same failures. What appears to be a self-sustaining cultural process is in reality a secondary adaptation to an adult inability to overcome structural constraints.

The debate between those who argue that ghetto culture is the product of **economic determinism** (through structural differentiation) and those who believe it is caused by **cultural determinism** (persistence of a culture of poverty) continues. A person's attitudes toward welfare, toward the urban poor, who are mostly racial and ethnic minorities, and toward different orientations to life all reflect the individual's beliefs about this issue. About the only common ground shared by the two schools of thought is their mutual support of increased employment and educational opportunities.

Scientific studies have failed to document an actual culture of poverty among ghetto residents.[45] Furthermore, no evidence exists of the presence of confused sexual identifications, delinquency, or other pathological conditions directly resulting from absence of a father.[46] Moreover, investigators often found evidence of great strength in poor black families, with an extended-family structure of several generations headed by competent and emotionally strong women maintaining family stability within a positive home environment.[47]

Yet some sociologists believe the economic determinist and cultural determinist positions can be reconciled. Hyman Rodman suggested that all social classes share the general values of a society but that the lower class, while not rejecting those values, adopts additional values representing realistic levels of attainment. The lower class does not reject the less attainable values of the majority society but adopts a value-stretch approach, or a wider range of values.

> Lower-class persons . . . do not maintain a strong commitment to middle-class values that they cannot attain, and they do not continue to respond to others in a rewarding or punishing way simply on the basis of whether these others are living up to the middle-class values. A change takes place. They come to tolerate and eventually to evaluate favorably certain deviations from the middle-class values. In this way they need not be continually frustrated by their failure to live up to unattainable values. The resultant is a stretched value system.[48]

L. Richard Della Fave adds that this **value-stretch** approach of the poor occurs when the gap between ideal value preference and achievement expectations becomes too great.[49] In other words the poor do not have different values but different behaviors resulting from coping mechanisms. Since they expect less, they become satisfied with less.

INTERGROUP CONFLICT

Is conflict inevitable when culturally distinct groups interact? Do structural conditions encourage or reduce the probability of conflict? Robert E. Park concluded in 1949 that a universal cycle of events repeatedly occurs in all countries, making conflict always a reality. In Park's day the term *race* referred to racial and ethnic groups, and his comments should thus be given the broader application.

Park saw an inevitable process that was irreversible and could take a long time. The stages of this cycle were contact between the groups, then competition, followed by some kind of adjustment or accommodation. The final stage was assimilation and amalgamation.

> The race relations cycle which takes the form, to state it abstractly, of contact, competition, accommodation, and eventual assimilation, is apparently progressive and irreversible. Customs regulations, immigration restrictions, and racial barriers may slacken the tempo of the movement; may perhaps halt it altogether for a time; but cannot change its direction, cannot, at any rate, reverse it. . . . It does not follow that because the tendencies to the assimilation and eventual amalgamation of races exist, they should not be resisted and, if possible, altogether inhibited. . . . Rising tides of color and oriental exclusion laws are merely incidental evidences of this diminishing distance. . . . In the Hawaiian Islands,

where all the races of the Pacific meet and mingle . . . the native races are disappearing and new peoples are coming into existence. Races and cultures die—it has always been so—but civilization lives on.[50]

Park's theory fit nicely into the prevailing assimilationist thinking of his time, but there are several problems with his race-relations cycle. By its very nature this hypothesis of an inevitable cycle is not testable.[51] Park could not cite any racial group that had passed through all four stages. Instead of seeing these negative data as refuting the theory, Park and other cyclical theorists explained the lack of assimilation as the result of obstacles or interference. As a result of such tautological reasoning, this theory lacks an essential element of empirical science: It cannot be proved or disproved.[52] Moreover, the universality of the cyclical theory falters because there are cases in which conflict and competition did not occur when different groups came into contact.

Conflict does not necessarily occur when different peoples make contact. Brazil and Hawaii are just two examples of places where relatively peaceful and harmonious interactions have existed among different peoples. In many other instances of intergroup relations, however, some form of stress, tension, or conflict does occur. In this chapter we have presented the major factors that may set the stage for such conflict: cultural and structural differentiation. Those factors may be applied to an understanding of conflict between dominant and minority groups.

Cultural Differentiation

When similarities between the minority group and the indigenous group exist, the probability is that the relationship will be relatively harmonious and that assimilation will eventually occur.[53] The greater and more visible the cultural differences, the greater the likelihood that conflict will occur. When large numbers of German and Irish Catholics came to this country in the mid-nineteenth century, Protestant America grew uneasy. As priests and nuns also arrived and as the Catholics built churches, convents, and schools, Protestant America became alarmed at what it considered a papal conspiracy to gain control of the country. Emotions ran high, and the result was unrest and violence.

Religion often is a basis for cultural conflict, as demonstrated by the examples of the treatment of Mormons, Jews, and Quakers, who have all suffered discrimination in this country. Yet many other aspects of cultural visibility also can serve as sources of contention. Cultural differences may range from clothing (for example, Sikh turbans and saris) to leisure activities (for example, Hispanic cockfights). Americans once condemned the Chinese as opium smokers, even though the British had introduced opium smoking into China and promoted it among the lower-class Chinese population.

Cultural differences do not necessarily cause intergroup conflict. Part of the explanation about variance in relations between culturally distinct groups comes from interactionist theory. As you will recall, this perspective holds that the extent of shared symbols and definitions between groups in mutual intercommunication determines the nature of interaction patterns. Although it is true that actual differences may provide a basis for conflict, interactionists say the key to harmonious or disharmonious relations lies in the definitions or interpretations of those differences. Tolerance or intolerance, acceptance or rejection of others thus depends on perceptions of others as threatening or nonthreatening, assimilable or nonassimilable, worthy or unworthy.

Structural Differentiation

Because they offer macrosocial analyses of a society, both functional theory and conflict theory provide a basis for understanding how structural conditions affect intergroup relations. Functionalists seek explanations in the adjustments needed in the social system to compensate for other changes. Conflict theorists emphasize the conscious, purposeful actions of dominant groups to maintain systems of inequality.

Functional Analysis

Sometimes economic and technological conditions facilitate minority integration. When the economy is healthy and jobs are plentiful, newcomers find it easier to get established and work their way up the socioeconomic ladder. In present-day America, however, technological progress has reduced the number of low-status, blue-collar jobs and increased the number of high-status, white-collar jobs, which require more highly skilled and educated workers. The result is that fewer jobs are available for unskilled, foreign, marginal, or unassimilated people.

Perhaps because of the importance of one's job as a source of economic security and status, **occupational mobility**—the ability to improve one's job position—seems to be an important factor in determining whether prejudice will increase or decrease. A number of studies have shown that downward social mobility increases ethnic hostility.[54] Bruno Bettelheim and Morris Janowitz report from seven studies that persons moving downward in status are not only more prejudiced than the group they left but also more prejudiced than the lower-status group they enter. Additionally, upwardly mobile people are generally more tolerant than nonmobile individuals.[55] It would appear that loss of status and prestige increases hostility toward outgroups, whereas upward gains enable people to be more magnanimous toward others.

Conflict Analysis

If one group becomes dominant and another becomes subservient, obviously one group has more power than the other. Social-class status partly reflects this unequal distribution of power, which also may fall along racial or ethnic lines. For ethnicity to become a basis for stratification, it appears that several factors must be present:

In their English as a Second Language class, these minority women learn word processing as a means to bolster their English proficiency. Such technological methodology also teaches job skills to aid the foreign-born in their cultural and structural assimilation into the mainstream of American society. (© 1992 Mark Ludak/Impact Visuals)

Ethnic stratification will emerge when distinct ethnic groups are brought into sustained contact only if the groups are characterized by a high degree of ethnocentrism, competition, *and* differential power. Competition provides the motivation for stratification; ethnocentrism channels the competition along ethnic lines; and the power differential determines whether either group will be able to subordinate the other.[56]

This **power differential** is of enormous importance in race and ethnic relations. If the stratification system is rigid, as in a slave or caste system, with no hope or means of improving status, then intergroup relations may be stable though perhaps far from mutually satisfactory. Dominant power, whether expressed in legalized ways or through structural discrimination, intimidation, or coercion, maintains the social system.

Even if the stratification system allows for upward mobility, some members of the dominant group may believe that the lower-class racial and ethnic groups are challenging the social order as they strive for their share of the "good life." If the dominant group does not feel threatened, the change will be peaceful. If the minority group meets resistance but retains hope and a sense of belonging to the larger society, the struggle for more power will be within the system (for example, by means of demonstrations, boycotts, voter-registration drives, or lobbying) rather than through violence.[57] The late nineteenth-century race-baiting riots on the West Coast against Chinese and Japanese workers, as well as the 1919 Chicago race riots against blacks entering the meat-packing industry, illustrate violent responses of a dominant group against a minority group over power resources. Similarly, the recent black–Korean violence in several urban neighborhoods, including during the 1992 Los Angeles riots, as well as the violence between blacks and Cubans in Miami in 1988, typify minority-group clashes over limited resources.

Social-Class Antagonisms

Conflict theorists, such as Ralf Dahrendorf, suggest that social class is an important variable affecting conflict. Dahrendorf maintains that a correlation exists between a group's economic position and the intensity of its conflict with the dominant society. The greater the deprivation in economic resources, social status, and social power, the more probable it is that the weaker group will resort to intense and violent conflict to achieve gains in any of these three areas. As the social-class position of a group increases, intergroup conflict will be less intense and less violent.[58]

Years earlier Max Weber argued that when economic resources become more evenly distributed among classes, relative status will become the issue of conflict, if conflict occurs at all.[59] Conflict occurs not only because a lower-class group seeks an end to deprivation but also because the group next higher on the socioeconomic ladder feels most threatened. Quite often the working-class group displays the most prejudice and most frequently engages in violence against the upward-striving minority group. Other factors may be at work, but status competition is significant in causing conflict.

Social-class antagonisms also influence people's perceptions of racial and ethnic groups.[60] Some social scientists maintain that the problem of black–white relations is more a problem of social class than of racism. James M. O'Kane illustrates this view:

> The gap exists between the classes, not the races; it is between the white and black middle classes on the one hand, and the white and black lower classes on the other. Skin color and the history of servitude do little to explain the present polarization of the classes. . . . Class differentials, not racial differentials, explain the presence and persistence of poverty in the ranks of the urban Negro.[61]

O'Kane suggests several parallels between Irish, Italian, and Polish immigrants and Southern blacks who migrated to Northern cities (the Chinese, some of the Japanese, and others also could be included). All came from agrarian poverty to industrial slums. Encountering prejudice and discrimination, some sought alternative routes of upward mobility: crime, ethnic politics, or stable but unskilled employment.[62] Other social scientists argue that the black experience does not equate with that of European immigrants. They hold, as did the Kerner Commission investigating the urban riots of the late 1960s, that the dominant society's colonization of blacks deprived them of the strong social organizations that other groups had. Moreover, today's labor market offers fewer unskilled jobs for blacks than it once offered for other immigrant groups, thereby depriving blacks of a means to begin moving upward.[63]

This debate about race versus social class as the primary factor in assessing full integration of blacks in America continues to rage, particularly among black social scientists. We shall devote more attention to this topic in a subsequent chapter on African Americans.

THEORIES OF MINORITY INTEGRATION _____

Over 60 million immigrants have come to the United States since its founding as a nation. During this extensive migration, three different theories have emerged concerning how these ethnically different peoples either should or did fit into American society. These schools of thought are (1) **assimilation,** or the majority-conformity theory; (2) **amalgamation,** or the "melting-pot" theory; and (3) **accommodation,** or the pluralistic theory.

The type of interaction between minority peoples and those of the dominant culture has been partly dependent on which of these ideologies was then accepted by those already established in the community. People formulate attitudes and expectations based on the values they hold. If those values include a clear image of how an "American" should look, talk, and act, then people who are different from that model will find their adjustment and acceptance by others a more difficult matter. Conversely, if those values allow for diversity, then a greater possibility exists that harmonious relationships will evolve.

Assimilation

Generally speaking, **assimilation** means the functioning of racial or ethnic minority-group members within a society without any marked cultural, social, or personal differences from the people of the majority group. Physical or racial differences may persist, but they do not serve as the basis for group prejudice or discrimination. In effect the minority groups no longer appear to be strangers because they have forsaken their own cultural traditions and successfully imitated the dominant group. Assimilation may thus be described as $A + B + C = A$.[64]

Anglo-Conformity
Because the majority of the people living in the United States during the eighteenth century were of English descent, English influence on the new

nation's culture was enormous—in language, institutional forms, values, and attitudes. By the first quarter of the nineteenth century, a distinct national consciousness had emerged, and many wanted to deemphasize their English origins and influences. However, when migration patterns changed the composition of the American population in the 1880s, the Yankees reestablished the Anglo-Saxon as the superior archetype.[65] Anglo-Saxonism remained dominant well into the twentieth century as the mold into which any newcomers must fit.

To preserve their Anglo-Saxon heritage, Americans often attempted, sometimes with success, to curtail the large numbers of non-Anglo-Saxon immigrants. For those who did come, social pressures demanded that they shed their native culture and attachments as quickly as possible and be remade into Americans along cherished Anglo-Saxon lines. The schools served as an important socialization agent in promoting the shedding of cultural differences.

Sometimes insistence on assimilation reached feverish heights, as evidenced by the **Americanization** movement during World War I. The arrival of so many "inferior" people in the preceding 30 years and the participation of the United States in a European conflict caused questions to be raised about those who were not "100 percent American." Governmental agencies at all levels, together with many private organizations, acted to implement more immediately foreigners' adoption of American practices: citizenship, reverence for American institutions, and use of the English language.[66] Because this policy required that all minority groups divest themselves of their distinctive ethnic characteristics and adopt those of the dominant group, George R. Stewart suggested that it be called the "transmuting pot" theory.[67]

Other assimilation efforts have not been very successful—for example, with people whose ancestral history in an area predates the nation's expansion into that territory. Most Indian tribes throughout the country as well as the Mexican Americans of the Southwest have resisted this cultural hegemony. In fact, some critics argue that assimilation has not yet occurred for most racial and ethnic groups.

Types of Assimilation

Milton Gordon has suggested assimilation has several aspects or subprocesses.[68] One early phase is **cultural assimilation** or **acculturation**, the change of cultural patterns to those of the host society. **Marital assimilation** or **amalgamation**, the large-scale intermarriage with members of the majority society, is another phase. Most important, cultural assimilation (acculturation) and **structural assimilation** (large-scale entrance into the cliques, clubs, and institutions of the host society on a primary-group level) best reveal the extent of acceptance of minority groups in the larger society.

Other types of assimilation are (1) **identificational assimilation**, the development of a sense of peoplehood or ethnicity based exclusively on the host society, not on one's homeland; (2) **attitude-receptional assimilation**, reaching the point of encountering no prejudiced attitudes; (3) **behavior-receptional assimilation,** reaching the point of encountering no discriminatory behavior; and (4) **civic assimilation**, the absence of value and power conflict with the native-born population.

Gordon states that "Once structural assimilation has occurred, either simultaneously with or subsequent to acculturation, all other types of assimilation will naturally follow."[69] Other sociologists disagree with Gordon, claiming that cultural assimilation does not necessarily result from structural assimilation. Some studies have shown that structural assimilation has not yet occurred to any significant degree.[70]

Louis Wirth maintained that situational variables are important in the assimilation of minority groups.[71] Wirth distinguished among pluralism, assimilation, secession, and militancy as successive minority responses to majority-group prejudice and discrimination. As groups begin to gain some power, they generally attempt to gain social tolerance of the group's differences *(pluralism)*, then go beyond this and become absorbed by the dominant society *(assimilation)*. Those groups who are prevented from assimilating eventually withdraw *(secession)*, but if conflict then ensues, they seek more extreme remedies *(militancy)*.

Assimilation may be both a majority-group and a minority-group goal, but it is also possible that one or both may view assimilation as undesirable. Accordingly, the preceding typologies are not always helpful when examining dominant-minority relationships. Gordon shows the complexity of the assimilation process; Wirth suggests that the dynamics of the situation shape the evolvement of dominant-minority relations throughout the assimilation process. The larger question, whether the assimilation process is linear, remains in all cases. Not all groups seek assimilation, and not all groups who seek assimilation attain it.

Assimilation—as a belief, goal, or pattern—helps explain many aspects of dominant-minority relations, particularly acceptance and adjustment. For many members of the dominant society, assimilation of minorities has meant their absorption into the mold, reflecting what Barbara Solomon calls "the Anglo Saxon complex."[72] For physically or culturally distinct groups (for example, blacks, Indians, Asians, or Moslems), such a concept has raised an often insurmountable barrier. Even without the Anglo-Saxon role model, assimilation has been preceded by a transitional period in which the newcomer has gradually blended in with majority-group members. In doing so the individual has acquired a new behavioral identity, perhaps at some personal cost.

The Melting Pot Theory

The democratic experiment in America fired many an imagination. Here a new society was being shaped, peopled by immigrants from different European nations and not slavishly dependent on the customs and traditions of the past. This set of circumstances generated a romantic notion of America as a melting pot. The **melting pot theory**, or the theory of amalgamation, states that all the diverse peoples blend their biological and cultural differences into an altogether new breed—the American. This concept may be expressed as $A + B + C = D$.[73]

Advocates

J. Hector St. John de Crèvecoeur, a French settler in New York, first popularized the idea of a melting pot. Envisioning the United States as more than just a land of opportunity, de Crèvecoeur in 1782 spoke of a new breed of humanity coming forth from the new society. That Crèvecoeur included only white Europeans partly explains the weakness of this approach to minority integration.

> What is an American? He is either a European, or the descendant of a European; hence that strange mixture of blood which you will find in no other country. I could point out to you a man whose grandfather was an Englishman, whose wife was Dutch, whose son married a French woman, and whose present four sons have now four wives of different nations. He is an American, who, leaving behind him all his ancient prejudices and manners, receives new ones from the new mode of life he has embraced, the new government he obeys and the new rank he holds. . . . Here individuals of all nations are melted into a new race of men, whose labors and posterity will one day cause great changes in the world.[74]

This idealistic concept found many advocates over the years. In 1893 Frederick Jackson Turner updated it with his frontier thesis, a notion that greatly influenced historical scholarship for more than 40 years. Turner believed that the challenge of frontier life was the catalyst that fused the immigrants into a composite new national stock within an evolving social order:

> Thus the Middle West was teaching the lesson of national cross-fertilization instead of national enmities, the possibility of a newer and richer civilization, not by preserving unmodified or isolated the old component elements, but by breaking down the line-fences, by merging the individual life in the common product—a new product, which held the promise of world brotherhood.[75]

In 1908 English author Israel Zangwill's play *The Melting-Pot* began an extraordinarily popular run, enthusiastically etching a permanent symbol on the assimilationist ideal:

> There she lies, the great melting pot. Listen! Can't you hear the roaring and the bubbling? There gapes her mouth—the harbor where a thousand mammoth feeders come from the ends of the world to pour in their human freight. Ah, what a stirring and a seething—Celt and Latin, Slav and Teuton, Greek and Syrian. America is God's Crucible, the great Melting Pot where all the races of Europe are melting and reforming!—Here you stand good folk, think I, when I see you at Ellis Island, here you stand, in your fifty groups, with your fifty languages and histories, and your fifty hatreds and rivalries. But you won't be long like that, brothers, for these are the fires of God you come to—these are the fires of God! . . . Germans and Frenchmen, Irishmen and English, Jews and Russians, into the Crucible with you all! God is making the American! . . . the real American has not yet arrived . . . He will be the fusion of all races, perhaps

the coming superman. . . . Ah, Vera, what is the glory of Rome and Jerusalem, where all races and nations come to worship and look back, compared with the glory of America, where all races and nations come to labor and look forward.[76]

Both the frontier thesis and the melting-pot concept have since come under heavy criticism. Although many people still pay homage to the melting pot concept, few social scientists still accept this explanation of minority integration into society. Nevertheless, many Americans still hold this view. Arguments against bilingual education, the "English-only" movement, and exclusive emphasis on Western heritage are but a few examples.

Did We Melt?

Over several generations intermarriages frequently have occurred between people of different nationalities and, to a lesser degree, of different religions and, to a still lesser degree, of different races. One could thus argue that a biological merging of previously distinct ethnic stocks, although not so much of different races, has taken place.[77] However, the melting pot theory spoke not only of intermarriages among the different groups but also of a distinct new national culture evolving from elements of all other cultures. Here the theory has proven unrealistic. This country, from its founding, has been dominated by an Anglo-Saxon population and thus by the English language and Anglo-Saxon institutional forms. Rather than a melting of various cultural patterns into a new American culture, what actually has occurred is a metamorphosis of elements of minority cultures into the Anglo-Saxon mold.

Milton Gordon suggests that only in the institution of religion have minority groups altered the national culture; the United States is now a land of three major faiths: Protestant, Catholic, and Jewish.[78] Some social observers have viewed the emergence of three major faiths as evidence that America was actually a "**triple melting pot**." Based on her studies in New Haven in 1944 and 1952, Ruby Jo Reeves Kennedy concluded that intermarriage was occurring between various nationalities but only within the three major religious groupings.[79] A few years later Will Herberg echoed this analysis, arguing that ethnic differences were disappearing as religious groupings became the primary foci of identity and interaction.[80] Subsequent studies have offered conflicting evidence of assimilation versus pluralism based on religion, national origin, social class, and residence. We shall examine some of these findings shortly.

In other areas the entry of many diverse minority groups into American society has not resulted in new social structures or institutional forms in the larger society. Instead, subcultural social structures and institutions have evolved to meet group needs, and the dominant culture has benefited from the labors and certain cultural aspects of minority groups within the already existing dominant culture. For example, minority influences are found in word usage, place names, cuisine, architecture, art, and recreational activities, as well as in jazz and Latin music.

Sociologist Henry Pratt Fairchild offered a physiological analogy for comprehending how the absorption of various cultural components or peoples explains assimilation and dismisses amalgamation.[81] An organism consumes

"Uncle Sam's Troublesome Bedfellows"
This cartoon pictures Uncle Sam annoyed by groups that were seen as unassimilable. Both racial differences (blacks, Chinese, and Indians) and religious differences (Catholics and Mormons) were cause for being kicked out of the symbolic bed. This cartoon appeared in a San Francisco illustrated weekly, *The Wasp,* on February 8, 1879. (*The Distorted Image, courtesy Anti-Defamation League of B'nai B'rith, John and Selma Appel Collection*)

food and is somewhat affected (nourished) by it; the food, though, is assimilated in the sense that it becomes an integral part of the organism, retaining none of its original characteristics. This is a one-way process. In a similar manner American culture has remained basically unchanged, though strengthened, despite the influx of many minority groups.

Most social scientists now believe that the melting pot theory is a myth and always has been. Its idealistic rhetoric has attracted many followers and still does. In reality, the melting meant Anglo-conformity, being remade according to the idealized Anglo-Saxon mold. Herberg offered some observations on the theory of Anglo-conformity as opposed to the idea of the melting pot:

> But it would be a mistake to infer from this that the American's image of himself—and that means the ethnic group member's image of himself as he becomes American—is a composite or synthesis of the ethnic elements that have gone into the making of the American. It is nothing of the kind; the American's image of himself is still the Anglo-American ideal it was at the beginning of our independent existence. The "national type" as ideal has always been, and re-

mains, pretty well fixed. It is the *Mayflower*, John Smith, Davy Crockett, George Washington, and Abraham Lincoln that define the American's self-image, and this is true whether the American in question is a descendant of the Pilgrims or the grandson of an immigrant from southeastern Europe.[82]

The rejection of the melting pot theory by many people, coupled with an ethnic consciousness, spawned the third ideology, cultural pluralism.

Pluralism

Pluralism recognizes the persistence of racial and ethnic diversity, as in Canada where multiculturalism is both recognized and official policy. Pluralist theorists argue that minorities can maintain their distinctive subcultures and simultaneously interact with relative equality in the larger society. In countries such as Switzerland and the United States, this combination of diversity and togetherness is possible in varying degrees because the people agree on certain basic values (see Box 2.1). At the same time minorities may interact mostly among themselves, live within well-defined communities, have their own forms of organizations, work in similar occupations, and marry within their own group. Applying our descriptive equation, pluralism would be $A + B + C = A + B + C$.[83]

Early Analysis

Horace Kallen is generally recognized as the first exponent of cultural pluralism. In 1915 he published "Democracy Versus the Melting Pot," in which he rejected the assimilation and amalgamation theories.[84] Not only did each group tend to preserve its own language, institutions, and cultural heritage, he maintained, but also the very nature of democracy gave them the right to do so. To be sure, minority groups learned the English language and participated in American institutions, but what the United States really had become was a "cooperation of cultural diversities." Seeing Americanization movements as a threat to minority groups and the melting pot notion as unrealistic, Kallen believed that cultural pluralism could be the basis for a great democratic commonwealth. A philosopher, not a sociologist, Kallen nonetheless directed scholarly attention to a practice that many Americans had long followed.

Pluralistic Reality

From its colonial beginnings the United States has been a pluralistic country. Early settlements were small ethnic enclaves, each peopled by different nationalities or religious groups. New Amsterdam and Philadelphia were exceptions, both heavily pluralistic within their boundaries. Chain migration patterns resulted in immigrants settling in clusters. Germans and Scandinavians in the Midwest, Poles in Chicago, Irish in New York and Boston, French in Louisiana, Asians in California, Cubans in Miami, and many others all illustrate how groups ease adjustment in a new country by re-creating in miniature the world they left behind. Current immigrant groups and remnants of past immigrant groups are testimony to the pluralism in American society.

As Gordon observes, "Cultural pluralism was a fact in American society before it became a theory—at least a theory with explicit relevance for the nation as a whole and articulated and discussed in the general English-speaking circles of American intellectual life."[85] **Cultural pluralism,** two or more culturally distinct groups living in the same society in relative harmony, has been the more noticeable form of pluralism. **Structural pluralism,** the coexistence of racial and ethnic groups in subsocieties within social class and regional boundaries, is less noticeable but also existent. Many minority groups lose their visibility because they have acculturated but may retain identification with and pride in their heritage and maintain primary relationships mostly with members of their ethclass. Despite this pluralistic reality in America, we need to remember that much intolerance of such diversity has been, and continues to be, a problem within our society.

Retrospect

Culture provides the definitions by which members of a society perceive the world about them. Language and other forms of symbolic interaction provide the means through which this knowledge is perceived and transmitted. Becoming acculturated requires learning both the language and the symbol system of the society. Unless it is isolated from the rest of the world, a society undergoes change through culture contact and the diffusion of ideas, inventions, and practices. Within large societies subcultures usually exist. They may be gradually assimilated (convergent subcultures), or they may remain distinct (persistent subcultures).

Structural conditions also influence people's perceptions of the world, whether they live in an industrialized or agrarian society, a closed or open social system, a growing or contracting economy, a friendly or unfriendly environment, or whether or not their homeland, friends, and relatives are accessible. Distribution of power resources and compatibility with the existing social structure will greatly determine majority–minority relations as well. Interactionists concentrate on the perceptions of cultural differences as they affect intergroup relations. Functionalists and conflict theorists emphasize the structural conditions.

The interplay between the variables of race, ethnic group, and social class are important for understanding how some problems and conflicts arise. What often gets mistaken for an attribute of race or ethnic groups may be a broader aspect of social class. Because many attitudes and values are situational responses to socioeconomic status, a change in status or opportunities will also bring about a change in those attitudes and values. Investigative studies have not supported the culture-of-poverty hypothesis of family disintegration and a self-perpetuating poverty value orientation.

Three theories of minority integration have evolved since the nation's beginning. The romantic notion of a melting pot, in which a new breed of people with a distinct culture would emerge, proved unrealistic. Assimilation, or majority-conformity, became a goal of many, both native-born and foreign-born; yet not all sought this goal or were able to achieve it. Finally, pluralism emerged as a school of thought in recognition of the persistence of ethnic diversity in a society with a commonly shared core culture.

Key Terms

Accommodation	Marital Assimilation
Acculturation	Melting Pot Theory
Amalgamation	Norms
Anglo-Conformity	Parallel Social Institutions
Assimilation	Persistent Subculture
Chain Migration	Pluralism
Convergent Subculture	Power Differential
Culture	Race
Culture-of-Poverty	Reputational Method
Cultural Assimilation	Social Class
Cultural Determinism	Social Structure
Cultural Differentiation	Structural Assimilation
Cultural Diffusion	Structural Conditions
Cultural Pluralism	Structural Differentiation
Cultural Transmission	Structural Pluralism
Economic Determinism	Thomas Theorem
Ethclass	Triple Melting Pot Theory
Ethnogenesis	Value Stretch
Marginality	Vicious-Circle Phenomenon

Review Questions

1. What is the relationship between culture, reality, and intergroup relations?
2. What are subcultures? What forms do they take? What significance do these forms have for intergroup relations?
3. What is the relationship between a society's structural conditions and intergroup relations?

4. What is meant by the culture of poverty? What criticisms exist about this thinking?
5. How do the functional, conflict, and interactionist perspectives approach factors likely to contribute to intergroup conflict?
6. Discuss the major theories of minority integration.

Suggested Readings

ABRAMSON, HAROLD J. "Assimilation and Pluralism," in *Harvard Encyclopedia of American Ethnic Groups,* Stephan Thernstrom, Ann Orlov, and Oscar Handlin (eds.). Cambridge, MA: Harvard University Press, 1980, 150–160.
    A fine essay discussing the two major elements affecting intergroup relations in a multiethnic society.

GORDON, MILTON M. *Assimilation in American Life.* New York: Oxford University Press, 1964.
    A highly influential and still pertinent book offering an analysis of the role of race and ethnicity in American life.

HALL, EDWARD T. *The Silent Language.* Garden City, NY: Doubleday, 1959.
    Excellent introduction to how nonverbal communication conveys cultural values and behavior characteristics, often leading to misunderstandings.

MORRIS, DESMOND. *Manwatching: A Field Guide to Human Behavior.* New York: Abrams, 1977.
    Helpful book, with extensive color photo illustrations, about importance of expressions, gestures, signals, and actions in human behavior.

NEWMAN, WILLIAM M. *American Pluralism.* New York: Harper & Row, 1973.
    A comprehensive analysis of pluralism in American society, synthesizing the contributions of other social scientists.

WILLIAMS, ROBIN M., JR. *American Society: A Sociological Interpretation.* New York: Random House, 1970.
    Useful examination of American culture, with influential analysis of impact of norms and values on social life.

YANKELOVICH, DANIEL. *New Rules.* New York: Random House, 1981.
    Summary evaluation of changed American norms and attitudes about cultural pluralism and self-fulfillment, based on national surveys.

3

Prejudice and Discrimination

When strangers from different groups come into contact with one another, the resulting interaction patterns may take many forms. So far we have discussed the role that ethnocentrism, social distance, culture, and social structure play in shaping perceptions of any outgroup. Prejudice and discrimination also emerge as major considerations in understanding intergroup relations. Why do they exist? Why do they persist? Why do certain groups become targets more frequently? How can we eliminate prejudicial attitudes and discriminatory actions?

PREJUDICE

The word *prejudice* is derived from the Latin word *praejudicium* and originally meant prejudgment. Thus some scholars defined a prejudiced person as one who hastily reached a conclusion before examining the facts.[1] However, this definition proved inadequate because social scientists discovered that prejudice often arose *after* groups came into contact and had at least some knowledge of one another. For that reason Louis Wirth described prejudice as "an attitude with an emotional bias."[2]

Because feelings shape our attitudes, they reduce our receptivity to additional information that may alter those attitudes. Ralph Rosnow had this fact in mind when he broadened the definition of prejudice to encompass "any unreasonable attitude that is unusually resistant to rational influence."[3] In fact, a deeply prejudiced person is one who is almost totally immune to information. Gordon Allport offers a classic example of such an individual in the following dialogue:

Mr. X: The trouble with the Jews is that they only take care of their own group.

Mr. Y: But the record of the Community Chest campaign shows that they gave more generously, in proportion to their numbers, to the general charities of the community, than did non-Jews.

Mr. X: That shows they are always trying to buy favor and intrude into Christian affairs. They think of nothing but money; that is why there are so many Jewish bankers.

Mr. Y: But a recent study shows that the percentage of Jews in the banking business is negligible, far smaller than the percentage of non-Jews.

Mr. X: That's just it; they don't go in for respectable business; they are only in the movie business or run night clubs.*

It is almost as if Mr. X is saying, "My mind is made up; don't confuse me with the facts." He does not refute the argument; rather, he ignores the new and contradictory information and moves on to a new area in which he distorts other facts to support his prejudice against Jews.

Prejudicial attitudes may be either positive or negative; however, negative prejudice is of primary concern to the sociologist studying minorities because only negative attitudes can lead to turbulent social relations between dominant and minority groups. Numerous writers, therefore, have defined prejudice as an attitudinal "system of negative beliefs, feelings, and action-orientations regarding a certain group or groups of people."[4] The status of the strangers is an important factor in the development of a negative attitude. Prejudicial attitudes exist among members of both the dominant and minority groups. When seeking to understand the nature of relations between dominant and minority groups, it is important to realize that the antipathy felt between groups is quite often prevalent on both sides.

Levels of Prejudice

Bernard Kramer suggests that prejudice exists on three levels: cognitive, emotional, and action orientation.[5]

Cognitive Level

The **cognitive level** refers to a person's beliefs and perceptions of a group as threatening or nonthreatening, inferior or equal (for example, in terms of intellect, status, or biological composition), seclusive or intrusive, impulse-gratifying, acquisitive, or possessing other positive or negative characteristics. Mr. X's cognitive beliefs are that Jews are intrusive and acquisitive. Other illustrations of cognitive beliefs are that the Irish are heavy drinkers and fighters, blacks are musical and lazy, and the Polish are thick-headed and unintelligent. Generalizations shape both ethnocentric and prejudicial attitudes, but there is a difference. *Ethnocentrism* is a generalized rejection of all outgroups based on an ingroup focus, whereas **prejudice** is a rejection of certain people solely on the basis of their membership in a particular group or groups.

In many societies majority-group members often believe that a particular low-status minority group is "dirty," "immoral," "violent," or "law-breaking." In the United States the Irish, Italians, blacks, Mexicans, Chinese, Puerto Ricans, and others have at one time or another been labeled with most, if not all, of these adjectives. In most European countries and the United States, the group that was lowest on the socioeconomic ladder has often been

*Gordon W. Allport, *The Nature of Prejudice* (Reading, MA: Addison-Wesley, 1954), 13–14.

depicted in caricature as also lowest on the evolutionary ladder. The Irish and blacks in the United States, and peasants and ethnic groups in Europe, have each been pictured at one time as apelike in cruel jokes and cartoons.

> The Victorian images of the Irish as "white Negro" and simian Celt, or a combination of the two, derived much of its force and inspiration from physiognomical beliefs . . . [but] every country in Europe had its equivalent of "white Negroes" and simianized men, whether or not they happened to be stereotypes of criminals, assassins, political radicals, revolutionaries, Slavs, gypsies, Jews or peasants.[6]

Emotional Level

The **emotional level** refers to the feelings that a minority group arouses in an individual. Although these feelings may be based on stereotypes from the cognitive level, they represent a more intense stage of personal involvement. The emotional attitudes may be negative or positive, such as fear, distrust, trust, disgust, sympathy, nonsympathy, contempt, admiration, envy, or anger. These feelings, based on beliefs about the group or groups, may come about through social interaction or the possibility of interaction. For example, whites might react with fear or anger to the integration of their schools or neighborhoods, or Protestants might be jealous of the life-style of a highly successful Catholic business executive.

Action-Orientation Level

An **action orientation** is the positive or negative predisposition to engage in discriminatory behavior. If someone harbors strong feelings about members of a certain racial or ethnic group, that individual may have a tendency to act for or against them—being aggressive or nonaggressive, offering assistance or withholding it. Such individuals would also be likely to want to exclude or include members of that group both in their close, personal social relations and in their peripheral social relations. For example, some people would want to exclude members of the disliked group from doing business with them or living in their neighborhood. Another manifestation of the action-orientation level of prejudice is the desire to change or maintain the status differential or inequality between the two groups, whether the area be economic, political, educational, social, or a combination. Note that an action orientation refers to a predisposition to act, not the action itself.

Stereotyping

One of the most common reactions to strangers is broad categorization of them. Prejudice at the cognitive level often is the result of false perceptions of others that are enhanced by either cultural or racial stereotypes. A **stereotype** is an oversimplified generalization by which we attribute certain traits or characteristics to any person in a group without regard to individual differences. Most cultural stereotypes emphasize variance from societal norms.

"Mutual: Both Are Glad There Are Bars Between 'Em!"
This visual stereotype of an apelike Irishman reinforced prevailing beliefs that the Irish were emotionally unstable and morally primitive. This cartoon appeared in *Judge* on November 7, 1891, and is typical of a worldwide tendency to depict minorities as apelike. (*The Distorted Image, courtesy Anti-Defamation League of B'nai B 'rith, John and Selma Appel Collection*)

Racial stereotypes suggest that there are peculiarities about certain traits or characteristics that are hereditary and will thus continue, regardless of what society does. Both forms of stereotypes are doubly abusive. Not only do they deny an individual the right to be judged and treated on the basis of merit, but also, by being applied to the image of the entire group, they become a justification for discriminatory behavior.

Negative stereotypes also serve as important reference points in people's evaluations of what they observe in everyday life. Following is an excellent illustration of how we attribute motives and causes that are consistent with our stereotypes to other people's behavior:

> Prejudiced people see the world in ways that are consistent with their prejudice. If Mr. Bigot sees a well-dressed, white, Anglo-Saxon Protestant sitting on a park bench sunning himself at three o'clock on a Wednesday afternoon, he thinks

nothing of it. If he sees a well-dressed black man doing the same thing, he is liable to leap to the conclusion that the person is unemployed—and he becomes infuriated, because he assumes that his hard-earned taxes are paying that shift-less good-for-nothing enough in welfare subsidies to keep him in good clothes. If Mr. Bigot passes Mr. Anglo's house and notices that a trash can is overturned and some garbage is strewn about, he is apt to conclude that a stray dog has been searching for food. If he passes Mr. Garcia's house and notices the same thing, he is inclined to become annoyed, and to assert that "those people live like pigs." Not only does prejudice influence his conclusions, his erroneous conclusions justify and intensify his negative feelings.[7]

Once established, stereotypes are difficult to eradicate, even among suc-ceeding generations. Evidence of the pervasiveness and persistence of ste-reotypes came by comparing responses of college students over several gen-erations. Provided with a list of 84 adjectives, the researchers asked the students to select five that they thought described the most characteristic traits of 10 racial and ethnic groups (see Appendix I).[8] Although each group became increasingly reluctant to make such generalizations, a high level of uniformity nonetheless marked their responses.

Notably, students either showed a tendency to agree on the same attributes others had chosen in earlier studies or picked a similar new adjective. Positive stereotypes regarding work achievement continued for Americans, Germans, Japanese, and Jews. Emotional stereotypes for Irish and Italians, a carefree image for "Negroes" (the acceptable word then), a negative stereotype for Turks, a positive and conservative image for English, and commitment to family and tradition for Chinese, all remained constant generalizations over the 35-year span. Other recent studies have reported similar findings.[9]

Both majority-group and minority-group members may hold stereotypes about each other. The ready acceptance of such generalized labeling often begins with some small basis in fact applying to just a few individuals, which is then erroneously applied to everyone in that group. Social barriers between the two groups, mass-media portrayals reinforcing the stereotypes (see Box 3.1), and societal pressures to conform to the stereotype combine to suggest the validity of such thinking, enabling people to ignore contrary evidence.

Ethnophaulisms

An **ethnophaulism** is a derogatory word or expression used to describe a racial or ethnic group. This is the language of prejudice, the verbal picture of a negative stereotype, reflecting the prejudice and bigotry of a society's past and present. Howard J. Ehrlich suggests that ethnophaulisms can be of three types: (1) disparaging nicknames (chink, dago, polack, jungle bunny, or honky); (2) explicit group devaluations ("jew him down" for trying to get something for a lower price, "luck of the Irish" suggesting undeserved good fortune, or "to be in Dutch" meaning to be in trouble); (3) irrelevant ethnic names used as a mild disparagement ("jewbird" for black cuckoos having

BOX 3.1 THE IMPACT OF THE MEDIA

As a reflector of society's values, the media have a tremendous impact on the shaping of our personal and group identities. Radio, television, films, newspapers, magazines, and comics can convey the rich textures of a pluralistic society or they can, directly or indirectly (by omission and distortion), alter our perception of other ethnic groups and reinforce our defensiveness and ambivalence about our own cultural backgrounds. As an Italian-American, I've realized this myself when comparing the ethnic invisibility of 50s television with modern shows that concentrate on Mafia hit men and multiple biographies of Mussolini. Having squirmed as I watched some of these portrayals, I can empathize with Arabs who resent being characterized as villainous sheikhs, Jews seen as mendacious moguls or even the current vogue for matching a Russian accent with a kind of oafish villainy. Although such stereotypes may or may not serve political ends, they share the cartoonlike isolation of a few traits that ignore the humanity and variety of a group's members.

What is the impact of ethnic stereotypes on TV and in film on how people feel about themselves and how they perceive other ethnic groups?

Although research in this area is limited, what is available suggests that TV and films's portrayal of ethnics does have a deleterious effect on perceptions of self and others. In my own clinical work, I have found that minority children and adults will often internalize negative stereotypes about their own group. Other studies have shown that ethnic stereotypes on television and in the movies can contribute to prejudice against a particular group—especially when the person is not acquainted with any members of that group. . . .

In studies of youngsters who commit hate acts—desecration of religious institutions, racial and anti-Semitic incidents—many youngsters apprehended reported they got the idea of performing vandalism from news coverage of similar acts (the copy cat syndrome). They saw media coverage as conferring recognition and prestige, temporarily raising their low self-esteem.

Add to TV fiction and news the rash of "truly tasteless" joke books, radio call-in shows that invite bigoted calls from listeners, late-night TV hosts and comedians who denigrate ethnic groups, and the impact on people's perceptions is considerable. While the media cannot be blamed for creating the bigotry, their insensitive reporting and encouragement of inflammatory comments establishes a societal norm that gives license to such attitudes and behavior.

SOURCE: Joseph Giordano, "Identity Crisis: Stereotypes Stifle Self-Development," *Media & Values* (Winter 1987), 13.

prominent beaks, "welsh" on a bet signifying failure to honor a debt, or "Irish confetti" for bricks thrown in a fight).[10]

Both majority and minority groups coin and use these ethnophaulisms, or ethnic slurs, for other outgroups. Such usage helps justify discrimination, inequality, and social privilege for the majority, and helps the minority cope with social injustices caused by others. *Them* versus *us* name-calling is not only divisive but indicative of the state of intergroup relations. Erdman Palmore, for example, concluded that all racial and ethnic groups use ethnophaulisms. He also observed that a correlation exists between the number of them used and the degree of group prejudice, and also that they express and support negative stereotypes about the most visible racial or cultural differences.[11]

Ethnophaulisms seem to appear most often during times of major social and economic change, such as migration or immigration waves, rapid urbanization or technological change, recessions and depressions, or war. Linguistic experts have identified about 1,200 ethnic slur-names or epithets used in historic American speech.[12] Most of them are obsolete today, although a few still remain and other new ones still appear almost yearly.

Sometimes members of a racial or ethnic minority group will use an ethnophaulism directed against themselves in their conversations with one another. On occasion they may use the term as a reprimand to one of their own kind for acting out the stereotype, but more often they mean it as a humorous expression of friendship and endearment. However, when an outsider uses that same term, they resent it because of its prejudicial derision.

Ethnic Humor

Why do some people find ethnic jokes so funny, whereas others find them distasteful? Studies show the response often reflects the listener's attitude toward the group being ridiculed. If you hold favorable or positive attitudes toward the group that is the butt of the joke, then you are less likely to find it funny than if you hold unfavorable or negative views. If you dislike a group about which a joke implies something negative, you will tend to appreciate the joke much more than others.[13]

Sometimes people tell or laugh at derogatory jokes about their own group. Jeffrey Goldstein suggests several reasons for such action. One is to strengthen ingroup cohesiveness by reminding members of the perceptions and threats of outgroups. Another is to dissociate oneself from stereotypes of one's group through self-disparaging group humor. A third possibility is that we use ethnic humor to affirm ourselves, point out the absurdity of our predicaments, and objectify our faults and make them laughable. The key to ethnic humor, then, lies in both the joker's and audience's attitudes.[14]

Television Influence

Virtually every American household owns at least one television set, with families averaging over seven hours of TV viewing daily. Does all this viewing make us think or act differently? Does it change our attitudes or shape our feelings and reactions about minority groups? Or is it only entertainment with no appreciable effect on perceptions and behavior? Abundant research evidence indicates television programming distorts reality; promotes stereotypical role models; and significantly shapes and reinforces our attitudes about men, women, and minority groups.

Perpetuates Stereotypes

Twice in the late 1970s, the U.S. Commission on Civil Rights charged the television industry with perpetuating racial and sexual stereotypes in programming and news.[15] Aside from the almost exclusively negative racial portrayals on police shows over the preceding six years, the report attacked the television industry for portraying "a social structure in which males are very much in control of their lives . . . older, more serious, more independent, and more likely to hold prestigious jobs. Women, on the other hand, were younger, often unemployed, more 'family bound,' and often found in comic roles. Those women who were employed were in stereotyped and sometimes subservient occupations."

In 1982 media expert George Gerbner continued the criticism, arguing that little had changed since the commission's reports.[16] A tiny percentage of black characters, for example, were "unrealistically romanticized," but the overwhelming majority of them were in subservient, supporting roles—such as the white hero's comic sidekick. Gerbner commented:

> When a black child looks at prime time, most of the people he sees doing interesting things are white. That imbalance tends to teach young blacks to accept minority status as naturally inevitable and even deserved.[17]

In the 1990s the blatant stereotypes have faded, but more subtle ones remain. Terrorists are likely to be Arabs, single mothers to be welfare black, gang members Hispanic, and gardeners Asian. The popular television show "In Living Color" gets denounced by some for perpetuating racial and gay stereotypes, although others disagree. Still, blacks, Asians, Hispanics, and women have made significant gains in television, both on and behind the camera.[18]

Influences Attitudes

Television influences attitudes toward racial or ethnic groups by the status of the parts assigned to their members, the kind of behavior they display within these parts, or even the type of products they promote. Television greatly influences children's attitudes in this area. Sheryl Graves, for example, found how positive and negative portrayals of black characters in cartoons affected black and white children's attitudes toward blacks. She found a positive attitude change among black children seeing either portrayal and among white children seeing a positive portrayal. The most dramatic change, however, was in a negative direction for white children exposed to even a single program showing blacks portrayed negatively. Conversely, the more a child watches

"Sesame Street," the less likely it is that that child will have negative attitudes toward blacks.[19]

"All in the Family," a popular comedy series in the 1970s and now in syndicated reruns, received an NAACP award for its contribution to race relations but divided critics as to its reducing or reinforcing racial bigotry.[20] Finding an explanation for both views, Neil Vidmar and Milton Rokeach reported findings that selective perception, prior attitudes determining reactions, governed viewers' affective responses.[21] Liberal viewers saw the program as satire, with son-in-law Mike effectively rebutting Archie's ignorance and bigotry or minority members besting Archie by the end of the program. In contrast, prejudiced viewers—particularly adolescents—were significantly more likely to admire Archie over Mike and to perceive Archie as winning in the end. Although most respondents indicated they thought Mike made better sense than Archie, highly prejudiced adolescents were significantly more likely to perceive Archie as making better sense. It appears the program was more likely reinforcing prejudice and discrimination than combating it.

Ingroup and Outgroup Perceptions

Two months before a 1986 racial attack in that area made national headlines, a study of 1,200 students at a public high school in the Howard Beach area of Queens in New York City revealed their attitudes toward race and ethnicity in real life and on television.[22] The school had been chosen because it contained a multiethnic population, with large numbers of black, Hispanic, and Italian American students and smaller groups of Irish and Asian descent.

One-fourth of these students said TV shows what life and people are really like and that TV influences their racial and ethnic attitudes. Their responses to 20 TV ethnic characters as positive or negative, as well as being realistic, revealed broad patterns of consistent responses (see Table 3.1). Generally, group members saw their portrayed group members more favorably and as typical than did nonmembers.

Causes of Prejudice

There appears to be no single cause of prejudice but, rather, many causes that are frequently interrelated. Because fear and suspicion of outgroups are so widespread, scholars and scientists once believed that prejudice was a natural or biological human attribute. Today, because of increased knowledge about the growth of prejudices in children and about the varying patterns of interaction throughout world history, behavioral scientists realize that prejudices are socially determined. A great many theories exist concerning exactly how we become prejudiced.

Socialization

In the **socialization** process individuals acquire the values, attitudes, beliefs, and perceptions of their culture or subculture, including religion, nationality, and social class. Generally, the child conforms to the parents' expectations in

TABLE 3.1	REASONS FOR WATCHING TV, BY ETHNIC GROUP (IN PERCENTAGES)						

	Ethnic group						
Reasons for watching	Asian	Black	Hisp.	Jew.	Ital.	Irish	All
It brings my family together.	18	23	20	10	14	13	18
I learn a lot from it.	35	51	36	24	28	31	40
It shows how others solve problems I have.	41	38	36	31	34	27	37
I get to know different people.	35	42	33	24	26	27	34
It teaches things I don't learn in school.	26	32	26	16	17	11	27
It shows what life is really like.	29	28	27	14	19	13	25
I learn how to act.	9	12	11	2	7	2	10
It keeps me from being bored.	94	86	78	86	88	89	85

SOURCE: S. Robert Lichter and Linda S. Lichter, "Television's Impact on Ethnic and Racial Images," American Jewish Committee, 1986. Reprinted by permission.

acquiring an understanding of the world and its people. Being young and therefore impressionable and knowing of no alternative conceptions of the world, the child usually accepts these concepts without questioning. We thus learn the prejudices of our parents and others, and they subtly become a part of our values and beliefs. Even if they are based on false stereotypes, prejudices shape our perceptions of various peoples and influence our attitudes and actions toward particular groups. For example, if we develop negative attitudes about Jews because we are taught that they are shrewd, acquisitive, and clannish—all-too-familiar stereotypes—as adults we may refrain from business or social relationships with them. We may not even realize the reason for such avoidance, so subtle has been the prejudice instilled within us.

People may learn certain prejudices because of their pervasiveness. The cultural screen that we develop and through which we view the world around us is not always accurate, but it does reflect shared values and attitudes, which are reinforced by others. Prejudice, like cultural values, is taught and learned through the socialization process. The prevailing prejudicial attitudes and actions often are deeply embedded in custom or law (for example, Jim Crow laws), and the new generation may accept them as proper, maintaining them in their adult lives.

Although socialization explains how prejudicial attitudes may be transmitted from one generation to the next, it does not explain their origin or why they intensify or diminish over the years. These aspects of prejudice must be explained in another way.

Herbert Blumer suggests that prejudice always involves the notion of group position in society.[23] Prejudiced people believe that one group is inferior to another, and they place each group in a hierarchical position in society. This perception of group position is an outgrowth of the individual's experiences and understanding of them. The group stereotypes are socially approved images held by members of one group about another.[24]

Self-Justification

Through **self-justification,** we denigrate a person or group to justify our maltreatment of them. In this situation, self-justification leads to prejudice and discrimination against another's group.

Some philosophers argue that we are not so much rational creatures as we are rationalizing creatures. We require reassurance that the things we do and the lives we live are proper, that good reasons for our actions exist. If we are able to convince ourselves that another group is inferior, immoral, or dangerous, then we can feel justified in discriminating against them, enslaving them, or even killing them.

History is filled with examples of people who thought their maltreatment of others was just and necessary: As defenders of the "true faith," the Crusaders killed "Christ-killers" (Jews) and "infidels" (Moslems). Participants in the Spanish Inquisition imprisoned, tortured, and executed "heretics," "the disciples of the Devil." The Puritans burned witches, whose refusal to confess "proved" they were evil. Indians were "heathen savages," blacks were "an inferior species," and thus both could be mistreated, enslaved, or killed. The civilians in the Vietnamese village of My Lai were "probably" aiding the Vietcong, so the soldiers felt justified in slaughtering the old men, women, and children they found there.

Some sociologists believe that self-justification works the other way around.[25] That is, instead of self-justification serving as a basis for subjugation of a people, the subjugation occurs first and the self-justification follows, resulting in prejudice and continued discrimination. The evolvement of racism as a concept after the establishment of the African slave trade would seem to support this idea. Philip Mason offers an insight into this view:

> A specialized society is likely to defeat a simpler society and provide a lower tier still of enslaved and conquered peoples. The rulers and organizers sought security for themselves and their children; to perpetuate the power, the esteem, and the comfort they had achieved, it was necessary not only that the artisans and labourers should work contentedly but that the rulers should sleep without bad dreams. No one can say with certainty how the myths originated, but it is surely relevant that when one of the founders of Western thought set himself to frame an ideal state that would embody social justice, he—like the earliest city dwellers—not only devised a society stratified in tiers but believed it would be necessary to persuade the traders and work-people that, by divine decree, they were made from brass and iron, while the warriors were made of silver and the rulers of gold.[26]

Another example of self-justification serving as a cause of prejudice is the dominant group's assumption of an attitude of superiority over other groups. In this respect establishing a prestige hierarchy—ranking the status of various ethnic groups—results in differential association. To enhance or maintain one's own self-esteem, one may avoid social contact with groups deemed inferior and associate only with those identified as being of high status. Through such behavior self-justification may come to intensify the social distance between groups. As discussed in Chapter 1, *social distance* refers to the degree to which ingroup members do not engage in social or primary relationships with members of various outgroups.

Personality

In 1950 T. W. Adorno and his colleagues reported a correlation between individuals' early childhood experiences of harsh parental discipline and their development of authoritarian personalities as adults.[27] If parents assume an excessively domineering posture in their relations with a child, exercising stern measures and threatening the withdrawal of love if the child does not respond with weakness and submission, then the child tends to be very insecure, nurturing much latent hostility against the parents. When such children become adults, they may demonstrate **displaced aggression,** directing their hostility against a powerless group as compensation for feelings of insecurity and fear. Highly prejudiced individuals tend to come from families that emphasize obedience.

The authors identified authoritarianism by the use of a measuring instrument called an F scale (the F standing for potential fascism). Other tests included the A-S (anti-Semitism) and E (ethnocentrism) scales, the latter measuring attitudes toward various minorities. One of their major findings was that people who scored high on authoritarianism also consistently showed a high degree of prejudice against all minority groups. These highly prejudiced persons were characterized by rigidity of viewpoint, dislike for ambiguity, strict obedience to leaders, and intolerance of weakness in themselves or others.

No sooner did *The Authoritarian Personality* appear than controversy began. H. H. Hyman and P. B. Sheatsley challenged the methodology and analysis.[28] Solomon Asch questioned the assumptions that the F scale responses represented a belief system and that structural variables, such as ideologies, stratification, mobility, and other social factors, do not play a role in shaping personality.[29] E. A. Shils argued that the authors were interested only in measuring authoritarianism of the political right while ignoring such tendencies in those at the other end of the political spectrum.[30] Other investigators sought alternative explanations for the authoritarian personality. D. Stewart and T. Hoult extended the framework beyond family childhood experiences to include other social factors.[31] H. C. Kelman and Janet Barclay demonstrated that substantial evidence exists showing that lower intelligence and less education also correlate with high authoritarianism scores on the F scale.[32]

Despite the critical attacks, the underlying conceptions of *The Authoritarian Personality* were important, and research on personality as a factor in prejudice has continued. Subsequent investigators have refined and modified the original study. Correcting scores for response bias, they have conducted cross-cultural studies. Respondents in Germany and Near East countries, where a more authoritarian social structure exists, scored higher on authoritarianism. In Japan, Germany, and the United States, authoritarianism and social distance were moderately related. Other studies frequently have shown that an inverse relationship exists between social class and F scale scores.[33]

Although the authoritarian-personality studies have been helpful in the understanding of some aspects of prejudice, they have not provided a causal explanation. Most of the findings in this area show a correlation, but the findings do not prove, for example, that harsh discipline of children causes them to become prejudiced adults. Perhaps the strict parents were themselves prejudiced, and the child learned those attitudes from them. Or, as George Simpson and J. Milton Yinger say:

> One must be careful not to assume too quickly that a certain tendency—rigidity of mind, for example—that is correlated with prejudice necessarily causes that prejudice. . . . The sequence may be the other way around. . . . It is more likely that both are related to more basic factors.[34]

For some people prejudice may indeed be rooted in subconscious childhood tensions, but we simply do not know whether these tensions directly cause a high degree of prejudice in the adult or whether other powerful social forces are the determinants. Whatever the explanation, authoritarianism is a significant phenomenon worthy of continued investigation. Recent research, however, has stressed social and situation factors, rather than personality, as important causes of prejudice and discrimination.[35]

Yet another dimension to the personality component is that people with low self-esteem are more prejudiced than those who feel good about themselves. Some researchers have argued that individuals with low self-esteem deprecate others to enhance their feelings about themselves.[36] A recent study suggests "low self-esteem individuals seem to have a generally negative view of themselves, their ingroup, outgroups, and perhaps the world," and thus their tendency to be more prejudiced is not due to rating the outgroup negatively in comparison to their ingroup.[37]

Frustration

Frustration is the result of relative deprivation in which expectations remain unsatisfied. **Relative deprivation** refers to a lack of resources, or rewards, in one's standard of living in comparison with others in the society. A number of investigators have suggested that frustrations tend to increase aggression toward others.[38] Frustrated people may easily strike out against the perceived cause of their frustration. However, this reaction is not always possible because the true source of the frustration is often too nebulous to be identified or too powerful to act against. In such instances the result may be a displaced or free-floating aggression; in this situation the frustrated individual or group usually redirects the aggressiveness against a more visible, vulnerable, and socially sanctioned target, one unable to strike back. Minorities meet these criteria and are thus frequently the recipients of displaced aggression by the dominant group.

Placing blame on others for something that is not their fault is known as **scapegoating.** The term comes from the ancient Hebrew custom of using a goat during the Day of Atonement as a symbol of the sins of the people. In an annual ceremony a priest placed his hands on the head of a goat and listed the people's sins in a symbolic transference of guilt; he then chased the goat out of the community, thereby freeing the people of sin.[39] Since those times the powerful group has usually punished the scapegoat group rather than allowing it to escape.

There have been many instances throughout world history of minority groups serving as scapegoats, including the Christians in ancient Rome, the French Huguenots, the Jews, the Chinese, the Irish, the Japanese, and the Quakers. Gordon Allport suggests that certain characteristics are necessary for a group to become a suitable scapegoat.[40] The group must be (1) highly visible in physical appearance or observable customs and actions; (2) not strong enough to strike back; (3) situated within easy access of the dominant group or, ideally, concentrated in one area; (4) a past target of hostility for whom latent hostility still exists; and (5) the symbol of an unpopular concept.

Some groups fit this typology better than others, but minority racial and ethnic groups have continually been a favorite choice. Irish, Italians, Catholics, Jews, Quakers, Mormons, Chinese, Japanese, blacks, Puerto Ricans, Chicanos, and Koreans have all been, at one time or another, the scapegoat in the United States. Especially in times of economic hardship, there seems to be a tendency to blame some group for the general conditions, often leading to aggressive action against the group as an expression of frustration. For example, a study by Carl Hovland and Robert Sears found that between 1882 and 1930, a definite correlation existed between a decline in the price of cotton and an increase in the number of lynchings of blacks.[41]

In several controlled experiments sociologists have attempted to measure the validity of the scapegoat theory. Neal Miller and Richard Bugelski tested a group of young men aged 18 to 20 working in a government camp about their feelings toward various minority groups.[42] They were reexamined about these feelings after experiencing frustration by being obliged to take a long, difficult test and denied an opportunity to see a film at a local theater. This group showed some evidence of increased prejudicial feelings, whereas a control group, which did not experience any frustration, showed no change in prejudicial attitudes.

Donald Weatherley conducted an experiment with a group of college students to measure the relationship between frustration and aggression against a specific disliked group.[43] After identifying students who were or were not highly anti-Semitic and subjecting them to a strong frustrating experience, he asked the students to write stories about pictures shown to them. Some of the students were shown pictures of people who had been given Jewish names; other students were presented with pictures of unnamed people. When the pictures were unidentified, no difference appeared between the stories of the

In 1989 former Ku Klux Klan leader David Duke narrowly won election to the Louisiana State Legislature, appealing to white voters frustrated at perceived minority gains at their expense. His 1992 presidential campaign fizzled early and he was an insignificant factor in states where his name was on the ballot. (© *1991 Rick Reinhard/Impact Visuals*)

anti-Semitic students and those of other students. However, when the pictures were identified, the anti-Semitic students wrote stories reflecting much more aggression against the Jews in the pictures than did the other students.

For over 20 years Leonard Berkowitz and his associates have studied and experimented with aggressive behavior. Their conclusions are that, confronted with equally frustrating situations, highly prejudiced individuals are more likely to seek scapegoats than are nonprejudiced individuals. Another intervening variable is that certain kinds of frustrations—personal (marital failure, injury, or mental illness) rather than shared (dangers of flood or hurricane)—make people more likely to seek scapegoats.[44]

Some experiments have shown that aggression does not increase if the frustration is understandable.[45] Other experimenters have found that people become aggressive *only* if the aggression directly relieves that frustration.[46] Still other studies have shown that anger is a more likely result if the person frustrating us could have acted otherwise.[47] Clearly, the results are mixed, depending on the variables within a given social situation.

Talcott Parsons suggests that the family and the occupational system are both likely to produce anxieties and insecurities that create frustration.[48] According to this view, the growing-up process (gaining parental affection and approval, identifying with and imitating sexual role models, and competing with others in adulthood) may involve severe emotional strain. The result is an adult personality with a large reservoir of repressed aggression that becomes **free-floating**—susceptible to redirection against convenient scapegoats. Similarly, the occupational system is a source of frustration: Its emphasis on competitiveness and individual achievement, its function of conferring status, its requirement that people inhibit their natural impulses at work, and its relationship to the state of the economy are but a few of the factors that generate emotional anxieties. Parsons pessimistically concludes that minorities fulfill a functional "need" as targets for displaced aggression and will therefore remain targets.[49]

Frustration–aggression theory, although helpful, is not completely satisfactory. It ignores the role of culture and the reality of actual social conflict, while failing to show a causal relationship. Most of the responses measured in these studies were of people already biased. Why did one group rather than another become the object of the aggression? Moreover, frustration does not necessarily precede aggression, and aggression does not necessarily flow from frustration.

Competition

People tend to be more hostile toward others when they feel their security is threatened; thus many social scientists conclude that economic competition and conflict breed prejudice. Certainly a great amount of evidence shows that negative stereotyping, prejudice, and discrimination increase strongly whenever competition for a limited number of jobs increases.

An excellent illustration concerns the Chinese sojourners in the nineteenth century. Prior to the 1870s the transcontinental railroad was being built, and the Chinese filled many of the jobs made available by this project in the sparsely populated West. Although they were expelled from the gold mines and schools and had no redress of grievances in the courts, they managed to convey to some whites an image of a clean, hard-working, law-abiding people. The completion of the railroad, the flood of former Civil War soldiers into the job market, and the economic depression of 1873 worsened their situation. The Chinese were even more frequently the victims of open discrimination and hostility. Their positive stereotype among some whites became more commonly a negative one: They were now "conniving," "crafty," "criminal," "the yellow menace." Only after they retreated into Chinatowns and entered specialty occupations not in competition with whites did the intense hostility abate.

One of the early pioneers in the scientific study of prejudice, John Dollard, demonstrated how prejudice against the Germans, which had been virtually nonexistent, came about in a small American industrial town when times got bad.

> Local whites largely drawn from the surrounding farms manifested considerable direct aggression toward the newcomers. Scornful and derogatory opinions

were expressed about the Germans, and the native whites had a satisfying sense of superiority toward them. . . . The chief element in the permission to be aggressive against the Germans was rivalry for jobs and status in the local woodenware plants. The native whites felt definitely crowded for their jobs by the entering German groups and in case of bad times had a chance to blame the Germans who by their presence provided more competitors for the scarcer jobs. There seemed to be no traditional pattern of prejudice against Germans unless the skeletal suspicion of all out-groupers (always present) be invoked in this place.[50]

Both experimental studies and historical analyses have added credence to the economic-competition theory. Muzafer Sherif directed several experiments showing how intergroup competition at a boys' camp leads to conflict and escalating hostility.[51] Donald Young has shown that, throughout American history, in times with high unemployment and thus intense job competition, strong nativist movements against minorities have existed.[52] This pattern has held true regionally—with the Asians on the West Coast, the Italians in Louisiana, and the French Canadians in New England—and nationally, with the antiforeign movements always peaking during periods of depression. So it was with the Native American Party in the 1830s, the Know-Nothing Party in the 1850s, the American Protective Association in the 1890s, and the Ku Klux Klan after World War I. Since the passage of civil rights laws on employment in the twentieth century, researchers have consistently detected the strongest antiblack prejudice among whites who are closest to blacks on the socioeconomic ladder.[53] It seems that any group applying the pressure of job competition most directly on another group becomes its prejudicial target.

Once again, a theory offers some excellent insights into prejudice—there is a correlation between economic conditions and hostility toward minorities—but it also has some serious shortcomings. Not all groups who have been objects of hostility have been economic competitors (for example, Quakers and Mormons). Moreover, why is there greater hostility against some groups than against others? Why do the negative feelings in some communities run against groups whose numbers are so small that they cannot possibly be an economic threat? It would appear that other values besides economic ones cause people to be antagonistic to a group perceived as an actual or potential threat.

Social Norms

Some sociologists have suggested that a relationship exists between prejudice and a person's tendency to conform to societal expectations.[54] **Social norms**—the norms of one's culture—provide the generally shared rules of what is and is not proper behavior; by learning and automatically accepting the prevailing prejudices, the individual is simply conforming to those norms. This theory says that there is a direct relationship between degree of conformity and degree of prejudice. If this is true, then people's prejudices would decrease or increase significantly when they move into areas where the prejudicial norm is either lesser or greater. Evidence supports this view. Thomas Pettigrew found that Southerners in the 1950s became less prejudiced against blacks when they interacted with them in the army, where the social norms were less prejudicial.[55] In another study Jeanne Watson found that people moving into an anti-Semitic neighborhood in New York City became more anti-Semitic.[56]

In 1937 John Dollard published his major study, *Caste and Class in a Southern Town*, providing an in-depth look into the emotional adjustment of whites and blacks to rigid social norms.[57] In his study of the processes, functions, and maintenance of accommodation, Dollard shows how the "carrot-and-stick" method is employed. Intimidation, or sometimes even severe reprisals for going against social norms, ensures compliance. However, such actions usually are unnecessary. The advantages whites and blacks gain in psychological, economic, or behavioral terms serve to perpetuate the caste order. These gains in personal security and stability set in motion a vicious circle. They encourage a way of life that reinforces the rationale of the social system in this community.

The problem with the social-norms theory is that although it explains prevailing attitudes, it explains neither their origins nor the reasons for the development of new prejudices when other groups move into an area. In addition the theory does not explain why prejudicial attitudes against a particular group continue to rise and fall in cyclical fashion over the years.

Although many social scientists have attempted to identify the causes of prejudice, no single factor has proven to be an adequate explanation. Prejudice is a complex phenomenon, and it is most likely to be the product of more than one causal agent. Sociologists now tend either to emphasize multiple-causation explanations or else to stress social forces at work in specific and similar situations, such as economic conditions, stratification, or hostility toward an outgroup.

Can Prejudice Be Reduced?

A great many organizations and movements whose prime objective was to reduce prejudice have existed over the years. Although they have varied in their orientation and focal point of activity, their techniques have basically been two: (1) to promote greater interaction between dominant and minority groups in all aspects of living, by either voluntary or compulsory means; and (2) to dispense information that will destroy stereotypes and expose rationalizations (self-justifications). Neither approach has been successful in all instances, probably because the inequalities that encourage such attitudes still exist.

Contact
Contact between people of different racial and ethnic backgrounds does not necessarily lead to friendlier attitudes. In fact, the situation may worsen, as has happened frequently when schools and neighborhoods experienced the influx of a different group of people. However, many instances show that

interaction reduces prejudice.[58] It would appear that a great many other variables determine the effect of contact, including the frequency and duration of contacts; the relative status of the two parties and their backgrounds; whether their meeting is voluntary or compulsory, competitive or cooperative; and whether they meet in a political, religious, occupational, residential, or recreational situation.[59]

A good example of the significance of the type of contact lies in the **jigsaw method** experiments of Elliot Aronson and his associates.[60] This research team observed that classroom competition for teacher recognition and approval often wreaked special hardship on minority children less fluent in English or less self-assured about participating in class. Creating interdependent learning groups of five or six children, each member charged with learning one portion of the day's lesson in a particular subject, the children then learned the complete lesson from one another, thereafter taking a test on all the material. This cooperative technique, highly structured and teacher facilitated, has successfully taught content and cooperative skills while enhancing self-esteem and peer liking (see Box 3.2).

Information

Many people have long cherished the hope that education would reduce prejudice. Some studies, such as that by Gertrude Selznick and Stephen Steinberg, have found a definite correlation between level of education and degree of tolerance,[61] but other studies have not.[62] Charles Stember's research led him to conclude that more highly educated persons were not more tolerant—they were simply more sophisticated in recognizing measures of bias and more subtle in expressing their prejudices.[63] In sum it appears that formal education is far from a perfect means of reducing prejudice. One reason for this failure is that people tend to use **selective perception;** that is, they learn information that accords with their own beliefs and rationalize away that which does not. Another reason is the almost quantum leap from the classroom to real-life situations. Dealing with prejudice from a detached perspective is one thing, but dealing with it in actuality quite another, because emotions, social pressures, and many other factors are all involved.

Despite these criticisms, courses in race and ethnic relations certainly have value because they raise the students' level of consciousness about intergroup dynamics. However, a significant reduction or elimination of prejudice is more likely to occur by changing the structural conditions of inequality that promote and maintain prejudicial attitudes. As Herbert Blumer suggests, the sense of group position dissolves and racial prejudice declines when major shifts in the social order overtake the current definition of a group's characteristics.[64] So long as the dominant group does not react with fear, instituting a countermovement, the improvement of a minority's social position changes the power relations and reduces the negative stereotypes. Therefore, continued efforts at public enlightenment and extension of constitutional rights and equal opportunities to all Americans, regardless of race, religion, or national origin, appear to be the most hopeful means of attaining a prejudice-free society.

| BOX 3.2 | THE JIGSAW METHOD |

The experience of a Mexican-American child in one of our groups serves as a useful illustration. We will call him Carlos. Carlos was not very articulate in English, his second language. Because he was often ridiculed when he had spoken up in the past, over the years he learned to keep quiet in class. He was one of those students . . . who had entered into an implicit contract of silence with his teacher, he opting for anonymity and she calling on him only rarely.

While Carlos hated school and was learning very little in the traditional classroom, at least he was left alone. Accordingly, he was quite uncomfortable with the jigsaw system, which required him to talk to his groupmates. He had a great deal of trouble communicating his paragraph, stammering and hesitating. The other children reacted out of old habits, resorting to insults and teasing. "Aw, you don't know it," Susan accused. "You're dumb, you're stupid. You don't know what you are doing."

One of the researchers, assigned to observe the group process, intervened with a bit of advice when she overheard such comments: "Okay, you can tease him if you want to. It might be fun for you, but it's not going to help you learn about Eleanor Roosevelt's young adulthood. And let me remind you, the exam will take place in less than an hour." Note how this statement brings home the fact that the reinforcement contingencies have shifted considerably. Now Susan does not gain much from putting Carlos down. And she stands to lose a great deal, not just from the teacher singling her out for criticism but because she needs to know Carlos's information.

Gradually, but inexorably, it began to dawn on the students that the only chance they had to learn about Carlos's segment was by paying attention to what he had to say. If they ignored Carlos or continued to ridicule him, his segment would be unavailable to them and the most they could hope for would be an 80 percent score on the exam—an unattractive prospect to most of the children. And with that realization, the kids began to develop into pretty good interviewers, learning to pay attention to Carlos, to draw him out, and to ask probing questions. Carlos, in turn, began to relax more and found it easier to explain out loud what was in his head. What the children came to learn about Carlos is even more important than the information about the lesson that they got from him. After a couple of days, they began to appreciate that Carlos was not nearly as dumb as they had thought he was. After a few weeks they noticed talents in him they had not seen before. They began to like Carlos, and he began to enjoy school more and to think of his Anglo classmates as helpful friends and interested colleagues rather than as tormentors.

SOURCE: Elliot Aronson and Neal Osherow, "Cooperation, Prosocial Behavior, and Academic Performance: Experiments in the Desegregated Classroom," *Applied Social Psychology Annual* 1 (1980), 174–175.

DISCRIMINATION _____

Discrimination is actual behavior, the practice of differential and unequal treatment of other groups of people, usually along racial, religious, or ethnic lines. The Latin word *discriminatus*, from which the English word is derived, means to divide or distinguish, and so its negative interpretation has remained relatively unchanged down through the centuries.

Levels of Discrimination

Actions, like attitudes, may have different levels of intensity. Discrimination may thus be analyzed at five levels.[65] The first level is *verbal expression*, a statement of dislike or use of a derogatory term. The next level is *avoidance*, in which the prejudiced person takes steps to avoid any social interaction with that group. This action could include choice of residence, organizational membership, activities located in urban centers, or primary relationships in any social setting.

At the third level *exclusion* from certain jobs, housing, education, or social organizations occurs. In the United States the practice of **de jure segregation** was once widespread throughout the South. Not only were children specifically assigned to certain schools to maintain racial separation, but also segregationist laws kept all public places (theatres, restaurants, restrooms, transportation, and so on) racially apart as well. **De facto segregation** may result from residential patterns and become embedded in social customs and institutions. Thus the standard practice of neighborhood schools in racially segregated communities creates segregated schools.

The fourth level of discrimination is physical abuse, the beatings and attacks on members of the disliked group. Unfortunately, this behavior still occurs often in the United States. A new term, **ethnoviolence,** has entered our vocabulary. The National Institute Against Prejudice and Violence identifies ethnoviolence as a range of behavior—verbal harassment and threats, vandalism, graffiti, swastika painting, arson, cross burning, physical assaults, and murder—committed against people targeted solely because of their race, religion, ethnic background, or sexual orientation.[66] Thousands of incidents of ethnoviolence occur each year against various minority groups throughout the nation on college campuses and in both suburban and urban areas.

The final level of discrimination is when massacres, genocide, or pogroms are conducted against a people. We sometimes still learn of such barbarous actions, as in South Africa in 1992.

Relationships Between Prejudice and Discrimination

Prejudice can lead to discrimination, and conversely, discrimination can lead to prejudice. Depending on the situation, either discrimination or prejudice may cause the other, but no certainty exists that one will follow the other. Although our attitudes and our overt behavior are closely interrelated, they are not identical. We may harbor hostile feelings toward certain groups without ever making them known through word or deed. Similarly, through our overt behavior we may *effectively* conceal our real attitudes.

It is true that prejudiced people are more likely than others to practice discrimination; discrimination is thus quite often the overt expression of prejudice. However, it is wrong to assume that discrimination is always the acting out of prejudice. It may be instead the result of a policy decision protecting the interests of the majority group, such as the curtailment of immigration for economic reasons. It may be due to social conformity, such as when people submit to outside pressures despite their personal views.[67] Discriminators may explain their actions with reasons other than prejudice toward a particular group, and those reasons may be valid to the discriminators. Sometimes the discriminatory behavior may precede prejudicial attitudes as, for example, when organizations insist that all job applicants take aptitude or IQ tests based on middle-class experiences and then judge negatively the lower-income people who do not score well.

Robert Merton formulated a model (see Figure 3.1) showing the possible relationships between prejudice and discrimination. Merton demonstrates that, quite conceivably, a nonprejudiced person will discriminate and a prejudiced person will not. In his paradigm Merton classifies four types of people according to how they accept or reject the American Creed, "the right of equitable access to justice, freedom and opportunity, irrespective of race or religion, or ethnic origin."[68]

The Nonprejudiced Nondiscriminator, or the All-weather Liberal
All-weather liberals are consistent. They are neither prejudiced nor practicers of discrimination. Accordingly, they are properly motivated to illuminate others and to fight against all forms of discrimination. However, says Merton,

Prejudiced	Discriminates	
	No	Yes
No	All-weather liberal	Fair-weather liberal
Yes	Timid bigot	Active bigot

FIGURE 3.1
Interrelationship Between Prejudice and Discrimination

they have their shortcomings in that they confuse discussion with action. They talk chiefly to others sharing their viewpoint, and so they deceive themselves into thinking that they represent the consensus of the community. Furthermore, because their "own spiritual house is in order," they feel no pangs of conscience pressing them to work collectively on the problem. A counterargument would be that some all-weather liberals are activists and do speak to others with different viewpoints, thereby transforming discussion into action.

The Nonprejudiced Discriminator, or the Fair-weather Liberal

Expediency is the byword for those in this category, for their actions often conflict with their personal beliefs. They may, for example, be free of racial prejudice, but they will keep silent when bigots speak out, they will not condemn acts of discrimination, and they will join in efforts to keep blacks out of their neighborhood for fear of its deterioration. These people frequently feel guilt and shame because they are acting against their beliefs.

The Prejudiced Nondiscriminator, or the Fair-weather Illiberal

Merton's term *timid bigots* best describes fair-weather illiberals. They believe in many of the stereotypes about minorities and definitely feel hostility toward these groups. However, they keep silent in the presence of those who are more tolerant; they conform because they must. If there were no law or pressure to be unbiased in certain actions, they would discriminate.

The Prejudiced Discriminator, or the All-weather Illiberal

Without doubt, such folks as the all-weather illiberals are active bigots. They have no conflict between attitudes and behavior. Not only do they openly express their beliefs, practice discrimination, and defy the law if necessary, but they also believe that it is their duty to do so.

The second and third categories, the nonprejudiced discriminator and the prejudiced nondiscriminator, are the most helpful classifications, showing us that social-situational variables often determine whether or not discriminatory behavior occurs. Individuals may act in a manner inconsistent with their beliefs because of the pressure of group norms.

Other Aspects of Discrimination

Discriminatory practices are frequent in the areas of employment and residence, although such actions often are covert and denied. Another dimension of discrimination, often unrealized, is **social discrimination,** or the creation of a "social distance" between groups. Simply stated, in their intimate primary relationships, people tend to associate with those of a similar ethnic background and socioeconomic level; the dominant-group members thus usually exclude minority-group members from close relations with them.

Hubert Blalock, offering conflict perspective reasoning, suggests extreme discrimination usually will result when the dominant group feels that its self-interests—such as primacy and the preservation of cherished values—are threatened.[69] Blalock believes that the dominant group will not hesitate to employ discriminatory action if it thinks that this will be an effective means of undercutting the minority group as a social competitor. Also, the dominant group will aggressively discriminate if it interprets minority variation from cultural norms as a form of social deviance threatening society's sacred traditions (for example, the large influx of Catholic immigrants in nineteenth-century America or the appearance of "dishonest" Gypsies among "decent, hard-working" people). Discrimination, in this view, is "a technique designed to neutralize minority group efforts."[70] (See Box 3.3 for an international example.)

BOX 3.3

THE INTERNATIONAL SCENE

Northern Ireland contains about 1 million Protestants with loyalties to Britain and about a half-million Catholics with a preference for unification with the Republic of Ireland. It is today a polarized society, its sporadic violence fed by centuries of deep-seated hostilities.

Sociologically, Catholics are the minority group, with some political power but only at the local level. They are more likely to be poor, to be unemployed longer than Protestants, and to live in substandard housing in segregated communities. Catholics tend to be in low-status, low-skill jobs and Protestants in high-status, high-skill positions. It is difficult, however, to determine whether these employment patterns result from overt job discrimination or from structural factors of community segregation, education, and class, or from both.

Although the degree of actual discrimination employed to maintain their dominance is uncertain, Protestants do rationalize about the situation through a set of negative beliefs about the Catholics. Many Protestants stereotype the Catholics as lazy welfare cheats who are dirty, superstitious, and ignorant. They also view them as being oversexed and brainwashed by priests, the "proof" being the typically large-sized Catholic family. Moreover, Protestants suspect that Catholics are intent on undermining the government. Most Protestants see no discrimination on the basis of religion in jobs, housing, and other social areas. Catholics "get what they deserve" because of their values, attitudes, and disloyalty.

For their part, most Catholics in Northern Ireland strongly believe that they experience discrimination as a direct consequence of their religion. They perceive Protestants to be narrow-minded bigots who stubbornly hold onto political power with no desire to relinquish any part of it.

Prospects for a solution are not very promising. A vicious circle of prejudice and discrimination intensifies Protestant resistance to sharing power and Catholic reluctance to offer any support to the central government.

The Concept of Justice

At what point do efforts to secure justice and equal opportunities in life for one group infringe on the rights of other groups? Is justice a utilitarian concept—the greatest happiness for the greatest number—or is it a moral concept—a sense of good that all people share? Is the proper role of government to provide a climate in which there is equal opportunity to participate in a competitive system, or is it government's responsibility to ensure equal results in any competition? These issues have engaged moral and political philosophers for centuries, and they go to the core of the affirmative-action controversy.

Over 2,300 years ago Plato wrote in the *Republic* that justice must be relative to the needs of the people who are served, not to the desires of those who serve them. For example, physicians are obliged to make the patients' health their primary concern if they are to be just. In *A Theory of Justice* John Rawls interprets justice as fairness, which maximizes equal liberty for all.[71] Society must eliminate social and economic inequalities in order to provide the greatest benefit to the least advantaged, placing minority persons in offices and positions that are open to all under conditions of fair equality of opportunity. Both men see the ideal society as well ordered and strongly pluralistic: Each of the component elements performs functionally differentiated roles in working harmony; society must arrange its practices to make this so.

Shift in Government Policy

Anticipating the emergence of the equal-protection-under-the-law clause of the Fourteenth Amendment as a major force for social change, Joseph Tussman and Jacobus tenBroek examined the problems of the doctrine of equality five years before the 1954 Supreme Court desegregation ruling.[72] Americans, they argued, have always been more concerned with liberty than with equality, identifying liberty with the absence of governmental interference.

> What happens, then, when government becomes more ubiquitous? Whenever an area of activity is brought within the control or regulation of government to that extent equality supplants liberty as the dominant ideal and constitutional demand.[73]

Tussman and tenBroek note that those who insist on constitutional rights for all are not so much demanding the removal of governmental restraints as they are asking for positive governmental action to provide equal treatment for "minority groups, parties, or organizations whose rights are too easily sacrificed or ignored in periods of popular hysteria."[74] Responsibility for promoting individual rights is increasingly being placed upon public authority.

In the 1960s and 1970s, the three branches of the federal government acted to promote minority rights in judicial decisions, legislative programs, and executive actions. As their impact was felt at state and local levels; in college and graduate school admissions; in hiring, training, and promotion policies; and in other facets of life, many white males reacted angrily, feeling that their

The 1992 acquittal of white Los Angeles police officers accused of beating Rodney King ignited riots and demonstrations throughout the country. People of all races were outraged by what they considered a miscarriage of justice. Many minority people have long believed the criminal justice system is biased. (© 1992 Ricky Flores/Impact Visuals)

own rights were now being denied. They charged reverse discrimination, that they were now deliberately excluded from or passed over for positions by "less qualified" minorities and females. As a ground swell of reaction set in by white males claiming they were being unfairly penalized for past societal wrongs, various court challenges brought the issue to a head.

Supreme Court Rulings

The issue was partially resolved with the *Bakke* decision in 1978. In what one observer termed a "Solomonic" compromise, the Supreme Court ruled 5 to 4 that it is illegal for a university to use racial or ethnic quotas in its admissions program but also that race may be used as a positive factor in admissions decisions. The principle of affirmative action, designed to improve educational and job opportunities for racial minorities and women, was thus upheld, although in refined form. The ruling was not definitive, however. In the same week as the *Bakke* decision, for example, the court ruled that the use of racial quotas at AT&T (American Telephone and Telegraph) was justified be-

cause of long-standing discriminatory practices in this corporation that required corrective action.

Two of the majority opinions from the *Bakke* decision seem to best summa-
rize the Court's assessment of this extremely complex matter. Justice Lewis F.
Powell stated: "The guarantee of equal protection cannot mean one thing
when applied to one individual and something else when applied to a person
of another color. If both are not accorded the same protection, then it is not
equal." Justice Harry A. Blackmun pointed out the other part of the problem:
"In order to get beyond racism, we must first take account of race. There is no
other way. And in order to treat some persons equally, we must treat them
differently. We cannot—we dare not—let the Equal Protection Clause perpetuate racial superiority."

What has been the subsequent influence of the landmark *Bakke* case? A
recent analysis by John Gpuhl and Susan Welch revealed relatively little impact on the application, acceptance, and enrollment of blacks and Hispanics
in medical and law schools, which had already leveled off two or three years
before the *Bakke* ruling.[75]

Another important case involved the United Steelworkers of America and
Kaiser Aluminum & Chemical Corporation, which reserved half of the positions in its skilled-craft training programs for minorities and women. Brian
Weber, a white Louisiana factory worker, filed a class action suit when two
blacks with less seniority were picked ahead of him for this program. When
the U.S. Supreme Court handled the case of *Weber v. Kaiser* in 1979, it further
upheld affirmative action in ruling that private employers may voluntarily
adopt quotas to remedy past discrimination, even if blameless themselves.
Considered by some analysts a potentially more significant decision than the
Bakke case, the court considered the spirit and intent of the law, the serious
racial imbalance among craft employees, and the fact that the temporary plan
did not deny promotions to, or cause firings of, whites.

Still other recent court decisions have echoed the rationale of the *Weber*
decision. In 1986 the court mandated that the New York City sheet-metal
workers' union meet a 29 percent minority membership within one year. In
1987 the court ruled that employers may favor minorities and women over
better qualified white males to achieve better balance in their work force.
Three times the court ruled on promotions: using race as a criterion for promotion of black police officers in Detroit: allowing temporary promotions of
black and Hispanic firefighters in Cleveland ahead of whites with more seniority and higher test scores; and endorsing racial quotas to achieve affirmative action goals among Alabama state troopers.

In contrast, the court in 1984 put a new limit on affirmative action, upholding the last-hired, first-fired principle. As long as seniority systems are unbiased, the court declared, they may not be disrupted to save jobs of newly
hired minority workers. By 1989 a more conservative U.S. Supreme Court
was ruling further against affirmative action measures. First it struck down
the use of fixed quotas in local and state minority set-aside laws. Benign racial
classifications, giving minority group preference a fixed share of government

contracts, cannot be used, the court ruled, even as a tool to remedy past discrimination unless detailed evidence of such exists. Next the court changed the guidelines in job-bias suits, requiring employees to prove their job discrimination charges, not simply to claim such and then have the courts decide. Future rulings are likely to reflect further the present court's position on affirmative action.

Retrospect

Prejudice may exist at three levels: cognitive, emotional, and action orientation. Stereotyping, difficult to erase once established, is found in the use of ethnophaulisms and ethnic humor. Television has a profound impact in shaping and reinforcing attitudes; unfortunately, it continues to perpetuate racial and sexual stereotypes instead of combating them.

No single cause can account for all instances of prejudice. Among the explanations social scientists offer are socialization, self-justification, personality factors, frustration, competition, and social norms. Each of these factors explains some cases of prejudice, and sometimes various combinations of them explain other cases. Social-situational variables, such as economic conditions, stratification, and hostility toward the outgroup, also are important in understanding the existence of prejudice.

Increased contact between groups and improved information as in courses about minorities do not necessarily reduce prejudice. The nature of the contact, particularly if it is competitive or cooperative, is a key determinant. Information can develop heightened awareness as a means of improved relations, but external factors (economic conditions and social pressures) may override rational considerations.

Discriminatory behavior operates at five levels of intensity: verbal expression, avoidance, exclusion, physical abuse, and extermination. Discrimination is not necessarily an acting-out of prejudice. Social pressures may oblige nonprejudiced individuals to discriminate or prevent prejudiced people from discriminating.

Reverse discrimination remains an emotionally charged issue. Is it a democratic government's responsibility to provide a climate for equal opportunity or to ensure equal results? If the latter, at what point do efforts to secure equality for one group infringe on the rights of other groups?

Key Terms

Action-orientation Level of Prejudice
Authoritarian Personality
Cognitive Level of Prejudice
Displaced Aggression

Emotional Level of Prejudice
Ethnophaulism
Ethnoviolence
Frustration

Institutionalized Discrimination   Selective Perception
Jigsaw Method   Self-justification
Prejudice   Social Norms
Relative Deprivation   Socialization
Reverse Discrimination   Stereotype
Scapegoating   Value Judgment

Review Questions

1. What is prejudice? What are some of its manifestations?
2. What are some of the possible causes of prejudice?
3. What role does television play in combating or reinforcing stereotypes?
4. What is discrimination? What are some of its manifestations?
5. What is the relationship between prejudice and discrimination?
6. What is reverse discrimination? Why is it so difficult an issue?

Suggested Readings

ALLEN, IRVING L. *Unkind Words: Ethnic Labeling from Redskin to WASP.* New York: Bergin & Garvey, 1990.
 Informative, highly readable insight into how ethnic animosities take many and devious forms in abusive slang.

BLALOCK, HUBERT M., JR. *Race and Ethnic Relations.* Englewood Cliffs, NJ: Prentice-Hall, 1982.
 A theoretical "roadmap" of race and ethnic relations offering a macrosocial view of prejudice and discrimination.

CLARK, KENNETH B. *Prejudice and Your Child,* 2d ed. Boston: Beacon Press, 1963.
 A thorough examination of the effects of race prejudice on children, both majority and minority group members, with specific suggestions to overcome prejudicial feelings in children.

FEAGIN, JOE R., AND CLAIRECE B. FEAGIN. *Discrimination American Style.* Englewood Cliffs, NJ: Prentice-Hall, 1978.
 An excellent overview of the forms and dimensions of discriminatory actions practiced in American society against various minority groups.

JONES, JAMES M. *Prejudice and Racism.* Reading, MA: Addison-Wesley, 1972.
 A comprehensive and helpful summary about racial prejudice determined by years of social scientific investigation.

MILLER, ARTHUR G. *In the Eye of the Beholder: Contemporary Issues in Stereotyping.* New York: Praeger, 1982.
 An anthology of articles discussing the nature and impact of stereotyping based on race, ethnicity, gender, age, mental illness, and appearance.

MILLER, RANDALL M. (ed.). *The Kaleidoscopic Lens: How Hollywood Views Ethnic Groups.* Englewood, NJ: Jerome S. Ozer, 1980.
 Stereotypical portrayals in film of racial and ethnic groups in America are discussed and illustrated.

PERLMUTTER, PHILIP. *A History of Ethnic, Religious, and Racial Prejudice in America.* Ames: Iowa State University Press, 1991.
 Comprehensive study of bigotry against various groups from colonial beginnings to the present.

PETTIGREW, THOMAS F., GEORGE M. FREDERICKSON, DALE T. KNOBEL, NATHAN GLAZER, AND REED UEDA. *Prejudice.* Cambridge, MA: The Belknap Press of Harvard University Press, 1982.
 A small paperback examining further the subject matter of this chapter on prejudice and discrimination.

4

© 1992 Ricky Flores/Impact Visuals

Dominant–Minority Relations

So far we have looked at behavioral patterns in relating to strangers, the role of culture and social structure in shaping perceptions and interactions, and the complexity of prejudice and discrimination. In this chapter we shall discuss response patterns that dominant and minority groups follow in their dealings with one another.

What we are suggesting in the following pages is that these patterns occur in varying degrees for most groups regardless of race, ethnicity, or time period. They are not mutually exclusive categories, and groups do not necessarily follow all these patterns at one time. Although each group has its own unique characteristics and many factors determine actual responses, the experiences of each minority and dominant group of a given society share these pattern commonalities in some fashion.

MINORITY-GROUP RESPONSES

Although personality characteristics play a large role in determining how individuals respond to unfavorable situations, behavioral patterns for the group in general will be similar to those of other groups in comparable circumstances. External factors play an important part, but social interpretation is also a critical determinant. The minority group's perception of its power resources—its power to change established relationships with the dominant group in a significant way—will, to a large extent, determine which response it will be more likely to make.[1]

Avoidance

One way of dealing with discriminatory practices is to avoid encountering them, if possible. Throughout history minority groups—from the ancient Hebrews to the Pilgrims to the Soviet Jews prior to 1991—have attempted to solve their problems by leaving them behind. One motivation for migration, then, is avoidance of discrimination. If leaving is not possible, minorities may turn inward to their own group for their social and economic activities. This approach serves to insulate minority groups against the antagonistic actions of the dominant group, but it also promotes charges of "clannishness" and "nonassimilation." However, lacking adequate economic, legal, or political power, avoidance may be the only choice open to the minority group.

By clustering together in small subcommunities, minority peoples not only re-created a miniature version of their familiar world in the strange land but also established a safe place in which they could live, relax, and interact with others like themselves who could understand their needs and interests. For some minority groups, seeking such shelter from the prejudices of others was probably a secondary motivation following a primary choice to live among their own kind.

Asian immigrants, for example, followed this pattern. When the Chinese first came to this country, they worked in many occupations in which workers were needed, frequently clustering together in neighborhoods close to their jobs. Prejudicial attitudes had always existed against the Chinese, but in the post–Civil War period they became even more the targets of bitter hatred and discrimination for economic and other reasons. Evicted from their jobs by race-baiting union strikes and limited in residential choice by restrictive housing covenants, many had no choice but to live in Chinatowns within the larger cities. They entered occupations not competitive with whites (curio shops, laundries, restaurants, and so on), and followed their tradition of settling their disputes among themselves rather than subjecting themselves to public law adjudication.

Deviance

When a group is continually rejected and discriminated against, some of the members find it difficult to identify with the dominant society and to accept its norms. People at the bottom of the socioeconomic ladder, particularly members of victimized racial and ethnic groups, may respond to the pressures of everyday life in ways they consider reasonable but that others view as deviant. In particular this situation occurs when laws represent an attempt to impose the moral standards of the dominant group on the behavior of other groups. Many minority groups in the United States—Irish, Germans, Chinese, Italians, blacks, Native Americans, and Hispanics—have been at one time or another arrested and punished in disproportionate numbers for so-called crimes of personal disorganization. Included among the outrages to the morality of the dominant group have been public drunkenness, drug abuse, gambling, and sexual "misconduct." It is a matter of dispute whether this is a function of the frequency of misconduct or of selective arrests. Also, some "deviance" is that only from the perspective of the majority group, whereas other types of deviance, such as wife-beating, may also be deviant within the minority community.

Part of the problem regarding law enforcement is its subjective nature and the discretionary handling of violations. Many people have criticized the American criminal justice system for its disparities in according fair and equal treatment to the poor and minority-group members as compared with the middle and upper classes.[2] The complaints have included (1) the tendency of police to arrest suspects from minority groups more than those from the majority group when discretionary judgment is possible; (2) the overrepresentation of certain dominant social, ethnic, and racial groups on juries; (3) the difficulty for the poor in affording bail; (4) the poor quality of free legal defense; and (5) the disparities in sentences for dominant and minority groups. Because social background constitutes one of the factors that the police and courts consider, those who belong to a racial or ethnic group with a negative stereotype are at a severe disadvantage.

When a particular racial or ethnic group commits a noticeable number of deviant offenses, such as delinquency, crime, drunkenness, or some public-nuisance problem, the public often extends a negative image to all members of that group even if it applies to only a few. Some common associations, for example, are Italians and gangsters, Irish and heavy drinking and fighting, Chinese and opium, blacks and street crimes such as mugging and purse snatching, Puerto Ricans and knife fighting. Even though a very small percentage of a group actually engages in such behavior, sometimes the entire group becomes negatively stereotyped. A number of factors—including values, behavior patterns, and structural conditions in both the native and adopted lands—help explain the various kinds of so-called deviance among different minority groups. The best means of stopping the deviance is a debatable issue between proponents of corrective versus preventive measures.

Deviant behavior among minority groups occurs not because of race or ethnicity, as prejudiced people would claim, but partly because of poverty and lack of opportunity. Clifford Shaw and Henry McKay, in a classic study of juvenile delinquency in Chicago, suggested that structural conditions, not membership in a particular minority group, determine crime and delinquency rates.[3] They found that the highest rates of juvenile delinquency occurred in areas with poor housing; few job opportunities; and the widespread incidence of prostitution, gambling, and drug use. The delinquency rate was consistently high over a 30-year period, even though five different ethnic groups had moved in and out of those areas during that period. Nationality was unimportant; the unchanged conditions brought unchanged results. Other studies have also demonstrated a correlation between higher rates of either juvenile or adult crime and income level and place of residence.[4]

Because many minority groups are heavily represented among low-income populations, studies emphasizing social-class variables provide insight into the minority experience. For example, Albert Cohen found that a lack of opportunities encourages delinquency by lower-class males.[5] Social aspirations may be similar in all levels of society, but opportunities are not. Belonging to a gang may give a youth a sense of power and help overcome feelings of inadequacy; hoodlumism becomes an expression of resentment against a society with norms that seem impossible to follow.[6] The large majority of racial-group and ethnic-group members do not join gangs or engage in criminally deviant behavior. Nevertheless, because some minority groups are represented disproportionately in such activities, despite the small percentage of the total group involved, the public image of the group as a whole suffers.

Some social factors, particularly parental attitudes about education and social ascent, appear to be related to delinquency rates. For example, parental emphasis on academic achievement may partially explain the low rate of juvenile delinquency among second-generation Jews compared with the high rate of juvenile delinquency among second-generation Italians, whose parents often viewed formal education as a frill.[7]

Defiance

If a minority group is sufficiently cohesive and conscious of its growing economic or political power, its members may act openly to challenge and eliminate discriminatory practices. When defying discrimination, the minority group is taking a strong stance regarding its position in the society. Prior to this time certain individuals of that group may have been in the vanguard (for example, by challenging laws in court).

Sometimes the defiance is violent and appears to be spontaneous, although it usually is the outgrowth of long-standing conditions. One example is the Irish draft riot in New York in 1863 during the Civil War. When its volunteer armies proved insufficient, the Union used a military draft to secure the needed troops. In those days well-to-do males could legally buy the military services of a substitute. Because the Irish were mostly poor and concentrated in urban areas, many of them were drafted. Their defiance of what they considered an unfair practice became a riot in which the blacks became the scapegoats, with lives lost and property destroyed or damaged. Similarly, the 1991 Washington, DC, Hispanic riot after a black female police officer shot a Salvadoran immigrant and the 1992 Los Angeles riot following the acquittal of police officers videotaped beating Rodney King may both have been spontaneous reactions but only within the larger context of smoldering, deepseated, long-standing resentments.

A militant action, such as the takeover of a symbolic site, is a moderately aggressive act of defiance. The late 1960s witnessed many building takeovers by blacks and other disaffected, angry, alienated students on college campuses. In many instances the purpose of the action was to call public attention to what the group considered indifference or discrimination accorded their people. Similar actions occurred in this period to protest the war in Vietnam. A small group of Native Americans took this approach in the 1970s to protest their living conditions; they seized Alcatraz Island in California, the Bureau of Indian Affairs in Washington, DC, and the village of Wounded Knee in South Dakota. The influence of the media helped to validate and spread the idea of using militant actions to obtain a group's ends.

Any peaceful action that challenges the status quo is less aggressive but is defiant nonetheless; parades, marches, picket lines, mass meetings, boycotts, and demonstrations are examples. Another form of peaceful protest is to deliberately break discriminatory laws and challenge their constitutionality or to break a discriminatory tradition. The civil rights actions of the 1960s—sit-ins, lie-ins, and freedom rides—challenged Jim Crow laws that restricted access by blacks to public establishments in the South. Shop-ins at stores that had previously catered to an exclusively white clientele illustrated deliberate efforts to break traditional store practices.

Acceptance

Many minority people, to the frequent consternation of their leaders and sympathizers, accept the situation in which they find themselves. Some do so stoically, even justifying it by subtle rationalizations. Others are resentful but accept the situation for reasons of personal security or economic necessity. Although this approach maintains the superior position in society of the dominant group and the subordinate position of minority groups, it does ease the open tensions and conflicts between the two groups. Others accept the situation through false consciousness, or because the dominant group controls information.

Conforming to prevailing patterns of interaction between dominant and minority groups also can be a subconscious action, the end result of social conditioning. Just as socialization can serve as a cause of prejudice, so too it can cause minority-group members to disregard or be unaware of alternative status possibilities. How much acceptance of lower status is of this nature and how much is characterized by resentful submission is a question that has not been completely answered. However, some sociologists believe that it is not uncommon for one to conform externally while rejecting the system mentally and emotionally.

Blacks, Mexican Americans, and Native Americans have experienced a multigenerational subordinate position in the United States. Until the 1960s a combination of structural discrimination, racial stratification, and a sense of powerlessness and the futility of trying to change things caused many to accommodate to the situation imposed on them. Similarly, Japanese Americans had little choice when, following the bombing of Pearl Harbor and the subsequent rise in anti-Japanese sentiment, the U.S. government in 1942 uprooted and imprisoned 110,000 of them in "temporary relocation centers."

Acceptance as a minority response is not as common in the United States as it once was. More aware of the alternative ways of living that are presented in the media, today's minorities are more hopeful of sharing in them. No longer do they passively accept the status quo, which denies them the comfortable living and leisure pursuits others have. Society—as evidenced by court decisions, legislation, new social services, and other efforts—has even created a more favorable climate for improvement of the status of minority groups. Perhaps televised news features and behavioral science courses have helped to heighten the public's social awareness.

Negative Self-Image

The apathy that militant leaders find among their own people often results from a negative self-image, a rather common consequence of prejudice and discrimination. Continual treatment as an inferior encourages a loss of self-confidence. If everything about a person's position and experiences—jobs with low pay, substandard housing, the hostility of others, and the need for assistance from governmental agencies—works to destroy pride and hope, that person may become apathetic. To remain optimistic and determined in the face of constant negative experiences from all directions is extremely difficult.

Kurt Lewin once observed that development of a negative self-image among minority-group members was a fairly general tendency.[8] The pervasiveness of dominant-group values and attitudes, which include negative stereotypes of the minority group, may cause the minority-group member to accept them. A person's self-image includes race, religion, and nationality; thus, individuals may feel embarrassed and inferior if they are aware that any of these attributes are held in low esteem within the society. In effect, minority-group members begin to perceive themselves as negatively as the dominant group originally perceived them.

This negative self-image, or self-hatred, manifests itself in many ways. People may try to "pass" as members of the dominant group and deny membership in a disparaged group. They may fully agree with the dominant group's prejudices and accept their state. They may also engage in ego defense by blaming others within the group for their low status.

> Some Jews refer to other Jews as "kikes"—blaming them exclusively for the anti-Semitism from which all alike suffer. Class distinctions within groups is often a result of trying to free oneself from responsibility for the handicap from which the group as a whole suffers. "Lace curtain" Irish look down on "shanty" Irish. Wealthy Spanish and Portuguese Jews have long regarded themselves as the top of the pyramid of Hebraic peoples. But Jews of German origin, having a rich culture, view themselves as the aristocrats, often looking down on Austrian, Hungarian, and Balkan Jews, and regarding Polish and Russian Jews at the very bottom.[9]

Negative self-image, then, can cause people to accept their fate passively. It also can cause a sense of personal shame for possessing undesired qualities or can create antipathy toward other members of the group for possessing them. Minority-group members frequently attempt to overcome their negative self-image by changing their name or religion, having cosmetic surgery, or moving into a locale where the stereotype is not as prevalent.

Portraying negative self-image as a fairly general tendency among minority-group members, as Lewin does, may be too broad a generalization. For example, members of tightly cohesive religious groups could draw emotional support from their faith and from one another. The insulation of living in an ethnic community, strong ingroup loyalty, or the determination to maintain their cultural heritage also may prevent minority-group members from developing a negative self-image.

The Vicious Circle

Sometimes the relationship between prejudice and discrimination is circular. Gunnar Myrdal refers to this pattern as **cumulative causation,** a vicious circle wherein prejudice and discrimination each causes the other.[10] The dynamics of the relations between dominant and minority groups set in motion an almost perpetual sequence of reciprocal stimuli and responses. For example, a discriminatory action in jobs leads to a minority reaction, poverty, which in turn reinforces the dominant-group attitude that the minority group is inferior, which leads to still more discrimination, and so on.

Myrdal points out that this pattern may be desirable or undesirable. The expectations held about the newcomers are the key to the nature of the pattern that develops.[11] If the dominant group makes the newcomers welcome, they in turn are likely to react in a positive manner, which reinforces their friendly reception. If the new group is ignored and made to feel unwelcome, the members may react negatively, which also reaffirms original attitudes and actions. As Allport says, "If we foresee evil in our fellow man, we tend to provoke it; if good, we elicit it."[12] In other words, negative expectations engender negative reactions. The reactions encourage greater prejudicial opinions, broaden the social distance between the groups, and cause the vicious circle to continue.

When the Jews were denied access to many vacation resorts in the nineteenth century, their reaction served to reinforce their negative stereotype in the minds of some, thus reinforcing the discrimination. Some Jews demanded the right of equal access, showing the resort operators that Jews were "pushy." As the Jews, because of this discriminatory policy, began going to their own resorts in the Catskill Mountains, they were then labeled "clannish." Similarly, the Irish encountered severe job discrimination in the mid-nineteenth century, and because of the poverty that resulted, many of them lived in urban slums and had trouble with the law. With this evidence of their "inferiority" and "undesirability," their job opportunities became even more limited. In the same way, white discrimination against blacks, based partly on their low standard of living, furthers the problems of poverty, thus fueling even more any white antipathy for blacks.

Marginality

Minority-group members sometimes find themselves caught in a conflict between their own identity and values and the necessity to behave in a certain way in order to be accepted by the dominant group. This situation usually is found when a member of a minority group is undergoing a transitional period. In an attempt to enter the mainstream of society, the *marginal* person internalizes the dominant group's cultural patterns but has not yet gained full acceptance. Such individuals are in an ill-defined role, no longer at ease within their own group but not yet fully a part of the *reference group,* the one to which they refer when evaluating themselves and their behavior.[13]

Over the years sociologists have differed in their interpretation of the effects of marginality. Robert E. Park, who gave this social phenomenon its name, believed it caused the individual a great deal of strain and difficulty. Such a person, he observed, is one "whom fate has condemned to live in two societies and in two not merely different but antagonistic cultures."[14]

According to Park's thesis, this situation can cause the marginal person to suffer anxiety over a conflict of values and loyalties. This inner conflict can occur among both adults and children. The adults leave the security of their cultural group, thereby risking being labeled renegades by their own people. They seek sustained social contacts with the dominant group, which may view them as outsiders. No longer comfortable with the old ways but influenced by them and identified with them nonetheless, the adults often experience feelings of frustration, hypersensitivity, and self-consciousness.

The children of immigrants also find themselves caught between two worlds. At home their parents attempt to raise them in their social heritage, according to the established ways of the old country. The children, through school and other outside experiences, become exposed to the American culture and want to be like the other children. Moreover, they quickly learn that the dominant group views the ways of their parents as inferior and that they too are socially rejected because of their background. Consequently, many young people may develop emotional problems and be embarrassed to bring classmates home.

Marginality, according to this view, is an example of cultural conflict, primarily due to the clash of values within the individual. However, many sociologists now believe that the reaction to marginal status depends in large measure on whether or not the individual receives reassurances of self-worth from the community. Thus defining the situation and adjusting to it are contingent on the individual's sense of security within the community.[15] In addition, ethnic subcommunities and institutions and a sense of solidarity among members of the ethnic group contribute to that sense of well-being. These observations have led some sociologists to emphasize stable individuals in a marginal culture rather than marginal persons in a dominant culture.[16] In other words individuals in a marginal culture share their cultural duality with many others in primary-group relationships, institutional activities, and interaction with members of the dominant society without encountering any dichotomy between their desires and actuality.

Whether this phase of the assimilation process represents an emotionally stressful experience or an insulated one, minority-group members nonetheless pass through a transitional period during which they are not fully a part of either world. An immigrant group may move into the mainstream of American society within the lifetimes of the first-generation members, or they may choose not to do so or simply be unable to. Usually marginality is a one- or two-generational phenomenon. After that, members of the minority group have either assimilated or formed a distinctive subculture. No matter which route they take, they are no longer caught between two cultural worlds.

Middleman Minorities

Building on theories of marginality, Hubert Blalock suggested the concept of "middleman" minorities.[17] This model, based on a dominant–subordinate stratification system, places middleman minorities in an intermediate rather than low-status position.[18] Feudal or colonial societies, with their ruling elite and large peasant masses, often have middleman minorities performing mediating commerce links between the two. Consequently, such minorities commonly are trading peoples whose history of persecution (Jews, Greeks, and Armenians) or sojourner orientation (Chinese, Japanese, and Koreans) obliged them to perform risky or marginal tasks that permitted easy liquidation.[19]

Middleman groups often serve as buffers, the target of hostility and conflict from both the top and bottom strata. Jews in Nazi Germany and Asians in Uganda in the early 1970s, for instance, became scapegoats for economic stresses in those societies. Their susceptibility to such antagonism and their sojourner self-definition of not remaining long in the host society promote among them high ingroup solidarity.

Systematic discrimination can make middleman minority status a rather permanent one, as in the case of European Jews in the medieval period. Sometimes the entrepreneurial skills developed in trade and commerce provide middleman minorities with highly adaptive capabilities and competitive advantages, enabling them to achieve upward mobility and assimilate more easily; this occurred for Jewish immigrants to the United States and also may occur for the Korean Americans. In other cases a group may emerge as a middleman minority because of changing residential patterns. One example is Jewish store owners in cities who once serviced their own people who have now moved away; unable to follow them these urban merchants now serve the new urban minority groups situated lower on the socioeconomic ladder.

DOMINANT-GROUP RESPONSES

Members of a dominant group may react to minority peoples with tolerance and compassion, although they may sometimes be condescending in their attitudes. This type of favorable response usually occurs when the minority is small in number, not perceived as a threat, or both. As the minority group increases in population, threatening the natives' monopoly on jobs and other claims to privileged cultural resources, the dominant group's attitude is likely to become suspicious or fearful. If the fear becomes great enough, the dominant group may take some form of action against the minority group.

Legislative Controls

If the influx of racial and ethnic groups appears too great for a country to absorb or if prejudicial fears prevail, that nation may act to regulate and

Here is an illustration of both the middleman minority concept and occupation patterning within minority groups. This Asian Indian newsstand owner in Manhattan typifies an occupational niche of his compatriots in most American cities, where many of their customers are members of other minority groups. (*Arvind Garg/Photo Researchers*)

restrict their entry. Australia, Canada, and the United States—the three greatest receiving countries in international migration—once had discriminatory immigration laws that either excluded or curtailed the number of immigrants from countries other than those in northern and western Europe. Following similar patterns of policy change, Canada (in 1962), the United States (in 1965), and Australia (in 1973) began to permit entry from all parts of the world.

To maintain a paternalistic social system, the dominant group frequently restricts the educational opportunities and voting of the subordinate group. This denial assures the dominant group of maintaining its system of control, whether over internal minorities such as the blacks in the Old South and the various ethnic minorities in the Soviet Union, or over colonized peoples such as those ruled by the Belgians, British, Dutch, French, Japanese, and Portuguese. Colonial powers have usually committed themselves to stability, trade, and tapping the natural resources of a country rather than to its development and self-governance. As a result, the usual experience of native populations under colonial rule has been leadership without real power in important matters, limited educational opportunities, and restricted political participation. Other means of denying political power have been disenfranchising voters through high property qualifications (British West Indies), high income qualifications (Trinidad), and poll taxes (United States), although none of these practices exists today in those areas. The most conspicuous recent example of rigid social control is in South Africa, where a legislated apartheid society denied blacks not only equal education and the ballot but also almost every other privilege.

Segregation

Through a policy of containment, by avoiding social interaction with members of a minority group as much as possible and keeping them "in their place," the dominant group can effectively create both spatial and social segregation.

Spatial segregation refers to the physical separation of a minority people from the rest of society. This most commonly occurs in residential patterns but also takes place in education, in the use of public facilities, and in the occupational area. The majority group may institutionalize this form of segregation by law (de jure segregation) or establish it as an ongoing practice through norms (de facto segregation).

Spatial segregation of minorities has been quite common for a long time. Since the days of the preindustrial city with its heterogeneous populations, the dominant group has relegated racial and ethnic minorities to special sections of the city, often the least desirable areas.[20] In Europe this medieval ecological pattern resulted in minority groups being situated on the city outskirts nearest the encircling wall. Because this pattern remains in much of Europe today, Europeans, unlike Americans, consider it a sign of high prestige to live near the center of the city.[21]

The dominant group may use covert or overt means to achieve spatial segregation of a minority group. Some examples of covert actions are restrictive covenants, "gentlemen's" agreements, and collusion between the community and real estate agents to steer "undesirable" minorities into certain neighborhoods only.[22] Overt actions may include restrictive zoning, segregation laws, or intimidation. Both covert and overt segregation actions have been targets of U.S. court rulings over the past 30 years.

An important dimension of spatial segregation is that the dominant group can also achieve it through avoidance, or residential mobility. Usually referred to as the **invasion–succession** ecological pattern, this process has been a common one, involving different religions and nationalities as well as different races. The most recognized example in the United States is previously all-white neighborhoods becoming black, but any study of most urban neighborhoods would reveal the same pattern as successive waves of immigrants came here over the years. Residents of a neighborhood may attempt to resist the influx of a minority group, eventually abandoning the area when their efforts are not successful. This pattern results in neighborhoods with a concentration of a new racial or ethnic group, a new segregated area.

Social segregation involves confining participation in social, service, political, and other types of activities to members of the ingroup. The dominant group excludes the outgroup from any involvement both in meaningful primary-group activities and in secondary-group activities. Organizations have screening procedures to keep out unwanted types, and informal groups also act to preserve their composition.

Segregation, whether spatial or social, can be either involuntary or voluntary. Minority-group members may choose not to live among the dominant group but by themselves instead; such a course of action is an avoidance response, discussed previously. On the other hand, minority-group members may have no choice at all about where they live because of economic or residential discrimination.

Whether by choice or against their will, minority groups form ethnic subcommunities, whose existence in turn promotes and maintains the social distance between the minority groups and the rest of society. Not only are minority-group members physically congregated in one area and thus spatially segregated, but also they are not engaging in any social interaction with others outside of their own group.

Under the right conditions, frequent interaction often lessens prejudice, but when interaction is severely limited, the acculturation process is slowed considerably. Instead, a reinforcement of values occurs concerning what is regarded as normal or different, paving the way for stereotyping, social comparisons, and prestige ranking.

Expulsion

When other methods of dealing with a minority group fail, and sometimes not even as a last resort, an intolerant dominant group may persecute or expel the minority group from the territory in which it resides. Henry VIII banished the Gypsies from England in the sixteenth century, Spanish rulers drove out the Moors in the early seventeenth century, and the British expelled the Acadians from Nova Scotia in the mid-eighteenth century. A more recent example is Idi Amin, the former authoritarian ruler of Uganda, who decreed in 1972 that all Asians must leave his country.

The United States also has its examples of mass expulsion. In colonial times the Puritans forced Roger Williams and his followers out of Massachusetts for their nonconformity, and they settled in what became Rhode Island. The forcible removal of the Cherokee from rich Georgia land and the subsequent "Trail of Tears," in which 4,000 perished along the thousand-mile forced march, is another illustration.

Mass expulsion is an effort to remove a group that is seen as a social problem rather than an attempt to resolve the problem. This policy often takes form after other methods, such as assimilation or extermination, have failed. Whether a dominant group chooses to remove a minority group by extermination or by the somewhat more humane method of expulsion depends in part on how sensitive the country is to world opinion. Sensitivity to world opinion often is related to the country's economic dependency on other nations.

Xenophobia

If the dominant group's suspicions and fears of the minority group become greatly heightened, they sometimes result in volatile, irrational feelings and actions. This overreaction is known as **xenophobia**, the undue fear of or contempt for strangers or foreigners. This almost hysterical response—reflected in print, in speeches and sermons, in legislation, and in violent actions—begins with ethnocentric views. Ethnocentrism encourages the creation of negative stereotypes, which in turn can lead to prejudice and discrimination and which can escalate through some catalyst into a highly emotional reaction.

The Federalists, fearful of "wild Irishmen" and "French radicals" and anxious to eliminate what they saw as a foreign threat to the country's stability, succeeded in passing the Alien and Sedition Acts in 1798. When a bomb exploded at an anarchist gathering at Chicago's Haymarket Square in 1886, many Americans thereafter linked foreigners with radicals. The Bolshevik Revolution in 1917 led to the Palmer raids, in which Russian Americans were illegally rounded up and incarcerated; some even were deported. Similarly in 1942 the placement in concentration camps of 110,000 Japanese Americans, many of them second- and third-generation Americans, was an irrational overreaction. All these are examples of a xenophobic reaction to people and events. (See Box 4.1 for a recent international example.)

Annihilation

The Nazi extermination of more than 6 million Jews brought the term *genocide* into the English language, but the practice of killing all the men, women, and children of a particular group goes back to ancient times. In warfare among the ancient Hebrews, Assyrians, Babylonians, Egyptians, and others, the usual practice was for the victor in battle to slay all the enemy, partly to prevent their children from seeking revenge. For example, preserved in Deuteronomy are these words of Moses:

> . . . when Sehon offered battle at Jasa, coming out to meet us with all his forces. . . . We made an end of him and of his sons and of all his people, took all his cities there and then, putting all that dwelt there, men, women, and children, to the sword, and spared nothing except the beasts we drove off for our use, and such plunder as captured cities yield.

| BOX 4.1 | **THE INTERNATIONAL SCENE** |

Under communist rule East Germany imported thousands of workers from other Marxist regimes, particularly Angola, Cuba, Mozambique, and Vietnam. With the fall of the Berlin Wall and communism itself, about two-thirds of the 90,000 sojourners returned to their homelands. Despite this, a wave of xenophobia swept eastern Germany in the early 1990s.

With high unemployment and an uncertain future, alienated German youths committed a series of violent attacks on Third World scapegoat targets. In April 1991, neo-Nazis in Dresden threw a Mozambican from a moving streetcar to his death. The following month they invaded a tenement in Wittenberg, forcing two Namibians off a fourth-floor balcony and critically injuring them. In July 1991, 50 skinheads in eastern Berlin besieged a center for asylum-seekers from Third World countries, smashing windows and assaulting residents. In 1992 over 1,800 attacks on foreigners and 17 deaths brought Germans to the frightening realization that this rampant xenophobia reflected much more than the random vandalism of a minority of alienated youth.

Politics also reflects the xenophobic mood of some Germans. In local elections in 1992, the anti-immigrant German People's Union and the Republikaner Party led by former SS officer Franz Schonhuber won seats for the first time in two state parliaments. In response the government has banned a 130-member, neo-Nazi group, the Nationalist Front, as well as the airing of extremist right-wing music. A survey taken at the end of 1992 revealed that 69 percent of Germans surveyed said that they rejected the "Foreigners Out!" slogan, up from 43 percent earlier in the year.

> . . . Og, that was king of Basan, came out to meet us with all his forces, and offered battle at Edrai. . . . So the Lord our God gave us a fresh victory over Og, king of Basan, and all his people, and we exterminated them, there and then laying waste all his cities. . . . We made an end of them as we had made an end of Sehon, that reigned in Hesebon, destroying all the inhabitants of their cities, men, women, and children, plundering their cattle and all the plunder their cities yielded.[23]

In modern times various countries have used extermination as a means of solving a so-called race problem. Arnold Toynbee once said that the "English method of settlement" followed this pattern.[24] The British, through extermination and close confinement of survivors, succeeded in annihilating the entire Tasmanian race between 1803 and 1876.[25] The Dutch considered South African Bushmen less than human and attempted to obliterate them.[26] When the Indians of Brazil resisted the settlement of Portuguese in their land, the whites solved the problem by systematically killing them. One of their favored means of doing so was to place the clothing of recent smallpox victims in their villages and allow the contagion to decimate the native population.[27]

In the 1890s and again in 1915, the Turks massacred hundreds of thousands of Armenians, events still solemnly remembered each year by Armenian Americans. One classic example in the United States was the massacre at Wounded Knee in 1890, when the Seventh Cavalry killed about 200 Native American men, women, and children.

Lynchings are not a form of annihilation, for the intent is not to exterminate an entire group but to set an example through selective and drastic punishment. Nonetheless, the victims usually are minority-group members, and often that fact is the reason they are hanged instead of receiving some other punishment. Although lynchings have occurred in the United States throughout its history, only since 1882 have reasonably reliable statistics been kept (Figure 4.1). Sources such as the *Chicago Tribune* and Tuskegee Institute, which have kept data on this subject, reveal that 5,000 lynchings have occurred since 1882. They have happened in every state except the New England states, with the Deep South (including Texas) claiming the most victims. In fact 90 percent of the lynchings in this period have occurred in the

FIGURE 4.1
Lynchings in the United States Since 1882

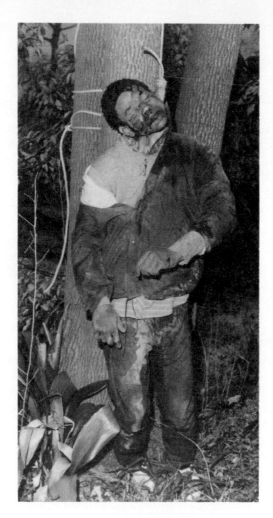

The gruesome scene of the 1981 Ku Klux Klan lynching of 19-year-old Michael Donald in Mobile, Alabama, has a more positive sequel. The Southern Poverty Law Center successfully prosecuted the murderers and brought civil charges against the KKK, winning for the victim's mother a $7 million judgment, effectively putting the Alabama Klan out of business. (*Giles Peres/ Magnum*)

Southern states; blacks have accounted for 80 percent of the victims and other minority-group members the remainder. The statistics do not, however, include lynchings during the nation's first 100 years, including those in the western frontier, when many Native Americans and Chicanos also met this fate.[28]

Annihilation sometimes is unintended, as when whites inadvertently spread their sickness to the American and Canadian Indians, Eskimos, and Polynesians. With such ailments as measles, mumps, chicken pox, and small-pox unknown to them, the native populations had little resistance and thus often succumbed to these contagious diseases. Other forms of annihilation, usually intentional, occur during times of mob violence; overzealous police actions; and the quiet, calculated actions of small groups.[29]

EXPLOITATION

Countless writings have enumerated instances of the exploitation of minority groups in all countries. Sometimes the perpetrators of this abuse are members of the same group, as, for instance, the crew chiefs of migrant workers and the *padroni* of old Italian immigrant communities, both of whom often benefited at the expense of their own people. Most often, however, members of dominant groups exploit minority groups, a practice emphasized by conflict theorists.

Although we shall be using functionalist, conflict, and interactionist theories throughout this book, three conflict analyses sometimes prove helpful in understanding ethnic antagonism: the power differential, internal colonialism, and the split labor market.

The Power Differential Theory

Stanley Lieberson suggested a **power theory** in which intergroup relations depend on the relative power of the migrant group and the indigenous group.[30] Because the two groups usually do not share the same culture, each will strive to maintain its own institutions. Which group becomes superordinate and which becomes subordinate governs what will follow.

If the newcomers are superior in terms of technology (particularly weapons) and social organization, then conflict may occur at an early stage, and there is likely to be a numerical decline as a result of warfare, disease, or disruption of sustenance activities. The local inhabitants find their institutions undermined or co-opted and may eventually participate in the institutions of the dominant group. In time a group consciousness may arise, and sometimes the indigenous group will even succeed in ousting the superordinate migrant group. In many former African colonies and in Southeast Asia, when this happened, interethnic fights among the many indigenous groups often led to new forms of superordination and subordination within countries (as was the case in Nigeria and Uganda).

Lieberson maintains that neither conflict nor assimilation is an inevitable outcome of racial and ethnic contact. Instead, the particular relationship between two groups determines which alternative will occur. Conflict between a superordinate migrant group and a subordinate indigenous group can be immediate and violent. If the relationship is the reverse and the indigenous group is superordinate, conflict will be limited and sporadic, and the host society will exert a great deal of pressure on the subordinate migrant group to assimilate, acquiesce, or leave. Additionally, the superordinate indigenous group can limit the numbers and groups entering, to reduce any threats of demographic and institutional imbalance. Restrictive immigration laws against the Chinese in 1882 and against all but northern and western Europeans in 1921 and 1924 illustrate this process. Violent union attempts to remove Asian workers, labor union hostility to blacks, and efforts to expel foreigners (such as Indians, Japanese, and Filipinos) or to revolutionize the social order (Indian boarding schools and the Americanization movement) all illustrate the use of power against minority groups.

Another sociologist, William J. Wilson, has suggested that power relations between **superordinate** and **subordinate** groups are different in paternalistic and competitive systems.[31] With **paternalism** (such as in South Africa and the Old South), the dominant group has almost absolute control over the subordinate group and can exert almost unlimited coercion to maintain societal order. In a competitive system, such as in the United States today, there is some degree of power reciprocity, and so society is somewhat vulnerable to political pressures and economic boycotts.

Rapid social change—industrialization, unionization, urbanization, migration, and political changes—usually loosens the social structure, leading to new tensions as both groups seek new power resources. If the minority group increases its power resources through protective laws and improved economic opportunities, it may foresee even greater improvement in its condition. This heightened awareness is likely to lead to conflict unless additional gains are forthcoming. For example, the civil rights movement of the mid-1960s brought about legislation ensuring minority rights and opportunities in jobs, housing, education, and other aspects of life, but this led to new tensions. In the late 1960s there were urban riots and burnings, protest demonstrations and human barricades to stop construction at low-income housing sites, school-busing controversies, and challenges against labor discrimination.

The Internal Colonialism Theory

When dealing with the issue of black militancy in the late 1960s, Robert Blauner attempted to integrate the factors of caste and racism, ethnicity, culture, and economic exploitation.[32] His major point was that American treatment of its own black population was comparable to the past European subjugation and exploitation of non-Western peoples in their own lands. Although he focused on American black–white relations, he did suggest that the Mexican Americans might also fit his internal colonialism model and that the Native Americans could be added as another suitable example.

> Of course many ethnic groups in America have lived in ghettoes. What makes the Black ghettoes an expression of colonized status are three special features. First, the ethnic ghettoes arose more from voluntary choice, both in the sense of the choice to immigrate to America and the decision to live among one's fellow ethnics. Second, the immigrant ghettoes tended to be a one and two generation phenomenon; they were actually way-stations in the process of acculturation

and assimilation. When they continue to persist as in the case of San Francisco's Chinatown, it is because they are big business for the ethnics themselves and there is a new stream of immigrants. The Black ghetto on the other hand has been a more permanent phenomenon, although some individuals do escape it. But most relevant is the third point. European ethnic groups like the Poles, Italians and Jews generally only experienced a brief period, often less than a generation, during which their residential buildings, commercial stores, and other enterprises were owned by outsiders. The Chinese and Japanese faced handicaps of color prejudice that were almost as strong as the Blacks faced, but very soon gained control of their internal communities, because their traditional ethnic culture and social organization had not been destroyed by slavery and internal colonization. But Afro-Americans are distinct in the extent to which their segregated communities have remained controlled economically, politically, and administratively from the outside.[33]

Several of these statements need to be modified. Chinatowns have persisted not because of any business advantage but because of racial discrimination. In proportion to the Chinatown population, only a few Chinese actually benefit from the tourist trade. Second, the Chinese and Japanese *always* had "control of their internal communities," although they differ greatly from one another with respect to their structure and cohesiveness.

Blauner sees the exploitation that was limited for other groups as being more permanent for blacks and possibly Chicanos. He believes that conflict and confrontation, as well as real or apparent chaos and disorder, will continue, because this may well be the only way in which an internally colonized group can deal with the dominant society. This conflict orientation suggests that the multigenerational exploitation of certain groups creates both a unique situation in comparison with the situation of other groups and a basis for the conflict—often violent—that sporadically flares up in our cities.

The Split Labor Market Theory

Edna Bonacich theorizes that ethnic antagonism is the result of a combination of economic exploitation by employers and economic competition between two or more groups of laborers that produces a wage differential for labor.[34] She contends that much of the ethnic antagonism is based not on ethnicity and race but on the conflict between higher-paid and lower-paid labor.

> Ethnic antagonism is specifically produced by the competition that arises from a price differential. An oversupply of equal-priced labor does not produce such antagonism, though it too threatens people with the loss of their job. However, hiring practices will not necessarily fall along ethnic lines. . . . All workingmen are on the same footing, competing for scarce jobs. When one ethnic group is decidedly cheaper than another (i.e., when the labor market is split), the higher paid worker faces more than the loss of his job; he faces the possibility that the wage standard in all jobs will be undermined by cheaper labor.[35]

If the higher-paid labor group is strong enough, it may be able to stop the real or potential cheaper competition through an exclusion movement or caste

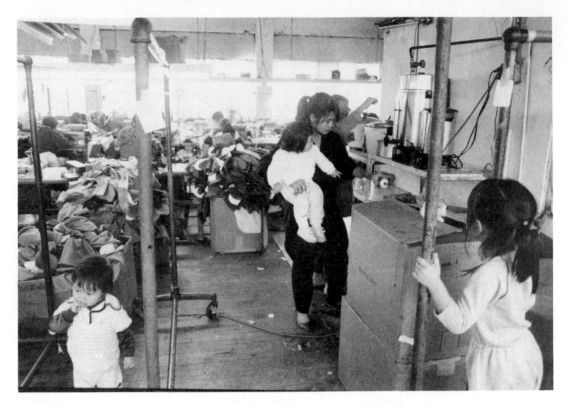

Sweatshops today remain a form of economic exploitation just as they did three generations ago. One difference is the children in the shops alongside their working mothers. Many Asian and Hispanic newcomers, many of them undocumented aliens, work under appalling conditions for long hours and low pay (© *1990 D. Steele/Impact Visuals*)

system. To some degree America's restriction of Chinese and Japanese immigrant labor and Australia's restriction of Asian and Polynesian immigrants are victories for organized labor against lower-paid competition. In a caste system, higher-paid labor controls certain high-paying jobs exclusively and limits the minority group to other, lower-paying jobs often lacking health benefits and pension plans. This creates an aristocracy of labor and submerges the labor-market split by stratifying the differentially priced workers. This phenomenon can be seen in the job differentials between blacks and whites in certain trade unions.

Some factors lowering the price of one group's labor might be their exploitation by management, their unfamiliarity with wage standards, their language and customs, and their lack of economic resources, all of which force them to take either low-paying jobs to survive, to make contractual commitments before emigrating, or to seek political support from a labor organization or government.

> Governments vary in the degree to which they protect their emigrants. Japan kept close watch over the fate of her nationals who migrated to Hawaii and the Pacific coast. . . . In contrast Mexican migrant workers to the United States have received little protection from their government, and African states were unable to intervene on behalf of slaves brought to America.[36]

When a labor market splits along ethnic lines, racial and ethnic stereotyping becomes a key factor in the labor conflict, and prejudice, ethnic antagonism, and racism become overt. The conflict is not the result of religious differences, and it is not a matter of which group was first to move into the area, because there are examples of ethnic antagonism in which these variables have been controlled. Bonacich argues that the one characteristic shared by all societies high in ethnic antagonism is that they have an indigenous working class that earns higher wages than do immigrant workers. Not everyone agrees with this theory. In the case of the anti-Chinese movement led by labor unions, racism was the motivating factor, and white workers offered to work for lower wages if this meant that the Chinese would be removed from their jobs.[37]

When applying the split labor market theory to the history of the Chinese in America between 1848 and 1882, Hilton suggested several modifications.[38] If the economy is expanding and labor shortages occur, ethnic antagonisms are disarmed. Most important, an ethnic bourgeoisie necessarily evolves because of the existence of an ethnic labor force.

> Native capitalists are seldom equipped to locate and reproduce that ethnic labor force by themselves. Unfamiliarity with the language and customs of Chinese workers made it necessary that white capital rely on an intermediary class of Chinese businessmen for two purposes. First, locating and hiring an adequate number of Chinese workers required that capital act through an intermediate class of Chinese compradors. Second, once obtained, the Chinese labor force had to be provisioned according to their accustomed tastes. This requirement fostered the development of a class of Chinese merchants.[39]

Hilton also indicates that ethnic bourgeoisie is both exploitative, in that it benefits from the ethnic worker, and benevolent, in that it solidifies the ethnic community and provides for its social needs. The ethnic bourgeoisie can affect a split labor market because its stronger economic and political base and often higher educational level enable it to act on behalf of the ethnic group. Although it does not always do so, the ethnic bourgeoisie can articulate the injustices of a caste system and challenge restrictive institutions.

A bourgeoisie arises from within the ranks of any ethnic group at some stage in their readjustment to life in America. Most notable are the *padroni* among the Italian and Greek immigrants and the *padrinos* among Puerto Rican and Mexican laborers.

For a brief summary of each of these theories, see Box 4.2.

BOX 4.2   **THREE CONFLICT THEORIES**

The Power Differential Theory

1. Neither conflict nor assimilation is inevitable.
2. Relative power of indigenous and migrant groups determines events.
3. If the migrant group is superordinate, early conflict and colonization will occur.
4. If the indigenous group is superordinate, the results are occasional labor and racial strife, legislative restrictions, and pressures on the minority to assimilate.
5. In a paternalistic society the dominant group has almost absolute control to maintain societal order.
6. A competitive society is somewhat vulnerable to political pressures and economic boycotts.

The Internal Colonialism Theory

1. American treatment of its black population is comparable to the past European subjugation and exploitation of non-Western peoples.
2. Black ghettos are more permanent than immigrant ghettos.
3. Black ghettos are controlled economically, politically, and administratively from the outside.
4. Continual exploitation means conflict and confrontation.
5. Mexican Americans and Native Americans also may fit this model.

The Split Labor Market Theory

1. Ethnic antagonism results more from conflict between higher- and lower-paid workers than from ethnicity and race.
2. Racial and ethnic stereotyping and prejudice emerge as key factors in labor conflicts.
3. Native labor presses for exclusion of the ethnic group or for a caste resolution restricting ethnic laborers to lowest-paying jobs.
4. An expanding economy creates labor shortages, which disarm labor antagonism.
5. An ethnic bourgeoisie arises as middleman between capitalists and labor.
6. The ethnic bourgeoisie can help maintain or challenge the caste labor system.

Limitations of These Theories

The power theory offers one variable to explain conflict or acceptance patterns; this does not provide insight into all conflicts, however, such as those between a superordinate indigenous group and a subordinate migrant group. Blauner's internal colonialism theory applies to only three groups—blacks,

Chicanos, and Native Americans. Bonacich's emphasis on the labor market is helpful, but her theory does not attempt to deal with other sources of prejudice, such as racial or religious antipathy or culture clash. In short none of these theories can satisfactorily explain most dominant-minority interaction. Many situations are quite complex and defy a single causative explanation. Other instances do show recurring patterns; in these cases, given an understanding of their limitations, theories such as those proposed by Lieberson, Blauner, and Bonacich can provide some insights into the minority experience.

Retrospect

Minority-group responses to prejudice and discrimination may be acceptance, avoidance, deviance, or defiance, depending in large measure on the group's perception of its power to change the status quo. After continual treatment as an inferior, a negative self-image may result. Another consequence of continued inequality is its intensification through a vicious circle or cumulative causation process.

Marginality is a social phenomenon occurring during the transitional period of assimilation; it can be either a stressful or a sheltered experience, depending on the support system of the ethnic community. Some groups become middleman minorities because of their historical background or sojourner orientation; they can remain indefinitely in that intermediate place in the social hierarchy, the potential scapegoat target of those above and below them, or achieve upward mobility and assimilation.

Dominant-group actions toward the minority group also may take various forms, including favorable or indifferent responses. When the reaction is negative, the group in power may place restraints on the minority group (for example, legislative controls, segregation, or suppression). If the reaction becomes more emotional or even xenophobic, expulsion or annihilation may occur. Sensitivity to world opinion and economic dependency on other nations in the modern world may curtail such actions. When the dominant group reacts more favorably to the minority group, intergroup tensions may be resolved through genuine or token reform.

Whether the indigenous or migrant group possesses superior power determines the nature of intergroup relations. Another influence is whether the social system is paternalistic or competitive. Consideration of black and Hispanic ghettos or Native American reservations as examples of internal colonialism offers a second conflict perspective. A third is a split labor market view of differential wage levels sparking ethnic antagonism. A final consideration is the rise of an ethnic bourgeoisie that is both exploitative and benevolent.

Key Terms

Acceptance	Negative Self-Image
Annihilation	Paternalism
Avoidance	Power Differential
Cumulative Causation	Power Theory
Defiance	Social Segregation
Deviance	Spatial Segregation
Exploitation	Split Labor Market
Expulsion	Subordinate
Internal Colonialism	Superordinate
Marginality	Vicious Circle
Middleman Minority	Xenophobia

Review Questions

1. What are some common minority-group responses to prejudice and discrimination?
2. What are some common majority-group responses to minorities?
3. Explain marginality and why it may or may not be a stressful experience.
4. What are middleman minorities? How do they affect acceptance?
5. Discuss three conflict viewpoints about exploitation of minorities.

Suggested Readings

BLALOCK, HUBERT M., JR. *Toward a Theory of Minority Group Relations*. New York: Wiley, 1967.
   Still an influential work, describing conceptual frameworks for understanding dominant-minority relations, including self-serving discrimination and middleman minorities.

BONACICH, EDNA, AND JOHN MODELL. *The Economic Basis of Ethnic Solidarity*. Berkeley, CA: University of California Press, 1980.
   Building on middleman minority theory, an examination of Japanese cohesiveness leading to socioeconomic advancement.

CURRAN, THOMAS J. *Xenophobia and Immigration, 1820–1930*, Boston: Twayne, 1975.
   A detailed historical account of the persistence of the xenophobic spirit in America, and the fear that the stranger threatened American culture.

MASON, PHILIP. *Patterns of Dominance*. New York: Oxford University Press, 1970.
   Readable and comprehensive analysis of dominant-group actions to maintain their privileged position in society.

PART II

EUROPEAN AMERICANS

"America is God's Crucible, the great melting-pot where all the races of Europe are melting and re-forming."

— *Israel Zangwill, 1908*

Culver Pictures

5

Northern and Western Europeans

Although the Native Americans lived on this continent in rich cultures for centuries before the Europeans arrived, we deliberately begin with the northern and western Europeans. It is this group that established what became the dominant culture to which others had to adjust. If we are to understand fully the dynamics of intergroup relations involving not only Native Americans but also all other immigrants past and present, we must first discuss how the creation of a white, Anglo-Saxon Protestant society set the stage for potential conflict. As you will see, religion, nationality, and social class were causal factors for conflict even within this northern and western European grouping. A trickle of immigrants from almost all parts of the world arrived during the early history of the United States. The story of the colonial period and the first 100 years as an independent nation, however, is predominantly the experience of immigrants from the British Isles, France, Holland, Scandinavia, and Germany and their descendants.

SOCIOHISTORICAL PERSPECTIVE

At first all Europeans were strangers to these shores, and they responded with wonder and excitement in their journals and reports about the vastness, resources, and promise of the New World. In those early years, all shared in the adventure of creating a new society. First the necessity to survive, then pro- or anti-British sentiments dominated relations among diverse peoples. As life stabilized and a common culture evolved, many newcomers not only found themselves in strange surroundings but also were more quickly perceived as strangers in a society in which homogeneity had come to be taken for granted. Thus many Irish and Germans, with their cultural, religious, and social-class differences from the natives, often experienced open hostility on their arrival.

Before examining the connection between theory and the actual experience of any group, note that a pitfall is inherent in considering ethnic groups within only a limited historical framework. A tendency to do so results from the fact that immigration patterns have varied among countries and have peaked at different times. The word *peak* provides a clue to how the experiences of each racial or ethnic group should be viewed. Although each minority group usually has had a significant period of migration, thus providing a focal point for examination, each country has sent a continual flow of immigrants over the years. It follows, then, that the immigrants' experiences have varied with changing conditions and that each nationality has usually had a first-generation American grouping at any given time.

The Colonial Period

Members of each ethnic group came to the New World for economic, political, or religious reasons, or sometimes for the adventure of beginning a new life in a new land. As strangers, most encountered yet another ethnic group—the Native Americans—who at a much earlier time may have been immigrants to this land as well. Although limited social interaction between the European settlers and the natives occurred, their cultural differences frequently resulted in a xenophobic reaction from both sides. The story of their relations is usually one of misunderstanding, fear, suspicion, exploitation, hostility, and violence. Coming from vastly different cultural worlds, they quickly came into conflict with one another.

Cultural Diversity

From the moment the first Europeans settled in America, cultural differences existed throughout the land. The settlements were culturally distinct from one another in nationality or religion—for example, the Puritans in Massachusetts and the Congregationalists in Connecticut. Some settlements, even in their very early stages, were composed of a mixture of ethnic groups. To strengthen his Pennsylvania colony, the English Quaker William Penn recruited several hundred Dutch and many more German settlers. In fact the "Pennsylvania Dutch" are actually of German descent, the word *Dutch* being a corruption of *Deutsch*, which means German. The settlement of New Amsterdam in the colony of New Netherland was also a pluralistic community, reflecting the home country's positive attitude toward minorities and refugees within its borders.

> In 1660, William Kieft, the Dutch governor of New Netherland, remarked to the French Jesuit Issac Jogues that there were eighteen languages spoken at or near Fort Amsterdam at the tip of Manhattan Island. . . . The first shipload of settlers sent out by the Dutch was made up largely of French-speaking Protestants. British, Germans, Finns, Jews, Swedes, Africans, Italians, Irish [quickly] followed, beginning a stream that has never yet stopped.[1]

Religious differences caused social problems more frequently than did nationality during this period. Many people who first crossed the Atlantic as immigrants had been religious dissenters in their native land and were seeking a utopia in the new land—a place with religious harmony. Unfortunately, they brought with them their own religious prejudices. Although they themselves came seeking religious freedom, they were intolerant of others with different religious beliefs. When the colonies were mostly Protestant, there was antagonism among the various denominations and sects. Later, when Catholic immigrants arrived, the old hostilities that had existed in Europe generations earlier manifested themselves once again in the United States.

Expulsion and Avoidance

The most frequently cited example of expulsion during the colonial period is that of the Puritans driving out the "heretic" Roger Williams and his followers, who settled in Rhode Island. Of course, the settlers also displaced the Native Americans, often forcibly. Many of the early settlers—for example, the Pilgrims, the French Huguenots, and the Sephardic Jews—had themselves been driven from their native lands in Europe.

With ample land available in the seventeenth and eighteenth centuries, religious, national, or racial groups experiencing prejudice and discrimination could move elsewhere if they wished. As long as there was open land, many did so, forming new societies or living in isolation in small family groups. Driven from New York State at gunpoint in the early nineteenth century, the Mormons exemplify both expulsion and avoidance. As they journeyed westward they frequently encountered intense hostility and violence because of their religious beliefs and their practice of polygamy. They crossed the country seeking a place of refuge until they were able to make their home in the still-unsettled regions of Utah, Nevada, and California.

Spatial Segregation

The early settlements of the seventeenth century—Jamestown (Virginia), Plymouth (Massachusetts), New Sweden (Delaware and New Jersey), New Amsterdam (New York), and Philadelphia (Pennsylvania)—were actually small ethnic enclaves. Immigrants from different countries and with differing religious beliefs settled among their own kind. Even in the pluralistic settlements in Philadelphia and New Amsterdam, members of the various ethnic groups sought to live near their own people. Each of these instances of residential clustering in a recognizable ethnic community was a voluntary act of spatial segregation. In the years to follow, other minority groups also would congregate within well-defined communities, either by choice or because of societal demands.

During the colonial period these Americans welcomed the newer immigrants as buffers along the frontier, but it was a "welcome tinged with misgivings."[2] The immigrants' good character and ability to support themselves were considered more important than their nationality; nevertheless, the Germans, French, and Scotch-Irish did encounter hostility from time to time.

The immigrants originally lived in scattered ethnic settlements. As the English came to dominate, they inhabited primarily the Eastern seaboard. Some minority peoples settled in ethnic pockets in this region, while others settled on the edge of the frontier. Most of this spatial segregation was voluntary because virgin land was available to all who wished to strike out on their own. The immigrants had come to the new land to start a new life, and found their own land to do so.

The Early National Period

Many new immigrants arrived during the immediate post-Revolution period, and an antiforeign attitude, sporadic and localized until then, asserted itself.

Both political factions feared that their opponents would benefit from the newcomers. The Jeffersonians were alarmed at the arrival of so many refugees, particularly the French, from the collapsing European aristocracies. The Federalists, the conservatives of their day, feared that the ranks of the anti-Federalists would grow, because poor immigrants, particularly the Irish, had no commitment to preserving a strong central government.

Whatever their motives, the dominant English Americans' beliefs about and actions toward the newly arriving northern and western European immigrants followed a familiar pattern in dominant-minority relations. Suspicious of those different from themselves, the members of the dominant culture felt threatened.

In a letter to John Adams in 1798, George Washington indicated his reservations about newcomers, especially when they settled in their own little communities. His words are similar to others to be uttered in the nineteenth and twentieth centuries:

> My opinion, with respect to immigration, is that except of useful mechanics and some particular descriptions of men or professions, there is no need of encouragement, while the policy or advantage of its taking place in a body (I mean the settling of them in a body) may be much questioned; for, by so doing, they retain the language, habits and principles (good or bad) which they bring with them.[3]

Xenophobia

Many Federalists, in fact, believed that the large foreign-born population was the root of all the evil in the United States. In letters, speeches, and newspapers they expressed the fear that

> coming from "a quarter of the world so full of disorder and corruption" as Europe, it was to be feared that immigrants would "contaminate the purity and simplicity of the American character"; warned "their principles spread like the leaven of unrighteousness; the weak, the ignorant and the needy are thrown into a ferment, and corruption threatens the whole mass." True some immigrants were industrious, peaceable, and voted the Federalist ticket—but for one such "good" European, lamented Noah Webster, "we receive three or four discontented, factious men—the convicts, fugitives of justice, hirelings of France, and disaffected offscourings of other nations." "Generally speaking," said a Federalist, "none but the most vile and worthless, none but the idle and discontented, the disorderly and the wicked, have inundated upon us from Europe." Clearly, the property and the virtue of the United States would not be secure until foreign immigration had been reduced to a mere trickle of hand-picked newcomers of approved political sympathies.[4]

William Smith Shaw, the young nephew of President John Adams, wrote to the First Lady in 1798: "The grand cause of our present difficulties may be traced . . . to so many hordes of Foreigners imigrating [sic] to America. . . . Let us no longer pray that America may become an asylum to all nations."[5]

Legislative Action

The Federalists attempted to limit all office holding to the native-born and to extend the period for naturalization from five to fourteen years. Although they succeeded in having the longer periods enacted, the states—faced with the problems of establishing a new nation—successfully evaded this legislation.

In 1798, with a volatile situation in Europe and a distinct possibility of war with France, the Federalists succeeded in passing a series of laws known collectively as the Alien and Sedition Acts. Many factors contributed to the successful passage of this notorious legislation. One factor was the presence of a large foreign-born population that was perceived as a threat to the stability of the country. Significantly, the legislation passed because of sectional block voting, with New England almost unanimously in favor of the bills. Few foreigners resided in New England, and hence little contact had occurred; nonetheless, widespread negative stereotyping existed in that region. Jefferson's election to the presidency in 1800 ended this xenophobia, and the acts were abrogated.

Population Composition

At this stage in history, the young nation possessed several distinct ethnic groups, differing in heritage, language, customs, and religion. Within the several states admitted to the Union lived the northern and western Europeans, dominated by the English Protestants. The French lived in the New Orleans region and gave the country its only ethnic flavor truly distinct from the English and the various Indian tribes. In the territories awaiting conquest and statehood were other Indian tribes and the Spanish. Of course, many other ethnic groups were present—though relatively small in numbers—and contributed to the growth and development of the young nation.

The Pre–Civil War Period

Not until 1820 did the national census include a person's country of origin as part of its data, and new regulations required shipmasters to submit passenger lists to customs officials. This census (which excluded the Indians) listed approximately 9.6 million Americans, of whom 20 percent were blacks and most of the remainder white Protestants from northern and western Europe. Between 1820 and 1860 over 5 million immigrants—more than half the U.S. population in 1820 and more than the entire population in 1790—would cross the Atlantic and Pacific oceans to disembark on American shores.

In these 40 years preceding the Civil War, the first great wave of immigrants produced still more arrivals from England and Scandinavia. Ireland and Germany, however, supplied the greatest numbers. In fact, so great was the Irish immigration that they accounted for 44 percent of all immigration in the 1830s and 49 percent of all immigration in the 1840s. Consequently, they accounted for 7 percent of the total population by the end of the Civil War. Not only was the arrival of so many foreigners overwhelming, but also many of the newcomers were Catholic—a religion to which many Protestant groups were openly hostile.

The rich, untapped earth of America's Midwest attracted many German and Scandinavian immigrant farmers in the nineteenth century. Owners of land for the first time in their lives, these former peasants labored hard and harvested bountiful crops. Their letters to family and friends in Europe, as well as the lavish advertisements of steamship and railroad companies, enticed still others to come. (*The State Historical Society of Wisconsin*)

Structural Conditions

The land the immigrants came to in the first half of the nineteenth century was quite different from that of past centuries. From rudimentary beginnings a nation had evolved, bursting with exuberance and confidence. A common culture now prevailed, marked by strong beliefs in Protestantism, individual enterprise, and political democracy. The institutions of society were strongly linked to an Anglo-Saxon heritage. Americans admired and emulated English writers. In a new country filled with nationalistic fervor, England was still the model for a civilization.

Along the East Coast and in the cities west of the Appalachian Mountains, life was stable and established. Although regional variations as well as differences in religion and social status existed, the prevailing cultural norms were relatively homogeneous.

Urban living conditions, particularly for the poor Irish immigrants, were very substandard, even for those days. The poverty-stricken newcomers, forced to live in a squalid environment, suffered high disease and mortality rates, as well as the condemnation of the dominant society for living the way they did. Like so many others in the generations that followed, such critics did not realize that their own attitudes and actions might well have helped to create the situation in the first place:

> Typical of overcrowded cellars was a house in Pike Street which contained a cellar ten feet square and seven feet high, with one small window and an old-fashioned inclined cellar door; here lived two families consisting of ten persons of all ages. The occupants of these basements led miserable lives as troglodytes amid darkness, dampness, and poor ventilation. Rain water leaked through cracks in the walls and floors and frequently flooded the cellars; refuse filtered down from the upper stories and mingled with the seepage from outdoor privies. From such an abode emerged the "whitened and cadaverous countenance" of the cellar dweller.[6]

Xenophobia

Americans perceived the large influx of immigrants between 1820 and 1860 as a threat to their institutions and their social order. Not only were many of the newcomers Catholic, but also they were from countries embroiled in political turmoil. Anxiety mounted over the imagined radical threat as well as the Catholic threat.

In the 1830s antiforeign organizations, calling themselves "native" Americans, originated in many cities. They frequently raised up "mobs to burn Catholic convents, churches and homes, assault nuns, and murder Irishmen, Germans, and Negroes."[7] These sporadic outbursts gradually coalesced into the powerful Know-Nothing movement of the 1850s. They unleashed a vicious hate campaign, frequently accompanied by brutal violence, particularly in the large cities where many immigrants lived. Surprisingly successful, the Know-Nothings "became the magnet for all dazed elements in the political whirlpool; they fed on pathological fears and fanned to white heat all the petty animosities that had bored into the public mind."[8]

A Whig presidential candidate, General Winfield Scott, waged an anti-Catholic, antiforeign campaign with Know-Nothing support but lost badly to Democrat Franklin Pierce in 1852. By 1854 the Know-Nothing Party was strong enough to elect 75 congressmen and many city, county, and state officials.[9] In 1855 the party elected six governors, and many contemporaries believed that this reactionary movement would capture the White House in the 1856 election.[10] A strong candidate, former President Millard Fillmore, sought to return to office on the Know-Nothing ticket. The conservative Whig party endorsed Fillmore, but a serious split within its ranks, with defections to Republican candidate John C. Fremont, enabled Democrat James Buchanan to win the three-way race. The bitter sectional rivalry of the Civil War period effectively ended this ethnocentric-turned-xenophobic movement.

Not all voices were raised against the European expatriates. In defense of the newcomers, Harriet Martineau answered some of the criticisms:

> It would certainly be better that the immigrants should be well-clothed, educated, respectable people (except that, in that case, they would probably never arrive). But the blame of their bad condition rests elsewhere, while their arrival is, generally speaking, a pure benefit. . . . Every American can acknowledge that few or no canals or railroads would be in existence now in the United States, but for the Irish labor by which they have been completed; and the best cultivation that is to be seen in the land is owing to the Dutch and Germans it contains.[11]

Ralph Waldo Emerson, an articulate literary figure of the times, was also a popular speaker on the lyceum lecture circuit. In those days many communities had a *lyceum*, or association, for discussion and popular instruction by lectures or other means. In his lectures Emerson tried to convince his listeners through an eloquent expression of deeply felt ideas. One of his journal entries in 1845 shows how he tried to combat the nativism movement by stressing the "smelting-pot" concept.

> I hate the narrowness of the Native American Party. It is the dog in the manger. It is precisely opposite of true wisdom. . . . Well, as in the old burning of the Temple at Corinth, by the melting and intermixture of silver and gold and other metals, a new compound more precious than any, called Corinthian brass, was formed; so in this continent—asylum of all nations—the energy of Irish, Swedes, Poles, and Cossacks, and all the European tribes—of the Africans, and of the Polynesians, will construct a new race, a new religion, a new state, a new literature, which will be as vigorous as the new Europe which came out of the smelting-pot of the Dark Ages, or that which earlier emerged from Pelasgic and Etruscan barbarism.[12]

Currents and countercurrents occurred then, as now. Not all members of the same ethnic group encountered problems, nor did all native-born Americans react so negatively to the newcomers. Yet patterns of harmony or conflict did exist, and they very often depended upon the degree of cultural and structural differentiation that existed in each region.

THE ENGLISH

Despite earlier explorations by other countries, the English were the first white ethnic group to establish permanent settlements in the New World. The first two successful ones were Jamestown and Plimmoth (Plymouth) Plantation (the word *plantation* was first used in the North).

These two settlements were culturally quite different from one another; they offer an excellent example of cultural diversity among the same nationality as opposed to a stereotyped concept of a people. Jamestown served as the seed from which the Southern aristocracy and slavery would grow. Plymouth was the forerunner of town meetings (participatory democracy), the abolition movement, and "Yankee ingenuity" (capitalistic enterprise). Many factors, such as the different purposes of the settlements, and different religions, climates, and terrains, played a role in determining the unfolding of events and life-styles.

The writings of William Bradford, the first governor of the Plymouth colony, provide evidence that the English were an ethnically conscious people. More than 370 years have passed since the time of the Pilgrims, but Bradford's words regarding their experiences could apply to many other immigrant groups—past, present, and future.

The Departure

Leaving one's native land for another country known only by reputation can be an awesome experience. For many it is a time of joy and sorrow, anticipation and trepidation. People know what they are leaving behind, but they are not certain what they will find. The Pilgrims first fled England for Holland, which opened its doors to all refugees, and later they journeyed to America. In the following passage, Bradford is speaking about the Pilgrims' journey to Holland, but the locale is only incidental to the expression of the immigrant's typical sensations:

> Being thus constrained to leave their native soil and country, their lands and livings, and all their friends and familiar acquaintances, it was much, and thought marvelous by many. But to go into a country they knew not but by hearsay, where they must learn a new language and get their livings they knew not how, it being a dear place and subject to the miseries of war, it was by many thought an adventure almost desperate; a case intolerable and a misery worse than death.[13]

Culture Shock

Arrival at one's destination brings with it culture contact. One's world of reality, that familiar way of life one accepts subconsciously, is jolted to some degree as the group encounters a different civilization. Bradford continues:

> Being now come into the Low Countries, they saw many goodly and fortified cities, strongly walled and guarded with troops of armed men. Also, they heard a strange and uncouth language, and beheld the different manners and customs of the people, with their strange fashions and attires, all so far differing from that of their plain country villages (where they were bred and had so long lived) as it seemed they were come into a new world.[14]

Resisting Assimilation

Not all immigrants desire to be full, participating citizens in the country to which they move. Many, in fact, do not become naturalized citizens. Although they are starting a new life, they do not necessarily intend to forsake their cultural heritage. More often, they seek to preserve that heritage as a familiar world in a strange land, and to pass it on to their children. Often the children become assimilated into the new ways despite their parents' efforts. The Pilgrims feared that their children would be assimilated into the Dutch culture, and viewed such an outcome as an evil to be avoided.

> But that which was more lamentable, and of all sorrows most heavy to be borne, was that many of their children, by these occasions and the great licentiousness of youth in that country, and the manifold temptations of the place, were drawn away by evil examples into extravagant and dangerous courses, getting the reins off their necks and departing from their parents. . . . So that they saw their posterity would be in danger to degenerate and be corrupted.[15]

English Influence

The English immigrants' major impact on American culture occurred during the colonial period. Settling in the 13 original colonies, they so established themselves that succeeding generations were culturally and numerically dominant by the time of the American Revolution. In 1790 about 78 percent of the population could claim nationality or descent from the British Isles (see Table 5.1). This large majority of English-speaking citizens made an indelible imprint on American culture in language, law, customs, and values. The wars of 1776 and 1812 notwithstanding, the descendants of English immigrants still prided themselves on their heritage, as indicated in their writings at that time. For example, in his *Sketchbook* Washington Irving encouraged Americans to pattern themselves after the English nation rather than any other.

After 1825, when the British Parliament repealed the ban on the emigration of artisans, many English, Scottish, and Irish mill hands came to southern

TABLE 5.1

U.S. WHITE ETHNIC POPULATION IN 1790

National Origin	Percentage
English	60.1
Scottish, Scotch-Irish	14.0
German	8.6
Irish	3.6
Dutch	3.1
French, Swedish	3.0
Other	7.6
Total	100.0

These estimates from the American Historical Association come from a surname analysis of the 3.9 million people listed in the 1790 census. Slaves accounted for approximately 20 percent of the total population.

Massachusetts and Philadelphia. There they found work in the textile factories, often at twice or more the salary they had been earning at home. As experienced mill operatives, the English continued to come throughout the nineteenth century, especially to the Massachusetts towns of Fall River and New Bedford. When the American silk industry clustered in Paterson, New Jersey, in the 1840s, many British immigrants moved there, several of them starting their own factories. British immigrants formed a solid base for the rising American textile industry, and many became managers and proprietors.[16]

Many British coal miners also came, but by the latter part of the nineteenth century they were being replaced by Slavic and Italian workers. Those who remained in the coal industry usually were supervisors and foremen. Some British farmers also emigrated to the United States, scattering throughout the Midwest. British immigrants of all occupations seldom concentrated in any one area, going instead wherever the job market led them.

As foreigners with the same language and cultural heritage as the dominant society, British immigrants seldom experienced prejudice or discrimination in the United States. Rowland Berthoff cites numerous studies and reports indicating that the English were rarely ridiculed on the vaudeville stage except as titled fops (an inaccurate representation). Ethnophaulisms did not exist, except for such inoffensive nicknames as "John Bull" or "limey," and even these were not widely used.[17]

Yet the British were not always comfortable in the new land. Ilja M. Dijour found similar results among immigrants to other countries and reported, "The return of British from Australia, South Africa, and Canada or of Portuguese from Brazil, or Spaniards and Italians from the rest of Latin America is incomparably higher than the re-emigration of say Japanese from Brazil, Slavic people from Australia or Canada, or others." Dijour explained that a major cause of these findings was that the first group had the exaggerated expectation of finding no differences in the new country, whereas the second group was psychologically prepared to find everything different in the new country.[18] Those not expecting to be strangers were unprepared when they realized that they actually were strangers.

During the first 100 years after American independence, many British immigrants found the new country less inviting than England. Comparing the criticisms of 75 returnees prior to 1865, Wilbur Shepperson found some common themes reflecting a failure of the new land to live up to their expectations:

> The Republic was peopled by men of action who cared little for the deeper meaning of life, who were blind to the beauties of their natural environment, and who were hostile to refinement and sensitivity.
> . . . Rather than vigorous, they found America boring; rather than questioning and vital, republican communities were suspicious and moribund. Although they were often unemployed, Americans boasted of their economic opportunities; although they condemned politicians, they defended the political system; although they advocated freedom, they enforced conformity. . . .
> Knowledge of the language allowed for rapid assimilation of English immigrants, but at the same time it permitted them to compare critically American

authors, newspapers, and theaters with those at home. Acquaintance with English government and legal traditions provided easy understanding of American law, but it sometimes provoked censure of political methods and frontier justice. Nearness to markets, cheap labor, and advanced technological methods in Britain often led immigrants of the entrepreneur class to despair of the New World's inefficient agricultural methods and unorthodox business practices. British workers once associated with the trade union or Chartist movements found American labor groups lacking in organization, leadership, and purpose.[19]

In the post–Civil War period, some degree of Anglophobia still prevailed, and British immigrants discovered that they had to exercise self-restraint to be accepted as Americans. An ethnic consciousness led many British to resent this necessity and to dislike the ways of the new country. Between 1881 and 1889 a total of 370,697 British and Irish aliens left the United States for their native land.[20]

> In fact, in all things but money and quick promotion, British-Americans thought the United States a debased copy of their homeland. Many seemingly familiar customs and institutions had lost their British essence. "The Land of Slipshod," one immigrant in 1885 called the country, its language not English but a "silly idiotic jargon—a mere jumble of German idioms and popular solecisms, savored by a few Irish blunders," the enforcement of its basically English legal code "totally farcical," and its children half-educated, spoiled, and unruly. . . . Many returned home discontented with "the manners and habits of the people."
>   . . . Although as the years passed the immigrants' personal ties came to be in America rather than in Britain, their fondness for and pride in the old country waxed. British travelers found them everywhere, "British in heart and memory, . . . always with a touch of the exile, eager to see an English face and to hear an English voice!"[21]

Despite certain similarities, enough differences and ethnic consciousness remained to restrain British immigrants from merging in a totally smooth fashion. Second-generation British Americans, however, had no such problem and identified with the United States as their country.

The United Kingdom has been the source of a great many immigrants over the years; between 1820 and 1990 a total of 5.1 million people came to the United States.[22] It ranks third in the list of nations that have supplied immigrants to the United States since 1820, and an average of 17,000 new British immigrants arrive yearly. Even though England was the largest European supplier of immigrants throughout the 1970s and 1980s, these immigrants are not a very visible ethnic group because they are not readily detected as strangers.

THE DUTCH

The two greatest periods of Dutch immigration were 1881 to 1930, with 1.6 million, and 1951 to 1970, with almost 829,000 new arrivals.[23] Since 1971 immigration from the Netherlands has been relatively low, averaging about 1,200 annually. Despite these statistics the major impact of Dutch influence on American society, which is quite significant, comes from a much earlier period.

In 1624, 30 Dutch families settled in Beverwyck, later called Albany, and in 1625 the Dutch built a moat and fort on Manhattan Island and called it New Amsterdam. A year later Governor Peter Minuit concluded his famous deal and bought the whole island from the Indians for 60 guilders—$24—worth of merchandise.

Pearl Street in present-day New York City marks the limit of dry land in the days of New Amsterdam, where palisades had been erected against Indian raiders. In Dutch these were called *de wal,* and thus the northern boundary gave its name to the Wall Street of today. Breukelen (later Brooklyn) became a town in 1646. Peter Stuyvesant's farm or *bouwerij* in Manhattan, where he lived after the English takeover in 1664 until his death in 1672, gave its name to the Bowery, a well-known street in New York.

Other Dutch settlements sprang up in the Bronx, on Staten Island, in New Jersey at Bergen (named after a town in Holland, and later known as Jersey City), at Ridgewood, at Hackensack, in the Raritan and Ramapo valleys, and in South Carolina at St. James Island. So widespread were the Dutch settlements and so strong was the Dutch imprint that Dutch remained a major language in American society for quite some time.

Structural Conditions

During the colonial period, few Dutch were willing to exchange the security at home for the hardships of the New World. With their stable economy and a harmonious society, the Dutch had little inducement to venture forth in great numbers as other ethnic groups had. Urban areas in Holland had heterogeneous populations because the Dutch had offered shelter to many refugees from other countries. When seeking to establish trading settlements in the New World, the Dutch therefore sought other minority-group members willing to journey to the New World. As a result, immigrant Dutch settlements became as heterogeneous as their counterparts in Holland.

The spirit of seventeenth-century Holland resulted in a cosmopolitan and tolerant atmosphere in New Amsterdam that outlasted Holland's rule. The somewhat more relaxed atmosphere of New Amsterdam contrasted with that of the English colonies to the north, restricted by their rigid blue laws. New York City, with its large number of places to eat, drink, and dance, seems to have inherited this New Amsterdam characteristic. Sports were popular too. The colonists loved boat and carriage races, and from Holland they imported the game of *kolf,* which later became golf.

The English takeover of New Amsterdam in 1664 caused no hardship for the Dutch settlers. They enjoyed a basically favorable social environment during the time of the American colonies, in the post-Revolutionary War period, and thereafter. A relatively tolerant people in an intolerant age, similar in physical appearance and religious beliefs to other Americans, the Dutch were generally accepted, though sometimes they were the butt of gentle humor, as illustrated in the writings of Washington Irving.

Holland's early support of the American Revolution and its status as the second country to give formal recognition to the United States further strengthened positive American attitudes toward the Dutch. In 1782 John Adams succeeded in securing the first loan for Congress from three Amsterdam banking houses; the loan was for 5 million guilders, or $2 million—a very substantial amount in those days. By 1794 the total amount loaned by Holland had risen to 30 million guilders, or $12 million. This amount comprised most of the foreign debt incurred by the United States.

In 1846 a group of religious separatists settled in what became Holland, Michigan. Spurred by religious and economic motives, a new wave of Dutch immigrants followed suit, settling mostly in Michigan, Iowa, Wisconsin, and Illinois because of their favorable soil and climate conditions. The social bond proved to be religion rather than nationality, and schisms ensued, resulting in the Dutch Reformed Church, the Christian Reformed Church, and the Netherland Reformed Church. The success of the first group's efforts to propagate the faith and achieve higher social standing rested partly on Hope College in Holland, Michigan. Their success encouraged the Christian Reformed Church, a more conservative group, to establish Calvin College in Grand Rapids to achieve the same objectives for their people.

Pluralism

The Dutch immigrants who came here, whether during the colonial period or the nineteenth century, found their liberal attitude toward other groups usually was reciprocated. They were a distinct ethnic group—in language as well as in other ways—but they generally found a friendly atmosphere wherever they went. Nonetheless, like many other nationalities yet to come, some of whom would not find such openness, they formed their own enclaves and tried to preserve their language and traditions through their own churches, schools, and associations.

For several reasons, Dutch culture and influence persisted for many generations despite the Anglo-Saxon cultural dominance. The Dutch were self-sufficient and enjoyed high social standing in the society. Their church, rather than American ways, formed the basis of their social life; the more orthodox they were, the more they resisted assimilation. A steady migration into concentrated residential communities reinforced the old ways. Finally, a friendly atmosphere enabled the Dutch to coexist in a pluralistic society.

The following passage gives some insight into the extensive use of the Dutch language and the resistance to the English language. Note, for example, that not until 1774 were the children taught English, more than 100 years after New York became an English colony:

In 1764 Dr. Archibald Laidlie preached the first English sermon to the Dutch Reformed congregation in New York City. Ten years later English was introduced in the schools. In Kingston, Dutch was used in church as late as 1808. A few years before, a traveler had reported that "on Long Island, in New York, along the North River, at Albany, how Dutch was in general still the common language of most of the old people." Francis Adrian van der Kemp, who had come to this country as a refugee in 1788, wrote that his wife was able to converse in Dutch, with the wives of Alexander Hamilton and General George Clinton. Much later, in 1847, immigrants from Holland were upon their arrival welcomed in Dutch by the Reverend Isaac Wyckoff of New York, a descendant of one of the first settlers in Rensselaerwyck, who only in school had learned to speak English; and until very recently many communities in New Jersey adhered to the tradition of a monthly church service in Dutch. As late as 1905 Dutch was still heard among the old people in the Ramapo Valley of that state.[24]

Although most of the Dutch immigrants came to the United States during the same period as the southern, central, and eastern Europeans, they did not encounter ethnic antagonism and they assimilated more easily. Their physical features, their religion, their comparatively small numbers, and their more urbanized background enabled them both to adapt to and to gain approval from the dominant society more easily than other groups.

THE FRENCH

French Americans fall into three population segments: migrants from France, migrants from French Canada (who settled primarily in New England), and French Louisianians brought under U.S. jurisdiction. (The French Louisianians, also known as Cajuns, were expelled from Acadia, French Canada, by the British in 1755, and by 1790 about 4,000 of them had resettled in Louisiana.) Each group's experiences have been somewhat different, illustrating different patterns in dominant-minority relations.

Marginality and Assimilation

In the seventeenth century, the Huguenots fled either to Holland or to America to escape religious persecution. It is often thought that because of their Protestantism, their willingness to work hard, their conversion to the Anglican Church, and their rapid adoption of the English language, the Huguenots assimilated easily into colonial society. However, the transition was not altogether a smooth one, and the second generation apparently agonized over their marginal status in the same way other groups did.

By 1706, sufficient time had elapsed since the Revocation [in 1685 Louis XIV formally eliminated religious liberty, causing the renewal of persecution and extermination of the Huguenots] to give rise to a younger generation unsatisfied with the adherence to old French forms, a generation adverse to a language not in general use in the province, clamoring for the new and the popular. . . . The children of many of the refugees were even ashamed to bear French names. The idea of remaining foreigners in a land in which they were born and reared was alien to their thought.[25]

Encountering distrust and some violence from the dominant society, partly explained by the frequent hostilities between England and France, the Huguenots tried to Anglicize themselves as quickly as possible to avoid further unpleasantness. They changed their names and their customs, learned to speak English, and soon succeeded in assimilating completely into American society. For them, assimilation and loss of ethnic identity was the desired goal. Not all Americans or ethnic groups agree with such a goal; many prefer instead a pluralistic society.

With time, attitudes changed. The Revolutionary War period made England an enemy and France an ally. The Marquis de Lafayette was a war hero, and such popular figures as Benjamin Franklin and Thomas Jefferson openly admired the French and their culture.

Francophobia

When the French Revolution was still in its moderately liberal stage, the Jeffersonians were French sympathizers and the Federalists were vehemently anti-French. Then came the celebrated XYZ Affair, in which French officials demanded bribes before permitting U.S. diplomats to secure desired conferences or agreements. This inflamed public opinion against the French and their sympathizers. The lives of French immigrants during those passionate times were at best uncomfortable and at worst filled with trouble and turmoil.

> The fear and detestation in which American "Jacobins" were held were no less powerful than the abhorrence felt for the French revolutionists themselves. "Medusa's Snakes are not more venomous," declared a Federalist, "than the wretches who are seeking to bend us to the views of France." "The open enemies of our country," declared the *Albany Centinel,* "have never taken half the pains to render our Government and our rulers infamous and contemptible in the eyes of the world, than those wretches who call themselves Americans, Patriots and Republicans." This "Gallic faction" was believed to be in close communication with Paris, "the immense reservoir, and native spring of all immorality, corruption, wickedness and methodized duplicity."
>
> . . . In the eyes of the Federalists, however, every Frenchman was a potential enemy; whether royalists or revolutionists, they were eager to extend French influence over the United States, and actuated by national pride, they might join a French army of invasion. Moreover, their notoriously loose morals and irreligion threatened to infect Americans.[26]

By 1801 the Republicans effectively ended the Federalists' political dominance. President Thomas Jefferson purchased the Louisiana Territory from France in 1803, and with it the French city of New Orleans, which retains much of its ethnic flavor to this day, including the famed Mardi Gras celebration.

Pluralism

The French subculture in southern Louisiana suggests ethnic homogeneity to the outsider, but the cultural variety of its communities includes French-speaking Native Americans, black Creoles and Acadians, or Cajuns. This once-persistent subculture was at one time so strong that it absorbed other ethnic groups in that area, as T. Lynn Smith and Vernon Parenton observed in 1938.

> The French assimilated the Germans while both were under Spanish rule and both subject to strenuous programs designed to stamp them with a Spanish cultural heritage. But the virile French culture was not content with this, even made a beginning at swallowing the politically dominant Spaniards themselves, a beginning which has been practically consummated during the American period while both were enveloped in the so-called melting pot which was heralded as bringing about Americanization. Under American rule the Louisiana French have, to the present time, perpetuated their language and culture and, at the same time, have absorbed most of the diverse Anglo-Saxon elements which have settled among them.[27]

Two years later these same observers noted some changes in the previously insulated subculture, although they believed that the march to the American mainstream was limited.

> Today, urbanizing influences are permeating the entire section. These include improved communication, mechanization of agriculture (with its concomitant social implications) and, particularly, mass media of education (radio, movies, and newspapers) as well as increased contacts outside French-speaking Louisiana. Nevertheless, the system of common values which was generated by language, national origin, settlement pattern, as well as familial, kinship, and religious ties, has thus far retained its societal integrative forces in this period of rapid and far-reaching technological changes now operative among these people.[28]

The emergence of television in the 1950s accelerated the process of ethnogenesis. Cajun children were now typically given "American" names and encouraged to go to college, their numbers doubling in the 1960s at South Louisiana universities.

> The resulting wave of Cajun college graduates tended to congregate in the college towns, where they came to constitute a notable segment of Acadiana's urban population. . . . [H]owever, these upwardly mobile urban Cajuns did not abandon their parent culture entirely. Indeed, like members of other minorities throughout the United States, many urban Cajuns found that their Anglo-Protestant neighbors simply would not let them forget their past, and many others became deeply disillusioned with homogenization into the great, rootless American mass. These young urbanites, by the late 1960s, came to resent the fact that they had ever been made to feel ashamed of their heritage.[29]

One outcome of the resulting backlash was a reaffirmation not only of Cajun identity but also of the French language, whose use had been declining. By

Three generations of Cajun women, displaying one form of extended family bonding, sit quilting under an old oak tree in Catahoula, Louisiana. This shared activity helps maintain a cohesive subculture through the cultural transmission of their traditional designs, skills, and time-honored practices. *(©1989 John Eastcott/Image Works)*

the early 1970s, French window signs and bilingual programs in the schools were commonplace. However, the oil depression that hit Louisiana in 1986 caused tens of thousands of Cajun workers to migrate to other jobs in Tennessee, Georgia, and Florida, where their mainstreaming is most likely.[30]

Those who remained behind in southern Louisiana find their culture, particularly their language, threatened. The importation of foreign nationals to teach metropolitan French in the schools made the Cajuns either apathetic or hostile to bilingual programs. That and budget cutbacks caused significant retrenchment in the 1980s, making the language's future at best uncertain.[31] Today Cajun music and cuisine remain resilient entities, as do nuclear family cohesiveness and extended family bonds. Nevertheless, most aspects of Cajun culture are becoming more Americanized.

A more durable persistent subculture can be found among the French Canadians living in New England. Today the French Canadians comprise 34 percent of Vermont's population, 30 percent of New Hampshire's, 28 percent of Maine's, and 17 percent of the Massachusetts population.[32]

Although French Canadians emigrated to the United States prior to the Civil War, their largest movement came after the Civil War. The Industrial Revolution brought rapid expansion to the New England factories, and the owners actively recruited labor in French Canada. Many French Canadians flocked from Quebec to the mill towns, competing with the Irish and others for jobs. The heaviest migration occurred in the 40-year period from 1841 to 1880. By 1873 approximately 400,000 French Canadians were living in the United States, half of them in New England and most of the remainder in the Midwest, primarily Illinois and Michigan.[33]

As in Louisiana, the family and the church have served as strong cohesive units in retaining language and culture. French parochial schools also have had a unifying effect on the community. The French Canadians still remain a distinct ethnic group, and their loyalties to their institutions and to their original home, Quebec, suggest that they will continue to remain a strong subculture in the foreseeable future. Moreover, their proximity to Quebec— with its French press, radio and television stations, and cultural influences— all foster a vibrant ethnicity.

THE GERMANS

Germany has supplied the greatest number of immigrants, over 7 million since 1820. Today 58 million people, about one of four Americans, trace their bloodlines to Germany (see Table 5.2). In several earlier periods the large concentrations of German Americans raised nativist fears, but today's aver-

TABLE 5.2	U.S. POPULATION OF EUROPEAN ANCESTRY IN 1990	
	Million	**Percentage**
German	58	23
Irish	39	16
English	36	14
Italian	15	6
Scottish, Scotch-Irish	11	4
French	10	4
Scandinavian	10	4
Polish	9	4
Dutch	6	3
Russian	3	1

Note: The most dramatic changes since the 1980 census were a large increase in Americans of German ancestry and a significant decline in those of English ancestry. More than two-thirds of all Americans trace their bloodlines to northern and western Europe.

Americans claiming German, Polish, Scandinavian, or Dutch ancestry are most concentrated in the northern Midwest. Those of Irish, English, Italian, French, or Russian descent are most concentrated in the Northeast. Large Scottish, Scotch-Irish concentrations are scattered around the nation.

SOURCE: U.S. Bureau of the Census, 1990 Census Special Tabulations, 1990 CPH-L-89, p. 1.

age citizen no longer thinks of them as a distinct ethnic group even though over 10,000 new German immigrants arrive annually.

Early Reactions

William Penn was so successful in recruiting German immigrants to his Pennsylvania colony that by the outbreak of the Revolutionary War, they numbered over 100,000 —one-third of the colony's total population. England's deployment of Hessian (German) mercenary troops in this area may have been done in part to secure sympathetic German colonial assistance in such areas as supplies and intelligence reports.

The Germans' situation provides a good example of a dominant culture reacting to a perceived threat from a distinct minority group. They were different in language, customs, and religion (being primarily Lutherans), as were other groups, but their high visibility due to their numbers and settlement patterns brought them to public attention.

Many Germans also had the additional disadvantage of having been placed in a subservient position at the outset. A very popular system, particularly in Pennsylvania, was the use of indentured servants or "redemptioners." Through this plan persons unable to pay their passage would serve from three to seven years as laborers, artisans, domestics, or tutors. On their arrival in the harbor, such persons were advertised for sale in the newspapers, and the ship became a market because the ship captain or entrepreneur was paid for advancing the passage money. Occasionally families were separated. Such a situation could not help but encourage ethnocentric feelings of superiority among native-born Americans over such "poor foreigners."[34] Some English immigrants also came to the New England colonies as indentured servants, but in Pennsylvania the Germans represented a different ethnic group as well.

By 1750 the influx of German immigrants had become so great that Benjamin Franklin became quite disturbed and asked:

> Why [should] the Pennsylvanians . . . allow the Palatine Germans to swarm into our settlements, and by herding together to establish their Language and Manners to the exclusion of ours? Why should Pennsylvania, founded by the English, become a colony of Aliens, who will shortly be so numerous as to Germanize us instead of our Anglifying them?[35]

These expressed fears were to be repeated by others at a later time, about other immigrant groups. Franklin's worries about the duality of language display a marked similarity to some twentieth-century concerns regarding the Spanish-speaking populace and bilingual education. Franklin particularly opposed the Mennonites, fearing that members of this religious sect were pacifists. Maurice Davie reports that Franklin had misgivings about the Germans also because of their clannishness, their meager knowledge of English, their separate German press, and their increasing need for interpreters. Speaking of the latter, Franklin said, "I suppose in a few years they will also be necessary in the Assembly, to tell one-half of our legislators what the other half say."[36] Franklin was not arguing for restriction on immigration but rather for rapid assimilation (Anglo-conformity).

The Second Wave: Segregation and Pluralism

The German immigrants of the eighteenth century settled first in Pennsylvania and then in other mid-Atlantic states, but the nineteenth-century immigrants went to the Midwest, settling in the Ohio, Mississippi, and Missouri river valleys. They became homesteaders, preserving their heritage through their schools, churches, newspapers, language, mutual aid societies, and recreational activities. Also, various colonization societies in Germany sent thousands of German settlers to the St. Louis region in the 1830s, to Texas in the 1840s, and to Wisconsin in the 1850s.

The failure of the liberal German revolution brought many political refugees to the United States in 1848. Known as "Forty-eighters," these Germans settled in the large cities of the East and Midwest. Most settled in Baltimore, New York, St. Louis, Milwaukee, and Minneapolis. Having been political activists in their homeland, the Forty-eighters quickly became active in American politics. Many Germans even gave serious thought to an all-German state within the union with German as the official language; some considered creating a separate German nation, believing that the slavery issue would cause the dissolution of the Union.

Although more dispersed throughout the country than the Irish, in the cities they concentrated in "Germantowns." Here most of the businesses were owned and operated by Germans, with German as the principal spoken language. The parallel social institutions of their fraternal and mutual aid societies, newspapers, schools, churches, restaurants, and saloons, like those of other immigrant groups, aided their newly arrived compatriots in adjusting to their new country.

The Turnvereine were gymnastic societies and cultural centers that provided libraries, reading rooms, discussion groups, and singing and dramatic groups for German Americans. However, they became controversial for their radical reform proposals and political activism on behalf of social welfare legislation, direct popular election of all public officials, tax and tariff reform, abolition, and militant opposition to prohibition.

An often-overlooked ethnic footnote to American history is Abraham Lincoln's astute realization of the value of German American political activism. With a sizable German population in Illinois before the Civil War, Lincoln tried to master the German tongue and became owner of a German-language newspaper.[37] His efforts earned rich dividends as the Forty-eighters, who had adopted the Republican Party, persuaded thousands of their compatriots to do the same. They also exerted considerable influence in 1860 to secure the nomination for Lincoln and to elect him to the presidency.

The subcommunities of Germans in the cities were similar to the separate German communities in the agrarian regions. In both situations the Germans were physically and socially segregated, mostly by their own choice. In a city such as Milwaukee, Germans at one time were in the absolute majority; the 1850 census showed 6,000 Germans and 4,000 native-born Americans. Today the Germantown sections of most of these cities still retain some vestige of their ethnic identity.

Societal Responses

Tensions were increased by the large numbers of Germans, most of them Catholics and Jews, and by the mid-nineteenth century, many violent confrontations had occurred with native-born Americans. During the height of the Know-Nothing movement in the 1850s, the Germans often were victims of verbal abuse, open discrimination, and even mob violence. On August 5, 1855, a day long remembered in Louisville, Kentucky, as Bloody Monday, a mob of Know-Nothings—incited by fiery articles in the Louisville *Journal*—

| BOX 5.1 | THE ETHNIC EXPERIENCE |

"When I got to Ellis Island, we all had to line up and they would examine us. Some people could pass and they marked their coat. Some they marked on the left and some they marked on the right lapels. Those that were marked on one side could go through right away. Maybe they had been here before, I don't know. But I got a mark—'This is back.' So they let us through a big hall and we had to strip naked. And we met two fellas, they were doctors with stethoscopes. I didn't know what a stethoscope was—I learned that after. They tapped us on the chest and on the back and then I had to run around. I was the only one they examined.

"All of a sudden one raised his fist. He was gonna knock the other fella down, the other doctor. I didn't know what it meant, I was told afterward. One said I had consumption and the other doctor said there was nothing wrong with me—all I needed was a bellyful of food for a couple of months, I was undernourished. Well, finally, I got passed. And when I got out, I had to go before an examiner. My brother had arranged for relatives that lived in Brooklyn. The examiner said to my cousin, 'You will have to put up $50,000 bail so this young man will not become a burden of the United States.'

". . . Then the examiner said, 'You are free to go.' And [voice breaking] when I—I tell the news 'you are free,' I choke up. The judge says, 'The boy [pause, tears streaming] may be undernourished [Pause, then very emotionally] but he has a wonderful mind.' And he said again, 'You are free to go,' and we went out."

SOURCE: German immigrant who came to the United States in 1910 at age 16.

stormed into the German section of the city. When the riot was over, 22 men had been killed, several hundred were wounded, and 16 houses had been burned.

German immigrants assimilated fairly rapidly, but because of the large, continual flow of newcomers, a significant ethnic subculture was always in evidence. Some 230 years after the arrival of the first German settlers, this continuing subculture came under xenophobic attack. Becoming embroiled for the first time in 1917 in a European war so traumatized Americans that a strong wave of anti-German feeling prevailed for several years. Patriotic hysteria brought intense pressure on the Germans to eliminate their cultural manifestations. This Americanization movement, which was sometimes brutal, did succeed in eliminating distinct "Little Germany" subsocieties. This was one instance where forced assimilation succeeded, because the Germans wanted to identify with the land of their children, not the land of their forebears.

Cultural Impact

American speech, eating, and drinking reflect German influence. Frankfurters, sauerkraut, sauerbraten, hamburgers, wiener schnitzel, pumpernickel bread, liverwurst, pretzels, zwieback, and lager beer were introduced by German immigrants. The words *stein* and *rathskeller* also are of German origin, as are the concepts of the kindergarten and the university. Germans almost exclusively dominated the brewing industry, founding Anheuser-Busch, Coors, Schaefer, Schlitz, Schmidt's, Pabst, Ruppert, and many others.

Some leading German industrialists were George Westinghouse, electrical engineering; Frederick Weyerhaeuser, lumber; John Jacob Astor, fur trade; Bausch and Lomb, optical instruments; Chrysler, Studebaker, and Kaiser, car manufacturers; Steinway and Wurlitzer, piano makers; and Heinz, food canning. A German immigrant, Thomas Nast, was America's first great caricaturist and political cartoonist, and he created the Democratic donkey, the Republican elephant, and the "I Want You" Uncle Sam recruiting poster of World War I vintage.

The Germans no longer predominate as a distinct ethnic minority, even though some remain unassimilated. Their earlier experiences, particularly those of mid-nineteenth-century German Catholics and of German Americans during World War I, were a forerunner of the types of conflict certain other minority groups also would encounter.

THE IRISH _____

Prerevolutionary immigration from Ireland was mostly by the Ulster Irish, Presbyterians who were descendants of Scottish immigrants who had migrated to Northern Ireland a generation earlier. Settling mostly in New England at first around 1717, they clustered together, preserving their ethnicity and seldom mingling with the Anglo-Americans. The latter regarded these newcomers with contempt, labeling them ill-tempered ruffians who drank and fought too much. Soon the friction escalated into Boston newspaper denunciations, destruction of an Irish Presbyterian meetinghouse, and a mob blocking the disembarkation of Irish ship passengers.[38]

William Penn's recruitment in Europe for his colony soon led to the Scotch-Irish choosing Pennsylvania as their most common destination. However, the tendency of the newcomers to be land squatters without paying for the land and their frequent conflicts with the Germans living there resulted in Pennsylvania authorities discouraging further immigration. Afterward Scotch-Irish immigration flowed to the frontier regions of Virginia and the Carolinas.[39] By the end of the eighteenth century, cultural assimilation had occurred, but structural and marital assimilation lagged behind.

Unlike the Scotch-Irish Protestants, the religion, peasant culture, and rebelliousness against England by Irish Catholics not only marked them as strangers to the Americans but also set the stage for the most overt discrimination and hostility any ethnic group had thus far encountered. Originally made unwelcome in the New England settlements, most of the early Irish immigrants settled in Pennsylvania or in Maryland, which had been founded as an English Catholic colony in 1634 but which had become Protestant-controlled by the mid-eighteenth century. By 1790 the Irish accounted for 3.6 percent of the total population of 3,172,444. Their numbers became a source of increasing concern to the Federalists, especially during the presidency of John Adams. Fearing that the "wild Irish" rebels would attempt to turn the United States against England and also that they would join the Republican party, the Federalists were strongly against the incoming "hordes of wild Irishmen." Rufus King, American minister in London, was one of the foremost opponents of Irish emigration to the United States. He expressed to Secretary of State Timothy Pickering his fear that the disaffected Irish would "disfigure our true national character," which was purest in untainted New England. Massachusetts-born John Quincy Adams agreed that the United States had "too many to these people already."[40]

After 1830 emigration to America became increasingly essential to the Irish, whose oppression under British rule prevented their becoming successful in their native land. The successive failures of the potato crop and the resulting famine in the late 1840s accelerated the exodus. Approximately 1.2 million people emigrated between 1847 and 1854, the peak year being 1851, when almost a quarter of a million Irish came to the United States.

Settling mostly in the coastal cities, the living conditions in these overcrowded "Dublin Districts" were deplorable. With many families living in poorly lighted, poorly heated or ventilated tenements, contagious, deadly diseases—such as cholera—were widespread. Also drawn elsewhere to work in the mines or to build the canals and railroads, Irish shantytowns sprang up in many locales, their presence a symbol to native-born Americans of an "inferior" people in their midst.

Cultural Differentiation

The Irish attracted attention because of their sheer numbers and also because they were Catholic and had strong anti-British feelings. Both factors weighed heavily against them in Anglo-Saxon Protestant America. In addition, they were a poverty-stricken rural people who settled in groups mainly in the slum areas of cities on the East Coast. Because they could find only unskilled jobs, they began life in America with a lower-class status, bearing that stigma at a time when America was becoming increasingly class conscious.

The Irish were the first ethnic group to come to the United States in large numbers as a minority very different from the dominant culture of the country. They were to be the harbingers of the "new" immigrants yet to come. As Charles Marden and Gladys Meyer point out:

> This was America's first confrontation with a peasant culture. The English, Scandinavians, or Germans who came to America in the nineteenth century came from towns or from freehold farming patterns. The Irish had been long exploited by the English landholding system. The unchallenged position of the Catholic church cemented bonds of identity. A history of famine, a family and inheritance system that led to late marriage and many unmarried men and women, the ambivalent situation of being English-speaking but not part of English-derived institutions, and migration in large numbers put the Irish in a peculiar relationship to dominants. Some welcomed them as a necessary working-class contingent; others engaged in flagrant discrimination.[41]

Even when they were welcomed as people who would fill the working-class jobs, it was with an ethnocentric attitude of superiority over a lowly breed of people, typified by these comments of a Massachusetts senator in 1852:

> That inefficiency of the pure Celtic race furnishes the answer to the question: How much use are the Irish to us in America? The Native American answer is, "none at all." And the Native American policy is to keep them away.
>
> A profound mistake, I believe. . . . We are here, well organized and well trained, masters of the soil, the very race before which they have yielded everywhere besides. It must be, that when they come in among us, they come to lift us up. As sure as water and oil each finds its level they will find theirs. So far as they are mere hand-workers, they must sustain the head-workers, or those who have any element of intellectual ability. Their inferiority as a race compels them to go to the bottom; and the consequence is that we are, all of us, the higher lifted because they are here.[42]

Societal Reaction

The "native" American movement, which had briefly been evident in the immediate post–Revolutionary War period, now swept across the land in a shameful display of bigotry and intolerance. The growth of anti-Irish feeling was strongly linked to anti-Catholic feeling. Fears of "Popery" arose, strengthened by the influx of priests to minister to the needs of the Irish Catholics. The Irish were brutalized by this movement far more than the Germans were by Know-Nothing violence; destruction of property, beatings, and loss of life occurred in the Irish sections of many cities. In addition to frequent street brawls, the mob violence sometimes resulted in the burning of churches and convents. In an ironic twist of fate, the Irish later tended to dominate some urban police forces, and they would be the ones to either control or arrest unruly Know-Nothing mobs, thus maintaining the American way of life that the Irish had once been accused of destroying.

Antagonism toward the Irish was manifested most strongly in social and job discrimination. For a long time job advertisements in Boston and elsewhere included the line "No Irish need apply."

THE AMERICAN RIVER GANGES.

"The American River Ganges"

Many consider this the most vicious anti-Catholic, anti-Irish cartoon ever printed in a mass-circulation magazine. It illustrates the belief that Irish Catholics were endangering public education (symbolized by the upside-down American flag). Notice the Irish harp and papal tiara flying above Tammany Hall, the teachers being led to the gallows, and the children being thrown to the river bank by Democratic politicians. One Protestant teacher (the Bible tucked into his jacket) is protecting children from the crocodiles, which represent Catholic bishops. Their jaws are mitres, their scales are vestments, and their faces are Irish stereotypes. This cartoon by German immigrant Thomas Nast appeared in *Harper's Weekly* on September 30, 1871. *(The Distorted Image, Courtesy Anti-Defamation League of B'nai B'rith, John and Selma Appel Collection)*

Indeed, they suffered severe discrimination in the new land and most often found employment only in the lowest-paying and hardest-working jobs: as ditchdiggers, or dockers, or "terriers" working on the railroads and in the canal beds. In some respects (clearly not in all), the urban experience for Blacks in the twentieth century—in terms of the attitudes of others and in terms of occupations—has its parallel in the Irish experience in the middle of the previous century.[43]

Cultural Impact

Irish labor played a key role in the industrial expansion of the United States, particularly in building the great systems of canals, waterways, and railroads. As Roman Catholicism evolved into a major faith in a Protestant country, through increased membership and the power of the church hierarchy, Irish Americans exerted a great moral force on the nation. As the Irish began to assimilate, they often served as a middleman minority, aiding new European immigrant groups in work, church, school, and city life.[44] The Irish were not so hospitable to the Chinese, however, often clashing with them in the cities and in railway labor disputes.

Minority Response

The Irish experience was the prototype for the experiences of later immigrants, not only in their hostile reception by the dominant culture but also in their reaction to the prejudice and discrimination that they frequently encountered. One should not underestimate the hardship involved in leaving one's native land—alone or with family—journeying far to another country, feeling both anxieties and hopes, and then finding oneself an unwanted stranger in a strange land.

Actions and Reactions

Irish responses were both retreatist and aggressive, as demonstrated through their social behavior and their involvement in the labor movement and in the urban political machine. Because these activities frequently offended American norms of behavior, they reaffirmed the suspicions of native-born Americans, thereby reinforcing the stereotypes of the Irish and prolonging the vicious circle.

> Unable to participate in the normal associational affairs of the community, the Irish felt obliged to erect a society within a society, to act together in their own way. In every contact therefore the group, acting apart from other sections of the community, became intensely aware of its peculiar and exclusive identity.[45]

The small degree of intermarriage both reflected and buttressed the distinction between the Irish and other Americans. Among the Irish, religious and social considerations encouraged a tendency to mate with their own

---

BOX 5.2	THE ETHNIC EXPERIENCE

"Like many more immigrants like myself, I came to this country to seek a living because living over there was very, very poor. Work was scarce and hard. I decided that I ought to try the United States to make a living.

"I left home in Ireland on a Friday morning. I went to a place then called Queenstown in County Cork. I was there for the greater part of Friday and Saturday because you had to go through quite a number of tests and screening to be allowed to board ship. On Sunday morning around eight o'clock I boarded the ship.

"We arrived in the United States a week from that Monday, around two o'clock in the afternoon in the harbor of New York. The nicest thing I saw after being so seasick—and I might say I was very, very seasick—the nicest thing I ever experienced was seeing the Statue of Liberty. It meant we were here and we were all right. We had landed and we were safe. Then, of course, I had to go through customs and things like that.

"I had heard a great deal about the United States, that it was a good country, and I might very well say that it was a good country, although all that time I was disappointed because I wasn't the one to find the gold in the streets. I really had to go out and look for a job. I worked for awhile in a doctor's office and from there I went to work for a chemical company. There was disappointment. There were loans from my family and my friends. It's something you wonder if you can make it. Thank God I did."

SOURCE: Irish immigrant who came to the United States in 1920 at age 18.

---

kind. As Catholics they were repeatedly warned that union with Protestants was tantamount to loss of faith, and the great majority of non-Irish in the city considered marriage with them degrading. As a result, the percentage of Irish intermarriage was extremely low.

The number of Irish households headed by women, mostly widows, was fairly high in the mid-nineteenth century, about 18 percent in 1855 and dropping to only 16 percent in 1875.[46] Such high percentages normally resulted from the men either marrying younger women or meeting an early death in their dangerous occupations. An expanded household to include other relatives was quite common, as was the taking in of boarders to help meet living expenses.

In building their parallel social institutions, the Irish succeeded in helping one another. Besides offering informal aid for kin and neighbors, the Irish created their own mutual-welfare system through their trade associations (the predecessor of labor unions), fraternal organizations, and homes for the aged that were staffed by nuns. These efforts assisted and protected the Irish from societal indifference and hostility but also isolated them and slowed their acculturation.[47] The Irish community was further united through family, church, and school, as well as through their social and recreational activities. Such "clannishness" only added fuel to the fires of resentment among the American assimilationists, even though the Anglo-Saxon community had helped to cause the situation. Jewish immigrants would later experience similar problems when their community was subject to charges of clannishness.

Quite often some members of a low-status minority group are arrested more frequently than members of other groups for certain crimes, particularly those of personal disorganization. The Irish, for example, were disproportionately represented in arrests and convictions for brawling, drunkenness, disturbing the peace, and more serious crimes during the nineteenth century. These occurrences reinforced the dominant society's stereotyped attitudes toward them.

Labor Conflict

Irish labor was diversified, but it was concentrated in low-status unskilled or semiskilled occupations. The Irish worked at the hard, physical jobs in the cities, in the mines of Appalachia, or in railroad construction from the Alleghenies to the Rockies. With their knowledge of the English language, the Irish provided strong, articulate membership and leadership in such early labor movements as the Knights of Labor. The greatest notoriety surrounded the violence and murders committed by the Molly Maguires, a secret terrorist group that aided the Irish miners in their struggle with the mine owners. Following infiltration of their group by a secret agent for the Pinkerton Detective Agency and a highly questionable court proceeding, the Molly Maguire movement ended in the hanging of 20 men, the largest mass execution in the nation's history.

Bonacich's split labor market theory helps explain much of the conflicts involving the Irish. Irish–German conflict, particularly in Pennsylvania, was intense in the late eighteenth and early nineteenth centuries, because of economic competition and use of Germans as strikebreakers.[48] On the West Coast Irish workers held meetings and demonstrations, demanding curtailment of further Chinese immigration, viewing those lower-paid ethnics as a serious economic threat.[49] The Irish also fiercely resisted abolition, fearing labor competition from released slaves. Antiblack riots in Chicago, Cincinnati, and Detroit followed.[50] Most notorious was the so-called Draft Riot of 1863 in New York City, in which about 400 rioters were killed, as well as dozens of blacks, police, and soldiers. This riot, the worst in American history, was led by Irish longshoremen, angry over the recent use of black strikebreakers to undermine efforts to secure better wages.[51]

Upward Mobility

Grassroots politics speeded along Irish upward mobility, triggering a nativist concern over Catholic priests controlling American politics. Through political machine organization, the Irish controlled Tammany Hall in New York by the 1860s, and the Brooklyn Democratic party by the 1870s.[52] By the 1890s they also controlled Boston, Buffalo, Chicago, Philadelphia, St. Louis, and San Francisco. Through a paternalistic patronage system, the boss-controlled urban political machine offered economic and political opportunities, as well as social-welfare provisions for the Irish community.[53]

Irish Catholics made slow but steady progress in entering the societal mainstream. Antipathy against them gradually lessened as their command of English, improved economic position, and physical appearance made them less objectionable to Anglo-American Protestants than the new immigrants arriving from other parts of Europe.

The New Irish

With half its population under the age of 28 and a fairly constant 18 percent unemployment rate since 1982, Ireland has experienced a new wave of emigrants leaving their native land. Almost 32,000 Irish entered the United States legally in 1981–1990, but with a two-year waiting list, perhaps 50,000 more came illegally. Only 1,300 of these Irish illegals applied for amnesty because most have not been here long enough to meet residency requirements.[54] Legal Irish newcomers have increased significantly due to legislation reserving 48,000 Irish immigrant visas over a three-year period that began in October 1991.

Like their predecessors, the new Irish cluster in the big cities, working in construction or homes, for the care of children and the elderly. Reflecting the chain migration pattern, Boston receives immigrants from the west of Ireland, whereas those from Donegal, Fermanagh, and other northern counties go to Philadelphia. Cleveland attracts newcomers from Achill Island off the coast of Mayo. Other Irish settle along Bainbridge Avenue in New York's Bronx, known as the "Irish Mile."

Well represented in the professions, in financial services, and in the executive suites of corporate America, the old Irish—the descendants of earlier immigrants—are now mostly in suburbia, enjoying higher incomes and status. Reminded of their roots by the flourishing Irish ethnicity visible once again in urban neighborhoods and desirous of helping the newcomers, the old Irish are nonetheless embarrassed by the radicalism of the new Irish with their fervent Brits-out nationalism.[55] Such an experience is quite similar to that of assimilated German Jews distressed by the large influx of East European Jewish immigrants, many of them ardent socialists, at the turn of the century.

THE SCANDINAVIANS _____

Some Swedes and Finns came to what is now the United States as early as 1638, making their landfall at the mouth of the Delaware River. They estab-

Current St. Patrick's Day parades are primarily times to celebrate pride in one's cultural heritage. Past parades were likely to serve as militant demonstrations of Irish power and ethnic resiliency and to inspire ethnic pride despite the harsh value judgments against them by an often hostile society. *(Michael Dwyer/Stock, Boston)*

lished a colony, New Sweden, a land of promise encompassing parts of modern-day Delaware, Pennsylvania, and New Jersey. Combating the Dutch and the English as well as the heat and the mosquitoes, these settlers constructed the first log cabin in the New World.

Although small numbers of Norwegians, Swedes, and Danes continued to emigrate to the United States, they did not come here in substantial numbers until after 1865. Thereafter, motivated by religious dissension, voting disenfranchisement, crop failures, and other economic factors, the Scandinavians emigrated in large numbers.

A great many of these immigrants settled in the northern region of the Midwest, in rural communities where the soil was highly fertile and where they could enjoy social and political equality and yet retain their ethnicity. Their settlements in the farmlands of the northern Middle West became strongholds of church-centered Norwegian and Swedish traditions. Isolation from the dominant drift of American social patterns permitted their widespread and long-lived retention of indigenous lifeways, which continue in some measure to this day.[56] Ole Rolvaag presented an eloquent and poignant saga of late-nineteenth-century Norwegian pioneers in the Dakota Territory in *Giants in the Earth*, a vivid social-psychological portrait of pioneer life. Capturing the exuberant hopes, fears, despair, struggles, and interactions of the immigrants in the heartland of America, this monumental work offers vivid testimony to the human quest of a dream.

> And it was as if nothing affected people in those days. They threw themselves blindly into the Impossible, and accomplished the Unbelievable. If anyone succumbed in the struggle—and that happened often—another would come and take his place. Youth was in the race; the unknown, the untried, the unheard-of, was in the air; people caught it, were intoxicated by it, threw themselves away, and laughed at the cost. Of course it was possible—everything was possible out here. There was no such thing as the Impossible any more. The human race had not known such faith and such self-confidence since history began. . . . And so had been the Spirit since the day the first settlers landed on the eastern shores; it would rise and fall at intervals, would swell and surge on again with every new wave of settlers that rolled westward into the unbroken solitude.[57]

Copper and iron mining in northern Michigan and eastern Minnesota attracted the majority of emigrating Finns. By 1920, 52 percent of all Finnish Americans lived in these two states. Another 25 percent lived in the West, working in mining, lumber, and fishing industries. The great concentration of Finns in Astoria, Oregon, earned it the nickname "the Helsinki of the West." In the East Finns settled mostly in small Massachusetts towns or in the Red Hook section of Brooklyn in New York, near a Norwegian community.[58]

Peter Kivisto suggests that Finns were perhaps the most radical ethnic group to come to the United States. Between 25 and 40 percent of the Finnish immigrants participated in national leftist organizations, including the Finnish Socialist Federation of the Socialist Party as well as the International Workers of the World (IWW).[59] By 1920 marital assimilation was increasingly the norm among Finnish Americans, except in the western Great Lakes region and Astoria, where endogamy remained high. Decline of ethnic institutions and upward mobility further Americanized Finnish Americans and simultaneously brought about the decline of the Finnish American left.[60]

Ingroup Solidarity

Like other immigrant groups, the Scandinavians attempted to resist Americanization and to cling to their Old World traditions. Intermarriage was frowned on, often far into the twentieth century. An ethnic newspaper's 1897 lament about exogamy illustrated the concern "that the national spirit is not particularly strong among the Danes of this region" and that intermarriage would "strike out our mother tongue and all we received as a heritage from our fathers."[61]

As greater numbers of Norwegians settled in Minnesota and Wisconsin, they eventually outnumbered the native-born population, creating social tensions and political competition. A typical example occurred in 1878 in Trempealeau County, Wisconsin, a beautiful region of wooded hills and valleys. When the Norwegians practiced their custom of picnicking and drinking on Sunday afternoons—the Continental Sabbath—their American neighbors increasingly censured them. When a Norwegian running as an independent was elected sheriff on a vote split along party lines, the Sunday custom continued without further interference; political party leaders also realized they could no longer ignore or antagonize this ethnic majority.[62]

Ethnicity, however, is an ever-changing dialogue between immigrants and the host society. When Presidents Theodore Roosevelt and Woodrow Wilson launched attacks prior to U.S. entry into World War I, on hyphenated Americans for their language retention, ethnic press, and ethnic organizations, local attacks on Scandinavian ethnicity followed. In 1915 the *Minneapolis Journal* published an editorial, "The Hyphen Must Go!" It argued that in the upper Midwest the melting pot was not doing its job because immigrant communities were retaining too much of their Old World cultures, and too many "hyphenated" newspapers, schools, and societies were still using the immigrant languages.[63]

Ethnic Identity

Norwegians, Swedes, and Danes have come to the United States from lands with different governments, different traditions, and different languages. Because of the physical similarities among the three groups and because they frequently settled together in the new land, use of the term *Scandinavian* to designate all three groups became common throughout American society.

> The common use of the term *Scandinavian* to describe Swedes, Norwegians, and Danes in a broad and general way is one of the products of the commingling of these three peoples on the American side of the Atlantic. The word really fits even more loosely than does the word *British* to indicate the English, Welsh, and Scotch. It was applied early in the history of the settlements in Wisconsin and Illinois, to groups which comprised both Norwegians and Danes on the one hand, or Norwegians and Swedes on the other hand, when no one of the three nationalities were strong enough to maintain itself separately, and when the members of one were inclined . . . to resent being called by one of the other names; for example, when a Norwegian objected to being taken for a Swede. The Scandinavian Synod of the Evangelical Lutheran Church, organized in 1860, included both Norwegians and Danes.
>
> . . . The use and acceptability of the word steadily grew; the great daily paper in Chicago took the name *Skandinaven;* in 1889, the editor of *The North* declared: "the term has become a household word . . . universally understood in the sense in which we here use it to designate the three nationalities. . . ."[64]

In addition to farming, the Scandinavians primarily worked as lumberjacks, sailors, dock workers, and craftsmen in the building and machine trades. Because they came from countries with compulsory education, their literacy rate was very high, and a large percentage of them acquired U.S. citizenship. Danes tended to spread out more and to downplay the role of the church and fraternal organizations, in comparison to Norwegians and Swedes. For that reason the Danes assimilated more quickly, although all groups succeeded in blending into the American social fabric fairly easily. The Swedes hit their peak year of immigration in 1913, and the Norwegians hit their peak in 1924. The total number of Scandinavians who have emigrated to the United States is now approximately 2.5 million.

THE SCOTS

The first wave of Scottish migration occurred during the colonial period; by 1790 they were second in number only to the English, totaling 221,562, or 7 percent of the population, compared with the 2,605,699 English, who made up 82 percent. Consequently, Scottish Americans played a prominent role during the formative years of the new nation. As an illustration, 11 of the 56 signers of the Declaration of Independence were Scottish Americans. Almost 80 percent of all Scottish emigrants came to America later, however; between

Ship building offered many job opportunities for nineteenth-century immigrants, particularly from Scandinavia and Ireland. Many East Coast seaport cities had shipyards, such as this one in East Boston. The skeletons of these sailing vessels are in the process of receiving their planking, decks, and finishing. *(The Bettmann Archive)*

1871 and 1930 more than 640,000 Scots arrived. This group was primarily from the working class, and they entered various semiskilled occupations.

The Scots should not be confused with the Scotch-Irish, who were mostly Lowland Scots who came from the Irish city of Ulster. Before the Revolution, 50,000 of them had settled on the southern frontier and in the central Appalachians. They were concentrated primarily in North Carolina and Pennsylvania. Living on the American frontier, the Scotch-Irish did not mingle with outgroup members, interacting and marrying within their group boundaries.[65] They often took the law into their own hands when they felt their interests were threatened, rebelling violently against taxation, massacring Indians, and forming lynch mobs. Numerous recorded incidents attest to their involvement in ethnic conflict and community violence.[66]

Although the Scotch-Irish activity supported the rebel cause, the Scots from the Highlands of Scotland were loyalists throughout the Revolutionary War. They settled in established areas rather than along the frontier and insisted upon maintaining their ethnic identity even though they were easily assimilated almost from the outset.

The rigid discipline of Scottish church life—either Presbyterian or Episcopalian—was reflected in their life-style. Deeply religious, they adhered to a strict moral code; the Protestant Ethic of hard work, frugality, and honesty was as evident among them as among Calvinist New Englanders. Like many other communities, they also sought to preserve their culture and to duplicate the way of life from the old country.

Scottish emigration did not maintain its magnitude after 1936. Lack of new Scottish immigrants in sizable numbers reduced their proportional representation in the total population, and the assimilation process mostly removed their visibility. Maintaining their ethnic identity was a losing battle. The Scots did continue, however, to wear disguises on Halloween (a practice now followed by many children in the United States on this holiday) and to celebrate regularly the January 25 birthday of Robert Burns, the Scottish poet. In western North Carolina there are the annual Highland Games with pipe bands, and a formal ball afterwards, with the men in formal evening kilts and the women in white ball gowns with their clan tartan sashes over their shoulders.

THE WELSH

Although frequently lumped together with the English, the Welsh are a distinct ethnic minority in the United States, and there were sufficient numbers during the pre–Civil War period to warrant the printing of newspapers and some books in Welsh.

Welsh immigrants came here with the early colonists, settling together to a much greater degree than did the English. They were very active during the Revolution, and five Welsh Americans—William Floyd, Button Gwinnett,

Thomas Jefferson, Francis Lewis, and Lewis Morris—were signers of the Declaration of Independence.

As with other immigrants, economic and religious motives lured the Welsh to the United States. They were of different Protestant denominations; Baptists and Quakers came first, followed later by Anglicans and Presbyterians. Primarily farmers and miners, many settled in Cambria County, Pennsylvania, where they exerted a strong social and political influence; others settled in Oneida County, New York, a region in which "Welsh butter" became famous. By the late nineteenth century many Welsh miners—like their English counterparts—had become superintendents and foremen of coal mines in many states, including Ohio, Illinois, and Washington.

BOX 5.3

THE INTERNATIONAL SCENE

Throughout the 1970s and 1980s, hundreds of thousands of Turks entered West Germany, filling an important need for workers during the nation's booming economic growth. Their migration for industrial jobs was similar to that of the southern, central, and eastern Europeans to the United States in the late nineteenth and early twentieth centuries. The similarity did not end there. Visually distinct in dress, language, and religion, the Turks usually clustered together, forming ethnic communities with recognizable parallel social institutions within their subculture.

Their presence, although a boon to the economy, was not entirely welcome. Germans expressed widespread anti-Turkish prejudice in numerous ways, including incendiary press reports, letters in newspapers, tauntings, ethnophaulisms, neighborhood protests, fights, and disproportionate arrests of Turks.

By 1990, though, the 1.6 million Turks living in western Germany had become more accepted. They had achieved economic security, paying more into the German social welfare and pension system than they took out. Many Turks had become entrepreneurs, investing almost $3 billion in the country by opening new businesses and creating over 100,000 jobs. Their upward mobility into a respectable social class had lessened the ethnic prejudice against them.

In the United States, Europeans had faced the antiforeign militancy of the Ku Klux Klan and its legacy of violence. In Germany, following reunification and the subsequent impact of the global recession on the German economy, the Turks faced in 1992 the militant violence of antiforeign neo-Nazis. Beatings and firebombings, sometimes to the cheers of other Germans watching from their apartment balconies, sporadically occurred. In November 1992 neo-Nazis firebombed a Turkish apartment in Molln, killing two little girls and a grandmother. In May 1993 they struck again in Solingen, killing five Turkish women and children. Both acts prompted protests by Turkish immigrants and Germans, but the situation remains volatile.

SOCIOLOGICAL ANALYSIS _____

In our study of the northern and western European immigrants, we have discussed their experiences within a sociohistorical context, as well as the specific patterns of dominant-minority interaction. To understand better the meaning of those patterns, we shall now place them within conceptual frameworks of the three major sociological perspectives.

The Functionalist View

With their emphasis on a societal network of interrelated parts working together for survival or stability, functionalists see the arrival of large groups of people to forge a civilization out of a vast, undeveloped country rich in natural resources as highly desirable. The New World offered the newcomers economic opportunity and freedom from religious and political oppression, while benefiting from their presence. The unskilled newcomers helped build the cities, canals, and railroads; clear the land for farming; and create demand for goods and services. Others used their entrepreneural skills or craftsmanship to supply the growing nation with needed commerce. The evolution of an independent American society and of poor immigrants Crevècoeur had called "useless and withered plants" that "have taken root and flourished" was the outgrowth of a smoothly functioning social system.[67]

Sometimes the large numbers of Irish and Germans entering the country created dysfunctions; the society could not absorb them that quickly. They clustered together, culturally distinct from the dominant Anglo-American model, a situation that generated prejudice and discrimination against them. The ensuing conflict, like that involving French Americans in earlier years, disrupted the social system, preventing cooperative efforts toward common goals and denying attainment of personal goals to many newcomers. In time the necessary adjustments occurred; education and upward mobility through economic growth and the Civil Service (in the case of the Irish) allowed both acceptance and assimilation.

The Conflict View

The beginning point of this theoretical perspective is the dominance of Anglo-Americans in the new nation. Not only did they influence the adoption of language, customs, and social institutions derived from Great Britain, but also they held economic and political power. In this context the Federalist hostility toward the French and Irish becomes more than ethnic antagonism. The propertied elite saw the influx of so many "common" people and the possible spread of Jacobin revolutionary ideas as threats to their power, and they took various actions to safeguard their interests (Alien and Sedition Acts, Native American party, and so on). Political considerations also weighed heavily in dealings with the Irish and Germans. The rise in power of Irish city politicians and the political activism of the Forty-eighters caused nativist reactions through mob violence, political movements, and state legislative countermeasures.

Economic exploitation, particularly in the case of the Irish, brought prosperity to the owners of mines, factories, and railroads. Often working under brutal conditions in physically demanding jobs, many Irish struggled to survive in the slums where their low wages obliged them to reside. The captains of industry, when confronted with strikes or labor organization efforts, used their power to thwart such efforts through the courts, law-enforcement personnel, or vigilante groups to break up demonstrations, or by hiring other workers. Much of the industrial expansion in the nineteenth century, conflict theorists maintain, was at the expense of the immigrant workers who made it possible. The resultant conflict did eventually bring about change, as Irish and Germans organized and gained a greater share of the nation's wealth.

Lieberson's power theory seems quite appropriate for the Irish in particular. As unskilled, peasant migrants, the Irish were the subordinate group to the Anglo-Americans. The conflict was sporadic and limited, with the Irish kept in their subordinate role until they too gained their share of power.

The Interactionist View

Understanding how people perceive and define the strangers in their midst is the basis of interactionist analysis. The Dutch in New Amsterdam and the Quakers in Philadelphia, for example, were receptive to cultural pluralism, and so harmonious relations ensued between them and the diverse peoples in their respective colonies. In contrast the Puritans were intolerant of anyone different, resulting in the expulsion of such religious dissidents as Roger Williams and Anne Hutchinson and their followers. Long-standing violent conflict in Europe between the English and Irish and between the English and French partially explains negative Anglo-American perceptions of French Americans and Irish Americans; cultural prejudices, transmitted from generation to generation, helped foster ethnic antagonism in the United States, often on a reciprocal basis.

In a country predominantly Protestant throughout its colonial and early national periods, the arrival of large numbers of Irish Catholics and German Jews disturbed the native population. They interpreted the presence of these groups as a threat to the "American" way of life, labeling them as inferiors and worse. Note the use of "hordes" (William Shaw) and "swarm" and "herding" (Benjamin Franklin)—words used frequently by others as well. Words are symbols, and here they connote both animalistic qualities and massive numbers, the latter often perceived as a contaminating menace to society. With this social interpretation of reality, confrontations and conflict were inevitable.

Retrospect _____

Structural and cultural differentiation played important roles in determining the nature of intergroup relations among northern and western Europeans in the United States. Generally, as long as the social structure was in its forma-tive period and thus very fluid, the ethnic groups did not experience discrim-ination or low status for long. Relative isolation from European influences and sharing the commonality of forging a new life in the wilderness helped reduce any nationalistic biases. Although sporadic flareups occurred due to nationalistic rivalries, the different ethnic groups were usually hospitable to one another, welcoming strangers coming to settle because they themselves would benefit from the community's growth.

As life became more settled, residential patterns more densely clustered, and the social structure more solidified, recently arrived strangers became more conspicuous. Their cultural differences were often accentuated by their less fortunate economic circumstances. German and Irish immigrants of the nineteenth century, for example, encountered hostility not only because of their religion and culture but also because of their lack of power. Many settled in established areas and thus started a new life in a region already dominated by others who looked on them with scorn. Those who kept to themselves by settling in rural areas—the Scandinavians, the French, and some of the Ger-man immigrants—fared better than those who tried to settle in already ur-banized areas.

Prevailing attitudes were of critical importance to a minority group's experience. The Dutch and Quakers, tolerant of those who were different, encouraged religious and cultural diversity within their settlements. Cultural diffusion and assimilation were least likely among the religiously orthodox. This was true not only for dominant groups in most New England colonies—who expelled or denied welcome to dissenters, Quakers, Catho-lics, and Jews—but also for minority groups who resisted intermarriage and assimilation, such as the nineteenth-century Dutch, Scandinavians, and Irish.

Cultural diversity was a reality from the outset. Each settlement was an ethnic enclave in which people of similar beliefs and values clustered together and helped one another to adjust in a new land. As the settlements became more populated, growing into towns and cities, the ethnic enclaves formed by the newer immigrants were actually subcommunities within a larger soci-ety. Although they were not as physically isolated as earlier ethnic groups, they were, nonetheless, socially and spatially segregated, often voluntarily, from those unlike themselves.

All immigrants in varying degrees faced hardships in adjusting to the strangeness of a new land and people. To ease that adjustment, they tried to re-create the familiar old world here in the new, through their churches, schools, newspapers, and fraternal and mutual-aid societies. Their efforts to preserve their language and culture helped to bring them a measure of secu-rity, but the attempts also often led to suspicion, dissension, and hostility between the dominant and minority cultures.

Discrimination and xenophobia occur especially when the superordinate group views the size and influence of the subordinate group as a threat to the stability of the job market, the community, or the nation itself. The nativist movements against the French and the Irish during John Adams's presidency, and against the Germans and the Irish in the mid-nineteenth century, testify to that pattern. Through legislative efforts and violent actions, the dominant-group members sought to justify their discriminatory behavior as appropriate to preserve the American character.

For the "old" immigrants the Civil War brought to an end the difficulties they had encountered because of their background, for they were now comrades-in-arms for a common cause. Then too a new threat loomed on the horizon as "new" immigrants—shorter and swarthier, with unfamiliar dress, foods, and customs—began the second great wave of migration to the United States. These new immigrants seemed to be totally unlike all that Americans were or should be. People found a new target for their fears, distrust, prejudices, and discrimination in these "undesirable" aliens.

The functionalist perspective stresses the young nation's need for newcomers and problems arising from large numbers of Irish and Germans hampering more rapid absorption. Conflict theorists emphasize Anglo-American dominance and the economic exploitation of other nationalities. Interactionists discuss how differing social interpretations of strangers—Dutch toward Puritan, Federalists toward foreigners, Protestants toward Catholics—set the stage for ethnic conflict.

Review Questions

1. What are some examples of cultural pluralism among the Dutch, French, German, Irish, Scandinavian, and Scottish peoples in the United States?
2. What significance attaches to the fact that English Americans comprised 82 percent of the population at the nation's beginning?
3. What similarities of dominant-minority patterns were shared by most northern and western European immigrants?
4. Apply the sociological concepts about strangers to those immigrant groups suffering from the xenophobic reactions of dominant groups toward them.
5. Apply the three major theoretical perspectives to the experiences of the immigrant groups discussed in this chapter.

Suggested Readings

ANDERSON, CHARLES H. *White Protestant Americans.* Englewood Cliffs, NJ: Prentice-Hall, 1970.
   A readable, comprehensive account of the cultural dominance of Anglo-Americans and their role in interethnic relations.

BEALS, CARLETON. *Brass Knuckle Crusade,* rev. ed. New York: Hastings House, 1960.
   Enlivened with graphic anecdotes, a fine portrait of mob violence and political activism during the days of the Know-Nothings.

BILLIGMEIER, ROBERT H. *Americans from Germany: A Study in Cultural Diversity.* Belmont, CA: Wadsworth, 1974.

A thorough coverage of German immigrants, its title referring to both the differences among those immigrating and their subcommunities.

DOLAN, JAY P. *The Immigrant Church: New York and German Catholics, 1815–1865.* Baltimore: Johns Hopkins Press, 1975.

A penetrating insight into the immigrant Catholic Church as it encountered many forms of Anglo-Saxon Protestant attack.

FALLOWS, MARJORIE R. *Irish Americans: Identity and Assimilation.* Englewood Cliffs, NJ: Prentice-Hall, 1979.

Overview of the Irish American experience, from rejection to acceptance, with analysis of subcultural values and behavior.

HIGHAM, JOHN. *Strangers in the Land.* New York: Antheneum, 1973.

An excellent historical narrative of the patterns of American nativism from 1860 to 1925.

KLEPPNER, PAUL. *The Cross of Culture: A Social Analysis of Midwestern Politics, 1850–1900.* New York: Free Press, 1970.

Solid analysis of the German and Scandinavian role in local and state politics, showing ethnic solidarity as a means to political power.

LEYBURN, JAMES G. *The Scotch-Irish: A Social History.* Chapel Hill, NC: University of North Carolina Press, 1962.

One of the better books about this ethnic group, from the pre-Revolutionary years to modern times, providing subcultural analysis and history.

6

Southern, Central, and Eastern Europeans

During the colonial period, immigrants also came to the United States from southern, central, and eastern Europe. Many, in fact, played important roles in the Revolutionary War and during the early years of the new nation. Not until the late nineteenth century, however, would immigrants come from this part of the world in any significant numbers. The same economic changes that had earlier caused emigration from northern and western Europe (now growing in industrial employment), spread south and east, creating in that region agrarian difficulties, famine, and unemployment, thereby causing a significant shift in the source of European emigration to the United States.

SOCIOHISTORICAL PERSPECTIVE

In the late nineteenth century a noticeable shift occurred in the kind of immigrant coming to America. The 1870s saw a dramatic increase in the number of Russians, Italians, and Austro-Hungarians arriving (see Appendix II). By 1896 the turning point was reached: The number of immigrants from northern and western Europe was surpassed by the number of immigrants from the rest of Europe. Their physical and cultural differences made the newcomers easier to identify as strangers, and they often were broadly categorized as being alike, despite their many intrinsic differences as individuals and as separate ethnic groups. They arrived in large enough numbers to be able to preserve their culture and social boundaries within an urban subcultural setting, but this also increased the probability of prejudice and discrimination against them.

The Push–Pull Factors

A number of reasons accounted for the great wave of immigration from 1880 to 1920 (Figure 6.1). During that time American industry was growing rapidly, requiring ever larger numbers of workers. Improved transportation— quicker, sturdier steamships with their highly competitive rates for steerage dropping to $10 or less—encouraged an ocean crossing.

Peasant life was especially harsh in Europe. The ruling classes and local estate farmowners exploited the common people. They crushed most peasant revolts and protests instead of reforming the basic agricultural economy. Peasants saw their sons drafted into the army for periods of 12 to 31 years. Trying to eke out an existence amid poverty, unemployment, sickness, and tyranny, some of Europe's poor looked elsewhere for a better life.

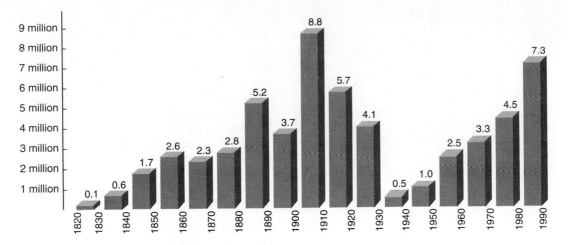

FIGURE 6.1
Total Immigration to the United States from 1820 to 1990, by Decades
SOURCE: U.S. Immigration and Naturalization Service.

Letters from friends or relatives already in America were eagerly read and circulated among villagers. Newspapers, books, pamphlets, and transportation and labor recruiting agents all stimulated what contemporaries came to call "America fever." Following a familiar minority pattern of avoidance, Europe's poor and persecuted peoples fled their homelands for the promise of "Golden America."

Political and economic unrest in Europe also encouraged the exodus. Governments faced the pressures of overpopulation, chronic poverty, the decline of feudalism, dissident factions, and a changing agrarian economy. For them large-scale emigration to America was an expedient solution to many problems, so they sponsored emigration drives, further increasing the European migration.

And so they came—Italians, Portuguese, Greeks, and Armenians from the southern part of the continent; Hungarians, Poles, Czechs, Slovaks, and others from the plains of central Europe; Byelorussians, Ukrainians, Ruthenians, and others from the western regions of Czarist Russia; Jewish emigrants, whose religion and Yiddish culture had frequently made them targets of discrimination and persecution, from all parts of eastern and central Europe, particularly Russia. All these different peoples came, leaving behind their familiar world and seeking a new destiny.

Structural Conditions

The America the immigrants came to was far different from the one earlier immigrants had found. The frontier was rapidly disappearing; industrialization and urbanization were changing the life-style of the nation. The immigrants, mostly illiterate, unskilled, rural peasants, were plunged into a new cultural and social environment.

Because they had virtually no resources, many of these immigrants settled in the cities that had been their ports of entry or in the inland cities along railroad lines, such as Chicago. At the turn of the century, living conditions in the cities were far worse than they are today. Overcrowding, disease, high mortality rates, crime, filth, and congestion were commonplace. Crowded into poorly ventilated tenements and cellars, the immigrants often lived in squalor.

Settling in the oldest city sections, the immigrants formed ethnic subcommunities, re-creating the nationality quilt of Europe. Although these groups were neighbors because of necessity, intermarriage or joint organizational activities were rare. In an effort to find security in a strange land, they repeated the adjustment patterns of the "old" immigrants. They sought and interacted with their own people, establishing their own churches, schools, and organizations to preserve their traditions and culture.

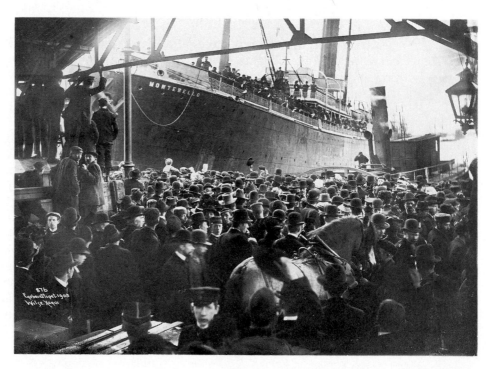

A throng of European male immigrants surging toward the gangplank of a steamship bound for America was a common scene at all the continent's seaports in the early twentieth century. "America fever" reached such heights by 1907 that 5,000 immigrants a day were being processed at Ellis Island, where three-fourths of all European immigrants arrived. *(Courtesy of Norsk Folkemuseum)*

BOX 6.1	THE ETHNIC EXPERIENCE

"Working conditions were terrible, terrible. If you have to sit two—three hours overtime for ten cents, what can I explain you? It don't get worse. But these ten cents I need. Whenever it was overtime, I was the first one to raise my hand.

"The boss watches you. You shouldn't talk to one another. He watches you between lunch and supper, you know. So you want something, you have something in your drawer like candy. He watches. No, no, no, nothing. You can't eat while you're working. So, you watch, you put the candy in your mouth.

"It was so hot in the shop, the sweat was running from the body and from the hand and the material got stained. The boss didn't care, the foreman didn't care. Once two policemen came in. They stopped the power. They said we couldn't work in such a heat. You haven't even got a fan here to have a little coolness. Nothing! People used to faint. Big people used to faint.

"In winter—it was such a hard winter. When I opened the door in the morning to go to work, I couldn't take away my hand from the knob—the frost. Terrible, terrible. At work in the big shop in the middle was a stove. It kept us a little warm. But, you know, young people, young blood—we put on a sweater. Yeah, the conditions was terrible. Can't be worse. Can't be worse. It was terrible. And the boss had a fresh mouth always for the workers."

SOURCE: Austrian Jewish immigrant who came to the United States in 1914 at age 17.

As unskilled workers, most found employment in the low-status, manual labor jobs in the factories, mines, needle trades, and construction. At that time the worker had no voice in working conditions, for labor unions had not yet become effective. The fourteen-hour day, six-day week for low wages was common. There were no vacations, sick pay, or pension plans. Child labor was the norm, and entire families often worked to provide family income. Lighting, ventilation, and heating were poor; in the factories moving pieces of machinery were dangerously exposed. There was no workers' compensation if, as was likely, someone was injured on the job. A worker who objected was likely to be fired and blacklisted. Exploited by the captains of industry, the immigrants became deeply involved with the labor union movement, so much so that to tell the story of one without the other is virtually impossible:

It is true that many immigrants embraced the industrial ethos and found fulfillment in it. But many could not adjust to the new work discipline required of them and drifted from job to job; a good percentage returned to the Old Country, defeated and disillusioned. Some tried and failed to find work for which their skills and previous experience equipped them. Others turned to collective action—temperance societies, workers' educational associations, fraternal benefit societies, cooperatives, and unions—either to protect themselves from a system that was often pitiless, or to try in a small way to change the social and economic environment in which they found themselves. Still others resorted to radical and "direct" action to forcibly change a system which did not yield what they had crossed the Atlantic to find.[1]

Despite the adverse conditions, many immigrants worked hard and made sacrifices. Things were still better than what they had left behind. More important, America gave them hope and a promise of better things—if not for themselves, then surely for their children.

Societal Reactions

Although the immigrant groups kept themselves socially segregated from one another, outsiders mostly saw them as un-American strangers and tended to lump them all together. Italians and Jews stood out from the others because of their large numbers, residential clustering, religion, language, appearance, and cultural practices. Although many people viewed all "new" immigrants as both undesirable and unassimilable, American society directed the greatest antagonism against the more visible Italians and Jews.

Racism

A negative reaction to incoming minority groups had occurred many times before. This time, however, it developed a new dimension—actions based on physical features:

> The arrival on American shores of these darker swarms of migrants—the so-called "new immigration"—was countered by the development of a new note in American nativism: the racist claim of ineluctable biological superiority for those with lighter skins, fairer hair, and earlier debarkation dates. Together with the older nativist themes of anti-Catholicism, fear of "foreign radicalism," and general xenophobia, this newer development in collective hatred, along with an awakening anti-Semitism, combined to produce the onslaught on the immigrant's culture, social organization, and self-regard known as the Americanization movement—a development which . . . was brought to its highest pitch by the events of World War I and the immediate post-war period.[2]

Probably the most significant blending of the nativist and racist thinking of this period came from Madison Grant's influential book, *The Passing of the Great Race,* which appeared in 1916. Relying on what he considered scientific truth, Grant used race as the key factor determining culture and behavior. He argued that racial hybridism can only lead to a reversion to the "lower type." As his pessimistic title suggests, Grant saw the vastly superior Old American stock as disappearing (through "racial suicide") as a result of lower birth rates because they chose not to contaminate their racial purity:

As an Ellis Island doctor checks for eye disease, other immigrants anxiously await their turn. Earlier, other doctors had watched at the top of steps to stop anyone who was limping or showing shortness of breath. Because any form of disability resulted in deportation, many immigrants believed only healthy people lived in America. *(Courtesy of Brown Brothers)*

[Native Americans of colonial stock] will not bring children into the world to compete in the labor market with the Slovak, the Italian, the Syrian and the Jew. The native American is too proud to mix socially with them and is gradually withdrawing from the scene, abandoning to these aliens the land which he conquered and developed. The man of the old stock is being crowded out of many country districts by these foreigners just as he is today being literally driven off the streets of New York City by the swarms of Polish Jews. These immigrants adopt the language of the native American, they wear his clothes, they steal his name and they are beginning to take his women, but they seldom adopt his religion or understand his ideals; and while he is being elbowed out of his own home, the American looks calmly abroad and urges on others the suicidal ethics which are exterminating his own race.[3]

Grant's book was highly influential with other writers and congressional leaders. Popular magazines, such as the *Saturday Evening Post,* quoted and praised Grant. Other "scholars" followed with eugenic explanations to show a correlation between racial physique and culture:

> Previously vague and romantic notions of Anglo-Saxon peoplehood were combined with general ethnocentrism, rudimentary wisps of genetics, selected tidbits of evolutionary theory, and naive assumptions from an early and a crude imported anthropology (later, other social sciences, at a similar stage of scientific development added their contributions) to produce the doctrine that the English, Germans, and others of the "old immigration" constituted a superior race of tall, blonde, blue-eyed "Nordics" or "Aryans." Whereas the peoples of Eastern and Southern Europe made up the darker Alpines or Mediterraneans—both inferior breeds whose presence in America threatened, either by intermixture or supplementation, the traditional American stock and culture.[4]

Ronald M. Pavalko maintains that racism was the fundamental basis for the negative response to the "new" immigrants, and that any economic argument for immigration restrictions was a smokescreen.[5] He cites economist Isaac A. Hourwich, who reported that in reality unemployment rates tended to be lowest in years of *high* immigration and highest during years of *low* immigration.[6] However, "specific economic and political events—industrial conflict, World War I, and the Russian Revolution—contributed to [a] redefinition" of these groups in nonracial terms.[7] As the emphasis shifted to national loyalty and stability, the Americanization movement marked a "crucial turning point."

> The transformation of the new immigrants from a stigmatized racial entity to a threat to economic and political order represents a shift in the definition of them as *unassimilable* to one emphasizing the point that they *must be assimilated.* We can only speculate on whether the new immigrants would have continued to be the focus of a racist ideology if this redefinition had not occurred. It does seem clear that the conscious and explicit emphasis on "Americanization" did not represent a rejection of racist assumptions about them as much as the substitution of economic and political concerns as more pressing.[8]

Americanization

Without any assistance from government agencies, and with little or no knowledge of the language or customs, the immigrants were expected to fit into the society quickly. Moreover, Americans expected them to speak only English, strip away their old culture, and avoid any ethnic institutions or organizations. These demands often led to ethnic self-hatred or a negative self-image because of the newcomers' ambivalence, or their inability or slowness to assimilate.[9]

To preserve the stability of the country, many people attempted to hasten the assimilation of the new immigrants already here. They looked on the schools as agents of socialization, one of the key forces in effecting Anglo-conformity. The following quotation, by an educator of the early twentieth century, is representative of the prevailing dominant-group attitudes of that period:

> These southern and eastern Europeans are of a very different type from the north Europeans who preceded them. Illiterate, docile, lacking in self-reliance and initiative, and not possessing the Anglo-Teutonic conceptions of law, order, and government, their coming has served to dilute tremendously our national stock, and to corrupt our civic life. The great bulk of these people have settled in the cities of the North Atlantic and North Central states and living, moral and sanitary conditions, honest and decent government, and proper education have everywhere been made more difficult by their presence. Everywhere these people tend to settle in groups or settlements, and to set up here their national manners, customs, and observances. Our task is to break up these groups or settlements, to assimilate and amalgamate these people as a part of our Amer-

"An Interesting Question"

"How long will it be," asked the caption, "before the rats own the garden and the man gets out?" This cartoon shows Uncle Sam asleep in his garden, unaware of the invasion of foreign rats. Their faces are stereotyped depictions of Jews, Russians, Italians, Greeks, and other immigrants from southern and eastern Europe. This cartoon by E. M. Ashe appeared in *Life* on June 22, 1893. *(Courtesy of Library of Congress [LC-USZ62-7386])*

ican race, and to implant in their children, so far as can be done, the Anglo-Saxon conception of righteousness, law and order, and popular government, and to awaken in them a reverence for our democratic institutions and for those things in our national life which we as a people hold to be of abiding worth.[10]

The children of the immigrants felt the conflicts between majority-group expectations and their minority perspective more keenly than did their parents. They were truly marginal people, caught between two worlds. The schools were promoting the shedding of cultural differences, and the children were growing up in a society contemptuous of foreigners. Because the land they knew was America and because they wanted to be accepted, the children began to be self-conscious. Many, for example, were embarrassed to bring friends to their homes, where a foreign language, foreign cooking, and a different atmosphere prevailed.

Xenophobia

Historians often cite the Haymarket Affair as the single most important factor in causing a xenophobic reaction against all immigrants. In Chicago in May 1886, at the height of a general strike for an eight-hour work day, the anarchist organizers—almost all of them immigrants—held a rally in Haymarket Square. As nervous police approached the peaceful gathering, someone threw a bomb at them. It exploded in their midst, killing one officer and wounding 70. The bomb thrower's identity was never discovered, but the courts sentenced six immigrants and one native-born American to death; another immigrant received a long prison term. Newspapers fostered a negative stereotype of the immigrant and attacked immigrants on this basis. National hysteria and fear of anarchy built up, particularly in the large cities of the Northeast and Midwest:

> The current social scene presented a troubling contrast to the image of America that Anglo-Saxon intellectuals cherished. The tradition of racial nationalism had always proclaimed orderly self-government as the chief glory of the Anglo-Saxons—an inherited capacity so unique that the future of the mid-eighties cast doubt on the survival of a free society. The more anxious of the Anglo-Saxon apostles knew that the fault must lie with all the other races swarming to America. Did they not, one and all, lack the Anglo-Saxon's self-control, almost by definition? So, behind the popular image of unruly foreigners, a few caught sight of unruly races; and Anglo-Saxon nativism emerged as a corollary to antiradical nativism—as a way of explaining why incendiary immigrants threatened the stability of the republic.[11]

Reflecting public hostility about these other "different" groups, one editorial writer said:

> These people are not Americans, but the very scum and offal of Europe . . . long-haired, wild-eyed, bad-smelling, atheistic—reckless foreign wretches, who never did an honest hour's work in their lives . . . crush such snakes . . . before they have time to bite.[12]

A magazine writer warned Americans that anarchy was a "blood disease" unknown to the Anglo-Saxons but common to the "darker swarms" from Europe:

> I am no race worshipper but . . . if the master race of this continent is subordinated to or overrun with the communistic and revolutionary races, it will be in grave danger of social disaster.[13]

For a long time after the Haymarket Affair, the words *foreign* and *radical* were linked in American culture. Negative stereotyping and nativistic move-

"Spoiling the broth!" ran the caption to this February 1921 cartoon, which first appeared in the *Los Angeles Times* and was reprinted elsewhere. This sentiment of inundation and nonassimilation of immigrants led to the passage of a restrictive immigration law later that year, effectively reducing the number of immigrants to the United States. (*The Distorted Image, Courtesy Anti-Defamation League of B'nai B'rith, John and Selma Appel Collection*)

ments increased. Calls for restrictions on immigration mounted and continued until the Immigration Law of 1921 was passed.

Legislative Action

In 1907, in response to public pressure, Congress established a joint Senate–House commission to investigate the entire immigration situation. Chaired by Senator William P. Dillingham of Vermont, the commission issued a voluminous report in 1911. This report was the first to use the concept of "old" versus "new" immigration. The Dillingham Commission reported that the "new" immigrants tended to congregate, slowing the assimilation process, unlike the "old" immigrants, who had dispersed. Also, "new" immigrants were less skilled and less educated, had greater criminal tendencies, and were more willing to accept lower wages and a lower standard of living. As a solution the commission suggested that either a literacy test be required of immigrants or immigration be restricted based on a percentage of the immigrants from a given country already here.

Although it supposedly used social-science statistics, the commission made several major errors. First, by using two simplistic categories, it failed to take into consideration vast differences in ability, opportunity, and social organization among the various ethnic groups. Second, it overlooked the longer period the "old" immigrants had had to achieve economic stability. Released during a time of economic recession, the report further encouraged calls for restrictions on immigration.

Congress's first response, in 1913, was to pass a literacy bill requiring all immigrants over 16 to be able to read some language. President Taft vetoed the bill, however, just as President Cleveland had vetoed a similar proposal in 1896. Finally, in 1917, Congress overrode President Wilson's veto of a new literacy bill similar in content to the earlier bills that had been vetoed. This law did little to stem the tide of immigrants, however, for it exempted those fleeing religious persecution, of whom there were a great many. Also, the literacy rate in Europe had risen since 1900 (Table 6.1), so the literacy test was not a serious obstacle for many people. Because of the continual flow of immigrants from war-ravaged Europe, the fear that such political upheavals as the Bolshevik revolution would spread to the United States, and the general mood of isolationism that swept over postwar America, pressures for immigration restrictions mounted.

Although outgoing President Wilson vetoed the congressional bill dealing with immigration, it became law after it was reintroduced in a special session of Congress and signed by President Harding. The National Origins Quota Act of 1921, adopting a proposal that the Dillingham Commission had made 10 years earlier, limited the numbers of immigrants. It imposed for three years a quota system under which the number of new immigrants allowed was only 3 percent of the number of people of that nationality already in the United States in 1910. The effect of this legislation was to reduce the number of southern, central, and eastern European immigrants from the 780,000 annual average in 1910–1914 to about 155,000 annually.

| TABLE 6.1 | ILLITERACY AMONG SOUTHERN, CENTRAL, AND EASTERN EUROPEANS ARRIVING FOR THE YEAR ENDING JUNE 30, 1920 |

Group	Percentage Illiterate
Armenians	24
Bohemians, Moravians	3
Bulgarians, Serbians, Montegrins	36
Croats, Slovenians	37
Dalmatians, Bosnians, Herzegovinians	33
Finns	3
Greeks	17
Jews	23
Italians	47
Lithuanians	32
Magyars	17
Poles	32
Portuguese	60
Rumanians	25
Russians	29
Ruthenians	49
Slovaks	28
Spaniards	5
Turks	75

SOURCE: Stanley Lieberson, *A Piece of the Pie* (Berkeley: University of California Press, 1980), 171.

When the act expired, it was replaced by the even tougher Johnson-Reed Act of 1924, which reduced each country's annual quota to 2 percent of its emigrants already in the United States in 1890, thereby discriminating even more strongly against the "newer" immigrant countries, as the worldwide quota dropped to almost 165,000. In 1929, however, the quota of 3 percent was restored with a total ceiling of 150,000.

Henry Pratt Fairchild, a sociologist, summed up the ethnocentric attitudes of his time when he said:

The highest service of America to mankind is to point the way, to demonstrate the possibilities, to lead onward to the goal of human happiness. Any force that tends to impair our capacity for leadership is a menace to mankind and a flagrant violation to the spirit of liberalism.

Unrestricted immigration was such a force. It was slowly, insidiously, irresistibly eating away at the very heart of the United States. What was being melted in the great Melting Pot, losing all form and symmetry, all beauty and character, all nobility and usefulness, was the American nationality itself.[14]

BOX 6.2	MAJOR IMMIGRATION ACTS

1875   First direct federal regulation of immigration, barring criminals, prostitutes, "coolie" labor.

1882   Established system of central control of immigration through state boards under Secretary of the Treasury.

1891   Established Bureau of Immigration.

1921   Limited immigration to 3 percent of foreign-born persons of that nationality living in the United States in 1910.

1924   Temporarily set limit to 2 percent of foreign-born persons of that nationality living in the United States in 1890; in 1929 returned to 3 percent in equal ratio to a total ceiling of 150,000.

1952   Set annual quota of one-sixth of 1 percent of ancestry or national origin recorded in 1920, with minimum quota of 100 and ceiling of 2,000 for countries in Asia–Pacific triangle.

1965   Abolished national origins quota system; numerical limitations of 120,000 from Western Hemisphere and 170,000 from Eastern Hemisphere, with a 20,000 per-country limit for latter only; excluded spouses, children, parents from numerical restrictions.

1976   Added 20,000 per-country limit to Western Hemisphere.

1978   Combined separate hemisphere ceilings into one worldwide limit of 290,000.

1986   Granted amnesty and eligibility for permanent resident status to illegal aliens residing in the United States before 1982.

1990   Set immigrant ceiling of 700,000 for 1992 through 1994, dropping to 675,000 thereafter.

SOURCE: U.S. Immigration and Naturalization Service, *1990 Statistical Yearbook*, Washington, DC, U.S. Government Printing Office, December 1991, Appendix I.

Although an exception was made to receive approximately 400,000 displaced persons following World War II, the 1929 legislation remained in effect until the McCarran-Walter Act of 1952 was passed. This new law, passed over President Truman's veto, still reflected nativist biases. It simplified the quota formula to one-sixth of 1 percent of the foreign-born population from each country in the 1920 census.

The Immigration and Nationality Act of 1965 ended the quota system, coming into effect in 1968. Numerical limits of 120,000 from the Western Hemisphere and 170,000 from the Eastern Hemisphere were set, based on a complicated preference system stressing job skills and close family kinship. In 1976 a 20,000-per-country annual limit was established, followed in 1978 by replacement of hemisphere quotas, with a single worldwide ceiling of 290,000, then changed in 1980 to 270,000, excluding refugees. Immediate relatives of U.S. citizens were admitted above the 270,000 limit, however, bringing annual legal immigration totals to over 500,000 annually in the 1980s. Then 1990 legislation set a new ceiling of 700,000 until 1994, when it would drop thereafter to 675,000.

THE SLAVIC PEOPLES

Often included under the general classification "Slavic peoples" are the Poles, Russians, Ukrainians, Ruthenians, Bulgarians, Rumanians, Czechs, Serbs, Croats, Slovaks, and Slovenians. The first four groups came to the United States in much greater numbers during the 1880–1920 mass migration period. Because these were more visible minorities, more information is available about their experiences, allowing separate discussions. However, American public opinion during the 1880–1920 period usually made no distinctions among these groups, and as a result their experiences in this country were frequently similar.

Slavic people had been in the New World since colonial times. New Amsterdam and New Sweden, for example, received Protestant refugees from this region in the seventeenth century, and Moravians fled to the Quaker colony of Pennsylvania in the eighteenth century. In the mid-nineteenth century many political refugees came to America, and almost all of them remained. In the post–Civil War period, however, Slavic people began to come in steadily increasing numbers, and this influx continued until the Immigration Act of 1921 sharply curtailed it.

These "new" immigrants scattered throughout the country, although a good many tended to concentrate in the mining and industrial areas in Pennsylvania and the Midwest. Beginning as unskilled workers, they formed the large majority of the workers in the coal fields, the iron and steel factories, and the slaughterhouses of Chicago. By 1917 they outnumbered all other ethnic groups in those places of occupation. The normal pattern was for the males to come first and their families later, if at all. Like many Greeks and Italians, numerous Slavic males merely came as sojourners to earn money for land, dowries, or just a better life, returning to their native land after a year or two. These three nationalities were the majority of the more than 2 million aliens who returned to Europe between 1908 and 1914.

In his book *The Slavic Community on Strike*, Victor R. Greene offers many vivid pictures of the immigrant experience in the mining industry. In the following excerpt he portrays the anxiety and arrival of a newcomer to the Pennsylvania coal region:

> The typical greenhorn would have alighted from the immigrant train in the Pennsylvania hard-coal region undoubtedly apprehensive if he had not yet met his correspondent. With luck, one or both had a photograph to aid in recognizing the other. Otherwise, the weary traveler at the depot asked or shouted the name of his sponsor. One can imagine the tears of joy on both sides when to the

immigrant's call his countryman responded, and their relief was expressed in a demonstrative embrace. . . .

The sponsor then led his charge to a group of shacks usually at the edge of town. This ghetto was separated from the rest of the populace, just as in other places in America where the East Europeans lived. Here in the coal country inhabitants term the foreign nest the Slavic mining "patch." If he arrived at night, the bundle-laden traveler would have to grope through the darkness, as no street illumination, paved roads or signs (even if he could have read them) facilitated this last, short trip.[15]

Here we can visualize the social segregation and the resulting ethnic enclave so common to all the immigrant groups. Although their languages and customs varied, the Slavic peoples commonly experienced economic hardship. Children were often put to work to help the family survive, instead of being sent to school. This not only deprived these immigrant children of a "normal" childhood but also delayed upward mobility by at least a generation.

The sight of so many children employed in mining along with their fathers appalled many Americans. The Slav would give a ready answer when accused of practising child labor—economic necessity. Popular American abhorrence of the evil forced through minimum age laws, but to little avail, as parents and employers violated them with rare penalty. Some child labor reformers announced that they had found boys as young as six working at the mines; nine or ten was probably the actual minimum. A leading reformer sympathized with the East European youngster as the "helpless victim of the frugality, ignorance, and industrial instincts of his parents." The value placed by Americans on educating the young little interested the Slav, for the valuable child was the working one. Above a minimum education was useless, and the pressing need for income forced sons into the pits at or before their teens. . . . All of the workers here, men and boys, labored the normal ten-hour, six-day week, when at full time.[16]

In the case of the Slavic immigrants, a combination of factors—their peasant background, economic deprivation, child labor, and little education—slowed their rise up the socioeconomic ladder. A high proportion of second- and third-generation Slavic Americans, for example, have had lower income and educational levels than the Greek and Jewish Americans[17] Among the reasons for these differences was the fact that the latter groups often came from more urbanized areas and were able to establish effective community organizations in the United States more quickly. Many Slavic Americans today are blue-collar workers whose income and standard of living have been improving as a result of the bargaining power of their unions.

Recent Immigrants

About 20,000 refugees fled to America from Hitler-occupied Czechoslovakia, most of them professionals, scholars, and artists. When the communists seized control in the postwar era, thousands more sought refuge in the United States. Still other refugees were admitted into the United States in

Child labor was once a sad reality in America and an economic necessity among East European immigrants. These breaker boys at a coal mine would work a full 10- or 12-hour day at one-tenth an adult's wages. Some fell asleep and into the chutes from which they extracted slag from the coal and would be maimed or killed. Others developed black lung disease like many adult miners. The rest usually became miners themselves when they were old enough. *(Culver Pictures)*

1968 after the Soviet invasion ended that country's brief flirtation with liberalization. Since 1961 about 40,000 Czechs have migrated here.

In previous editions of this book, I said of the immigrants from Yugoslavia:

> The south Slavic peoples continue to think of themselves as one of six distinct nationalities and so have not set aside their cultural, religious, and language differences to achieve any united ethnic grouping. They have little interest in becoming a political entity except in fragmented endeavors regarding their homeland.[18]

With the subsequent breakup of Yugoslavia, the tragic civil war that raged among Serbians, Croats and Bosnians around Sarajevo in 1992 and 1993 is vivid testimony to that reality. Some refugees from this strife-torn land have fled to the United States, although most have sought refuge in nearby European countries. Immigrants from Yugoslavia to the United States numbered over 30,000 in the 1970s and almost 19,000 in the 1980s.

THE POLES _____

Included among other Slavic groups until 1899, when they began to be counted separately, the Poles constituted the third-largest ethnic group of the "new" immigration. With their homeland under the divided control of Germany, Russia, and Austria-Hungary, 1 million Poles came here between 1899 and 1914, fleeing poverty and seeking economic opportunity. In fact the desire for economic improvement was so common to almost all the new immigrants that the expression to be "after bread" is found in the vocabularies of most central and eastern Europeans.

A 30-year-old Polish, Nobel Prize–winning writer, Henryk Sienkiewicz, visiting the United States from 1876 to 1878, illustrates this point in his classic observation of the difficulties his people first encountered here. Note also the traces of ethnocentrism in his observation of Americans:

> Their lot is a severe and terrifying one and whoever would depict it accurately would create an epic of human misery. . . . Is there anyone whose hand is not against them? Their early history is a tale of misery, loneliness, painful despair and humiliation. . . . They are primarily peasants and workers who have come in quest of bread. Thus you will easily understand that in a country inhabited by a people who are not at all sentimental, but rather energetic, industrious, and whose competition it is difficult to survive, the fate of these newcomers, poorly educated, unfamiliar with American conditions, ignorant of the language, uncertain how to proceed, must be truly lamentable.[19]

Although Sienkiewicz recorded his observations before the large influx of Polish immigrants, which peaked in 1907, he found a great many Polish immigrants in the United States. At that time there were Polish communities at Radom, Illinois; Krakow, Missouri; Polonia, Wisconsin; and Panna Maris, Texas.[20] Buffalo, Detroit, Milwaukee, and Chicago—the chief Polish center— all had very sizable Polish populations also.

Culture Shock

The effects of culture shock—bewilderment and disorganization, particularly in family life—can be seen in many immigrants' writings and in the records of courts and social-service agencies. This initial immigrant reaction has received considerable attention from sociologists. One of the early sociological classics, *The Polish Peasant in Europe and America* by William I. Thomas and Florian Znaniecki, explored this theme, and the framework they used subsequently influenced other studies of Polish American life.[21]

Leaving behind a *gemeinschaft* society, where behavior was regulated by custom and habit, the Polish immigrants found themselves isolated, surrounded by unsympathetic and even hostile people whose language and customs they did not comprehend. Thomas and Znaniecki maintained that even if active demoralization and antisocial behavior did not occur, those who made the transition suffered a "partial or general weakening of social interests, a growing narrowness or shallowness of the individual's social life." The authors showed how many immigrant families found the adjustment too difficult, and how crime, delinquency, divorce, desertion, prostitution, and economic dependency were often the by-products of family disorganization. Such tendencies could often be found in immigrant communities caught in a web of economic and social instability.

Community Organization

The values and forms of village life in rural Poland were reintegrated, although not completely, in the parish structure of the urban American Roman Catholic Church.[22] For example, St. Stanislaus Kostka Church in Chicago in 1899 became the world's largest parish. The church blended staunch Roman Catholicism, Polish culture, and a full range of social services to help the immigrants become Americanized.

Not all Poles wanted to become Americanized, however, and many wanted the church to reflect Polish culture. Many were also frustrated by vain attempts to have Polish priests elevated in a church hierarchy dominated by the Irish and Germans. Consequently, representatives from various "independent" parishes formed the Polish National Catholic Church; Lithuanians formed a similar movement. Both church groups used their native languages in the Mass rather than Latin. They also added other elements of their culture (patriotic songs, patron saint feast days) to their church activities.

The peasants of pre–World War I Poland had negative attitudes toward education. Summarizing the numerous scholarly references to this point, Helena Znaniecki Lopata reported:

> The attitudes of the Polish peasants toward education—which defined it as a waste of time at best, and as a dangerous thing undermining the traditional way of life at worst—were transplanted to the American soil. Ideally, the children of Polonia began working at an early age to help the family in its endless struggle for money. The United States Immigration Commission, which undertook an intensive study of immigrants in 17 American cities in 1911, found the children of Poles following this typical educational career: parochial school from the ages of 8 to 12, first communion, public school for two years, and then work.[23]

At that time all the Polish immigrant wanted education to do was to provide children with a strict moral upbringing in a well-disciplined atmosphere.

The Polish community did not fall into complete family disorganization and demoralization, as predicted by Thomas and Znaniecki. Its immigrant peasant culture was not a rigid set of norms subject to collapse from constant attack but were as receptive to ethnogenesis as any other ethnic community. Poles formed some of the earliest and strongest ethnic associations, such as the Polish National Alliance.

"Looking Backward"

"They desire to ban the newest arrivals at the bridge over which they and theirs arrived." Five wealthy men—from left to right, an Englishman, a German Jew, an Irishman, a German, and a Scandinavian—prevent the new immigrant from coming ashore and enjoying the same privileges that they now enjoy. The shadows of the five wealthy men are representations of their social status before immigration: the Englishman's shadow is a stableman, the German Jew's is a notions peddler, and the others' are peasant farm workers. *(This cartoon by Joseph Keppler appeared in* Puck *on January 11, 1893.)*

> The history of Polonia over the years, locally or as a superterritorial community, indicates that its cultural fabric was much more flexible and viable, based on the social structure and gradually changing, bending, and modifying as new norms were introduced purposely or through unconscious diffusion by its members.[24]

Several studies in the 1960s showed the rate of Polish upward mobility to be below that of other ethnic groups.[25] While this was true of the first two generations, by the mid-1970s a change could be seen. The older Polish Americans were at the top of the blue-collar world, and most of their offspring were entering the professions and the white-collar world.[26]

Examining the Polish American community in Los Angeles, Neil C. Sandberg found a lessening in cultural ethnicity among the third- and fourth-generation members.[27] Because successive generations had experienced upward mobility, he found an inverse correlation between social class and ethnicity.[28] In other words, greater individualism and less group cohesiveness accompanied social mobility. Lopata also suggests that the Polish communities could dissolve through continued assimilation but that a Polish national cultural base could conceivably replace the organizational and institutional base of the immigrants.[29]

Polonia Today

Of the roughly 12 million Americans claiming Polish ancestry in 1990, about 80 percent are clustered in nine northeastern and midwestern states. Chicago still claims the largest concentration outside Poland, about 1 million. However, there and elsewhere, traditional inner-city Polish neighborhoods have yielded to other minority groups, as the better-educated and more successful Polish Americans have moved to the suburbs. St. Stanislaus Kostka Church, for example, still stands, but the second language of the mass is no longer Polish but Spanish.[30]

New Polish immigrants still arrive, more than 83,000 in the 1980s. In 1990 about 7,500 of the 18,300 new arrivals chose Chicago as their intended settlement area.[31] Like their predecessors, many struggled to survive in a depressed U.S. economy.

THE HUNGARIANS

In the nineteenth century the Hungarians, or Magyars, were a minority in control of the Kingdom of Hungary. They began a campaign of "Magyarization"—imposing the Magyar language and culture—on all peoples living within their boundaries. As emigration to the United States increased, the Hungarian government financed both Catholic and Protestant churches and various immigrant societies in an effort to maintain its influence over Hungarians living in America. The government was not successful, for many of the immigrants sought their own identity and attempted to preserve their own languages and culture.

Like others before and after them, the Hungarians congregated in their own ethnic clusters. Most settled in New Jersey, New York, Ohio, Pennsylvania, Illinois, Indiana, and West Virginia. Cleveland and New York City attracted the greatest concentration of immigrants. With more than 76,000 Hungarians living in New York City in 1920, it was the "third largest Hungarian city in the world."[32]

In each such ethnic community the Hungarians established their own institutions and organizations, embodying the same religious division among Catholics, Protestants, and Jews as in their homeland. They established their own social and fraternal organizations to provide sick benefits and to pay for funerals. They also founded their own newspapers and nationalistic cultural groups.

Labor Conditions

America was seeking industrial workers, and so the Hungarians forsook farming and worked instead in the mines, steel factories, and other heavy industries. The labor agitation of the late nineteenth century often included Hungarian as well as Lithuanian and Slavic workers. These confrontations frequently were violent and bloody:

The most violent episode occurred outside of Hazelton, Pennsylvania in 1897. A posse, headed by a sheriff who was a former mine foreman, fired several vollies [sic] into an unarmed group of 150 strikers, mostly Hungarian, who were marching to a nearby town to urge other miners to join the strike. Twenty-one immigrants were killed and another forty wounded. There was general agreement among other mine foremen that there would have been no bloodshed if the strikers had not been foreign-born.[33]

The prominence of Hungarian immigrants in such brawny occupations as mining and steel, as well as in the labor unrest, led to whites using the ethnophaulism *hunky,* an alteration of their proper name, to refer generally to all Central European laborers. By the turn of the century, *hunky* had evolved into a universal term for a white, roughneck laborer—a redneck— and blacks simply extended it to all whites, using the dialectal pronunciation *honky. Hunky* is now a term rarely heard, but *honky* lingers on as a racial epithet.[34]

A sizable portion of these turn-of-the-century immigrants originally came as sojourners, but most eventually stayed. Consequently, their becoming U.S. citizens was a slower process. Those in the Hungarian American community who were naturalized citizens totaled only 15 percent before World War I, 21.1 percent by 1920, and 55.7 percent by 1930.[35]

The number of Hungarians who came to America is somewhat difficult to determine exactly, since the U.S. government did not distinguish Hungarians from Austrians until 1905, and even the Poles living in that country were included with the Hungarians until 1919. However, on the basis of immigration records and the research of Emil Lengyel, it is estimated more than 2 million Hungarians came to the United States between 1871 and 1920, many from the middle Danube region. As many as half may have returned to their homeland once they had saved enough money to buy their own farms or for some other purpose.

Political Refugees

In the mid-1950s an entirely different group of Hungarians came to America for political rather than economic reasons. When the Soviet Union crushed the Hungarian rebellion in 1956, Congress passed special legislation to circumvent the restrictive national quotas of the McCarran-Walter Bill of 1952. The United States airlifted the refugees—families, minors unaccompanied by parents, and students—and gave them temporary shelter at Camp Kilmer, New Jersey. Many voluntary agencies and Hungarian Americans assisted the 30,000 newcomers, who, after the initial shock of displacement, quickly adjusted to America and began to rebuild their lives.

Although more than 56,000 Hungarians have come to the United States since 1951, only a trickle now arrive, about 800 to 900 a year. Those numbers suggest a gradual decline of ethnicity in Hungarian American communities, except for instances of situational or symbolic ethnicity as now occur, for example, among Irish Americans.

THE GYPSIES

Gypsies are perhaps America's most elusive minority. Although more than 5,000 books have been written about them, many of these books are fictional and few are based on close observation. Although Gypsies number somewhere around 500,000 or more in the United States, they have been studied less than some Native American tribes with one-hundredth their population.[36] Several reasons account for this: Census and immigration authorities have never kept official statistics on them, Gypsies actively discourage any form of "snooping," and they are frequently on the move.

Who are the Gypsies? Because they are nomads and without territorial confinement, their major distinguishing characteristics are language and culture. They speak Romany, a form of Sanskrit, which has enabled researchers to trace their origins to northern India.[37] There are the *Rom* (Gypsies) and the *gadje* (others). Words that distinguish between the ingroup and the outgroup in this way are quite common in tribal societies. When individual Gypsies assimilate into the dominant culture, they are no longer considered to be Gypsies. Thus we must view the Gypsies as a persistent subculture, maintaining a unique cultural system.

Throughout the second half of the seventeenth century, Gypsies from Scotland came to work the Virginia plantations. Records indicate that Gypsies also settled among the French in New Amsterdam.[38] In the 1840s, because of repressive actions against them in England, Gypsies began migrating to the United States in substantial numbers.[39] Because the Nazis exterminated somewhere between 300,000 and 500,000 Gypsies, and they remained generally unwelcome throughout Europe afterward, many legal and illegal Gypsy immigrants undoubtedly came to the United States during the postwar period. Our only evidence for this, however, is their increased visibility at that time.

At the core of Gypsy culture is the family (the *familia*), which is actually a functional extended family. Parents, siblings, aunts, uncles, cousins, assorted relatives, and adopted children all live and work together, caring for one another in times of joy and sorrow.[40] The *familia* is an effective support institution for all problems, offering also a safe refuge from the *gadje*. The second unit of identity for the *Rom* is the *vitsi*, a clan or band of a few to more than 100 *familiyi*, forming a cognitive kinship group of affiliation through which Gypsies classify one another.[41]

The *familia* is strongly patriarchal, with the males working for short spans of time in a variety of trades: roofing, driveway blacktopping, auto body repair, scrap metal, and carnival work.[42] Women also provide a valuable source of income, usually from fortune-telling, which the *Rom* practice only with the *gadje,* not among themselves.[43] Although parents do not force matches, they are the principals in the mate selection process, encouraging marriages within the *vitsa* beyond first-cousin relationships. A bride price, or *daro,* ranging from under $1,000 to $10,000, goes toward the bride's trousseau, the wedding festivities, and household articles for the new couple.[44]

Most marry between the ages of 12 and 16, seldom over 18 for a first marriage, their young ages no doubt contributing to the high rate of failed Gypsy marriages. The wife traditionally lives with her husband's family and is known as a *bori,* subject to the supervision of her in–laws.[45]. Elopements have increased and romantic love is more accepted preceding still-arranged marriages, but *Rom–gadje* intermarriages comprise fewer than 6 percent of all Gypsy marriages.[46]

Rom culture has as its linchpin the concept of *marimé,* which extends to all areas of life. The term means *defilement* or *pollution,* referring to rigid lines between good and bad, clean and unclean, health and disease, *Rom* and *gadje.*[47] Most notable is its application to the upper and lower halves of the human body. The pure and clean upper portion cannot come into contact in any way with the lower portion, which is *marimé,* or with objects that have been in contact with it. For example, each person uses soaps and towels of different colors for the two body portions.[48] A woman brings shame on herself for exposing too much leg, but breasts are unashamedly squeezed by both men and women.[49] A *marimé* woman—one who has recently given birth or is having her monthly period—cannot cook or serve food to men, step over anything belonging to a man, or allow her skirts to touch his things.[50]

> The *gadje* are conceived as a different race whose main value is economic, and whose raison d'être is to trouble the Rom. The major offense of the *gadje,* the one offense the Rom can never forgive, is their propensity to defilement. *Gadje* confuse the critical distinction between the pure and the impure. They are observed in situations which the Rom regard as compromising; forgetting to wash in public bathrooms; eating with the fork that they rescued from the floor of the restaurant; washing face towels and tablecloths with underwear at the laundromat; relaxing with their feet on the top of the table.
>
> Because they do not protect the upper half of the body, the *gadje* are construed as *marimé* all over, head to foot.[51]

Both honest and dishonest Gypsies exist, but their negative attitudes toward the *gadje* make them "fair game" as targets of prejudice. Depending on chance and opportunity, some Gypsies do make individuals or companies targets for *bujo,* a flimflam or swindle. Other *Rom* disapprove of the *bujo* because it brings down community wrath on them all.

Most Gypsies cannot read or write. They have little faith in formal education, believing it will "de-Gypsy" them. Special schools for Gypsy children have been set up in California, Washington, DC, Philadelphia, Chicago, Seattle, and Camden, New Jersey, but they have had very limited success, given Gypsy opposition to formal schooling.[52]

Gypsies have always been remarkably adaptable to their cultural environment, however, although they adapt without losing their cultural identity. Ever distrustful of bureaucracy, they nonetheless use it to their advantage, including the use of banks, credit cards, and charge accounts.

> No gypsy likes to be pinned down on anything. Real birth certificates, for example, are anathema to him. If he needs a passport or otherwise requires proof

of date and place of birth, he will obtain an affidavit for this purpose supplied and sworn to by other gypsies, or he will get a "delayed" certificate of birth one way or another from a cooperative doctor or midwife. The main thing is to be flexible about such matters, since he never knows what kind of potential bureaucratic booby trap lies in wait for him, and he always operates on the theory that it is best to expect the worst. . . .

In thwarting the great computer numbers game that pigeonholes the rest of us, any self-respecting gypsy carries at least three social security cards, a handful of driver's licenses and a revolving collection of credit cards in a variety of names.[53]

Although most Gypsies have a home base, they maintain a fondness for travel. This mobility orientation rests partly on their association of travel with freedom, health, and good luck and of settling down with illness and bad luck. Job opportunities, social visits, and evasion of *gadje* authorities are other reasons. Part of their avoidance pattern includes posing as non-Gypsies.

Gypsies deliberately conceal their ethnicity to avoid confrontations with and harassment by truant officers, landlords, the police, and the welfare department. They pass as Puerto Ricans, Mexicans, Armenians, Greeks, Arabs, and other local ethnics in order to obtain jobs, housing, and welfare. Gypsies usually report themselves as members of other groups to census takers, causing Gypsy census statistics to be extremely unreliable. Gypsies have developed these skills so well that many Americans are unaware that there are any Gypsies in America.[54]

Gypsy sexual mores concerning intimacy are very strict, an outgrowth of their normally confined living arrangements and their social structure. Premarital chastity remains highly regarded, and Gypsy women rarely resort to prostitution. Birth control and abortions are rare, and as a result the birth rate is very high. Because Gypsies do not officially record these births, our only information on the birth rate comes from case studies. Peter Maas, for example, reports on one couple that had 14 children and 76 grandchildren, most under 30 years of age; these grandchildren had already produced 183 children, with more likely to come.[55]

The safety valve within the social organization is the *kris,* or Gypsy court. Through an effective grapevine, Gypsies send word to the different tribes of the time and place of the *kris.* Much like Indian chieftains at a powwow, the tribal leaders confer, settle disputes, and place restraints on more powerful members. The most potent social sanction is shunning, no longer acknowledging someone as a *Rom.* Because Gypsies spend virtually all their waking moments in group activities with other *Rom,* shunning is a feared social death keeping the *Rom* effectively in line.[56] The *kris* operates with ceremonial dignity; it forms the social cement that binds Gypsy society together. Once it is over the *kris* becomes an occasion for general feasting, renewal of friendships, bartering, and bride-buying, because such large gatherings are not very frequent.

The Gypsies have kept their tribal codes and morals virtually unchanged in an urbanized and industrialized society by remaining outside the educational institutions and being passively antagonistic to the larger society. Although they are highly conscious of ritual, Gypsies survive through adaptation to their environment. Despite enormous pressure from every society in which Gypsies have lived, they have retained their identity and resisted assimilation. Gypsies live mostly in cities, about 10,000 in Chicago and 15,000 in Los Angeles. Residing in all states, their largest concentrations are in New York, Virginia, Illinois, Texas, Massachusetts, and on the Pacific Coast.[57]

THE RUSSIAN PEOPLES

Of the more than 3 million Russian immigrants who came to the United States between 1881 and 1920, approximately 43 percent were Jewish.[58] In Chapter 12 on religious minorities, we shall examine the Jewish experience in America. This section primarily focuses on the non-Jewish Russian immigrants.

BOX 6.3   **THE ETHNIC EXPERIENCE**

"Finally in 1949 we were given permission to come to the United States as Displaced Persons, to be taken by sponsors who were to provide for us in America, where food and clothing were plentiful and freedom was everyone's right. The D. P. families boarded a huge ship where the men stayed in one part and the women and children remained in another. There were no separate compartments, but one large barrack filled with beds. Because the passengers were not used to the ocean, most of them spent their trip in sick bay or on deck trying to survive the voyage.

"On July 7, 1949, our ship landed in Baltimore, Maryland, where we were greeted by the Red Cross. We were taken to a depot and given blankets which were to be placed on the cement floor for the purpose of sleeping. At that time food and old clothes were distributed while we waited for the arrival of our sponsors. An American man bought me a Coca-Cola from a vending machine. I had never tasted anything so delicious before and to this day I can still recall the incident so vividly that I can actually taste that first Coke although all others lack that particular flavor.

". . . My sister and I were sent to a public school in the local town. This experience was devastating to me since I did not know one word of English. The teacher, who seemed like a friendly person, must have tried with much frustration to communicate with me, but I was frustrated too, and so did what most children do under those circumstances—I turned her off and did what my imagination led me to do. I colored, cut, played imaginary games and had an all-around good time till I finally started to put some of the sounds together and began to realize the meaning of a few English words.

"... Because we lived in Maryland, race prejudice was the first unpleasant and embarrassing situation which my family had to encounter. My father was the only white man to work in the fields. During the lunch break he was allowed to come into the farmhouse to eat while the others ate their lunch outside. Soon my father learned that dark-skinned men were not allowed to eat with fair-skinned men. I heard my parents discussing this problem. Since they did not know American history and did not speak English, they had to figure that for some reason the dark people were not liked in this country. We did not even know what they were called except that the farmer sometimes called them 'niggas', which later I learned was niggers.

"One day the farmer became very angry because he learned that we were entertaining the other farm hands in our home. My mother, being a good neighbor, invited the other workers to our house for supper. We had pirogis and the men drank corn liquor. The Negro families reciprocated and we were invited to their homes. It seemed a very natural thing to do and we could not understand why the farmer became so excited. During our first six months stay in Maryland, our home must have been the first case of integration in the South and we were not even aware of it.

"Although I was only seven years old at the time, my observations of the treatment which the Whites inflicted on the Blacks had a lasting effect on me. While riding in the all-white school bus, I was shown the shabby school for the 'niggas.' I could not understand why two schools were needed in the first place. While stopping for food in the town, I saw only Whites were served in most stores. No matter where I went, the Blacks were excluded. ... Looking back, I guess that my education in Maryland did not take place in the segregated public school but on the farm, where I learned more about human behavior than any college course could ever offer."

SOURCE: Ukrainian refugee who came to the United States in 1949 at age 7.

Included among the peoples of Russia who came to the United States were the Ukrainians, who sometimes called themselves Carpatho-Russians or Little Russians; the Ruthenians, whose homeland is now a part of Slovakia; the Jews; the "Great Russians" from the medieval Duchy of Muscovy; the Byelorussians, or White Russians, from the western region; and to a lesser extent the Finns, Estonians, Latvians, and Lithuanians. In its efforts to "Russianize" its empire and to solve its problems with political dissidents and poverty, the Czarist government openly encouraged its ethnic minorities to leave.

Contact and Conflict

Although a few Ukrainians settled in the western United States and Canada and became farmers, most settled in the urban industrial centers of the Northeast and Midwest, working in the factories and coal mines. Wasyl Halich offers a good example of one Ukrainian group's early contacts with Americans and their fights with Irish miners who saw them as a serious economic threat:

> The experience of the first Ukrainian group in America contains some of the basic elements of that of other pioneers on this continent. When they landed in New York, they did not understand a word of English; their colorful attire attracted much attention, and they were regarded as a curiosity. Being unable to get lodgings, they had to leave the city. They walked to Philadelphia, being forced to sleep outdoors because people were afraid to give shelter to such curious strangers. . . .
>
> This group of immigrants arrived in the mining communities during a labor strike. Not understanding the conditions, or probably because of necessity, they went to work as strike-breakers; consequently they brought upon themselves the hatred of old miners, mostly Irishmen. There were frequent assaults on the strike-breakers which ended in riots. The influx of fresh immigrants tended to keep the wages low, and this prolonged the racial and labor antagonism between the Ukrainian and Irish groups. In connection with this racial animosity not infrequently the newcomer became a victim of "accidental" injury in the mine, or even death.[59]

Based on census data, church records, and immigration reports, historians believe that about 700,000 Ukrainians and several hundred thousand Ruthenians had emigrated to the United States by 1914.

Like the Ukrainians and other nationality groups, the Ruthenians settled mostly in large industrial cities, taking whatever industrial jobs they could find. By 1880 about 100,000 Ruthenians were in America, and their experiences paralleled those of other immigrant groups, as shown by this excerpt from Jerome Davis's *Russians and Ruthenians in America* concerning their spatial and social segregation and their first taste of America at Ellis Island:

> The majority of Russians and Ruthenians are almost as completely isolated from the American people as if they were in the heart of giant Russia. They have no points of contact with the sound elements of American life. The dream of the Russian as he leaves his native shore is that everything is beautiful in America. It is the land of liberty and equality but he begins to feel that perhaps he has been hoodwinked almost as soon as he reaches Ellis Island. The Russians claim that the coarse and brutal treatment they received at the immigrant stations is far worse than that in the Russia of the Tsars. Certainly, the wholesale tagging of the immigrant, the physical inspection, the turning back of the eyelids, rushed through with machine-like regularity resembles more the inspection of cattle than of thousands of human souls.[60]

Cultural Differentiation

The great majority of Russian Americans are members of the Russian Orthodox Church, but in other respects they differ from one another. In addition to ethnic distinctions based on regional residence, the emigrants also came from all levels of society.

The first wave of Russian immigrants were Mennonites, who actually were of German origin and had maintained the German language and German customs within the Russian borders for a century. As they became targets of forced assimilation, military conscription, and persecution in the 1870s, they began to emigrate to the Great Plains of the United States. Although there were never a substantial number—only 30,000 to 40,000 in total by 1900— they made a significant contribution to American agriculture by introducing Turkish wheat, a hard winter wheat that had become the leading first-class wheat product by the turn of the century.

The peak Russian migration occurred between 1881 and 1914, with poor, illiterate peasants emigrating for economic reasons and others seeking political or religious freedom. In America they had to make the transformation from a rural to an industrial environment. They settled in the industrialized regions, joining other immigrants in the grueling labor in the mines and factories of America. They were heavily exploited and often complained about the harshness of their work situation. Not at all passive, they were active in the labor movement and sought to improve their working conditions.

Following the Bolshevik revolution, a new type of Russian immigrant sought asylum in the United States. Czarist army officers, landowners, professional people, and political activists all fled from the new regime. Thereafter Soviet restrictions sharply curtailed Russian emigration, except for those Russians who succeeded in coming to the United States as displaced persons after World War II.

Life in America

During the boom immigration period, the Russian peasants were at the bottom of the socioeconomic ladder in their newly adopted country. Two excerpts, although referring to Russian immigrants, are excellent illustrations of the recurring pattern of any minority experience. They could just as easily be applied to other groups who live or have lived in the urban slums. In the first the editor of a religious newspaper tells of the toll exacted by the long working hours under wretched conditions in 1916:

> Each working day shortens the worker's life for a few months, saps the living juice out of him, dries out the heart, dampens the noblest aspirations of the soul; transforms a living man into a sort of machine, embitters the whole life. The ragged soul and body of the worker bring forth to the world half-sick children, paralytic, idiotic—therefore the factory's poison kills not merely the unfortunate workers, but also whole generations.[61]

Closely related to working conditions were poor living conditions because of low wages. This timeless commentary by a social worker of that period analyzes the effects of the squalor and apathy in the urban ghettos on the Russian immigrants:

> Parental neglect, congestion of population, dirty milk, indigestible food, un-cleaned streets, with the resulting contaminated atmosphere, the prevalence of infectious diseases, multiplied temptations to break the law. . . . Add a twelve-hour day, and a seven-day week, irregular, casual employment, sub-standard wages, speeding processes which have no regard to human capacities or nervous strains for which the system is unprepared, indecent housing, unsanitary conditions both in home and factory, and we have an explanation amply adequate to account for sub-normal wage earners.[62]

Xenophobia

Many Russian Americans who had worked hard to achieve some economic security in America found themselves jobless and unable to find work after the Bolshevik Revolution in 1917. Employers, fearful of any threat to capitalism in the United States, removed all Russian workers from their labor force lest they be Bolsheviks. Most Russian peasant immigrants were probably ignorant of the ideology of Bolshevism or, in the case of second-generation Americans, more attuned to American values and attitudes, but they were identified as "Bolsheviks" simply because of their nationality. Some may have been sympathetic to the Bolshevik regime but only because it had overthrown the hated Czarist government. The thought of spreading that revolution to the United States, where the political, labor, and social conditions were very different, appears to have been in the minds of only a very small percentage.[63]

Nevertheless, labor unrest and radical agitation during that period caused a strong xenophobic reaction against many foreigners. A. Mitchell Palmer, a new attorney general, stepped into the federal power vacuum caused by the incapacity of President Wilson. His first target was the Union of Russian Workers, and his men raided 11 of their meeting places in various cities. About a month later, 249 immigrants were deported, many forced to leave their wives and children behind in most dire circumstances. The Palmer raids continued with a vast dragnet of East Europeans, primarily Russians:

> Officers burst into homes, meeting places, and pool rooms, as often as not seizing everyone in sight. The victims were loaded into trucks, or sometimes marched through the streets handcuffed and chained to one another, and massed by the hundreds at concentration points, usually police stations. . . . Many remained in federal custody for a few hours only; some lay in crowded cells for several weeks without a preliminary hearing. For several days in Detroit eight hundred men were held incommunicado in a windowless corridor, sleeping on the bare stone floor, subsisting on food which their families brought in, and limited to the use of a single drinking fountain and single toilet. Altogether, about three thousand aliens were held for deportation, almost all of them eastern Europeans.[64]

BOX 6.4   **THE ETHNIC EXPERIENCE**

"The closer we came to the United States the better we felt after being so dizzy and nauseous. The trip took us ten days and we landed in Ellis Island in 1924. We saw a big, big building. It was like an armory and, yes, we went through inspection. Before we went on the boat we went through inspection and the physical, and when we came to Ellis Island it was the same thing. They inspected all the clothing of ours and the physical too. Everything was all right with us. Some people didn't pass the inspection and they had to go back, with their health and all.

"All the immigrants were holding their bundles, the baggage, by them. Also we ate by huge tables and most of the food they served was herring. There were some young immigrant boys and they played the mandolin and I was dancing and I didn't think about anything. We were laughing and dancing. I didn't understand what they were saying but we had a lot of fun. We stayed in Ellis Island three days because we came in on a Friday and on the weekend they didn't let anyone out. So we stayed there three days.

"When my father came in—they told me it's my father, of course, but I didn't know him because I hadn't seen him in ten years—I was thrilled to see him. And, of course, as a young girl, I was very happy and I was giggling a lot and that worried my father because he heard a lot of girls came here in this country and they got in trouble. He asked me, 'My dear daughter, why are you giggling so much?' I didn't have an answer for him then. I never saw my father and yet I saw him worry for me and giving me orders what to do, what not to do. It was very strange to me, but we were all very happy to see him and finally he took us on a subway. The subway was very new to me. This I didn't see in Europe.

"When we came to America I was not of age yet to go to work, so from the Board of Education they came and they told me I must go to day school, and so my brother and I did. When I went into the school all the children spoke English and the teacher—whatever she said to me—I didn't understand. When it came to arithmetic I was tops but as far as language, she couldn't teach me much because she was busy with all the children.

"But I saw my father was struggling very much and he didn't make too good of a living here, so I went on my own and I took out working papers and I found a job. I was working in a silk mill and I went to night school.

"All the immigrants who came here were there and the teacher was teaching us, 'Open the door,' 'Close the door,' and so everyone had these advantages to learn how to speak.

"Now I see it wasn't such a big palace my father took us in. It was four rooms but everything looked so nice. It was a piece of carpet on the floor with a victrola with the letters, chairs, and a little sofa, and I thought we came into a palace and I used to correspond with my girlfriends overseas and I told them what beautiful things we have. But now when I look back it wasn't really so beautiful."

SOURCE: Russian immigrant who came to the United States in 1923 at age 15.

Opposition to these brazen and illegal actions arose, and many of the immigrants were freed. Yet more than 500 of them actually were deported. Expulsion was still an effective weapon of the government in America. Eventually the growing strength of the Congress of Industrial Organizations (CIO) within the labor movement would bring these people a measure of economic security and domestic tranquility.

Recent Immigrants

After World War II there were thousands of Ukrainian displaced persons in Europe. In 1948 Congress passed the Displaced Persons Act, allowing homeless people from war-ravaged Europe to enter, in addition to the annual quota under existing immigration laws. Under this special legislation and with the assistance of many Ukrainian Americans, about 85,000 Ukrainian refugees came to America. The new arrivals were better educated, more politically oriented, and better able to adapt to American life than the older immigrants; they were refugees, not "economic" immigrants, and, significantly, structural conditions in their homeland had changed.

Ukrainian immigrants, with a language and culture distinct from the Russians, have always maintained their own identity among themselves, even though officially included among Russians. Ukrainian American parallel social institutions not only reflected this fact but became even stronger after World War II to preserve their unity and heritage among American-born generations. With the advent of the separate Ukraine republic in 1992, we can expect continuance of this ethnic group identity.

Russian immigration dropped sharply while the communists were in power. Only about 107,000 new immigrants came to the United States between 1921 and 1990, but about 109,000 refugees, mostly Jewish, arrived in the United States between 1988 and 1990.[65] With the changed political climate in the former Soviet Union, about 20,000 immigrants from the former Soviet republics, primarily Russia, are now entering yearly.

Among the many settlement locations of first-generation Russian Americans throughout the country, large concentrations can be found in Boston, Minneapolis, and Rockville, Maryland. In a 25-block section of Brooklyn called Brighton Beach, nicknamed "Little Odessa" after the Black Sea port, lives the nation's largest Russian population, about 50,000 of the New York City area's 120,000 Soviet Jews. Here the emigrés have settled just outside the central shopping district in regional ethnic neighborhoods with people from Kiev in one area, for example, and those from Georgia in another. The community itself is distinctly Jewish and so thoroughly Russian in flavor in its sights, sounds, smells, window signs, and spoken language that the outsider can quickly be either charmed or disoriented.

About 4 million descendants of Russian immigrants are members of the Russian Orthodox Church, which has more than 400 parishes in the United States. Seventy to 80 parishes consist mainly of 100,000 Russian-speaking emigrés.[66] Found in virtually every profession and occupation, they preserve their heritage with their history centers, newspapers, publishing houses, and organizations. Recent arrivals sometimes are overwhelmed by the freedom of choice they have here but usually adjust to the greater complexities that life in America offers.

THE ITALIANS

Although few in number, the first Italians to come to the New World were significant among the early explorers. Cristoforo Colombo (Columbus), Giovanni Cabotto (John Cabot), Amerigo Vespucci, and Giovanni de Verrazano all explored and charted the new land. Father Marcos da Nizza explored Arizona in 1539, and other Italians were among the settlers throughout the colonies. Filippo Mazzei was an influence on the writings and the farming of his neighbor, Thomas Jefferson. Many Italians fought in the Revolution, the Civil War, and the other wars that followed. Antonio Meucci invented the first primitive version of the telephone 26 years before Alexander Graham Bell, and Constantino Brumidi painted the frescoes in the rotunda of the U.S. Capitol building.

Throughout the nineteenth century, the parallels and relationship between Italians and blacks were somewhat unusual. In some pre–Civil War Southern localities, futile efforts were made to replace black slaves with Italian workers. In other areas Southerners barred Italian children from the white schools because of their dark complexions. General Edward Ferraro commanded an all-black combat division during the Civil War. In 1899 five Sicilian storekeepers were hanged in Tallulah, Louisiana, for the unforgivable crime of treating black customers the same as whites.

The Great Migration

The major story of the Italian immigrants began after great numbers of them arrived between 1880 and 1920. Of the more than 5 million Italians who have come to the United States throughout its history, 80 percent came during this 40-year period. Many Italian males engaged in "shuttle migration," going back and forth between America and Italy. Fleeing abject poverty and economic disaster in the harsh "Mezzogiorno" east and south of Rome, they quickly became so visible to American society that they were subject to vicious anti-Italian bigotry.

Most Italian immigrants were peasants from rural areas who were ill prepared for the occupations of an industrial nation. They therefore labored in low-status, low-paying manual jobs as railroad laborers, as miners, and on the waterfront; in construction they dug ditches, laid sewer pipes, and built roads, subways, and other basic structures in urban areas.

Societal Hostility

Strong negative attitudes against the Italians sometimes resulted in violence and even killings. Several Italians were lynched in West Virginia in 1891. In

BOX 6.5   **THE ETHNIC EXPERIENCE**

"We came here on a large ship in 1910. We had a rough time coming here with storms and all, and my big sister was deadly sick. She never lifted her head up from her berth. It was a very long trip, about thirteen days, and the waters were rough. And when we got to Ellis Island, we were so happy to get out of that ship.

"When we got there my daddy was waiting for us and we got some nice gifts from the attendants in Ellis Island. Who got a doll, who got a jumping jack. But the funniest part was when they were selling bananas in the room, and my brother thought they were peppers and he wanted a pepper and discovered they were bananas.

"When my father took us down to the street, we heard a different language. We looked at each other. We went to my mother. We didn't know what they were saying, maybe they were talking about us. My father said, 'Don't worry. That's the language they speak here and you'll learn it yourself very fast.'

"Then my dad took us on a train to Old Forge, Pennsylvania, where he had rented rooms for us and we lived there six months. They were mostly all Polish people and German, and my mother didn't feel at home with no Italians around. My mother wanted to move to Paterson, New Jersey, because there were more Italian people there, but here she didn't understand anybody. And that's what we did. There were all Italians on the street where we lived. My dad was a musician but the other Italian immigrants worked on the trolley tracks, digging trolley tracks or to make streets.

"I got in right away with all the kids. They were all very friendly with me. As soon as recess used to come, they used to be in a playground. They would all come around me and they would talk to me in English, which helped me pick it up right away."

SOURCE: Italian immigrant who came to the United States in 1910 at age 8.

the same year, when 10 Sicilians were tried and acquitted of killing the New Orleans police chief, an angry mob that included many of the city's leading citizens stormed the prison and executed them, adding an eleventh victim who had been serving a minor sentence for a petty crime. Four years later coal miners and other residents of a southern Colorado town murdered six Italians. The following year three Italians were torn from a jail in Hahnsville, Louisiana, and hanged. After a street brawl in 1914, in a southern Illinois mining town, that left one Italian and two native-born Americans dead, a lynch mob hanged the only survivor, an Italian, with the apparent approval of the town's mayor. A few months later another Italian was lynched in a nearby town because he had been arrested on suspicion of conspiracy to murder a mining supervisor. Actually there was no evidence to substantiate the charge other than his nationality.

In Massachusetts Nicola Sacco and Bartolomeo Vanzetti—an immigrant shoe factory worker and a poor fish peddler—were charged with and convicted of robbery and murder in 1920. The prosecutor insulted Italian defense witnesses and appealed to the prejudices of a bigoted judge and jury. Despite someone else's later confession and other potentially exonerating evidence, their seven-year appeals fight was futile, and they were executed in 1927. At his sentencing in 1927, Vanzetti addressed presiding Judge Webster Thayer, at one point in his moving speech he said:

> I would not wish to a dog or a snake, to the most low and misfortunate creature of the earth—I would not wish to any of them what I have had to suffer for the things that I am not guilty of. . . . I have suffered because I was an Italian, and indeed I am an Italian.[67]

These incidents are extreme examples of society's reaction to the Italian immigrants. Because they came in sizable numbers, the public became increasingly aware of their presence, and they quickly became the stereotype of all that was objectionable in the "swarm" of immigrants coming here. When an Italian got into trouble, newspaper headlines often magnified the event and stressed the offender's nationality.[68] Italians, like Jews, found certain occupations, fraternities, clubs, and organizations closed to them; and they were excluded from certain areas of the city and suburbs by restrictive covenants.

Social Patterns

The Italians mainly settled in the eastern cities in "Little Italys," the North End of Boston and Mulberry Street on the Lower East Side of New York City being two of the better-known areas. In the west, San Francisco's North Beach area became and still remains an Italian enclave. Often groups from the same village would live together in the same tenement. Earning poor wages because they were part of the unskilled labor force, they moved into rundown residential areas vacated by earlier immigrants whose children and grandchildren had moved up the social ladder and were out of the slum. Because of their numbers they were able to create an Italian community replete with Italian stores, newspapers, theaters, social clubs, parishes, and schools. However, because of their village, family, and communal orientations, they failed to establish group-wide institutions.[69]

A variant of the extended-family system of southern Italian society was adapted to Italian life in America. Relatives were the principal focus of social life, and non-Italians were usually regarded as outsiders. True interethnic friendships rarely developed. Moreover, individual achievement (an American tradition) was not heavily encouraged. What mattered most were family honor, group stability, and social cohesion and cooperation. Each member of the family was expected to contribute to the economic well-being of the family unit.

In the old country absentee landowners usually had exploited Italian tenant farmers, and priests and educators had silently supported this less-than-equitable system. Peasant children were rarely welcome in the schools. Land-owner resistance to the political unification of Italy, which finally came about in 1870, further increased the hardships of tenant farmers and small land-holders. Consequently, Italian immigrants generally distrusted priests and educated people.[70] In America, as in Italy, there was little involvement with the church, especially among males, and schooling was regarded as of only limited practical use. Children were permitted to attend school, for the most part, only as long as the law demanded; then they were sent to work to increase the family income. A few children were exceptions, but most second-generation Italian Americans attending college did so in conflict with their families.

> The studies of the immigrant would suggest that the move to America resulted in little change in the pattern of adult life. The social structure which the immigrants brought with them from Italy served them in the new country as well. Those who moved to the cities, for example, settled in Italian neighborhoods, where relatives often lived side by side, and in the midst of people from the same Italian town. Under these conditions, the family circle was maintained much as it had existed in Southern Italy.
>
> The outside world continued to be a source of deprivation and exploita-tion. . . . Situated on the lowest rung of the occupational hierarchy, they were exploited by their employers and by the "padrone," the agent who acted as middleman between the immigrants and the labor market. Moreover, the churches in the immigrant neighborhoods were staffed largely by Irish priests, who practiced a strange and harsh form of Catholicism, and had little sympathy for the Madonna and the local saints that the Italians respected. The caretaking agencies and the political machines were run by Yankees and other ethnic groups. As a result of the surrounding strangeness, the immigrants tried to retain the self-sufficiency of the family circle as much as they could. They founded a number of community organizations that supported this circle, and kept away from the outside world whenever possible.[71]

Marginality

First-generation Italian-Americans, reinforced by so many of their compatri-ots, retained much of their language and customs. The second generation became more Americanized, producing a strain between the two generations. Those Italians who did not settle or remain long in the "Little Italys" assim-ilated much more quickly. Some changed their names and religion to accel-erate the process.

In his study *Street Corner Society*, William Foote Whyte commented on the problems of marginality experienced by Italian American boys:

> Some ask, "Why can't those people stop being Italians and become Americans like the rest of us?" The answer is that they are blocked in two ways: by their own organized society and by the outside world. Cornerville people want to be good American citizens. I have never heard such moving expressions of love for this country as I have heard in Cornerville. Nevertheless, an organized way of

life cannot be changed overnight. As the study of the corner gang shows, people became dependent upon certain routines of action. If they broke away abruptly from these routines, they would feel themselves disloyal and would be left helpless, without support. And, if a man wants to forget that he is an Italian, the society around him does not let him forget it. He is marked as an inferior person—like all other Italians. To bolster his own self-respect he must tell himself and tell others that the Italians are a great people, that their culture is second to none, and that their great men are unsurpassed.[72]

Social Mobility

Upward mobility occurred more slowly for the Italians than for other groups coming at about the same time, such as the Greeks, Armenians, and Jews. Many factors already discussed contributed to this situation—a retreatist lifestyle, disregard for education, negative stereotyping, and overt hostility protracted by the continuing flow of new Italian immigrants. Sheltered within their ethnic communities in many large U.S. cities, the Italians adapted to an industrial society. They joined the working class and encouraged their children to do likewise as soon as they were able.

In the early stages of immigration from a particular country, labor agents served as the middlemen for employers seeking immigrant workers. Friends and relatives soon replaced them, sending specific information about job opportunities, often introducing them to that workplace, teaching them specific work tasks, and working alongside them. *(Courtesy of the New York Public Library.)*

Second-generation adults, although drawn to *la via nuova*—the new way—through the schools, movies, and other cultural influences, still adhered to a social structure centered on the extended family. Expected to contribute to the family's support early, they followed their parents into working-class occupations without benefit of extended education to secure higher-status jobs. Today the picture has changed. Third and fourth generations, attaining educational levels comparable to that of other white ethnic groups, are mostly middle class and well represented in the professional fields.

Intermarriage, or marital assimilation, is a primary indicator of structural assimilation, the last phase of minority group mainstreaming. Exogamy among Italian Americans, especially the third and fourth generations, exceeds 40 percent, similar to that of most European American groups.[73] As structural assimilation becomes more apparent, Richard D. Alba suggests we are witnessing "the twilight of ethnicity" not only for Italians but also for all Americans of European ancestry. Twilight, says Alba, is an appropriate metaphor, because ethnic community remnants and differences still remain, with occasional flareups of ethnic feelings and conflicts, but this ethnicity is "little more than flickers in the fading light" as social assimilation increases.[74]

THE GREEKS

Most of the Greeks who came to this country in the early twentieth century did not expect to stay long. They came as sojourners, planning to make money and then return to Greece. For many the dowry system was an important "push" factor. Fathers and brothers found they could earn more money in the United States than in their homeland, and so these Greek men journeyed here to earn the money to provide substantial dowries for the prospective brides in their families. The fact that 95 percent of all Greek immigrants were male encouraged them to return home to their women.

Occupational Distribution

Many Greeks worked as laborers on railroad construction gangs or in factories. Those who did often were under the control of a *padrone* who, like the Italian *padroni*, acted as a labor agent and paternal figure. Abuses were common in such a system. Other Greek immigrants operated their own small businesses of many types, although Greeks came to be identified particularly with candy stores and restaurants:

> The association of Greeks with candy and food was proverbial. Chicago became the center of their sweets trade, and in 1904 a Greek newspaperman observed that "Practically every busy corner in Chicago is occupied by a Greek candy store." After World War II the Greeks still maintained 350 to 450 confectionary shops and eight to ten candy manufacturers in the Windy City. Most Americans

still connect the Greeks with restaurants and for good reason. Almost every major American city boasts of its fine Greek eating establishments, a tradition that goes back more than half a century. After World War I, for example, estimates were that the Greeks owned 564 restaurants in San Francisco alone.[75]

For many Greeks the restaurant provided a more stable economic base and a higher social status. Restaurant owners enjoyed more esteem than peddlers or manual laborers. Because so many immigrants sought a career in the restaurant business (and still do), they were continuously interacting with the general public. A 1901 government survey showed Greeks faring better than Poles; at present most Greeks, except for the newest arrivals, are economically secure, and many are in the upper middle class.[76] Greek Americans are found in most middle-class occupations, although the restaurant business holds appeal mostly for the first generation only.

Social Patterns

Although they came from a mostly agricultural country, the Greeks settled primarily in the cities. Like so many other ethnic groups, they resided in ethnic enclaves or "Greek colonies" within the major cities. A *kinotis,* or community council, served as the governing body; it was responsible for establishing and staffing schools and churches and for the general welfare of the community. The *kaffeneion,* or coffeehouse, played a very important role, as Theodore Saloutos reports:

> It was to the coffeehouse that the immigrant hurried after his arrival from Greece or from a neighboring community. It was in the coffeehouse that he sought out acquaintances, addresses, leads to jobs, and solace during the lonely hours. . . .
> The coffeehouse was a community social center to which the men returned after working hours and on Saturdays and Sundays. Here they sipped cups of thick, black Turkish coffee, lazily drew on narghiles, played cards, or engaged in animated political discussion. Here congregated gesticulating Greeks of all kinds: railroad workers, factory hands, shopkeepers, professional men, the unemployed, labor agitators, amateur philosophers, community gossips, cardsharks, and amused spectators.[77]

Because of the favorable working conditions, many Greek males chose to remain in America. Because they preferred endogamous marriage, these men returned home to marry a Greek woman or else sent money home to pay for the passage of a wife or wife-to-be. Like other immigrant peoples of this period, family ties among the Greeks in America were very close. The father was the unchallenged head of the household. Children were raised to be strictly obedient and had specific chores assigned to them. They studied Greek in addition to their regular studies in American public schools and were frequently admonished to work hard and take advantage of the opportunities their parents had not had. The Greeks placed a high value on education and encouraged their children to enter the professions.

The Greek church—the Eastern Orthodox Church—and the Greek press bolstered Greek American solidarity. Additionally, many organizations encouraged cohesiveness. The most notable of these was the American Hellenic Educational Progressive Association (AHEPA), founded in 1922. Its purpose was both to preserve the Greek heritage and to help the immigrant understand the American way of life.

In their ethnogenesis process, Greek Americans have blended certain aspects of pluralism (fierce love of homeland, pride in their heritage, slowness to become citizens, endogamy, and institutional agencies) with some aspects of assimilation (geographic and occupational dispersion, low visibility, and relatively high socioeconomic status). Cultural pluralism has been an important element in their adaptation to American society.

Societal Reaction

Not all Greek immigrants adjusted to American society smoothly. Many young males, away from family discipline and village controls, got into trouble with the law. Sociologist Henry Pratt Fairchild held a prejudiced and stereotyped view of the Greeks and other foreigners in America. He was concerned about the large overrepresentation of Greek immigrants among law violators and was pessimistic about the possibility of their assimilating or even being a benefit to American society. His comments about the effects of concentration in Greek colonies contain elements of the culture-of-poverty thesis developed in the 1960s with respect to Puerto Ricans, Mexicans, and blacks. Fairchild states that the negative values within the community are not likely to be overcome unless there is effective interaction with members of the better (that is, middle) class. He also favored deconcentration and dispersal of Greeks.

> It seems likely that the presence of this race (Greeks) in the country will add to, rather than diminish, the growing indifference to law as such, which is one of the most threatening signs of the times. This lack of reverence for law, and every form of authority, seems to be characteristic of every race. But the Greeks appear to have it when they come. What the character of their children will be in this respect we can only conjecture. . . . It has been frequently remarked in the course of the preceding discussion, that the evil tendencies of Greek life in this country manifest themselves most fully when the immigrants are collected into compact, isolated, distinctively Greek colonies, and that when the Greek is separated from the group and thrown into relations with Americans of the better class, he develops and displays many admirable qualities.[78]

Today few negative comments about Greek Americans are heard. When Greeks are singled out as an ethnic group at all, the reference usually is positive or neutral. They often serve as a model of a nationality group that has been accepted, has achieved economic security, and has become Americanized, yet also has retained a strong pride in their ethnicity. Reinforced by the arrival of 3,000 to 4,000 new immigrants annually, the Greek American community retains its ethnic vitality, with its church and festivals continuing sources of ethnic pride and identity.

THE PORTUGUESE

Although it is a relatively small country, Portugal has provided the United States with a half million immigrants of varying economic and cultural backgrounds. Whether their manner of adaptation was assimilationist or nonassimilationist has depended on the part of the United States to which they migrated.

Early Immigrants

The fondness of many Portuguese for the sea was reflected in their early contributions to the United States. In the sixteenth century, Portuguese mariners explored the California coast. In the eighteenth and nineteenth centuries, immigrants, primarily from the Azores Islands, settled in New England and became an important part of the fishing industry. Mostly of Flemish stock, these Portuguese had been whalers and fishermen for many generations. Recruited by business agents to bring their expertise to America, they came and settled in such coastal port cities as New Bedford and Newport. Although the Portuguese were predominantly Catholic, the Jews among them erected one of the first synagogues in the United States in Newport in 1763. Other Portuguese, some from the mainland and of Moorish lineage, worked on farms and in dairies. They started as farm laborers, then rented and eventually bought the old New England farms that became available. As the Portuguese continued to come and American industry grew, the newcomers turned to factory work; the majority of New England's Portuguese were working in factories shortly after the turn of the century.

A few Portuguese went to California, lured by the gold rush. Others followed in typical chain-migration fashion. Thousands of other Portuguese went to the Hawaiian Islands in the late nineteenth century. By 1920 about 84,000 Portuguese lived in New England; the rest lived in California and Hawaii. Since transportation for laborers and their families was guaranteed and since they had labor contracts from the plantation owners, they were willing to make the long journey. Those in Hawaii assimilated, whereas those in California, encountering little conflict, retained their ethnic identity and sense of community to a much greater degree. The reason for this difference appears to be that the Portuguese quickly became a sizable working force on the Hawaiian pineapple and sugar plantations—about 12 percent of the population. The dominant group, from northern Europe, identified themselves separately through a special census classification and stereotyped the Portuguese as inferior. The Portuguese reacted by continuing to work hard, moving into crafts and skilled trades that paid better, and intermarrying and surrendering the usual accouterments of ethnic visibility—language, customs, residential clustering, and sometimes even their names—to achieve a respected status.

> There is a wide cultural differentiation between the Portuguese in the Island setting and those in California today [1941]. Four decades of separation have shown the influence that environment can have in remolding a people. Although there have been changes in the cultural patterns of the Portuguese in California, it is in Hawaii, where the Portuguese people have gone through the processes of competition, conflict, and accommodation, and assimilation and have broken down social distance, that the distinction from old-world family patterns [is most evident.][79]

As the experiences of other groups have already shown, the adaptation of strangers in a new land moves along a continuum that may or may not end in total assimilation. The Portuguese in Hawaii and California exemplify two successful patterns under differing structural conditions.

Later Immigrants

As with other immigrant groups, the Portuguese were encouraged to migrate here by the Industrial Revolution. Beginning in the late nineteenth century and peaking in 1921, after which immigration quotas restricted their numbers, 200,000 came, many to work in the mills of Massachusetts and Rhode Island. Their adaptation as rural peasants in an urban setting parallels that of other ethnic groups. They clung to the old ways and restricted their social relations to their own kind.

In an analysis of two Portuguese communities in New England in the late 1920s, Donald Taft noted a high rate of infant mortality and a low level of educational achievement. This lack of interest in education may have been due to their occupational preference for farming and fishing as well as to their high rate of illiteracy.[80] In the following passage, note the ethnocentric outlook, patronizing tone, and stereotyping:

> There seems no doubt that for the majority of Portuguese, immigration to New England has meant an improved status. Granting that they are poverty-stricken here, that they live far below our standards of comfort and decency, that women often work outside the home and that children leave school as soon as the law allows, that homes are unattractive and wages low; nevertheless their lot is far better than in the homeland, except perhaps in its picturesqueness. America gives the Portuguese a small wage but a higher one, a poor house but a better one, a meager sixth grade education but more than they know enough to want, and it is universal and compulsory.
> . . . The presence of these people undoubtedly handicaps the public health organizations, increases the births where they should be fewest, and the death rates of all ages but especially of little children. It also makes possible economic and political exploitation whether by unscrupulous natives or by their own leaders. Indeed the presence of the Portuguese goes far to account for the poor

record of our two communities [Fall River and Portsmouth] in official statistics and for the not altogether enviable reputation which they may have among sociologists.[81]

Although they are scattered throughout the nation, Portuguese Americans are concentrated in Massachusetts, Rhode Island, California, Hawaii, and Newark, New Jersey, where *Luso-American,* the only Portuguese national weekly newspaper, is still published. A steady flow of new immigrants from Portugal has replenished the Portuguese communities. In the 1960s the numbers of arrivals increased sharply because of political unrest and worsening economic conditions in Portugal, reaching a total of about 76,000. Chain migration and continuing push–pull factors contributed to the number of Portuguese immigrants increasing to about 102,000 in the 1970s. Totals for the 1980s, however, dropped to about 40,000 (see Appendix II).

THE ARMENIANS

Armenian immigrants settled in Jamestown in 1619. In that year Armenian workers, together with some Germans and Poles, struck to secure the political rights being denied them as "inferiors." The Virginia House of Burgesses granted them their freedom in response to this early civil rights protest in America.[82]

Confusion over Refugee Identity

A number of factors appear to have initiated Turkish persecution of the Armenians, who had come under the rule of the Ottoman Empire after 1375. As Christians in a Moslem country, the Armenians became a special target for the authoritarian, religiously intolerant rulers. Moreover, they often were better educated and more prosperous than the Turks, who therefore suspected them of wanting political power. Over the years Armenians migrated for religious, political, and economic reasons, but the Turkish government's genocidal campaign against them between 1894 and 1916 was the primary reason for their movement to America. In 1915–1916 alone the Turks killed 1 million Armenians.[83]

Because they traveled with Turkish passports and the U.S. government identified immigrants by country of origin, Armenian and Syrian Christians were classified as Turks. It is therefore difficult to determine exactly how many Armenians came here in the late nineteenth century. However, government estimates placed the number of Armenian immigrants between 1895 and 1899 at 70,982. The Turkish government then cut off further emigration until 1915. Because of the war only a few thousand came until the 1920s, when 26,000 Armenians arrived in America.[84] After that, although Armenians continued to emigrate, their actual numbers were further obscured because the U.S. government identified them by their points of departure:

usually Egypt, France, Lebanon, Iraq, Iran, Turkey, or Syria. Despite their high degree of ethnic consciousness, church records, and special censuses, the number of Armenians remained only an estimate.

Societal Reaction

As indicated in the social-distance scales of Emory Bogardus, American public opinion and stereotypes of the Turks were quite negative, partly as a result of the atrocities committed against the Armenians.[85] Still, when Armenians attempted to become United States citizens, the federal government tried to stop them. The issue was resolved in 1925 in the U.S. District Court with the case of Tatos O. Cartozian, an Armenian rug merchant in Portland, Oregon. The government argued that Armenians were of Asiatic descent and thus not eligible for citizenship under the 1790 Naturalization Act, which allowed only whites to become citizens. By this time Asians were the only group ineligible for citizenship; persons of African descent were given the right to citizenship by the Fourteenth Amendment and changes in the naturalization laws. After hearing expert testimony to the effect that they were Indo-European in language and origin, the court ruled in favor of the Armenians.

Cultural Differences

Armenians have had a long, continuous history because of their resiliency in maintaining their cultural identity. Two contributing factors have been language and religion. Not only do Armenians have their own language; they have their own alphabet, increasing ingroup solidarity. A second source of ethnic cohesion among the Armenian people, both in their homeland and in America, has been the Armenian Apostolic Church. As the first national Christian church in the world, dating from the third century, it never sought converts among other nationalities and functioned as much more than a religious institution. As Gary Kulhanjian reports:

> The Armenian Church was and still is a fortress for preserving the cultural identity of Armenians in the world. Religion, social organizations, ethnocentrism, family life, and endogamy had all been potent social forces by which Armenians or Americans of Armenian descent have been culturally identifiable.[86]

Armenian art, architecture, literature, philosophy, and music are heavily interwoven within the fabric of the church.

Another important factor in Armenian cohesiveness has been family life. But, as Kulhanjian observes, the assimilation process appears to be weakening some traditional influences:

> The patriarchal family life of Armenians has played a major part in the cultural identification of these people throughout the world. Family life has traditionally advocated endogamy of the young generation. The young people have rebelled against many traditional ways of doing things, including endogamy. Americans

BOX 6.6	THE INTERNATIONAL SCENE

Italy, accustomed for generations to seeing its people emigrating, has experienced a large influx of immigrants in recent years. The nation's brand-new Ministry of Immigration registered in 1991 over 662,000 foreign residents outside the European Community and estimated that probably another 600,000 were there illegally. They come by small boats from northern Africa, across the mountains from poverty-stricken Albania, or aboard inexpensive flights from Asia.

Africans and Asians are visible everywhere, selling cheap merchandise on the streets, trying to clean windshields at intersections, or pumping gas. Italians disparagingly refer to the newcomers by the ethnophaulism *vu cumpra*, which is a slang version of the phrase *Vuoi comprare* (Do you want to buy?).

The presence of so many physically and culturally distinct newcomers in so short a period has created an anti-immigrant backlash, turning Italy from a relatively open country into a closed one. In 1990 it passed tougher immigration laws and has since expelled thousands of illegal aliens and turned back tens of thousands of migrants from its borders.

In August 1991 about 18,000 Albanian "boat people" arrived in the Italian port of Bari. Within two weeks all were forcibly sent back, after being held under what were described as appalling conditions. Observers believed the harsh treatment was intended to deter other Albanian refugees.

Racial incidents are now commonplace. A group of Somalians demonstrated in Rome in May 1991 in protest against overcrowded and substandard housing. A few months earlier an arsonist torched an immigrant shelter near the Colosseum. Sengalese complain that when they board buses, Italians move away from them. A national poll taken in 1991 showed that 75 percent of Italians surveyed oppose further immigration.

of Armenian descent have drifted away from marrying within their minority, although some do; however, a great many still retain their subcultural identity with the Church, although they have married Americans from various backgrounds. This young group of second- and third-generation Armenian Americans has not been as ethnocentrically minded as their parents or grandparents, who are foreign-born Americans. Cultural differentiation has been predominant among the older foreign-born Armenian Americans.[87]

Armenians Today

Armenians place a high value on education. A 1991 survey found that 45 percent of Armenian Americans had earned at least one college degree, and that 57 percent were in professional or management jobs. They have established their own state-approved American-Armenian International College at LaVerne, in Los Angeles, and two chairs in Armenian studies at UCLA.[88]

The major 1988 earthquake in Soviet Armenia and the political unrest there three years later sparked a new wave of refugees and immigrants. Of the almost 1 million Armenians now living in the United States, about 40 percent live in California. Other areas of large concentration are New England, New York, New Jersey, and Michigan.

SOCIOLOGICAL ANALYSIS

With so many millions of immigrants from diverse backgrounds discussed in this chapter, our study of them has necessarily covered a wide range of material. By applying the three major sociological perspectives, however, we can find unifying themes of common experiences in dominant-minority interrelations.

The Functionalist View

From this viewpoint the arrival of significant numbers of immigrants served the rapidly industrializing nation well. Immigrants provided a valuable labor pool to meet the needs of an expanding economy, enabling the United States to emerge as an industrial giant. Unemployment was not a problem, and the poor of Europe were able to build a better life for themselves in their adopted land. Despite nativist fears, the freedom and economic opportunities created fervent patriotic converts among the newcomers. Later political and war refugees, many of them talented and skilled people, increased this hard-working, freedom-loving population. The American social system evolved into a complex, interdependent, and prosperous society, in large measure through the efforts of its first- and second-generation European Americans.

Accompanying problems of overcrowded tenements, social disorganization, crime, harsh working conditions, labor strife, and ethnic antagonism can all be understood within the context of rapid social change. For the mostly poor immigrants unable to afford better housing, the tenements at least offered a place to begin life anew, while also providing a dense concentration of compatriots for a social support system. For many the abrupt change of life—language, customs, and urban living—brought problems of adjustment resulting in various pathologies of behavior. The abuses of the industrial age—child labor, poor wages and working conditions, and lack of security—did cause severe hardship for many workers, but these factors were overcome in time through legislative safeguards and labor union organization. Massive immigration, especially in the first two decades of this century, further strained society's absorption capabilities, prolonging the assimilation process and thereby fostering negative reactions from native-born Americans. Gradually the necessary adjustments occurred: labor regulations, housing codes, acculturation, and upward mobility. With the corrective actions, harmonious interrelations ensued, restoring the social system to a stage of equilibrium.

The Conflict View

Use and abuse of power, not societal inability to cope with rapid change, marks the conflict approach. American industrialists exploited immigrant workers, maximizing profits by minimizing wages and maintaining poor working conditions. When workers protested or went out on strike, employers blacklisted them, hired other ethnics as strikebreakers, secured court injunctions, or used vigilantes, police, or state militia to break up the demonstrations. Employers held absolute economic power to curtail worker agitation, since their position was reinforced by the other social institutions aligned with the powerful against the powerless. The power theory suggested by Lieberson places such actions in a conceptual framework consistent with earlier experiences of the Irish. Bonacich's split labor market theory becomes applicable, for example, in the use of Hungarians and Italians as strikebreakers, generating interethnic conflict as employers sought to thwart the "troublemakers."

Upward mobility for these "white ethnics" occurred not from gradual societal adjustments, say conflict theorists, but from an organized worker movement in opposition to the power structure. First- and second-generation American workers fought hard through the labor union movement—often at great risk and with great sacrifice against strong pressures—to secure their share of the American Dream. The change resulted from conflict, from class consciousness, and an unrelenting social movement against the entrenched economic interests. With economic gains came stability and respectability, enabling these ethnic groups to gain acceptance and overcome prejudice and discrimination against them.

The Interactionist View

Imagine yourself a native-born American living in a northeastern or midwestern city at the turn of the century. You would find your city filled with from two-thirds to three-fourths foreign-born people who were mostly dark-skinned and dark-haired or else physically distinctive because of their clothing. Everything about them—their religion, life-style, and behavior—seemed so different, so "un-American." The people you associated with did not live clustered together in such crowded slums. And there were so many of these people! You constantly read about them getting arrested for breaking some law or another. The city had changed, and not for the better! You worried that the country itself would lose its "authentic" identity as it was overrun by these European "misfits" who had little appreciation for American values and democratic principles.

Such a mental picture is not that difficult. Industrialization, urbanization, social disorganization, economic exploitation, and a host of other factors may have created the social problems regarding immigrants then, but the native-born mostly saw only the symptoms manifest in the immigrant communities. Believing such conditions had not existed until "these people" came, Americans defined the problems as inherent in the "new" immigrants. Indeed, everything the typical American saw or heard only reinforced the perception that the current floodtide of immigrants threatened the entire social fabric. The cries for immigration restrictions, eventually enacted, and the acts of avoidance, discrimination, and occasional violence all reflected the negative stereotyping of those who appeared "different."

Retrospect

The period from 1880 to 1920 was the greatest immigration epoch in American history thus far; 23 million persons left everything behind for the promise of "Golden America." Social and economic forces at work on both continents combined to encourage this mass migration. Europe's inability to offer a decent standard of living and America's need for great quantities of industrial labor were the major push–pull factors. Recruited or attracted to America because of its rapid industrialization, European immigrants fulfilled an important need in the growth and development of the United States.

Yet the "new" immigrants were hardly welcomed with open arms. Ethnocentric preconceptions of how an "American" should look and behave prejudiced large segments of the society against them. Their physical and cultural differences identified them as strangers and heightened nativist fears of an undesirable element populating America. By 1900 one-third of the total population were first- or second-generation Americans, a fact that spurred demands to close the "floodgates" to stem the "immigrant tide." Finally, in 1921 the first restrictive legislation against Europeans was enacted. Not until the late 1960s would the discriminatory quota system based on national origin be terminated entirely.

Many of the theoretical considerations in majority–minority relations apply to the European immigrants. Their cultural and structural differences set the stage for stereotyping, all three levels of prejudice, and discrimination. Progressive stages of culture shock, community organization, development of subcultural areas, and marginality often were the norm. Dominant patterns of nativism, antagonism, social and spatial segregation, and legislative controls were common, as were the minority responses of avoidance, deviance, defiance, and acceptance.

The immigrants settled in ethnic clusters and established their own institutions, and they generally followed the broad patterns of earlier groups of immigrants. The various new peoples differed from one another in language, customs, and value orientations, although Americans frequently found those who were not Italians or Jews indistinguishable and lumped them all together. Not all of them wanted to stay, and not all of those who did stay assimilated. The immigrants in their ethnic clusters exhibited the same sort of cultural pluralism as, in more isolated settings, the "old" immigrants had shown. But the times were different. Urbanization had brought about a greater degree of functional interdependence, a reliance on one another for exchange of goods and services. Thus the newcomers were not as isolated as the earlier immigrants had often been. Their numbers were great, and the dominant society wanted them to assimilate, although it also feared they could not do so.

For many immigrants, the transition from an agrarian to an industrial society was difficult. Those who had either come from an urban background or had to adapt to being a subordinate minority group in Europe, such as the Greeks, Jews, and Armenians, were able to adjust to city life more easily. They took advantage of educational opportunities, climbed the socioeconomic ladder when they or their children could, and adjusted to American society. Others, being mostly illiterate peasants, took longer to get established. Not all the immigrants became citizens, and not all were successful. Some did not learn English. Today the poorer areas of the cities, which originally housed newcomers, contain a number of poor and aged immigrants for whom the American Dream, in economic terms at least, has proved elusive.

American industry employed the immigrants because it needed them. The work was hard, the hours long, and the pay low, but most believed that the opportunities were better in America than in their homelands. Exploitation of workers led to labor unrest and the growth of the union movement. Some immigrants were attracted to radical movements, others returned home, but most toiled, indoors or outdoors, to succeed in their adopted land for themselves and their children.

Review Questions

1. How had structural conditions in America changed for the "new" immigrants?
2. What factors aroused dominant antagonism against the newcomers? In what ways was this hostility expressed?
3. Were there any similarities in the ways in which the various ethnic groups adapted to American society?
4. Apply the concepts of stereotyping and the vicious circle to the immigrant experience during this period.
5. How does the power differential relate to these immigrants' experiences and the labor union movement?
6. How do the three major sociological perspectives explain the experiences of southern, central, and eastern Europeans?

Suggested Readings

ALBA, RICHARD D. *Italian Americans: Into the Twilight of Ethnicity.* Englewood Cliffs, NJ: Prentice-Hall, 1985.

An excellent study of the immigration, settlement, and assimilation of Italians into the social fabric of American society.

DAVIS, JEROME. *The Russian Immigrant,* reprint ed. New York: Arno Press and *The New York Times,* 1969.

A classic work still considered pertinent to understanding the Russian American acculturation experience.

GAMBINO, RICHARD. *Blood of My Blood.* Garden City, NY: Doubleday, 1974.

Comprehensive and readable, a moving account of the Italian American experience over the years.

GANS, HERBERT. *The Urban Villagers,* 2d ed. New York: Free Press, 1983.

An excellent community study of an Italian American neighborhood, examining its cohesive social network.

HALICH, WASYL. *Ukrainians in the United States,* reprint ed. New York: Arno Press and *The New York Times,* 1970.

Originally published in 1937 but still the definitive study of early Ukrainian immigrants.

LENGYEL, EMIL. *Americans from Hungary,* reprint ed. Westport, CT: Greenwood Press, 1974.

First published in 1948, a fine study of the Hungarian American subculture and immigrant adjustment to the United States.

LOPATA, HELENA Z. *Polish Americans: Status Competition in an Ethnic Community.* Englewood Cliffs, NJ: Prentice-Hall, 1976.

A concise, well-written study of the Polish American community, with a primary focus on its multigenerational changes.

SOLOUTOS, THEODORE. *The Greeks in the United States.* Cambridge, MA: Harvard University Press, 1964.

A thorough study of the Greek Americans, their economic mainstreaming, and their retention of ethnic solidarity.

PART III

PEOPLE OF COLOR

"I have a dream that my four little children will one day live in a nation where they will not be judged by the color of their skin but by the content of their character."

— *Martin Luther King, Jr., 1963*

7

Joel Gordon

The Native Americans

Different in race, material culture, beliefs, and behavior, the Europeans and the Native Americans at first were strangers to each other. The Europeans who first traded with and then conquered the natives showed little interest in or understanding of them. Brutalized and exploited, the Native Americans experienced all the dominant-group response patterns—legislative action, segregation, expulsion, xenophobia, and, for some tribes and groups, annihilation. In turn they reacted with varying patterns of avoidance, defiance, and acceptance, steadfastly remaining a numerous and persistent subculture leading a marginal existence.

SOCIOHISTORICAL PERSPECTIVE

From the first European contact with the original population in the New World to the present day, the Native Americans usually have not been understood. Columbus called them Indians because he thought he had reached the islands off the coast of Asia known as the Indies. Today some object to this word, preferring to use *Native American* or a tribal name such as Cherokee, Shoshone, or Lakota.

Perhaps up to 8 million Native Americans lived in what was to become the United States before European colonization. Divided into several hundred tribes with discrete languages and life-styles, these original inhabitants had cultures rich in art, music, dance, life-cycle rituals, belief systems, social organization, coping strategies, and instruction of their young. Although the tribes varied in their values, customs, beliefs, and practices, their cultures primarily rested on living in harmony with the land.

Early European explorers and settlers, reflecting ethnocentric views, condemned those aspects of Native American culture that they did not understand and related to other aspects only in terms of their own culture. Some considered the Native Americans to be savages, even though Native American societies had a high degree of social organization. Others idealized them as uncorrupted children of nature who spent most of their time engaging in pleasurable activities. In Europe intellectual debate raged over how the presence of people so isolated from other human beings could be explained. Were they descended from the inhabitants of Atlantis, Carthage, ancient Greece, East Asia? Were they the Lost Tribes of Israel?[1] Were they no better than beasts, or were they intelligent, capable beings?

In colonial and frontier America, the stereotype of the Native Americans often was negative, especially when they were an obstacle to those Europeans who wanted to use the Native Americans' land. As a result of *self-justification*, the denigration of others to justify maltreating them, some whites viewed Native Americans as cruel, treacherous, lying, dirty heathens. Although that very negative stereotype no longer prevails, even today Native Americans are portrayed in films, television, and comic strips as colorfully dressed but unemotional, humorless, and uncommunicative individuals ("Dances with Wolves" a notable exception). Supposedly all they desired during the frontier period was scalps, firearms, and "firewater." Native Americans often are stereotyped as backward, lacking ambition, or continually drunk, or they are regarded as romantic anachronisms.

Some people overgeneralize about Native Americans, thinking of the many tribes as one people even though the various tribes have always been quite different from one another in language, social structure, values, and practices. Of the approximately 300 different Native American languages spoken in 1492 in what is now the United States, only about half that number still exist. At present there are 314 Native American reservations, and the Bureau of Indian Affairs recognizes 506 different tribal entities in the United States.[2] Figure 7.1 shows the principal Native American tribes living in the United States today.

Native Americans share several distinguishing physical characteristics. Most Native Americans have thick, black, straight hair but very little facial or body hair. They tend to be dark-eyed with rather prominent cheekbones. Beyond these similarities they generally vary greatly in physical stature and features. The term *redskin* is not at all accurate; their skin coloring ranges from yellowish to coppery brown.

The Native Americans' experiences in the American colonies were unique in one respect: The whites, not the Native Americans, were the newcomers, and the whites were the minority for many years. The relationship between Native Americans and whites often was characterized either by wariness and an uneasy truce or by violent hostilities. Even in colonial Massachusetts and New Netherland, where peaceful coexistence initially prevailed, the situation deteriorated.

As the two peoples interacted more fully, each group became more disenchanted with the other. The Native Americans could not understand the European settlers' use of beatings, hangings, and imprisonment as means of social control. The settlers could not understand the Native Americans' resistance to Christianity and to the whites' more "civilized" way of life. These were but peripheral considerations, however; the major issue was whose way of life would prevail and whether the land would be further developed or allowed to remain in its natural state, abounding with fish and wildlife.

The disenchantment grew as the settlers encroached more and more on Native American lands. Eventually hostilities broke out. Large-scale fighting that resulted in many killings broke out in Virginia in 1622 and in Connecticut

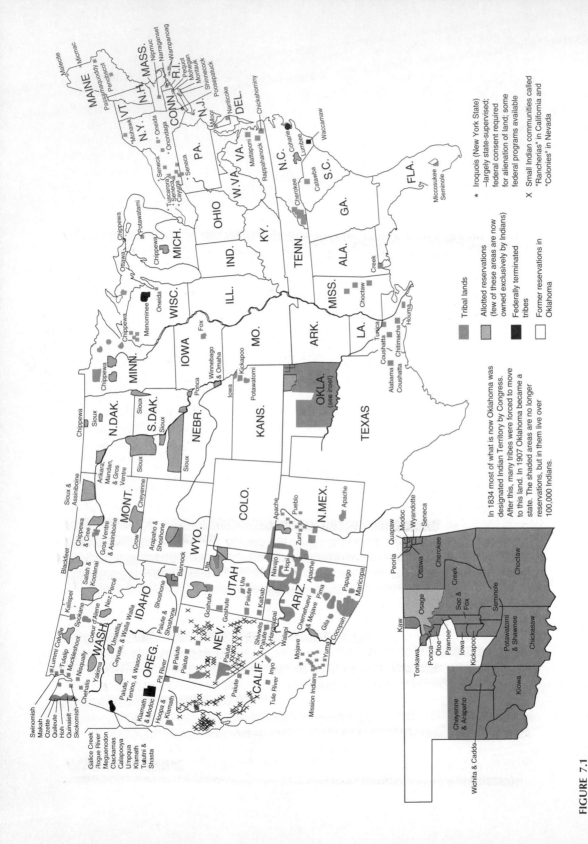

FIGURE 7.1

Principal Native American Tribes in the Continental United States (where they live today)

SOURCE: Based on data from "Indian Land Areas, General" (map), U.S. Department of the Interior, Bureau of Indian Affairs, U.S. Government Printing Office, 1986.

in 1637. Metacom, the leader of the Wampanoag, who was known as King Philip, united the Nipmuc and Narraganset behind him in 1675 and attacked 52 of the 90 New England settlements, completely destroying 12 of them. The colonies seemed in danger of total defeat, but in 1676, Philip was killed and the Native American bands were wiped out one by one. Fighting between Native Americans and whites continued sporadically and locally throughout the westward movement until the 1880s.

In the mid-nineteenth century the government embarked on a policy of containment as a means of controlling the Native Americans and encouraging westward expansion. The government used military force to displace the many tribes and resettle them on wasteland reservations, where they remained unless new settlement plans or the discovery of oil and valuable minerals resulted in further displacement. This program of forced segregation and dependency, compounded by attempts at forced "Americanization," reduced the Native Americans to the status of a subordinate colonized people—wards of the government—living at a subsistence level. Reflecting changing attitudes and interests in the late nineteenth and early twentieth centuries, Congress enacted various pieces of legislation ostensibly designed to help the Native Americans. These laws, to be discussed shortly, actually worked to the Native Americans' disadvantage and worsened their already low and dependent status.

One short-lived Pan-Indian association of the twentieth century, the Society of American Indians, which existed from 1910 until 1920, failed to unify the tribes into an effective pressure group or to draw much outside support. In 1944 a group of World War II veterans formed the National Congress of American Indians (NCAI). In the early 1960s another organization, the National Indian Youth Council (NIYC) came into existence. New moves toward unity began in the 1960s, and new legislation and greater government sympathy helped the Native Americans' cause. The most significant factor in the Native Americans' new success, however, was the impact of the civil rights movement, for it created a greater social consciousness in the country and inspired the Native Americans to strive harder for self-determination. Although they had never been silent, they now became more vocal and organized, and they found non-Indians more receptive. They became more militant, as demonstrated by the occupation of Alcatraz Island in 1969; the takeover of the Bureau of Indian Affairs in Washington, DC, in 1972; the long confrontation in 1973 at Wounded Knee, site of the 1890 massacre, and the March on Washington in 1978. A new generation of Red Power advocates took up the fight for Native American rights. Some attempted to achieve their goals through a national or Pan-Indian movement, whereas others preferred an emphasis on individual tribal culture and practices.

Throughout the 500-year history of Native American–white relations, the Native Americans have frustrated whites by their general refusal to believe that the whites' religions and life-styles are better. To understand the nature of these relations between dominant and majority groups is to understand the important role of ethnocentrism, stereotyping, cultural differences, and power differentials in intergroup relations.

EARLY ENCOUNTERS

To appreciate the significance of the first encounters, it is important to note that two human races were seeing each other's physical distinctions for the first time but also that the vast differences in culture, knowledge, and lifestyle made each a source of wonder to the other. Columbus's first impressions of the Arawak Tribe in the Caribbean reflected ethnocentrism:

> I knew they were a people who would better be freed and converted to our Holy Faith by love than by force . . . they are all generally of good height, of pleasing appearance and well built. . . . They must be good servants and intelligent . . . and I believe that they would easily become Christians, as it appeared to me that they had no sect.[3]

Although he admired the Native Americans, Columbus essentially saw them as "creatures." He looked upon them as potential servants, and he assumed that they had no religious convictions because he found no trappings of religion or written codes such as he was accustomed to seeing in Europe.

As Europeans became more curious about Native Americans, an idealistic concept of the Native American as the Noble Savage took hold. Michel de Montaigne, a sixteenth-century French philosopher, after reading ethnocentric comments in many travelers' journals and talking with explorers, wrote that the Native Americans were indeed Noble Savages, for they

> [have] no kind of traffic, no knowledge of letters, no intelligence of numbers, no name of magistrate, nor of politics, no use of service, or riches, or of poverty; no contracts, no successions, no partitions, no occupation but idle, no apparel but natural, no manuring of lands, no use of wine. The very words that impart a lie, falsehood, treason, covetousness, envy, detraction, were not heard among them.[4]

While some Europeans were romanticizing Native Americans and a positive mystique about the Native Americans swept Elizabethan England and other parts of Europe, others viewed the Native Americans as bloodthirsty barbarians and cruelly exploited them. The early phases of Spanish military activity, particularly in Mexico, Peru, and the American Southwest, included Native American enslavement, plunder, rape, and slaughter. The Spanish put the peaceful Arawak Tribe of the Caribbean islands into forced labor, using them in land clearing, building, mining, and plantation work. Because they had no weapons comparable to those of their conquerors, the subjugated peoples often responded by committing mass suicide and mass infanticide. The Native American population began to decline rapidly as a result of disease, warfare, and self-destruction.

The dichotomy of views of the Native American either as a Noble Savage or as a bloodthirsty barbarian was epitomized in the great debate between Bartolomé de las Casas, a bishop serving in the New World, and Juan Ginés de

Sepúlveda, a Renaissance scholar. The latter considered the Native Americans no better than "beasts" who should be enslaved. Las Casas presented a picture of the Native Americans as innocent children, both artistically and mechanically inclined, with intellectual capabilities for learning and a willingness to coexist with the Spanish intruders.[5] In 1550 King Charles V appointed the Council of the Indies, a panel of distinguished theologians and counselors, which met at Valladolid. The council heard the arguments of the two antagonists, agreed in large measure with Las Casas, and thereby redirected Spanish policy toward the Native Americans.

As part of his long struggle to protect the Native Americans, Las Casas had returned to Spain in 1517 to plead their case directly to the king. In doing so he revealed the extent of their decimation: "At my first arrival in Hispaniola [1497], it contained a million inhabitants and now there remain scarce the hundredth part of them." He felt that the Native Americans could survive only if another labor force replaced them. By convincing the Spanish authorities that Africans were sturdier and better adapted to agricultural operations, he opened the doors for the subsequent massive slave trade of blacks to the Spanish possessions in the New World. It is cruelly ironic that the humane efforts of Las Casas on the Native Americans' behalf led to the brutalization and exploitation of black people and racial discrimination against them for over 400 years.

The Native American populations in the United States and Latin America differ in their social, economic, and political status. Nevertheless, they are an indigenous people to the land, regardless of present-day national boundaries (such as the Mohawk in New York State and Canada). Several factors, including habitability of terrain, migration patterns, degree of industrialization, and especially different attitudes in the various countries, have accounted for these differences. In the United States the nineteenth-century policy of removal, containment, and Native American dependency on the federal government prevented most tribes from becoming full participants in American society. In Latin America, however, Spain adopted a more benevolent policy toward the Native Americans in 1550, following the recommendations of the Council of the Indies, and greater interaction, intermarriage, absorption, and gradual acculturation occurred among the Native Americans and the Spanish. Except for those living in the central Andes and other remote areas, the Native Americans became fuller participants in their society than their counterparts in the United States and lived in relative cultural and racial harmony with the white, black, *mulatto* (of mixed black and white ancestry), and *mestizo* (of mixed Native American and white ancestry) populations. Along with the other nonwhite groups, they were part of the large low-ranking social class, in sharp contrast to the small high-ranking class. Despite racial harmony they have had very little opportunity for upward mobility, and most Latin American nonwhites live in economic stagnation. In contrast, most North American tribes have experienced both economic stagnation and a lack of racial harmony.

Native American populations in Latin America and North America were decimated by various sicknesses that had resulted from earlier contact with white explorers or traders. When the early settlers in New England found deserted Native American villages, they rejoiced; they considered this to be mute testimony of the judgment of Divine Providence on these "heathens" as well as on their own undertaking. The Lord had smitten the pagan to make way for the righteous! This accidental annihilation had often resulted from a serious contagion such as smallpox, tuberculosis, or cholera. The Native Americans also were often fatally susceptible to such diseases as measles, mumps, and chicken pox because they had not developed immunities to these European illnesses.

Cultural Strains

When the white settlers were few in number and depended on Native American assistance, the Native Americans were hospitable and the whites were receptive to them. The Native Americans along the Eastern Seaboard helped the colonists to get settled by teaching them what to plant and how to cultivate it as well as imparting to them the knowledge and skills they would need to survive in the wilderness. As the settlements became stabilized, the relations between the two races became more strained, as the following excerpt from Douglas Edward Leach's study of seventeenth-century New England reveals:

> Ever since the coming of the white men there had been economic intercourse between Indians and English traders. At first it had seemed that the flourishing trade in furs, tools, cloth, and foodstuffs was as beneficial to the Indians as to the colonists, but as time went on and the English extended their activities the Indians grew more and more dissatisfied with the situation. It became apparent that they were gradually sinking into a position of complete economic subservience. Indian villages which had once enjoyed almost total sulf-sufficiency were now increasingly dependent upon products of English manufacture. Individual Indians became enmeshed in debt, which degraded them still further in the eyes of the English. The wiser leaders among the Indians saw that if the trend were not reversed, the time would soon come when the natives of New England would be completely stripped of their independence.
>
> In the meantime, some of the Indians were exchanging their forest ways for the security and comfort of English habitations by engaging themselves as servants or laborers to the settlers, whose ambitious expansionism was fostering a continual shortage of labor. This meant that members of the two races were now being brought into frequent contact with each other on the streets of colonial villages, producing still more interracial friction. Furthermore, the migration of individual Indians to the English plantations was disturbing to the other Indians who chose to cling to their old independence, and who saw with dismay the weakening of tribal and family bonds. . . .
>
> At the same time, the English colonists were being hardened in the conviction that the Indians were a graceless and savage people, dirty and slothful in their personal habits, treacherous in their relations with the superior race. To put it bluntly, they were fit only to be pushed aside and subordinated, so that the land could be occupied and made productive by those for whom it had been destined

by God. If the Indians could be made to fit into a humble niche in the edifice of colonial religion, economy, and government, very well, but if not, sooner or later they would have to be driven away or crushed.[6]

Throughout the westward movement, if contact led to cooperation between the two cultures, the resulting interaction and cultural diffusion usually worked to the disadvantage of the Native Americans. They lost their self-sufficiency and became economically dependent on whites. The whites, in turn, demanded full compliance as the price of continued peaceful relations. Even if the Native Americans complied with the whites' demands, however, many whites continued to regard Native Americans as inferior, destined for a subservient role in white society.

Differing Values

Benjamin Franklin offered a classic example of different values in his account of a treaty signed between the whites and the Iroquois in 1744:

> After the principal Business was settled, the Commissioners from Virginia acquainted the Indians by a Speech, that there was at Williamsburg a College, with a Fund for Educating Indian youth; and that, if the Six Nations would send down half a dozen of their young Lads to that College, the Government would take care that they should be well provided for, and instructed in all the Learning of the White People. . . . [The Indians'] Speaker began . . . ''We are convinc'd . . . that you mean to do us Good by your Proposal; and we thank you heartily. But you, who are wise, must know that different Nations have different Conceptions of things; and you will therefore not take it amiss, if our Ideas of this kind of Education happen not to be the same with yours. We have had some Experience of it; Several of our young People were formerly brought up at the Colleges of the Northern Provinces; they were instructed in all your Sciences; but, when they came back to us, they were bad Runners, ignorant of every means of living in the Woods, unable to bear either Cold or Hunger, knew neither how to build a Cabin, take a Deer, or kill an Enemy, knew our Language imperfectly, were therefore neither fit for Hunters, Warriors, nor Counsellors; they were totally good for nothing. We are however not the less oblig'd by your kind Offer, tho' we decline accepting it; and, to show our grateful Sense of it, if the Gentlemen of Virginia will send us a Dozen of their Sons, we will take great Care of their Education, instruct them in all we know, and make *Men* of them.''*

Almost 100 years later, George Catlin offered insight into another manifestation of differing value orientations. Catlin, a nineteenth-century artist famous for his paintings of Native Americans and his sensitivity to their ways, observed in the following passage how each of the two cultures viewed the other:

*Excerpt from *Benjamin Franklin,* edited by Chester E. Jorgenson and Luther Frank Mott. Copyright © 1962 by Hill and Wang, Inc. Reprinted by permission of Hill and Wang, a division of Farrar, Straus & Giroux, Inc.

The civilized world look upon a group of Indians, in their classic dress, with their few and simple oddities, all of which have their moral or meaning, and laugh at them excessively, because they are not like ourselves—we ask, "why do the silly creatures wear such great bunches of quills on their heads?—Such loads and streaks of paint upon their bodies—and bear's grease? abominable!" and a thousand other equally silly questions, without ever stopping to think that Nature taught them to do so—and that they all have some definite importance or meaning which an Indian could explain to us at once, if he were asked and felt disposed to do so—that each quill in his head stood, in the eyes of his whole tribe, as the symbols of any enemy who had fallen by his hand—that every streak of red paint covered a wound which he had got in honourable combat—and that the bear's grease with which he carefully anoints his body every morning, from head to foot, cleanses and purifies the body, and protects his skin from the bite of mosquitoes, and at the same time preserves him from colds and coughs which are usually taken through the pores of the skin.

At the same time, an Indian looks at the civilized world, no doubt, with equal, if not much greater, astonishment, at our apparently, as well as really, ridiculous customs and fashions; but he laughs not, nor ridicules, nor questions—for his natural good sense and good manners forbid him,—until he is reclining about the fireside of his wigwam companions, when he vents forth his just criticisms upon the learned world, who are a rich and just theme for Indian criticism and Indian gossip.

An Indian will not ask a white man the reason why he does not oil his skin with bear's grease, or why he does not paint his body—or why he wears a hat on his head, or why he has buttons on the back of his coat, where they can never be used—or why he wears whiskers, and a shirt collar up to his eyes—or why he sleeps with his head towards the fire instead of his feet—why he walks with his toes out instead of turning them in—or why it is that hundreds of white folks will flock and crowd round a table to see an Indian eat—but he will go home to his wigwam fireside, and "make the welkin ring" with jokes and fun upon the ignorance and folly of the knowing world.[7]

These two selections are excellent illustrations of how culture shapes an individual's view of reality. When people use their own group as a frame of reference in judging another group, the resulting ethnocentric judgments declare the outgroup to be strange and inferior.

One Native American nation, the Iroquois, had a pronounced influence on some of the provisions of the U.S. Constitution. Iroquois is a name given to five Native American tribes located in New York State and the Ohio River Valley—the Cayuga, Mohawk, Oneida, Onondaga, and Seneca—who united in a league in 1570. They added a sixth tribe—the Tuscarora—in 1722, and also took other groups, including the Delaware, under their protection. The League had not yet reached its full extent when it was curtailed by the white settlers; by 1851 it had virtually disappeared.

In its time the League's democratic processes were so effective that romanticists called the Iroquois the "Greeks in America," and many aspects of their system served as a model for the colonists. Called the Great Law of Peace, the Iroquois constitution gave each of the five tribes an equal voice, guaranteed freedom of political and religious expression, and had amendment and impeachment processes.[8]

NATIVE AMERICAN VALUES AND SOCIAL STRUCTURE

Although there were, and still are, a great many tribes whose cultures differ from one another, some marked similarities have existed among them. For one thing, the Native Americans have lived in a close and intimate relationship with nature, respecting and not abusing the land. They maximize the use of any animal prey—using its skin for clothing and shelter, its bones for various tools and implements, its sinews for thread, its meat for food, its bladder for a container, and so on.

Native American attitudes toward possession of the land itself ranged from single to joint to tribal ownership, depending on the tribe. More frequently the land belonged to the tribe; as tribal members, individuals or families could live on and possibly farm certain portions. Land no longer cultivated by one Native American could be cultivated by another. However, the nominal owner could not dispose of the property without considering the land-use rights of the current user (see Box 7.1). More emphasis was thus placed on the rights of the user than on the rights and power of the nominal owner.[9] This practice is somewhat comparable, at least in terms of shared access, to a law in present-day Sweden that roughly translates to "every person's right." In that country a landowner cannot deny others access to the land, since all are entitled to enjoy its beauty. Thus campers or hikers do not encounter no-trespassing signs; because all respect the land, littering and other forms of abuse are quite rare.

Concerning personal interaction, Native Americans established primary relationships either through a clan system (descent from a common ancestor) or through a friendship system, much like other tribal societies:

> Kin relationships were the basic building blocks of Indian society. These blocks were formed into social and political structures ranging from nuclear families to vast empires. The Indians, in their initial attempts to establish a basis of cooperation with the immigrant whites, attempted to incorporate the newcomers into the familiar kinship system. When proffered marriage alliances were turned down by the whites, the Indians sought to establish relationships based on the reciprocal responsibilities of brother to brother, nephew to uncle, and, finally, children to father. The white man refused the proferred relationships, misinterpreted Indian speech as weakness, and increasingly imposed his will on the disheartened remnants of once proud Indian nations.[10]

Native American children grow up under the encouragement and discipline of the extended family, not just the nuclear family. A generalized love of all children in the tribe, rather than just their own progeny, has been common

BOX 7.1   **THE ETHNIC EXPERIENCE**

The Great Chief in Washington sends word that he wishes to buy our land. How can you buy or sell the sky, the warmth of the land? The idea is strange to us. Yet we do not own the freshness of the air or the sparkle of the water. How can you buy them from us? Every part of this earth is sacred to my people.

We know that the white man does not understand our ways. One portion of the land is the same to him as the next, for he is as a stranger who comes in the night and takes from the land whatever he needs. The earth is not his brother but his enemy, and when he has conquered it, he moves on. He leaves his fathers' graves, and his children's birthright is forgotten.

There is no quiet place in the white man's cities. No place to hear the leaves of spring or the rustle of insect wings. But perhaps because I am savage and do not understand, the clatter only seems to insult the ears. And what is there to life if a man cannot hear the lovely cry of the whippoorwill or the arguments of the frogs around the pond at night?

The whites too shall pass, perhaps sooner than other tribes. Continue to contaminate your bed and you will one night suffocate in your own waste. When the buffalo are all slaughtered, the wild horses all tamed, the secret corners of the forest heavy with the scent of many men, and the view of the ripe hills blotted by talking wires. Where is the thicket? Gone. Where is the eagle? Gone. And what is it to say goodbye to the swift and the hunt? The end of living and the beginning of survival.

SOURCE: Chief Seattle to President Franklin Pierce, 1855.

among the Native Americans.[11] This factor may help explain the permissive and indulgent child-rearing practices many Europeans reported.[12] Whether the Native American tribe was a hunting, a fishing, or a farming society, social scientists have found that the children were raised in a cooperative, noncompetitive, and affectionate atmosphere. Considered from the outset as an individual, the child developed a sense of responsibility and interdependency at an early age. Unrestrained displays of affection or temper and the use of corporal punishment have rarely been part of traditional Native American child-care practices. Instead, the means of social control are shame and ridicule, and the Native American matures into an individual keenly aware of any form of conduct that would lead other members of the tribe to have such reactions. Sometimes the price of emphasizing these forms of social control is heavy, for a great deal of psychological harm can be caused by shame and ridicule.

Closely related to the sensitivity to shame and ridicule is the Native American concept of personal honor, including the honor of one's word. Once pledged, whether to a white person or to another Native American, that word was never broken. Exceptions existed, for, Albert Britt reports, chiefs "lied only as a war measure, personal or tribal—later, in an attempt to please the white."[13] Some tribes had no word for *thief*, although an enemy's goods were always fair game. Sometimes, as among the Sioux, Crow, and Blackfoot, young men of one tribe would steal from another tribe as a form of sport or a joke, but normally they would not steal from one another.[14]

The Native American woman's role differed from the man's. Women's functions were to work and to raise children. However, the traditional view that women held a subservient position and labored long and hard while the men idled away their time is not completely accurate. Actually there was a cooperative but not egalitarian arrangement between the sexes, with the men doing the heavy work and the women doing tasks that would not conflict with their child-rearing responsibilities. In hunting and fishing societies, the men would be away from the village for extended periods searching for food. In farming societies the men cleared and cultivated the land, and the women tended the crops, collected edible foods, and gathered firewood while the men sought a fresh meat supply. Each member of the tribe according to sexually defined roles, had responsibilities to fulfill for kin and tribe.

STEREOTYPING OF NATIVE AMERICANS _____

One popular misconception was that the Native American was a bloodthirsty savage. Some tribes, such as the Apache and Ute, were more warlike, but most sought to avoid conflict if they could. Rivalries did exist among various tribes, however, and the French, English, and Americans often exploited these rivalries for their own advantage. The Native Americans did believe strongly in retributive justice: a wrong had to be repaid, even if it took years, but not to a greater degree. Scalping, often depicted in films as a common Native American practice, in fact was not common. Even those tribes that did scalp frequently did so because of their belief in retributive justice. Some historians argue that the Native American first learned about scalping from white settlers:

> Whatever its exact origins, there is no doubt that scalp-taking quickly spread over all of North America, except in the Eskimo areas; nor is there any doubt that its spread was due to the barbarity of White men rather than to the barbarity of Red men. White settlers early offered to pay bounties on dead Indians, and scalps were actual proof of the dead. Governor Kieft of New Netherland is usually credited with originating the idea of paying for Indian scalps, as they were more convenient to handle than whole heads, and they offered the same proof that an Indian had been killed. By liberal payment for scalps, the Dutch virtually cleared southern New York and New Jersey of Indians before the English supplanted them. By 1703 the colony of Massachusetts was paying the equivalent of about $60 for every Indian scalp. In the mid-eighteenth century, Pennsylvania fixed the bounty for a male Indian scalp at $134; a female's was

Throughout the American Southwest, Native Americans selling handcrafted jewelry is a common sight, at numerous roadside stands or at sidewalk bazaars such as this scene in Santa Fe. With limited occupational choices available, utilizing artistic skills of one's heritage preserves the past and meets present needs. *(M.B. Duda/Photo Researchers)*

worth only $50. Some White entrepreneurs simply hatcheted any old Indians that still survived in their towns.*

Another side of the Native American stereotype is the portrayal of the Native American as silent or aloof. This image probably grew out of normal Native American behavior in ambiguous situations, such as those faced by Native Americans transported to Europe for exhibition, transported to Washington, DC, for treaty negotiations, or interacting with strangers. Because they had developed from childhood a sensitivity to acting in any way that might bring about shame or ridicule, Native Americans often remained silent for fear of speaking or acting improperly. This practice is still common in courtship; in the greeting offered to children returning from boarding school; and in the face of harsh, angry words from a white. In each instance the practice among most tribes is to allow some time, perhaps days or months, to elapse before the uncertainty is sufficiently reduced to permit conversation.

*From *Man's Rise to Civilization as Shown by the Indians of North America from Primeval Times to the Coming of the Industrial State* by Peter Farb, p. 158. Copyright © 1968 by Peter Farb. Reprinted by permission of the publishers, E. P. Dutton.

THE ETHNIC EXPERIENCE

"I had heard marvelous things of this people. In some things we despised them; in others we regarded them as *waken* [mysterious], a race whose power bordered upon the supernatural. I learned that they had made a 'fire-boat.' I could not understand how they could unite two elements which cannot exist together. I thought the water would put out the fire, and the fire would consume the boat if it had the shadow of a chance. This was to me a preposterous thing! But when I was told that the Big Knives had created a 'fire-boat-walks-on-mountains' [a locomotive] it was too much to believe.

"I had seen guns and various other things brought to us by the French Canadians, so that I had already some notion of the supernatural gifts of the white man; but I had never before heard such tales as I listened to that morning. It was said that they had bridged the Missouri and Mississippi rivers, and that they made immense houses of stone and brick, piled on top of one another until they were as high as high hills. My brain was puzzled with these things for many a day.

"Certainly they are a heartless nation. They have made some of their people servants—yes, slaves! We have never believed in keeping slaves, but it seems these *Washichu* [white men] do! It is our belief that they painted their servants black a long time ago, to tell them from the rest, and now the slaves have children born to them of the same color!

"The greatest object of their lives seems to be to acquire possessions—to be rich. They desire to possess the whole world. For thirty years they were trying to entice us to sell them our land. Finally the outbreak gave them all, and we had already spread over the whole country.

"They are a wonderful people. They have divided the day into hours, like the moons of the year. In fact, they measure everything. Not one of them would let so much as a turnip go from his field unless he received full value for it. I understand that their great men make a feast and invite many, but when the feast is over the guests are required to pay for what they have eaten before leaving the house [restaurant].

"I am also informed, . . . but this I hardly believe, that their Great Chief [President] compels every man to pay him for the land e lives upon and all his personal goods—even for his own existence—eve   year! I am sure we could not live under such a law."

SOURCE: Sioux youth during the 1870s.

Native American silence is a cautionary device to preserve respect and dignity on both sides.[15] The silence does not represent aloofness, and it is temporary, continuing only until the situation lends itself to speaking.

Hollywood has established the false Native American stereotype in the minds of many Americans. Ignoring their many ethnic identities, the movies have created a single fictional identity, often called "Sioux" or "Apache," and have portrayed "the Indian" as either a noble redskin or a vicious savage, either of whom denies the "white man his proper Christian right to this continent."[16] As Will Rogers once said, "The problem ain't ignorance, but everyone knowing something that ain't true."

CHANGES IN GOVERNMENTAL POLICY _____

Official government policy toward the Native Americans has changed frequently over the years. In 1763 the King of England issued a proclamation declaring henceforth that the Native American tribes would be treated as independent nations and denying the colonies all jurisdiction over them. Thereafter if the colonists wanted to obtain additional Native American land or negotiate any trade pacts, they had to do so through the English government and not directly with the Native Americans. Historians cite enforcement of this policy as an indirect cause of the American Revolution. In addition to the delay in gaining approval caused by drawing up petitions, making ocean crossings, and waiting for bureaucratic processing, the colonists fumed over heathens being accorded higher official status than they, loyal British subjects. Yet when the colonies declared their independence from England, they adopted the same policy in 1778, and the tribes had quasinational status. Congress reaffirmed this policy with passage of the Northwest Territory Ordinance in 1787, declaring itself responsible for Native American property, rights, and liberty.

Indian Removal Act

Under the sponsorship of President Andrew Jackson, Congress passed the Indian Removal Act in 1830 by a close vote. This act called for the expulsion of all Native Americans from the southeastern states to the west of the Mississippi River. This legislation was prompted in part by the state of Georgia, which for several years had been annexing the fertile land of the Cherokee for its expanding cotton industry. The Cherokee had rejected Georgia's claim to jurisdiction and petitioned the U.S. Supreme Court for protection under their "foreign nation" status and treaties with the federal government.

Combining two cases, *Cherokee Nation v. Georgia* and *Worcester v. Georgia,* Chief Justice John Marshall delivered the majority opinion on February 28, 1832, establishing the foundation that has shaped U.S. Native American policy ever since. The Cherokee were not a foreign nation, the court ruled, and therefore could not sue Georgia. They were instead a "domestic dependent nation," a "distinct community, occupying its own territory." Because of this definition, the court said, the laws of Georgia had no jurisdiction, and the court thus ruled in favor of the Cherokee keeping the land.

President Jackson's reported response was, "John Marshall has rendered his decision, now let him enforce it." Indeed, two of the three branches of government favored removal, and Jackson interpreted his overwhelming re-election in November as a mandate from the electorate. Jackson thus decided to ignore the court ruling and instead enforce the Indian Removal Act, launching one of the ugliest episodes in the nation's history.

Expulsion

Under forced signing of the Treaty of Dancing Rabbit Creek (1830), the Choc-taw of Mississippi went first. The government removed 20,000, with 5,000 dying from famine and disease along the march to Indian Territory in Okla-homa. In 1836 the army moved against the Creek in Alabama, forcing 17,000 westward; 2,000 died from exposure, famine, and disease en route, with another 3,500 dying within three months of arrival. About 1,000 Chickasaw in Mississippi died during their forced march.[17] The Seminole in Florida successfully used guerilla warfare tactics in the Everglades, killing almost 2,000 soldiers and costing the U.S. Army over $20 million before being left alone.[18]

The Cherokee

About 1790 the Cherokee, after some 14 years of warfare with the Americans, decided to adopt American customs and culture. In other words, they em-barked on an active program of assimilation in an effort to live harmoniously with a different civilization. Over the next 40 years their success in achieving this goal was remarkable. They converted their economy to one based on agriculture and commerce, strengthened their self-governing political system, and prospered. They cultivated farmlands in the fertile soil of the tristate region of Georgia, Tennessee, and North Carolina, and reaped bountiful har-vests. The Cherokee patterned themselves after the whites, setting up churches, schools, sawmills, grist mills, and blacksmith shops. They acquired spinning wheels, looms, plows, and all the other implements of white society.

Most extraordinary of all was the achievement of one Cherokee of part-white ancestry named Sequoyah. In 1821, after a 12-year struggle, this crip-pled genius succeeded in inventing a phonetic syllabary notation system for the Cherokee language. This immense accomplishment was unprecedented in world history. An untrained man had been able to write a language by himself, and to do so in a way that could be easily learned. What quickly followed is also remarkable. Within three years almost all the Cherokee could read and write their own language. By 1828 the tribe had its own newspaper and had adopted a written constitution, a code of laws, a bicameral legisla-ture, and an appellate judiciary.

By American standards the Cherokee were the most "civilized" tribe in the country. Driven by the desire for self-improvement, they had educated themselves, converted to Christianity, and learned the whites' ways of agriculture, business, and government. They had successfully acculturated. Just one problem remained: The whites wanted their rich land for cotton growing, and the Cherokee too now faced eviction.

With public opinion against the Cherokee, the voices of John Marshall, Daniel Webster, Henry Clay, Sam Houston, Davy Crockett, and others could not help the Cherokee cause. Georgia confiscated Cherokee land and redistributed it through land lotteries, with the state militia stationed in the region to preserve the peace should the Native Americans resist:

> The premeditated brutality of the militia's daily conducts suggested their commanders' hope of provoking a Cherokee reaction which might provide an excuse for their immediate physical expulsion. The carefully disciplined Cherokee instead patiently submitted even when the provocations extended to the burning of their homes, the confiscation of their property, the mistreatment of their women, the closing of their schools, and the sale of liquor in their churches.[19]

The Cherokee retreated into the forests and continued their desperate legal maneuvering to avoid removal. Although federal troops removed the Choctaw and Chickasaw in Mississippi and the Creek in Alabama, they did not move against the Cherokee, who had won worldwide sympathy and whose legal efforts to prevent removal were still successful. Instead, the federal government intensified its efforts to promote disunity among the Cherokee through bribery, jailings, persecution, and denial of the services and support guaranteed under treaties. Most of the Cherokee remained loyal to their president, John Ross, and rejected the proposed treaty of removal and its $5 million compensation payment.

Government officials finally succeeded in getting the treaty signed on December 29, 1835, by convening an ad hoc council of Ross's Cherokee opponents. Fewer than 500 of the 17,000 Cherokee appeared, but they signed the treaty, and the Senate ratified it on May 18, 1836. Ross and the Cherokee people fought this pseudolegitimate treaty, and in January 1838 Ross presented the Senate with a petition signed by 15,665 Cherokee repudiating the treaty. The Senate rejected the petition by a 37 to 10 vote. A new wave of public protest in the North, including an impassioned open letter to President Van Buren from Ralph Waldo Emerson, had no result. On April 10, 1838, the president ordered General Winfield Scott to remove the Cherokee immediately, using whatever military force was necessary. The U.S. government, through its military forces, acted against an entire people who had willingly adapted to the changing world around them. Soldiers forced them at gunpoint from their homes, first to stockades and then westward, far from all that had been theirs:

> Families at dinner were startled by the sudden gleam of bayonets in the doorway and rose up to be driven with blows and oaths along the weary miles to the

stockade. Men were seized in their fields or going along the road, women were taken from their wheels and children from their play. In many cases, on turning for one last look as they crossed the ridge, they saw their homes in flames, fired by the lawless rabble that followed on the heels of the soldiers to loot and pillage. So keen were these outlaws on the scent that in some instances they were driving off the cattle and other stock of the Indians almost before the soldiers had fairly started their owners in the other direction. Systematic hunts were made by the same men for Indian graves, to rob them of the silver pendants and other valuables deposited with the dead. A Georgia volunteer, afterward a colonel in the Confederate service, said: "I fought through the Civil War and have seen men shot to pieces and slaughtered by thousands, but the Cherokee removal was the cruelest work I ever knew."[20]

The Cherokee suffered extensively during this mass expulsion. Beginning in October 1838, army troops marched the Cherokee westward along what the Cherokee later called the Trail of Tears: Ten to 20 Native Americans died each day from exposure and other miseries. By March 1839 fewer than 9,000 out of 13,000 survived to reach the Indian Territory, which is now Oklahoma. At the midpoint in this sad episode—December 3, 1838—President Van Buren's message to Congress announced:

> It affords me sincere pleasure to apprise the Congress of the entire removal of the Cherokee Nation of Indians to their new homes west of the Mississippi. The measures authorized by Congress at its last session have had the happiest effects. . . . They have emigrated without any apparent reluctance.[21]

Reservations and Dependency

A shift in government policy in the mid-nineteenth century changed Native American life-styles to such an extent that one can see its aftereffects today on any reservation. Instead of using annihilation and expulsion as means of dealing with the Native Americans, the government embarked on a policy of segregation and isolation. Between 1850 and 1880 it established most of the reservations, of which there are now more than 300.

In 1871 Congress tacked onto an appropriations bill a rider that ended federal recognition of the Native American tribes as independent, sovereign nations and made them wards of the government instead. Bureaucrats were now responsible for the welfare of the Native Americans, issued them food rations, and supervised every aspect of their lives. The results were devastating. Proud and independent people who had been taught self-reliance at an early age were now totally dependent on non-Native American government agents. Many of the tribes had been nomadic, and did not easily adjust to reservation life. Moreover, such problems as inadequate administration by the Native American agents and irregular delivery of food, supplies, and equipment only made matters worse.

The government was still not through restructuring the Native Americans' life-styles, for leaders at the time believed that what they were doing was "for the best." Americanization became the goal. This meant destroying tribal

"The Trail of Tears"

Forcibly removed from their land in the East in 1838 by federal troops, despite their peaceful assimilation efforts, the Cherokee trekked westward to Oklahoma under heavy guard. More than 4,000 died during the winter journey. This dominant act of expulsion occurred despite a U.S. Supreme Court ruling in favor of the Cherokee. *(Woolarac Museum)*

organizations, suppressing "pagan" religions and ceremonies, allowing only the English language in the schools, requiring "white" hair and clothing styles, and teaching only American culture and history.

> Most of the attention of the Americanizers was concentrated on the Indian children, who were snatched from their families and shipped off to boarding schools far from their homes. The children usually were kept at boarding school for eight years, during which time they were not permitted to see their parents, relatives or friends. Anything Indian—dress, language, religious practices, even outlook on life (and how that was defined was up to the judgment of each administration of the government's directives)—was uncompromisingly prohibited. Ostensibly educated, articulate in the English language, wearing store-bought clothes, and with their hair short and their emotionalism toned down, the boarding-school graduates were sent out either to make their way in a white world that did not want them, or to return to a reservation to which they were now foreign. The Indians had simply failed to melt into the great American melting pot.[22]

The Dawes Act

One value that was promulgated was the rugged individualism of white society, rather than the cooperative, noncompetitive approach of the Native American. This was the purpose of the General Allotment Act of 1887. Its sponsor, Senator Dawes, genuinely believed that it would create in the Native

American that spirit of self-interest that he considered the major force in white civilization.

What this legislation actually did was deprive the Native Americans of even more land. Its intent was to break the backbone of Native American culture by ending the communal ownership of reservation lands and giving each Native American a share. Many of the Native Americans had no technical knowledge of farming and neither the cash nor credit to obtain farm implements. Some Native American peoples believed it was sacrilegious to plow open the earth. Loopholes in the Dawes Act enabled unscrupulous whites to plunder the Native American land, either through low-cost long-term leases or by convincing the Native American owners to write wills leaving their property to white "friends." This practice was widespread, and a suspicious increase in the number of Native American deaths followed; some of these deaths actually were proven to have been murders.[23]

When tribes refused to accept the allotment policy, the government passed the Curtis Act in 1898. This law terminated the tribal governments of those tribes resisting allotment and made their tribal chiefs presidential appointments thereafter. By 1914 the 138 million acres of Native American land had been reduced to 56 million acres, all of it eroded and of poor quality.[24]

Indian Reorganization Act

After 1933 the Roosevelt administration shifted from a policy of forced assimilation to one of pluralism. Secretary of the Interior Harold L. Ickes and Bureau of Indian Affairs Commissioner John Collier, in particular, were deeply sympathetic to the Native American cause. One outcome was the Indian Reorganization Act of 1934, which ended the land allotment program, encouraged tribal self-government, extended financial credit to the tribes, gave preference to Bureau of Indian Affairs (BIA) employment of Native Americans, and permitted consolidation of Native American lands split up through inheritance. Furthermore, the Native Americans were encouraged to revive their ancient arts and crafts, their languages, their religions and ceremonies, and their customs and traditions. In keeping with an administrative philosophy of treating the Native Americans with dignity, the act was permissive, not mandatory; each tribe could vote to accept or reject the new law. Most chose to accept it.

In the 1950s new top administrative personnel in the Interior Department and the BIA who had a different philosophy caused a shift back to attempts at assimilation. Some critics of the 1934 legislation had thought it regressive. Now these people, believing that the only way to end the chronic poverty, disease, overpopulation, and hopelessness among the Native Americans was to end the isolation of reservation life, tried some new approaches.

The Relocation Program

Beginning in 1952 the Bureau of Indian Affairs attempted at least partially to resolve the problem of overpopulation on the reservations. The BIA provided financial and other assistance to individuals or families who wanted to secure jobs and living accommodations in urban areas. For many Native Americans the word *relocation* had terrible connotations. That was the euphemism that had been used for the prison camps in which 110,000 Japanese Americans had been placed during World War II. Furthermore, Dillon S. Myer, the government administrator who had been in charge of those camps, was now in charge of the Native American relocation program.

Most of the Native Americans who used this program (about 40,000) went to work in low-status unskilled or semiskilled jobs and to live in the poorer sections of the cities. Some adjusted and became acculturated; others felt uprooted and were driven to alcoholism. More than one-fourth of the total number returned to the reservations. The program tapered off after 1960, mostly because of other efforts to improve Native American life.

The Termination Act

A series of bills passed in 1953–1954 sought to end federal responsibility for the Native Americans by ending all federal services and federal liaison with tribal organizations and by dispensing receipts from sale of reservation land among all tribal entities. Medical care, schools, road maintenance, and other federal services provided under treaty obligations were immediately stopped instead of gradually withdrawn to allow transitional adjustments. Tribes such as the Menominee of Wisconsin were forced to sell lakefront property to maintain these services. The termination acts affected 109 tribes and bands, a total of 13,263 Native Americans, and over 1.3 million acres of trust land.[25]

Two of the more prosperous tribes, the Klamath of southern Oregon and the Menominee of Wisconsin, both of whom owned considerable tracts of valuable timberland, some Paiute and Ute in Utah, and several other tribes were the first to be affected by this legislation. For the Klamath, a tribe of 668 families totaling some 2,000 individuals, termination even threatened to end their tribal identity. In the spring of 1968, when 77 percent voted to withdraw from the tribe and receive a cash payment for their share of the land holdings, many government and business officials feared that liquidating tribal assets when the lumber market was already depressed would threaten the Pacific Northwest economy. Instead of selling the lumber, Congress voted to purchase the land, creating the Winema National Forest. A federal trusteeship for adults declared incompetent to handle their own affairs and for minors kept the government involved in 48.9 percent of the tribe members' affairs.[26]

In the case of the Menominee, the new policy brought economic disaster.

> Almost overnight, many millions of dollars of tribal assets disappeared in the rush to transform the Menominee reservation into a self-supporting county. The need to finance the usual hospital, police, and other services of a county and pay taxes imperiled the tribe's sawmill and forest holdings, alienated tribal lands, threatened many Indians with the loss of their homes and life savings, and saddled Wisconsin with a huge welfare problem which it could not underwrite

BOX 7.3

GOVERNMENT ACTIONS TOWARD MAJOR NATIVE AMERICANS

1763   Royal Proclamation: Tribes accorded independent nation status; all land west of Appalachian mountains is Native American country; royal government must be a party to all land purchases.

1778   Continental Congress: Reaffirms former British policy as American policy.

1787   Northwest Territory Ordinance: Opens Midwest for settlement; declares government responsible for Native American property, rights, and liberty.

1824   Bureau of Indian Affairs created under jurisdiction of the Secretary of War.

1830   Indian Removal Bill: Mandates all Native Americans must move west of Mississippi River.

1830–43   Except for Iroquois and Seminole, over 100,000 Native Americans forcibly removed; about 12,000 die on the "Trail of Tears."

1850–80   Most reservations established as forced segregation becomes the new Native American reality.

1871   Appropriations Bill Rider: Tribes declared no longer to be independent nations; legislation, not negotiation, to determine any new arrangements.

1887   Dawes Act: Reservations to be surveyed, divided in tracts and allotted to individual tribal members; surplus land to be sold.

1898   Curtis Act: Terminates tribal governments refusing allotment; president to appoint tribal chiefs hereafter.

1906   Burke Act: Eliminates Native American's right to lease one's land, with intent to force Native Americans to work the land themselves.

1924   Indian Citizenship Act: Grants U.S. citizenship to the American Indians.

1934   Indian Reorganization Act: Ends allotment; encourages tribal self-government; restores freedom of religion; extends financial credit; promotes revival of Native American culture and crafts.

1952   Relocation Program: Moves Native Americans at government expense to urban areas for better job opportunities.

1953   Termination Act: Authorizes elimination of reservation systems with immediate end of federal services and tax immunity.

1973   Menominee Restoration Act: Revokes termination and restores Menominee reservation and tribal status.

1974   Indian Finance Act: Facilitates financing of Native American enterprises and development projects through grants and low-cost loan funds.

1975   Indian Self-determination and Education Assistance Act: Expands tribal control over reservation programs; provides funding for new public schools on or near reservations. (Other tribal restoration acts follow.)

1976   Indian Health Care Improvement Act: Provides funds to build or renovate hospitals, add more personnel, give scholarships to Native Americans to enter Indian Health Service.

1978   Education Amendments Act: Gives substantial control of education program to local Native American community.

1978   Tribally Controlled Community College Assistance Act: Provides grants to tribal community colleges.

1978   Indian Child Welfare Act: Restricts placement of Native American children by non-Native American social agencies in non-Native American homes.

and which had to be met by desperate appeals for help from the same federal government that had thought it had washed its hands of the Menominees.[27]

The standard of living had dropped sharply as the tribe lost its ability to furnish water, electricity, or health care. Shortly after termination, a tuberculosis epidemic swept through the Menominee. Washington's blunder cost the Menominee their hospital, their sawmill, and some of their best land, which they had to sell because they could not afford the taxes on it. President Nixon officially repudiated the termination policy in 1970, and Congress reversed the termination of the Menominee in December 1973. The Restoration Act re-created their reservation, but nobody gave the Menominee back their hospital or their sawmill. The following year the Menominee took over the abandoned 64-room Alexian Brothers monastery to serve as their hospital. It had been built on Menominee land at a time when any church group could take as much Native American reservation land as it needed to build religious structures. Local whites, who had bought tribal land cheaply when the tribe had to sell, objected, although the Alexian Brothers did not. When bloodshed seemed imminent, the governor of Wisconsin called out the National Guard to maintain order. A peaceful accommodation was reached, and the Menominee retained permanent possession of the building. Between 1977 and 1990, most of the other tribes that had been terminated also had federal recognition restored (see Table 7.1) but in many cases not their land.

TABLE 7.1	**FORMERLY TERMINATED NATIVE AMERICAN TRIBES NOW RESTORED**		
Tribe or Band	**State**	**Population**	**Acres**
Menominee	Wisconsin	3,270	233,881
Klamath	Oregon	2,133	862,662
Western Oregon (61 tribes and bands)	Oregon	2,081	3,158
Alabama–Coushatta	Texas	450	3,200
Southern Paiute	Utah	232	42,839
Lower Lake Rancheria	California	n/a	n/a
Wyandotte	Oklahoma	1,157	94
Peoria	Oklahoma	640	n/a
Ottawa	Oklahoma	630	n/a
Coyote Valley Ranch	California	n/a	n/a
California Rancherias (37–38 rancherias)	California	1,107	4,315
Catawba	South Carolina	631	3,388
Ponca	Nebraska	442	834

SOURCE: Bureau of Indian Affairs.

Self-Determination

For the first time in the twentieth century, a Native American became Commissioner of Indian Affairs—first, Robert L. Bennett, an Oneida from Wisconsin in 1966 and then Louis R. Bruce, a Mohawk–Sioux. However, paternalistic federal bureaucrats continued. An important turning point occurred with President Richard Nixon's message to Congress on July 8, 1970, repudiating termination and laying the groundwork for contemporary Native American policy.

> The story of the Indian in America is something more than the record of the white man's frequent aggression, broken agreements, intermittent remorse and prolonged failure. It is a record also of endurance, of survival, of adaptation and creativity in the face of overwhelming obstacles. It is a record of enormous contributions to this country—to its art and culture, to its strength and spirit, to its sense of history and its sense of purpose.
>
> It is long past time that the Indian policies of the Federal government began to recognize and build upon the capacities and insights of the Indian people. Both as a matter of justice and enlightened social policy, we must begin to act on the basis of what the Indians themselves have long been telling us. The time has come to break decisively with the past and to create the conditions for a new era in which the Indian future is determined by Indian acts and Indian decisions.
>
> . . . Of the Department of the Interior's programs directly serving Indians, for example, only 1.5 per cent are presently under Indian control. Only 2.4 per cent of HEW's Indian health programs are run by Indians. The result is a burgeoning Federal bureaucracy, programs which are far less effective than they ought to be, and an erosion of Indian initiative and morale.
>
> . . . This, then, must be the goal of any new national policy toward the Indian people: to strengthen the Indian's sense of autonomy without threatening his sense of community. We must assure the Indian that he can assume control of his own life without being separated involuntarily from the tribal group. And we must make it clear that Indians can become independent of Federal control without being cut off from Federal concern and Federal support.

Since that message Presidents Nixon, Carter, Reagan, and Bush made concerted efforts, usually through Justice Department advocacy in the courts or lobbying for legislation, to secure Native American rights. Although successful in a few instances, they did not much improve the quality of Native American life, as the following sections reveal.

PRESENT-DAY NATIVE AMERICAN LIFE _____

Of all the minorities in America, according to government statistics on income, employment, and housing, the Native American is "the poorest of the poor." It is cruelly ironic that most of the Native Americans' problems are due not only to their subordinate position as a result of conquest but also to their insistence on their right to be different, to continue living as Native Americans. In a society that has long demanded assimilation, this insistence has not been popular.

Population

The 1990 census showed a 38 percent increase in the Native American population, rising from 1.4 million in 1980 to almost 2 million. One major reason for this growth is a Native American birth rate almost twice the national average.

As Figure 7.2 indicates, the age stratification of Native Americans and Alaska Natives is greater in the younger years than for the total U.S. population. The greater ratio of childbearing age groups suggests continued faster rates of population increase among Native Americans. They are far from the "vanishing American" others have claimed. Yet half live on reservations that cannot offer adequate economic support for those already living there.

Employment

Chronic unemployment is a serious problem, often over 50 percent on most reservations and sometimes as high as 80 percent. As many as 75 percent of

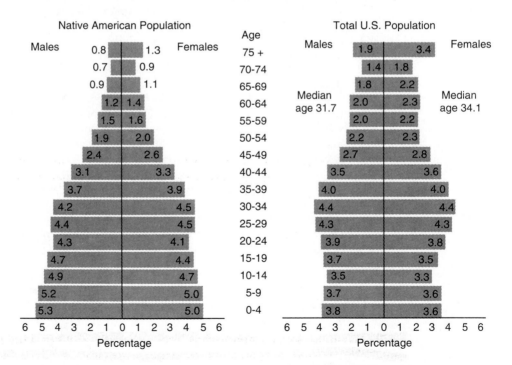

FIGURE 7.2
Native American Population, 1990
SOURCE: U.S. Bureau of the Census.

those who do work are on federal payrolls, providing education, health care, and social services to their fellow tribespeople. Others eke out an existence from fishing, raising a few head of sheep or cattle, or from a small garden if they are lucky enough to have water.

Government Efforts

In the 1980s the federal government invested $30 billion to lift reservations out of poverty.[28] Efforts to attract light industry and business to the reservations have had only limited success. The Economic Development Administration built 37 "industrial development parks on Native American lands but in 1989, five stood empty and only two had even achieved a 50 percent occupancy rate."[29] Imposed from above by bureaucracies and owned by outsiders, the businesses experienced high employee turnover. Preferring to hire women at lower wages, these businesses did little to aid the male unemployment problem.

Tribal Enterprise

Some tribes have been successful through their own efforts. The Mississippi Choctaw are one of the 15 largest employers in the state with five auto-parts factories and one greeting-card operation, and they have an 80 percent employment rate.[30] Similar successful operations can be found among the Salt River Pima Maricopa of Arizona, New Mexico's Jicarilla Apache, and the Devils Lake Sioux of North Dakota. The Oklahoma Cherokee now receive half of their funds from commercial ventures, including Cherokee Nation Industries, which constructs military components. Most successful have been the Maine Passamaquoddy, whose diversified investments from a land claims settlement have netted a $60 million profit from sale of a cement plant in 1988. Owning the rights to an antipollution technology known a recovery scrubber, which turns harmful sulphur dioxide and dust into limestone and fertilizer, the tribe has an assured financial future.[31]

Some tribes have improved their financial situation with casinos. They are allowed by federal law to offer any versions of gambling that are not specifically prohibited in other parts of the state. Most of these casinos are little more than glorified bingo halls, some permitting poker. About half of the 314 reservations now have casinos of some sort. Most successful are the Florida Seminole just outside Miami and the Cabazon tribe near Palm Springs, California.

Life Expectancy

The demographic statistics (see Table 7.2) testify to the harshness and deprivation of reservation life and the despair accompanying it.[32] The average life span in some tribes is 45 years.[33] Nationally, the Native American life span is about 10 years less than the national average. Leading causes of death among Native American adults are accidental deaths (particularly involving motor vehicles), chronic liver disease and cirrhosis, diabetes, homicide, and suicide—all higher than the national average.[34]

| TABLE 7.2 | AGE-ADJUSTED DEATH RATES IN THE UNITED STATES PER 100,000 POPULATION: 1986–1988 |

Cause of Death	Native Americans	All Races	Ratio
Cardiovascular disease	169.8	210.6	0.8
Malignant neoplasms	88.7	132.9	0.7
Motor vehicle accidents	56.1	19.5	2.9
All other accidents	42.4	15.2	2.8
Chronic liver disease and cirrhosis	28.3	9.1	3.1
Diabetes mellitus	26.4	9.8	2.7
Pneumonia, influenza	18.6	13.1	1.4
Suicide	17.8	11.7	1.5
Homicide	16.4	8.6	1.9
Tuberculosis	2.9	0.5	5.8

SOURCE: U.S. Mortality Rates: Monthly Vital Statistics Report, NCHS, DHHS Pub. No. (PHS)89–1120, Vol. 38, No. 5, Supplement, September 26, 1989, Table 12.

Suicide deaths among Native American youth are more than twice (26.3 per 100,000) that of the general population (12.4 per 100,000).[35] Recent studies reveal that teens who take their lives typically belong to tribes with loose social integration that are undergoing rapid socioeconomic change. Groups with a high risk of suicide are more likely to be substance abusers, had or caused a pregnancy, believed their family didn't care, and experienced death by suicide among family and friends.[36] A possible related factor is that 11 percent of native teens reported that at least one of their parents was dead, compared with 5 percent of teens in a comparison survey of white teens in rural Minnesota.[37]

Alcohol Abuse

The most serious social problem facing Native Americans today is alcohol abuse, which is a major factor in their high mortality rate. Death from alcoholism is five times the national average. Native American people 25 to 34 years old have a terminal liver cirrhosis rate nearly 15 times the national rate.[38] Seventy-five to 80 percent of Native American suicides involve the use of alcohol. Crimes related to alcohol and other drugs occur up to 20 times more often among Native Americans than among whites in the same geographic areas.[39]

Despite popular misconceptions about Native American susceptibility to alcohol problems, no research to date has found Native Americans to be different from other people regarding the physiology of alcohol metabolism.[40]

Reservation gambling casinos offer Native Americans employment opportunities and a source of tribal revenue. This Lakota Sioux gambling casino with slot machines, blackjack and roulette tables is much more sophisticated than many other reservation casinos which are usually limited to bingo and perhaps poker. *(Rick Gerharter/Impact Visuals)*

Moreover, some recent evidence suggests that tribal people may actually drink less than the total U.S. population. Surveyed tribes had a 40 percent drinking rate compared to the national rate of 70 percent.[41]

Problem drinking sets in early among Native American youth. A 1992 report from a nationwide survey identified high emotional stress and no sense of a future among adolescents correlating with a dramatic rise in heavy drinking that triples between the seventh and twelfth grades to 27.3 percent. Although white youths' alcohol consumption begins to diminish after age 22, no comparable decline occurs for Native American youth.[42]

Michael Nofz suggests that cultural marginality is a key factor in understanding problem drinking among Native Americans.[43] On the one hand Native Americans seek to maintain a tribal identity and traditional cultural heritage, even though they are not always certain what their heritage means in the context of modern life; on the other hand they desire the success in the world of work and careers, the respect, and standard-of-living goals set by the dominant society. Inner conflict results because the standards of the two worlds within which the Native American attempts to adapt are not always consistent. What mainstream society deems appropriate may be undesirable according to tribal values, or vice versa.

A reservation man, for example, who works at an off-reservation business must engage in compartmentalized behavior strategies to avoid scorn in either world. At work he must display individual competitiveness and strive to obtain recognition and reward. But if he carries this behavior into his tribal setting, traditional tribal members will scorn him as an "apple" or a "white Indian." Alcohol soon emerges as a solution to temporarily ease frustrations and to minimize a growing sense of inadequacy when negative judgments of personal conduct are made by either group.[44]

Education

Some significant changes have occurred since 1969 when a Special Senate Subcommittee on Indian Education issued a scathing report on the BIA school system, particularly its boarding schools. This report, which was largely ignored, offered powerful arguments supporting Native American self-determination:

> We are shocked at what we discovered. . . .
>
> We have developed page after page of statistics. These cold figures mark a stain on our national conscience, a stain which has spread slowly for hundreds of years. They tell a story, to be sure. But they cannot tell the whole story. They cannot, for example, tell of the despair, the frustration, the hopelessness, the poignancy, of children who want to learn but are not taught; of adults who try to read but have no one to teach them; of families which want to stay together but are forced apart; or of 9-year-old children who want neighborhood schools but are sent thousands of miles away to remote and alien boarding schools.
>
> We have seen what these conditions do to Indian children and Indian families. The sights are not pleasant.
>
> We have concluded that our national policies for educating American Indians are a failure of major proportions. They have not offered Indian children—either in years past or today—an educational opportunity anywhere near equal to that offered the great bulk of American children. Past generations of lawmakers and administrators have failed the American Indian. Our own generation thus faces a challenge—we can continue the unacceptable policies and programs of the past or we can recognize our failures, renew our commitments, and reinvest our efforts with new energy.
>
> . . . Creative, imaginative, and above all, relevant educational experiences can blot the stain on our national conscience. This is the challenge the subcommittee believes faces our own generation.[45]

In 1976 the American Indian Policy Review Commission issued a report on education criticizing the BIA for not acting to remedy any of the problems the subcommittee had pointed out.[46] Particularly singled out were the 19 boarding schools, which the Commission called "dumping grounds for students with serious social and emotional problems" that "do not rehabilitate" but "do more harm than good."[47]

The commission reported that the official BIA policy of sending students to the school closest to home is in reality not practiced.[48] Alaskan Native American children have been sent to Fort Sill, Oklahoma. Others who are classified as "problems," such as the girl in Washington State who objected to a history test that called her ancestors "dirty savages," also are sent to distant boarding schools. In another report the commission also criticized the locations of the schools:

> The sites of these schools were determined not merely by financial considerations of the Government, but by the conscious intention of forcing a separation between Indian parents and children and between Indian children and the idea of the reservation.[49]

Others have frequently commented on the teaching of American culture and history in reservation schools and on insensitivity and nonreceptivity to Native American culture and history. One typical example is a composition given to Chippewa children at a reservation school in the Northwest: "Why we are all happy the Pilgrims landed."

The Educational Amendments Act of 1978 gave substantial control of Native American education programs to the local Native American communities. With policy setting and program guidance being the responsibility of local school boards and local school authorities, a curriculum that considers the unique aspects of Native American culture and heritage now exists. Bilingual Native American language programs in 17 states both help preserve the ancestral language as well as teach English to those children raised learning only their tribal language.

Today 12 percent of Native Americans are aged 10 to 19, compared to 9 percent of other U.S. racial-ethnic groups. Yet compared to those same minority groups, fewer Native American teens will graduate from high school (55.4% vs. 66.5%), fewer still will complete college (7.4% vs. 16.2%).[50] Put differently, if 100 Native American students enter the ninth grade, only 55 will graduate from high school. Of these graduates, fewer than half will enter college, and only about seven of these will earn a degree.

Approximately 80 percent of Native American students attend public schools. The rest, about 40,000 students, attend 180 BIA-operated schools in 23 states, two-thirds of which are boarding schools and one-third on reservations.[51] Isolated reservation students often rise quite early to catch a school bus and spend long hours traveling long distances when weather permits such travel. Similarly, many secondary students continue to be bused over long distances to continue their education.

Another 1978 legislative act, the Tribally Controlled Community College Assistance Act, provides federal grant money to 24 tribally controlled colleges in 11 western and midwestern states. Enrolled are about 10,000 Native Americans, a full-time equivalent of about 4,500 students.[52]

Housing

One of the most visible signs of deprivation is reservation housing, called "open-air slums" by some. Mostly located down back roads unseen by reservation visitors, the various tribes live in small, overcrowded western-style houses, in mobile homes, or in hogans—traditional, one-room, eight-sided log houses with sod roofs. One in four Native American homes lacks indoor plumbing. Native Americans without a convenient water supply are obliged to haul it from a mile or more away. One in seven homes lacks electricity.[53] Because many Native Americans live in crowded dwellings without running water, infectious diseases spread more rapidly. A 1990 study of New Mexico Native Americans found their mortality rate from such infectious diseases as tuberculosis, influenza, pneumonia, kidney infection, meningitis, and parasitic diseases to be greater than that for other population groups.[54]

NATURAL RESOURCES

Trappers, settlers, oil drillers, and large companies have continually encroached on Native American territory to obtain natural resources or fertile land. The situation is no different today. The need for water and energy has led government and industry to look covetously at reservation land once considered worthless. In July 1978 2,000 Native Americans participated in a 2,700-mile march to Washington, DC. There they demonstrated against several proposed bills that would have allowed strip mining and siphoning of ground water from tribal land, issues still pertinent today.

Exploitation and Emerging Control

The 53 million acres held by 22 western tribes contain much of the nation's richest reserves of natural gas, oil, coal, and uranium, worth billions of dollars. In fact, one-third of the nation's low-sulfur coal and at least half the uranium deposits are on tribal land. For some tribes, such as the oil-rich Osage in Oklahoma, benefits are being realized. Yet only 14 percent of Native Americans live on reservations that receive natural resource revenues equal to $500 or more annually per reservation resident.[55]

Even when a tribe thinks its timber, mining, or fishing royalties have secured it a measure of financial stability, that may not be the case. A 1982 federal audit, for example, found that decades of sloppy bookkeeping by the Bureau of Indian Affairs had left the Red Lake band of Minnesota Chippewa more than $800,000 short in their trust fund. In 1989 the BIA simply deducted $1.2 million from their account to adjust for accounting mistakes, forcing the tribe to sue for recovery of its money. Federal auditors in September 1991 warned that fiscal mismanagement of the $2 billion in BIA trust funds may cost the taxpayers untold millions to cover hundreds of tribal claims.[56]

Sometimes BIA ineptitude results in significant underpayment to the tribes from mining and lumbering companies. The government's own watchdog, the General Accounting Office, has also criticized the BIA for frequently failing to protect Native American interests when encouraging and approving

On most reservations, Native Americans live away from areas where tourists are permitted. This small, cluttered village on the Navajo reservation in Moenkopi, Arizona, is typical of clustered housing sites in the Southwest. Northwest tribes often live in substandard housing in isolated wooded areas. *(M.B. Duda/ Photo Researchers)*

extraction of natural resources. The following examples are but a few of many present-day efforts to victimize the Native Americans for the sake of their land's riches.

Northern Cheyenne

Much of the 440,000-acre Cheyenne Reservation in Montana sits atop a 60-foot-deep deposit of high-quality coal. At BIA urging the tribe approved a vaguely worded agreement that gave industry virtual carte blanche to use 243,808 acres—more than half the reservation.[57] The company was free to strip-mine and to build railroad lines, vast industrial complexes of power and conversion plants, and non-Native American towns for its workers. As the mammoth consequences became known to the Cheyenne and to environmentalists, organized opposition arose to contain this development and to protect the land. The struggle continues to this day, as the tribe battles coal miners and railroad companies on its lands.

Navajo

More than 180,000 Navajo live on the nation's largest Native American reservation; its 16 million acres in the four corners where Arizona, New Mexico, Colorado, and Utah meet exceeds the size of West Virginia. This is a harsh, barren land where 2.5 billion tons of coal and 55 million pounds of uranium deposits remain in the ground waiting to be mined.[58] Ironically, high-voltage wires run across vast tracts of the Navajo Nation carrying electricity to California but not to thousands of the Navajo living beneath them.

Like most Western tribes the Navajo have an agricultural economy. An 1868 treaty guaranteed them basic water rights, but the U.S. Bureau of Reclamation and the Army Corps of Engineers built a dam upstream, diverting their water to non-Native American users. Water levels dropped, fish died, and the Navajo farmland suffered. After years of protest, a massive federal irrigation project, begun in 1976, now brings water to part of the Navajo arid land in northwestern New Mexico.

Lake Superior Chippewa

In northern Wisconsin the Chippewa fight an annual battle on the shores of Lake Minocqua when they exercise their fishing rights. Resentful local fishermen stage vocally abusive and sometimes violent protests at the site, fearful that the Native Americans' spearfishing will deplete the supply of walleyed pike and drive away sport fishermen. Although the Chippewa have voluntarily limited the size of their annual catch, the protesters' animosity continues. Bumper stickers appeared in 1989, reading, "Save a walleye. Spear a pregnant squaw." Antifishing protesters carried spears topped with fake Native American heads and hurled rocks and insults.[59] A bulletin board at a bowling alley in the northern Wisconsin town of Eagle Rock in 1990 warned against shooting Native Americans:

> That will only get more sympathy for them, but if you put holes in their boats, they can't spear and holes in their tires they can't get to the lakes. Stop being wimps. Yelling or simply watching will not intimidate anyone. . . . Force confrontation and overreactions, escalate. . . . Nothing will change until you escalate.[60]

Claiming "the exercise of treaty rights is not in tune with contemporary society," northern Wisconsin protesters have aligned with the Citizens Equal Rights Alliance (CERA), a national anti-Native American organization. Stop Treaty Abuse (STA) claims 3,000 members and has publicly dedicated itself to pursuing a course of disruption until all citizens can equally use resources on Native American lands. Understandably, large development corporations support these organizations.

Council of Energy Resource Tribes

Twenty-five Native American tribes formed the Council of Energy Resource Tribes (CERT) in 1975. Modeled after the OPEC oil cartel, Native American leaders believed this new organization could prevent further exploitation and secure far greater revenues for tribal mineral resources. Aided by a $2 million federal grant, CERT hired technical experts to negotiate with the private corporations. An early spectacular success was a contract with Atlantic Richfield (ARCO) for $78 million in tribal royalties over a 20-year period, after the company had opened negotiations with a $300,000 offer.

CERT has doubled in the number of tribes represented and has expanded its services to include advisement on monitoring nuclear-waste management on tribal lands. An apparently effective economic coalition, CERT also seeks to increase Native American youth employment through increasing their engineering and technical skills and by developing proposals to industrialize reservations by using royalties from resource development. Critics, including other Native Americans, worry about environmental destruction and disruption of traditional values and culture through extensive mining operations.

"Dances with Garbage"

With landfills filling up or shutting down because pollutants are leaching into groundwater, disposal companies are looking for new cheap sites for the 320 billion tons of solid waste and 3 billion tons of toxic waste materials produced annually in the United States.[61] Native American lands are not subject to the same set of environmental regulations as the rest of the country. Poor, but possessing large tracts of isolated land areas, Native Americans in recent years have thus seen their reservations become targets of proposed toxic dumping grounds. More than 100 tribes have been approached, with most of them rejecting the disposal companies' cash offers and employment promises.[62]

In contrast the Rosebud Sioux tribal council in South Dakota voted to allow O&G Industries of Connecticut to build a 6,000-acre mega-regional trash site on the reservation. Previously rejected at the neighboring Pine Ridge Reservation, the huge dump would hold millions of tons of garbage, incinerator ash, coal ash, sewage sludge ash, and shredded tires. Despite company promises of financial riches for its 18,000 members, tribal activists are leading a major opposition drive to reverse the decision.[63]

Another tribe had little choice about its contact with waste. The St. Regis Mohawk Reservation on the St. Lawrence River near Massena, New York, has been inundated with chemical garbage for decades. Located downstream, downwind, and downgradient in an industrial corridor extending 100 miles west to Lake Ontario, the reservation suffers from both aquatic poisoning and airborne toxins and has experienced a high number of birth defects. Its water and land food chain is permeated with PCBs discharged by General Motors, Reynolds Metal, and other corporate polluters. Although the Environmental Protection Agency in 1983 fined GM $507,000 for illegal use and disposal of PCBs, the largest fine ever levied for violations of the Toxic Substance Control Act, problems remain. Noxious odors, dead marine life along 1,000 feet of shoreline, and high toxicity everywhere have ravaged the ecosystem.[64]

Water Rights

Nevada's Pyramid Lake, a spectacular 30-mile expanse of water, belongs to the Paiute, whose water rights the government is supposed to protect. Instead, in 1906 it developed an irrigation project diverting 9.8 billion gallons of water each year before it reaches the lake. By the 1940s the water level had dropped 80 feet, killing the trout on which the Paiute depended. In 1944 the U.S. Supreme Court decided the water rights case, awarding the tribe $8 million in damages. However, in settling the case on their behalf, the Justice Department did nothing about the fish crisis, the water level in the lake, or restrictions for future irrigation. Finally, the Justice Department, formally confessing its "breach of faith with the Indians," petitioned the Supreme Court to reopen the case to allow the Paiute to refill their lake.[65]

Water rights cases are rather complex, however. The McCarran Amendment of 1952 waived the sovereign immunity of the United States for Native American water rights in general stream adjudications, granting state courts the power to decide. Also, although the U.S. Supreme Court has been reluctant to deny to Native Americans prerogatives to water rights, it has occasionally denied Native American claims if the case had previously been adjudicated. Such was the case with Pyramid Lake; the court rejected the Paiute claim because of an earlier decision in 1940.[66]

Water disputes are sharpest in the Southwest, where the water table is the lowest. Urban sprawl and agribusiness have prompted whites to sink deep wells around reservations in Arizona siphoning off the water reserves of several tribes. In New Mexico, for example, farmers simply "appropriated a viable water system the Pueblo Tribe had built two hundred years before Cortes set sail," leaving that tribe without an adequate supply.[67]

Water rights are the Western tribes' most valuable rights, providing a basis for achieving economic independence. Loss of water dooms them to an even worse existence. On the bright side, 10 water rights cases were settled in the 1980s at a total cost of $600 million. In 1990 Congress approved payment of $25 million to the Mojave Apache of the Fort McDowell Reservation near Phoenix. In 1992 a $56.5 million settlement with the Northern Cheyenne in Montana was delayed for budgetary reasons. Another 14 disputes are under negotiation.[68]

RED POWER

As Alvin M. Josephy, Jr. has noted, the Native Americans have never been silent about their needs and wishes.[69] Beginning with Seneca Chief Red Jacket's visit to Washington in 1792, Native Americans have repeatedly tried to tell the federal authorities what their people wanted and what was acceptable to them. Because they were seen as savages, the Native Americans found that government representatives usually ignored their views. When the forced removal programs and the bloodshed came to an end in the late nineteenth century, the government began trying to change the reservation Native Americans' way of life, to eliminate their poverty, and to encourage further integration. In the twentieth century Native American militancy was quite rare until the 1960s. In the mid-1960s the Native Americans changed their approach, partly because the social climate was different. Many social forces were at work—the civil rights movement, the Vietnam protest, the idealism of the Great Society, and a growing social awareness in society itself. Perhaps taking their cue from other movements, a new generation of Native American leaders asserted themselves.

Pan-Indianism

This recent social movement, which attempts to establish an American Indian ethnic identity instead of just a tribal identity, has its roots in the past. The growing Iroquois Confederation of the seventeenth century, the mobility and social interaction among the Plains Tribe in the nineteenth century, and the spread of the Ghost Dance religion were all early examples of Pan-Indianism. As Native American youths found comfort in one another's presence, first in boarding schools and later in urban areas, they found a commonality in their identity as Native Americans.

From this emerging group consciousness evolved several organizations dedicated to preserving Native American identity and gaining greater political clout. The Society of American Indians (SAI) and the National Congress of American Indians (NCAI) were the first twentieth-century attempts to organize. More recently the National Indian Youth Council (NIYC) and the American Indian Movement (AIM) have attracted many young people who object to discrimination and white domination. The NIYC staged fish-ins to protest treaty violations of Native American rights in Washington State. In the ensuing legal battle, the Supreme Court ultimately ruled in favor of the Native Americans.

The Pan-Indian movement has not been completely accepted, however, even among young people. Many Native Americans are anxious to preserve their tribal identities and prefer to work for the cultural enrichment and social betterment of their own tribe rather than to engage in a national movement. As part of this tribal emphasis, these individuals also learn and teach their people silversmithing, pottery and blanket making, and other crafts that are part of their heritage. In an effort to increase tribal pride and economic welfare, they also establish cultural centers to exhibit and sell their artistic works and wares.

Alcatraz

On November 20, 1969, a group of 78 Native Americans under the name "Indians of All Tribes" occupied Alcatraz Island, a former federal prison. This move, the first militant Native American action in the twentieth century, was both symbolic and an effort to establish a cultural center. The sarcasm in this excerpt from their proclamation attacks the paternalism, neglect, and deprivation fostered on American tribes past and present:

> We will give to the inhabitants of this island a portion of that land for their own, to hold in perpetuity—for as long as the sun shall rise and the rivers go down to the sea. We will further guide the inhabitants in the proper way of living. We will

offer them our religion, our education, our life-ways, in order to help them achieve our level of civilization and thus raise them and all their white brothers up from their savage and unhappy state. We offer this treaty in good faith and wish to be fair and honorable in our dealings with all white men. We feel that this so-called Alcatraz Island is more than suitable for an Indian Reservation, as determined by the white man's own standards. By this we mean that this place resembles most Indian reservations in that:

1. It is isolated from modern facilities, and without adequate means of transportation.
2. It has no fresh running water.
3. It has inadequate sanitation facilities.
4. There are no oil or mineral rights.
5. There is no industry and so unemployment is very great.
6. There are no health care facilities.
7. The soil is rocky and nonproductive; and the land does not support game.
8. There are no education facilities.
9. The population has always exceeded the land base.
10. The population has always been held as prisoners and kept dependent upon others.

Further, it would be fitting and symbolic that ships from all over the world, entering the Golden Gate, would first see Indian land, and thus be reminded of the true history of this nation. This tiny island would be a symbol of the great lands once ruled by free and noble Indians.[70]

This militant action did not succeed. The group's cohesiveness collapsed when the 12-year-old daughter of its leader, Michael Oakes, a Mohawk, accidentally fell down an elevator shaft on the island and died. Oakes, the unifying and motivating force, left Alcatraz with his daughter's body. Federal authorities then stepped in and removed the Native Americans. Oakes himself was later shot to death in California, supposedly mistaken for a trespasser. Today Alcatraz Island is a tourist attraction as a former prison, and its conversion to a gambling casino has been discussed.

Wounded Knee

On February 27, 1973, about 200 members of the American Indian Movement seized control of the village of Wounded Knee, South Dakota, taking 11 hostages. The location was symbolic because Wounded Knee had been the site of the last Native American resistance in 1890, when 150 Sioux, including men, women, and children, were massacred by the U.S. Cavalry. Many were killed from behind, and the wounded were left to die in a blizzard the following night.[71]

A 71-day siege following the seizure was a staged media event aimed at directing national attention to the plight of the Native Americans. Some Native American leaders criticized the action as rash, but most Native Americans appeared to be in sympathy with it. The holdout ended May 8, 1973, with two

Native Americans killed, injuries on both sides, including a U.S. marshal paralyzed, and $240,000 in damages to property.[72]

Several months later the leaders—Dennis Banks, a Chippewa, and Russell Means, a Sioux—were brought to trial on charges directly related to the siege at Wounded Knee. The presiding judge dismissed all charges, severely criticizing the FBI and the Justice Department for misconduct in withholding or doctoring documents, conducting illegal wiretaps, and spending money on liquor and women for a Native American progovernment witness. Later Banks and Means were imprisoned on related charges.

Among other things the militants had demanded that the government deal with the Sioux on the basis of an 1868 treaty that guaranteed them dominion over the vast Northern Plains between the Missouri River and the Rocky Mountains, land that the U.S. government confiscated in 1876. That Native American land claim has been described by Sioux representatives as the "largest, most historically and socially significant and, in terms of time taken in the courts, the oldest Native American land claim on record."

THE COURTS

With more than 700 Native Americans as lawyers by 1990, legal efforts to honor treaty rights have been more numerous and successful. In 1980 the U.S. Supreme Court reaffirmed a lower court's award of $105 million for illegal seizure of the Black Hills to 60,000 Sioux living on eight reservations in South Dakota, Montana, and Nebraska. Native American activist Russell Means urged Sioux chiefs to reject the U.S. offer and demand the land instead, claiming the Black Hills land was "our graveyard, our church, the center of our universe and the birthplace of our people . . . everything we hold sacred and dear, and this is the reason it is not for sale."[73] The Oglala Sioux then filed suit for return of the western half of South Dakota and for $1 billion in damages for "hunger, malnutrition, disease, and death" caused by loss of the land, also asking for tribal hunting rights on the land, a ban on removal of natural resources, and a ban on federal interference with Sioux use of the land for "subsistence and religious purposes."[74] In June 1981 the U.S. Court of Appeals rejected the suit, saying it had no jurisdiction in the matter because Congress had created the Indian Claims Commission, since disbanded, as the sole remedy for Black Hills claims.[75] In 1987 Senator Bill Bradley of New Jersey took up the Sioux cause, introducing a bill to return 1.3 million federally owned acres in South Dakota to the Native Americans. The land, most of it part of the Black Hills National Forest, would become a national park operated by the Sioux. Heavy opposition from South Dakota political leaders has stopped the bill's passage.

The cash settlement for the Black Hills partially rested on a 1950 precedent, when the U.S. Court of Claims awarded $31.2 million to the Colorado Ute for lands illegally taken from them. This amounted to about $10,000 for each tribal adult and child. A precedent also existed for return of land. The Taos

Pueblo of New Mexico had regarded the lands at and near Blue Lake as sacred since the fourteenth century. Demanding the land back from the Forest Service instead of a cash settlement, the Taos did regain 48,000 acres in 1970 through Congressional action at President Nixon's urging.

In spring 1977 the Passamaquoddy and Penobscot laid claim to about 5 million acres, or nearly one-third of Maine. The Carter administration threw its support behind the Native Americans and in 1978 reached an out-of-court settlement: $25 million cash, $1.7 million a year for 15 years, and 300,000 acres at $5 an acre. The basis for these claims was that the Native American land had been bargained away in violation of the Nonintercourse Act of 1790, which reserved to Congress the power to negotiate with Native American tribes. With professional advice the tribes developed an investment portfolio that included manufacturing plants for audiocassettes and videocassettes and the largest cement factory in New England. Unemployment among the two tribes has dropped from 50 to 8 percent since the investments began.[76]

Elsewhere, after losing 76 out of 80 court battles with various Native American tribes, the State of Washington broke new ground, dealing with the tribes as if they were governments. Reaching agreement on salmon management, they are now also cooperating on health policy, child-welfare agreements, and water rights. Wyoming, Colorado, and New Mexico have also negotiated directly with tribes in their borders to avoid costly and possibly losing court battles.[77] In New York State, the Mohawks, Oneida, Cayuga, Onondaga, Seneca, and Tuscarora Nations of the Iroquois Confederacy all have sizable land claims the state is trying to resolve. The state needs to do so because the U.S. Supreme Court ruled in 1985 that New York's treaty with the Oneida violated the Nonintercourse Act, setting the precedent ruling for its treaties with the others. As of 1993 no resolution had been reached.[78]

BUREAU OF INDIAN AFFAIRS (BIA) _____

The BIA, a government agency, can trace its origin to 1824. It has many critics, among Native Americans as well as among federal officials, sociologists, and anthropologists. Some view it as a bureaucracy staffed by some able, dedicated people who are restricted and frustrated by an inefficient organization, and others see it staffed by self-serving, unsympathetic people who simply do not belong there. A 1969 Special Report to the President stated:

> There are undoubtedly weak, poor, and inefficient men within the Bureau. Some enter the system, especially at the area level, by patronage: some should never have been employed by the Bureau; some are poor because of inadequate training and orientation after they were employed; and some were good originally but, after many frustrations and defeats, gave up. . . . One of the scores of "weaknesses," with which it appears unable to cope, is the continued presence within the Bureau of key personnel who long since should have been removed from it. . . . Many members of Indian communities are driven to desperation, some even to suicide, as a result of ineptitude, indifference or lethargy on the part of a poor superintendent or area official. Yet the record of the 1960's con-

tains documentation of Commissioner Nash turning down Indian appeals to relieve them of intolerable agency personnel by telling them he would not remove a man while he was under fire, and of Commissioner Bennett answering tribal complaints of frustration and negativism with the retort that he was not interested in discussing "criticism of the BIA."[79]

Native American hostility toward the BIA goes beyond complaints about unsympathetic, incompetent, or even patronizing personnel; it is directed against its very structure. Although different government agencies touch all Americans in some ways, few non-Native Americans realize how totally the BIA dominates Native Americans' lives. The agency is in charge of everything, from tribal courts and schools to social services and law enforcement on the reservation. It must approve virtually every tribal decision on the use of tribal resources—even the disposition of cash settlements that the Navajo and other tribes have won in lawsuits against the BIA itself.[80]

A BIA official's mere supposition that certain individuals cannot properly handle their money or their personal affairs is sufficient to require formal BIA approval of any transactions those persons make. Only by comprehending the total pervasiveness of this bureaucracy can one begin to fathom the dependence, despair, and frustration the system engenders.

In the early 1970s there was a slight shakeup at the BIA, ostensibly to increase Native American self-determination. However, little really changed, as the American Indian Policy Review Commission, made up of 10 executives from private industry, indicated in its report to Congress in 1976. It concluded that every area of personnel management in the BIA was "inadequate" and recommended a massive restructuring to bring decision-making closer to tribal level.[81] Recent laws have made some of these recommendations official policy.

A 1984 Presidential Commission Report reported that the BIA spent two-thirds of its $1 billion annual budget on itself and contracted only 27 percent of its programs to the tribes. Noting that the BIA moved too slowly in assisting tribes to gain more economic independence, the commission concluded that the BIA should be disbanded.[82]

Yet the BIA has continued with a sorry record of waste, corruption, and choking red tape. Its fiscal mismanagement mentioned earlier has reached epic proportions in other areas. According to estimates by the Interior Department and Congress, the BIA is losing the tribes $1 billion annually in oil and gas royalties.[83] A 1991 survey of government executives ranked the BIA the least respected of 90 agencies.[84]

URBAN NATIVE AMERICANS

Only 808,000 Native Americans, or 41 percent, live on reservations, with another 400,000, or 20 percent, living in nearby communities.[85] For the remaining 39 percent, an urban area is their place of residence (see Figure 7.3). Los Angeles claims the largest concentration (more than 87,000), although

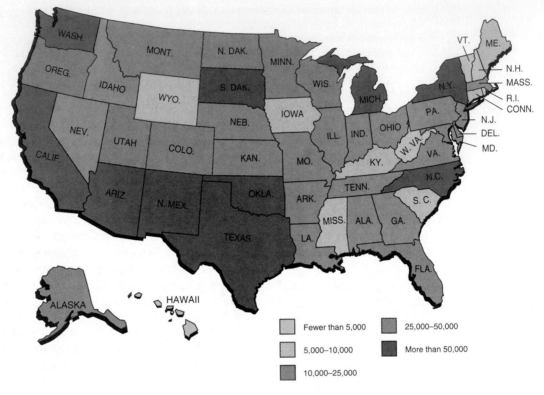

FIGURE 7.3
Where Native Americans Live
SOURCE: U.S. Bureau of the Census.

that constitutes but 0.6 percent of the city's total population. San Francisco's Native American population is almost 44,000, or 0.7 percent of the total. Other cities with sizable numbers, usually exceeding 16,000, are Boston, Chicago, Cleveland, Dallas, Detroit, Denver, Houston, St. Louis, Miami, Minneapolis–St. Paul, New York, Omaha, Philadelphia, Phoenix, San Diego, and Seattle.[86]

Although they are more scattered in residence than are the blacks or Chicanos, approximately three-fourths of the urban Native Americans live in poverty in the poorer sections of the cities. For example, 40 percent of the 14,000 Native Americans living in New York City in 1986 were unemployed, and eight out of nine families were living below the poverty level.[87] Usually lacking job skills and adequate education, Native Americans generally experience the same poverty they left behind but without the familiar environment and tribal support system. Researchers have found that urban migration does not immediately improve Native American well-being. Findings consistent with other studies show that although they are more likely to be working than those who remain behind on the reservations, urban Native Americans do not gain any improved income earnings until after five years of residence in the city.[88]

Even though urban Native Americans are not gathered in ethnic enclaves, all their other behavior patterns are similar to those of European immigrants. Situated in a social arena where they are the minority, they experience the culture shock of urban living away from the solidarity of the tribe. This shock sometimes leads to personal disorientation, and Native Americans seldom get relief or assistance from the dominant society.

> A recent incident in Los Angeles highlights the problem of adjustment. A newly-arrived Navaho, who spoke no English, became quite ill, and on the street approached a woman wearing a white uniform, in the belief that she was a nurse. The woman, a beautician, thought she was being attacked and had the Indian arrested. Unable to communicate with the man, the police placed him in a hospital where he was classified as an insane Mexican-American.[89]

The newcomers often seek out other Native Americans, usually of the same tribe, and frequent the same bars. Drunkenness is as serious a problem in the cities as on the reservations. The Native Americans suffer from lack of preparedness, disorientation, and lack of job skills, and as a result seek solace in drink from the harshness of the "cement prairies." In an in-depth study of Navajo migrants in Denver, Theodore D. Graves found drunkenness to be common as a result of structural and psychological variables. The Navajo had great difficulty adjusting to city life because their parents had not been role models for urban employment and because their cultural attitudes were dysfunctional for the work environment.[90] Custom and tradition, peer pressure, and drinking role models help to explain why they take out their frustration in drink.

Although urban Native Americans interact with whites, these relationships tend to be superficial and functional rather than intimate. Bruce A. Chadwick and Joseph H. Strauss, for example, found a fairly low level of assimilation among urban Native Americans in Seattle, especially in terms of political participation and conflict with the dominant power structure. They found no relation between length of time lived in the city and degree of structural assimilation. For almost all, assimilation was quite low.[91]

Native Americans who succeed in adapting to urban living, usually over a two- to five-year period, settle into semiskilled or skilled jobs. Once they have gained some economic security, they frequently move out of the city to racially mixed suburban areas. While this shows some degree of acculturation and convergent social adaptation, other evidence suggests this trend is limited. Many middle-class urban-adapted Native Americans form their own ethnic institutions, including churches, powwow clubs, social centers, and athletic leagues.[92]

One interesting Eastern public image of the urban Native American is that of the Iroquois ironworkers, who regularly work high atop the structural steel frames of skyscrapers being built in the urban centers. Although this group has a colorful image, most urban Native Americans are less visible to the non–Native American society. Consequently, they have not received as much

| BOX 7.4 | THE INTERNATIONAL SCENE |

In 1990 near Oka, a small town of 1,800 residents in Quebec Province near Montreal, a dispute erupted between Mohawk Indians and municipal officials who had approved building a tract of houses and expanding a nine-hole municipal golf course on land claimed by the tribe. On March 11 a heavily armed Mohawk group barricaded an access road.

After a four-month standoff, about 100 members of the Sûreté du Quebec (SQ) tactical force used assault rifles, concussion grenades, and tear gas to storm the barricade. Well-prepared in manpower and weapons, the Native Americans waged a fierce three-hour battle, successfully driving back the police and shooting one officer to death. Both sides erected three sets of barricades facing each other at different access points.

Within hours a second group of Mohawk blockaded the Mercier Bridge, the main access to Montreal from several suburban communities on the south shore of the St. Lawrence River. Other Indians across Canada mounted demonstrations and brief blockades in support of the Mohawk. As pressure escalated, Mohawk leaders warned in August that any raid would result in far more violence than last time.

Police refused to allow deliveries of food and medical supplies, even from the Canadian Red Cross. Mohawk leaders charged that the government planned to starve them into submission and asked the U.N. Working Group on Indigenous Populations to investigate alleged human rights abuses in Oka.

Faced with a public relations disaster and the adamant Mohawk stance, the federal government in Ottawa intervened in September to purchase the disputed property for the Mohawk to claim as their own.

Canadian Indians everywhere looked beyond Oka, some saying the tactics of confrontation offered their people a last chance to escape decades of poverty, despair, and social disintegration. "If we don't do anything in the nineties," said Regina Crowchild, president of the Indian Association of Alberta, "we will be finished. Our leaders will be gone and our younger generation will be lost."

attention from sociologists as have those on reservations.[93] Urban living, however, helped to spawn the Pan-Indian movement. Contact with members of other tribes raised a group consciousness of being Native American, which led to an attempt to improve the lot of all by united action.

From the Pueblo, the first penthouse dwellers in the United States, to the city-dwelling Native American of today, urban living does not appear to have encouraged more rapid movement into the mainstream of American society. Today's urban Native Americans are relatively invisible, but that does not necessarily mean they have assimilated. There may have been some degree of acculturation, but most urban Native Americans attempt to preserve their ethnic identity and do not interact socially with non–Native Americans to any noticeable degree.

CULTURAL IMPACT

Perhaps no other ethnic group has had as great an impact on American culture as have the Native Americans, primarily because they were already here, and the whites, who had to adapt to a new land, found it advantageous to learn from them. Cities, towns, counties, states, rivers, lakes, mountains, and other geographic entities by the thousands bear Native American names today. More than 500 words in our language are Native American, including *wigwam, succotash, tobacco, papoose, chipmunk, squash, skunk, toboggan, opossum, tomahawk, moose, mackinaw, hickory, pecan, raccoon, cougar, woodchuck,* and *hominy.*[94]

The Native Americans' knowledge of herbs and the more than 80 plants they domesticated brought whites a wide variety of new tastes. Native Americans introduced the Europeans to corn, white and sweet potatoes, kidney beans, tomatoes, peanuts, peppers, pumpkins, avocados, pineapples, maple sugar, chicle, and cacao, as well as tobacco and long-fiber cotton. The Native Americans' knowledge of medicinal plants is also part of their legacy:

> At least fifty-nine drugs, including coca (for cocaine and novocaine), curare (a muscle relaxant), cinochona bark (the source of quinine), cascara sagrada (a laxative), datura (a pain-reliever), and ephedra (a nasal remedy), were bequeathed to modern medicine by the Indians.[95]

The Native Americans also made various other objects that many Americans still use today. Some of these are canoes, kayaks, snowshoes, toboggans, moccasins, hammocks, pipes, parkas, ponchos, dog sleds, and rubber syringes. Native American influence on jewelry, clothing, art, architecture, literature, and Scouting is substantial. "Iron Eyes" Cody, a Native American actor, appeared in a 1980s television campaign against littering and symbolized the likeness between traditional Native American reverence for the land and the positions that conservationists support today. The Iroquois influence on the Constitution for House–Senate conferences has already been mentioned. Additionally, a new appreciation and adaptation of Native American child-rearing practices, group-directed activities, cooperatives, and ministrations to a patient's mental state are occurring.[96]

SOCIOLOGICAL ANALYSIS

Both Hollywood and the BIA use general Native American stereotypes in their treatment of Native Americans, even though extensive differences have always existed among tribes. In this chapter we have looked at their similarities and differences, noting the changes in attitude and public policy toward them over the years. Our three theoretical frameworks not only offer us a coherent approach to understanding the Native American experience but also provide insights into their problems.

The Functionalist View

Whites may never have fully understood the Native American social system, but anthropologists have found that their tribal societies functioned with a high degree of social organization. Kin relationships, from the nuclear family to a vast clan system, formed the basis of interaction. Clearly defined, interdependent work roles for young and old, male and female, in cooperative tasks of living gave them a rather stable society. Living off the land, their pantheist belief system made them practicing conservationists, maintaining a harmonious relationship with their natural environment. They were self-sufficient people with institutionalized practices of gift-giving and property control—such as willful destruction of one's property in a competitive display of wealth among some Pacific Coast tribes—which helped sustain a fairly equitable society without great extremes of poverty or riches.

Even early contacts with white explorers, trappers, and settlers usually were harmonious, both sides benefiting from what each had to offer the other. Dysfunctions occurred as Native Americans slipped into economic subservience, their way of life further threatened by encroachment on their land by steadily increasing numbers of white settlers. Whites saw the Native Americans as a hindrance to their making the land productive, forcibly removing the Native Americans as a nonvaluable part of their expanding society. Forced segregation on nonproductive reservations completely destroyed Native American society as a self-sufficient entity while reinforcing their culture. This systemic disorganization has been entrenched for over 100 years, restricting life opportunities and continuing the poor education, income, housing, health, alcoholism, and other pathologies that are costly to the society and the people who endure them.

Functionalists stress that the most effective method of resolving these problems is to reorganize our social institutions to put the Native American social system back into balance. However, the plight of the Native Americans is functional to the few reservation Native Americans employed by government agencies to provide services and to BIA employees whose jobs rest on continued paternalistic control, as well as to whites living near reservations who dominate that region's economy. These individuals, Native American and white alike, would find adjustments in the system dysfunctional to themselves and so do not advocate such changes.

The Conflict View

Lieberson's power theory provides an obvious model for studying Native American–white relations. As discussed in Chapter 4, here is a case of the white newcomers, superior in technology compared to the indigenous population, engaging in early conflict. The native population suffered numerical decline from warfare, disease, and disruption of sustenance activities, and their social institutions were undermined. Westward expansion, the nation's "Manifest Destiny," occurred by pushing aside the people whose land it was, without regard for their rights or wishes. Formal government agreements and treaties became meaningless to those in power if further land confiscation or exploitation for natural resources offered profits.

What about today? Who benefits from Native American deprivation now? The battle over the precious commodity of water in the Southwest offers one answer. Water is about the only entity these tribes possess that might be developed in order for them to achieve economic independence, but it has been literally stolen out from under them by mining companies, farmers, and land developers. Prolonged court battles enable powerful business interests to maintain their dams, wells, and aqueducts at the expense of the Native Americans. You have read of abuses of other natural resources as well. Why doesn't Congress do something? Legislators respond to public pressure. Those not living near Native Americans are not motivated or sufficiently concerned to insist that corrective action be taken. Those living near the Native Americans have a vested interest in maintaining the status quo, and they are the constituency with the power to influence their district's or state's national legislative representatives.

Yet Native Americans have achieved some positive results. They did so through an emerging group consciousness, whether tribal or Pan-Indian. Protest marches and demonstrations, militant acts of defiance—the Alcatraz, Wounded Knee, and BIA occupations—and class-action lawsuits have all brought public attention to their situation and some remedy. Conflict theory suggests that organized social movements by the exploited can bring about social change. Native Americans are increasingly discovering that redress of their grievances will not occur without concerted public pressure.

The Interactionist View

Consider again the words of Columbus, Franklin, and Catlin given earlier in this chapter. Ethnocentric views of Native American culture prompted a definition of the native population as inferiors, savages, even nonhumans! Once you create such social distance between groups by dehumanizing them, it is easy to justify any action taken against them. Compounding the negative labeling process was the racial differentiation. European Americans even viewed the acculturated Native Americans working as servants or laborers in colonial villages, or the entire Cherokee people, as members of an inferior race fit to be subordinated and relegated to a noninterfering, humble role in society.

For their part the Native Americans at first found white customs, fashions, and behavior amusing and astonishing. Later they perceived the whites as threats to their existence, and as liars and treacherous people. The ensuing hostilities reaffirmed each group's negative view of the other, the conflict ending with total subjugation of the Native Americans.

Government national policy today mistakenly interprets the needs of all tribes and treats all tribes alike: the biggest and smallest, the agrarian and fishing, the ones with economic land bases and the ones without. Many Americans view the Native Americans as perpetuating their own problems by remaining on reservations, depending on government support, and refusing to blend in with white society. Growing up on a reservation, Native Americans find security in tribal life, viewing the outside world as alien and without promise. Now the strangers in their own land, they believe it is their right to preserve their culture and to receive government assistance because of past abuses and broken treaties. With so many different interpretations of the current situation, the problems of the reservation appear difficult to resolve.

Retrospect

The white strangers who came among the Native Americans eventually outnumbered them, overpowered them, and changed their way of life. Once a proud and independent people, they were reduced to a state of poverty, despair, and dependency. The land they had known so well and roamed so freely was no longer theirs. Forced to live within an alien society that dominated all aspects of their lives, the Native Americans became strangers in their native land. Misunderstood and categorized as savages, they observed the taken-for-granted world of the whites more keenly than most whites did theirs.

Physical and cultural differences quickly became the basis for outgroup hostility as the groups competed for land and resources. Like other groups, the Native Americans faced the familiar patterns of stereotyping, prejudice, discrimination, and conflict because of their alleged inferiority and actual lack of power. Isolation on the reservations not only prevented the assimilation that most Native Americans did not desire anyway but also created for them a world of dependency and deprivation. Subsequent efforts at forced assimilation—boarding schools, relocation, and termination—failed because of Native American resiliency and the BIA's lack of thoroughness in personal preparation, assistance, and follow-through.

The Native Americans are still misunderstood and exploited. One, two, or three hundred years ago, those who did not live near the Native Americans idealized them, and those who were closest often abused and exploited them. It is no different today. Many people are oblivious to the Native Americans' problems and consider them quaint relics of the past, and others find them either undesirable or in the way. Some still want their land and will use almost any means to secure it. Native Americans still encounter discrimination in stores, bars, and housing, particularly in cities and near the reservations. They are frequently beaten or killed, and their property rights are infringed upon.

Since the 1960s, some Native Americans have become more aggressive. Many young, better-educated Native Americans are forgetting tribal differences and finding a common bond—Pan-Indianism—uniting in the struggle to protect what they have and to restore what they have lost. Others prefer a more individualist approach within the tribe. Some gains have been made and more non–Native Americans are becoming aware of the facts, but at present the Native Americans still are one of the poorest American minorities.

Review Questions

1. Why do some social scientists call the Native Americans the first victims of racism? Is racism an integral part of their experiences? Why?
2. Cite some examples of ethnocentrism and stereotyping regarding Native Americans.
3. Why is the power differential so crucial in understanding the Native Americans' past and present problems?
4. Why have most government efforts to "help" the Native Americans failed?
5. In what ways can it be said that little has changed in the exploitation of the Native Americans?

Suggested Readings

BAHR, HOWARD M., BRUCE A. CHADWICK, AND ROBERT C. DAY, EDS. *Native Americans Today: Sociological Perspectives*. New York: Harper & Row, 1972.
An excellent anthology covering studies and analyses of modern social problems among various Native American peoples on and off the reservation.

BROWN, DEE. *Bury My Heart at Wounded Knee*. New York: Bantam, 1972.
A Native American viewpoint of past Native American–white interrelations, offering a valuable corrective to traditional historical coverage.

DELORIA, VINE, JR., AND CLIFFORD M. LYTLE. *American Indians, American Justice*. Austin: University of Texas Press, 1983.
A fine sociohistorical examination of how judicial definitions and decisions have affected Native Americans from past to present.

FARB, PETER. *Man's Rise to Civilization*. New York: E. P. Dutton, 1968.
A fine, comprehensive study of North American tribes, from Pre-Columbian years to the industrial age, written in a very readable style.

JOSEPHY, ALVIN M., JR. *Now That the Buffalo's Gone: A Study of Today's American Indians*. New York: Alfred A. Knopf, 1982.
Excellent essays discussing changing Native American–government relations and current problems, such as tribal autonomy and water rights.

LAZARUS, EDWARD. *Black Hills, White Justice*. New York: HarperCollins, 1991.
A thorough chronicle of the ongoing legal battle of the Sioux nation for its land, from colonial times to the present.

PEROFF, NICHOLAS C. *Menominee Drums.* Norman: University of Oklahoma Press, 1982.
   Profiles the Wisconsin tribe in its successful efforts to overturn the termination of its reservation.

WAX, MURRAY L. *Indian Americans: Unity and Diversity.* Englewood Cliffs, NJ: Prentice-Hall, 1971.
   A succinct overview of Native Americans, from their past to the present, with emphasis on Pan-Indianism and tribal variation.

8

Kathy Sloan/Photo Researchers

East Asian Immigrants

Perceived as strangers because of their physical and cultural differences, Asian immigrants have often been broadly categorized as a single entity despite their diversity of nationality, history, language, customs, religion, politics, socioeconomic and educational background, or even subgroup variances within each nationality. With high immigration doubling their numbers from 3.5 million in 1980 to 7.3 million in 1990, Asians and Pacific Islanders are transforming the face of America.[1] In California one in 10 residents is now Asian; in San Francisco County 29 percent are Asian.[2] Throughout the United States the Asian American population is noticeably increasing, sometimes generating resentful, even hostile, reactions from other local residents (Figure 8.1).

SOCIOHISTORICAL PERSPECTIVE

Asians had some contact with the land and peoples of the Western Hemisphere before the beginning of recorded emigration in the mid-nineteenth century. Pottery and other archaeological finds suggest Japanese contact with Ecuador and Peru in 3000 B.C., and Chinese settlements in Mexico can be dated from the latter part of the Ming Dynasty (1368–1664). China played a role in early U.S. history, as New England merchants sought a monopoly on the lucrative China trade, an issue that became important in the struggle for American independence. Chinese sailors served on U.S. ships in the early 1800s, and a short-lived Chinese colony was established at Nootka Sound in 1792.[3] The first U.S. consul outside the Western Hemisphere was Samuel Shaw, assigned to Canton in 1794.

The Chinese first came to the United States during the gold rush (1849). Japanese, Koreans, and Filipinos came to the West Coast from 40 to 60 years later to seek their fortune. Some came to stay, but many came as sojourners, intending to return home after a limited work engagement. This view of America as a temporary overseas job opportunity, together with the white racism they faced and, in the case of the Chinese, a tradition of separate associations wherever they went, led the early Asian immigrants to form subsocieties. Throughout the first third of the twentieth century, when many Asians sought permanent residence in the United States, structural discrimination sharply limited their work and life opportunities.

The Chinese encountered racist hostility almost as soon as they arrived in California, despite the overwhelming need for manual labor in the mid-nineteenth century. They were often expelled from the mining camps, forbidden to enter schools, denied the right to testify in court, barred from obtaining citizenship, and even occasionally murdered. After the Civil War, anti-Chinese tensions increased, culminating in the Chinese Exclusion Act of 1882. The Japanese, Koreans, and Filipinos who came to the West Coast later encountered racism and discrimination similar to that which the Chinese had faced. Many of them went to work as farm laborers in rural areas or as unskilled workers in urban areas.

A major social problem affecting most Asian immigrants through the 1940s was the shortage of women. Not only was this imbalance in the sex ratio significant in their personal, social, and community life, but it was also the basis for racist complaints about prostitution or miscegenation. For the Chinese the sojourner orientation and the custom that wives should remain in the household of the husband's parents, and subsequent immigration restrictions mostly account for this disproportionate sex ratio. By the turn of the century the shortage of women had led to the rise of brothels in Chinatowns, and the Chinese were condemned for resorting to prostitutes. The Filipinos

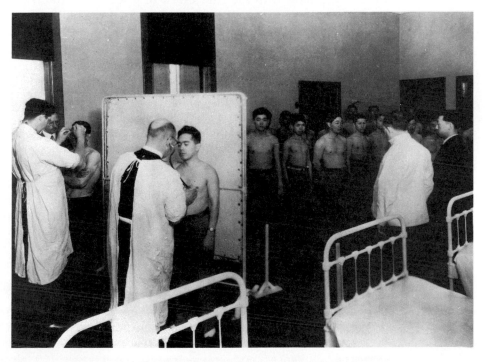

These Asian immigrant hopefuls receive medical exams at the Angel Island Immigration Station. Situated in San Francisco Bay, this western counterpart to Ellis Island was the primary processing center for Asian immigrants. Experiencing the same societal hostility as many Italian immigrants at Ellis Island, a large proportion of Asians were detained at Angel Island and/or rejected for admission into the country. *(Southern Pacific Transportation Corporation)*

also were mostly male and thus affected by the shortage of women. Whether the Asians patronized prostitutes or sought the company of white women, racists expressed moral indignation, and negative racial stereotypes resulted. Legislators in 14 states passed laws against miscegenation to keep Asians from marrying whites.

By 1920 the Japanese sex ratio was largely balanced. Following World War II, a greater number of females migrated to the United States, and the sex ratio for other Asian immigrant groups improved. Refugees and war brides from the Japanese, Korean, and Vietnamese wars account for part of the change, as do the brides of servicemen stationed overseas during the intervening years. The Immigration Act of 1965, in its relative-preference provisions, first ensured both sexes equal opportunity to enter the United States.

After World War II immigrants from these countries and from other parts of Southeast Asia were entering a much more industrialized American society. Many also came from lands that had been somewhat affected by Western influence. Some were political refugees, better educated and more skilled than earlier Asian immigrants. Many continued to prefer living in California, while others moved to the East Coast or elsewhere. Entering various occupations these postwar immigrants were spared the violent hostility of previous times, although they still encountered resentment and discrimination.

CULTURAL ATTRIBUTES

Because of greater social distance due to racial and cultural differences, white Americans often have viewed the Asians as a homogeneous group. They are not. Not only are they very different in their nationalities, languages, religions, and cultures, but also they are a diverse people within each of their own cultures. Consequently, no single model can explain the wide disparities in occupational choices or acculturation and acceptance experiences.

Although recognizing the need to look beyond racial stereotypes to understand the different Asian immigrant groups more fully, we can nonetheless identify certain cultural hallmarks most Asians tend to share. The degree to which these norms and values are shared significantly depends on social class, length of residence in America, and acculturation.

Generally, traditional Asian values place great emphasis on appropriate behavior, the strict control of aggressive or assertive actions, and a self-conscious concern for what one does in the presence of others. Sibling rivalry is discouraged, and older children are socialized to set an example for younger siblings in politeness, gentleness, and unselfish sacrifices for another's pleasure. Unlike American children's exposure to an inner sense of guilt as a social-control mechanism, Asian children experience the external sanctions of shame, or losing face, of bringing disgrace or dishonor to the family name.

Within the family, open displays of emotion or affection are rare, except with infants or small children. Uniting the family is the important value of filial piety. Elders in the family, even those only slightly older, command respect and obedience; one never talks back to them. Traditional sex-role definitions require the men to provide for and protect the women and the women to be subordinate to the men. Fathers and eldest sons are thus the most dominant family members.

As with most immigrant groups, the Asian extended family is predominant. A cohesive structure exists, partially encouraged by the sense of duty and responsibility arising out of filial piety but also from values stressing ancestor worship and the importance of the family name. Loneliness and isolation for the unmarried or aged seldom occur because the extended family system embraces and absorbs them. No one typical Asian family model exists, however, and the blending of American and Asian cultures affect the family structure, especially allowing a more egalitarian role for women.[4]

Asian Americans stress educational achievement as the means to upward mobility. Although this value orientation results in Asian Americans being among the nation's highest-educated minority groups, the down side is that this parental pressure can lead instead to drug use, mental illness, and suicide.[5]

THE CHINESE

Americans on both sides of the continent knew something about the Chinese long before they first came to the United States. The United States had established trade relations with China as early as 1785, and a great many Protestant missionaries had been sent there after 1807. Newspaper reports and magazine articles, inspired by the Anglo-Chinese War (1839–1842) and subsequent rebellions and incidents, gave lurid descriptions of filth, disease, cruel tortures, and executions. The American people gradually developed an unfavorable image of the Chinese based on these ethnocentric distortions and exaggerations. In 1842, seven years before the gold rush, the *Encyclopedia Britannica* gave this unflattering portrait of the Chinese people:

> A Chinaman is cold, cunning and distrustful; always ready to take advantage of those he has to deal with; extremely covetous and deceitful; quarrelsome, vindictive, but timid and dastardly. A Chinaman in office is a strange compound of insolence and meanness. All ranks and conditions have a total disregard for truth.[6]

Structural Conditions

Most of the Chinese who came to the United States in the nineteenth century were farmers, artisans, craftsmen, political exiles, and refugees. The discovery of gold in California proved to be an opportunity not only for easterners and Europeans but also for the Chinese from Kwangtung, who could get out easily and who sought to recoup their losses from flood, famine, and the Tai

Ping Revolution (1850–1864). A combination of push–pull factors thus brought the Chinese to the United States. Chinese males set out alone, often leaving wives and children in the village and the kinship circle of the extended family. The first wave of migrants came as sojourners, intending to earn some money and then return home.

The Chinese were visible because of their race, and their appearance and behavior aroused both curiosity and suspicion. The sounds and characters of their language seemed most peculiar to the non-Chinese, as did their religions. Their "strange" clothes and hair worn in queues also seemed out of place in the crude pioneer surroundings. Since they had little or no command of English, kept mostly to themselves, and viewed California as a temporary workplace, the Chinese remained an enigma to most Americans.

When the Chinese began arriving in greater numbers in the late 1850s, the surface gold deposits were becoming exhausted. The white miners left these low-yield diggings to the Chinese, who in the 1860s moved on to become railroad construction workers, ranch hands, farm laborers, domestic servants, unskilled workers in the factories that had started to spring up, and anything else at which they could find work. Back in 1852 their industriousness had prompted Governor John MacDougall to praise them before the California legislature as the "most desirable of our adopted citizens" and to call for a land grant system to encourage more to come. However, the Chinese were not permitted to become U.S. citizens, and their reception in the years that followed could hardly be called a welcome.

By 1860 California's population had a large and varied ethnic segment. About 38 percent were foreign-born, and many others were Spanish-speaking natives or children of European immigrants.[7] The Chinese constituted about 9 percent of the state's population in 1860, but because they were mostly adult males, they represented close to 25 percent of the labor force at that time.[8] As the general population increased, the percentage of the total and working population that they represented decreased.

Hired as laborers who worked in gangs, the Chinese at this time helped to build the western portion of the transcontinental railroad for the Central Pacific. As many as 9,000 Chinese a year toiled through the High Sierra country, digging tunnels and laying tracks, and the task was completed sooner than expected. Leland Stanford, then president of the Central Pacific Railroad, described the Chinese as "quiet, peaceable, industrious, economical." Although Chinese laborers received the same wages as non-Chinese, they fed and housed themselves, unlike the white workers, thereby costing the railroad company only two-thirds as much as whites.[9] The Chinese did not, however, pose an economic threat to the non-Chinese workers, who found their jobs upgraded.

> Hiring Chinese resulted not in displacement of non-Chinese but in their upgrading. To the unskilled white railroad laborer of 1865, the coming of the Chinese meant his own advancement into that elite one-fifth of the labor force composed of straw-bosses, foremen, teamsters, skilled craftsmen. And one final reason was perhaps more cogent than all the others. No man with any choice

would have chosen to be a common laborer on the Central Pacific during the crossing of the High Sierra.[10]

At the same time the railroad was being built, West Coast manufacturing was increasing. Wartime demands on eastern industries and the high cost of transporting eastern goods encouraged this growth.[11] A shortage of available women and children prompted the textile industry to hire many Chinese.[12] The end of the Civil War brought veterans seeking jobs and Eastern manufacturing concerns seeking West Coast markets, helped by efficient, low-cost shipment of goods over the transcontinental railroad. Fired when their work was completed, Chinese railroad laborers sought other jobs, but the economic conditions worsened, culminating in the Panic of 1873. Labor supply exceeded demand, and racist arguments of laborers, union organizers, and demagogues mounted against Chinese "competition."

Some of the ethnophaulisms directed against the Chinese during this period of labor agitation dealt with their being "dirty" and "disease-ridden." These epithets had originated decades earlier. In the 1840s Americans first became aware of the relationship between germs and dirt and disease. Negative stereotypes about the supposed Chinese preference for eating vermin and crowded, unsanitary Chinatowns caused the Chinese to be associated with leprosy, cholera, and bubonic plague. By the 1870s the labor

These Chinese laborers in 1877 worked on the 1,100-foot trestle over the Secretown Ravine, about 64 miles east of Sacramento, California. They were among the 12,000 Chinese who helped build the Central Pacific Railroad and open the West for other settlers. By this time anti-Chinese feeling was increasing, particularly in the growing western cities. *(Culver Pictures)*

issue had become predominant, but as the labor unions joined together against the Chinese, they labeled them a menace to both the economy and the health of the society. The *real* issue by 1877 was race, disguised as labor conflict.

Societal Reactions

Racist attacks against the Chinese continued throughout the second half of the nineteenth century. Some compared their "racial inferiority" with that of the blacks, and others attacked the "vices" of the Oriental race. In the 1850s one antislavery Southerner had attempted to draw parallels among several groups that were supposedly inferior:

> No inferior race of men can exist in these United States without becoming subordinate to the will of the Anglo-Americans. . . . It is so with the Negroes in the South; it is so with the Irish in the North; it is so with the Indians in New England; and it will be so with the Chinese in California. . . . I should not wonder, at all, if the copper of the Pacific yet becomes as great a subject of discord and dissension as the ebony of the Atlantic.[13]

Cries for restrictions on Chinese immigration increased as racial antagonism rather than economic competition became the issue. In 1865 *The New York Times* viewed with alarm the effect of the increase in Asian immigration on American civilization, religion, morals, and political institutions:

> Now we are utterly opposed to the permission of any extensive emigration of Chinamen or other Asiatics to any part of the United States. There are other points of national well-being to be considered beside the sudden development of material wealth. The security of its free institutions is more important than the enlargement of its population. The maintenance of an elevated national character is of higher value than mere growth in physical power.
>   . . . We have four millions of degraded negroes in the South . . . and if there were to be a flood-tide of Chinese population—a population befouled with all the social vices, with no knowledge or appreciation of free institutions or constitutional liberty, with heathenish souls and heathenish propensities, whose character, and habits, and modes of thought are firmly fixed by the consolidating influence of ages upon ages—we should be prepared to bid farewell to republicanism and democracy.[14]

In 1867 California Democrats used an anti-Chinese platform to such advantage that they swept the state elections, including the gubernatorial chair. Democrats elsewhere saw a bonanza in this subject because many Republicans were identified with the railroads and with companies that recruited and employed the Chinese, and because the Democrats—identified with the defeated Confederacy and slavocracy—could not use Negro-baiting effectively after 1865. Republicans secured the Burlingame Treaty of 1868 between China and the United States, providing for free immigration and emigration to both countries "for the purpose of curiosity, or trade, or as permanent residents." Still, public hostility against the Chinese continued.

To some the Chinese also posed the first real immigrant threat to the idealized concept of the melting pot. Individuals who held this belief argued that German and Irish Catholics at least were physically similar to the Protestant northern and western Europeans. An 1868 *New York Times* editorial offered this incredible display of racist bigotry:

> Although they are patient and reliable laborers, they have characteristics deeply imbedded which make them undesirable as part of our permanent population. Their religion is wholly unlike ours, and they poison and stab. The circumstance would need be very favorable which would allow of their introduction into our families as servants, and as to mixing with them on terms of equality, that would be out of the question. No improvement of race could possibly result from such a mixture.[15]

As the prejudices of the 1850s developed into the sinophobia of the 1870s and 1880s, the negative stereotype of the "yellow peril" broadened. Senator James G. Blaine of Maine, a party leader and presidential hopeful, attacked even the Chinese family structure, since the Chinese, as sojourners, had temporarily left their families in China. His erroneous comments not only ignored the typical cohesiveness of Chinese family structure, but also the common practice of European males to come to the United States ahead of their families.

> The Asiatic cannot go on with our population and make a homogeneous element. This idea . . . comparing European immigration with an immigration that had no regard to family, that does not recognize the relation of husband and wife, that does not observe the tie of parent and child, that does not have in the slightest degree the enabling and civilizing influence of the hearthstone and the fireside.[16]

Legislative Action

Several hundred thousand Chinese came to the United States between 1820 and 1882. As Chinese sojourners both came to America and returned to China in steady numbers, steamship companies found passenger trips a very profitable operation and so encouraged Chinese immigration. In 1881, 11,890 Chinese disembarked, and in 1882 the number jumped to 39,579.[17] Economic woes and labor agitation against the Chinese led to increasing pressures for restrictions. President Arthur vetoed the first restriction bill, which would have barred all Chinese immigration for 20 years. A few months later he signed a revised bill, barring Chinese laborers for a 10-year period but permitting Chinese businessmen, clergy, students, and travelers to enter. The Chinese Exclusion Act of 1882 marked a significant change in national policy toward immigrants. For the first time the federal government had enacted a human embargo on a particular race of laborers. There were still sufficient exceptions to allow 8,031 legal Chinese immigrants in 1883, but legislative action in 1884 tightened the restrictions further, and the number of immigrants in 1885 dropped to 22.[18]

The exclusion law had a pronounced effect on public opinion. Now that a ban on immigration of Chinese laborers was official policy, people's negative attitudes toward the Chinese became more and more evident in the media and in people's actions. Violence and killings, which had occurred prior to the legislation, continued. In 1871 21 Chinese had been massacred in Los Angeles, and there had been anti-Chinese riots in Denver in 1880. Hostile actions became much more widespread after 1882. For example, at Rock Springs, Wyoming, in September 1885, a mob attacked and murdered 28 Chinese, wounded many others, and drove hundreds from their homes. What appeared to be a carefully organized plan against the Chinese was put into effect by labor unions and politicians in the western United States. In Tacoma, Seattle, Oregon City, and many smaller towns, angry mobs expelled hundreds of Chinese residents, with considerable loss and destruction of property.

Congress renewed the exclusion act for another 10 years in 1892 and extended it indefinitely in 1902. Other Anglo-Saxon countries on the Pacific Rim also restricted Chinese immigration. Australia passed legislation in 1901, but

THE ARGUMENT OF NATIONALITY.

EXCITED MOB—" *We don't want any cheap-labor foreigners intruding upon us native-born citizens.*"

Using stereotyped images to denote nationalities, this 1878 editorial cartoon perceptively identifies the anger of working-class ethnic Americans against Chinese laborers. This antagonism resulting from economic competition illustrates the split labor market theory. *(The Library of Congress)*

Canada did not take such action until 1923. Americans frequently criticized Canada, especially British Columbia, because Chinese entered the United States from that province. The reverse migration also occurred after 1858, when the United States served as a point of entry into Canada for many Chinese.

Organized labor's creation and instigation of the anti-Chinese issue is illustrated in an 1893 American Federation of Labor (AFL) convention resolution, which held that the Chinese brought to America "nothing but filth, vice, and disease." It also maintained they had corrupted "a part of our people on the Pacific Coast to such a degree that could it be published in detail the American people would in their just and righteous anger sweep them from the face of the earth."[19] These wild racist charges had little basis in fact except that filth and disease did exist in some Chinatown districts, just as in Irish, Italian, and other ethnic urban slums.

Segregation

How did the Chinese react to all this abuse, vilification, and discriminatory legislation? Some reluctantly returned to China. Some sought redress in the courts, winning all cases involving state immigration restrictions but few involving assault or property damage complaints, because from 1854 to 1870, California courts did not allow Chinese to testify against whites. Expelled from various trades and occupations as well as from many residential areas, the Chinese had little choice but to congregate in Chinatowns and rely on the benevolent and protective associations for assistance. A large number congregated in San Francisco, but others moved to the larger eastern and midwestern cities, forming ethnic enclaves there. These Chinatowns were in low-rent ghetto areas, usually situated near major means of transportation, which at least allowed the Chinese to be readily accessible to friends and relatives. For example, in New York City and San Francisco they are in close proximity to the docks, and in Boston, Pittsburgh, and St. Louis they are near the railroad stations.

The Chinese sought redress of grievances through the courts, petitioning for equal rights. They won for their children the right to attend public schools; then they fought to desegregate the schools. Housing codes kept them in the ghetto, and they found themselves segregated both socially and spatially. Securing jobs through the associations or from Chinese merchants, most entered occupations either not in competition with whites (such as art and curio shops or Chinese restaurants) or serving only their own people. They settled disputes among themselves, partly because this was their custom and partly because they distrusted the white people's court. The traditional associations and the family clan offered them the familiarity and protection they needed. Chinese temples, newspapers, schools, and Old World festivals all were efforts to preserve their cultural and traditional practices.

Examining the early growth of the Chinatowns, and analyzing the modern status of New York's Chinatown, D. Y. Yuan suggested that there was a four-stage process of development.[20] The first stage was marked by involuntary choice in response to societal prejudice and discrimination. Defensive insulation came next, as a mutual protection against racial hostility. As a group consciousness emerged, voluntary segregation became the third stage, sharing culture and problems of adjustment. The final stage is gradual assimilation, a process markedly slowed down by voluntary segregation and social isolation.

Albert Palmer drew from first-hand experience as a white boy growing up near San Francisco's Chinatown in the late nineteenth century in his social analysis of the stereotyped dominant view of these "foreign settlements":

> Those who know only the picturesque Chinatown of today can hardly realize what the Chinatown of the eighties and nineties was like. It was dirty, overcrowded, rat-infested, and often diseased. It was poorly built with narrow alleys and underground cellars and secret passages, more like a warren of burrowing animals than a human city. It seemed uncanny because inhabited by a strange yellow race who wore "pigtails," talked an outlandish lingo in high falsetto voices, were reputed to eat sharks' fins and even rats, and to make medicine out of toads and spiders, and who sprinkled garments for ironing by sucking their mouths full of water and then squirting it out over the clothes. And Chinatown was accounted vicious because it was the haunt of gambling, opium smoking, lotteries, tong wars and prostitution, where helpless little slave-girls were bought and sold. . . .
>
> Now, fear is a great disturber, and it largely created the old Chinatown. It did this partly, in fact, by herding Chinese into narrow, squalid quarters and surrounding them by hatred and suspicion; and partly in imagination, by creating the weird and distorted picture of their outlandish character. . . . Chinatown was never quite so bad as the prejudice and fear imagined it![21]

In an analysis of organizational life within San Francisco's Chinatown between 1850 and 1910, Stanford M. Lyman found that the traditional associations quickly came in conflict with one another.[22] As the clans (lineage bond), *hui kuan* (ethnic or regional bond), and secret societies (outlaw or protest bond) fought to secure the allegiance of immigrants and to dominate the community, the Chinese faced strife from both inside and outside their community:

> The organizational developments and internecine fights that took place in Chinatown from 1850 to 1910 indicate that forming an overseas Chinese community was not an easy task. Principles of clan solidarity, barriers of language and dialect, allegiance to rebellious secret societies, and their own competitive interest in making enough money to permit retirement in China divided the loyalties of the Chinese immigrants. Yet during the same period the depredations of anti-Chinese mobs, the difficulties and indignities imposed by restrictive immigration legislation, the occupational discrimination created by state and local laws prohibiting or limiting the employment of Chinese, and the active opposition of the American labor movement to the Chinese workingman all seemed to call for a community united in the face of its enemies. What emerged out of this condition of pressures from without the ghetto and divisions within was a

pattern alternating between order and violence. By 1910 this pattern had assumed a complex but recognizable sociological form: that of the community whose members are bound to one another not only because of external hostility but also because of deadly internal factionalism.[23]

The Chinese continued to encounter discrimination and hostility in the Caucasian world:

> During most of this period, the lives of average Chinese in the United States were difficult and irregular. No matter how well educated they were, in their living quarters they were confined to a crowded Chinatown. . . . College training in engineering or other technical subjects did not guarantee decent positions to Chinese. If one should go out, dressed casually for a walk, or go to a club, or even to a church, he was liable to be picked up by the immigration officers on suspicion of illegal residence. For many years officials made a practice of picking up persons in the street or in public places on the suspicion that they were aliens illegally in this country. Such arrests were reported to be very common, especially in the late 1920s. . . . It was up to the Chinese to prove he was not an illegal alien or even an illegal citizen. But proof is sometimes difficult and takes time. Eventually he would solve his difficulty, but only after suffering much trouble and anxiety.[24]

Not all Chinese migrated to the crowded Chinatowns of the cities. A few hundred, many of whom became merchants, settled in the Mississippi Delta. Chinese grocers sold mostly to blacks, extending them credit and providing other essential services (such as assisting illiterate rural blacks with government forms and making telephone calls). Some Chinese married black women; others brought their families over from China. In this transition from sojourner to immigrant, the Chinese men with families tried to evade their "black" status and avoid discrimination against their children, who were attending white public schools. In the 1920s, however, as a result of segregationist actions, Chinese children were expelled from the white schools, and the action was upheld by the courts "to preserve the purity and integrity of the white race, and prevent amalgamation." Separate schools for Chinese were established, as the Mississippi Chinese developed parallel institutions when they were excluded from the white prototypes. By 1950 their status had improved, and white churches and schools were opened to them. Recently the second-generation Mississippi Chinese have been migrating to other parts of the United States.

Social Factors

Perhaps the most tragic element in Chinese life in the United States was the scarcity of Chinese women. In the nineteenth century, single Chinese women usually did not venture forth alone seeking economic opportunity, and Chinese tradition demanded that the wife remain with her husband's parents, even if he worked far from home. About half the Chinese sojourners were married.[25] The imbalance in the male–female ratio was very significant:

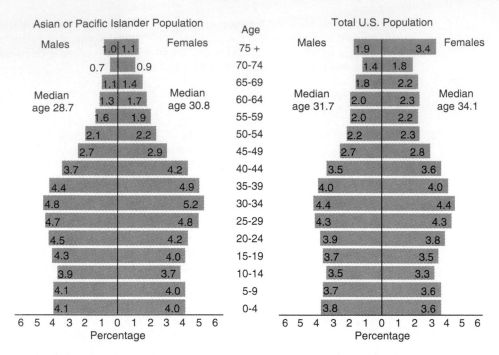

FIGURE 8.1
Asian and Pacific Islander Population, 1990

SOURCE: U.S. Bureau of the Census.

1,858:1 in 1860; 1,284:1 in 1870; 2,106:1 in 1880; 2,678:1 in 1890; and 1,887:1 in 1900. The 1890 ratio converts to 102,620 Chinese males and 3,868 females. By 1920 the sex ratio, while still very much out of balance, had lessened to 695:1.[26] This ratio steadily declined thereafter. By 1990 Chinese immigration had reached parity in sex distribution: 49 percent male and 51 percent female from mainland China and 47 percent male and 53 percent female from Taiwan.[27] In earlier years, however, this overabundance of Chinese males and scarcity of Chinese females led to organized prostitution in Chinatowns. Numerous brothels dotted the Chinatowns, some of them run or protected by the secret societies and staffed with girls kidnapped from their villages, sold by impoverished parents, or lured abroad by the deceit of a proxy marriage.[28]

> With the vast Pacific Ocean separating him from domestic joys and companionship, the Chinese sojourner relied on the tong-controlled brothels for sex, attending the gambling and opium dens for recreation and respite from the day's toil, and paid homage and allegiance to his clansmen, *Landsmänner,* and fraternal brothers to secure mutual aid, protection, and a job.[29]

Intermarriage also was generally impossible for the Chinese, since 14 states had passed laws forbidding miscegenation. Furthermore, in 1884 a federal court ruled that only wives of those males exempt from the Chinese Exclusion Act of 1882, namely merchants and businessmen, could emigrate to the United States. For nearly all the Chinese laborers in America, establishing a family was impossible. By 1890, 40 years after the Chinese had first arrived, only 2.7 percent of the total Chinese population was American-born. The figure climbed to 30 percent by 1920. Legislation in 1943 allowed Chinese women to enter the country, enabling the American-born Chinese population to pass the halfway point in 1950. By 1960 the American-born Chinese were approximately two-thirds of the total.[30]

Recent Patterns

Congress ended the ban on immigration from China in 1943 and began a quota system. But first there was a dispute that reflected the lingering anti-Chinese feeling in America. Speaking against repeal, Congressman White of Idaho in 1943 condemned the Chinese as a race unable to accept American standards, as he used the actions of a few to create a false stereotype of an entire group.

> The Chinese are inveterate opium-smokers most of the day. They brought that hideous opium habit to this country. . . . There is no melting pot in America that can change their habits or change their mentality. . . . If there are any people who have refused to accept our standard and our education, it is the Chinese.[31]

Actually the 1943 legislation permitted only 105 Chinese to enter per year, and that quota included anyone in the world of Chinese descent, not just those from China. Special and separate legislative acts covering refugees, displaced persons, and brides allowed more Chinese to enter. However, not until the Immigration Act of 1965 would the Chinese be able to enter under regular immigration regulations.

Since 1965 the Chinese American population has been rapidly increasing, almost quadrupling since 1970 to 1.6 million in the 1990 census (see Table 8.1). As a result, the Chinatowns in San Francisco, Los Angeles, and New York have themselves almost doubled, spilling over their traditional boundaries into adjacent neighborhoods. The arrival of so many "FOB" (fresh off the boat) immigrants and refugees has raised commercial rents, squeezing out old-line shops. With the Chinatowns unable to absorb all the newcomers, Chinese are flourishing in nearby areas as well—in the Corona, Flushing, and Jackson Heights sections of Queens, New York, and in the Richmond and Sunset districts outside San Francisco.[32] Chinese is now the third most common language in the United States, ranking behind English and Spanish.[33]

The San Francisco, Los Angeles, and New York Chinatowns, paradoxically, are both tourist attractions and slum communities. They are filled with overcrowded, dilapidated buildings and troubled by the problems of youth gangs and high tuberculosis rates, but they retain historical, picturesque, and commercial importance. Less evident to tourists are the Chinese garment shops or

TABLE 8.1	ASIAN AMERICAN POPULATION		
Nationality	1970	1980	1990
Chinese	435,000	806,000	1,645,000
Filipino	343,000	775,000	1,407,000
Japanese	591,000	701,000	848,000
Korean	70,000	355,000	799,000
Vietnamese*	n/a	262,000	615,000
Hmong*	n/a	5,000	90,000
Laotian*	n/a	48,000	149,000
Cambodian*	n/a	16,000	147,000
Thai*	n/a	45,000	91,000

*Virtually all have entered the U.S. since 1970.

SOURCE: U.S. Bureau of the Census, *Press Release CB91–215*, June 12, 1991, Tables 3A and 3B, pp. 5–6.

sweatshops, notorious for their long hours and meager compensation. Also hidden above and behind the street-level storefront facades is the population density, 10 to 12 times the city average, and a tuberculosis risk rate 13 times that of the general population.[34]

Chinese Americans present a bipolar occupational distribution. Thirty percent are in professional and technical positions as against 15 percent of the white labor force; but the Chinese are heavily overrepresented as low-skilled service workers, with 24 percent, as compared to 7 percent of the white labor force. Such employment characteristics partly reflect educational and immigration patterns. Also notable is a higher median family income for Chinese Americans than for other Americans. However, because over 60 percent of Chinese families have more than one wage earner compared to the 51 percent of the total population of families, that fact may account for the difference more than higher-paying positions.[35]

A Chinatown concern in recent years has been the increasing rebelliousness, criminality, and radicalism of many Chinese youth. The formation of delinquent gangs, particularly in New York and San Francisco, has resulted in a growing number of gang wars and killings. The growing problem of youthful militancy and delinquency appears to reflect the marginal status of those in the younger generation, who experience frustration and adjustment problems in America. Recent arrivals from Hong Kong are unfamiliar with the language and culture, they are either unemployed or in the lowliest of jobs, and they live in overcrowded, slum-like quarters with no recreational facilities. For some youth, gang behavior serves as an alternative and a means of filling status and identity needs.[36]

In a scene photographed around 1912, American flags fly in New York City's Chinatown. This blend of the distinctive features of an ethnic community and the American influence illustrates the ongoing processes of both acculturation and ethnogenesis, the absorption of some cultural elements of the host society while retaining or adapting elements from one's cultural heritage. *(National Archives)*

THE JAPANESE

When Commodore Perry sailed into Tokyo Bay in 1853, his arrival marked the beginning of a new era for Japan. For more than 200 years, the Japanese had lived in government-enforced isolation. The emperors had prohibited travel and foreign visitors, although castaways were treated hospitably and allowed to leave. No one was permitted to build large boats, and any Japanese attempt to emigrate was punishable by death.

The situation began to change in 1860 when the Japanese government sent its first official emissaries to Washington:

> With their first major debarkation in the New World, the Japanese appeared to Americans to lack emotional expression. [A San Francisco reporter observed:]

"This stoicism, however, is a distinguishing feature with the Japanese. It is part of their creed never to appear astonished at anything, and it must be a rare sight indeed which betrays in them any expression of wonder."

In the 85 years which passed between the arrival of Japan's first embassy and the end of World War II, this "distinguishing feature" of the Japanese became the cardinal element of the anti-Japanese stereotype. Characterized by journalists, politicians, novelists, and film-makers as a dangerous enemy, the Japanese were also pictured as mysterious and inscrutable.[37]

Beginning in 1868 the Japanese began emigrating, first as laborers and eventually as permanent settlers. Their numbers on the U.S. mainland were small at first. U.S. Census records show only 55 in this country in 1870 and 2,039 in 1890. After that they came in much greater numbers, reaching 24,326 in 1900, 72,157 in 1910, and 111,010 in 1920.

Economic Competition

Because many families in Japan still followed the practice of primogeniture (the eldest son inheriting the entire estate), many second and third sons came to the United States to seek their fortunes. They settled in the western states, where anti-Chinese sentiment was still strong, most of them becoming farmers or farm laborers. Their growing numbers, their concentration in small areas, and their racial visibility led to conflict with organized labor, vegetable growers, and shippers in California.

Early Japanese immigrants entered various manufacturing and service occupations. Hostility from union members, who resented Asians' willingness to work for lower wages and under poor conditions, produced the inevitable clashes. Members of the shoemakers' union attacked Japanese cobblers in 1890, and members of the union for cooks and waiters attacked Japanese restaurateurs in 1892. Finding work difficult to get, most Japanese gravitated to the outlying areas and entered agricultural work, first as laborers and eventually as tenant farmers or small landholders; other Japanese became contract gardeners on the estates of Caucasians.

The Japanese, whose industriousness and knowledge of cultivation placed them in serious competition with the native farmers, encountered further discriminatory actions. In 1913 the California legislature passed the first alien land-holding law, prohibiting any person ineligible for citizenship from owning land and permitting such persons to lease land for only three years. Under the United States Naturalization Act of 1790, then still in effect, citizenship was available to "any alien, being a free *white* person [italics mine]." In 1868 the government had modified this law to extend citizenship to persons of African descent (the recently freed slaves), but the Japanese were still excluded.

Because their children, having been born in this country, were automatically U.S. citizens, the Japanese held land in their children's names, either directly or through land-holding companies in which they collectively owned the stock. After World War I new agitation arose against the Japanese. In 1920 the California legislature passed a law prohibiting aliens from being guardians of a minor's property or from leasing any land at all. The U.S. Supreme Court upheld this law in 1923, and New Mexico, Arizona, Louisiana, Montana, Idaho, and Oregon passed similar laws. Because their opportunities were still best in agriculture, many Japanese continued in tenant or truck farming. Morton Grodzins suggests that their immense success (they raised 42 percent of California's truck crops by 1941) helps to explain why Caucasian vegetable growers and shippers pressed for their evacuation during World War II.[38]

National Policy

Most non-Californians had no strong feelings about Japanese immigrants, but they were quite aware of Japan's growing military power after the Japanese defeated Russia in 1905. The catalyst that finally triggered a change in national policy toward the Japanese was a local incident. In 1906 the San Francisco Board of Education passed a resolution transferring 93 Japanese children scattered throughout the city's 23 schools into a segregated Oriental school in Chinatown. This action made national headlines and had international ramifications. Under pressure from the Japanese government, President Theodore Roosevelt instructed the attorney general to initiate lawsuits challenging the constitutionality of this action.

As a compromise, the school board rescinded its resolution, the government dropped its legal action, and Roosevelt issued an executive order, which remained in effect until 1948, barring the entry of Japanese from a bordering country or U.S. territory. Thus, Japanese who stayed even briefly in Hawaii, Canada, or Mexico could no longer enter the mainland United States. In addition, President Roosevelt secured the so-called Gentlemen's Agreement of 1908, whereby Japan agreed to restrict, but not eliminate altogether, the issuance of passports. The big loophole in the Gentlemen's Agreement was permission for wives to enter. Many Japanese married by proxy and then sent for their "picture brides." Several thousand Japanese a year came until World War I, and almost 6,000 a year came after the war. As men brought their wives here and children were born, fearful nativists made exaggerated claims that the Japanese birthrate could create a danger of the Japanese "overrunning" the country. Questions about Japanese immigration began to shift from their economic competition to their "assimilability" because of their race, life-style, and alleged birthrate. The anti-Japanese stereotype, long a part of dominant-group attitudes, played a key role:

> The anti-Japanese stereotype was so widespread that it affected the judgements of sociologists about the possibilities of Japanese assimilation. Thus, in 1913 Robert E. Park was sufficiently depressed by anti-Japanese legislation and popular prejudice to predict: "The Japanese . . . is condemned to remain among us an abstraction, a symbol, and a symbol not merely of his own race, but of the Orient and of that vague, ill-defined menace we sometimes refer to as the

'yellow-peril.' " Although Park later reversed his doleful prediction, his observations on Japanese emphasized their uncommunicative features, stolid faces,
and apparently blank character.[39]

The Immigration Law of 1924, which severely restricted the number of
southern, central, and eastern Europeans who could enter, specifically barred
the Japanese, since it denied entry to all aliens ineligible for citizenship. The
bill passed by large majorities (323 to 71 in the House and 62 to 6 in the
Senate), indicating widespread support for limiting immigration to the supposedly "assimilable" peoples. The Japanese government vehemently denounced this legislation, taking it as a personal affront, a violation of the
terms of the Gentlemen's Agreement, and an insult to a nation only recently
courted by the United States. Nevertheless, the legislation remained in effect
until 1952.

Expulsion and Imprisonment

By 1940 there were about 127,000 Japanese in America, 94,000 of them in
California. About 63 percent were American-born, and only 15 percent were
of voting age. Japan's attack on Pearl Harbor in 1941 and the subsequent war
led to what is now referred to as "our worst wartime mistake."[40] More than
110,000 Japanese, many of them second- and third-generation Americans
with as little as one-eighth Japanese ancestry, were removed from their homes
and placed in what were euphemistically called relocation centers in Arkansas, Arizona, California, Colorado, Idaho, Utah, and Wyoming.[41]

> The evacuees loaded their possessions onto trucks. . . . Neighbors and teachers
> were on hand to see their friends off. Members of other minority groups wept.
> One old Mexican woman wept, saying, "Me next. Me next."
>   . . . People were starting off to 7 o'clock jobs, watering their gardens,
> sweeping their pavements. Passers-by invariably stopped to stare in amaze-
> ment, perhaps in horror, that this could happen in the United States. People
> soon became accustomed to the idea, however, and many profited from the
> evacuation. Japanese mortgages were foreclosed and their properties attached.
> They were forced to sell property such as cars and refrigerators at bargain
> prices.[42]

This mass expulsion of the Japanese from the West Coast was unnecessary
for national security, although that was given as the primary justification. The
traditional anti-Asian sentiment on the West Coast, fear of the "perfidious"
character of the Japanese, and opposition to Japanese producing a sizable
share of the area's agricultural products may all have been factors. There was
no mass evacuation of the 150,000 Japanese in Hawaii, which was much more
strategic and vulnerable to attack because of its location. The differences in
the Japanese experience in Hawaii and on the mainland can perhaps best be
understood by looking at the differences in structural discrimination. In Hawaii the Japanese were more fully involved in economic and political endeav-

At the Santa Anita reception center, these Japanese-American evacuees—most of them born in the United States—file into the dining hall for lunch, where more than 2,000 meals were served in less than an hour. From here the government transferred the evacuees to "relocation centers" for the duration of the war. Only in 1988 did the government begin making token reparations payments to these people for the financial losses they sustained by this imprisonment. *(The Library of Congress)*

ors, partly because they lived in an environment of greater racial harmony. On the West Coast the Japanese were more isolated from most of American society, and certain labor and agricultural groups saw them as an economic threat. Also, anti-Oriental attitudes and actions had prevailed in that area for almost 100 years.

Besides the trauma that resulted from being uprooted and incarcerated, the Japanese had to make many cultural adjustments to their new surroundings. Instead of their preferred deep hot baths, they had only showers and common washrooms. Central dining halls prevented families from eating together intimately as a family unit. Outside and sometimes distant toilet facilities, not partitioned in the early months, were a hardship for the old and for the parents of small children. Almost 6,000 babies were born while these centers were in existence, and proper hospital facilities were not always available. There were only partial partitions between rooms occupied by different families in the same barracks, and this did not allow for very much privacy. Ted Nakashima, a second-generation Japanese American, offered a frightening portrait of what the early months of life in the Tule Lake camp were like:

> The resettlement center is actually a penitentiary—armed guards in towers with spotlights and deadly tommy guns, fifteen feet of barbed wire fences, everyone confined to quarters at nine, lights out at ten o'clock. The guards are ordered to shoot anyone who approaches within twenty feet of the fences. No one is allowed to take the two-block-long hike to the latrines after nine, under any circumstances. The apartments, as the army calls them, are two-block-long stables, with windows on one side. Floors are . . . two-by-fours laid directly on the mud, which is everywhere. The stalls are about eighteen by twenty-one feet; some contain families of six or seven persons. Partitions are seven feet high, leaving a four-foot opening above. . . .
>
> The food and sanitation problems are the worst. We have had absolutely no fresh meat, vegetables or butter since we came here. Mealtime queues extend for blocks; standing in a rainswept line, feet in the mud, waiting for the scant portions of canned wieners and boiled potatoes, hash for breakfast or canned wieners and beans for dinner. Coffee or tea dosed with saltpeter and stale bread are the adults' staples. Dirty, unwiped dishes, greasy silver, a starchy diet, no butter, no milk, bawling kids, mud, wet mud that stinks when it dries, no vegetables—a sad thing for the people who raised them in such abundance. . . .
>
> Today one of the surface sewage-disposal pipes broke and sewage flowed down the streets. Kids played in the water. Shower baths without hot water. Stinking mud and slops everywhere.
>
> Can this be the same America we left a few weeks ago? . . . What really hurts most is the constant reference to us evacuees as "Japs." "Japs" are the guys we are fighting. We're on this side and we want to help.
>
> Why won't America let us?[43]

Although the harsh physical conditions and sanitation problems improved, the Japanese Americans remained prisoners because of their background. They tried to make life inside the barbed wire fences a little brighter by fixing up their quarters and planting small gardens. However, these "residents" of the "relocation centers" still lived, for the most part, in concentration camps. About 35,000 young Japanese Americans had left these centers by the end of 1943, going voluntarily to the East and Midwest for further schooling or a job. For those obliged to remain in the camps, life was monotonous and unproductive. The evacuation brought financial ruin to many Japanese families; they lost property, savings, income, and jobs for which they were never adequately compensated.

By weakening Japanese subcommunities and institutions, the evacuation program encouraged acculturation. The traditional authority of the first-generation Japanese Americans (Issei) lessened, family structure and husband–wife roles underwent changes and became more equal because of camp life, and those second-generation Japanese (Nisei) who resettled found new opportunities. The Japanese relocated to the Midwest and to the East Coast, but later many families returned to the West. Many became more a part of American society in the postwar period because they had been forced to do so.

At first the Supreme Court in 1944 upheld the Japanese evacuation by a 6 to 3 vote, although the dissenting justices gave strong minority opinions. Justice Francis Murphy called approving the evacuation "the legalization of racism." Justice Robert H. Jackson, who would later prosecute the Nazi war criminals at Nuremberg, wrote:

> Once a judicial opinion rationalizes such an order to show it conforms to the Constitution, or rather rationalizes the Constitution to show that the Constitution sanctions such an order, the Court for all time has validated the principle of racial discrimination in criminal procedure, and of transplanting American citizens. The principle then lies about like a loaded weapon ready for the hand of any authority that can bring forward a plausible claim of an urgent need. Every repetition imbeds that principle more deeply in our law and thinking and expands it to new purposes.[44]

Soon thereafter another case, *Endo v. United States*, brought an end to this forcible detention as of January 2, 1945, when the Supreme Court unanimously ruled that all loyal Japanese Americans be set free unconditionally. In 1976 President Ford signed an executive order officially closing the camps, but such mass evacuations could conceivably recur because of the judicial precedent set by the U.S. Supreme Court in upholding the action.

Justice Jackson's 1944 dissenting opinion seemed prophetic 35 years later when the seizure of American hostages at the U.S. Embassy in Iran prompted calls from some politicians for the roundup of Iranian students then attending U.S. colleges and their detention in the very same concentration camps.

Recent Patterns

While they were internees and during the years following this mass incarceration, Japanese Americans sought vindication and a redress of grievances through the Japanese American Citizens League (JACL). They fought to obtain frozen bank deposits, receive compensation for land, and restore lost retirement benefits to Civil Service workers. The Evacuation Claims Act of 1948 brought token repayment of about 10 percent of actual Japanese American losses.[45] In 1988 another bill was passed, offering a formal apology to the former internees for violating their "basic civil liberties" because of "racial prejudice." The bill also agreed to award a tax-free payment of $20,000 to each of the 60,000 surviving detainees.[46] However, only a fraction of that amount has since been appropriated and paid out.

Because homeland influences are important in understanding immigrant orientations, changes in Japan since World War II are worth mentioning. American occupation of the country and foreign aid led to significant and rapid social change in Japan. The westernization and industrialization affected Japanese values and life-styles; it also altered American attitudes. The 25,000 war brides who accompanied returning GIs originally encountered suspicion and hostility, but such attitudes eventually disappeared. Some were not accepted by the Japanese American ethnic community, but Japanese wives of Caucasians were usually looked on as exotic by the dominant group.[47]

Traditionally, Japanese parents have encouraged their children to get a good education, and since the 1940s, Japanese American males and females have been well above the national norms of those completing high school and college. Japanese emphasis upon conformity, aspiration, competitiveness, discipline, and self-control help to explain their high educational attainments.[48] Encouraged by their parents, the upwardly mobile *Nisei* (second generation), *Sansei* (third generation), and *Yonsei* (fourth generation) have increasingly entered the professional fields, especially engineering, pharmacy, electronics, and other technical fields. Most Japanese Americans, in fact, are American-born, and their higher education levels translate into their having incomes above any other ethnic group, including white Americans.[49]

The social organization and social controls within Japanese culture have long been strong enough to overcome any problems of marginality, as evidenced by their low rates of divorce, crime, delinquency, mental illness, and suicide. Harry H. L. Kitano, a Japanese American sociologist who was interned during World War II, has observed the following:

> The ability of the Japanese family and community to provide ample growth opportunities, to present legitimate alternatives, to provide conditions of relative tolerance and treatments, to provide effective socialization and control, as well as the relative congruence between Japanese culture and middle-class American culture, has aided the group in adapting to acculturative changes with a minimum marginal population. Relatively few Japanese seek social friendships in the social cliques and organizations outside their own ethnic group. And those who do seek outside contacts appear to have many of the necessary requisites for such activity—high education, good training, and adequate income.[50]

Since the mid-1970s, things have changed somewhat because half of all Japanese Americans are now native-born Americans.[51] Japanese Americans have become arguably the best assimilated Asian American group as well.[52] Structural assimilation, for example, is evident among the *Sansei* and *Yonsei*, where outgroup dating and exogamy have significantly increased, surpassing 50 percent or more according to some studies.[53]

Japanese immigration to the United States in the 1980s totaled 47,000, far fewer than that of other East Asian countries.[54] Consequently, the Japanese American population represents a steadily declining proportion of the Asian American community. Two out of every three Japanese Americans live either in California (37 percent) or Hawaii (29 percent). About half of all new arrivals are skilled and professional workers who find many similarities between American society and their homeland. Most are Buddhists, a religion growing in membership in the United States because of the continuing entry of Japanese and other Asian believers in this faith.

One special group in the United States is commonly called the *Kai-sha*— business people and employees of large corporations on two- or three-year assignments with their companies' U.S. branch offices. Their presence is more noticeable in the New York metropolitan region than ever before. Many suburban towns near New York City, particularly those along the Metro train line north into Westchester County and northeast along the New Haven line have experienced a large influx of Japanese *Kai-sha* and their families. Long-time residents of such communities as Scarsdale, Hartsdale, Larchmont, and Mamaroneck, unaccustomed to Asian neighbors, have seen their neighborhoods extensively integrated in a short time.[55]

THE FILIPINOS

The Filipinos came to this country with a unique status. After 1898 the Philippines had become an American possession and the inhabitants were considered nationals, although not U.S. citizens. Consequently, they were not designated as aliens, and there was no quota restriction on their entry until 1935. Their Spanish heritage confused their status, however, because the federal government held that they were not Caucasians. The U.S. Supreme Court upheld this official position in a 1934 ruling on a case challenging the 1790 naturalization law limiting citizenship to foreign-born whites:

> "White persons" within the meaning of the statute are members of the Caucasian race, as Caucasian is defined in the understanding of the mass of men. The term excludes the Chinese, the Japanese, the Hindus, the American Indians and the Filipinos.[56]

Early Immigrants

Like so many other immigrant groups, the early Filipino immigrants did not think of themselves in nationalist terms. Instead they placed themselves in one of several native language subgroupings: the Tagalogs, Visayans, or Ilocanos. Their social hangouts—the clubhouse, bar, or poolroom—often reflected that separation. American society lumped them all together, however, and soon societal hostility would forge a common ethnic identity among them.

After the Gentlemen's Agreement of 1908 curtailed Japanese emigration, the Hawaiian Sugar Planters' Association recruited laborers from the Philippines to work the plantations. The modest number of Filipinos in the continental United States (there were only 5,603 here in 1920, according to census records) began to increase in 1923. Why? California growers, faced with the loss of Mexican labor because of quota restrictions in the pending Immigration Act of 1924, turned to the Filipinos as an alternative labor source. By 1930 their numbers had increased to over 45,000, with more than two-thirds of them living in California.

Many Filipinos worked in agriculture at first, particularly in California and Washington. However, the promise of educational opportunities and the lure of the big city attracted many young Filipino males to urban areas, where they sought jobs. Discrimination and their lack of education and job skills resulted in their getting only low-paying domestic and personal service work in hotels, restaurants, businesses, and residences. They were employed as bellboys, waiters, cooks, bus boys, janitors, drivers, house boys, elevator operators, and hospital attendants. By 1940 their employment in these areas peaked, with nine out of 10 Filipinos so employed.[57] Feeling that they were being exploited by their employers, they often joined unions, or formed their own unions when denied membership in existing unions, and went on strike, which only intensified management resentment. Ironically, the union hierarchy also disliked them and later joined in efforts to bar them from the United States.

As the Depression of the 1930s worsened and jobs became scarcer, increased objections were made to the presence of the Filipinos. Race riots erupted in Exeter, California, on October 24, 1929, and in Watsonville, California, on January 19, 1930, when one Filipino was killed. In both instances several hundred white men beat Filipinos, shattered windows in cars and buildings, and wrecked property. Other clashes occurred in San Jose and San Francisco. Then on January 28, 1930, someone bombed the Filipino Federation of America Center in Stockton—called "the Manila of California" because of its large Filipino population.

The Scarcity of Filipino Women

Of every 100 Filipinos coming to California between 1920 and 1929, 93 were male; almost 80 percent were single and between 16 and 30 years of age. Because there were few Filipino women available, these males sought the company of women of other races. This situation enraged many Caucasian men, as the following racist statement illustrates:

> The Filipinos have . . . demanded the right to run dance halls under the alias of clubs, with white girls as entertainers. And the excuse they have openly and brazenly given for their demand is that the Filipinos "prefer" white women to those of their own race and that besides there are not enough Filipino women in the country to satisfy their lust. . . . If that statement is not enough to make the blood of any white man, of any other decent man boil, then there is no such thing as justified indignation at any advocacy of immorality.[58]

This prejudicial, demagogic statement reflects the sort of sexually oriented charges often directed against racial groups. Association with Caucasian women through intermarriage, dance halls, and affairs led to increased tensions in Filipino–Caucasian relations. The Filipinos' reputation as great lovers emerged as a stereotype, causing a San Francisco judge to comment:

> Some of these boys, with perfect candor, have told me bluntly and boastfully that they practice the art of love with more perfection than white boys, and occasionally one of the girls has supplied me with information to the same effect. In fact, some of the disclosures in this regard are perfectly startling in nature.[59]

Filipino responses were quick to follow. Sylvester Saturday, editor of the Filipino Poets League in Washington, DC, stated:

> We Filipinos are tickled at being called "great lovers." Surely, we are proud of this heritage. We love our women so much that we work ourselves to death to gain and keep their affections.[60]

Another Filipino from Chicago chided:

> And as for the Filipinos being "great lovers," there is nothing surprising about that. We Filipinos, however poor, are taught from the cradle up to respect and love our women. That's why our divorce rate is nil compared with the state of which Judge Lazarus is a proud son. If to love and respect our womenfolks [sic] is savagery, then make the most of it, Judge. We plead guilty.[61]

White America was not amused. Several western states passed laws prohibiting marriages between Filipinos and Caucasians. The Tyding-McDuffie Act in 1935 granted deferred independence to the Philippines and imposed an immediate rigid quota of 50 immigrants a year. Repatriation efforts from 1935 to 1937 succeeded in returning only 2,190 to the Philippines.[62]

Because of the lack of Filipino women and legal restrictions on intermarriage, many Filipino males remained single. These early immigrants became lonely old men with no family ties, living in poverty after years of hard work, although a small number did intermarry among Mexicans, Indians, mulattos, Asians, and Caucasians.[63]

Unlike the Chinese, who had a tradition of being sojourners and who formed benevolent and protective associations, the Filipinos did not establish the institutions usually found in immigrant communities. Their lack of families and the seasonal, transitory nature of their employment were primary reasons for this. As a result of housing discrimination, they lived in hotels and rooming houses in less desirable sections of town. The pool hall and taxi-dance hall became their recreational outlets.[64]

Postwar Immigrants

With the Philippines an ally during World War II, the social climate on the mainland became more liberal for Filipinos. In January 1942 legislation was passed enabling Filipino residents to become naturalized American citizens. They could buy land in California, and many did, often from Japanese Americans who were being removed from certain areas, such as Los Angeles. Many Filipinos bought farms in the San Fernando Valley and the San Joaquin Valley as well as in the Torrance–Gardena area.[65]

Since the Immigration Act of 1965, Filipino immigration has been quite high. An unstable political situation at home prior to the end of the Marcos regime in 1986 and continuing economic limitations in the Philippines since then serve as the major push factors. Like the Japanese, new Filipino arrivals tend to have better educational and occupational skills than most of their ethnic cohorts born in the United States. Over two-thirds are professional and technical workers in medicine, law, engineering, and education. However, because of licensing and hiring problems, many are underemployed, unable to secure jobs comparable to their education, skills, and experience.[66]

Filipinos are fragmented socially, linguistically, and politically. Unlike the Koreans, few are entrepreneurs, and seldom do Filipinos form cooperative credit associations to raise business capital. Because of America's need for nurses, Filipino women often come first, reversing the usual immigration pattern, and after saving enough income, they then send for their husbands and children. Filipino youth, unlike other Asian Americans but similar to the Indochinese, often reject traditional family discipline. Household earnings are fairly good because everyone in the family who can work, does.[67]

The largest concentration of Filipinos living outside the Philippines is in Hawaii, where they comprise 60 percent of all hotel maids and porters. On the mainland Filipinos tend to settle on either the West Coast or East Coast. Mostly Roman Catholics with a strong loyalty to family and church, today's Filipino Americans are otherwise very diverse in the various socioeconomic characteristics of education, occupation, income, and residence. Time of immigration and age appear to be the key variables. The oldtimers, retired laborers, usually are single males with meager incomes. Second or third generations born in America usually share such problems as lack of social acceptance, low income, low educational achievement, and negative self-image. In contrast new arrivals often are college graduates seeking the economic mainstream.[68]

Filipino Americans more than doubled in number between 1970 and 1980, going from 343,000 to 775,000. By the 1990 census they had exceeded 1 million, becoming the largest Asian and Pacific Islander ethnic group in the United States.

THE KOREANS

Because of its strategic location, Korea has been a pawn in the expansionist efforts of several nations. Voyagers visited Korea frequently from the late seventeenth century onward. By the middle of the nineteenth century, English, French, and Russian whaling ships sailed Korean waters, and many Catholic missionaries had come to Korea. The United States, however, in 1882 became the first Western nation to sign a treaty with Korea when it formalized a relationship of friendship and trade. Other nations quickly followed suit, and all attempted to remove the Chinese influence from Korea. In 1910 Japan gained control of Korea as a result of a conflict with China.

Although various treaties and declarations by the different nations guaranteed Korea's independence, Japanese encroachment, both political and economic, continued. Japan's victory over Russia in 1905 solidified Japanese domination of Korea, and Japan retained colonial control until the end of World War II. Korea still did not gain national independence, however, for the

Allied military strategy in 1945 was that Soviet troops would accept the Japanese surrender north of the thirty-eighth parallel and U.S. troops would do the same south of it. This temporary line, created out of military expediency, became a permanent delineation that still exists.

Early Immigrants

The Hawaii Sugar Planters' Association, needing laborers to replace the Chinese excluded by the 1882 legislation, recruited 7,226 Koreans, 637 of them women, between 1903 and 1905.[69] This was the first large group of Koreans to migrate to the United States. The Koreans, mostly peasants, sought economic relief from the famines plaguing their country at the turn of the century. In Hawaii they worked long hours for meager wages under harsh conditions.[70] Of this original group, about 1,000 returned to Korea, 2,000 males and 12 women went on to the mainland United States, and the rest remained in Hawaii.[71] The males were almost all between the ages of 20 and 40.[72] (See Box 8.1)

Between 1907 and 1924 several thousand more Korean immigrants, mostly "picture brides," political activists fighting Japanese oppression, and students, migrated to the United States. As a result of the age disparity between the picture brides and the older males, many second-generation Korean Americans spent a good portion of their formative years with non-English-speaking widowed mothers who had had limited formal schooling.[73]

Recent Immigrants

Not until the Korean War and passage of the Refugee Relief Act in 1953 did Koreans migrate in substantial numbers. As refugees or as war brides, Koreans came to the United States in growing numbers beginning in 1958. The continued presence of U.S. troops in South Korea and the cultural influence that resulted were constant inducements to the Koreans to intermarry or think about living in America. Also, the liberalized immigration law of 1965 opened the doors to Asian immigrants and allowed relatives to join family members already in the United States. This chain migration pattern resulted in an impressive fivefold population increase in 10 years, from 70,000 in 1970 to 355,000 in 1980, and by 1990 it reached 799,000. The proportion obtaining U.S. citizenship is higher than that of immigrants from China, India, Japan, and Mexico.

The Role of the Church

Almost 70 percent of the Korean American population identifies itself as Christian, a significantly higher proportion than the 30 percent Christian population living in Korea. Mostly Presbyterian and Methodist, Korean American churches numbered 1,624 in 1986, compared to fewer than 75 in

BOX 8.1	THE ETHNIC EXPERIENCE

[The following comments, through the courtesy of Harold and Sonia Su-noo, are a composite of interviews with three Korean women who were among the first 12 women to come to the mainland.]

"We left Korea because we were too poor. We had nothing to eat. . . . There was absolutely no way we could survive.

"At first we were unaware that we had been 'sold' as laborers. . . . We thought Hawaii was America in those days. . . . We cut sugar canes, the thing you put in coffee. . . .

"I'll never forget the foreman. No, he wasn't Korean—he was French. The reason I'll never forget him is that he was the most ignorant of all ignoramuses, but he knew all the cuss words in the world. . . . [I] could tell by the sound of his words. He said we worked like 'lazy.' He wanted us to work faster. . . . He would gallop around on horseback and crack and snap his whip. . . . He was so mean and so ignorant!

". . . If all of us worked hard and pooled together our total earnings, it came to about fifty dollars a month, barely enough to feed and clothe the five of us. We cooked on the porch, using coal oil and when we cooked in the fields, I gathered the wood. We had to carry water in vessels from water faucets scattered here and there in the camp area. . . .

"My mother and sister-in-law took in laundry. They scrubbed, ironed, and mended shirts for a nickel apiece. It was pitiful! Their knuckles became swollen and raw from using the harsh yellow laundry soap . . . but it was still better than in Korea. There was no way to earn money there."

[On the mainland the Koreans encountered even worse problems than in Hawaii because of the more highly charged racial tension and the severe weather conditions, as the following account indicates.]

"We had five children at that time—our youngest was three and a half. I was paid fifteen cents an hour for weeding. Our baby was too young to go to school, so I had to take him along with me to the fields—it was so early when we started that he'd be fast asleep when we left so I couldn't feed him breakfast. Returning home, he'd be asleep again because he was so tired. Poor child, he was practically starved. He too suffered so much. . . . [In February] the ground . . . was frozen crisp and it was so cold that the baby's tender ears got frozen and blood oozed from him. . . . For all this suffering, I was paid fifteen cents an hour. . . ."

SOURCE: Three Korean immigrants, ranging in age from 19 to 25, who came to Hawaii between 1903 and 1905.

1970. In the New York metropolitan area alone, more than 180 Korean congregations are concentrated in neighborhoods such as Flushing, Elmhurst, and Woodside in Queens.[74]

The dramatic increase in these ethnic churches was aided by the abundant supply of Korean ministers with pioneering spirits who immigrated to the

United States.[75] For example, 67 percent of the Korean immigrant churches in the Los Angeles area were established by ministers, with only 28 percent founded by congregations and 5 percent founded by denominations.[76]

Ethnic churches, including the Korean, make important contributions to the immigrant community, serving more than religious purposes. The church becomes a social organization, providing religious and ethnic fellowship, a personal community, and a family atmosphere within an alien and urban American environment.[77]

In a recent study of the role of Korean churches in the ethnic community of Chicago, where over 50,000 Koreans live, researchers found patterns reminiscent of earlier European immigrants.[78] Church affiliation was 57 percent compared to 12 percent in Korea. This heightened interest in church membership and frequent attendance at worship services is common among new immigrant groups seeking a communal bond in their ethnic identity. Not surprisingly, the study found that religious involvement was the primary motive, but over 95 percent listed "loneliness and seeing friends and relatives" as the secondary reasons for involvement in church activities. Because the greater the participation, the greater their identification with their homeland and culture, the Korean American church, like other ethnic predecessors, serves as a focal point for enhancing ethnic identity.

The Korean immigrant population is extremely heterogeneous in its economic, educational, and social backgrounds, making it inevitable that cliques and factions would form within their congregations based on shared interests and backgrounds. However, that process has caused some fierce factional struggles and even church schisms within the Korean American community. Because of marginality, underemployment, and possibly discrimination, some Korean Americans experience "status anxiety." Seeing church leadership positions as elders, deacons, or deaconesses as an achievement of status recognition and high esteem, competition for these positions often has evolved into a fierce struggle and factional strife.[79]

Occupational Adaptation

In Los Angeles County, where more than 200,000 Korean Americans live, 40 percent of the males operate their own businesses.[80] Nationwide, their 11.9 percent self-employment rate is the highest of all ethnic or racial groups, including whites. Whereas better than one in 10 Korean Americans is a business owner, the figure for blacks is one in 67 and for nonminorities one in 15.[81] So deeply entrenched is self-employment in the Korean immigrant ethos that a recent survey revealed that 61 percent of South Koreans planning to emigrate to the United States expected to go into business for themselves even though most had never been self-employed in their homeland.[82]

In many cities and exurbs, these small Korean family-operated businesses are especially conspicuous. In Los Angeles, Korean Americans have cornered the wig and liquor businesses. In Washington, DC, Philadelphia, and New York City, Korean Americans are especially visible as grocery-store owners and fruit-stand operators. In New York City, Korean greengrocers now sell more than three-fourths of the city's produce.[83]

Many other Korean Americans are employees of these small stores and firms that penetrate the black and Hispanic markets.[84] Because the Koreans, themselves a minority group, occupy an intermediate position in trade and commerce between producer and consumer, elite and masses, the role they play is that of a middleman minority.[85] As we shall discuss later, sometimes their visibility in other racial or ethnic neighborhoods has sparked violence.

Widespread use of rotating-credit associations has greatly aided the Koreans in establishing their own businesses. Similar to the *hui* among the Mandarin Chinese, the *tanomoshi* among the Japanese, and the *susu* in the patois of the Caribbean, the Koreans provided startup funds for their ethnic entrepreneurs through the *kye* (pronounced keh). In its simplest form, each member contributes a fixed amount monthly to a fund and has rotating access to the pot. The first borrowers pay extra loan interest. Dating back to Korean farming villages of the sixteenth century, the *kye* helps many newcomers get started in business while simultaneously functioning as a social club to bind immigrants together.

Overall, Koreans are more highly educated than most other nonwhite groups. Their income, in proportion to their number of college graduates, lags

About 12 percent of all Korean Americans are self-employed, more than any other minority group. This store owner's family lives above his deli and also works in the store—common patterns among many immigrants of no separation of work and residence and of the necessity of combined family work efforts. (*Corky Lee*)

behind that of native-born Americans, although their earnings are similar to those of other Asian American groups.[86] Koreans have not fared so well in social as in economic status. If recent studies are any indication, Korean Americans have never scored high in any measures of social distance, an important indicator of structural assimilation. In studies conducted in 1956 and 1966, Emory S. Bogardus found Koreans at or near the bottom in preference ranking, below other Asian peoples.[87] In a small replication study at Western Illinois University in 1976, Won Moo Hurh also found a near-bottom social distance ranking for Koreans.[88]

THE VIETNAMESE

In April 1975 the Vietnam War ended, and 127,000 Vietnamese and 4,000 Cambodian refugees entered the United States. As they waited in relocation centers at military bases for sponsors, public opinion polls showed that the majority of Americans, especially the working class, were convinced the refugees would take jobs away from Americans. Labor and state officials raised serious objections to "flooding" the labor market and welfare rolls with so many aliens at a time when the economy was in a recession. Yet all the refugees were resettled within seven months in all 50 states.

Like the Cuban exiles, many of these Vietnamese were middle class, migrating for political rather than economic reasons. Many were well educated, with marketable skills, and nearly half spoke English.[89] They were a cosmopolitan people, mostly from the Saigon region, and many had previously lived elsewhere, particularly in North Vietnam. A 1978 study of 350 refugees scattered in nine localities in Alabama, Florida, or California found that 76 percent of household heads were male, their average age was 37, and 68 percent were employed in a full-time job.[90]

In 1979 tens of thousands of Vietnamese "boat people," many of them actually Chinese living in Vietnam, sought refuge in other countries, setting sail in flimsy, overcrowded boats. Many drowned or were killed by pirates, but several hundred thousand reached refugee camps in other countries (see Box 8.2). President Carter authorized 14,000 refugees a month for 15 months, bringing in over 200,000 additional Indochinese refugees. Since September 1975, more than 1 million Southeast Asian refugees entered the United States. Most of these newcomers—from Laos, Cambodia, and Thailand as well as Vietnam—spoke little English and had few occupational skills, making their adjustment and attainment of economic self-sufficiency more difficult.

Cultural Differentiation

Unlike Americans, who commonly believe in the ability to establish one's own destiny, many Vietnamese believe life is essentially predetermined, with individual control over what occurs partial at best.[91] Two of the more impor-

| BOX 8.2 | THE ETHNIC EXPERIENCE |

"Our boat was kind of lucky, 'cause 70 percent of boats get captured by Vietnamese Coast Guard. That day there was no moon. It was totally dark. . . . Luckily we make it. . . . After one day and one night we get out of the control of the Vietnamese. Now we know we're free! . . . Our boat was thirty feet long and about seven feet wide and, totally, we had about 103 people. It was so crowded, almost like a fish can, you know? Can you imagine?

. . . "There was only enough water for one cup for each person in one day. So we rarely drank the water for, if we don't have water, we're going to die in the sea. The first day everyone got seasick. Nobody got used to it, the kind of high waves and ocean. So everyone got seasick and vomited. . . . But by the second day and the third day, we felt much better.

"We kept going straight into the international sea zone and we met a lot of ships. We tried to get signal for help, we tried to burn our clothes to get their attention. We wrote the big S.O.S. letter in our clothes and tried to hang it above the boat. No matter how we tried, they just passed us by. I think they might feel pity for us, have the good compassion, but I think they're afraid their government going to blame them because the law is, if you pick up any refugee in the ocean, your country got to have responsibility for those people. So finally we so disappointed because we got no help from anybody and our boat is now the only boat and we have only 3 h.p. motor.

"We have too many people and the wave is extremely high, about five feet. It is so dangerous. You can see the boat only maybe like one feet distant from the sea level. But we got no choice. We decide to keep going straight to Malaysia. The fifth day, the sixth day, we saw nothing. The only thing we saw is water, sun, and at night the stars. It's just like upside-down moon. And the sea. If you look down into the ocean, you get scared, because the water—color—is so dark. It's like dark blue. If you look down into the water, you had the feeling like it invite you, say "Go down with me." Especially at night, the water—it's black, like evil waiting for you. Say, "Oh, 103 people, I was waiting for you. Come down with us." We kept going, but we don't know where we're going to be, if we have enough food and water to make it. . . . We don't even know if we're going the right way . . . we just estimate by looking at the sun and the stars.

. . . "The sixth day we saw the bird and a couple of floating things, so we are hoping we are almost come to the shore. We had some hope and we kept traveling one more day, the seventh day. That day is the day—our water—we have only one more day left. And the gasoline is almost gone. And we saw some fire, very little fire, very far away. And we went to that fire. One hour, two hours. And finally we saw that fire offshore drilling platform of Esso Company. Everybody's screaming and so happy because

> we know at least we have something we can turn to. . . . We know we
> cannot go any further. Most of the women and children in my boat are
> exhausted, and some of the children unconscious. Some of the children
> had been so thirsty, they just drank the water from the sea. And the water
> from the sea is terrible. The more you drank, the more you got thirsty. And
> the children, starving, got a bad reaction from the seawater. We all got skin
> disease and exhausted. . . . They took us in their boat to the refugee camp
> in Malaysia.
>
> *SOURCE:* Vietnamese refugee who came to the United States in 1980 at age seventeen.

tant aspects of existence that the Vietnamese believe determine one's destiny
are *phuc duc* and astrology. These are core elements within the family infrastructure of filial piety and ancestor worship, and they provide important
insights into the Vietnamese ability to adapt to a new society with a minimal
amount of emotional anxiety.

The concept of *phuc duc* refers to the amount of good fortune that comes
from meritorious or self-sacrificing actions. This accumulation of rewards,
primarily secured by the women for their family, also affects the lives of
succeeding generations into the fifth generation. *Phuc duc* is quantifiable in
that improper conduct diminishes the amount one has, whereas the nature of
one's actions and one's degree of personal sacrifice determines the amount of
phuc duc one acquires.

> To a great extent *phuc duc* acts as the social conscience of the nation, a collective
> superego. The children are conscientiously instructed in the ways of living that
> result in phuc duc. It is, in great part, related to the Confucian concept of Li,
> although it is actually Buddhist-Confucian in origin and unique to Vietnam. It
> has its place in future reincarnations but primarily it relates to the family and to
> future generations of the family. Thus the responsibility that it represents is
> impressively exacting: the future destiny of one's loved ones and those yet
> unborn depends upon one's conduct.[92]

So strong is the Vietnamese belief in horoscopes that parents accept no
responsibility for a child's personality, believing that the configuration of the
celestial bodies at the moment of conception has fixed the character of that
individual. At the time of birth a Vietnamese astrologer specifically predicts
the personality and events to come for the newborn infant. This often becomes a self-fulfilling prophecy because the predictions influence actual be-

Beginning in 1979 tens of thousands of Vietnamese refugees fled their country in over-crowded boats on the open sea. These "boat people" took a heavy gamble against capture, robbery, rape, and death from brutal pirates or against capsizing and drowning in a storm. Unlike these fortunate ones, a great many never made it. Those who did went to refugee camps in nearby friendly countries until a sponsor could be found in Australia, Canada, the United States, or Europe. *(Magnus Barlett/Woodfin Camp)*

havior (parental child-rearing practices as well as the child's own actions, including mate selection as an adult). Thus the prophecy is confirmed by its result.

The important thing here is that the Vietnamese way of life includes belief in a deterministic life force over which one has minimal control. This concept has greatly influenced the accommodation of the Vietnamese to the United States:

> For many this is the second or third time that they have been refugees. It is not something that one ever gets used to, but there is a philosophic acceptance of fate. And this the Vietnamese can accept. It is assigned to bad phuc duc, to the heavens, to the land on which one's ancestors are buried, or whatever. The cause, however, is externalized and inasmuch as this is universally concurred in by one's peers, these adverse events are integrated into one's psychic apparatus with a minimum of emotional dislocation.[93]

Han T. Doan points out that Vietnamese believe human nature is basically good but corruptible.[94] Diligence is thus necessary in all activity: One must exercise caution, self-control, meditation, honor, modesty, and moderation. Vietnamese are strongly tradition-bound, revering their ancestors, homeland, and family traditions. They tend to live in harmony with nature rather than to dominate it. Instead of favoring individualism, Vietnamese culture is oriented toward achievement of group goals, primarily within the extended family.

> The doctrine of the "Golden Mean" of Confucius and that of the "Middle Path" of Buddha have been ingrained in the Vietnamese thinking and have dominated Vietnamese thoughts. These doctrines account for the harmony maintained in social relationships among Vietnamese and between Vietnamese and other peoples. In their relations with others, Vietnamese, in order to maintain the "just middle," try to avoid injuring others and hurting their susceptibility; they compromise. They are also delicate and tactful, gentle, polite, and flexible: what belongs to others is pretty and what belongs to them is ugly. Also, it is desirable for Vietnamese to show respect to their superiors and kindness to their inferiors. The desire to please others can be found in old folk sayings that "since one does not have to buy nice words, one should choose those pleasant to others' ears." To make others happy, one sometimes has to bend low and to live up to their expectation.[95]

According to Confucian thinking a hierarchical system is the natural order of things. It is necessary, therefore, that individuals know their position in the system, and behave as befits that position.[96] Thus these cultural values of courage and stoicism in the face of adversity, as well as adaptation through conformity, helped make the refugees' adjustment somewhat easier. Peter I. Rose adds that other cultural values also were effective: a strong sense of family; a high value on education; high motivation to achieve, especially for a better life for their children; and an emphasis on discipline, responsibility, and hard work.[97]

Acculturation

Although very few entire families succeeded in leaving Vietnam, enough members of Vietnamese extended families did arrive to enable continuance of traditional family structures. Although this arrangement would seem to ease their adjustment, early studies revealed that immersion in the automated, specialized American culture caused tension between the vivid, persistent extended-family image and emotional reality.[98] "Vietnamericans" established separate households, often at a considerable distance from other relatives, making contacts, visits, and shared responsibility for older adult family members more difficult.

Refugee adaptation to American life appears to vary. One study found that a higher education level and degree of Americanization prior to immigration eased the acculturation process.[99] A contradictory finding in another study was that higher education meant poorer adjustment because of underemployment.[100] Both studies agreed, however, that those Vietnamese with the most traditional point of view faced the greatest culture shock and difficulty in adaptation.

An ongoing study by behavioral scientists at the University of Washington in Seattle, begun in 1976, uses the Cornell Medical Index to document the physical and mental health status of Vietnamese refugees.[101] Among their findings are that adaptation problems continued into the third and fourth year after arrival. Physical complaints often are the result of psychological stresses and are psychosomatic. Women are more likely than men to suffer from depression, anxiety, and tension. A greater frequency of feelings of inadequacy, anger, tension, and sensitivity occurs among the refugees than in the general population. Principal causes of mental stress are loneliness, lack of community life, breakup of the family, uncertainty about the future, home-sickness, grief over losses of fleeing one's homeland, and frustration in coping with American life. As found in earlier studies of Cuban and Hungarian refugees, hostile and aggressive attitudes toward the host society or fellow refugees often proves to be an effective adaptive style. This emotional arousal helps Vietnamese to overcome the passivity of their cultural values, discussed earlier in this section, and to seek out and find better ways to survive and surmount their problems.

Contributing to the adjustment problem was the federal government's policy of scattering the refugees throughout all 50 states. Intended as an integration program to accelerate acculturation, it instead denied the Vietnamese the social and emotional support network of an ethnic community such as used by past immigrant groups. Initially no mutual assistance organizations formed, and early studies showed varying degrees of success in refugee adaptation to American life.

Gradually the Vietnamericans began to relocate near one another, particularly in California, Texas, Virginia, and Louisiana. Here their concentrations led to the development of ethnic neighborhoods and social networks so characteristic of first-generation Americans. "Little Saigon" has blossomed in Orange County, California, for example, where the language, signs, shops, offices, and music all convey a distinct Vietnamese atmosphere.[102] Similarly, Anaheim now has its own little Saigon.[103] In Texas and Louisiana, ethnic communities also are visible, especially near the Gulf Coast, where many Vietnamericans have entered the fishing industry.

As with most immigrant groups, age determines the degree of acculturation. The elderly come to be with their families but show little interest in giving up their cultural values or assimilating. Youth find their traditional family values inconsistent with those in American society. Traditionally, Vietnamese parents play a major role in determining their adolescents' situations. Vietnamese culture places emphasis on achieving one's identity and sense of worth through close relationships with family adults and being a member of the extended family. American adolescents are more autonomous, self-determining, and concerned about peer approval. American ways seem more attractive to Vietnamese youth, and so they often refuse parental guidance and enter into situations without parental consent. Intergenerational conflict is thus exacerbated by the cultural values of the adults and those learned by their children.[104]

OTHER SOUTHEAST ASIANS

Cambodians and Laotians, like the Vietnamese, were also once a part of French Indochina. For centuries, however, these three groups have been linguistically, culturally, and ethnically distinct from one another, and differences exist within each nationality group as well. Of the approximately 1 million Indochinese Americans identified by the 1990 census, about 24 percent were from Laos, 15 percent were from Cambodia, and 61 percent were from Vietnam.

Thailand, formerly Siam, is another nation in this part of the world that has sent a significant number of immigrants to the United States. Over 91,000

In a wonderful example of ethnogenesis, these immigrants from Thailand gather together on a suburban back patio for a typical American weekend barbecue, using a shish kebab recipe from their homeland. Their hairstyles and clothing reflect the mixture of cultural influences from their native and adopted lands. (*Bob Daemmrich/The Image Works*)

Thai now live in the United States. Relatively little has been written about this group so far, except in grouping them with other Southeast Asians.

The Laotians

About 240,000 Laotians now call the United States home. These refugees include several groups, including over 3,000 Tai Dam living prosperously in Iowa. Most of the refugees from Laos, however, are the Hmong (pronounced *mung* and meaning "free people").

A mountain people living north of the Plain of Jars in Laos, the Hmong had lived a marginal existence, practicing slash-and-burn farming on hilltops, attributing disease to evil spirits, and relying on the stories of their parents and grandparents for their education. Their belief in spirits includes the idea that a frightening or shameful experience results in illness caused by the individual spirit fleeing the body. To lock the soul to oneself so it cannot leave, the Hmong wear copper or silver bracelets, anklets, and necklaces as special protective jewelry.[105]

Recruited as American allies during the secret war in Laos in the early 1970s, thousands of Hmong men and boys went to work for the CIA by rescuing downed American pilots, sabotaging communist war supplies, and gathering intelligence on North Vietnamese troop movements. About 15,000 Hmong were killed in combat with the Vietcong. When the Pathet Lao took control of Laos, they systematically attempted to wipe out the Hmong, forcing them to flee. Many Americans felt a special concern and commitment to the Hmong, and tens of thousands were admitted into the United States as refugees. Coming from a society that had no written language until 40 years ago, a society without a cash economy, one in which the concept of "getting a job" was unknown because one simply lived off the land and provided for one's family, the Hmong have faced enormous difficulties in making the quantum leap to living in American society.

The Hmong are from a patrilineal society in which the traditional role of the wife is devotion to her husband. An extremely strong extended family and clan system binds the individuals together. This is why, after initially being scattered across the country by the U.S. government, many Hmong have resettled near kin and clan members. Eighty-nine percent of the Hmong population living in the United States now reside in three states: California (47,000), Minnesota, (17,000), and Wisconsin (16,000).[106] Although problems of language, economic naivete, and virtually no job skills initially plagued the Hmong, placing a large percentage on welfare, some recent studies suggest their gradual, successful acculturation.[107]

As the children become Americanized adolescents, cultural dissonance typically affects the Hmong family. Parents lack personal experience and role models with the adolescent experience because adolescence as such did not exist in Laos. There, one married young and assumed parental responsibilities early. Dating without an adult chaperone, and any overt public display of

BOX 8.3	THE ETHNIC EXPERIENCE

"I came to the U.S. for the adventure. I had heard much about this country and seen many American films. My parents are Chinese and migrated to Thailand about twenty years before I was born. My father is a very successful businessman, having his own lumber business and a few hotels. So I really came here only to satisfy my own curiosity, but I stayed here for my undergraduate and graduate course work and I haven't returned yet.

"It's almost as if I sensed this before I left. I was going to America because I wanted to see that country, but before my parents took me to the airport, I cried. At the airport a lot of people came to say farewell to me and I just waved to them. I had the feeling I would never come back here. Especially when I got into the airplane, I felt that I was losing the things that I really love, and I wanted to get off. It's a very lonely and scary feeling. . . .

"Things seemed strange to me at first. Oriental people all have dark hair. Here I saw many people with different features, with blond hair, brown hair, and so on. At that time they looked funny to me. I had seen some American soldiers in Thailand, but they were a small minority. Now everyone around me was so very different. Another thing was being driven [so fast] on the highways. . . . We have few good highways in Thailand and this was a new experience.

"I can't describe to you how lonely and depressed I was in this country. I at first wished I had never come. The family I stayed with in New Hampshire was friendly and tried to teach me about America, but the language and cultural barriers were overwhelming in those first six or eight months. I was withdrawn because I was afraid of the people and didn't know how to do. Most people were impatient with me and so avoided me. I was sad and didn't like this country, but I felt obliged to my parents to stay for the year even though I was very homesick.

"At the end of the school year I went back home. I discovered I had changed. I was more independent and stubborn, and I enjoyed doing some things that Thai people thought were silly, like getting a suntan. Also, I really wanted to be somebody and make my parents proud, and I thought the best way was to get an education in the U.S. So I came back here and earned my bachelor's degree. This summer I'll finish my master's degree and then I'll go back home to my parents and give them my diplomas. They really belong to my parents because they gave me material and emotional support. I'll come back here . . . and maybe someday be a college professor."

SOURCE: Thai immigrant who came to the United States in 1971 at age 19.

affection such as kissing or holding hands in public, violate Hmong tradition. Attracted to the American way of life, Hmong teenagers often challenge their parents' authority on these matters.[108]

Although the Hmong have suffered from poverty since their arrival in the United States, their severe destitution earlier in the refugee camps in Thailand appears to have helped them cope. Moreover, they do not expect to stay poor, because they encourage many family members to work, and they show a strong commitment to educating their children.[109]

ETHNOVIOLENCE

A 1986 report of the U.S. Commission on Civil Rights concluded that violence against Asians had become a national problem, with a 62 percent increase in anti-Asian incidents over the previous year.[110] Does this rash of anti-Asian actions exemplify *isolate discrimination*—a term coined by Feagin referring to the actions of individuals against other individuals?[111] Kitano and Daniels think so, calling them acts of discrimination that have a minor impact on society, without the far-ranging effects of institutionalized discrimination, such as the anti-Asian immigration legislation or the 1942 evacuation of Japanese Americans.[112]

Individually each violent outbreak may seem to be a local incident, but it also may be a symptom of a more pervasive xenophobic fear escalating into a pattern of violence. Vietnamese fishermen have been beaten and their boats torched in Texas and California. Tire slashings, windshield smashings, and attempted porch firebombings against Cambodians have occurred in Revere, Massachusetts. In Seattle, shots were fired into homes of Southeast Asian refugees. In Detroit in 1982 an unemployed auto-industry foreman vented his frustration and anger on a scapegoat by mistaking a 27-year-old Chinese American for a Japanese person and beating him to death with a baseball bat while his 23-year-old son held the helpless victim. Subsequently, the men received lenient sentences and were acquitted of federal civil rights charges. A local incident only? Perhaps. But what of the baseball-bat slaying of an Asian Indian in Jersey City? Or the baseball-bat beating of a Laotian in Philadelphia or of a second Asian Indian in Jersey City? Were these copycat crimes only?

What then about the popular black disk jockey in Philadelphia in December 1986 who reportedly said on the air that Koreans "suck our blood" and that blacks should "use kerosene" to stop them. That incident led to a public apology by the radio station, but dozens of firebombings of Korean stores in Harlem, Philadelphia, and Washington, DC, and in other inner-city neighborhoods occurred in the late 1980s.

By the time of the May 1992 Los Angeles riots, when about 2,300 Korean-owned stores were damaged or destroyed, with estimated losses exceeding $400,000, a nationwide pattern of black–Korean conflict had been established.[113] Like Jewish and Italian immigrants before them, thousands of Koreans had become owners of inner-city retail stores, serving as a middleman minority to blacks and Hispanics in virtually every major American city. Working long hours and using low-paid family labor, they succeeded in neighborhoods where many area residents live a marginal existence.[114]

Black resentment stems partly from the Koreans' ease in borrowing through the *kye* and their mercantile success in black neighborhoods. Blacks accurately complain that Koreans take money out of the community but rarely hire non-Koreans. They also interpret Koreans' limited English and cultural interactions with customers as rudeness. Social distance, economic frustration, envy, alienation, and a sense of being exploited all help explain the racial tensions that erupt into ethnoviolence. An increase in inner-city black entrepreneurs and outreach by Korean merchants into the community they serve would do much to lessen the problem.

Other incidents of harassment, intimidation, graffiti, vandalism, and assault continue to serve as painful reminders of the continuing presence of racism, bigotry, and discrimination. The violent episodes may be the familiar patterns of similar actions taken against earlier immigrant groups, but that is hardly comfort for the victims or for an American-born generation that considers itself more sophisticated and tolerant than past generations.

THE MODEL MINORITY STEREOTYPE _____

Since the early 1980s, when William Petersen first praised Asian Americans as a "model minority," the term has become entrenched in the public mind.[115] Images of Chinese engineers, Japanese financiers, Filipino nurses, Korean entrepreneurs, and Vietnamese restaurateurs abound, helping to reinforce this positive stereotype. Asian American educational and economic successes apparently demonstrate that people of color can realize the American Dream through hard work and self-reliance. Their achievements are testimony, it would seem, to the opportunities for a color-free, problem-free, government-interventionist-free integration into American society. Like all stereotypes, however, that of the model minority is misleading and ignores the diversity of the Asian American population:

> Beneath a thick crust of scientists, professionals, and entrepreneurs are thicker layers of struggling families—peddlers and waiters and office cleaners and sweater stitchers who eke out a bare living by dint of double jobs and the presence of multiple wage earners.[116]

Other examples contradict the stereotype. Many Southeast Asian refugees remain on welfare; some obviously will be long-term recipients. Not all Asian American students are strong academically. The criminal activities of major Asian drug rings, smaller-scale Asian extortion gangs, and Asian youth gangs are an often brutal menace. Some Asian Americans live in crowded dwellings, suffer from tuberculosis or depression, and even some live without hope.

BOX 8.4   THE INTERNATIONAL SCENE

After decades of Japanese refusal to let in unskilled foreigners, tens of thousands of Bangladeshis, Pakistanis, Thais, and other Asians entered Japan in the 1980s on tourist visas and stayed illegally. Worried that it might be flooded by foreigners as France and Germany had been, Japan enacted tougher immigration curbs on unskilled workers in 1989 and began expelling the estimated 100,000 illegal Asians. Still needing a labor pool and not wanting to open its doors to outsiders, Japan next changed its immigration laws in 1990 to encourage immigration of foreigners with parents or grandparents in Japan, expecting a homogeneous blending.

About 150,000 unskilled, ethnic Japanese fleeing the troubled economy of Brazil quickly entered Japan to take the dirty, difficult, and dangerous jobs at construction sites, factories, and foundries or low-status jobs in restaurants and shops unwanted by native-born Japanese. However, what seemed to be a mutually beneficial arrangement to help the newcomers find work the Japanese needed done created numerous adjustment problems for both sides, who were unprepared for the culture shock each experienced.

The Japanese expected the Brazilians to be Japanese, but culturally they were not. They spoke Portuguese, little or no Japanese, when they arrived and for a long time afterward. They dressed differently, talked more noisily, laughed and embraced one another in public, all unlike the native-born Japanese. Their ethnicity became more visible with the advent of numerous Portuguese-language radio programs and newspapers, restaurants, stores, and social clubs. Brazilian street festivals in Tokyo flavored with samba and salsa attract large crowds.

The immigrants complain they are looked down on and treated with suspicion. They say they suffer discrimination in stores and restaurants, where they are either made to feel unwelcome or treated as probable shoplifters. Another problem they face is the lack of health benefits and workmen's compensation if injured at work. The government, meanwhile, has opened a dozen centers to assist the foreign laborers.

The idea of a model minority also does harm. The public often unfairly criticizes other minority groups for failing to attain comparable levels of achievement. Besides the enormous pressure this image places on Asian American youth to excel, their success is partly attributable to the fact that many are children of professionals. Coming from lands where an intellectual elite rose to power through stringent tests, their cultures have traditionally placed a high value on educational meritocracy. Moreover, through thousands of interviews with Asian Americans, researchers agree that fear is a compelling motive for their increased academic effort; they seek protection against discrimination through academic success.[117]

SOCIOLOGICAL ANALYSIS _____

Some of our discussion of Asian immigrants has covered events in previous generations; other parts of this chapter have focused on the contemporary scene. If we apply the sociological perspective to these individual group chronologies, we find that the time span is irrelevant in understanding the continuing patterns of intergroup relations.

The Functionalist View

Chinese in the nineteenth century filled important social needs—working on railroads, farms, ranches, and in stores and factories. Their work effectively contributed to the building of a transportation system, the manufacture of needed goods, and the provision of valuable services. Although racial antagonism had existed earlier, nationwide economic hard times in the 1870s worsened the situation. Economic dysfunctions set off intensified labor antagonism, culminating in a system adjustment of immigration restrictions. The withdrawal of Chinese into their Chinatowns, despite occasional internal strife, helped to promote ethnic solidarity and to offer a social network for interaction in a hostile white society. Later these Chinatowns would function as absorption centers for tens of thousands of new arrivals, once the immigration restrictions were lifted.

Japanese, Korean, and Filipino farm laborers, both in Hawaii and on the mainland, helped agriculture expand and prosper. An urbanizing West Coast needed many domestic and personal service workers, jobs filled mostly by Filipinos who liked city life and its educational opportunities. Major societal dysfunctions—the trauma of a war begun with a surprise attack and a severe, long-lasting depression—triggered negative actions against the Japanese and Filipinos, respectively. Eventually a restoration of system balance enabled these minority groups to overcome past discrimination and become more fully assimilated. Problems remaining with Filipino immigrants stem from their unemployment or underemployment and rapid increase in population, compounded by the recent recession and changing occupational structure of society.

Cultural traditions and family cohesiveness have been positive functions easing the adjustment of most East Asian immigrants into American society. Family dysfunctions have also occurred though, particularly with Americanized Asian adolescents. These difficulties range from disputes over dating to problems with self-identity and esteem, leading some Asian youth—unsupervised due to their parents' working long hours—into gangs.

Korean, Vietnamese, and other Indochinese refugees allowed Americans to act on one of their commonly held values—humanitarianism—by opening our doors to people from war-ravaged lands. Just as the host society provides freedom and opportunity to these Asian peoples, so too does the society gain from their labors and contributions to the American culture.

The Conflict View

From this perspective, when employers—railroads, farmers, urban businesses, Hawaiian plantation owners—needed inexpensive alien labor, they recruited it and reaped the profits. When times turned bad, those with power used it to protect their interests. So it was that the series of electoral victories by the anti-Chinese Workingmen's Party in California caused the Republican and Democratic political parties to coopt the anti-Chinese cause to defuse this new political movement. Similarly, the California growers advocated Japanese removal in 1942 to eliminate their competition. Labor organizations campaigned against the Chinese in the 1870s and against the Filipinos and other groups in the 1930s to prevent their taking increasingly scarce jobs.

Originally based on the labor antagonism against the Chinese, the split labor market theory applies to several of the Asian groups. Coming from low-income countries, the wages Asian workers accepted, while reasonable by their standards, undermined the wage scale of the native workers. For instance, when the Chinese entered the shoemaking trade extensively in the 1870s, weekly wages dropped from $25 to $9. Complaints about unfair competition of Japanese farmers included their "willingness" to work for less than whites, or to accept payment in crops or land instead of wages. More recently, white shrimpers burned Vietnamese-owned boats in Galveston Bay, blacks in Harlem urged boycotts of Korean stores, Hispanics in Denver housing projects attacked Indochinese refugees, and black–Filipino animosity on the East Coast occasionally manifested itself among medical service workers competing for certain hospital jobs.

Economic exploitation or competition generates other forms of ethnic antagonism. The Chinatown sweatshops exploit immigrant labor and undermine the unionized garment workers, who are further affected adversely by imports from places like Taiwan and Hong Kong. Auto workers and steel workers experience layoffs and job insecurity because of Japanese products. As black, white, and Hispanic workers treat Asians as the enemy, conflict theorists point out that the real culprits are those benefiting—the sweatshop employers, the corporations that avoided capital modernization expenditures to maximize profits, and the America-based multinational corporations that establish factories in low-income countries, marketing their products in the United States and elsewhere for higher profits.

The Interactionist View

Americans have used the word *inscrutable* almost exclusively to describe the Asians, especially the Chinese and Japanese. This concept that Asians defied understanding rested on their marked non-Western differences in physical appearance, language, belief systems, customs, stoicism, and observable behavior. If you will recall our discussion in Chapter 1 about the perceived similarity factor and acceptance of strangers, the extreme social distance between native-born Americans and Asian immigrants becomes understandable. As the groups furthest from the dominant group's increasingly distant interaction patterns, Asians thus offered easy targets for negative stereotyping, prejudice, scapegoating, and discrimination. Cultural differences became intertwined with physical differences in the minds of many Americans, allowing racism to predominate in value judgments and avoidance–dominance responses.

Asian immigrants in the late nineteenth and early twentieth centuries gave the West Coast its immigrant experience in similar fashion to the European migration in the eastern United States. Spanish Americans and Native Americans were already indigenous to the West, and so it was the Asians who created the new subcommunities, worked for low wages, and received the scorn and resentment of others. The Asian newcomers were replicating patterns of European immigrants in the eastern United States, but the Westerners interpreted these as threats to economic security and the American way of life. This social interpretation of reality set in motion the interaction problems that followed. As attitudes translated into actions, setting off reactions and reinforcing attitudes on both sides, the vicious circle intensified and perpetuated the ingroup's perception of the outgroup.

Recent Asian immigrants offer a bipolar model. Those who are preliterate and wedded to a tradition of the land face a bewildering leap into an urban society. Schutz's observation, discussed in Chapter 1, that every taken-for-granted situation for the native presents a crisis for the stranger, is overwhelmingly true for many Indochinese. Their adjustment and integration into society may be long and difficult. Others come with education and skills that enable them to enter the economic mainstream more easily. However, their racial and cultural differences presently curtail their social integration or structural assimilation.

Retrospect

As a result of a combination of racial and non-Western cultural differences, a great many Asian immigrants from 1850 to 1940 remained outside the American mainstream all their lives. Lack of acceptance and social interaction in the dominant society and frequent hostile actions directed against them made the Asians acutely aware of the differences in the people and culture around them. Each succeeding wave of Asian immigrants, from whatever country, encountered some degree of hostility because of racial and cultural visibility. To some Americans the Asians posed a serious challenge to the cherished notion of a melting pot because of their race, their non-Christian faith (though some were Christians), their language and alphabet, and the customs and practices. That many chose to settle on the West Coast near their port of entry, much as European immigrants had in the East, only accentuated their presence and led whites to overemphasize their actual numbers. Many also believed that these immigrants posed an economic threat to American workers, and this further encouraged racist reactions.

Many white Americans came to accept negative stereotypes, first about the Chinese and later about the Japanese and Filipinos. Normal ethnocentric judgments about a culturally distinct people, coupled with racial visibility that served as a distinct link to the stereotype, caused a generalized societal antagonism toward the Asians. The vast differences in culture and physical appearance, augmented by imagined racist fears of threats to economic security or to white womanhood from "lascivious Orientals," led to frequent hostility.

The Japanese were mostly concentrated in rural areas on the West Coast until 1940. On the mainland racist antagonisms and fears culminated in 1942 with the removal of Japanese Americans from their homes and jobs. Although a few Japanese Americans were rounded up in Hawaii, there was no mass evacuation because the Japanese lived in a less racist environment, with fuller political and economic participation. Filipinos also encountered overt racial discrimination prior to 1940. Since the changes in the immigration law in 1965, over 350,000 Filipinos have migrated to the United States. Although many are underemployed, they and the Chinese and Japanese encounter less hostility today than did their predecessors.

Koreans, Vietnamese, Cambodians, Laotians, and Thais are more recent Asian immigrants. Some are war refugees, but all are from non-Western cultures and are racially distinct from white and black Americans. They enter an America far less racially hostile toward Asians than it was in the past. Many are either dependents of U.S. servicemen or individuals with marketable job skills. Most come from a region of the world where patience, stoicism, quiet industriousness, and the cohesiveness of the extended family are long-standing traditions. These traditional values aid the newcomers' transition to a new life.

Asia is presently the major supplier outside this hemisphere of immigrants to the United States. Approximately 40 percent of all immigrants now come from Asia. Obviously, that part of the world is having a profound effect on the composition of our population. In the years ahead America will become even more a land of racial and cultural diversity.

Review Questions

1. Discuss the interrelationship between labor conflict and racism with regard to the Chinese, Japanese, and Filipinos.
2. How did the Chinese of the late nineteenth century respond to hostility and discrimination?
3. How can we explain the different treatment of Japanese Americans in Hawaii and on the mainland during World War II?
4. How do the concepts of the ethnic church and middleman minority apply to the Korean Americans?
5. What are some cultural characteristics of Vietnamericans?
6. Discuss the legislation and court rulings directed against Asian Americans.

7. How do today's Asian immigrants differ from their predecessors? How and why does society respond to them differently?

8. How do the three major sociological perspectives approach the Asian experience in the United States?

Suggested Readings

BULOSAN, CARLOS. *America Is in the Heart.* Seattle: University of Washington, 1973.
A moving autobiography of what it was like to be a Filipino in California in the 1920s.

DANIELS, ROGER. *The Politics of Prejudice.* New York: Atheneum, 1972.
A fine analysis of the use of political power against Asians in general, Japanese in particular.

HURH, WON MOO, AND KWANG CHUNG KIM. *Korean Immigrants in America.* Rutherford, NJ: Farleigh Dickinson University Press, 1984.
Good theoretical analysis based on empirical studies of Korean Americans living in Chicago and Los Angeles.

KIM, HYUNG-CHAN (ED.). *The Korean Diaspora.* Santa Barbara, CA: Clio Press, 1977.
An excellent collection of writings about Korean Americans and their organizations and enterprises.

KITANO, HARRY H.L. *Japanese Americans: The Evolution of a Subculture,* 2d ed. Englewood Cliffs, NJ: Prentice-Hall, 1976.
Succinct yet comprehensive overview of the Japanese experience in America over four generations.

_____ , AND ROGER DANIELS. *Asian Americans: Emerging Minorities.* Englewood Cliffs, NJ: Prentice-Hall, 1988.
A thorough sociohistorical profile of each of the different Asian peoples who have migrated to the United States.

LYMAN, STANFORD M. *Chinese Americans.* New York: Random House, 1974.
An excellent sociohistorical analysis of Chinese Americans, written in an effective, comprehensive manner.

_____ . *The Asian in North America.* Santa Barbara, CA: Clio Press, 1977.
A comprehensive overview of major Asian immigrant groups in North America, the similarities and dissimilarities of their experiences.

PIDO, ANTONIO J. A. *The Filipinos in America.* New York: Center for Migration Studies, 1986.
A detailed sociological study of the experiences of both the early and recent immigrants from the Philippines.

TAKAKI, RONALD. *Strangers from a Different Shore: A History of Asian Americans.* Boston: Little, Brown, 1989.
Presents a historic overview of the settlement and acculturation experiences of various Asian American groups.

Joel Gordon

9

Central and West Asian Immigrants

West Asian immigrants come from a part of the world situated between the area of Western thought and history on one side, and the area of Eastern thought and philosophy on the other. From Turkey through the Middle East to India, the Muslim religion is predominant, but the cultures are as diverse as elsewhere in the world.

Although some of these peoples migrated before 1965 and had encounters similar to those of other racial and ethnic groups of earlier times, most have come since the 1965 Immigration Act. Their acceptance as strangers and their adjustment to American life has differed from those of pre-1920 immigrants because structural conditions in both the sending and host countries have changed. Because of the occupational preference ranking of the 1965 legislation, many of those who have come are professional, managerial, or technical workers. Some are underemployed, but others are accepted in their occupational roles. Either way, most are generally isolated from informal social contact with others outside their nationality group. As with many East Asians, the social distance between most first generation West Asian Americans and native-born Americans is considerable.

SOCIOHISTORICAL PERSPECTIVE

Aside from special legislation allowing political or war refugees to enter, the immigration regulations before 1965 effectively limited the number of immigrants from the non-Western world. Eliminating the restrictive national origins quota system opened the door to America to many different peoples who had previously been denied entry. Because few had migrated to the United States prior to 1890, the year on which the 1924 immigration legislation based its quotas, very few non-Western immigrants had been able to gain approval to migrate to the United States.

Since the change of the immigration laws in 1965, a third major wave of immigration has been underway, once again creating dramatic changes in the composition of the nation's population. For example, immigration from India in the 1980s exceeded 250,000, compared to about 191,000 from Germany, Ireland, and Italy combined, previously three of the top suppliers of immigrants.[1] The 1990 census count of over 315,000 foreign-born Arab Americans exceeds the combined foreign-born population from Greece and Spain.[2]

The Push–Pull Factors

For many non-Western immigrants, overpopulation and poverty have so seriously affected the quality of life in their homelands that they have sought a better life elsewhere. Sometimes restrictive governmental actions or limited socioeconomic opportunities have pushed the people to look elsewhere. America, with its cultural diversity, economic opportunities, and higher living standards, is influential throughout the world and is a powerful lure to those who are dissatisfied with their situation. For others, the United States offers educational or professional or career opportunities. Rapid air travel and instant communications, which reduce the psychological distance from one's native country, have been further inducements.

Structural Conditions

The non-Western immigrants discussed in this chapter have followed the same patterns as other ethnic groups who have emigrated to the United States. They usually settle in urban areas in close proximity to their compatriots, with whom they develop close, primary social contacts. Because many are trained professionals or skilled technicians, however, their job situation is quite different from that of the unskilled poor who made up the majority of the 1880–1920 immigrant groups. They usually do not settle in decaying sections of cities, because with their income they can find better places to live. The economic profile of these non-Western Americans ranges from the older and more affluent to the newer and struggling. Some are suburbanities, some live in working-class urban neighborhoods, and still others cope with poverty. Wherever they congregate to live and work, one can find the various support facilities: church or temples, food stores and restaurants specializing in their native victuals, social clubs or organizations, and perhaps their own schools and newspapers. They soon send for other members of their family or write home telling of their good fortune, and this stimulates others to come to the United States. The chain migration pattern of earlier immigrants is once again in evidence.

A great many of the new immigrants do not fit the acculturation patterns that worked so well for other immigrant groups. For instance, Middle Eastern prosperity and the new international image of the Arabs have not only strengthened that group's ethnic solidarity in the United States but also encouraged some to plan to return to their native country eventually. A Saudi Arabian, for example, might return from the United States after acquiring an advanced education or experience that would be preparation for a better life back home. Saudi Arabia collects no taxes whatsoever and offers free education and medical care, and its standard of living is improving rapidly. Although immigration from Saudi Arabia may be extremely low, a greater number of newcomers from other Arab countries are seeking permanent residence here, as indicated in Table 9.1.

TABLE 9.1	MIDDLE EASTERN IMMIGRANTS ADMITTED TO THE UNITED STATES		
Country		**1971–1980**	**1981–1990**
Egypt		25,495	34,259
Iran		46,152	165,267
Iraq		23,404	22,211
Jordan		29,578	36,032
Lebanon		33,846	45,770
Morocco		4,431	7,158
Saudi Arabia		700	4,180
Syria		13,339	22,230
Yemen (Sanaa)		5,170	5,634

SOURCE: Adapted from U.S. Immigration and Naturalization Service Annual Report, *Statistical Yearbook* 1990, Table 3.

Because many of this group of non-Western immigrants have marketable skills, they can get professional and salaried jobs without first having to play a subservient role in the economy. They need not yield to pressures to conform to the American way of life in order to gain middle-class respectability. Their income is high enough to enable them to enjoy the life-style they want, and they are thus free to continue their own cultural behavior patterns. Some Americanization will undoubtedly occur, but these immigrants do not have to make substantial adaptations in order to "make it" in American society.

Another sizable segment of non-Westerners in the United States is that of the nonimmigrant students, workers, and business people. Although they usually remain for only two to five years, their growing numbers make their presence of significant concern in the field of race and ethnic relations. In 1990, for example, 178,000 Asian students arrived in the United States to study, and over 638,000 Asians came to this country as temporary business visitors.[3]

In many respects these temporary visitors, although visible to others in work, residential, shopping, and entertainment settings, are similar to Americans who work for a multinational corporation overseas. Even if assigned to another country for a considerable number of years, they seldom lose their sense of ethnic identity. They live within the culture and enjoy the available opportunities without any thought of abandoning their own cultural ties and becoming assimilated in the country in which they work. Many aliens working here have the same orientation, whether they work for one of their own country's multinational corporations or for some American employer. U.S. citizenship and assimilation are not part of their plans. Many of today's sojourners may be more sophisticated than their predecessors, but their resistance to assimilation is just as strong.

Societal Reaction

About 5,000 Asian Indians, and 325,000 Middle Easterners migrated to the United States between 1880 and 1920. They encountered far more prejudice and discrimination than their compatriots experience in America today. Americans are now more tolerant of what may seem to them to be the strange appearance and customs of the non-Western immigrants. Tolerance, though, is not the same thing as acceptance. People do categorize others and make judgments based on visible impressions, which often lead to stereotyping. Racial distinguishing features and distinctive apparel, such as a dashiki, turban, or sari, set these newcomers apart. Although little overt discrimination occurs, only limited social interaction is common.

In recent surveys of social distance among various minority groups, the racially distinct non-Western immigrants have all scored at the bottom.[4] Many newcomers find themselves accepted in their professional, managerial, and technical occupational roles by members of the dominant society, but they are not usually included in outside social activities. Once the workday or work-week ends, they seldom receive social invitations from dominant-group members; thus they interact mostly with family and compatriots. Economic mainstreaming may have occurred for many non-Western immigrants, but they have yet to achieve social integration.

THE ASIAN INDIANS ⸻⸻⸻⸻⸻⸻⸻⸻⸻⸻

Emigration from India to the United States took place in two distinct phases. In the early twentieth century several thousand poorly educated Indian agricultural laborers migrated to the West Coast and settled in rural regions in Washington (lumbering) and California (agriculture). Almost all the early immigrants were Sikh males who came from the Punjab region in northern India. Distinctive in their traditionally worn beards and turbans, they soon experienced hostile racism and violent attacks. Since 1965 a second group of immigrants—many Hindus who are better educated, more urbanized, and affluent—has come to the United States.

Early Immigrants

Between 1820 and 1900 fewer than 800 immigrants came to the United States from India. In the next two decades a small wave of almost 7,000 agricultural laborers from northern India journeyed to the West Coast of the United States, and still others chose Canada. Almost entirely male, this group—like so many other immigrant groups—intended to accumulate some savings and

These early-twentieth-century farm workers in California were mistakenly called Hindus, probably because that is the religion of most people from India. However, their turbans reveal these men to be Sikhs, a minority people from northern India. Nevertheless, "Hindu" was the racial epithet commonly used by nativists to inflame public opinion against their growing numbers. *(Brown Brothers)*

then return home. Between 1908 and 1920 a total of 1,656 did leave, and another 249 were deported as undesirable aliens.[5]

Societal Reaction

Even though the Japanese, Chinese, and Filipinos far outnumbered the Asian Indians, the latter group also experienced discrimination and aggression because of their visibility and identification as Asians. Near a lumber camp in Bellingham, Washington, several hundred whites raided the living quarters of Indian workers on September 5, 1907, forcing about 700 of them to flee across the Canadian border. Two months later, in Everett, Washington, several hundred whites drove the Indian workers out of town. Racial prejudice manifested itself in Port Angeles, where real estate brokers published in the local newspaper the terms of their covenant not to sell to "Hindoos or Negroes." They justified their action on the grounds that wherever these groups settle, they "have depreciated [the] value of adjacent property and injured the reputation of the neighborhood, and are generally considered as undesirable."[6]

The San Francisco–based Asiatic Exclusion League quickly included the Asian Indians among their targets and warned the public that they were a "menace." League officials declared that the East Indians were untrustworthy, immodest, unsanitary, insolent, and lustful.[7] These pressures against the Asian Indians were effective from 1908 to 1910, when immigration officials rejected 1,130 immigrants at their ports of entry. Pressure from the Western Pacific Railroad in 1910 enabled 1,462 to enter between 1911 and 1920, but another 1,762 were denied entry, mostly on the grounds that they would become public charges.[8] The popular magazine *Collier's,* influenced by the Asiatic Exclusion League's exaggerated claim that there were 10,000 Asian Indians living in California, printed an article warning its readers about the "Hindu invasion."[9] *Hindu* was a popular racial term in those days, no doubt reflective of the fact that 93 percent of India's population is Hindu. However, these immigrant victims were mostly Sikhs, a minority people comprising just 2 percent of their country's population.

> In this atmosphere of marked hostility toward Asians, the few thousand East Indians gradually established themselves primarily in California and relied chiefly on agriculture as a means of livelihood. Typically the Indians sought work in groups with a leader serving as their agent in negotiating with employers. Owing in part to the desire of many farmers to break the Japanese monopoly on the labor supply in those areas, they had little difficulty finding employment in the Sacramento and San Joaquin valleys. Also, Indians moved into the Imperial Valley, another rapidly growing agricultural area.[10]

In 1923 the U.S. Supreme Court reversed previous lower court decisions and ruled that Asian Indians were nonwhites and thus ineligible for citizenship under the terms of the 1790 naturalization act. The government then canceled the naturalization certificates that had previously been granted to 60 or 70 Asian Indians. This decision also prevented the Asian Indians from owning or leasing land in their own names because of state legislation against alien land-holding. The Asian Indians thus became itinerant farm laborers. Few of them had any family life because of the itinerant nature of their work and the lack of women they could marry.

Minority Response

Juan Gonzales, Jr., points out that the social and economic restrictions of discriminatory immigration and miscegenation laws created the social isolation of the early immigrants. Unable to travel, send for wives or future brides, or marry Anglo women, they could neither participate fully in American society nor produce a second generation of American citizens to aid their movement into the mainstream of American life.[11]

About 3,000 Asian Indians returned home between 1920 and 1940. A few hundred more were deported. The population dwindled from 5,441 in 1920 to 3,138 in 1930 and to 2,405 in 1940.[12] A few of those who remained married Mexican women. Most, however, lived in communal groups apart from the rest of society. Some congregated in Stockton, California—site of a large Filipino community—and built a temple there for worship.

In July 1946 the Luce-Celler Bill brought relief to the Asian Indian community. Removed from the "barred zone" established in 1917 to prevent most Asians and Pacific Islanders from immigrating to the United States, 100 Asian Indians now could enter annually. Males already living here could also now bring over their wives and children or make marital arrangements with women living in the Punjab. Finally, Asian Indians were permitted to become naturalized American citizens, an opportunity taken by 1,772 of them between 1948 and 1965.[13]

Gary R. Hess reports that by the mid-1950s the Asian Indian community in Sutter County in north-central California numbered about 900 and had grown stronger and more unified.[14] This had come about because the men preferred to marry Asian Indian women and because the caste system in India had a negligible influence in the United States, except perhaps in terms of status. Because of the small amount of intermarriage and the retention of important aspects of their culture, the rural Asian Indians, Hess concluded, remained only slightly acculturated even though they had adopted certain material comforts, dress, and other features of American life.

Physical appearance was an important factor setting these immigrants apart. In the early twentieth century, the long hair and full beards prescribed by the Sikh religion were not fashionable. Moreover, all the men wore turbans and were sometimes castigated as "ragheads." Those Indian women who had come before the Depression, as well as those who have come since the more liberal Immigration Act of 1965, were quite distinct in their wearing of the *sari*, a lightweight outer garment with one end wrapped about the waist and the other draped over the shoulder or covering the head. Most of the cultural differences—appearance, food taboos, and social interaction—were an integral part of either caste system or the religions of India. Therefore the Asian Indians not only seemed strange to the Americans but also had difficulty assimilating because they were reluctant to abandon their customs and practices.

Recent Immigrants

Statistics reveal the dramatic change in the number of immigrants from India. Only 15,513 entered the United States over the 65-year period from 1901 to 1965. In the next five years that total was easily surpassed when 24,587 immigrated between 1966 and 1970. Then the immigrant totals dramatically increased: 164,134 in the 1970s and 250,786 in the 1980s.[15] The Asian Indian presence is now significant, with 815,447 counted in the 1990 census, more than twice their numbers 10 years earlier. With over 28,000 additional immigrants arriving each year, they will soon surpass Japan to become the third largest Asian American population, behind China and the Philippines.[16]

Of the post-1965 immigrants from India, the largest number have been Hindi speaking, followed by Gujarati, Punjabi, and Bengali speakers. Asian

Indian immigrants have also been arriving from East Africa and Latin America, particularly the Caribbean and British Guyana, where earlier generations had first gone as indentured plantation laborers.[17]

Since 1965 the immigration laws have allowed in an increased number of Asian immigrants, but this alone does not explain the increase in migration. Conditions in India are an important factor. India is the world's second most populous country after mainland China, with 15 percent of the world's population on 2.5 percent of the world's land mass. This means that the population density is seven times greater than that of the United States.

The problem of overpopulation is quite serious. India's population has grown from 439 million in 1960, to 550 million in 1971, to over 820 million in 1990. The rapid growth is not due to any spurt in the birth rate but to a decline in the mortality rate. Even so, 3 million of the 23 million babies born in India each year die before they reach their first birthday, and another million die before they complete childhood. Of the remaining 19 million, nearly 9 million will become adults with physical and mental impairments and reduced productivity because of serious undernourishment and poor health. Another 7 million will suffer milder malnutrition and less striking physical and mental impairment.[18] The population is nevertheless increasing by about 1.2 million people each month.

With over two-thirds of the population engaged in agriculture, a literacy rate of only 30 percent, and problems of severe poverty, hunger, and inadequate resources, India does not have very much to offer in terms of economic security. However, many of the recent immigrants have been professional workers—physicians, surgeons, dentists, teachers, and skilled workers—providing the United States with the very people India needs most to retain if the quality of life there is to improve. This "brain drain" problem is one faced by most developing nations.

With their education and occupational skills, these newcomers can achieve economic security, but there are cultural strains. For example, they are uneasy with America's sexual mores. Parents have considerable difficulty convincing their children that the Indian custom of not dating before marriage has merit. As a result of societal pressures, many either wear American clothes or rarely venture out alone. Immigrants may also be lonely at holiday times and may feel guilty when their compatriots in India accuse them of having sold their skills to an already rich country.[19]

More than half of the Asian Indians are physicians, engineers, architects, or surveyors.[20] The other half are found most often operating convenience stores, gas stations, or family-managed hotels and motels. In fact, with Indian ownership of such establishments now approaching 20 percent across the land, they have found a family-labor economic niche as ubiquitous as the Korean greengrocery.[21]

Racial ambiguity marks the Asian Indian acceptance pattern. Their skin color ranges from light brown to almost black, although most of the immigrants in the United States are of a light hue. Americans perceive them as racially different but have difficulty categorizing them. Defined as "white" sometimes, "Asian" other times, and "brown" or "black" still other times, Asian Indians tend to classify themselves "white" and identify with the majority group.[22]

The New York–New Jersey region has the largest percentage of Asian Indians, over one-fourth of the nation's total. California has the second largest concentration, about 20 percent. Other states with significant Asian Indian American populations are Illinois, Texas, Pennsylvania, Michigan, Maryland, and Ohio.[23]

ARAB AMERICANS

Arab is a broad term covering people of diverse nationalities, religions, and socioeconomic backgrounds. Although Arab Americans may now share a sense of peoplehood, many cultural differences still separate them from one another and their ethnic identities remain fixed on their nationalities and specific homelands.

Approximately 3 million Arab Americans live in the United States, about half descended from immigrants who arrived between 1880 and 1940 and the rest from those who arrived after World War II. Over 250,000 Arab Americans live in southeastern Michigan, making it one of the largest concentrations of Arabs outside the Middle East.[24]

Dearborn, Michigan, a suburb of Detroit, became a favorite destination of many working-class Arab immigrants after the 1967 Arab–Israeli war. Several thousand Muslim Palestinians, Yemenis, and southern Lebanese arrived there, making it today the largest Muslim community in the United States. Because of the concentration of so many first-generation Arab Americans, Dearborn today resembles more completely a "Little Syria" than any other Arab American community. Nearby Detroit suburbs, such as Livonia, house large numbers of middle-class Arab Americans.

Despite the major settlement of Arab Americans in the Midwest (Cleveland, Chicago, and Toledo in addition to the Detroit metropolitan area), a greater proportion live in the Northeast. About 40 percent of all Arab Americans live in the Northeast, compared to about 28 percent in the Midwest, 20 percent in the South, and 12 percent in the West. Arab Americans in the Northeast are more likely to be U.S.-born, whereas those in the West are more likely to be immigrants. A fairly even settlement dispersion exists among the different Arab subgroups, although Saudi Arabians concentrate in the West, Assyrians in the Midwest, and Syrians in the Northeast.[25]

Cultural Attributes

Many of today's Arab Americans are a sophisticated, cosmopolitan people whose life-style is comparable to that of other middle- or working-class Americans. Among other Arab Americans—those first-generation arrivals adhering to traditional Arab values—Edward Hall identified four principal areas of cultural differentiation: rights to body space, privacy, facing, and olfaction.[26]

To these traditional Arabs, observes Hall, all individuals have rights in their moving about, no one more than another. For example, pushing and shoving in public places is not considered rude or intrusive. What the Arab does consider rude or aggressive is an American's cavalier regard for moving space, such as some drivers' callousness toward pedestrians. All have rights in their movement. Physical privacy is rare in the Arab world; there is no Arabic word for the concept. Arabs enjoy lots of space within their homes, avoiding partitions so as not to be alone. Personal privacy is being alone with one's thoughts, not talking to others. Using the "silent treatment" on an Arab to show anger will not work, for the Arab will simply feel that the silent party wants to be in thought and not in conversation. Arabs consider it impolite to converse in one's peripheral view. Thus speaking while walking side by side is not acceptable; the Arab will probably edge ahead, turn, and stop to see and to be involved in face-to-face contact. Perhaps most intriguing to Westerners is the prominent place of olfaction in traditional Arab life.

> Not only is it one of the distance-setting mechanisms, but it is a vital part of a complex system of behavior. Arabs consistently breathe on people when they talk. However, this habit is more than a matter of different manners. To the Arab good smells are pleasing and a way of being involved with each other. To smell one's friend is not only nice but desirable, for to deny him your breath is to act ashamed. Americans, on the other hand, trained as they are not to breathe in people's faces, automatically communicate shame in trying to be polite. . . . Smell is even considered in the choice of a mate. When couples are being matched for marriage, the man's go-between will sometimes ask to smell the girl, who may be turned down if she doesn't "smell nice." Arabs recognize that smell and disposition may be linked.
>
> In a word, the olfactory boundary performs two roles in Arab life. It enfolds those who want to relate and separates those who don't. The Arab finds it essential to stay inside the olfactory zone as a means of keeping tab on changes in emotion. What is more, he may feel crowded as soon as he smells something unpleasant.[27]

Arab Americans, like many other past and present immigrant groups, have established institutions to help preserve their cultural heritage, strengthen their ethnic identity, and unite the community. More than four dozen Arabic newspapers are published, and about 50 Arabic radio programs are broadcast in such cities as Chicago, Detroit, New York, and San Francisco. Religious and community organizations provide important emotional, social, and even financial services to help sustain the Arab community. Among professional organizations, two of the better-known are the National Association of Arab Americans and the Association of Arab American University Graduates.

Sociologist Ayad Al-Qazzaz notes the importance of kinship links in stabilizing community life.[28] Exchanges of letters, gifts, and family visits help maintain the bond between the immigrants and their relatives back home. Another important aspect is belief in an integrated economic family unit.

This Middle Eastern provision store in Brooklyn has its counterparts in Arab American communities throughout the U.S. Such stores, regardless of the ethnic group, not only supply immigrants with familiar products from the old country, they are also social gathering places and advice centers (*Tom McKitterick/Impact Visuals*)

Family members pool their income and resources into a common fund for all to share even if the family is dispersed. Each month Arab Americans send vast amounts of money overseas to their relatives, helping them to purchase land, build homes, or purchase modern agricultural equipment such as tractors, plows, and irrigation pumps.[29]

Residential Patterning

Arab Americans are repeating the pattern of earlier European immigrants by settling almost exclusively in urban areas. Whereas only three out of every four Americans live in urban areas, 91 percent of all Arab Americans are urban. Arab immigrants are even more likely to reside in urban areas (97 percent) than are U.S.-born Americans of Arab ancestry (87 percent).[30] Some first-generation Arab Americans live in recognizable ethnic territorial neighborhoods in close proximity to one another, but others tend to live in slightly more dispersed residential patterns.

In an extensive field study of 5,973 Arab immigrants living in the Paterson, New Jersey, metropolitan area, Vincent N. Parrillo and his investigators found them to be a religiously diverse group: 34.2 percent Moslem, 30.2 percent Orthodox Christian, 25.4 percent Melkite Catholic, and 10.2 percent Protestant.[31] Lebanese refugees, mostly of the middle class, tended to live in nearby suburbs, and Circassians, Jordanians, Palestinians, and Syrians lived on the northern and southern peripheries of the city, spilling over into adjacent exurbs. This settlement patterning of Arab immigrants on the edge of cities instead of in historic inner areas or zones in transition has been found in other American cities also.[32]

In the Paterson area a few families lived fairly close to one another, but one had to journey several blocks to find the next grouping. Nevertheless, a shared sense of community and frequent interactional patterns existed. Ethnic solidarity was maintained through a cosmopolitan network of communication and life-cycle rituals, homeland concerns, political activism, or limited social situations (work, school, and nearby families). Instead of a territorial ethnic community like that of past immigrants, Arab immigrants maintain an interactional community.

Racial composition of the neighborhood did not appear to be a factor in choice of residence or desire to relocate. No interracial tensions or conflicts were reported; Arab Americans shared a common assumption that those who lived where they did—white or black—were respectable people. Coming from a part of the world steeped in religious rather than racial prejudices, Arab Americans appear to be unconcerned about racial differences in this more secular society.

Media Stereotypes

Rarely do films or television shows portray Arabs as the ordinary people most of them are. Instead, they usually are shown as billionaires or terrorists. They are cartoonlike TV wrestling villains, such as Abdullah the Butcher, or else cartoon villains, such as Ali Boo-Boo, the Desert Rat, in a Heckle and Jeckle animated feature. In their comedy series, Laverne and Shirley prevented Sheik Ha-Mean-Ie from conquering the United States. In a 1987 movie, *Wanted Dead or Alive*, starring Gene Simmons of the rock group Kiss, an Arab terrorist comes to Los Angeles, where he conspires with other Arab Americans to poison the people of that city. When several Arab terrorists were arrested for bombing the World Trade Center in New York City, the Arab American community experienced much anxiety about the American public stigmatizing all of them for the violent act of just a few radicals.

To see these common themes of Arab villains and war against Arabs, one might falsely conclude they are our enemy. In fact the United States maintains friendly relations with 19 of 21 Arab countries, and most were allies during Operation Desert Storm in 1991. The more than 2 million Arab Americans living here are normal human beings, but you seldom learn that from the media. Failure to grasp the humanity within the Arab people increases the social distance between non-Arab and Arab.

THE SYRIAN LEBANESE _____

A number of factors have contributed to a confusion of ethnic identities and a lack of accurate official statistics covering the immigrants from Syria and Lebanon. In the late nineteenth and early twentieth centuries, the Arabian peninsula was part of the Ottoman Empire; its inhabitants were Turkish citizens until the end of World War I. Although there was a great deal of cultural diversity in this single geographic region, all the inhabitants spoke Arabic and, except the Egyptians, used the term *Syrian* to identify themselves. Still, the immigrants had Turkish passports, and so United States officials identified them as Turkish until 1899, when a separate category for Syrians was begun. Although approximately 85 percent of the immigrants came from the area known as Lebanon, only in the 1930s did the term *Lebanese* gain acceptance. Some Lebanese resisted, preferring to continue calling themselves Syrians, while some authentic Syrians began calling themselves Lebanese.

Ethnic Identity

Arabs tended to identify themselves by family name, religious sect, and village of origin. Rarely did they cross religious or village lines to set up common organizations. Instead, social clubs and fraternal organizations had a clannish focus, often leading to factionalism within the community. Neither political authority nor specific regional residence determined group affinity; rather, religion defined the goals and boundaries of the "Syrian" community, as here indicated:

> Theological differences of Jews, Christians and Moslems have become translated into social and structural realities with each community becoming socially separate from the others. What the people believe is not so important as the fact that people who believe similarly are considered to belong to some social order qualitatively different from that of the rest. Since religion deals with things of primary importance, a different religious persuasion turns others into members of a somewhat distinct society or "nation."
>
> . . . Since the religions of the Middle East were all structurally and socially separate from one another, the Jewish community and the immigrant Moslem and Christian community continued this pattern of separation in the United States.[33]

Migration and Settlement

Although religious differences kept the three groups separate, the push–pull factors that led them to emigrate to the United States affected them similarly. Essentially, a combination of harsh living conditions—hunger, poverty, and disease—and Turkish oppression, particularly against the Christians, led many Syrians to leave. The pull of the United States was the result of reports by missionaries and steamship agents of economic opportunities and religious and political freedom. Emigration to the United States began in the 1870s, reaching an estimated 100,000 between 1890 and 1914 as Turkish oppression increased. The peak years were 1913 and 1914, when more than 9,000 migrated to avoid conscription into the Turkish army, then being prepared for combat in World War I.

A seven-block area on Washington and Rector streets in lower Manhattan became an early thriving Syrian community in the late nineteenth century. Other Syrians settled in downtown Brooklyn and elsewhere throughout the entire country. Most Syrian immigrants came either from cities or from densely populated villages; they usually located in American cities of 100,000 or more and had little difficulty adjusting to urban life.

Between 1890 and 1895 the New York community established three Arab Christian churches: Melkite, Maronite, and Eastern Orthodox. Before then Syrians had simply joined American churches. Maronites and Melkites usually became Roman Catholics; members of the Eastern Orthodox Church generally became Episcopalians.[34]

Culture Conflicts

Syrians often replaced the Irish in old city neighborhoods. This is an example of the sociological concept of *invasion–succession,* in which one group experiencing vertical mobility gradually moves out of its old residences. It is then replaced by another group at the previous residents' original socioeconomic level. Sometimes there may be hostility between the old and new groups. In the case of Syrians, religious tension resulted in a clash with the Irish, as this 1920 account about the Dublin District of Paterson, New Jersey, reveals:

> When the Syrians came to live there, the rentals became higher. This caused hard feelings between the Irish and the Syrians, which developed into a feud between the two nationalities. The fight started in the saloon on Grand and Mill Streets, first with bitter arguments and harsh words, and then threatening fist fights. From the saloon, the fight came out to the streets. It was like two armies in opposition facing each other. . . . The police force was called in to put an end to this fight. All they could do was to throw water on them to disperse them. These fights continued for three days in the evening. Finally, a committee of Syrians went to talk to Dean McNulty of St. John's, explaining to him that they were Christians coming from the Holy Land, not Mohammedans or Turks, as the Irish used to call them. They were good Catholics and they wanted to live in peace with everybody. Then the good Dean, at Sunday masses, urged the Irish to stop fighting with the Syrians, who were like them, Catholics. He succeeded in stopping this fighting better than the police.[35]

Another problem the Syrian immigrants encountered before World War I was racial classification. In 1909 the U.S. District Court in St. Louis ruled them ineligible for naturalization on the basis of the 1790 legislation, declaring them to be nonwhite. Many Syrian Christians were blond and blue-eyed, but the racial barrier was determined by country of origin. The Circuit Court of Appeals reversed this decision. Shortly thereafter the matter was again raised, this time in the U.S. District Court in New York, which ruled that they could be naturalized.

Early Patterns

Syrian males usually came alone and then sent for their wives and children. Although poor they mostly were literate and insisted that their children complete primary school. The wife was more emancipated and less dependent on her husband than her counterparts in other ethnic groups at that time. She and the children, after they completed grade school, all worked together for the family's economic welfare. The family structure proved to be an important factor in the Syrians' economic success.

Generally Syrians preferred to work at trade and shopkeeping because trading was a time-honored occupation in their native land. Many Syrians became peddlers and traveled throughout the country, bringing both essential and exotic goods to many Americans. In the late nineteenth and early twentieth centuries, the peddler filled an economic need and was a welcome visitor to the home and community. About one out of three Syrian men became peddlers; others tried various ventures in commerce, started restaurants, or, in a few cases, worked in factories.

The choice of peddling by so many Syrians expedited their acculturation. It took them into American homes, quickly teaching them the language and customs. It prevented their cultural isolation by way of ghetto settlement patterns and instead dispersed them throughout the country. By 1914 the Syrians turned from peddling to becoming shopkeepers, with the majority operating dry-goods or grocery stores.

Upward Mobility

The Syrians achieved economic security quickly, often in the first generation. This is especially significant because fewer than one-fourth of those who came were professional or skilled workers. Aiding them in their adjustment, acceptance, and upward mobility were (1) wide dispersal, negating any significant opposition to their presence; (2) business expertise and selection of self-employment, which allowed them greater rewards; and (3) cultural values of thrift, industriousness, and investment that were comparable to the middle-class values of the host society.

> Even while they were still in the lower income brackets and in working class occupations, the "Syrians" displayed the social characteristics of the middle classes in American urban centers. Studies of these Arab immigrants in Chicago, Pittsburgh and the South reveal a common pattern: low crime rates, better than average health, higher I.Q.'s, and more regular school attendance among the children, few intermarriages and divorces.[36]

Coming from a country in which nearly every man owned the house he lived in, determined to be independent, and highly motivated to succeed, the

BOX 9.1	THE ETHNIC EXPERIENCE

"I am of Circassian origin, having been born in Syria. My father worked in government with the interior ministry. When the government changed from a moderate socialist to a radical socialist government following the Arab–Israeli War in 1968, my father was arrested as a pro-Western sympathizer. He escaped from jail, and we all fled to Jordan, where we received asylum. We migrated to West Germany, but very few Circassians live there, and so we came to the U.S. where other Circassians who had fled from Russia now lived.

"Before we came here, the idea I had about America was that the people were the same, that everybody was an American except the Blacks because they were different in color. I thought everybody would be an American, but when we came here—especially as soon as I went to high school—I found everyone identified with their parents' origin. In other words, they would call themselves Italian-American, Dutch-American, and so on. It was a little confusing to me because I expected them to say they were Americans. Instead they said their nationality first and then said American.

"Most Circassians live in northern New Jersey or in California, and so we settled in New Jersey where my father already knew some people. I did have a lot of trouble with the language here. I spoke two languages—Circassian and Arabic—but starting as a sophomore in high school I had trouble relating to the people. You know how high school kids are. They're immature. Sometimes in class I might say something with a super-heavy accent, and perhaps even say it completely wrong, and they would laugh at me. I didn't have many friends in high school because I worked after school, and besides, we didn't interact very much with the Americans because the Circassian community had its own activities and clubs. Our language and culture were different and the Americans weren't so friendly. Besides, once you know you have an accent, that does stop you from even trying to make friends. It's a barrier. You're still trying to learn a language and it's hard. With my brothers I spoke Arabic, with my parents who were so nationalistic we had to speak Circassian, and in school I had to learn English, and it was all very confusing."

SOURCE: Syrian immigrant who came to the United States in 1968 at age 15.

Syrians accumulated money rapidly and invested it either in property or in business ventures. By 1911 there were Syrians in almost every branch of commerce, including banking and import–export houses, and the government reported that their median income was only slightly lower than the $665 annual income of the adult native-born male.

Unlike other immigrant groups who had to wait two or three generations to exert their independence from ghetto life and to satisfy their desire for mobility, it was the Syrian immigrants (first generation) who amassed the wealth that

This early-twentieth-century Syrian-Christian peddler near Williston, North Dakota, was one of thousands of his countrymen who chose this occupation. Serving an important economic need, the Syrian peddlers acculturated quickly and encountered very little discrimination. *(Smithsonian Institution)*

their sons used as a lever for bringing themselves into wider contacts with society.[37]

Rapid economic success and lack of either unfavorable stereotypes or discrimination barriers once they were known as Syrians, not Turks, allowed the Syrian–Lebanese to assimilate into American society quite easily, so that they did not need to duplicate the host society's institutions. True, they had social organizations and their own newspapers, but their mobility, wide dispersal, differing religions, and emphasis on the extended family rather than on ethnic organizations resulted in their being assimilated rather easily.

By the mid-1950s the Syrian Americans had completely abandoned their "nomadic" occupations. They had entered the mainstream of American economic and social life and were represented in virtually every industry and profession.[38] Because they were prosperous, their children were able to enter the sciences, the professions, politics, and the arts, and many have distinguished themselves in each of these fields.

More than 80,000 Lebanese have left their war-ravaged country for the United States since 1971, yet they are not an ethnically visible group. Either joining friends and relatives already assimilated and dispersed, or coming as middle-class refugees, they usually blend in easily with the rest of American society in their work and residence. Lebanese Americans maintain a strong social network of communication and interaction in social events. Their extended families have tended to do things together, including vacationing and relocating to different geographical areas.[39] In recent years a countertrend of large-scale intermarriage has been occurring, which Milton Gordon asserts is the last stage of the assimilation process.[40] It remains to be seen whether a continued exodus from Lebanon creates an institutionalized ethnic subculture or whether the assimilation process evident among those Lebanese residing longer in United States quickly absorbs the newcomers as well.

THE PALESTINIANS

About 50,000 Palestinian Americans now live in the United States, with over 11,000 living in California.[41] Most Palestinian Americans are Muslims, although a large proportion are Christian, mostly members of the Antiochian Orthodox Church.

Homeland Influence

Until recently most Palestinian Americans tried to get on with their lives, trying to keep a low profile. Fighting stereotypes that labeled them as terrorists, they became disheartened by the actions of Palestinian extremists in their homeland. Yet they also felt bitterness over violent acts against their people, such as when Irgun, the underground army led by Menachem Begin, massacred 254 Arab men, women, and children at Deir Yassin in 1948 and stuffed their bodies in a well.

Feeling isolated in a country with a strong pro-Israeli policy, Palestinian Americans complain about the injustices in their homeland, where their people must carry identification cards, cannot vote, and are restricted by curfews and travel limits. Unlike Jewish Americans, who have the freedom to visit friends and relatives in Israel, Palestinian Americans say that they themselves are denied the privileges of other Americans to travel there and go to the houses of their parents.[42]

When the Palestinian uprisings occurred in 1988, the Palestinian Americans took a strong interest in the cause, watching network news telecasts and listening to their shortwave radios. Inspired by the demonstrations and the Arab League's recognition of an independent Palestinian state, second- and third-generation Palestinian Americans have gained a new sense of ethnic identity and belonging. Changes in Israeli leadership and government policy, coupled with direct negotiations beginning in 1992, have raised their hopes.

The American Federation of Ramallah

Many of the recent arrivals lack advanced education or occupational skills for various white-collar positions, so they work in a variety of working-class trades. One means of assistance comes from the American Federation of Ramallah, named after a town of 25,000 inhabitants just north of Jerusalem. It is a nationwide ethnic organization, with local and regional social clubs designed to help those of Palestinian heritage adjust to life in the United States. The organization provides financial assistance, guaranteed bank loans, and expertise to enable the newcomers to start mom-and-pop grocery, liquor, and variety stores. The newcomers repay the loans, adding a small percentage to help others who follow them. One estimate places Palestinian ownership of San Francisco's small convenience stores at more than 25 percent. With these stores the Ramallahans are earning money to prepare their children for more sophisticated businesses, building their future with help from the past.[43]

The Federation also conducts many social activities such as parties and picnics through its local branches. These events help maintain ethnic bonding and provide socializing opportunities for young people to meet potential marriage partners. A youth department offers summer-camp programs and cultural heritage classes.

Community Life

For middle-class Palestinian Americans, the mosques and churches serve many purposes. Here religious needs are met, of course, but they also are ethnic centers for social occasions, temporary hostels for new arrivals not yet situated, cultural learning centers for youth, meeting places for Arab organizations, and reception centers for visiting dignitaries.

Working-class Palestinian American males, often living in urban neighborhoods, usually congregate in coffeehouses in their free hours, much like earlier Greek immigrants. This neighborhood social center provides a place to relax, exchange gossip or information about the community or homeland, and perhaps learn of work opportunities.

THE IRANIANS _____

Iran, formerly called Persia, is not an Arab country. Its people speak their own language, Farsi, not Arabic, and their culture has its unique qualities setting it apart from neighboring Arab states. Immigration patterns and societal reaction to Iranian immigrants have fluctuated greatly in the past 30 years, depending on the political climate. Immigrants from Iran are relatively new to the United States. During the reign of Shah Mohammed Reza Pahlevi, about 50,000 Iranian students studied in the United States annually. They maintained a sense of community among themselves, forming associations and interacting with one another. Fear of political repression under the Shah kept many from returning to their homeland until after his fall from power in 1979. Other Iranians living in the United States then were skilled professionals working as sojourners, with no intention of remaining, or political refugees hoping to return home someday. At that time, except for the college students, Iranians did not maintain an ethnic community or network, keeping to themselves, partly in fear of the Shah's secret police agents (SAVAK) reporting something about them and bringing harm to relatives still in Iran. Minority emigrants from Iran—the Armenians, Bahais, Jews—showed great cohesiveness, intending to become U.S. citizens, but they comprised a very small percentage of all Iranian immigrants.

In a study of his fellow Iranian immigrants, Maboud Ansari found that the Iranian migration in the late 1970s consisted mostly of male, middle-class professionals. Although physically separated from his family, the typical Iranian immigrant still viewed the extended family at home as the only source of primary relations, usually through regular telephone calls. Here they did not form a territorially compact community or develop close ties with their compatriots.[44] Most remained physically and socially distant from other Iranians in the United States and did not come together except at Now-Ruz, the Iranian New Year, celebrated on the first day of spring.

> The Now-Ruz party (which takes place in many major American cities) is the only major national event for Iranians in America. As the only publicly visible ceremony, it creates an atmosphere of national identity and a sense of belonging. However, it seems that somehow the ceremony has lost the meaning originally attached to it. For example, one of the most important aspects of Now-Ruz is to review or to extend friendships. The Iranians who attend the festivities in America are apt to come together as strangers and leave without exchanging any addresses or gaining any new friendships. Most of the festivities are characterized by a lack of intimacy and excessive self-consciousness in maintaining of social distance.[45]

Ansari found that Iranians fell into five self-designated categories. Only about 20 percent called themselves *mandegar* (settlers), or Persian Yankees. Many are older, former exchange students who opted to stay permanently. The majority are in the second category, the *belataklif,* or ambivalent Iranians. Torn by a nostalgic love and guilt feeling for what has been left behind yet growing attached to what lies ahead here, the *belataklif* remain undecided about staying or returning. Yet the longer one remains, the less likely one is to return, thus becoming a *mandegar.* The other two categories are the *siyasi,* or political exiles who view their host society only as a necessary refuge, and the *cosmopolitan,* committed to one's profession not nationality, a citizen of the world at home anywhere.[46]

Anti-Iranian feelings ran high in the United States throughout 1980 when the hostage crisis at the U.S. Embassy in Iran remained unresolved. Verbal abuse, boycotts, and arson against Iranian American businesses, and physical attacks against Iranian students on several college campuses occurred. Iranian Americans, with no anti-American feelings themselves, became the scapegoats of American frustration, suffering indignities and discrimination. Even into the 1990s residual hostility was still much in evidence all through the "Irangate" controversy in Washington, DC, with revelations about weapons-for-hostages secret arrangements in 1980.

Iranian immigration in the 1980s totaled 116,172, up significantly from 45,136 in the 1970s.[47] Almost 60 percent choose California as their state of intended residence.[48] With more than 216,000 Americans now claiming Iranian ancestry, their presence is more readily noticed by outsiders.[49] Although found in most major cities, distinct Iranian neighborhoods now exist in Queens, New York, and Beverly Hills, California. As in the Washington, DC–Arlington, Virginia area, classes in Farsi, the Iranian language, take place in these enclaves. Located in these four areas also are Islamic centers and mosques, further evidence of the emerging Iranian community.

Born to mostly middle-class professional parents, today's second-generation Iranian Americans grow up in a child-centered family with equalitarian norms, quite unlike the patriarchal and authoritarian character of families in Iran.[50] Yet of major concern to many parents is the preservation of the Iranian heritage, and efforts are made to preserve the positive aspects of the culture, despite the inevitable Americanization process.

Living as a despised and persecuted religious minority in Iran, the Baha'ii have emigrated to the United States, establishing centers in several major American cities. The population of Baha'ii in the United States is greater than anywhere else in the world, including its cradle, Iran.[51]

THE IRAQIS

It is necessary to distinguish between the immigrants from Iraq who came here before and after World War II because the political, social, and economic changes in the Middle East have made these groups of immigrants very different. Studying one Iraqi subcultural group of Chaldeans living in the Detroit metropolitan area, Mary Sengstock observed its pre- and postwar changes caused by the evolution of Iraq into a modern nation–state and the heightened Arab consciousness caused by Arab–Israeli tensions.[52]

The early immigrants had formed a community of village-oriented entrepreneurs with their religious traditions as their primary identification. They maintained a *gemeinschaft* subsociety within American society. Family orientations were strong, and a great many Iraqis were self-employed, operating grocery stores and other small businesses. They were, for the most part, a self-enclosed ethnic community.

Not only have recent Iraqi immigrants to Detroit had different value orientations from their predecessors, reflecting their increased education and their more urbanized backgrounds, but they also had an effect on the self-perceptions and behavior of the earlier immigrants. Although the Chaldeans are Christian, they feel the pull of Arab nationalist loyalties, and this national consciousness is infectious.[53] Most now think of themselves as Arabs or Iraqis, not as Chaldeans or Telkeffes, another Iraqi subcultural group. Recent immigrants are less likely to be self-employed and more likely to be involved in bureaucratic endeavors that bring them into contact with many persons of different backgrounds. Recent Iraqi immigrants thus rely more on formal organizations and interact more with outsiders. They are likely to join non-Chaldean organizations and to develop social relationships, including close friendship ties and marriage, with people from other backgrounds. With new immigrants arriving all the time (this particular community exceeds 6,000), these patterns may well continue and be the norm.

The 1990 census revealed 45,936 foreign-born Iraqis now living in the United States and another 23,212 American citizens claiming Iraqi ancestry.[54] From 1981 to 1990, a total of 19,553 Iraqi immigrants came to this country.[55] With an average of 2,000 newcomers arriving annually and following a chain-migration pattern of settlement, this ethnic group has had a slow, steady ethnic revitalization.

Interestingly, the Gulf War against Saddam Hussein's troops did not generate hostility against Iraqi Americans living in the United States. Several factors probably contributed to this lack of societal animosity. Iraqi Americans are not that visually distinct, given their relatively small numbers and tendency to live within the larger Arab American community. Furthermore, they were mostly supportive of the brief military action against their homeland's dictator.

THE TURKS

The U.S. Immigration and Naturalization Service reports that a total of more than 412,000 Turkish immigrants have come to the United States since 1820.

Supporters of the 1991 Kurdish uprising demonstrate in front of the White House calling for U.S. action to assist fleeing refugees in northern Iraq. Most first-generation Americans, with strong ties to their homeland, direct their political activism toward political situations in their nation of origin. (*Ira Schwartz/Reutters/Bettmann*)

Ordinarily, that number would place Turkey in the top 20 suppliers of emigrants. However, if you recall our discussion on the Syrian–Lebanese, subjugated peoples of different languages and cultures left the Ottoman Empire with only Turkish passports prior to World War I. Over 300,000 people, three-fourths of the total "Turkish" immigration, entered the United States during this period (see Appendix II). Although immigration officials identified them as Turkish by their passports, they really were Armenians, Syrians, Lebanese, or other nationalities. Almost 86,000 Turks have immigrated since 1921, over 36,000 of these in the past 20 years.

Factors Against Immigration

Several factors explain this low level of emigration from Turkey itself in comparison with other poor, undeveloped nations during the great migration period. Perhaps foremost, Moslem Turks had waged a relentless campaign against the Christians within their empire and would hardly be favorably inclined toward settling in an almost exclusively Christian country. Second, the Turks had traditionally always migrated in large groups. Consequently, there was little outside the country to attract families or individuals. In 1923 Turkey barred any emigrant from ever returning, even as a visitor. This law remained in force until 1950. With laws against emigration, few Turks decided to seek a better life elsewhere. Since 1965, however, an increasing flow of Turkish immigrants have migrated to the United States because Turkey has been a friendly ally of the United States for several generations.

Societal Attitudes

Although relatively few Turks emigrated to the United States before World War I, feelings toward the Turks in this country were mostly negative, primarily because of the Ottoman Empire's political and religious repression:

> Such sentiment towards Turkey as existed in America was largely anti-Turkish. We had of course inherited the ordinary western European prejudice against the Turks as champions of Islam. In addition, many groups in America had espoused the cause of one or another of those Ottoman subject peoples who in the nineteenth century were fighting to gain their independence from the Empire. Immigrants from that Empire had helped foster pro-Greek or pro-Macedonian or pro-Bulgarian sentiments in this country. What had principally aroused American interest in Turkey, however, and what had especially directed that interest towards the non-Turks were certainly the long-standing presence and activities of American missionaries in the Ottoman world. It was chiefly the Armenians' aspirations and woes to which those missionaries gave currency.[56]

The Ottoman Empire was often brutal in its attempts to suppress the Armenian and Syrian–Lebanese Christians. Annihilation of enemies was frequent, and Turkish massacres of thousands of Armenians in the 1890s and again in 1915 stirred the wrath of many Americans. To this day many Americans of Armenian descent mark the anniversary of these Turkish pogroms. American hostility toward the Turks was common during those times, and this helps explain further the initial hostility the Syrian–Lebanese encountered in this country when they were confused with Turks. In his survey of social distance in 1926, Emory S. Bogardus found that Turks ranked twenty-seventh out of 30, above only Chinese, Koreans, and Indians from India. In 1946, 1956, and 1966, Turks shifted a position or two, finishing twenty-sixth in 1966, above Koreans, Mexicans, blacks, and Asian Indians.[57] In the same surveys Armenians ranked from five to eleven positions higher than Turks.

BOX 9.2   **THE INTERNATIONAL SCENE**

Of the 31.4 million people living in South Africa, about 1 million are Asian Indians. They are mostly descendants of laborers recruited since the 1860s to work the sugar estates or of traders who migrated before enactment of restrictive immigration laws in the early twentieth century.

Their heritage of struggling against white oppression began a century ago with the arrival of a young lawyer named Mahatma Ghandi. His efforts to improve the circumstances of his compatriots living in South Africa led to the development of his strategy of *satyagraha*, or mass defiance of discriminatory laws, later used in India's independence struggle. In 1894 Ghandi became the first secretary of the Natal Indian Congress (NIC), and before returning to India in 1914, he won concessions from Afrikaner leaders on taxes, marriage law, and rights of movement. The NIC became the model for the African National Congress (ANC), under whose banner Nelson Mandela later became a powerful leader.

The infamous Group Areas Act in 1950 forced 75,000 Indians and 8,500 "Coloured" (mixed-race) to vacate what had become valuable inner suburban land for more distant settlements with rudimentary services. When the ANC was banned in 1960 and its leadership arrested or exiled, Indian leaders and the NIC played a key role in keeping the ANC together. By the 1980s their political alliance was indicated by the presence of eight Indians on the 50-member ANC executive council.

As a middleman minority, the Indians have fared better than the Africans. They have moved into middle-echelon jobs in accounting, sales, banking, and factory management, as well as becoming owners of many business and service enterprises. Their success has generated some African resentment and hostility. Violent attacks in 1992 against Indian businesses in black areas has forced their owners to sell out and move back to major cities.

Finding themselves both courted and pressured by various black and white political factions, South Africa's Indians guardedly approach an uncertain future in a turbulent land.

Immigrant Patterns

When the Balkan War of 1912 began, many young unmarried males came to the United States to avoid military service. When war-ravaged Europe was at peace again in 1918, more than 30,000 of them returned to Turkey. The few thousand who remained settled primarily in New York, Massachusetts, Michigan, Illinois, and Indiana.

Most of the Turkish immigrants who came before World War II were illiterate and secured jobs as unskilled laborers. They settled mostly in New York City and Detroit, and they kept to themselves. Some gradually became acculturated, while others remained socially segregated within American society.

The more recent Turkish immigrants have been much better educated than their predecessors. Many are professionals or experienced businesspeople who have settled in a more dispersed pattern. Others are working-class tradesmen and laborers who usually have clustered together in urban areas in sufficient numbers to induce the establishment of bilingual programs in neighborhood schools. Annual immigration to the United States now approximates 3,000 annually, helping maintain ethnic vitality, although structural assimilation appears to continue to be a two-generation process.

THE PAKISTANIS

Immigrants from Pakistan have also become a significant presence. Their foreign-born presence, as documented in the 1990 census, totaled 93,663, or 0.4 percent of the nation's population.[58] In the 1980s Pakistani immigration reached a record 61,364, and the 1990s should see a much higher total.[59] One in four are white-collar workers or professionals, and the rest are craftsmen, service workers, or laborers.[60] Pakistani Americans have a widespread settlement pattern, although one in four settles in the New York metropolitan region. The Chicago and Washington, DC, metropolitan areas are other areas of residential clustering.[61] The Pakistanis' acculturation and assimilation patterns are similar to those of other groups discussed in this chapter.

SOCIOLOGICAL ANALYSIS

The immigrants from the countries discussed in this chapter have mostly arrived since 1965. Because they have lived in the United States less than one generation, their experiences lack the perspective of time for full analysis. Furthermore, as we said at the beginning of the chapter, because most are educated with marketable occupational skills, they do not completely fit the theoretical framework of past immigrants. How well do they fit into the three theoretical perspectives? As you shall see, each does provide a focus helpful to further understanding.

Onlookers await a Pakistani Day Parade. Many ethnic groups have utilized annual parades as a rallying event for group solidarity. This popular activity effectively instills ethnic pride in the younger generation, helping negate any marginality they may experience growing up as a member of a minority group. (*Michael Dwyer/Stock, Boston*)

The Functionalist View

Has the social system been able to adapt smoothly in absorbing the newcomers, so many of them racially and religiously different? Functionalists would point to the immigration laws ensuring either sufficient earning power in occupational preference or a support system in relative preference. These better educated, better skilled individuals quickly adjust, contribute to the economy, and appear to integrate into society with a minimum of problems. Most rank low on the social-distance scale at this time, but they do become functionally integrated fairly easily. Their economic power allows them to live in middle-class neighborhoods, accessible through fair-housing laws. Some may even integrate areas, their comparable values and life-style making their native-born neighbors more receptive to them as a racially or culturally distinct people.

Less skilled non-Westerners have helped fill a population void in urban and exurban neighborhoods. Although some minor problems may occur, these newcomers bring stability to neighborhoods, preventing their decline and helping maintain a racial balance. Urban density provides easy contact with one another, enabling ethnic solidarity to develop and be sustained. Living in close proximity to their work, these newcomers find jobs other Americans are unwilling to take, yet they fulfill societal needs. As they struggle to make it in America, they find better opportunities than they had known in their home countries, while society benefits from their work, purchasing power, and cultural contributions.

The Conflict View

Early non-Western immigrants provide grist for the analytical mill of conflict theorists. Industrialists often used Syrian–Lebanese as strikebreakers in the Northeast, particularly during the intense labor unrest in the early twentieth century. Just as the Syrian Lebanese offered factory owners a cheaper labor alternative, so did Asian Indians on the West Coast enable farmers, lumber companies, and railroads to benefit from their low-cost labor. Other workers resented their presence, fearing their growing numbers would jeopardize their own positions. Once again the split labor market theory would seem applicable. Economic competition between two wage-level groups generated ethnic antagonism and violence.

More recent arrivals suggest a different analysis. Tensions arise among American blacks and Hispanics at the bottom of the socioeconomic ladder who see foreign-born Africans and Middle Easterners leapfrogging over them. Resentment builds against these newcomers whose hiring appears to deny upward mobility for native-born minority groups. Foreigners are benefiting at the expense of Americans, they think. Additionally, the movement of Third World immigrants into white, middle-class apartment complexes and suburban neighborhoods changes the prior racial or cultural homogeneity, which sometimes stirs hostilities among the old-timers against the newcomers.

Although conflict may be less intense regarding these groups, an undercurrent of tensions and resentment can exist, as evidenced by occasional eruptions of public protest over the building of a Sikh temple in a suburban community or providing bilingual education for a group of Turkish American children in an urban school (two actual incidents).

The Interactionist View

Because visual clues are a major means of our categorizing strangers, those with different clothing or physical characteristics get classified as dissimilar types. Is it really surprising to learn that the racially different (Africans and Asians) and the religiously different (Buddhists and Muslims) score so low on the social-distance scale? If this perception of others as being very different is coupled with a sense of overwhelming numbers of newcomers, fears of a "Hindoo invasion" or whatever the case may be can easily lead to acts of exclusion, expulsion, and violence. Consider the case of the Irish in Paterson who attacked the Syrians moving into their neighborhood, thinking them to be Turks or "Mohammedans." Only when a respected religious leader redefined the situation for the Irish did the fighting stop. In recent years Palestinian Americans have struggled against Americans presuming they are all terrorists because of a few extremists. Misinterpretations about an ethnic group often have caused problems, and the peoples in this chapter are no exception.

Because recent immigrants often can mainstream economically, their coworkers or neighbors assume they have integrated socially as well. Interaction may occur in work-related relationships, but socially the middle-class newcomers tend to become "unknown ethnics," at least in primary relationships. Socially isolated except on rare occasions, the non-Westerners by necessity interact with compatriots, remaining a generalized entity in the minds of Americans. This social segregation appears to result more from an attraction toward similarly perceived others than overt avoidance. Whatever the reason, non-Westerners are mostly social outcasts in American leisure activities. We may say, "Variety is the spice of life," but we do not apply that principle to racial and ethnic personal relationships.

Retrospect

Relatively few members of the racial and ethnic groups mentioned in this chapter came to the United States before 1940. The experiences of those who did were generally similar to those of other non-Western peoples here and depended on the then-prevailing American policies and regional attitudes.

For the most part, the immigrant experience of people from this part of the world is current. Although they are still identifiable because of physical and cultural differences, they usually have little difficulty with Americans because of their occupational status, their urban locale, and the relaxation of American norms about newcomers. Nevertheless, as strangers they are keenly aware of the society in which they find themselves, and Americans generally tend to avoid interacting with them in meaningful primary relationships. The non-Westerners are somewhat unusual in that many are able to secure a respectable social status in terms of education, occupation, income, and residence, but because of their cultural differences and their resistence to assimilation, they have little social participation with native-born Americans. This often is a two-way arrangement.

As larger numbers of immigrants from the non-Western world come to the United States, they are making their presence felt more and more. One aspect of this impact is in religion. Waves of immigrant peoples have changed the United States from an almost exclusively Protestant country to one of three major faiths. Now this Judeo-Christian population composition, if present trends continue, may be modified further as the numbers of Muslims, Hindus, Buddhists, and adherents of other Eastern religions swell.

As the United States becomes culturally diverse in the areas of religion, physical appearance, and value orientations, more Americans are becoming conscious of the differences in the people around them. Some argue that Americans today are more tolerant because of a resurgence of ethnicity and a more liberal government attitude toward cultural pluralism. Others contend that the past nativistic reaction to Asians in the West and to southern and eastern Europeans in the East is being replicated today against the non-Western immigrants. There may not be riots and violent confrontations, but there are more subtle and sophisticated acts of discrimination in keeping with the changing times.

How accurate this analysis is has not yet been determined. What is known is that recent non-Western immigrants are better educated and better trained; they often speak English before they arrive; and thus they enter American society at a higher socioeconomic level than earlier immigrants did. Their ethnic community is more interactional than territorial for the most part, although some groups are more clustered and visible than others. They seem to adjust fairly easily to American life, although ingroup socializing is quite common, as with past immigrant groups. Perhaps we are still a generation away from being able to measure the full impact of their role within American society.

Review Questions

1. Explain why the differences in economic power between non-Western immigrants and earlier immigrants make assimilation less necessary now than before.
2. What parallels are there between the Asian Indian and Asian immigrant experiences, both past and present?
3. How have structural conditions in the home countries reshaped ethnic identity and attitudes among Arab immigrants to the United States?
4. Discuss problems of stereotyping and prejudice encountered by non-Westerners because of outgroup perceptions and the media.
5. What insights do the three sociological perspectives offer about non-Western immigrants?

Suggested Readings

AL-QAZZAZ, AYAD. *Transnational Links Between the Arab Community in the U.S. and the Arab World.* Sacramento, CA: Central Press, 1979.
    A small study offering background information on the Arab American community and its six links with the Arab world.

ANSARI, MABOUD. *Iranian Immigrants in the United States.* New York: Associated Faculty Press, 1988.
    A fine and authoritative sociological study of Iranian emigrés and immigrants, their values and acculturation patterns.

CHANDRASEKHAR, SRIPATI (ed.). *From India to America*. La Jolla, CA: Population Review Publications, 1982.

A collection of articles providing detailed information on the Asian Indian immigrant experience, from their earliest years in the United States.

EKLHOLY, ABDO A. "The Arab American Family," in Charles H. Mindel and Robert W. Habenstein, (eds.), *Ethnic Families in America,* 3d ed. New York: Elsevier, 1988.

A brief, well-written portrait of family structure, customs, and behavior patterns of Arab American families.

KAYAL, PHILIP M., AND JOSEPH M. KAYAL. *The Syrian–Lebanese in America*. New York: Twayne, 1975.

An excellent sociohistorical account of both early and recent Syrian–Lebanese immigrants and their encounters and accomplishments.

NAFF, ALIXA. *The Arab Americans*. New York: Chelsea House Publishers, 1988.

A clear, well-written introduction to Arab Americans, examining their culture and acculturation experiences in the United States.

10

F. M. Kearney/Impact Visuals

African Americans

Most Africans who arrived in America from 1619 until the end of the slave trade in 1808 were unwilling immigrants, but twentieth-century African voluntary emigration to the United States has been substantial. Between 1899 and 1922, 115,000 African blacks and over 25,000 West Indian blacks were admitted. The restrictive immigration law of 1924 reduced the number of new immigrants from these groups; Africans, for example, were limited to only 122 annually.[1] In recent years Africa has been averaging over 26,000 immigrants a year, while over 90,000 West Indians are now emigrating to the United States each year.

Differences in culture have prevented any unifying racial bond from forming between black immigrants and native-born blacks. The newcomers are strangers in a new land; many native-born blacks—like the American Indians—are strangers in their own land; and both groups are strangers to each other. The new arrivals have come from an area where their race was the majority, or where a tripartite color system prevailed, or where color was not a primary factor in group life, into a society where color is an important determinant. They find that white Americans identify Africans with a partially assimilated and socially restricted native black population that itself does not accept or relate well to them.

The role of blacks in American society, together with the recurring racial problems of prejudice and discrimination, often has been discussed, particularly in the past two decades. This chapter attempts to place black–white relations in perspective by showing the similarities in, and differences from, the patterns of dominant-minority interaction of other racial and ethnic groups. Other major themes are the long-lasting impact of cultural conditioning and the changes wrought by the civil rights movement.

SOCIOHISTORICAL PERSPECTIVE _____

During the age of exploration, black crew members served under Columbus and sixteenth-century Spanish explorers such as Balboa, Cortez, Pizzarro, and de Soto. The first known group of African immigrants were 20 voluntary immigrants who landed in Jamestown in August 1619, a year before the Pilgrims landed at Plymouth Rock. They came as indentured servants, as did many whites, worked off their debt, and became masters of their own destiny. They were the fortunate few, for the labor demands of the Southern colonies soon resulted in the enslavement of millions of other Africans and their forced migration to the United States. Slavery replaced indentured servitude in the South. Blacks were forcibly taken from their African homelands and sold into a lifetime of slavery in a land they did not choose and in which they had no opportunity to advance themselves because they were not free.

The Years of Slavery

To ease the transition other ethnic groups re-created in miniature the society they left behind, but the Africans were not allowed to do so. Other groups could use education to give themselves and their children a better future, but Southern state laws made the education of black slaves a criminal offense. Other groups may have encountered various degrees of hostility and discrimination, but through hard work and perseverance many were able to overcome nativist fears and prejudices. For the blacks, however, 200 years of master–slave relations did much more than just prevent their assimilation; they shaped values and attitudes about the two races that are still visible today.

As the industrial North and the slaveholding, agrarian South evolved into different societies, they developed different norms. Because norms are shared expectations of what does and does not constitute proper behavior, intergroup relations in these two regions might be expected to vary greatly. They did, but not in the way many Americans assume. To be sure, the institution of slavery created an inferior status for blacks and led to much prejudice and discrimination. Yet there were free blacks in the South too (nearly half a million by 1860)—those who had been set free by their owners, those who had purchased their freedom, or those who were descendants of free mothers. They lived in such urban areas as New Orleans, Mobile, and Charleston; in the tidewater regions of Virginia and Maryland; or in the Piedmont mountains of North Carolina and Virginia. Those who lived in the Southern cities worked in a wide variety of skilled and unskilled occupations; some were architects, teachers, store and hotel managers, clerks, and milliners. In the North, although there was some variance, the blacks faced considerable discrimination in education, housing, employment, and voting rights. Because in the North no operative caste system delineated norms and interaction patterns, many whites reacted more strongly to blacks in their midst. As a result, Northern blacks had considerable difficulty achieving economic security.

Racism and Its Legacy

Although some ancient civilizations considered themselves superior to others, they did so on the basis of culture, not race. Most historians agree that racism did not emerge until the sixteenth and seventeenth centuries.[2] This was the period of European exploration and imperialism, during which Europeans were brought into contact with many physically different, less technologically advanced peoples. Their physical characteristics, values, and ways of life were different, and so the Europeans naively concluded that there must be some relationship between how the people looked and how they behaved. This was another instance in which prejudices and stereotyping resulted from ethnocentric rationalization.

Myths about black racial inferiority emerged as a rationalization of slavery. Although slavery had existed under earlier systems, the ancient civilizations did not link skin color and social status. Statues and paintings from ancient Egypt, for example, depict slaves and rulers alike as both white and black.[3] Speculation about the causes of the rise of racism includes the rise of seagoing power among European nations and increased contact with red, brown, black, and yellow peoples; the influence of Christianity, linking slavery and skin color with the Curse of Ham; and European technological and military superiority over native peoples throughout the world. In the nineteenth century, evolutionary theory was also used to support racist thinking, for some argued that the white race was more highly evolved than the others.

W. E. B. DuBois interpreted this rise of racism as follows:

> Labor was degraded, humanity was despised, the theory of "race" arose. There came a new doctrine of universal labor: mankind were of two sorts—the superior and the inferior; the inferior toiled for the superior; and the superior were the real men, the inferior half men or less. . . . Luxury and plenty for the few and poverty for the many was looked upon as inevitable in the course of nature. In addition to this, it went without saying that the white people of Europe had a right to live upon the labor and property of the colored peoples of the world.
>
> In order to establish the righteousness of this point of view, science and religion, government and industry, were wheeling into line. The word "Negro" was used for the first time in the world's history to tie color to race and blackness to slavery and degradation. The white race was pictured as "pure" and superior: the black race as dirty, stupid, and inevitably inferior; the yellow race as sharing, in deception and cowardice, much of this color inferiority; while mixture of the races was considered the prime cause of degradation and failure in civilization. Everything great, everything fine, everything really successful in human culture, was white.
>
> In order to prove this, even black people in India and Africa were labeled as "white" if they showed any trace of progress; and, on the other hand, any progress by colored people was attributed to some intermixture, ancient or modern, of white blood or some influence of white civilization.[4]

Although an extremely small percentage of white Southerners actually owned slaves, they were the most influential, and other Southern whites were strong supporters of the system. The total separation of American slaves from the rest of society, unlike the partial separation of slaves in Latin American countries (where they had greater family stability and gradated freedom conditions), had important social consequences. As the dominant element of the Southern economy, plantation slavery affected the cultural life-style and the shape of societal institutions. Illiteracy, nonexistent social and economic organizations, itinerant preachers, only local white law enforcement and protection, lack of medical and learning facilities, isolation, and dependency were the lot of the blacks.

As a result of the racial ideology, stereotyping, and social isolation that survived the end of slavery, blacks in the United States—despite their adaptability, willingness, and competence—were more excluded from participation in the free community than were the ex-slaves of Latin America. Once established, the impact of a master–slave social system and the concomitant theory of racial inferiority conditioned values, attitudes, and development of capacities that were to last well beyond the Civil War. Treated as if they were biologically inferior, the blacks became socially inferior, first as a result of slavery and then as a result of discrimination in jobs, housing, and education.

Overcoming 200 years of social conditioning is not easy. A generation after the close of the Civil War, many blacks were making economic progress in the South, but the whites still held deep-seated beliefs of racial superiority. Previous discussions of the vicious circle and the long-lasting effects of stereotypes help explain the continuance of institutionalized racism long after the end of slavery.[5]

In 1876, when Reconstruction ended and the status of blacks became a Southern question rather than a national matter, blacks were given a formalized inferior status. Segregation, disfranchisement, "black codes," job discrimination, and occupational eviction took place. Not until the 1960s did many deliberate segregationist practices end in the South.

Although there are now many laws to protect people against discrimination, racist beliefs continue to exist; they can be seen in the reasons people give for moving out of racially changing neighborhoods or for their attitudes toward cities, crime, and welfare. Even though fear of crime, violence, and other evils of the inner city is justified, some individuals attribute such problems to race. Deviance, it must be remembered, occurs among all groups who are poor, powerless, and victims of discrimination.[6]

The problem with racism is twofold: its legacy and its subtlety. *Legacy* here refers not only to its institutionalization within society but also to its transmission from one generation to the next. Slavery may end, segregation may end, but some people still believe blacks are inferior. This is part of the subtlety of racism, because people usually draw such conclusions from their observable world. They are not aware that this "objective" reality has been socially constructed over generations. The alleged inferiority is a myth, except as a social product. One sees primarily the effects of prolonged racist attitudes and actions. Even one's own attitudes, actions, and reactions may unwittingly contribute to the existence of racism.[7]

THE QUESTION OF RACIAL SUPERIORITY _____

Belief in white supremacy has existed for a long time in the United States. There have been, and still are, people who believe that blacks are biologically inferior to whites. This was the justification for segregation and for the Jim

Crow laws, and this is the reason for many of the social problems of today. It is not only uneducated people who feel this way; some scientists and scholars also believe there are innate differences among the races. For example, in 1928 the noted American sociologist Pitirim Sorokin observed:

> That there are mental differences among races seems to be definitely established. . . . No partisan of a belief in the uniformity of all races can disregard the differences in the historical role and in the cultural achievements of the different races. . . . The difference in the cultural contributions and in the historical roles played by different races is excellently corroborated by, and is in perfect agreement with, the experimental studies of race mentality and psychology. . . . So far as I know, all studies of the comparative intelligence of the contemporary Negro and the white races . . . have unanimously shown that the I.Q. of the blacks, or even the Indians, is lower than that of the white or yellow.
>   The only conclusion which it seems possible to make from the above and similar studies is that the mentality of various races . . . is different.[8]

Scientific attempts to prove racial superiority and inferiority have traditionally followed three primary approaches: anatomical, historical (or comparative achievement), and psychological.[9]

The Anatomical Approach

It has been mentioned elsewhere in this text that in many parts of the world, the group lowest on the socioeconomic ladder often is viewed as lowest on the evolutionary ladder as well. Some scientists have tried to use physical characteristics to show that whites are further evolved than blacks. The blacks, they argue, most resemble the ape; they have a receding forehead, prognathous jaw, and broad, flat nose. What these proponents conveniently ignore is that the hair, texture, body hair, and lip form of whites are closer to apes than are those of blacks. Also, underneath their fur most simians have white skin. Using physical characteristics to rank the races in any evolutionary order is simply impossible, because no race is consistently more simian than another.

Whites generally have larger brains than blacks, and some people have contended that this proves they have superior intellectual capabilities.[10] However, physical size or cranial capacity is not in itself an indicator of mental capacity. Not only is there a wide range of size among all groups, but also some peoples not particularly noted for their intellectual achievements (preliterate Eskimos and Neanderthals) have possessed large brains. Physical characterizations of skin pigmentation, hair texture, and brain size do not correlate with a comparative evolution of the human races.

The Comparative–Achievement Approach

In other attempts to prove racial superiority, the achievements of different races have been compared. Some argue that because not all races have made "important" contributions to the world's culture and produced gifted artists, inventors, philosophers, geniuses, explorers, and conquerors, or built great civilizations and vast empires, they are not all equal. After all, they argue, a race that has produced all the engineering feats of today in architecture, computers, electronics, medicine, and space-age technology surely surpasses a primitive, illiterate, underdeveloped race of people, such as the Australian aborigines or Amazon jungle natives or African villagers.

Stanford M. Lyman attacks any attempt to measure the "contributions" of any ethnic group, because this involves a retrospective analysis of what has and has not been widely adopted or popularly acclaimed:

> The uselessness of contributions as a sociological concept is clear because its designative capacity is always post hoc. It forces a bifurcation of a natural class— the activities of a minority group—at an unnatural joint: those that are contributions and those that are not. When a minority is evaluated according to its contributions, its activities are classified in accordance with a concept that cannot be derived from their actual context. A people's activities should be regarded as contributions only when it can be shown that they were intended as such. Sociology should be faithful to the actual nature of its subject matter—people in active and creative existence.[11]

Another problem with this line of reasoning is that one should not confuse performance with potential. To do so is to misunderstand the dynamics of civilization as well as to lack perspective and to be ignorant of the history of culture. How, for example, do we measure achievement? Most of us would measure it by our standards, that is, using an ethnocentric approach. We may boast of our scientific knowledge and accomplishments, failing to realize that other people may not admire these things or consider them to be criteria for excellence. As Berry and Tischler point out:

> We would not come out so well in proving our superiority if our opponents insisted on using as criteria, not science and machines, but ability at sand painting, physical endurance, complexity of grammar, multiplicity of taboos, respect for the aged, ability in hunting, closeness to nature, fear of the deity, reverence for the soil, freedom from authority, disregard for material goods, the absence of neuroses, or peace of mind. The fact is that no racial or ethnic group excels in all things, but each has its own interests and values, goals toward which it strives, and channels into which its efforts are directed.[12]

Even if someone were to argue that some peoples are superior because of the flowering of their civilization, time would show that attainment also to be relative. Some civilizations have exceeded others, only to be surpassed in later years by those very ones thought to be inferior. The history of some world civilizations—those of the Sumerians, Egyptians, Greeks, Romans, and English—is testimony to this fact. From the ninth century, when marauding tribes were still roving through parts of Europe, through the fifteenth century, various African kingdoms were building such sophisticated and affluent cities as Timbuktu, the intellectual capital of Western Sudan, with its stone palaces, many-windowed homes, city university, and busy marketplace; or Benin, Nigeria, with wide streets and civic splendor and a huge, magnificent palace; or the numerous tall stone towns on the East African coast. Early explorers noted some of these achievements, but ethnocentric misconceptions and the debilitating effects of enslavement distorted, dulled, and destroyed this knowledge of the Africans and their varied social systems. In the following passage Basil Davidson presents an undistorted picture of African civilizations:

> Some of these systems produced societies whose standard of living—in terms of food, personal safety and freedom—equaled that of contemporary societies in Europe. In some instances they were even more advanced: African societies practiced a simple but effective social welfare in their concern for widows and orphaned children.
>
> This is the Africa . . . that Europeans began to see for themselves in the latter half of the fifteenth century. Instead of a primeval wilderness, these visitors found prosperous, self-contained cities linked to each other by a busy, carefully ordered trade. Their inhabitants—merchants, artisans, laborers, clerks—lived comfortable lives. . . .
>
> Though far behind Europe in their technical knowledge, Africans developed tropical farming techniques that have scarcely been bettered to this day. They were good miners and metalworkers. . . . They were astute businessmen. . . . They operated political systems of considerable flexibility and sophistication. They were superb sculptors. . . .
>
> But the record of achievement is not confined to big political systems alone. In the shadow of their pomp and glory rests the modest but impressive achievement of village-level Africa. In community attitudes that join man to man in a brotherhood of equals, in moral rules that guided social behavior, in beliefs that exalted the spiritual aspects of life above the material, the African village achieved a kind of social harmony that often functioned without any need for centralized authority. This, in fact, was where Africa best displayed its real genius—in its capacity for social organization.[13]

In the United States and Africa, the subjugation of the African people and the creation of a social structure in which they were assigned a dependent, inferior status effectively hindered their further achievements. Civilizations flourish and wane for a variety of social, economic, political, and military reasons, not because of the "superiority" of a race or an ethnic group.

Like all civilizations the African civilization ebbed, partly as a result of imperialism, colonialism, and slavery. The subjugation of blacks in the United States, first through slavery and then through continued discrimination and denial, effectively limited their advancement and thereby kept them from having as substantial an impact on American society as they might have had until the mid-1950s. Individual black poets, authors, inventors, craftspeople, engineers, actors, and others flourished under slavery and in the following period, but black people as a whole had little or no education, poor-paying jobs and poor housing, and little upward mobility. Life for them was survival; there was not much opportunity for anything else.

Another counterargument to this historical approach to racial superiority is cultural diffusion. Each civilization is the beneficiary of the inventions and discoveries of others, and white civilizations are no exception; they have evolved further from the contributions of nonwhite civilizations. Whatever the United States has accomplished in world leadership and in achievement as a nation, it owes much to various other peoples for many of the elements within its culture.[14]

The Psychological Approach

The intelligence test, first developed by Alfred Binet in 1905, became a popular means of comparing the intelligence of different racial and ethnic groups, although that was not Binet's intention. Supposedly this objective, scientific instrument would measure innate intelligence and not be influenced by any beneficial or detrimental effects of environment. Any question or claim of one group's intellectual superiority could now be determined. Early studies showed that northern and western Europeans, and often the Chinese and Japanese, scored consistently and decidedly higher than southern and eastern Europeans, blacks, Mexicans, and American Indians.[15] Conveniently ignoring the results for Asians, nativists and segregationists seized on these studies as arguments for immigration restrictions against "inferiors," for the Americanization of Native American Indians, and to justify Jim Crow laws in the South.

Gradually, as nativist antipathy against the "new" immigrants abated, the argument shifted primarily to intelligence differences between blacks and whites. The disparity in the test results, actually reflecting a cultural bias within the tests, now became a basis for claiming white intellectual superiority.

In 1958 Audrey Shuey's book *The Testing of Negro Intelligence* appeared and caused a furor. Shuey surveyed some 240 studies of 60 different intelligence tests that had been given over a 44-year span to hundreds of thousands of servicemen from World Wars I and II and thousands of school children of all ages through college, from all regions of the country. She concluded the following:

> The remarkable consistency in test results, whether they pertain to school or preschool children, to high school or college students, drafts of World War I or World War II, to the gifted or mentally deficient, to the delinquent or criminal; the fact that the colored–white differences are present not only in the rural South and urban South, but in the border and northern areas; the fact that relatively small average differences are found between the I.Q.'s of northern-born and southern-born Negro children in northern cities; the evidence that the tested differences appear to be greater for abstract than for practical or concrete problems; the evidence that the differences obtained are not due primarily to a lack of language skills, the colored averaging no better on non-verbal tests than on verbal tests; the fact that differences are reported in all studies in which the cultural environment of the whites appeared to be no more complex, rich, or stimulating than the environment of the Negroes; the fact that in many com-

parisons (including those in which the colored appeared to best advantage) the Negro subjects have been either more representative of their racial group or more highly selected than are the comparable white subjects; all point to the presence of some native differences between Negroes and whites as determined by intelligence tests.[16]

For any scientist, interpretation of findings is as critical as the findings themselves and the methods employed to obtain them. Shuey was accurate in observing the consistent lower scoring of blacks on intelligence tests. However, many disagreed with her conclusion that this was due to intellectual inferiority of the race. This conclusion of innate or generic differences was a quantum leap from her findings, which did not prove any such thing.

In the late 1960s the IQ controversy then centered around two California professors: Arthur R. Jensen, an educational psychologist at the University of California (Berkeley), and William B. Shockley, a Nobel Price–winning physicist at Stanford University. Jensen argued that the 10- to 20-point IQ differential between blacks and whites involved only certain mental functions. He pointed out that blacks and whites test equally well in such brain functions as rote learning and memory but that blacks test poorer in problem-solving, in seeing relationships, and in abstract reasoning. Because this material does not depend on specific cultural information, he maintained, the only conclusion is that the blacks' lower scores are due to their genetic heritage.[17] Shockley also declared in the mid-1960s that the conceptual intelligence of blacks, as measured by many different IQ tests, is significantly lower than that of whites, and that some of this variance is genetically caused and therefore cannot be corrected.

Refuting this position, Thomas Sowell argued that white ethnic groups, such as the Poles, Jews, and Italians, scored in the 80s during the tests of the 1920s but gained 20 to 25 points by the 1970s after experiencing upward mobility.[18] Those groups of European ancestry who have not experienced upward mobility, as well as the Mexican Americans and the Puerto Ricans, continued to score in the 80s on IQ tests. Most significantly, at various times and places other low-IQ groups have also done poorly on the abstract portions of mental tests. Studies of immigrant groups in 1917, of white children in isolated mountain communities, of working-class children in England, and of early Chinese immigrants all show marked deficiencies on the abstract sections. Concerning the Chinese Americans, recent studies show them to be strongest on the abstract portions of the mental tests, suggesting that upward mobility helps to improve powers of abstract reasoning. Other patterns— children's IQ scores declining as they become adults, and females consistently scoring higher than males—also are common among low-IQ groups, not just blacks. Again, these results change once the group achieves a higher socioeconomic status.

Another problem with IQ tests is that they measure only some forms of intelligence—analytical, conceptual, and verbal (see Box 10.1). We are only beginning to understand how and why the brain functions as it does. Until

| BOX 10.1 | **BLACK INTELLIGENCE TEST OF CULTURAL HOMOGENEITY**
BY ROBERT L. WILLIAMS, Ph.D. |

The purpose of a tongue-in-check "test" such as this was to demonstrate both the subcultural language or understandings of a group and the unfairness of culture-loaded IQ tests on low-income people. Many of you will probably do badly on these questions, regardless of your ability, if the questions are alien to your cultural background, and that is the point of demonstrating cultural bias in tests. Note the acronym formed by the first letters of the test title.

1. **Alley Apple is a a) brick, b) piece of fruit, c) dog, (d) horse.**
2. **CPT means a standard of a) time, b) tune, c) tale, d) twist.**
3. **Deuce-and-a-quarter is a) money, b) a car, c) a house, d) dice.**
4. **The eagle flies means a) the blahs, b) a movie, c) payday, d) deficit.**
5. **Gospel Bird is a a) pheasant, b) chicken, c) goose, d) duck.**
6. **"I know you, shame" means a) You don't hear very well. b) You are a racist. c) You don't mean what you're saying. d) You are guilty.**
7. **Main Squeeze means a) to prepare for battle, b) a favorite toy, c) a best girlfriend, d) to hold up someone.**
8. **Nose Opened means a) flirting, b) teed off, c) deeply in love, d) very angry.**
9. **Playing the dozens means a) playing the numbers, b) playing baseball, c) insulting a person's parents, d) playing with women.**
10. **Shucking means a) talking, b) thinking, c) train of thought, d) wasting time.**
11. **Stone fox means a) bitchy, b) pretty, c) sly, d) uncanny.**
12. **T.C.B. means a) that's cool baby, b) taking care of business, c) they couldn't breathe, d) took careful behavior.**

Answers: 1-a, 2-a, 3-b, 4-c, 5-b, 6-d, 7-c, 8-c, 9-c, 10-d, 11-b, 12-b.

we know more, any assumption of intellectual superiority or inferiority based on IQ scores is conjecture. Moreover, the only proven value IQ scores have is in predicting how well students will do in a traditional school setting. They do not predict performance in nontraditional approaches to education or in any job situation. Does a professor with a 135 IQ teach better than one with 120? Not necessarily, and that is another reason why IQ scores should not be a factor in questions of social interaction.

LANGUAGE AS PREJUDICE

Words are symbols connoting meanings to the world about us. That the very words used to describe the two races—*white* and *black*—usually convey positive and negative meanings, respectively, is unfortunate. For example, *white* often symbolizes cleanliness, purity, or heroes (clothes, armor, hats, and horses), and *black* often stands for dirty, evil, or villains. A snow-covered landscape is beautiful, but a sky laden with black smoke is not. Black clouds are seen as threatening, but white clouds are not.

The power of words is such that the pervasiveness of such meanings for these two words can easily influence minds and attitudes. Ossie Davis had such concerns in mind when he said:

> A superficial examination of Roget's *Thesaurus of the English Language* reveals the following facts: the word "whiteness" has 134 synonyms, 44 of which are favorable and pleasing to contemplate. For example: "purity," "cleanness," "immaculateness," "bright," "shiny," "ivory," "fair," "blonde," "stainless," "clean," "clear," "chaste," "unblemished," "unsullied," "innocent," "honorable," "upright," "just," "straightforward," "genuine," "trustworthy," and only 10 synonyms of which I feel to have been negative and then only in the mildest sense, such as "gloss-over," "whitewash," "gray," "wan," "pale," "ashen," etc.
>
> The word "blackness" has 120 synonyms, 60 of which are distinctly unfavorable, and none of them even mildly positive. Among the offending 60 were such words as "blot," "blotch," "smut," "smudge," "sullied," "begrime," "soot," "becloud," "obscure," "dingy," "murky," "low-toned," "threatening," "frowning," "foreboding," "forbidding," "deadly," "unclean," "dirty," "unwashed," "foul," etc. In addition, and this is what really hurts, 20 of these words—and I exclude the villainous 60 above—are related directly to race, such as "Negro," "Negress," "nigger," "darkey," "blackamoor," etc.
>
> If you consider the fact that thinking itself is subvocal speech (in other words, one must use words in order to think at all), you will appreciate the enormous trap of racial prejudgment that works on any child who is born into the English language.[19]

When *black* has so many negative connotations—blackening the reputation, being black-hearted, blacklisting or blackballing someone, being a blackguard, using black magic, running a black market, and so on—it is easy to see how language by itself can precondition a white person's mind against black people and can lead a black person's mind into possible self-hatred.

INSTITUTIONALIZED RACISM _____

Institutionalized racism, when laws legitimize differential racial treatment, took a new form after slavery was abolished. At first, though, it appeared racial equality might evolve. During the Reconstruction period and almost to the end of the nineteenth century, Southern blacks generally had greater access to stores, restaurants, public transportation, bars, and theaters than in the first half of the twentieth century. A typical pattern was for whites to live on one street in large homes, while behind them on the parallel street were the lesser dwellings of blacks, many of whom worked as domestics. Although there was a clear status distinction, in most places, no severe social distance occurred between the two races. Blacks lived in close proximity to whites and

BOX 10.2	THE ETHNIC EXPERIENCE

"I had heard so much talk about New York. People would say things were so good in New York until I felt that if I would get to New York, I would find money on the streets and wouldn't have no more worries. All my problems would be solved. When I got to New York, things were much different than that. Jobs were very hard to find, and the people were very different than in West Virginia.

"Finally I did get a job through the State Employment Office, working as a cook in the Brooklyn Navy Yard in a private canteen. I stayed there a year and then the war closed up—was over. Then I got another job in a seafood house on 34th Street and 3rd Avenue and I stayed there a year. Then a friend of mine and I went into our own business selling raw fish. Opened a store in Brooklyn selling raw fish. And, of course, it didn't pan out that way. The problem with that business was that we didn't have enough capital to carry us over the rough spots. And then my wife started having babies and so I had to give up that job and seek another, which I did, and finally I got a job right away at another seafood house.

"In the South we had whites live here, colored live there and everybody would speak to you whether they knowed you or not. But when I got to the North, I'd be out on the street, maybe walking around, before I got the jobs, looking around, trying to find my way around, and I would be saying, 'Good morning,' and 'Good evening,' whichever way the situation was, and people would look at me as if I was some dope or something. People would say, 'What's wrong with him?' People are not as friendly up here.

"And I also found out when we bought a house here, that the whites started right away moving out. They started selling their houses, putting up signs for sale. That didn't bother me any. Only thing was that I was just saying to myself that I thought New York was so great. Why should this be happening? And in the South, where I was living, it didn't happen that way. Blacks and whites lived side-by-side there, and we didn't have no problems with that. That kind of upset me that in New York, after hearing so much about it, this did go on."

SOURCE: Black migrant from West Virginia who came North in 1944 at age 26.

frequently interacted with them in secondary relationships through their occupational roles as domestic or service workers. In education, marriage, political participation, and major economic enterprises, however, blacks did not share a commonality with whites.

Immigration and Jim Crow

The change in black–white relations in the late nineteenth and early twentieth centuries is an example of *cultural drift*, a gradual and pervasive change in a people's values. Economic problems, scandals, and frustrations on the part of Southern whites appear to be some of the factors that reshaped Southern attitudes. In a region in which they had long been considered inferior, many blacks were achieving socioeconomic respectability and becoming economic competitors. Resentment of black upward mobility that flowed from the historical undercurrent of racist attitudes was increased by economic troubles (declining cotton prices and unemployment). Because they were racially distinct, the blacks were a convenient scapegoat for the frustrations and hostility of Southern whites.

Less liberal attitudes in the North also were a factor increasing the number of racist acts of discrimination in housing, labor, associations, unions, schools, and churches in both North and South.[20] What caused this change in the North? It is not just coincidence that this change in racial attitudes occurred just when great numbers of southern and eastern European immigrants were settling in Northern urban areas. The arrival of so many dark-eyed, dark-haired, dark-complexioned newcomers set in motion a nativist reaction culminating with restrictive immigration laws. Northerners became more sensitive to the influx of foreigners and "anarchists" as well as to Southern blacks coming to the North to seek work. There were racial overtones to the North's ethnocentric reaction to the "new" immigrants, and the South's reaction to the blacks received greater sympathy from Northern nativists. The North ceased to pressure the South regarding blacks and allowed the Jim Crow laws to emerge without a challenge.

In the 1870s and 1880s, Californians succeeded in making the Chinese question a national issue and cleverly related it to that of the blacks whenever necessary. Political deals were made, and later, Southern representatives voted overwhelmingly in favor of the Chinese Exclusion Act of 1882 and the 1921 immigration bill restricting southern and eastern Europeans, most of whom were settling in the North.

In 1896 the Supreme Court ruling on *Plessy v. Ferguson* upheld the principle of "separate but equal" railroad accommodations and education for blacks and whites. Only a few Southern states had had mandatory segregation laws covering train passengers before the turn of the century. Between 1901 and 1910 most Southern states passed many different **Jim Crow laws.** What followed was the "snowball effect" of such legislation. Segregation became the norm in all areas of life—bars, barber shops, drinking fountains, toilet facilities, ticket windows, waiting rooms, hotels, restaurants, parks, playgrounds, theaters, and auditoriums. Through literacy tests, poll taxes, and other measures, the Southern states also succeeded in disfranchising black voters.

Effects of Jim Crow

The segregation laws, mostly of twentieth-century vintage, reflected racist attitudes that were still current throughout the South decades after slavery had ended. When the 1954 Supreme Court ruling overturned school segre-

This black family arriving in Chicago from the South in 1910 represented a small vanguard of those migrating before World War I. Most left to avoid the discriminatory Jim Crow laws and to seek better educational and economic opportunities. Black migration northward increased somewhat after 1919 but significantly so after 1945. *(Historical Picture Service)*

gation laws, 17 states had mandatory segregation: Alabama, Arkansas, Delaware, Florida, Georgia, Kentucky, Louisiana, Maryland, Mississippi, Missouri, North Carolina, Oklahoma, South Carolina, Tennessee, Texas, Virginia, and West Virginia. Four other states—Arizona, Kansas, New Mexico, and Wyoming—permitted segregation as a local option.

The South

It is impossible to exaggerate the impact on a society of legalizing such discriminatory norms. These laws existed for two generations. During that time both white and black children grew up in a society in which the two races were distinguished from one another and treated differently simply because of that racial difference. Because the white world of reality was one in which differential treatment was the norm, the inferior status of blacks was taken for

For the first six decades of the twentieth century, Jim Crow laws maintained a racially segregated society in the South. All aspects of public interaction, including the entrance and seating accommodations of this movie theater, determined use and accessibility by race. Such pervasive norms socialized many people into accepting a world of institutionalized discrimination as "normal." *(Bern Keating/Black Star)*

granted. For most whites growing up in such an environment and in turn transmitting values and attitudes to their children, this was objective reality.

Structural discrimination in the South was pervasive. Despite challenges by the NAACP and by other groups and individuals, most blacks and whites appeared to accept the situation. To whites the inferior status of blacks in Southern society appeared to justify continued differential treatment. It was, as Gunnar Myrdal concluded in his study of American race relations, a perfect example of the vicious circle in which "discrimination breeds discrimination."[21] Because blacks' education and job opportunities were restricted, the end result of that action was to reinforce the attitude supporting the action. Thus suffering the consequences of deprivation and limited opportunity only aggravated the blacks' situation. They were an easily recognizable group that did not hold better-paying jobs or become educated; they lived in squalor amidst poverty, disease, crime, and violence; and they were not "good enough" to use the same facilities as whites. This gave whites more reason for their aversion to blacks and increased their prejudicial attitudes and discriminatory actions. Myrdal calls this intensification a cumulative causation, in which there is an almost perpetual sequence of reciprocal stimuli and responses.[22]

The North

But what about the North, where few segregationist laws existed? Although there had been some migration to the North earlier, prior to 1914 almost all blacks resided in the South; but then large numbers of blacks began to migrate to the Northern urban areas. Clearly the Jim Crow laws and poor economic conditions were the major push factors for moving north, and better wages, education, and political freedom were the primary pull factors.

> By 1915, the North needed labor. The war was under way in Europe and Northern industry was reaping the benefits from it. The large supply of foreign immigrant labor was rapidly dwindling. In the fourteen years after 1900, over twelve million immigrants found their way to the United States. More than one million immigrants reached the United States in 1914 alone. The next year this figure was cut to about one third, in 1916 to about one fourth, and, by 1918, only 110,618 new arrivals landed on the shores of the United States, while 94,585 left. Other sources of labor were needed and Southern Negroes appeared as an available and willing substitute. . . .
>
> The larger pay and increased economic opportunities in the North were heady inducements to migrants. But it was not only for economic reasons that the desire to come North existed in so many. . . . The desire of adults to see their children able to obtain an education caused many to move North. . . . According to a *New York Times* editorial (January 21, 1918), higher wages would have been far less attractive if the colored man had not felt, and felt for a long time and bitterly, that in the North and West he would not, as in his southern home, be reminded of his black skin every time he met a policeman, entered a street car, railway station or train, and in a hundred other less conspicuous ways in the course of a day.[23]

So the existence of Jim Crow in the South was an important cause of migration to the North. By 1925 there were over 1.5 million blacks living in the North, three fourths of them concentrated in the following metropolitan regions:

New York	251,300
Philadelphia	248,300
Chicago	131,600
St. Louis	102,600
Columbus–Cincinnati	89,600
Pittsburgh	88,300
Kansas City	65,400
Cleveland–Youngstown	58,800
Detroit–Toledo	55,900
Indianapolis	47,500[24]

As their counterparts on the West Coast had done in response to Asian immigrants, the labor unions in the North organized against the blacks. Seeing them either as an undesirable element or as economic competition, many workers quickly became antagonistic toward them. It was one more instance of people being liberals from a distance but reactionaries at close range. Although there was greater freedom in the North, the animosity led to majority patterns of avoidance and discrimination.

Race riots, basically an urban phenomenon reflecting the growing animosity in the North, swept through a number of cities during World War I. In 1917 in East St. Louis, Illinois, 39 blacks and eight whites were killed and hundreds seriously injured in one of the worst riots. In 1919 the situation became even worse, with returning war veterans seeking jobs and more blacks moving north:

> That year there were race riots large and small in twenty-six American cities including thirty-eight killed in a Chicago riot of August, from twenty-five to fifty killed in Phillips County, Arkansas; and six killed in Washington. For a day, the city of Washington, in July, 1919, was actually in the hands of a black mob fighting against the aggression of the whites with hand grenades.[25]

The riots intensified the hostile racial feelings even more. The South had de jure segregation, but Jim Crow—as a cause of black migration and a model for Northern attitudes and actions—played an important role in the development of de facto segregation in the North. With race the determinant for various life opportunities in both the North and the South, succeeding generations of blacks encountered the same obstacles to upward mobility. So the effects of Jim Crow on black assimilation into the mainstream of American society went beyond the South and lasted longer than just the first half of the twentieth century.

The Ku Klux Klan

Once an organization primarily designed to intimidate blacks, the Ku Klux Klan (KKK) reorganized in the twentieth century with a broader range of target groups. As a social organization, the Klan has experienced several phases of popularity and decline and several different sets of goals and objectives. Ex-Confederates had organized the original Klan during the Reconstruction period to frighten and discourage blacks and carpetbaggers. In 1915 William J. Simmons resurrected the movement, formalized its rituals and organization, and dedicated it to white supremacy, Protestant Christianity, and Americanism.

Protest or reactionary groups generally do not become popular unless there is a shared awareness of the problems or concerns to which the group addresses itself within a segment of the society. The Klan was no exception, both in the 1870s and again in the 1920s, when a combination of factors—the agricultural depression, Prohibition, immigration, and isolationism—brought it to a period of rapid expansion. By 1923 the Klan claimed 3 million enrolled members and operated in virtually every state in the union, with public ceremonies and parades.

BOX 10.3

THE ETHNIC EXPERIENCE

"I came to the North not because of a lack, not being able to cope with economic situations in the South, because I was doing all right economically. I came, more or less, for a change of environment and for a higher income for the work I was doing.

"I was educated in the South and by the time I left I was not sharecropping any longer, I was teaching and so my standard of living was different from back when I was a child growing up. I had heard many rumors about the North when I was a child. I had heard there was no segregation in the North. You were at liberty to ride buses, use all facilities, no discrimination in jobs. And I found all of this was, more or less, a fairy tale in a lot of respects. As an adult, I had a more accurate picture of what the North was all about since I had relatives living in Detroit, Washington, and New Jersey.

"I worked at different jobs—office worker, in a nursery school, a dietician—before going to grad school and becoming a public school teacher as I was in the South.

"The biggest adjustment to me going from a rural to an urban setting was getting accustomed to rushing, rushing, rushing city life. To me the people were always running instead of walking. There was always the hustle-bustle to catch the buses and catch subways and this kind of thing. And this was the hardest thing for me to get accustomed to, and the rate at which people worked. The people in the North move much, much faster than people in the South.

"I lived in an apartment with my sister four months, got married and moved to another apartment with my husband. We lived there a year and then moved to the suburbs where we bought our house. Now things here have deteriorated to the extent we have higher unemployment in the North than we do in the South. The overcrowding situation and your housing situation is badly in need of improvement too."

SOURCE: Black migrant from South Carolina who came north in 1954 at age 22.

At first the Klan concentrated on maintaining white supremacy by intimidating white employers as well as black workers and potential voters. Although this remained an important theme, as the Klan spread northward, its racist orientation broadened into a more general nationalism and nativism. Fears and condemnation of Jews and foreigners, especially Catholics, led the Klan into a campaign of promoting an Anglo-Saxon version of Americanism with evangelical zeal. In almost puritanical fashion the hooded Klansmen used mass raids, tarring and featherings, floggings, and other strong-arm tactics aimed at either moral regulation or a stabilization of the old order. In reality they accomplished neither because their actions only fomented additional strife and cruelty.

After a series of internal struggles, exposés of corruption, and mounting anti-Klan opposition, the Klan empire came apart. Although it retained some influence in rural regions of New York, Pennsylvania, Indiana, Texas, and North and South Carolina, its heyday ended in the mid-1920s. It is still very active, however, particularly during times of racial troubles. Ironically, in the 1970s the Klan sought to recruit Catholics—one of its major targets in the past—from the South Boston area who were against school busing.

The Ku Klux Klan, then, evolved into a multixenophobic organization in which southern and eastern European Catholics and Jews, as well as blacks, were seen as a threat to the American character. The Klan's enormous popularity in the early 1920s is a reflection of the times, since these minority peoples were felt to present an economic threat. As prosperity increased and immigration decreased, thereby reducing the tensions, support for the Klan also ebbed. Its success, like the success of the Native American Party and the Know-Nothing Party of the nineteenth century, indicates that many people were receptive to its philosophy and goals.

The Ku Klux Klan is not just a relic from the past, for it is active today. Wherever racial strife occurs, there they will be. They have harassed and intimidated blacks in southern California and Vietnamese along the Texas Gulf Coast. They have sought to recruit Catholics (once also their targets) in South Boston and Louisville, scenes of forced busing conflicts. Where unemployment rises, they seek out the vulnerable victims, offering a convenient black scapegoat for their troubles. In the backwoods of several states, they run paramilitary camps, practicing riflery and battle tactics for what they see as an inevitable racial war. Klan members indoctrinate their children at these camps, passing on a legacy of hate. Meanwhile, on equal-access local cable channels, they telecast programs promoting their bigotry.

THE WINDS OF CHANGE

In the past blacks had made many concerted efforts to improve their lot. The Colored National Farmers' Alliance claimed 1,250,000 members in 1891 but had faded from the scene by 1910. In the twentieth century several black leaders arose to rally their people: Booker T. Washington, W. E. B. DuBois, Marcus Garvey, and A. Philip Randolph. In the 1920s, 1930s, and 1940s, the National Association for the Advancement of Colored People (NAACP) and other groups filed court cases that had limited success but laid the basis for the 1954 desegregation ruling. None of these attempts, however, resulted in as massive a restructuring of black–white relations as the events of the mid-century.

Desegregation: The First Phase

Having experienced life outside their cultural milieu, many blacks who fought in World War II returned home with new perspectives and aspirations. The GI

Bill of Rights, Veterans Authority, and Federal Housing Authority offered increased opportunity for education, jobs, and housing. Expectations increased, and the growing popularity of television sets brought into more and more homes insights into life-styles that previously could only be vaguely imagined.

Several court cases challenging the school segregation laws in Delaware, Kansas, South Carolina, and Virginia reached the U.S. Supreme Court in 1954. Consolidating the several suits, the Justices ruled unanimously on May 17, 1954, that the "separate but equal" doctrine was unconstitutional. Social-science data, through amicus curiae briefs, played an important role in the decision.[26] The following year the court established means of implementing its decree by giving the federal district courts jurisdiction over any problems relating to enforcement of the ruling. The court insisted that the states move toward compliance with "all deliberate speed," but this guideline was vague enough to allow the states to circumvent the ruling at first.

Although the NAACP quickly began a multipronged challenge to school districts in the 17 states in which school segregation existed, their efforts met with mixed success. Many whites, seeing their values, beliefs, and practices threatened by outsiders, resisted desegregation. State legislatures passed bills to stave off integration, whites used economic and social pressures to intimidate any blacks who attempted to integrate local schools, and the school districts themselves procrastinated in dealing with the problem. For three years the battle of wills resulted in continuation of the status quo despite the Supreme Court ruling.

On another front an event occurred in Montgomery, Alabama, in 1955 that foreshadowed other minority actions in the 1960s. Mrs. Rosa Parks, a tired black seamstress on her way home from work, refused to give up her bus seat in the section reserved for whites and was arrested. Through the organizing efforts of Martin Luther King, Jr., in the black community, a successful bus boycott occurred. Four months later the NAACP argued the case in the Federal District Court, which ruled against segregated seating on municipal buses. The U.S. Supreme Court upheld the decision.

The confrontation in the fall of 1957 at Little Rock Central High School in Arkansas was a watershed in desegregation. Here the state's defiance of the Supreme Court could not be ignored because the governor called out the National Guard to forcibly block a concerted effort to integrate the high school. President Eisenhower, who had personally been against the 1954 ruling, acted decisively by federalizing the National Guard and sending regular army troops to assure compliance.

With all legal avenues of appeal exhausted and the federal government insisting that all citizens, including black children, be accorded equal rights, Southern resistance ebbed. Desegregation in the public schools, although sometimes merely tokenism, became the norm throughout the Southern states. That is not to say that everything was harmonious. Some whites established private academies to avoid sending their children to integrated schools, and some Southern leaders publicly committed themselves to up-

Enduring open harassment from white students and adults, Jefferson Thomas stands alone after school as he waits for transportation. One of the first black students to integrate Central High School in Little Rock, he was part of the civil rights movement in its first phase of desegregation. *(UPI/Bettmann Newsphotos)*

holding Southern tradition at all costs. Still, Jim Crow had been dealt a severe blow, and opponents readied themselves for the next assault.

Desegregation: The Second Phase

In the 1960s the civil rights movement gained momentum, attracted many more followers, and moved against all other Jim Crow legislation. Sit-in demonstrations began in Greensboro, North Carolina, on February 1, 1960, when four freshmen from the all-black Agricultural and Technical College sat at the all-white lunch counter at the local Woolworth's store and refused to leave. During the spring of 1960, there were sit-ins throughout the South. From the sit-ins evolved a fourth social organization—the Student Nonviolent Coordinating Committee (SNCC, pronounced *snick*)—to compete with the NAACP, the Congress on Racial Equality (CORE), and the Southern Christian Leadership Conference (SCLC), which Dr. King had formed after the bus boycott.

The success of the sit-ins convinced many people that direct action was a quicker and more effective means of achieving total desegregation. James Farmer of CORE organized Freedom Rides from Washington, DC, to selected Southern locations in 1961 to challenge the segregated facilities in bus terminals. These were followed by freedom marches, voter registration drives, and continued attacks on Jim Crow legislation.

All the movements were symptomatic of the times. Kennedy's election as president in 1960 and his speaking of "a new generation of leadership" had inaugurated a period of high hopes and ideals. It was a time of commitment and change, of Vista and the Peace Corps, of promise and reachable goals. As the civil rights movement grew, "We Shall Overcome" became the rallying theme song, and Bob Dylan's "Blowin' in the Wind" captured the spirit of the times.

Civil rights activity met with fierce resistance. Dr. King urged nonviolence, but younger black activists grew impatient with such an approach:

> Nonviolence was for him [King] a philosophical issue rather than the tactical or strategic question it posed for many younger activists in SNCC and CORE. The aim was "to awaken a sense of moral shame in the opponent." Such a philosophy presumed that the opponent had moral shame to awaken, and that moral shame, if awakened, would suffice. During the 1960's many civil rights activists came to doubt the first and deny the second. The reasons for this did not lie primarily in white Southern terrorism as manifested in the killing of NAACP leader Medgar Evers, of three civil rights workers in Neshoba, Mississippi, of four little girls in a dynamited church in Birmingham, and many others. To a large extent, white Southern violence was anticipated and expected. What was not expected was the absence of strong protective action by the federal government.
>
> Activists in SNCC and CORE met with greater and more violent Southern resistance as direct action continued during the sixties. Freedom Riders were beaten by mobs in Montgomery; demonstrators were hosed, clubbed, and cattle-prodded in Birmingham and Selma. Throughout the South, civil rights workers, Black and White, were victimized by local officials as well as by nightriders and angry crowds. It was not surprising, then, that student activists in the South became increasingly disillusioned with nonviolent tactics of resistance.[27]

Two events in 1963—the March on Washington and the integration of the University of Alabama—gave two civil-rights activists—King and Kennedy—the opportunity to express the mood of the times. On August 28, 1963, tens of thousands of marchers of all races from all over the country and many walks of life gathered before the Lincoln Memorial. King addressed them (in part) as follows:

> There are those who are asking the devotees of civil rights, "When will you be satisfied?" We can never be satisfied as long as the Negro is the victim of the unspeakable horrors of police brutality. We can never be satisfied as long as our bodies, heavy with the fatigue of travel, cannot gain lodging in the motels of the highways and the hotels of the cities. We cannot be satisfied as long as the Negro's basic mobility is from a smaller ghetto to a larger one. We can never be satisfied as long as a Negro in Mississippi cannot vote and a Negro in New York believes he has nothing for which to vote. No, no, we are not satisfied, and we will not be satisfied until justice rolls down like waters and righteousness like a mighty stream. . . .
>
> I say to you today, my friends, that in spite of the difficulties and frustrations of the moment I still have a dream. It is a dream deeply rooted in the American dream.

Martin Luther King, Jr.—flanked by other civil rights activists, including Ralph Abernathy, A. Philip Randolph, and Medgar Evers—makes a freedom march to Birmingham, Alabama, in 1962. Such public actions often produced jeers, taunts, insults, and physical attacks, as challenges to generations of racial discrimination drew strong resistance from many Southern whites. *(Dan Budnik/Woodfin Camp & Associates)*

> I have a dream that one day this nation will rise up and live out the true meaning of its creed: "We hold these truths to be self-evident; that all men are created equal." . . . I have a dream that my four little children will one day live in a nation where they will not be judged by the color of their skin but by the content of their character.

On April 4, 1968, an assassin's bullet prevented Martin Luther King from seeing his dream move closer to reality. President Kennedy was assassinated on November 22, 1963, before the passage of the civil rights legislation he proposed after sending troops to enforce the integration of the University of Alabama in that same year. When explaining his actions, Kennedy had told the American public in a television address:

> This nation was founded by men of many nations and backgrounds. It was founded on the principle that all men are created equal, and that the rights of every man are diminished when the rights of one man are threatened. . . .
>
> It ought to be possible, therefore, for American students of any color to attend any public institution they select without having to be backed up by troops. It ought to be possible for American consumers of any color to receive equal

service in places of public accommodation, such as hotels and restaurants, and theaters and retail stores without being forced to resort to demonstrations in the street.

And it ought to be possible for American citizens of any color to register and to vote in a free election without interference or fear of reprisal.

It ought to be possible, in short, for every American to enjoy the privileges of being American without regard to his race or his color.

In short, every American ought to have the right to be treated as he would wish to be treated, as one would wish his children to be treated. But this is not the case. . . .

One hundred years of delay have passed since President Lincoln freed the slaves, yet their heirs, their grandsons, are not fully free. They are not yet freed from the bonds of injustice; they are not yet freed from social and economic oppression.

And this nation, for all its hopes and all its boasts, will not be fully free until all its citizens are free.

The Civil Rights Act of 1964 was the most far-reaching legislation against racial discrimination ever passed. It provided for equal standards for all voters in federal elections. It prohibited racial discrimination and refusal of service on racial grounds in all places of public accommodation, including eating and lodging establishments and places of entertainment, recreation, or service. It gave the attorney general broader powers to intervene in private suits regarding violation of civil rights. It banned racial discrimination by employers or unions or by any recipient of federal funds, and it directed federal agencies to monitor this and to withhold funds from any recalcitrant state or local agency. Unfortunately, black workers still meet resistance from many unions when they apply for membership.

Congress passed additional legislation in 1965 to simplify judicial enforcement of the voting laws and to extend them to state and local elections. In 1968 further civil rights legislation barred discrimination in housing and gave the Native Americans greater rights in their dealings with courts and government agencies at all levels. Congress also set stiff federal penalties for those convicted of intimidating or injuring anyone who was exercising any of the civil rights provided by congressional action.

In 1966 Stokely Carmichael, the head of SNCC, advanced the slogan "Black Power," which became subject to many interpretations because it was never clearly defined. For many it was not a wild cry of radicals but a declaration that civil rights goals could be achieved only through concerted black efforts. It symbolized the attainment of what Kurt Lewin called a "sense of peoplehood," and Franklin Giddings identified it as a "consciousness of kind." The word *black* rather than *Negro* became the accepted way of referring to this racial group in the early 1970s.

One generation later we can readily see the gains in black power in the political arena. Black elected officials increased dramatically, from about 170 in 1964 to over 7,400 in 1991, two-thirds of these in the Southern states. By 1992 blacks served as mayors in 224 cities—among them such urban centers as Los

Angeles, Chicago, Philadelphia, Detroit, Washington, Atlanta, Oakland, New Orleans, New York, Birmingham, and Richmond.[28] Jesse Jackson's two presidential bids succeeded in increasing black voter registration by several million, further strengthening their ballot power. In other areas to be discussed shortly, blacks also improved their rate of participation. Perhaps "stateways" will change "folkways," as legislation opens doors to blacks, thereby providing long-term opportunities for the social conditioning of people's attitudes toward racial harmony.[29]

URBAN UNREST

As the civil rights movement gained momentum, it spread northward as well. Protests against discrimination in employment and housing and against de facto segregation in the schools began in the early 1960s in New York and Philadelphia and quickly spread:

> None of the problems of the blacks in the North—slum schools, unemployment or residential segregation—were new, but an intensified awareness of them had grown. Part of this new awareness reflected the economic cramp that developed during the latter part of the fifties, particularly in the burgeoning ghettoes of northern and western cities. Ideological cramp was being felt outside the South, too. The promise of a new equality for all blacks, the struggle of southern blacks to realize this promise, and the complacency of white America as the white South turned the new equality into token equality spread disillusionment into black neighborhoods all over the nation. Ironically, the plaintive and oft-repeated plea of white southerners that the problem of race relations was not just a Southern problem finally began to be heard—but only because it was now sounded by black voices.[30]

In the North ideological support for the black cause waned as the distance from the conflict diminished with increasing percentages of blacks in Northern cities. Changes were demanded nearer home, in particular open housing and busing. By 1964 Charles Silberman observed:

> And so the North is finally beginning to face the reality of race. In the process, it is discovering animosities and prejudices that had been hidden in the recesses of the soul. For a brief period following the demonstrations in Birmingham in the spring of 1963—a very brief period—it appeared that the American conscience had been touched; a wave of sympathy for the Negro and of revulsion over white brutality seemed to course through the nation. But then the counteraction set in, revealing a degree of anti-Negro prejudice and hatred that surprised even the most sophisticated observers.[31]

As blacks experienced some gains and some frustrations, a pattern of increased alienation, cynicism, hostility, and eventual violence ensued. When a social movement achieves some goals, its expectations are increased and so are its frustrations, leading to greater militancy.[32] Militant leaders such as Malcolm X, Eldridge Cleaver, Huey Newton, and Bobby Seale emerged to speak of the grievances of Northern blacks. New organizations, such as the Black Panthers, and older ones, such as the Black Muslims, attracted many followers as they set out to meet the needs of Northern blacks in the ghettos.

The 1960s Riots

In the summer of 1964 blacks rioted in the tenement sections of Harlem, Philadelphia, and Rochester, attacking both police and property. The following summer, the violence and destruction were more massive; outbursts occurred first in the Watts section of Los Angeles and then in Chicago, Springfield, Massachusetts, and Philadelphia. Ghetto violence continued; in the summer of 1966 there were 18 different riots, and in the summer of 1967, 31 cities experienced riots, of which those in Newark (26 killed) and Detroit (42 killed) were the worst.

The increase in the number and intensity of riots in 1967 prompted an in-depth study of 75 of the disorders, including those in Newark and Detroit, by the National Advisory Commission on Civil Disorders. It found that, although specific grievances varied somewhat from city to city, there were consistent patterns in who the rioters were, how the riots originated, and what the rioters wanted. The most intense causal factors were police practices, unemployment and underemployment, and inadequate housing. In its 1968 report the so-called Kerner Commission warned that the United States was "moving toward two societies, one black, one white—separate and unequal."[33]

The assassination of Martin Luther King, Jr., in April 1968 caused violence to erupt anew in 125 cities. The Justice Department reported 46 people killed in a week of unrest. Several years of civil rights legislation now set changes in motion. Government action at all levels sought to correct the conditions that encouraged the violence, and America's cities experienced no further major disturbances for several years.

Two factors contributed to the cooling of black urban violence. First, a new social movement protesting the war in Vietnam, to which many black youths were being sent, became a focus for public concern. Second, many black leaders were either assassinated (King, Evers, and Malcolm X) or imprisoned (Carmichael, Newton, and Seale) or went into exile (Cleaver). Many blacks redirected their energies toward community self-help programs, as other leaders were co-opted in leadership roles within the system and many blacks began to strive for the Black Power goal Carmichael had enunciated.

The 1980s Riots

In Miami in May 1980, though, black economic frustrations and resentment against the growing Cuban community—sparked by an all-white jury's acquittal of four white police officers accused of bludgeoning to death a black man—set off three days of the worst outbreak of racial violence in 13 years. When it ended, 18 were dead, more than 400 injured, and property damages exceeded $200 million.[34] In January 1989, violence erupted in Miami again, in the Overtown section, after a policeman shot and killed a black motorcycle rider.

The 1992 Los Angeles Riot

In late April and early May 1992 there were five days of rioting in Los Angeles after the acquittal of four white city police officers in the videotaped beating of black motorist Rodney King. Officials reported 58 deaths, 4,000 injuries, 11,900 arrests, and damage ranging as high as $1 billion.[35] The events seemed like a flashback to the 1960s, but in the intervening years American society had moved past the Kerner Commission's portrait of two separate black and white societies. Most of the 30 million African Americans did not take to the streets. Those who did were part of a relatively small urban underclass clearly distinct from the 40 percent of all African American families now middle class or upwardly mobile working class. Moreover, the 1965 Watts riot was black versus white, but the 1992 riot was multiracial warfare: blacks preying on other blacks, Latinos on whites, blacks and Latinos on Koreans and other Asian Americans.[36] The Rodney King verdict was only the spark that lit a powder keg built from the pathologies resulting from poverty—squalid living conditions, frustration, alienation, anger, and family disintegration.

In Chapter 8 we discussed some aspects of the black–Korean conflict. Part of that animosity stems from the growing presence and economic success of Korean merchants in black neighborhoods where poverty and unemployment are widespread. As previously mentioned, one in 10 Korean Americans is self-employed, compared to one in 67 African Americans. African Ameri-

In the April, 1992 aftermath of the Rodney King verdict, Los Angeles rioters surround an overturned car. This multiracial riot left 58 people dead, 4,000 injured, and $1 billion in property damage. Like other riots, it left area residents worse off economically and prompted the relocation of those able to leave. *(Reuters/Bettmann)*

cans are more likely to be in public sector employment.[37] Limited education is not a barrier to self-employment for Korean Americans because of their informal networks of assistance and advice. Poorly educated blacks, however, lack similar support networks and are less likely to become entrepreneurs in the central city.[38] Witnessing the economic gains of strangers in their midst while they themselves are mired in a limbo of deprivation, their resentment sometimes reaches the flashpoint of violence when it is triggered by an incident.

How do we prevent the violence? The primary answer lies in eliminating the economic despair that fuels riots. We must overcome such conditions as depressed urban economies, chronic unemployment, a poorly skilled and educated labor force, substandard housing, and unsafe streets.

Reducing the social distance among urban residents through community interaction is another approach. When "we" replaces "us" versus "them," violence is far less likely. Still another approach is increasing the number of black entrepreneurs in the central city. Black proprietors would be positive role models and could provide initial employment opportunities to urban black youth. These local mom-and-pop stores could become bonding anchors in the neighborhood, reinforcing community life around work, thereby helping generate and sustain informal associations.[39]

Post-Violence Exodus

For several complex reasons, a significant white middle-class migration from cities to suburbs began in the 1950s, and urban violence has clearly been a major factor (see Figure 10.1). The 1960s riots gave added impetus to white flight, with many stores and businesses following close behind. Because major cities also experienced population decline, this resulted in a larger concentration of people of color in those cities.

The latest riots are inducing a corollary effect. Experts note that the recent riots have caused many middle-class minorities from the embattled neighborhoods in south-central Los Angeles and elsewhere to leave.[40] Violence, burning, and looting thus destroy the neighborhood economy, stability, and potential as its middle class departs in fear.

SOCIAL INDICATORS OF BLACK PROGRESS _____

As Figure 10.2 shows, a larger percentage of blacks are younger than whites. This demographic fact suggests both a more rapid future population growth for blacks and the importance of the socioeconomic environment in which young people grow up. The more enriched their childhood socialization, the greater their adult life opportunities. The more deprived their environment, the more limited will be their adult life opportunities.

Where are we today? How far have we gone toward true equality for blacks as well as whites? Sociologists use quantifiable measurements or social indicators to identify specifically a group's achievements in comparison with

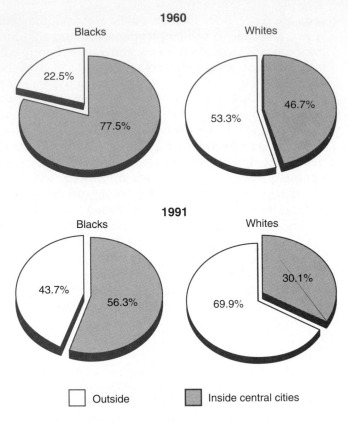

1960

FIGURE 10.1
**Population Living Inside and Outside Central Cities,
Blacks and Whites: (1960 and 1991)**

SOURCE: U.S. Bureau of the Census.

others, as well as its mobility within the stratification system. Three of the most common variables—education, income, and occupation—offer an objective portrait of what gains have been made, of how much the gap between the two races has been narrowed.

Education

Most impressive have been the considerable gains in level of education. Even though the national average for years of completed schooling has been rising, blacks have made such dramatic gains that they have narrowed the gap in median years of schooling completed from a three-year differential in 1950 to a few months' differential in 1991 (Table 10.1). Part of this success has been the "play it cool, stay in school" campaigns, which have effectively reduced the dropout rate (Table 10.2). The dropout rate among black students dropped

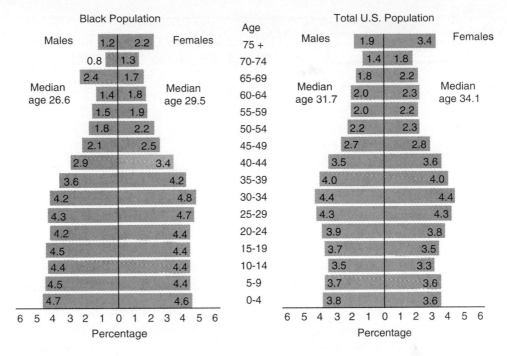

FIGURE 10.2
Age-Sex Composition of the Black Population, 1990
SOURCE: U.S. Bureau of the Census.

from 22.2 percent in 1970 to 11.3 percent in 1991. White students, excluding Hispanics, decreased sightly in the same period, from 10.8 percent to 10.5 percent.

If we look more closely at those students completing four years of high school or more, we find a slightly different picture. As Table 10.3 illustrates,

TABLE 10.1	MEDIAN YEARS OF SCHOOLING COMPLETED: SELECTED YEARS, 1950–1991				
	1950	1960	1970	1980	1991
Black males	6.4	7.7	9.4	12.0	12.4
White males	9.3	10.7	12.1	12.5	12.8
Black females	7.1	8.6	10.0	12.0	12.4
White females	10.0	11.2	12.1	12.6	12.7

SOURCE: U.S. Bureau of the Census, *Current Population Reports*, series P-20, No. 403 and *Statistical Abstract of the United States*, 1992, Table 220, p. 144.

TABLE 10.2	**HIGH SCHOOL DROPOUTS BY RACE AND AGE, BY PERCENTAGES: 1970–1991**		
Race and Age	1970	1980	1991
White	10.8	11.3	10.5
16–17 years	7.3	9.2	5.9
18–21 years	14.3	14.7	13.9
22–24 years	16.3	14.0	14.6
Black	22.2	16.0	11.3
16–17 years	12.8	6.9	7.4
18–21 years	30.5	23.0	16.6
22–24 years	37.8	24.0	14.0

Includes other age groups not shown separately.

SOURCE: U.S. Bureau of the Census, *Statistical Abstract of the United States,* 1992, Table 253, p. 161.

the percentages for both blacks and whites completing four years of high school have been steadily increasing, certainly a positive sign. However, despite the fact that blacks went from 12.9 percent completing four or more years of high school in 1960 to 37.7 percent in 1991, a gap remains. Figure 10.3 shows the heart of the problem. Of those entering high school, 87 percent of the whites and 83 percent of the blacks graduated. Only 32 percent of the blacks entered college compared to 39 percent of the whites. Completing

TABLE 10.3	**YEARS OF SCHOOL COMPLETED: 1960 TO 1991 (BY AGE, RACE, AND PERCENTAGES)**					
Years of School Completed	Black			White		
	1960	1970	1991	1960	1970	1991
Under 5 years	23.8	14.6	4.7	6.7	4.5	2.0
5–7 years	24.2	18.7	6.4	12.8	9.1	3.4
8 years	12.9	10.5	4.1	18.1	13.0	4.5
High School 1–3 years	19.0	24.8	18.0	19.3	18.8	10.2
4 years	12.9	21.2	37.7	25.8	32.2	39.1
College 1–3 years	4.1	5.9	17.5	9.3	11.1	18.6
4 years or more	3.1	4.4	11.5	8.1	11.3	22.2
Median years completed	8.0	9.8	12.4	10.9	12.1	12.8

SOURCE: U.S. Bureau of the Census, *Statistical Abstract of the United States,* 1992, Table 220, p. 144.

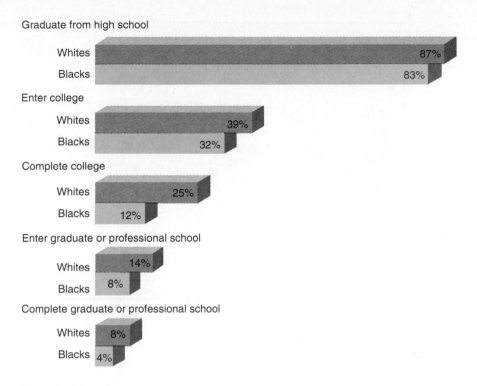

Graduate from high school
Whites — 87%
Blacks — 83%

Enter college
Whites — 39%
Blacks — 32%

Complete college
Whites — 25%
Blacks — 12%

Enter graduate or professional school
Whites — 14%
Blacks — 8%

Complete graduate or professional school
Whites — 8%
Blacks — 4%

FIGURE 10.3
Education Attainment Levels of Blacks and Whites
SOURCE: Basic data: Bureau of the Census, *Current Population Reports,* Series P-20, Nos. 443, 444.

college were 12 percent of the blacks, less than half the 25 percent white college graduates. Given current trends, we may expect this situation to improve each succeeding year, continuing a positive picture for this social indicator.

Another barometer of improvement is comparative test scores. The College Board, which runs the national Scholastic Aptitude Test (SAT), found a narrowing of the traditional black–white gap in test scores in the 1980s. A more expansive study of scores on the verbal skills section of the National Assessment of Education Progress, SAT, and Graduate Record Exam over a seven-year period revealed a consistent reduction in the black-white average difference on all three tests.[41]

Income

Historically, black family income has always been significantly lower than white family income. The civil rights legislation and the War on Poverty began a slow steady improvement until the 1980s when the economic problems of American society eroded some of the gains. As indicated in Table 10.4, the

TABLE 10.4	MEDIAN FAMILY INCOME: 1950 TO 1990			
Year	White	Black	Black Income as a Percentage of White Income	Actual Income Gap
1950	$ 3,445	$ 1,869	54.3	$ 1,576
1955	$ 4,605	$ 2,549	55.4	$ 2,056
1960	$ 5,835	$ 3,230	55.4	$ 2,602
1965	$ 7,251	$ 3,993	55.1	$ 3,258
1970	$10,236	$ 6,279	61.3	$ 3,957
1975	$14,268	$ 8,779	61.5	$ 5,489
1980	$21,904	$12,674	57.9	$ 9,230
1985	$29,152	$16,786	57.6	$12,366
1990	$36,915	$21,423	58.0	$15,492

SOURCE: Adapted from Statistical Abstract of the United States, 1992, Table 702, p. 449.

1990 median family income was $36,915 for whites and $21,423 for blacks. Put differently, black families earned 58 cents for every $1 white families earned. During the 1980s, the white–black income disparity was greatest in the South and improved in the Northeast and West. Industrial decay in the Midwest hit black households particularly hard because many were in entry-level, labor-intensive kinds of work most susceptible in a slumping economy.[42]

A frustrating social indicator has been the poverty rate among blacks. Significantly dropping from 48.1 percent in 1959 to 27.1 percent by 1975, it has since fluctuated up and down, depending on the economy. After rising a few percentage points as a result of the 1980–1982 recession, it then steadily declined from 1983 to 1989. A more serious economic downturn in 1990–1992 sparked another increase in the poverty rate among all Americans, with the black rate in 1991 revealing that one in three African Americans was living in poverty. Through good times and bad, the black poverty rate has constantly remained about three times that of the white rate (see Figure 10.4).

A significant factor has been the "feminization of poverty," with the rise in female-headed families.[43] Because many women lack education and job skills, their poor earning potential is limited further by unavailable or unaffordable child-care centers, making female-headed families the fastest growing segment of the population living in poverty. One in three (31.1 percent) female-headed families lives in poverty. An astonishing 63.9 percent of all black youngsters lived in a single-parent home in 1990, a matter of grave concern to African American leaders and government officials alike.[44]

For black America both progress and regression have been occurring simultaneously. A larger segment than ever before has been able to secure better-paying positions and greater economic stability. At the same time, we have

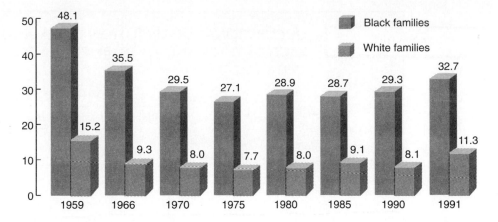

FIGURE 10.4

Black and White Families Below Poverty Level in Selected Years, 1959 to 1991, by Percentage.

SOURCE: U.S. Bureau of the Census, *Current Population Reports,* Series P-60, No. 158 and unpublished data.

witnessed the growth of a multigenerational, poor underclass that is mired in urban ghettos and habitually unemployed or underemployed.

In 20 years the percentage of blacks in the middle class has doubled, and a black male college graduate now earns approximately the same income as a white male college graduate.[45] At the same time we have witnessed the collapse of inner-city neighborhoods. Entry-level urban manufacturing jobs are mostly gone, as are black, middle-class role models in those areas. Emerging instead is a welfare and underground economy, where the only successful people with money are drug pushers, pimps, and prostitutes. It is a world where the men are often without jobs and the women without husbands. One-third of the approximately 10 million blacks living in poverty in 1991 made up this hard-core poor, trapped in an apparently unending cycle of broken homes, joblessness, welfare, drugs, crime, and violence.

Blauner's internal colonialism theory seems very applicable to this trapped segment of the black population. The segregated black ghetto does appear to be a more permanent phenomenon than that of European immigrants, with few individuals able to escape it. Until some sweeping action occurs, and none seems imminent, our urban ghettos remain sinks of despair, decay, and fear.

Occupation

Because the nature of one's work provides an important basis for societal esteem, the occupational distribution of an entire group serves as a comparative measurement of its status in the larger society. Table 10.5 offers this insight. Although slow, steady gains have been made in African American representation in managerial, professional, technical, and white-collar occupations, significant differences remain.

TABLE 10.5	OCCUPATIONAL DISTRIBUTION BY SEX AND RACE, 16 YEARS AND OVER, BY PERCENTAGES, 1991			
		Male		Female	

Classification	Black	White	Black	White
Managerial, professional	13.9	27.3	18.8	28.1
Technical, sales, administrative support	17.4	20.2	39.0	44.7
Service occupations	18.8	9.0	27.6	16.6
Precision production, crafts, repair	15.2	19.5	2.2	2.1
Operators, fabricators, laborers	31.2	19.2	12.2	7.5
Farming, fishing, forestry	3.5	4.7	0.3	1.2

SOURCE: Bureau of the Census, "The Black Population in the United States: March 1991," *Current Population Reports,* Series P-20, Table 2.

Black men were more likely to be employed as operators, fabricators, or laborers than in any other occupational group (31.2 percent). In contrast, white men were more likely to be employed in managerial and professional specialty occupations (27.3 percent). Black men were also twice as likely to work in service occupations than white men (18.8 percent vs. 9.0 percent). Service occupations include police, firefighters, food services, health aides, public transportation, social welfare aides, and cleaning and building service positions.

Both black and white women were more likely to be employed in technical, sales, and administrative support occupations than elsewhere (39.0 percent and 44.7 percent respectively). Black women were more likely to work in service occupations (27.6 percent vs. 16.6 percent), whereas over one-fourth (28.1 percent) of white women were employed in managerial and professional specialty occupations compared to almost one-fifth (18.8 percent) of black women.

Housing

To a large extent the quality of housing is a reflection of one's occupation and income. Following the previous discussion of other social indicators, one should not be surprised to learn that by 1990 housing units occupied by black owners were approximately 44 percent of all black housing.[46] However, racial discrimination has continued to affect both urban neighborhoods and population distribution. The 1968 Fair Housing Act made it "unlawful . . . to refuse to sell or rent . . . a dwelling to any person because of race, color, religion, or national origin," but a quarter century later de facto segregation persists in U.S. metropolitan areas.

Redlining

One continuing problem is **redlining,** the unwillingness of some banks to make loans on property in lower-income minority neighborhoods indicated on city maps with red pencil lines. Such a practice accelerates the deterioration of older housing because owners have difficulty obtaining funds for improvements to buildings and potential buyers are unable to secure mortgages. To overcome this problem, the Community Reinvestment Act (CRA) of 1977 stipulated that banks have an "affirmative obligation" to lend in lower-income neighborhoods. When it has been seriously applied, the CRA has proved to be effective in helping turn neighborhoods around, and thousands of lower-income people have discovered home ownership.[47] However, the CRA set no firm lending quotas, and a 1988 study revealed that in many cities (including Atlanta, Baltimore, Chicago, Philadelphia, and Washington) minority neighborhoods were unfairly denied mortgages in comparison to white neighborhoods.[48]

Residential Segregation

An increasing proportion of African Americans are living outside central cities (see Figure 10.1). Among blacks living in large metropolitan areas (more than 1 million population), 31 percent were living in suburbs in 1990 compared to 25 percent in 1980.[49] Despite this centrifugal shift, residential segregation has changed little since the 1950s. Blacks are more highly segregated than either Asians or Hispanics, having the highest levels of segregation found in the older industrial cities of the Midwest and Northeast. Residential segregation also exists among blacks living outside central cities because most have moved to outlying urban neighborhoods or suburbs that are mostly black or bordering on being mostly black areas.

RACE OR CLASS?

Despite economic gains made by many African Americans, one in three remains mired in poverty. The causes of this persistent gap, or bipolarization, within the black community has stirred heated debate. Is it the result of continuing racial discrimination or of socioeconomic conditions?

In his 1978 book *The Declining Significance of Race,* sociologist William J. Wilson touched off the debate by arguing that the life chances of blacks—their economic opportunities—are now determined far more by their social class than by their race.[50] If educated, blacks can compete equally with whites, enjoying unprecedented opportunities for better-paying jobs. At the same time, Wilson said, the increasing job qualifications in this high-technology age may well keep the black underclass permanently trapped in economic subordination. Although race is not insignificant, Wilson stressed that social class, not racial discrimination, denies upward mobility to the black poor. Affirmative Action helps middle-class blacks, not the poor. Until we recognize the dependency nature of welfare and the need to provide skills and education to the urban poor, we cannot effectively attack the problem of inequality.

Economist Thomas Sowell echoed this view, pointing out in *Ethnic America* the parallels between blacks and other ethnic groups in social class and upward mobility as key factors in their acceptance and socioeconomic mainstreaming.[51] Carl Gershman, a white civil rights activist and former research director of the A. Philip Randolph Institute, also called the current problem class-caused, suggesting that black leaders remained preoccupied with racial bias as the sole cause of ghetto poverty and ignored the reality of a bipolarization of American blacks.[52]

Other black social scientists do not agree with Wilson, Sowell, and Gershman. Sociologist Charles V. Willie in *Caste and Class Controversy* maintained that economics is but one facet of the larger society and should therefore not be considered in isolation. White racism permeates all social institutions, controlling entry to all desirable positions in education, employment, earnings, housing, and social status. By surrendering their blackness blacks may gain middle-class status, said Willie, but they become psychologically chained in a white world that permits only token entry while retaining actual power, control, and wealth.[53]

Psychologist Kenneth B. Clark called Wilson's position "wishful and premature optimism."[54] Death, retirement, and entry into judicial, political, or corporate careers have removed most effective civil rights leaders, preventing action for remedying continuing and worsening racial problems. Those blacks in corporate, government, or university life are less in genuine decision-making positions than in created positions of racial tokenism, with limited influence and a cautious attitude against jeopardizing their "personal gains and affable acceptance of their white colleagues." Institutionalized racism remains, said Clark, as seen in the failure of whites to resolve the problem of the urban ghettos and in the use of such racial code words as "busing," "quotas," "reverse discrimination," "meritocracy," and "maintaining standards," which imply that efforts to correct racial injustice weaken the fiber of society.

In 1987 Wilson argued further that, unlike the past, today's inner-city neighborhoods face social isolation.[55] The exodus of middle- and working-class black families from inner-city neighborhoods removes essential role models and undermines supportive social institutions. Furthermore, outsiders avoid these communities that are plagued by massive unemployment, crime, and schools that do not promote high achievement. Consequently, area residents—women and children on welfare, school dropouts, teenaged mothers, and aggressive street criminals—are cut off from the mainstream society.[56] Gary Orfield effectively noted the magnitude of this isolation:

> To a considerable extent the residents of city ghettos are now living in separate and deteriorating societies, with separate economies, diverging family structures and basic institutions, and even growing linguistic separation within the core ghettos.[57]

One false stereotype has African Americans living in poverty, and almost one in three do fall into that category. However, two out of three actually are part of America's working or middle class. This Oakland, California family enjoying their backyard is thus more representative of their race. *(Lawrence Migdale/Stock, Boston)*

Current social indicators about this segment of the black population do not provide any cause for optimism about any significant improvement in the near future. Until some bold, innovative action addresses the multiple problems of limited education and job skills, high unemployment, and the growing number of female-headed families dependent on welfare, the situation threatens to perpetuate the black underclass.

THE AFRICANS

Although many white Americans simply use Negroid racial features as the basis of group classification, there is much cultural diversity among blacks in America. Generalizing about them is just as inaccurate as generalizing about whites. Regional and social-class differences create distinctions among American blacks, and cultural differences make West Indian black immigrants unlike native-born blacks. Black immigrants from Africa are culturally distinct not only from the two former groups but also from one another when they have different countries of origin. Also, although many native-born American blacks call themselves Afro-Americans, in reality a wide cultural gulf separates them from the African immigrants.[58] This fact is often demonstrated at the student level when two separate groups form on college campuses. It has not been uncommon to see, for example, both a black student union and an African students association at the same college.

Value Orientations

Professor Muruku Waiguchu, himself an immigrant from Kenya, has contrasted some of the value orientations of black American and African college students in the United States.[59] He has found that African students tend to show some degree of contempt for and arrogance toward black-American students, commonly using such terms as "Negro" or "nigger" to refer to them. Africans are frequently more achievement-oriented, competitive, and opportunistic than black American students, partly because they have help from white supporters and no "history of denials and exclusion" from white America. The African student is also less racially conscious in the American sense and therefore is more likely to participate in interracial primary relationships (parties, dating, marriage) than black American college students. Waiguchu argues that the two black groups do not share a greater trust and understanding because both have been victimized by white social conditioning:

> Unlike any other people, much of our history, and therefore our cultural continuity, has been written by our detractors and oppressors. The inevitable consequence has been that we look at one another through the eyes given and provided to us through the education process and other forms of communication owned and operated by white people. . . . We do not articulate our interests collectively because we oftentimes do not understand one another and waste valuable time labelling one another with the stereotypes we have collected from the white man.[60]

Whether whites are the ultimate cause of black American–African misunderstanding is debatable. It is true, though, that differing cultural orientations and ethnocentrism play important roles. Just as dominant and minority white groups have often mistrusted each other, so different black groups may display an outgroup negativism despite racial similarity.

As Table 10–6 shows, African immigration has been significantly increasing in the past few decades. Chain migration, Americanization of foreign students enrolled in U.S. colleges, economic opportunities, and homeland events are the major push–pull factors at work.

African immigrants frequently face a double handicap when adjusting to American society. First, they encounter racial prejudice and discrimination in various social settings and on the job. For many this is a new experience because they were not a racial minority at home and they did not experience any of these problems there. Second, because of their own cultural distinctions, they do not identify with American blacks. Successful American blacks who are interested in helping the less fortunate usually concentrate on the American black poor, not on newcomers from Africa, obliging the African immigrants to seek out one another for mutual comfort and security.

TABLE 10.6	AFRICAN IMMIGRATION TO THE UNITED STATES*
1901–1910	7,368
1911–1920	8,443
1921–1930	6,286
1931–1940	1,750
1941–1950	7,367
1951–1960	14,092
1961–1970	28,954
1971–1980	80,779
1981–1990	176,893

*Includes Egypt, Libya, and Morocco.

SOURCE: U.S. Immigration and Naturalization Service, Annual Report, U.S. Government Printing Office, Washington, DC, 1991, Table 2.

Grouping the immigrants from the African continent into one category is as much a mistake as generalizing about the southern, central, and eastern Europeans was two generations ago, yet few studies have been done of the individual nationalities. Perhaps because their homelands are relatively new as independent countries freed from decades of colonial rule and their numbers here are still fairly small, they find a greater sense of identity in pluralistic America as Africans, while simultaneously relating to a few nearby compatriots as fellow Kenyans, Nigerians, and so on (Table 10.7).

As a result of occupational preference classifications in current immigration law, many African immigrants are educated and possess occupational skills placing them at a middle-class socioeconomic level. If their upsurge in immigration continues, their increased visibility and economic position may make them a more viable ethnic group than heretofore. Like Arab immigrants, they do not cluster in recognizable territories but instead form interactional networks or "dispersed villages."[61]

SOCIOLOGICAL ANALYSIS

Blacks have been victims of slavery, restrictive laws, or racial discrimination for most of the years they have lived in the United States. Many changes have occurred in the past 30 years, but problems remain. Some argue that the unique experiences of black people in America require separate analysis, that their situation cannot be compared to that of other ethnic groups. Others maintain that, despite certain significant dissimilarities, sufficient parallels exist to invite comparative analysis in patterns of dominant-minority relations. Use of the three major perspectives incorporates both views.

| BOX 10.4 | **THE INTERNATIONAL SCENE** |

Like the United States, Brazil was colonized by Europeans who subjugated the native population and imported Africans as slave laborers. In fact Brazil today is second only to the United States in the number of its citizens of African descent outside the African continent itself. Despite these similarities, race relations in Brazil have followed a very different path from that in the United States.

The United States maintains a fairly rigid biracial system, classifying people as white or nonwhite. Such a simplistic "us" and "them" categorization has long been a breeding ground for racial prejudice, segregation, and hostility. Moreover, it is becoming increasingly unrealistic. In 1991 the Census Bureau identified almost 1 million mixed-race married couples, up from 310,000 in 1970. According to the Population Reference Bureau, the United States is presently experiencing an interracial baby boom. Births to mixed-race couples accounted for 3.4 percent of all births in 1989. With such increases, how well do U.S. racial categories serve an emerging multiracial society?

In Brazil a multiracial classification system exists. In its broadest categories, the society has three population types: *pretos* (blacks), *brancos* (whites), and *pardos* (mulattos). The 1990 census identified 50 percent white, 7 percent black, 42 percent mulatto, and 1 percent Asian.

Mulattos in the United States are classified with blacks, but they are a separate group in Brazil. Moreover, Brazilian mulattos comprise abut 40 subclassifications of color variations. To identify each of these separate racial categories, Brazilians use dozens of precise terms reflecting minute distinctions in skin shading, hair, and facial features.

Since the first days of Portuguese settlement, miscegenation has been common, although usually within similar color gradients than between couples at opposite ends of the color line. Brazil's more fluid color continuum deters formation of a racist ideology or segregated institutions, although whites remain traditionally in a higher social class than most of the people of color.

The Functionalist View

Inequality exists in all societies because people value more highly certain occupational roles and social positions over others. A value consensus develops about their functional importance in meeting the needs, goals, and priorities of society. Status, esteem, and differential rewards depend on this orientation and the availability of qualified personnel. As one example, slavery offered the South a practical and effective means of developing an agricultural economy based on cotton; slaves provided a cheap labor force to work long hours, requiring only physical endurance—no training, skills, tal-

	AFRICAN IMMIGRATION TO THE UNITED STATES, BY COUNTRY OF ORIGIN: 1971–1990	
TABLE 10.7		

Country	1971–1980	1981–1990
Algeria	1,123	1,511
Angola	1,437	1,078
Cape Verde	5,531	7,876
Ethiopia	3,881	27,214
Ghana	5,195	14,876
Kenya	4,505	7,853
Liberia	2,400	8,058
Nigeria	8,767	35,365
Sierra Leone	1,265	5,194
Republic of South Africa	11,459	15,738
Tanzania	2,989	4,181
Uganda	3,370	3,881
Zambia	1,331	1,286
Zimbabwe	1,311	1,696

SOURCE: Adapted from U.S. Immigration and Naturalization Service Annual Report. *Statistical Yearbook* 1990 (Washington, DC: U.S. Government Printing Office, 1991). Table 4.

ent, or intelligence. The system worked, leaving slave owners free for "genteel" artistic, intellectual, and leisure pursuits while reaffirming in their minds the "inferiority" of their toiling "darkies."

This value consensus survived the social disorganization of the postbellum South. A generation later the Jim Crow laws once again formalized a system of inequality through all social institutions. A new tradition of restricted opportunities and participation based on old values but feeding on itself for justification of the existing order became entrenched. In the North blacks filled a labor need but remained unassimilated. This lack of societal cohesion and a continued presence of blacks generated prejudice, avoidance, and reciprocal antagonism. In both the North and the South in the twentieth century, these system dysfunctions—the waste of human resources and lost productivity—produced social problems of poor education, low income and unemployment, crime and delinquency, poor housing, high disease and mortality rates, and other pathologies.

System corrections, in the form of federal judicial and legislative action, helped restore more of a balance to society, reorganizing our social institutions and eliminating barriers to full social, political, and economic opportunities. Other dysfunctions—the Vietnam War, rampant inflation in the 1970s, structural blue-color unemployment, and the 1980–1982 recession—curtailed some black gains. Further adjustments are necessary to overcome the remaining problems.

The Conflict View

Slavery is an obvious past example of economic exploitation of blacks, but more recent practices may be less obvious. Job discrimination, labor union discrimination—particularly in the building trades—and prejudices in educational institutions leading to low achievement and high dropout rates have together forced many blacks into low-paying, low-status, economically vulnerable jobs. For many years confinement of blacks to marginal positions preserved the better-paying job opportunities, exclusively for whites. Maintenance of a low-cost surplus labor pool that was not in competition for jobs sought by whites benefited employers and the dominant society, providing domestic and sanitation workers and seasonal employees, as well as job opportunities for whites in social work, law enforcement, and welfare agencies.

Both de jure segregation and de facto segregation illustrate the success of those with power in protecting their self-interests by maintaining the status quo. Control of all social institutions kept blacks confined to certain occupations and residential locations, away from participation in the political process and out of the societal mainstream. Although a black and mulatto elite did arise and some positive white actions occurred, such as President Roosevelt's 1941 executive order banning racial discrimination in defense industries, blacks mostly remained an oppressed minority.

Blauner's internal colonialism model is appropriate here: The outside control of black segregated communities is by employers, teachers, social workers, police, and politicians who represent the establishment, making the administrative, economic, and political decisions governing the ghetto. Unlike European groups, Blauner maintained, the blacks did not gain control and ownership within a generation of their own buildings and commercial enterprises, remaining instead a subjugated and dependent colonized population.[62]

The civil rights movement of the 1960s, a culmination of earlier actions and court decisions, fits Marxian analysis of social change. Blacks developed a group cohesiveness, overcoming a false consciousness that equality was an unattainable goal, and formed an effective social movement. Sweeping changes through civil rights legislation, punctuated by urban violence from 1964 to 1968, brought improved life opportunities to blacks and other minorities.

The Interactionist View

Just as our attraction to strangers is based on perceived similarities, our antipathy to strangers can be based on learned prejudices. In the United States skin color often has triggered negative responses about busing, crime, housing, jobs, and poverty. Where do such attitudes originate? Earlier we discussed multigenerational stereotyping and social isolation of blacks as the legacy of racism. If beliefs about a people, culturally transmitted and reinforced by external conditions, center on their differences or alleged inferiority, then avoidance, exploitation, or subjugation can become common responses.

Opposition to integration efforts usually comes from fear of these "unlike" strangers. Although expressed reasons may include preserving neighborhoods or neighborhood schools, the real reason often is concern that blacks will "contaminate" the school or area. Beliefs that the crime rate, school discipline, property values, and neighborhood stability will be adversely affected by their presence often prompts whites to resist the proposed integration. Similarly, beliefs that blacks are less reliable, less honest, and less intelligent than whites have frequently influenced hiring and acceptance decisions in the past and still sometimes today. What matters is not so much the unfairness or inaccuracy of such sweeping generalizations but that people act upon them. Too many white people have spun a gossamer web of false reality and believed it.

Black racism works much the same way, seeing all whites as the enemy, all blacks as right, and suspicious of any friendly white action or criticism of any black. Because both sides define a situation in a particular way, their interpretation usually results in reinforcing consequences. Upward mobility—in education, occupation, and income—does much to alter people's interpretations.

Retrospect

Through 200 years of slavery and 100 additional years of another form of subjugation, blacks have found society unresponsive to their needs and wants. Negatively categorized by skin color, they have seen clearly that there are two worlds in this country: the white and the nonwhite. Many blacks remain trapped in poverty and isolated in urban ghettos; others who have achieved upward mobility often find, at least in meaningful primary relationships, that they are often still not accepted in white society.

There are many similarities between the black experience in the United States and the experiences of other minority peoples. Like the Asians and Native Americans, blacks frequently have been judged on the basis of their skin color, not their individual capabilities. They have experienced, as have many immigrant groups, countless instances of stereotyping, scapegoating, prejudice, discrimination, social and spatial segregation, deprivation, and violence. When they have become too visible in a given area or have moved into economic competition with whites, the dominant group has seen them as a threat and reacted accordingly. All of this is a familiar pattern in dominant-minority relations.

More than 200 years of slavery exacted a heavy toll on the black people of America, and exploitation and discrimination did not end with the abolition of slavery. As a result of generations of social conditioning, many whites continued to have a master–slave mentality long after the Civil War. Two generations later, when blacks had made some progress, the Jim Crow laws eliminated those gains and reestablished unequal treatment and life opportunities, thereby increasing prejudice.

A change in values and attitudes became evident with the historic Supreme Court decision of 1954. Although school integration was slow, it did come about, and both blacks and whites were encouraged to seek even more changes. The growth of the civil rights movement—an idea whose time had come at last—peaked in the mid-1960s, when a broad range of laws was passed to offer black people a more equitable life experience.

More than a third of a century has elapsed since the 1954 decision. A great number of changes have taken place in the land, and there have been observable improvements in all aspects of life for many blacks. Still, many problems remain. A disproportionate number of nonwhite poor continue to be concentrated in the cities, frequently trapped in a cycle of perpetual poverty. Despite all the legislation and court decisions, most blacks still engage in primary relationships with other blacks only. Social distance between blacks and whites in informal and private gatherings is still great. De facto segregation is still a problem, with the majority of whites living in suburbs and the majority of blacks living in urban areas.

Greater interaction occurs between the two races in places of public accommodation, and this may eventually reshape white attitudes. That, together with improved educational opportunities, may lead to greater structural assimilation for blacks. One element crucial to black progress is the condition of the economy. Its ability to absorb blacks into those positions in the labor force that permit upward socioeconomic mobility will, in large measure, determine the future status of blacks in American society.

Review Questions

1. In what ways is the black experience in the United States unique?
2. What similarities exist among the experiences of the blacks, Native Americans, and Asians in the United States?
3. What similarities are there between the responses of blacks and of European immigrants to prejudice and discrimination?
4. What factors have delayed blacks in gaining economic and political power as European and Asian immigrant groups did?
5. What is the present status of blacks in America according to the leading social indicators?
6. How are the cultural orientations of African immigrants dissimilar to those of black Americans?
7. What insights into the black experience do the three major sociological perspectives provide?

Suggested Readings _____

BILLINGSLEY, ANDREW. *Black Families in White America*. Englewood Cliffs, NJ: Prentice-Hall, 1968.

A now-classic rebuttal to the Moynihan Report, detailing the wide range of black family structure and socioeconomic hierarchy.

BLACKWELL, JAMES E. *The Black Community: Diversity and Unity*, 3d ed. New York: HarperCollins, 1991.

Examines the institutional structure, status, and aspects of daily life among black Americans.

DAVIS, GEORGE, AND GLEGG WATSON. *Black Life in Corporate America: Swimming in the Mainstream*. New York: Anchor Press, 1982.

A profile of black executives entering the corporate world and their roles, acceptance, and power.

FARLEY, REYNOLDS. *Blacks and Whites: Narrowing the Gap*. Cambridge, MA: Harvard University Press, 1984.

A thorough analysis of social indicators, showing both progression and regression in black America.

FREEMAN, RICHARD B. *Black Elite*. New York: McGraw-Hill, 1976.

An analytical portrait of the success of this new group through education and the emergence of black professionals.

HACKER, ANDREW. *Two Nations: Black and White, Separate, Hostile, Unequal*. New York: Scribner's, 1992.

A data-extensive comparison of social indicators and power that assesses the relative status of blacks and whites.

PINKNEY, ALPHONSO. *Black Americans*, 3d ed. Englewood Cliffs, NJ: Prentice-Hall, 1987.

A good overview of both the history and contemporary situation of American blacks, emphasizing the role of power and social class.

WILLIE, CHARLES V. *A New Look at Black Families*, 2d ed. New York: General Hall, 1981.

Excellent study of black-American families, debunking myths yet identifying their problems engendered by poverty and racism.

WILSON, WILLIAM J. *The Declining Significance of Race*, 2d ed. Chicago: University of Chicago Press, 1980.

A controversial argument that the current bipolar status of blacks makes social class more important than race in their gaining status and power.

Donna DeCesare/Impact Visuals

11

The Hispanic Immigrants

Perhaps no group attracts more public attention these days than do the Hispanic people. Their large numbers, their residential clustering, and the bilingual programs and signs provided for them make them a recognizable ethnic group. Those Hispanics who live in poverty or are involved in gangs, drugs, or other criminal activity attract attention and generate stereotypes, but other Hispanic Americans live in the societal mainstream as working-class or middle-class citizens. Although there are many differences in their cultural background, social class, and length of residence in the United States, Hispanic Americans share a common language and heritage. Because of this commonality, people often lump them all together despite their many geopolitical, socioeconomic, and cultural differences.

SOCIOHISTORICAL PERSPECTIVE

Spanish influence has long been felt in the United States. Long before the English settled in their colonies in the New World, Spanish explorers, missionaries, and adventurers roamed through much of the Western Hemisphere, including Florida and the southwestern United States. In 1518 the Spanish established St. Augustine, Florida, and in the same year that the first permanent English settlement (Jamestown) was established (1609), the Spanish founded Santa Fe in what is now New Mexico. Spanish cultural influence was extensive throughout the New World in the areas of language, religion, customs, values, and town planning (for example, locating church and institutional buildings next to a central plaza).

Structural Conditions

The Hispanic American experience varies greatly, depending on the particular ethnic group, area of the country, and period. In the American Southwest, agricultural needs and the presence of Mexican Americans are crucial factors in dominant-minority relations. In the East industrial employment, urban problems, and the presence of Cubans or Puerto Ricans provide the focal points of attitudes and actions. Figure 11.1 shows the percentage of Hispanics living in the 50 states in 1990.

Most low-skilled groups, including such Hispanic peoples as the Puerto Ricans and Mexicans, have at first obtained jobs that have low status, low pay, and little mobility. Unlike past groups, however, recent Hispanic immi-

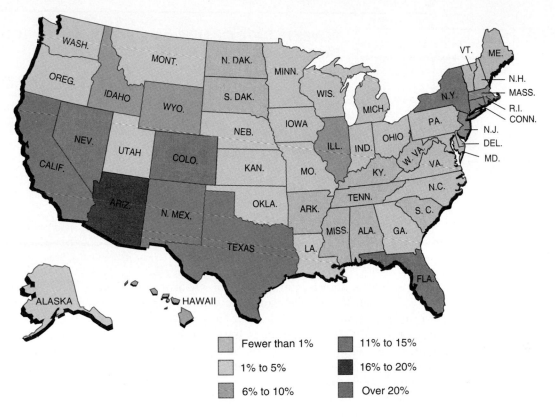

FIGURE 11.1
Hispanics in the United States by Percentage of State Population, 1990
SOURCE: U.S. Bureau of the Census.

grants have entered a post-industrial society in which the economy is no longer growing rapidly. Many Hispanic immigrants come from less industrialized nations and have few of the skills they need in order to adjust easily to working in America. Technological progress has eliminated many of the jobs earlier immigrants could obtain to achieve some degree of economic security (such as unskilled factory work). The suburbanization of industry has meant that in older cities, where poor immigrants have traditionally lived and worked out of economic necessity, there are no longer enough manufacturing jobs for the newcomers. Unions once helped European immigrants to obtain job security, better wages, and improved working conditions, but today's unions often exclude or restrict the "new" minorities.

Socioeconomic indicators offer mixed findings on the status of Hispanic Americans. The Hispanic–white poverty ratio has been steadily shrinking since 1975 (Table 11.1), but the income gap has been steadily growing (Table 11.3). An alarming indicator is the continuing high dropout rate of Hispanic

| TABLE 11.1 | POVERTY RATE OF HISPANIC, BLACK, AND WHITE FAMILIES: SELECTED YEARS, 1975–1990 |

Year	Percentage of Families Below Poverty Level			Ratio of Hispanic to White Poverty Rate
	Hispanic	Black	White	
1975	25.1	27.1	7.7	3.3
1980	23.2	28.9	8.0	2.9
1985	25.5	28.7	9.1	2.8
1990	25.0	29.3	8.1	2.6

SOURCE: U.S. Bureau of the Census, *Current Population Reports*, Series P–60, No. 175.

high school students, particularly of Mexican and Puerto Rican teens (Table 11.5). Puerto Ricans are more likely to be living in poverty than any other group including blacks, whereas Cuban Americans are the most successful (Table 11.2). Cuban Americans have the highest percentage of college graduates, and Mexican Americans have the lowest (Table 11.4). Such variances speak to the diversity found among Hispanic Americans and to the mistake of making generalizations about the group as a whole.

Overpopulation throughout Latin America is a highly significant factor in the continued migration of large numbers of Hispanics to the United States (Table 11.7). High birth rates, improved sanitation, reduction of child mortality, and negative attitudes toward birth control have led to population booms in countries with resources and habitable land that cannot support this many

| TABLE 11.2 | PERSONS BELOW POVERTY LEVEL, 1991, BY PERCENTAGES |

White	10.7
Black	31.9
All Hispanic	28.1
Mexican Americans	28.1
Puerto Ricans	40.6
Cuban Americans	16.9
Central and South Americans	25.4
Other Hispanic	21.5

SOURCE: U.S. Bureau of the Census, *Current Population Reports*, U.S. Government Printing Office, Washington, DC, P–60, No. 174 and P–20, No. 455.

| | TABLE 11.3 | MEDIAN INCOME OF HISPANIC, BLACK, AND WHITE FAMILIES: SELECTED YEARS, 1970–1990 |

	Median Family Income			Hispanic Family Income as Percentage of White Income
Year	Hispanic	Black	White	
1970	NA	$ 6,279	$10,236	NA
1975	$ 9,551	$ 8,779	$14,268	67
1980	$14,716	$12,674	$21,904	67
1985	$19,027	$16,786	$29,152	65
1990	$23,431	$21,423	$36,915	64

SOURCE: U.S. Bureau of the Census, *Current Population Reports*, U.S. Government Printing Office, Washington, DC, Series P-60, No. 174.

people. The total population of Latin America grew from over 285 million in 1970 to over 446 million by 1990. Current projections are that the population will reach about 537 million by 2000 and be over 624 million by the year 2010.[1] Suffering from poor living conditions, inadequate schools, limited job opportunities, and other aspects of poverty, many Latinos journey to the United States, legally or illegally, for a better life. The United States has a 2,000-mile border with Mexico and open migration for Puerto Ricans, and many other Hispanic nationalities use these routes to enter illegally. Each year U.S. government agents apprehend about 1 million illegal aliens; in 1991 the figure was nearly 1.2 million. Approximately 1.1 million, or 93 percent, were from

| | TABLE 11.4 | PERCENTAGE AGE 25 AND OLDER COMPLETING COLLEGE, 1991 |

White	22.2
Black	11.5
All Hispanic	9.7
Mexican Americans	6.2
Puerto Ricans	10.1
Cuban Americans	18.5
Central and South Americans	15.1
Other Hispanics	16.2

SOURCE: U.S. Bureau of the Census, *Current Population Reports*, U.S. Government Printing Office, Washington, DC, P–60, No. 174 and P–20, No. 455.

TABLE 11.5	HIGH SCHOOL DROPOUTS BY RACE AND HISPANIC ORIGIN, 1970, 1980, 1990, 1991, BY PERCENTAGES			

Race and Age	1970	1980	1991
White	10.8	11.3	10.5
16−17 years	7.3	9.2	5.9
18−21 years	14.3	14.7	13.9
22−24 years	16.3	14.0	14.6
Black	22.2	16.0	11.3
16−17 years	12.8	6.9	7.4
18−21 years	30.5	23.0	16.6
22−24 years	37.8	24.0	14.0
Hispanic	NA	29.5	29.5
16−17 years	NA	16.6	15.8
18−21 years	NA	40.3	35.1
22−24 years	NA	40.6	45.7

SOURCE: U.S. Bureau of the Census, *Statistical Abstract of the United States: 1992*, U.S. Government Printing Office, Washington, DC, Table 253, p. 161.

Mexico. Almost 17,000 were from El Salvador, and about 10,000 were from Guatemala.[2] The number of uncaught illegal aliens is conjecture, and estimates range from 2 to 4 million. These illegals, whatever their number, strain local and state social services, but they also make economic contributions as consumers and as workers with low skills.

Cultural Differentiation

The cultures of the peoples from the various Caribbean and Central and South American countries differ. Value orientations within a particular country also vary, depending on such factors as degree of urbanization, amount of outside contact, and social class. With these qualifications in mind, we shall examine some general cultural traditions, shared to a greater or lesser degree by most Hispanics, that differ from traditional American values. Before we do so, we should also note that in areas of considerable acculturation, such as New Mexico, some of these cultural traits are muted, and Hispanics have adopted many Anglo (the Hispanics' term for American) behavior patterns.

The Cosmic Race

One cultural concept that is associated with Hispanics—especially Mexicans—is that of *La Raza Cosmica,* the cosmic race. The Mexican intellectual José Vasconcelos coined the term to refer to the amalgamation of the white, black, and Indian races, that he believed was occurring in Latin Amer-ica.[3] In his old age he dismissed the idea as a juvenile fantasy, but the concept evolved into a group categorization similar to what Kurt Lewin calls a recog-nition of an "interdependence of fate." In essence *La Raza Cosmica* suggests that all the Spanish-speaking peoples in the Western hemisphere share a cultural bond and that God has planned for them a great destiny that has yet to be realized. Recent studies of Mexican Americans have found that this cultural belief is still significant, either directly or in terms of the behavioral values associated with it.[4] Reflecting centuries of European dominance, the concept is also one of fatalism; it implies that one should submit to the things of the present and not plan for the future. Younger Hispanics subscribe less to such fatalism than do their elders, and from their ranks evolved the polit-ical terms *La Raza Nueva* and *Chicano* to symbolize cultural unity, a positive self-image, and an activist movement that we shall discuss shortly.

Machismo

Overstated in the Anglo stereotype, *machismo* is a basic value covering various qualities of masculinity. To Hispanic males such attributes as inner strength in the face of adversity, personal daring, bravado, leadership, and sexual prow-ess are all measures of one's manhood.[5] The role of the man is to be a good provider for his family; to protect its honor at all times; and to be strong, reliable, and independent. He should avoid indebtedness or charity and any kind of relationship, formal or informal, that would weaken his autonomy. The culture and family system are male-dominated. The woman's role is within the family, and she is to be guarded against any onslaught on her honor.

Machismo may also find expression in such other forms as perceived sex-ual allure, fathering children, male dominance, and aggressive behavior. *Marianismo* is the companion value describing various qualities of femin-inity, particularly acceptance of male dominance and emphasis on family responsibilities.

The concept of machismo is not strictly a Latin American phenomenon; such traditional sex-role orientations have been common throughout most undeveloped countries, whether African, Eastern, Middle Eastern, Western, or in the Pacific islands. For the Latinos machismo diminishes with increasing levels of education, assimilation, and multigenerational residence in the United States.

The result of these values can be not only a double standard of sexual morality but also difficulty adjusting to American culture. Women have more independence in the United States than in most Hispanic countries. Instead of males being the sole providers, females can also find employment here, sometimes earning more money than the men of the family. The participation of Hispanic women in the labor force appears to be related to educational level. More highly educated Cuban and Central and South American women participate in the labor force at rates similar to those of all white women in the United States, whereas Mexican and Puerto Rican women have especially low rates. Overall, the participation of Hispanic females in the labor force is comparable to the national average for all women.[6]

Dignidad

The cultural value of *dignidad* is the basis of social interaction; it assumes that the dignity of all humans entitles them to a measure of respect. It is primarily "a quality attributed to all, regardless of status, race, color or creed."[7] Regardless of status, each person acknowledges others' *dignidad* in a taken-for-granted reciprocal behavior pattern. Therefore Hispanics—particularly Puerto Ricans—expect to be treated in terms of *dignidad*. Because it is an implicit measure of respect, one cannot demand it from others. Instead, one concludes that others are rude and cold if they do not acknowledge one's *dignidad*. More broadly, the concept includes a strong, positive self-image.

Racial Attitudes

In most Latin American countries skin color is less important as an indicator of social status than is social class. There seems to be a correlation between darker skin color and low social standing, but the sharp racial line between whites and blacks found in the United States is deemphasized in Latin America. A great deal of color integration takes place in social interaction, intermarriage, and shared orientations to cultural values. There is also a much wider range of color gradations, which helps to blunt any color prejudice. Still, in some places, such as Puerto Rico, color prejudice has increased, perhaps as a result of social and economic changes from industrialization.[8]

Color often is an unexpected basis of discrimination for Latinos coming to the United States. Being stereotyped, judged, and treated on the basis of one's skin color is essentially unknown to these brown-skinned peoples. Therefore, encountering prejudice and discrimination based on their skin color is a traumatic experience for them. Before long they realize the extent of this regrettable aspect of American society. Some adapt to it, others forsake it and return home, but practically all resent it.

Other Cultural Attributes

Hispanics, or Latinos, generally have a more casual attitude toward time and a negative attitude toward hurrying about. Another cultural difference that could easily lead to misunderstanding is their attitude about making eye contact with others. To them, not looking directly into the eyes of an authority figure such as a teacher or police officer is an act of respect, but Americans may interpret it as shyness, avoidance, or guilt. Like some Europeans, they regard physical proximity in conversation as a sign of friendliness, but Anglos are accustomed to a greater distance between conversationalists. One can envision an Anglo made uncomfortable by the "unusual" nearness of a Hispanic person and backing away, the latter reestablishing the physical closeness, the Anglo again backing away, and the Hispanic concluding that the Anglo is a cold or aloof individual. Each has viewed the situation from a different cultural perspective and thus interpreted the incident quite differently.[9]

Current Patterns

Hispanics are America's largest ethnic group and growing bigger all the time (see Figure 11.2). Their headcount of 22.3 million in the 1990 census was a 53 percent increase over their 14.6 million in 1980, becoming 9 percent of the total population, up from 7 percent in 1980.[10] Demographers predict that they will outnumber blacks by 2020 to emerge as the largest minority group, possibly comprising 15 percent of the total population.[11] This projection is based on their high birth rate, their low average age (half are under 21), and the fact that 44 percent of all legal immigrants come from Spanish-speaking lands (see Figures 11.3, and 11.4).

Nearly 14 percent of all American residents over five years of age spoke a language other than English at home in 1990. Spanish was spoken by 7.5 percent, making it the second most common language in the United States.[12] Many Hispanic Americans live outside the large concentrations in California, Florida, New York, and Texas. The Census Bureau reports that more Hispanics live in Illinois (904,000) than in New Mexico (579,000), and more in New Jersey (740,000) than in Arizona (688,000).[13] One in 10 among Chicago's 8

TABLE 11.6	OCCUPATION OF HISPANIC WORKERS AGES 16 YEARS AND OVER, 1980 AND 1991				
	Percentages in each Occupational Category				
	All Hispanics	Mexican	Puerto Rican	Cuban	Other Hispanic[a]
1980					
White-collar	35.0	31.0	35.3	NA	NA
Service	16.5	16.6	19.3	NA	NA
Agri/Forest	3.4	4.7	1.0	NA	NA
Blue-collar	45.2	47.7	44.5	NA	NA
1991					
White-collar	37.5	32.9	49.9	58.2	39.9
Service	20.3	18.9	17.5	12.0	27.0
Agri/Forest	5.7	8.4	1.2	1.4	1.8
Blue-collar	36.4	39.8	31.4	28.4	31.4

[a] Includes Central and South American and other Hispanic orign.

SOURCE: U.S. Bureau of Labor Statistics, *Employment and Earnings*, January issues, 1980, 1991.

TABLE 11.7	LEGAL HISPANIC IMMIGRATION TO THE UNITED STATES: BY DECADES, 1951–1990			
	1951–1960	**1961–1970**	**1971–1980**	**1981–1990**
Mexico	299,811	453,937	640,294	1,655,843
Caribbean	123,091	470,213	741,126	872,051
Central America	44,751	101,330	134,640	468,088
South America	91,628	257,954	295,741	461,847

SOURCE: U.S. Immigration and Naturalization Service, *Statistical Yearbook,* U.S. Government Printing Office, Washington, DC, 1992, Table 1, pp. 29–30.

million residents is Hispanic. One in five among Houston's 3.7 million and one in three among Miami's 3.1 million are Hispanic.

What do these growing numbers and extensive population clusters suggest for future dominant-minority relations? No simple answer can be given because of the variance in the education, socioeconomic background, and oc-

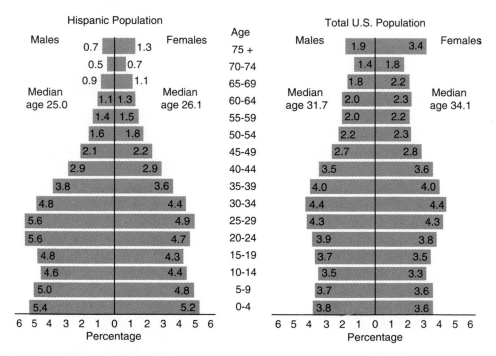

FIGURE 11.2

Composition of the Hispanic and Total U.S. Population, by Age and Sex, 1990

SOURCE: U.S. Bureau of the Census.

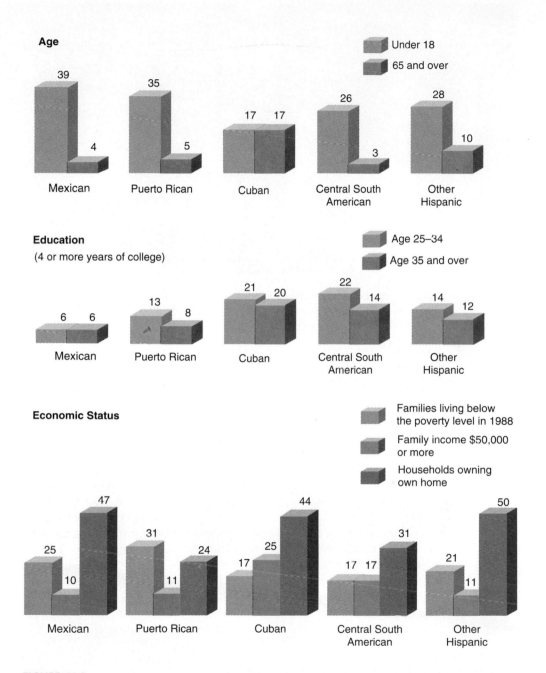

FIGURE 11.3

Differences Among Hispanic Subgroups in Age, Education, and Economic Status, by Percentages, 1990

SOURCE: U.S. Bureau of the Census.

When new immigration laws enabled undocumented aliens to obtain temporary protected status and work permits, up to 600 Salvadorans per night showed up and slept at this Spanish Catholic Center in Washington, DC. Over 17,000 were processed here as elsewhere thousands of other Hispanics sought amnesty. *(Donna DeCesare/Impact Visuals)*

cupational skills of the Hispanic newcomers. Despite nativist fears, however, English language mastery is a common goal of Hispanic parents for their children.[14] Concern about ethnic tribalism or English needing to be designated as the country's "official" language is unnecessary, as we shall discuss more fully in the last chapter.

Cultural vitality, long an attribute among Mexican Americans in the Southwest so near their homeland, will likely remain within other Latino communities also. The dynamics of cultural pluralism are fueled by the large Hispanic presence, current migration patterns, psychological ties to the homeland because of rapid transportation and communications, government policy, and societal tolerance. Acculturation and mainstreaming will no doubt occur for most Hispanics as it has for members of other groups, but the factors of cultural pluralism also suggest that the Hispanic influence will be long-lasting in American society. Hispanics will not just blend in with the rest of society. Rather, somewhat like French influence on the Louisiana region, Hispanic Americans will likely affect American culture itself.

THE MEXICAN AMERICANS

About 83 percent of the 13.5 million Mexican Americans in the United States live in the Southwest. Los Angeles, whose very name indicates its Spanish origin, has more than 2 million Mexican American residents, making it second only to Mexico City in Mexican population. A great deal of diversity exists among this ethnic group in terms of degree of assimilation and socioeconomic status. For example, there is a very small group of old-family Spanish Americans (*Hispanos*) in northern New Mexico and southern Colorado who follow the old traditions and speak very little English.

Throughout New Mexico, which, unlike Texas and California, has not had constant contact with Mexico through border crossings, the employment pattern is brighter. In fact Hispanic Americans there are heavily represented in civil service occupations at the local, state, and federal levels. In a sense they are like many recent non-Western immigrants in that they retain a cultural heritage (such as their diet, child-rearing philosophy, emphasis on the family, and extended family contacts) but hold economically secure occupational positions.

Second-generation Mexican Americans living in Los Angeles are far more likely to be assimilated than their counterparts in Corpus Christi.[15] However, most present-day Mexican Americans, whether they live in an urban or a rural area, lag far behind the rest of the U.S. population by every measure of socioeconomic well-being: education, income, and employment status.

When the United States secured the southwestern region after the Mexican-American War of 1846–1848 and then added a small boundary section through the Gadsden Purchase of 1853, there were a relatively small number of Mexicans living in these areas. Most of these, quickly outnumbered by Anglos, lost their lands through legal maneuvering and became a subordinated population.

Recruiting Mexicans

In the second half of the nineteenth century a great need for agricultural labor developed, and Mexicans from south of the border helped to fill it. Railroad lines were being built; cotton, fruit, and vegetable farms were expanding. The Chinese Exclusion Act of 1882 curtailed one source of laborers, and later the Immigration Acts of 1921 and 1924 curtailed another. But the demand for labor, especially for agricultural workers, increased, and the Mexicans left their poverty-stricken country for the economic opportunities available here.

It is important to understand the cultural milieu in their native land in order to understand the Mexicans' situation in the United States for more than 100 years. Most Mexicans were poor, illiterate peasants, virtually serfs, who eked out an existence laboring for the *haciendados*, the large landholding aristocracy of Mexico. Exploited by the hacienda owners and the Mexican government for years, and ignorant of the language and laws of this country, the Mexicans worked in the United States under servile conditions for meager wages. The degree of poverty in their native country is reflected in the fact that even though they worked for very low wages here, they were still earning a great deal more than they could at home.

Although there were restrictions on immigration, it was easy for Mexicans to cross the largely unpatrolled border and enter the country illegally, and many did so. They were known as "wetbacks" because they had crossed the Rio Grande. Some Mexican aliens also entered the United States legally as contract laborers. Under the *bracero* program Mexican aliens were temporarily brought into the United States, then returned to Mexico after the harvest. This system provided the needed workers without the accompanying expenses of educating their children, giving them welfare during nonworking periods, and providing other social services. The program lasted from 1942 until 1964, when farm mechanization, labor shortages in Mexico, and the protests of native Hispanics in the United States ended it.

Expulsion

Although cheap Mexican labor was a boon to the Southwestern economy, during a downturn in the national economy Mexicans usually were not welcome. One such time was the 1930s, when a great many Americans were jobless. Some Mexicans returned home voluntarily; others were pressured to do so by local residents. A great many more were rounded up and deported:

> During the depression the U.S. Government and public agencies, in what was called a "repatriation program," deported literally hundreds of thousands of Mexicans and Mexican Americans to cut down on welfare costs. Roundups extended through southern California, to most cities of the Southwest, and as far north as Chicago and Detroit.
>
> In Los Angeles, official trucks would grind into the barrios—the Mexican American neighborhoods—and the occupants would be herded into them. There was little or no determination of national origin. Citizenship or noncitizenship was not considered. Families were divided; the bringing of possessions was not permitted. . . .
>
> "They pushed most of my family into one van," one of the victims, Jorge Acevedo, remembers bitterly. "We drove all day. The driver wouldn't stop for bathroom nor food nor water. Everyone knew by now we had been deported. Nobody knew why, but there was a lot of hatred and anger. . . . We had always known that we were hated. Now we had proof."[16]

During the recession of the mid-1950s, the U.S. Immigration and Naturalization Service launched "Operation Wetback" to find and return all illegal Mexican aliens. Concentrating on California and Texas but ranging as far as Spokane, Chicago, Kansas City, and St. Louis, between 1954 and 1959 government officials found and expelled 3.8 million Mexicans, only 63,515 of whom had a formal hearing.[17] Not all were illegal aliens. Many American citizens, if they "looked Mexican," were stopped and questioned. If they could not immediately prove their legal status, they often were arrested and "sent home" without anyone even checking into their status.[18]

Violence

One infamous incident in which prejudices against the Mexicans erupted into violence is the Zoot Suit Riot of 1943. It was named thus because many

Mexican American youths at that time followed the then-current fad of wearing long, loose-fitting jackets with wide shoulders; high-waisted, baggy trousers with tight cuffs; and flat-topped hats with broad brims. The gamblers in the original show and the film version of *Guys and Dolls* dressed in this fashion.

On June 3, 1943, two events triggered the riot. Some Mexican boys, returning from a police-sponsored club meeting, were assaulted by a group of non-Mexican hoodlums from the neighborhood in Los Angeles. That same evening 11 sailors on leave were attacked, and one sailor was badly hurt. The sailors said that their assailants were Mexican youths who outnumbered them three to one. When the police, responding late, found no one to arrest in the area, about 200 sailors decided to settle the matter themselves the following evening. Cruising through the Mexican section in a caravan of 20 taxicabs, they savagely beat every Mexican they found. The police did nothing to stop this, and the press gave these events wide publicity:

> The stage was now set for the really serious rioting of June seventh and eighth. Having featured the preliminary rioting as an offensive launched by sailors, soldiers, and marines, the press now whipped public opinion into a frenzy by dire warnings that Mexican zoot-suiters planned a mass retaliation. To insure a riot, the precise street corners were marked at which retaliatory action was expected and the time of the anticipated action was carefully specified. In effect these stories announced a riot and invited public participation. . . .
>
> On Monday evening, June seventh, thousands of *Angelenos,* in response to twelve hours' advance notice in the press, turned out for a mass lynching. Marching through the streets of downtown Los Angeles, a mob of several thousand soldiers, sailors, and civilians, proceeded to beat up every zoot-suiter they could find. Pushing its way into the important motion picture theaters, the mob ordered the management to turn on the house lights and then ranged up and down the aisles dragging Mexicans out of their seats. Street cars were halted while Mexicans, and some Filipinos and Negroes, were jerked out of their seats, pushed into the streets, and beaten with sadistic frenzy. . . .
>
> Here is one of the numerous eyewitness accounts written by Al Waxman, editor of *The Eastside Journal:*

> > Four boys came out of a pool hall. They were wearing the zoot-suits that have become the symbols of a fighting flag. Police ordered them into arrest cars. One refused. He asked: "Why am I being arrested?" The police officer answered with three swift blows of the night-stick across the boy's head and he went down. As he sprawled, he was kicked in the face. Police had difficulty loading his body into the vehicle because he was one-legged and wore a wooden limb. . . .
> >
> > At the next corner a Mexican mother cried out, "Don't take my boy, he did nothing. He's only fifteen years old. Don't take him." She was struck across the jaw with a night-stick and almost dropped the two and a half year old baby that was clinging in her arms. . . .
> >
> > A Negro defense worker, wearing a defense-plant identification badge on his work clothes, was taken from a street car and one of his eyes was gouged out with a knife. Huge half-page photographs, showing Mexican boys, stripped of their clothes, cowering on the pavements, often bleeding

profusely, surrounded by jeering mobs of men and women, appeared in
all of the Los Angeles newspapers. . . .

When it finally stopped, the Eagle Rock *Advertiser* mournfully editori-
alized: "It is too bad the servicemen were called off before they were able
to complete the job. . . . Most of the citizens of the city have been de-
lighted with what has been going on."[19]

This bloody incident, like the Know-Nothing riots, the anti-Chinese race
riots, lynchings, and other past acts of violence, was the result of increasing
societal tensions and prejudices against a minority that erupted into aggression far in excess of the triggering incident. Whatever Mexicans thought
about Anglo society before this wartime incident, they would long remember
this race riot waged against them with official sanction from the police, the
newspapers, and city hall.

Urban Life

Most Mexican Americans live in cities. In some places, such as Los Angeles
and New Mexico, they often are better integrated into the mainstream of
society than their compatriots in rural areas. There they have higher intermarriage rates, nuclear instead of extended family residence patterns, and
less patriarchal male roles. They are entering more diverse occupations, and
many are attaining middle-class status and moving from the barrio to the suburbs and outskirts of the city. Yet in East Los Angeles and in other areas of the
Southwest, particularly in smaller cities and towns, Mexican Americans reside in
large ethnic enclaves, virtually isolated from participation in Anglo society. Even
those middle-class individuals whose families have lived in this country for
generations choose to live among their own people and interact only with them.

Many Mexican Americans live in substandard housing under crowded conditions. In the five Southwestern states their housing is more crowded than
that of nonwhites—in Texas, twice as many Mexicans as blacks live in overcrowded housing. Segregated in the less desirable sections of town, with their
children attending schools that warrant the same criticisms as inner-city
schools in the major cities, they experience many forms of discrimination.

Recent challenges to overt forms of discrimination have succeeded, but
covert methods still persist. One landmark case protecting the civil liberties of
Mexican Americans was the 1953 U.S. Supreme Court decision concerning
Peter Hernandez. This decision, which preceded the better-known *Brown v.
Board of Education* segregation case, held that a community's laws cannot be
written or applied against a particular class of people if this results in their
being treated differently. The ruling, which had a far-reaching impact on
discriminatory actions by public officials, was based on a case in which a
nonrepresentative jury (Mexican Americans never served on juries in that
region) convicted a Mexican American.

The large influx of Mexican Americans and their residential clustering in urban
areas have resulted in a high level of segregated schools. This trend toward
increased isolation of school children holds for most urban Hispanics but is

Ethnic murals, such as this one in Los Angeles, usually contain recognizable people, events, symbols, and hopes of the community within which they are located. Besides aesthetically enhancing the urban neighborhood, they serve as a stimulus for cultural identity, consensus, and pride. *(Peter Menzel/Stock, Boston)*

particularly pronounced in the American Southwest. For example, the percentage of white students in Los Angeles County high schools attended by Chicano students dropped from 45 percent to 17 percent between 1970 and 1985.[20]

Stereotyping

Negative stereotypes of Mexican Americans persist in American society. Such categorizations as their being lazy, unclean, treacherous, sneaks, or thieves have frequently appeared in the mass media. Currently, the two stereotypes that Mexican Americans have had to combat are those of illegal aliens and youth gangs. "Looking" Mexican often raises suspicions about legal residence or makes prospective employers wary of hiring a possible illegal alien, even if the individual is a legal U.S. resident. In the poor urban barrios of Los Angeles, San Antonio, and El Paso, youth gangs are an integral subculture within the community. The intergang fights and killings, particularly in East Los Angeles, as well as the drug scene, create a lasting, negative picture of Mexican Americans in the minds of many Anglos.

Sometimes scholarly works inadvertently contribute to the stereotype. Some people used Florence Kluckhohn's study of a remote village in New Mexico as the basis for generalizations about the values of all Mexicans.[21]

Thus such cultural attributes as present-time orientation, emphasis on intangible gratification rather than material rewards, and emphasis on enjoyment rather than working hard became synonymous with being Mexican.[22] In reality the values of most urban Mexican Americans are quite similar to those of other Americans: They want upward mobility, a better life for their children, and community interaction.[23]

Like blacks and Puerto Ricans, the Mexican Americans also suffer from the culture-of-poverty beliefs of the dominant society.[24] All too often they are blamed for their low socioeconomic standing because of their supposed cultural values. However, it is much more likely that their lack of education and job skills, and a lack of sustained dominant-minority interactions, rather than the minority's cultural variations, cause them problems in achieving economic security.

Chicano Power

The term *Chicano* was originally a derogatory name applied in Mexico to the "lower"-class Mexican Indian people rather than to the Mexican Spanish. Most Mexican American youths and the educated middle-class have now adopted the term as a symbol of pride and peoplehood. Chicanos look to the past to reaffirm their ethnic identity, but they also look to the future, aiming at becoming more organized, collectively independent within the system, and stronger in socioeconomic status.

In the 1960s leaders emerged—Cesar Chavez and his United Farm Workers Union, Rodolfo Gonzales and his La Raza Unida movement, and Reies Lopes Tijerina and his Alianza group seeking to recover land lost or stolen over the years, David Sanchez and his Brown Berets. They have left center stage now, and a new generation of Chicanos is making its presence known in a society that has previously either exploited or ignored the Chicanos. Today they are seeking to restore their people's pride and dignity, but they have had only limited success.

The very diversity of the Mexican American population makes it difficult to develop a unified, cohesive social or political action program that will appeal to the various classes within the community and to the diverse regional groupings within the nation, particularly in the Southwest. Mexican American political representation is fairly low at the local and state levels. Notable exceptions are the *Hispanos* throughout New Mexico, and Mexican American parity on the San Antonio city council. Elsewhere they are politically underrepresented, including the city council of Los Angeles, location of the largest Mexican American community in the country.

Current Patterns

In 1970 Mexican newcomers were mostly young males.[25] By 1990 the pattern had changed: The median age of new arrivals was almost 30, with males comprising 58 percent of the total and females 42 percent.[26] Although most Mexican Americans live in the five southwestern states, Illinois is now the third highest state of intended residence among new arrivals. In 1990, 420,377 Mexican immigrants settled in California, 130,813 in Texas, 48,618 in Illinois, and 18,350 in Arizona.[27] The 1990 census revealed 612,442 Mexican Americans living in Illinois, making it the fourth highest in Mexican American population behind California, Texas, and Arizona. Almost twice as many Mexican Americans live in Illinois than in New Mexico.[28]

Mexican immigration continues into both rural and urban areas, but most immigrants are settling in urban neighborhoods, although not necessarily in inner cities. About 91 percent live in metropolitan areas, although fewer than half reside inside central cities.[29] Many of those in central cities are of a low socioeconomic status and live in areas where the dropout rate of Mexican American youth runs as high as 45 percent and where drug use and gang violence are everyday realities.[30]

Another dimension of the Mexican American presence is the influx of illegal aliens. Mexico has more than 90 million people with high birth, poverty, and unemployment rates. These push factors send people over the border in significant numbers. Of the almost 1.2 million illegal aliens apprehended in 1990, 93 percent were from Mexico.[31] How many other illegals entered successfully is a matter of conjecture; current estimates range from 2 to 4 million.

THE PUERTO RICANS

Puerto Ricans frequently refer to their island as the "true melting pot," unlike the mainland, which has only claimed to be so. Originally inhabited by the Arawak and Caribe Indian tribes, Puerto Rico came under Spanish domination in 1493 and remained so for 400 years. When the Indian population was decimated, black slaves were imported. Miscegenation was quite common, resulting in a society that deemphasized race. The high degree of color integration discussed earlier is reflected in words such as *moreno, mulatto, pardo,* and *trigueño,* indicating a broad range of color gradations. Structural assimilation in the island's multiracial society extends to housing, social institutions, government policy, and cultural identity.[32] A high degree of intermarriage often means that people classified in one racial category have close kin relationships with other racial categories, either by bloodline or adoption.

> The racial scene in Puerto Rico has also been characterized by what I would call a high degree of two-way integration, while in the U.S. one-way integration has been and is the norm. That is, Blacks are usually sent to White schools, not vice-versa. Blacks integrate into White America, not Whites into Black America. . . . In this country it rarely happens that a Black couple adopts a White child. The number of White babies available for adoption and the limited income of

many Blacks tend to discourage this action. In most agencies the action is not permitted and the reverse is encouraged. In Puerto Rico, it is a fairly common occurrence to rear other people's children as one's own. These "hijos de crianza" come in all colors. Thus, a "White" couple may rear the darker, orphaned children of a neighbor and vice-versa.[33]

Joseph Fitzpatrick identified several cultural and historical factors that led to the more tolerant racial attitudes found in Puerto Rico (and other Latin American countries):

1. Spain's long experience with dark-skinned people (Moors) who often married white women.
2. In the wars of Christians against Moors and Saracens, captured whites also became slaves. Laws developed to protect all slaves, and this tradition carried over to the Spanish colonies.
3. Upper-class men in the Spanish colonies recognized their illegitimate children by women of color, frequently freeing the babies at their baptism.
4. Through the practice of *compadrazgo,* outstanding white members of a community became the godparents of a child of color at baptism. Even if the child's real father were unknown, the *padrino,* or *compadre,* was well known and became a significant person in the child's life.
5. A shared sense of community, by rich and poor, white and nonwhite, gave all a sense of place that was expressed in gatherings for fiestas, religious processions, and public events.[34]

Early Relations

In 1898, when the United States first annexed Puerto Rico after the Spanish-American War, there was an attempt at forced Americanization. The United States discouraged anything associated with the Spanish tradition and imposed the use of the English language. Presidents appointed governors, usually from the mainland, to rule the territory. The inhabitants were granted U.S. citizenship in 1917, but otherwise the island was virtually ignored and remained an undeveloped land with many poor people. Citizenship brought open migration because it eliminated passports, visas, and quotas, but it did not give the people the right to vote for president or to have a voting representative in Congress. By 1930 approximately 53,000 Puerto Ricans were living on the mainland. During the Depression and the war years, immigration virtually halted until the mass migration of the post–World War II era.

In the 1940s several improvements occurred. The Popular Democratic Party *(Partido Popular Democratico)* emerged as a powerful force on the island. Puerto Rico became a commonwealth, with the people writing their own constitution and electing their own representatives. In addition the island gained complete freedom in its internal affairs, including maintaining its Spanish heritage and not being required to use English. Another party, the *Partido Nuevo Progresista,* favors statehood and enjoys substantial public support. Questions in Washington about retention of Spanish as the official island language and the phasing in of federal income taxes have kept the statehood issue bottled up so far.

To help the island develop economically, the U.S. government launched "Operation Bootstrap" in 1945. Industries were given substantial tax advantages if they made capital investments in Puerto Rico. The tax breaks and abundant supply of low-cost labor resulted in 300 new factories being built by 1953, increasing to 660 by 1960 and creating over 48,000 new jobs. As a result Puerto Rico became the most advanced and industrialized land in the Caribbean and in most of Central and South America, with the highest per capita income. However, by the 1980s expiring tax exemptions prompted numerous industries to leave the island for cheaper labor and tax exemptions elsewhere, thereby reducing the available job opportunities. Puerto Rico's constant double-digit unemployment rate has regularly been twice that of the mainland and affected by mainland economic conditions. Following the 1980–1982 recession, the island's unemployment rate peaked at 23 percent in 1983, dropped thereafter with improved economic conditions on the mainland, then rose again during the 1990–1992 recession.[35]

The Push–Pull Factors

Despite the creation of thousands of factory jobs through Operation Bootstrap, the collapse of the sugar industry kept the unemployment rate around 13 percent, triggering the beginning of *La Migración*. In the 1950s one of the most dramatic voluntary exoduses in world history occurred, as one of every six Puerto Ricans migrated to the mainland. Many of the 480,000 who came in the 1950s were rural people who settled in metropolitan urban centers where jobs could be found. Encouraged by inexpensive plane fares and freedom of entry as U.S. citizens, they were driven from the island's stagnant agrarian economy by the promise of jobs. The greatest total period of Puerto Rican migration was 1946–1964, when a total of 614,940 moved to the mainland. Only the Irish migration of the mid-nineteenth century offers a close comparison, but that was forced in part by the Potato Famine.

Thereafter, a significant drop in Puerto Rican migration occurred. Many factors contributed to this. The pull factor lost its potency as cities, such as New York, lost hundreds of thousands of manufacturing jobs, no longer offering a promising job market. An island population of less than 2.4 million at that time and a declining fertility rate made sustaining a high exodus rate impossible. Furthermore, the earlier exodus relieved pressure on the home job market; increases in U.S. government welfare support, combined with remittances from family members on the mainland, encouraged many to stay on the island.[36] By the 1970s migration dropped to 65,900, then rose dramatically to 333,000 in the 1980s, prompted in large measure by the high unemployment rate mentioned earlier.

High migration and birth rates resulted in an increase in the Puerto Rican population living on the mainland from just over 2 million in 1980 to 2.7 million in 1990, a 35 percent increase.[37] Of all the Puerto Rican people living on either the island or mainland, 44 percent were living on the mainland.[38]

Like members of most ethnic groups, some Puerto Ricans return to their homeland to visit, others to stay. Close proximity to the island is an obvious inducement, although the reasons for the moving back vary.

> Reasons for the return migration appear to be retirement; schooling of children (young parents who wish to educate their offspring in an environment less violent, less hostile, and less drug ridden than that in areas where they live in large cities in the four States); homesickness (strong longing for the more family–friend oriented society in which no discrimination against Puerto Ricans exists, in which there is less apparent discrimination against darkness of skin, and in which the sociological and moral fabric of the community is not perceived to be as deteriorated as in the areas of the large cities in the four States where Puerto Ricans live [New York, New Jersey, Connecticut, and Illinois]); and rising expectations about prospects in Puerto Rico.[39]

The Family

In Puerto Rico, as in all Latin American countries, the individual's identity, importance, and security depend on family membership. There is a deep sense of family obligation that extends to dating and courtship; family approval is necessary because of the emphasis on a marriage joining two families, not just two individuals. An indication of family importance is the use of both the father's and mother's surnames but in reverse order to the American practice. José Garcia Rivera, whose father's last name is Garcia and whose mother's is Rivera, should be called Mr. Garcia, not Mr. Rivera. Fitzpatrick reveals that American confusion about use of these names is a constant source of embarrassment to Spanish-speaking people.[40] José's wife retains her family name and calls herself Maria Gonzalez de Garcia. On formal occasions she may use both sets of family names, such as Maria Gonzalez Medina de Garcia Rivera, while her husband would write his name José Garcia Diaz y Rivera Colon.[41]

Fitzpatrick identifies a fourfold typology among Puerto Rican families: (1) the extended family residing either in the same household or in separate households with frequent visits and strong bonds; (2) the nuclear family, increasingly common among the middle class; (3) the nuclear family plus other children of different names from previous union(s) of husband or wife, a not uncommon pattern among Puerto Ricans; (4) the female-headed household, with children of one or more men, but with no permanent male in the home.[42] The last type is frequently found among welfare families and is thus the target of much criticism.

Religion

The Catholic church has traditionally played an important role with immigrant groups, in succession assisting the French, Irish, Germans, Italians, Slavs, Poles, Syrians, Lebanese, and others.[43] This pattern was not repeated with the Puerto Ricans in terms of representation in the church hierarchy,

TABLE 11.8	HISPANIC IMMIGRATION INTO THE UNITED STATES, BY ETHNIC GROUP: 1950–1989			
	1950–1959		1960–1969	
Ethnic Group	Number of Migrants	Percentage of Total	Number of Migrants	Percentage of Total
Mexican	293,000	30.7	431,000	33.2
Cuban	71,000	7.4	249,000	19.2
Puerto Rican	480,000	50.2	222,000	17.1
Other Hispanic	112,000	11.7	397,000	30.6
	1970–1979		1980–1989	
Ethnic Group	Number of Migrants	Percentage of Total	Number of Migrants	Percentage of Total
Mexican	567,000	40.8	1,214,900	43.1
Cuban	278,000	20.0	197,000	7.0
Puerto Rican	65,900	3.0	333,000	11.8
Other Hispanic	503,000	36.2	1,074,500	38.1

SOURCE: Mexican, Cuban, Other Hispanic: Immigration and Naturalization Service annual reports 1950–1991, Table 9. Puerto Rican: U.S. Bureau of the Census, *Current Population Reports*, U.S. Government Printing Office, Washington, DC, Series P–25, No. 1009 and Puerto Rico Planning Board.

church leadership in the ethnic community, or immigrant involvement in the church. In 1970 Nathan Glazer and Daniel P. Moynihan observed:

> The Puerto Ricans have not created, as others did, national parishes of their own. Thus the capacities of the Church are weak in just those areas in which the needs of the migrants are great—in creating a surrounding, supporting community to replace the extended families, broken by city life, and to supply a social setting for those who feel lost and lonely in the great city. . . .
> Most of the Puerto Ricans in the city are Catholic, but their participation in Catholic life is small.[44]

Several factors have contributed to this break in the usual pattern. Because the island was a colony for so long, first Spanish and then American priests predominated within the church hierarchy on the island. Few Puerto Ricans became priests, and what few there were did not come to the mainland with the immigrants. The distant and alien nature of the church in Puerto Rico resulted in the Puerto Ricans having an internalized sense of Catholic identity without formally attending Mass and receiving the sacraments. Baptisms, weddings, and funerals all became important as social occasions, and the ceremony itself was of secondary importance. Throughout all of Latin America, Catholicism means personal relationships with the saints and a community manifestation of faith, not the individual actions and commitments expected in the United States. Another aspect of religious life in Puerto Rico, Brazil, and other parts of Latin America is the widespread belief in spiritualism and superstition. These practices undoubtedly are remnants of old folk rites, but they are still observed by various cults as well as by many Catholics.[45]

On the mainland a few other factors weakened any possibility that the Puerto Ricans would develop a strong ethnic church. Fitzpatrick indicates that the movement of other third-generation immigrants out of the city left behind clusters of old national churches with few parishioners.[46] Because of these existing church buildings and parochial schools, Cardinal Francis Spellman decided in 1939 that New York City parishes would be integrated to accommodate the newcomers. Instead of having their own churches, the Puerto Ricans had the services of one or more Spanish-speaking priests, with special masses and services performed in a basement chapel, school hall, or some other area of the parish. Although this practice was cost-effective for the Catholic church, it prevented the parish from becoming the basis for a strong, stable community because the group could not identify with it.

With the integrated parishes becoming more Hispanic over the years, the New York archdiocese added more Spanish-speaking priests. To aid their rapport with the people, the priests took a three-month summer course in Puerto Rico at the Institute of Intercultural Communication in Puerto Rico on Puerto Rican culture and acculturation problems on the mainland. Promotion of the annual *Fiesta de San Juan* each June became a widely observed religious festival in New York City. Religiocivic organizations such as the *Centro Católico Puertorriqueño* in Jersey City and the *Caballeros de San Juan* in Chicago became effective support organizations, further uniting the Puerto Rican community.

For many lower-class people of all racial and ethnic backgrounds, religion serves as an emotional escape from the harsh realities of everyday life. Pentecostalism is the fastest-growing religious movement among Puerto Ricans and throughout Latin America; it is the largest Protestant body both on the island and on the mainland. Storefront churches, with small and intimate congregations of about 60 to 100, offer their members a sense of community they cannot find elsewhere. Second-generation participation falls off sharply; Pentecostalism appears to be a first-generation phenomenon and perhaps of limited duration.[47]

Church estimates reveal that only 6 percent of the Puerto Rican population on the mainland are involved with any Protestant denomination, including Pentecostalism, and only 33 percent with the Catholic church.[48] It is doubtful, then, that religious identification will be an important factor in either assimilation or cultural pluralism, as it was for earlier immigrant groups.

Puerto Rican Communities

The New York metropolitan area emerged as the Puerto Rican center, at one time containing three-fourths of all Puerto Ricans living on the mainland. In the past two decades population dispersion has occurred. One in three Puerto Ricans still lives in New York City, but New York State's Puerto Rican population has dropped from 64 percent of the total mainland population in 1970, to 49 percent in 1980, and 39 percent in 1990. Puerto Ricans live in all 50 states, with other large concentrations found in New Jersey (11 percent); Florida (9 percent); Illinois and Massachusetts (6 percent); California, Connecticut, and Pennsylvania (5 percent).[49]

For many years the continuous shuttle migration kept an organized community life from fully developing. Hometown clubs—voluntary organizations based upon one's place of birth—offered social opportunities in providing a place for celebration of weddings, birthdays, first communions, and confirmations. Because they drew members from scattered New York neighborhoods, they did not serve as community centers, nor did any other social institution. Only the annual Puerto Rican Day Parade, begun in 1958, served as a focal point of group identity. By 1977, however, Clara Rodriguez was able to discern increased ethnic neighborhood organization.

> Note, for example, the growth of what are today Puerto Rican "cuchifrito" stands, social clubs, and after-hour clubs. These and other institutions did not exist years ago or existed in a very different form. Today they are identifying symbols of a Puerto Rican neighborhood. This same phenomena of change is also reflected in the speech of many second generation Puerto Ricans who no longer speak continuous Spanish, but whose English is decidedly "Rican".[50]

As with most ethnic communities, a great many social institutions have evolved. Some are informal, like the *bodega,* or local grocery store, which serves as more than a source of Hispanic foods. It is a social gathering place where social interaction, gossip, and neighborly community create an "oasis of Latin culture."[51] Here one can obtain advice on finding a home, getting a job, or buying a car.[52] The *bodega* thus functions as an important part of the community's infrastructure.

Other community institutions are civic and social organizations. Some, born out of the War on Poverty and dependent on federal funding, have declined, but others remain strong. Most notable is *Aspira,* founded in 1961. Through guidance, encouragement, and financial assistance, *Aspira* seeks to develop cultural pride and self-confidence in youth and to encourage them to further their education and enter the professions, technical fields, and the arts. Begun in New York City, its grass-roots program has achieved national fame and has expanded to other cities as well. A more direct community action group is the Puerto Rican Community Development Project, which attempts to promote a sense of identity among Puerto Ricans and to develop community strength. Another organization begun in New York is the Puerto

---

BOX 11.1   **THE ETHNIC EXPERIENCE**

"My husband and I bought our own house in Brooklyn after the Second World War, and a few years later we bought other property on Long Island, where we moved to raise our family. In 1956 we were employed by the U.S. Military Academy, West Point, and purchased a lovely home in a so-called exclusive area not too far away. This was a quaint neighborhood where custom-built homes ranged from $40,000 up to $100,000.

"Shortly after we moved in, we went down to Florida on vacation. When we came back, the house was empty. We slept on the floor and the following day our attorney by telephone searched every place high and low until he found our possessions in a warehouse in Nyack. Some of our neighbors had learned we were originally from Puerto Rico, were unhappy to have us as neighbors, and had plotted this against us.

"The harassment continued for a long time. They threw their garbage every night on our lawn. They even sent the police to intimidate us and even tried to buy us out. We told them they couldn't afford the luxury of buying us out. We felt we had all the rights in the world to enjoy all the privileges others had. We were honest, hard-working, respectable citizens too. So we took legal action and demanded for damages. The judge was fair and ruled for us."

SOURCE: Puerto Rican couple who came to the mainland in 1946 during their twenties.

Rican Family Institute, which provides professional social services to Puerto Rican families. Parent action groups, athletic leagues, cultural organizations, and social clubs also exist, providing services and fulfilling community needs.[53]

Socioeconomic Characteristics

Of all major racial or ethnic groups, Puerto Ricans have the highest poverty rate, averaging over 40 percent in recent years.[54] With three out of four living inside central cities, they live in old neighborhoods formerly inhabited by lower-class European immigrants. Unlike their predecessors, however, the Puerto Ricans cannot find work to match their limited job skills and educational background. Manufacturing and other blue-collar employment, most notably in the garment industry, has moved from the Snow Belt to the Sun Belt and from the city to the suburbs.[55]

Intensifying the ill effects of unemployment is the island ethic that women should not work. It is unusual to find the Puerto Rican female working in either a two-income family or in a female-headed household. Forty percent of all Puerto Rican households are headed by a female, significantly higher than all other Hispanic groups but slightly lower than for black families.[56] One

Puerto Rican business persons network at a monthly cocktail party of the National Puerto Rican Business Council. This organization, an example of a parallel social institution, enhances its members' business expertise and enables them to develop important contacts within the business community. *(Grant LeDuc/Monkmeyer Press Photo Service)*

reason for the poverty that had increased among Puerto Rican families while declining among black families is the far greater participation in the labor market by black women.[57] Puerto Rican families are twice as likely as black families to be on welfare and 50 percent more likely to be poor.

We need to keep in mind that Puerto Ricans, like all groups, include people with varying socioeconomic characteristics. Not all live in poverty. Almost 40 percent of all annual Puerto Rican family income exceeds $25,000; 11 percent exceeds $50,000. More than half of all Puerto Rican families, 57 percent, have both parents living together, a figure lower than for other Hispanic families but higher than for black families, which is 50 percent.[58]

Mexicans and Puerto Ricans: A Comparison

At first glance the statistics seem contradictory. Compared to Mexican Americans, most Puerto Ricans are less likely to have arrived recently, are better educated, and speak better English. Furthermore, employed Puerto Ricans, on average, earn more than employed Mexicans. However, fewer Mexican Americans live in poverty, and of those who do far fewer seek government assistance than do the Puerto Rican poor. The labor force nonparticipation rate, which shows those who have stopped looking for work, is far higher among Puerto Ricans.[59]

How do we account for this? Employed Puerto Ricans work in highly unionized labor markets that have favorable wages and working conditions. Mexican Americans work in states that are less well organized by unions and where continually arriving newcomers create an extensive labor supply, enabling exploitative practices by employers and depressing the wage scale. Another part of the answer lies in settlement patterns. Because more Puerto Ricans live inside central cities than do Mexican Americans, their economic well-being is dependent on economic conditions there, and the central cities have experienced a significant decline in low-skill jobs in recent decades. The Southwest, in contrast, has been experiencing rapid growth, making job prospects for less skilled jobs better there than in Northern cities.[60] Consequently, more Mexican Americans can find work but for less pay than Puerto Ricans get.

Another factor that has an impact on poverty is the difference in the number of families headed by females. In 1988 females headed 44 percent of Puerto Rican families compared to 18 percent of Mexican American families. Cultural values partly explain this phenomenon. Mexicans tend to stress the family unit, whereas rural Puerto Rico has a long tradition of out-of-wedlock childbearing. Many female immigrants tend to come out of this tradition, and they are more likely than those who do not emigrate to have recently gone through the breakup of a marriage or serious relationship.[61]

THE CUBANS

Although the United States granted Cuba its independence after the 1898 war with Spain, it continued to exercise control over the island. The United States had Cuba relinquish a naval base at Guantánamo, which it still maintains, and through the Platt Amendment it reserved the right to intervene in Cuba if necessary to protect American interests. The Cubans resented these infringements on their newly granted sovereignty. Later, in the 1930s, Franklin Roosevelt's Good Neighbor Policy helped to ease relations between the two countries.

Because the government listed Cuban immigrants among those from the West Indies until 1950, exact numbers prior to that time are impossible to determine. Almost 500,000 people came to the United States from the West Indies between 1820 and 1950. Cubans had little impact on the American scene during that period, although a Cuban community in northern New Jersey that dated back to 1850 did attract many refugees in the 1960s.

Cuban Migration

Since 1960 over 625,000 Cubans—more than came from the entire West Indies over a period of 130 years—have entered the United States. Touched off by Castro's rise to power, Cuban immigration surged in the first years of the

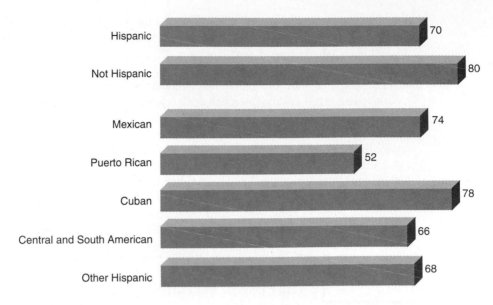

FIGURE 11.4
Percentages of Hispanic Married-Couple Families by Origin, March 1990
SOURCE: U.S. Bureau of the Census.

revolution, then ebbed and flowed with shifts in both U.S. and Cuban government policies.

In the 1960s and early 1970s, the first waves of postrevolutionary refugees had been "displaced bourgeoise"—well-educated, middle- and upper-class professionals and businesspeople alienated by the new regime.[62] Sympathetically received by the nation as resisters and refugees from the first communist regime in the Western Hemisphere, Cubans began to concentrate in several major cities, notably Miami and New York. Initial concern in those regions about overburdening the educational, welfare, and social service systems quickly dissipated as the Cubans made rapid economic progress and became a part of the community. By 1976 Cuban median income was $2,000 below the national norm but higher than that of other Hispanic groups and blacks, as well as in comparison to previous percentages of the national income of other newly arrived groups.

The largest single influx of Cubans occurred in late 1980, when the Mariel boatlift brought 125,000 Cubans to the United States in just a few months. Most were urban working-class and lower-class people, with at least several thousand hardened, vicious criminals among them. By 1990 the Cuban American population exceeded 1 million, with about 72 percent identified as first-generation Americans.[63]

Cuban Communities

In some instances Cubans at first found themselves treated disparagingly because non-Hispanic residents did not differentiate them from other, poorer

Spanish-speaking groups such as the Puerto Ricans and Dominicans. Although they had looked on such other Caribbean peoples with disdain in the past, the Cubans found that it was in their own best interests to work cooperatively with other Hispanic groups. In a pattern reminiscent of the Sephardic and Ashkenazic Jews, who first resisted and then were very helpful to the central and eastern European Jewish immigrants, the Cubans sometimes established closer relations with other Hispanic groups, particularly in New York. These cooperative efforts have helped to bring greater stability and visible progress to Hispanic neighborhoods.

Cubans often settled in blighted urban areas, but their motivation, education, and entrepreneurial skills enabled them to bring color, vitality, stability, and improvement to previously declining neighborhoods. Long-time residents of areas heavily populated by Cubans often credit them with restoring and increasing the beauty and vigor of the community.

BOX 11.2   **THE ETHNIC EXPERIENCE**

"I have to tell you that the Spanish-speaking people are always talking about brotherhood and the brotherhood of the Latin American countries. They say our brother country Mexico and our brother country Venezuela, and every time they mention a Latin American country, they say the brother country. Well, in reality, it is wrong. When we needed an escape from Cuba, we only had America. America was the only country that opened the door. America is the only place where you can go for freedom and where you can live as a human being.

"I love Cuba very much but I can tell you that we never had the freedom that we have here. I can sincerely say that the opportunities in this country—America—are so great and so many, that no matter how bad they say we are as far as economics right now—they're talking about recession and everything—no matter how bad they say, it will never be as bad as it was and it is, actually, in Cuba.

"America took us in and we are grateful to America and to the Americans. And remember, when we came over, we were looking for freedom and liberty. Now we have freedom, we have liberty, and we have the chance to make money. Many Cubans are doing very well, better than me. I make enough to support my family and to live decently. I am very happy and grateful.

"Believe me, I am not only speaking for myself, but for a large group of Cubans who feel the same way I feel. We are happy here. We miss Cuba. Sometimes we get tearful when we think about the old friends and the old neighborhoods, but we are lucky. We are lucky because we still can say what we want to say, and we can move around wherever we want, and be what we want to be."

SOURCE: Cuban refugee who came to the United States in 1960 at age 18.

Miami offers an excellent example. Its climate and closeness to Cuba made it the ideal choice of many exiles, thereby increasing the fears of residents about so large an ethnic group in their midst. Yet, by 1966 an observer could comment:

> Though some ill-feeling still persists in Miami, by and large the city has come to count its new Cuban community as its own good fortune. . . . There is even something of a real-estate boom in Miami—one of the few cities in the U.S. where housing markets are strong—and an estimated 30 percent of the new FHA commitments there are to Cubans. Enterprising Cubans have been credited with bringing a new commercial vigor to much of the downtown area, especially the former commercial center of Flagler Street, which had been rapidly running down. Many of the former Havana cigar manufacturers and their employees have set up nearly a dozen companies in Miami, helping the city to displace Tampa as the hand-rolled-cigar capital of the U.S. At least one cigarette company, Dorsal & Mendes, is thriving; there are also sizable and prosperous Cuban-owned garment companies, shoe manufacturers, import houses, shopping centers, restaurants and night clubs. To the northwest of Miami, Cuban entrepreneurs have set up sugar plantations and mills.[64]

Despite a few instances of ethnic-related traumas in the early 1980s after the arrival of the Marielitos (voter approval of a harsh Dade County antibilingual ordinance and four days of anti-Cuban rioting by blacks), changes quietly reshaped Miami's political, social, and professional landscape. With dozens of flashy new towers designed by Cuban American architects, even Miami's urban landscape changed. Cuban Americans integrated very quickly, becoming an important influence within the established system. In fact it is very difficult to find disgruntled Anglos complaining about Cubans' not speaking English. Instead, young Anglo executives are more likely to be studying Spanish to gain bilingual skills to enhance their chances for promotion.[65]

Because two out of every three Cuban Americans live in Florida, the Cuban impact on Miami, now dubbed "Little Havana," has been significant. More than 60 percent of all Cuban Americans live in the Miami area, where the Cuban influence has transformed Miami from a resort town to a year-round commercial center with linkages throughout Latin America and made it into a leading bilingual cultural center. Two-thirds of Miami's population is now Hispanic.

Northeastern New Jersey has the second largest Cuban American concentration, with another 87,086, or 8 percent, of the Cuban American population. New York and California each contains 7 percent of the Cuban American population at 77,016 and 75,034, respectively.[66] Other Cuban Americans are scattered among all the remaining states.

Because Cubans have had a high status throughout the Caribbean for a long time, their presence in Hispanic American neighborhoods has brought a new dimension in intracommunity relations, expectations, and cohesion:

> In the Caribbean, the Dominicans, Puerto Ricans and Jamaicans are all highly regarded as entrepreneurs. However, even they acknowledge, sometimes rue-

In Miami's "Little Havana," some older Cuban American men spend the afternoon playing dominoes. This daily activity is an institutionalized form of ethnic solidarity and social interaction, similar to the card games once found in European immigrant social clubs and coffeehouses in most American cities. *(Anita Bartsch/Design Conceptions)*

fully, that it is the Cubans who are to the tropics what the Parisians are to France and the Genoans to Italy: People who possess that special admixture of diligence and brashness, making the shrewd and prudently risky decisions that are the difference between high success and just making a living.[67]

Cultural Values

In addition to a commonality of values shared with other Latinos discussed earlier in this chapter, Cubans also share certain subcultural values that differ from those of the dominant American culture.[68] Among these are attitudes toward work, personal qualities, and the role of individuals in society.

American values stress hard work as a means of achieving material well-being, whereas the Cuban orientation is that material success should be pursued for personal freedom, not physical comfort. Work is not considered to be an end in itself, that one should live in order to work, as Cubans believe Anglos do. Instead, one should work to enjoy life. Intellectual pursuits are highly valued, idleness is frowned on.

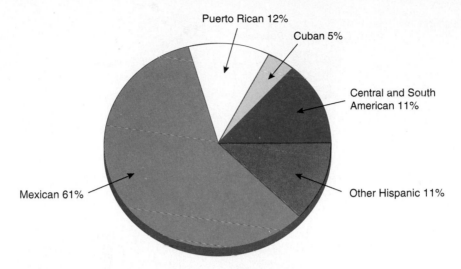

FIGURE 11.5
Hispanic Americans by Origin (Percentages of All Hispanics), 1990
SOURCE: U.S. Bureau of the Census.

Unlike the American Puritan value of thrift and frugality, Cubans are fervent believers in generosity. Common group traits include a sharing of one's good fortune, a warm open-house policy, and an extensive social outreach to others. Cubans believe one of the worst sins is to be a *tacaño,* a cheapskate who does not readily show affection and friendship through kindnesses and hospitality.

Individualism is a value best shown through national and personal pride, which Anglos often misperceive as haughtiness. Yet Cubans believe that individualism is not so much self-assertiveness as it is attitudes and actions oriented toward a group, sometimes a large number of people. Hostility needs to be directed through *choteo* and *relajo,* the continuous practice of humor, jokes, and wit, and accepted by others in good part. This is because one should avoid being a *pesado*—someone unlikeable, diagreeable, and without wit—which is the worst of all cultural sins.

Socioeconomic Characteristics

The population pyramid for Cubans (see Figure 11.6) shows the significant difference of this Hispanic group compared to others. The bulges at ages 40–59 and 15–24 reflect the young and middle-aged Cubans who arrived in the 1960s and early 1970s and their children. The narrow base shows their low current fertility.

Although still the most metropolitan of the Hispanic Americans, Cubans are now just as likely to live in such well-groomed suburbs as Coral Gables or

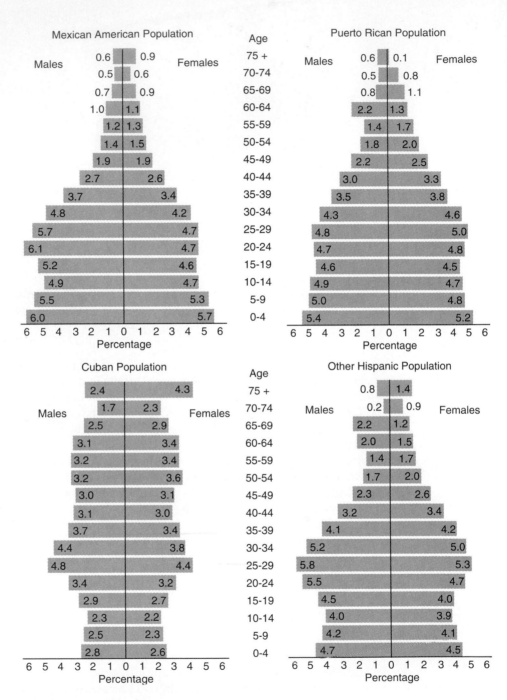

FIGURE 11.6

Age–Sex Composition of the Hispanic Population, 1990

SOURCE: U.S. Bureau of the Census.

Hialeah in Dade County, Florida—or others in California, New Jersey, or New York—as they are to live in the nearby cities. Cubans have a lower fertility rate, lower unemployment rate, higher median family income, greater education, and greater middle-class population composition than other Hispanic groups. As Table 11.6 shows (see p. 407), 58 percent are in white-collar occupations, a significantly higher proportion than any other Hispanic group.

CENTRAL AND SOUTH AMERICANS

Three push factors—overpopulation, economic hardship, and political turmoil—have triggered the significant increase in emigration from several Latin American countries. After Mexico, the largest contingents come from Cuba, Dominican Republic, Colombia, Argentina, and Ecuador, joined in recent years by growing numbers of refugees from El Salvador, Nicaragua, and Peru (see Table 11.9). From 136,379 Central and South American immigrants in the 1950s, their numbers expanded to 359,284 in the 1960s, 430,381 in the 1970s, and then leaped to 929,935 in the 1980s.[69] Included in the 1980s total are illegal aliens who applied for permanent residence under the amnesty provision in the Immigration and Reform Act of 1986. About 13 percent of the total applications were from Central America, being led by El Salvador (143,070) and followed by Guatemala (52,544), Colombia (26,363), the Dominican Republic (18,273), and Nicaragua (16,012).[70]

About a half million Central Americans live in Los Angeles. Substantial numbers also reside in San Francisco, Houston, Washington, DC, New York,

TABLE 11.9	WESTERN HEMISPHERE IMMIGRANTS FROM LEADING COUNTRIES, 1971–1990
1. Mexico	2,296,137
2. Cuba	409,441
3. Dominican Republic	400,170
4. Jamaica	345,725
5. Canada	326,877
6. El Salvador	247,975
7. Colombia	200,196
8. Haiti	194,714
9. Guyana	142,851
10. Ecuador	106,392
11. Trinidad and Tobago	101,334
12. Peru	93,501

SOURCE: U.S. Immigration and Naturalization Service. *Statistical Yearbook: 1991*, Washington, DC: U.S. Government Printing Office, 1992, pp. 28–30.

Chicago, New Orleans, and Miami. As the largest Central American group in the United States, Salvadorans usually constitute the majority of Central Americans in most cities, followed by Guatemalans (see Table 11.10). However, Nicaraguans predominate in Miami and Hondurans in New Orleans among Central Americans.[71]

The Dominicians

More than 400,000 Dominican immigrants have arrived in the United States since 1971, their numbers averaging about 27,000 annually, then jumping to 42,136 in 1990. Two of every three Dominicans live in New York, for a total of 357,868, according to the 1990 census. Most live in New York City, particularly in Washington Heights in Manhattan as well as in the South Bronx. Other primary areas of residence are New Jersey (52,807), Florida (34,268), and Massachusetts (30,177).[72]

Dominicans are more likely to live and interact within their own ethnic neighborhoods instead of integrating into a mixed Hispanic neighborhood. A common pattern is to coexist alongside Puerto Ricans, each ethnic group keeping mostly to itself. In the South Bronx, however, where Dominican

TABLE 11.10	CENTRAL AND SOUTH AMERICANS LIVING IN THE UNITED STATES, 1990
Central American	1,323,830
Costa Rican	57,223
Guatemalan	268,779
Honduran	131,066
Nicaraguan	202,658
Panamanian	92,013
Salvadoran	565,081
Other Central American	7,010
South American	1,035,602
Argentinean	100,921
Bolivian	38,073
Chilean	68,799
Colombian	378,726
Ecuadorian	191,198
Paraguayan	6,662
Peruvian	175,035
Uruguayan	21,996
Venezuelan	47,997
Other South American	6,195

SOURCE: U.S. Bureau of the Census.

immigration is primarily male and the Puerto Rican family predominantly female-headed, Dominican–Puerto Rican marriages and liaisons are becoming common.[73]

Most of the Dominicans are dark-skinned people who have fled the poverty of their land. Because of lack of skills, they have a high unemployment rate. Many live in poor urban neighborhoods, suffering the deprivation and family disruption so common among those with low levels of education and job skills. Racial discrimination further compounds their problems, and some find work as migrant farm laborers, away from urban troubles.

The Salvadorans

Several push factors account for the large-scale Salvadoran emigration to the United States.[74] Agricultural modernization and expansion by the landowning oligarchy displaced tens of thousands of rural peasants. Relocating to such urban centers as San Salvador, many could not find work despite the growing industrialization. Conditions deteriorated when protests and demonstrations were met by government repression. Death squads comprised of members of the ruling elite and the security and military forces targeted peasant leaders, union militants, and political activists. Revolutionary movements arose, and guerilla offensives in the 1980s caused escalating violence by the security and military forces as well as by the death squads. Attacks against civilian populations in rural areas occurred, including massacres of entire villages believed to be sympathetic to the guerillas.

As a stream of undocumented Salvadorans fled into the United States, immigration agents sought to apprehend and return them, denying them refugee status. The State Department ruled that although El Salvador might be a war-torn country, none of those leaving had been specifically singled out for persecution and thus did not really have a well-founded fear of persecution. Out of this conflict was born the sanctuary movement in the United States; clergy defied the government, hiding Salvadoran refugees in churches and homes. The clergy and members of their congregations provided food, shelter, and clothing before secretly aiding the refugees in getting to a safe location. It is these individuals who comprised the 143,070 Salvadoran applicants for amnesty and permanent residence in the United States.

Although the political situation has improved in El Salvador, most Salvadorans in the United States are remaining, putting down roots and enjoying the support system within their evolving ethnic communities. Through chain migration, other relatives and friends join them, continuing a steady migration flow.

The Nicaraguans

Nicaraguans have entered the United States as immigrants, refugees, asylees or illegals. A *refugee* is someone outside one's country unable or unwilling to

Reverend John Steinbruck counsels some 1980s Salvadoran refugees in a Washington, DC church involved in the Sanctuary Program. Both clergy and congregations throughout the country, defying the U.S. government, were actively involved in hiding refugees from immigration officials and in helping to relocate them. *(Budd Gray/Stock, Boston)*

return because of persecution or a well-founded fear of persecution. The definition of an *asylee* is the same as that of a refugee, except that the alien is physically in the United States or at a port of entry. After the Sandinistas came to power, 46,476 middle-class Nicaraguans emigrated from their communist-ruled homeland between 1980 and 1990.[75] As the Contras led a guerilla movement against the government, a second wave of new arrivals began arriving in September 1988. Between 1988 and 1990, more than 1,000 refugees arrived each year. During these three years, another 79,000 Nicaraguans streamed into Texas, filing asylum applications.[76] In that period, only 11,094 were granted asylum, however.[77] Those denied often entered the country illegally.

Most of the new arrivals, unlike their predecessors, were poor, unskilled, and illiterate *campesinos* from the countryside. Some had lived for months in refugee camps in Honduras and in other Central American countries that pressed the United States to accept the refugees.

Drawn by the Latin American population and the already established Nicaraguan communities in Miami and southern California, most refugees chose one of those two destinations. Miami–Dade County schools, for example, almost quadrupled their Nicaraguan student enrollment in 1988–1989. With no previous educational experience, most of the 13- to-15-year-olds could not read and had to be taught the basics of reading and arithmetic.[78] Sweetwater, a western suburb of Miami, became almost completely Nicaraguan, earning the nickname "Little Managua."

When the Sandinista regime came to an end in February 1990, the 11-year exodus of refugees also ended, although immigrants continue to arrive. Some Nicaraguans returned to their homeland, but most chose to stay in the United States. The 1990 census identified 202,658 Nicaraguans, of whom 79,056 were in Florida and 74,119 in California. Other states with sizable population concentrations were New York (11,011), Texas (7,911), New Jersey (4,226), Maryland (4,019), and Virginia (3,471).[79]

The Colombians

Colombia is the South American country supplying the most immigrants, more than 200,000 since 1971.[80] Population pressures, better economic opportunities, and chain-migration networking have increased the annual immigration totals recently, now averaging over 14,000 yearly. Eighty percent of the 378,726 Colombians tallied in the 1990 census were foreign-born.[81] Most of the remainder were children born to these first-generation Americans.

Colombians are mostly a light-tan-skinned people, making them less susceptible to racial discrimination than some Caribbean Hispanics. They are a mixture of educated professionals and low-skilled peasants seeking a better life. Living mostly in urban neighborhoods near other Hispanics, they too form their own social clubs and institutions, attempting to preserve their culture through ethnic folk-dance groups and holiday celebrations. In 1990 Colombian Americans were mostly found in New York (85,600), Florida (68,609), New Jersey (42,339), and California (32,024).[82]

A very small percentage of Colombians are heavily involved in the cocaine trade and the drug war killings. This high profile of a minute number of criminals unfortunately smears the rest, just as Italian Americans have suffered a guilt by nationality stereotype because of the Mafia. In reality almost all Colombian Americans are decent, law-abiding people who are working hard to make a life for themselves in their adopted country.

OTHER CARIBBEAN PEOPLES _____

English- and French-speaking Caribbean people have also emigrated to the United States in substantial numbers. Although they come from the same region, their languages and cultures set them apart from each other and from the Hispanic peoples as well. Most of them are dark-skinned; encountering racial discrimination in housing, jobs, and other social interactions is a common, though new, experience for them.

BOX 11.3   THE ETHNIC EXPERIENCE

"The Colombians here are the poor people. They are the ones who had no chance for an education in Columbia. They are the ones who—because they had no education—their pay was very meager. And so over here they have a better life than they would in Colombia. So over here they really—if you can call it the American Dream—has been fulfilled in them.

"Emotionally they're very attached to their country. See, this is the thing that is very hard for people to understand. They want them to become American and to forget everything. You can't! The ties—the blood ties—are too strong! You just can't become—as I said, I cannot even become an American. I can't! Even if I wanted to. You would have to make me all over again. And I love this country and I choose to stay in this country.

"Now with these people—take some of them. They have come because of necessity—sheer necessity. We criticize them because they don't love America, but I don't think that is the fact. Also, if you notice the kind of people that come here. For instance, I had students who were the children of my father's workers on the coffee plantation. Now in my country they were tilling the soil. You know, the children of the owner go to school. The children of the worker go to till the soil. They had no chance of an education. They had huts up in the mountains where they had no running water, no electricity. Now they come here and they have all the conveniences. If they live poorly, Americans criticize them but they don't realize where they were living before. If they're not clean and spotless and they don't keep the shades the right way—but these people have been doing this for a hundred years! The people who just came in never even had a shade to talk about. They never had a venetian blind. They never even had a window to talk about!" (Laughs.)

"I think we have to be careful because we often make the mistake of imposing our way to the people. Now you could say, we're not going to them, they're coming here. But if you accept them in the country, I think you also have to accept a big risk. I think the melting pot idea is not the prevalent idea. It is not a workable idea. Each one has a culture. Each people has a culture and if you want them in America, if you allow them to stay here, you have to work something by which each one is able to live. I don't mean to say that we have independent little countries, but that they are comfortable. Because you cannot remove—those are strong things that you cannot remove from a person."

SOURCE: Colombian immigrant who came to the United States in 1952 at age 16.

Guadeloupe, Martinique, and French Guiana send very few immigrants. English-speaking immigrants from the Bahamas, Bermuda, the British Virgin Islands, Dominica, and other small islands also send a few hundred or less each year. Barbados, Trinidad, and Tobago average several thousand immigrants yearly, and they may become larger suppliers when the chain-migration process intensifies. The two major suppliers are Haiti and Jamaica, whose immigrants we shall now briefly discuss.

The Haitians

In the first wave of more than 4,000 Haitian immigrants in the 1950s, most were well-educated members of Haiti's upper class who were fleeing the harsh regime of President François Duvalier. In the 1960s almost 35,000 Haitians, mostly of the middle class, arrived in the United States. The third wave, primarily illiterate peasants and unskilled urban workers with little or no education, including the "boat people," has been emigrating since the mid-1970s. A total of 56,335 legal immigrants entered the United States in the 1970s, and 138,379 came in the 1980s.[83]

Haiti is the poorest country in the Western Hemisphere, its people still suffering under a repressive government in 1992. Driven by desperation, thousands of undocumented Haitians flee to the United States, but federal policy has been to deny them refugee status, discourage their entry into the United States, and to deport them. The courts have impeded this policy, usually on procedural grounds, and many Haitians have eventually been included in the legalization process.

When they arrive, many of the Haitians in the third wave do not speak French, only Haitian Creole. French is the language of the educated elite in Haitian government, commerce, and education. Fluency in one language does not enable understanding in the other. Nevertheless, because of the prestige attached to things French and the assumption by many Americans that all Haitians speak French, Haitians often pretend to be able to speak it to enhance their status.[84]

Most Haitians are Roman Catholics, with an increasing segment attracted to evangelical Protestantism. A significant minority practice *voudou,* a religion with African roots combining belief in the existence of a *bon Dieu* or good God, and *lwas,* spirits who offer protection, advice, and assistance to resolve spiritual and material problems.[85]

Alex Stepick and Carol Dutton Stepick found that Haitian immigrants in south Florida lived in tightly clustered neighborhoods, with 86 percent reporting little or no interaction with Anglos.[86] Their social isolation partly results from their belief that both white and black Americans discriminate against them and from their inability to speak English. Only 20 percent in the Stepicks' extensive study claimed to speak English at least reasonably well.

In Florida, where more than 105,000 Haitians live, as well as in New York, where there are more than 107,000, their unemployment rate is four times the national average.[87] Living in crowded, substandard housing, they find work in low-paying jobs in service industries. About one-third of all migrant farm laborers on the East Coast are Haitians.

The Jamaicans

Another fairly recent group, the Jamaicans, constitute the largest non-Hispanic immigrant population from the Caribbean. Seventy-nine percent of

Repatriated Haitian "boat people" await clearance at Port-au-Prince harbor in March, 1992 upon return from Florida detention camps. Government policy has consistently been to deny refugee status to Haitians. Recently the Coast Guard turned back Haitian boats before entering U.S. territorial waters. *(Teun Voeten/ Impact Visuals)*

the 435,024 Jamaican Americans living in the United States in 1990 were foreign-born. Although California claimed over 19,000 Jamaican Americans by 1990, giving it by far the largest concentration west of the Appalachian Mountains, most Jamaicans are settling on the East Coast in urban environments. According to the 1990 census, the leading states with Jamaican Americans were New York (186,429), Florida (86,231), New Jersey (26,690), and Connecticut (20,219).[88]

With annual Jamaican immigration figures exceeding 23,000, the continual large influx augments their ethnic communities and cultural vitality. Their presence is perhaps most visible to other Americans through West Indian food stores and reggae music. Speech is another indicator, for Jamaicans speak English but with rapid speech patterning and a clipped accent, sometimes causing difficulty for a first-time listener.

Jamaica itself is a plural society, with three layered sections: a small white section at the top, at the bottom a black section comprising about four-fifths of the population, and a brown section in between.[89] Within this "hierarchically arrayed mosaic of total communities," each provides its members with the entire range of life experience.[90] Most of the immigrants coming to the

United States, reflecting their nation's population composition, are blacks. On the island they practice a folk culture containing numerous elements reminiscent of African societies and Caribbean slavery.[91]

Economic opportunity is the primary motivation for immigration. Tourism and the limited economy cannot support the growing population base. Adapting quite easily to American society, first-generation Jamaican Americans find their initial encounters with racism to be bitter and difficult experiences. Some become disillusioned and return home, but most remain to pursue their goals. Second-generation Jamaican Americans appear to be integrating into society as black Americans. It remains to be seen whether the present Jamaican communities become more structured, encouraging cultural pluralism through the continuing arrival of newcomers, or if a short-term integration process continues.

SOCIOLOGICAL ANALYSIS

Like other immigrant groups before them, the new arrivals from the Caribbean and Latin America are beginning to change the face of America, making their distinctive contributions to the neighborhoods in which they live. But with their growing numbers they also are encountering the hostility historically accorded almost all newly arriving ethnic groups. Application of sociological perspectives can thus place their current experiences in a comparative context.

The Functionalist View

Rapid population growth has been a mixed blessing for these newcomers. They have been able to develop supportive ethnic subcommunities, providing social institutions and an interactive network that ease readjustment to a new country. Cuban settlement in deteriorated urban neighborhoods has both revitalized those areas and brought, out of necessity, interethnic assistance to other Hispanic groups. Because 86 percent of all Hispanics live in nine states (California, Arizona, Colorado, New Mexico, Texas, Illinois, New York, New Jersey, and Florida), they are quickly realizing their potential political power, enabling them to make their presence felt for improvement of their life situation. Concern exists that their numbers and common language may be dysfunctional, delaying assimilation and creating a "Hispanic Quebec" within the United States.

Most of the newcomers lack sufficient education and job skills to escape a below- or near-poverty existence (see Figure 11.7). Yet the existence of a dual economy—industries on the periphery such as garment factories, restaurants, and hotels dependent on low-skill workers, even illegals or minors—provides barrio residents with job opportunities.[92] Illegals or low-skilled legal immigrants even promote domestic employment, keeping alive some manual labor

| BOX 11.4 | THE INTERNATIONAL SCENE |

Honduras is a Central American republic slightly larger than Pennsylvania. Its population of 4.7 million is about 90 percent *mestizo* (Spanish–Indian), 7 percent Amerindian, 2 percent black, and 1 percent white. Almost half of its labor force is in agriculture, and its primary exports are bananas, coffee, lead, zinc, shrimp, and lobsters.

One-third of Hondurans age 25 and over have no formal schooling at all, and another 51 percent have less than an eighth grade education. The per capita Gross National Product of Honduras is third from last among Central and South American nations, ahead of Nicaragua and Bolivia. As such it holds little attraction for immigrants. Yet few Hondurans leave, either. Emigration to the United States is fairly low; only 114,603 foreign-born Hondurans lived in the United States in 1990.

Something else turned Honduras into an international focus of migration. Two of its neighboring nations are El Salvador and Nicaragua, lands ravaged in the 1980s by bloody civil wars. Its location thus made Honduras a sanctuary for tens of thousands of refugees fleeing their homelands. Unable to care for so many people, Honduras turned to the United States for financial assistance and to the UN High Commissioner for Refugees (UNHCR), whose office aids the 17 million global refugee population.

Honduras emerged as an important sending country but not of its own people, for thousands of refugees successfully sought asylum in the United States. More than 100,000 others remained in camps within the reluctant host country. By 1988 conditions had improved to allow the repatriation of 2,500 Salvadorans and almost 8,000 Miskito and Sumo from the Honduran Mosquito Coast. In 1989, the UNHRC was able to close two camps in western Honduras that had been in operation for 10 years by returning the remaining 8,300 Salvadoran refugees. More than 15,000 Nicaraguans, including demobilized and repatriated *contras* and their families, also returned to their homeland. After the UNHRC repatriated another 45,000 Nicaraguans in 1990, the role of Honduras as a temporary shelter for its neighbors drew to a close.

that might otherwise be automated. Although they take poor-paying jobs other U.S. workers do not want, they have a dysfunctional impact in that they tend to hold wages down. Furthermore, by condoning the existence of an underclass, legal or illegal, we undermine fundamental concepts of personal rights, equality of opportunity, and tolerance of cultural diversity.

Rapid social change is the keystone to functional analysis of existing problems. The influx of large numbers in a short period and the changing occupational structure of American society have prevented the social system from absorbing so many low-skill workers right away. How can we ease Hispanic and Caribbean newcomers into the societal mainstream? We can either take a

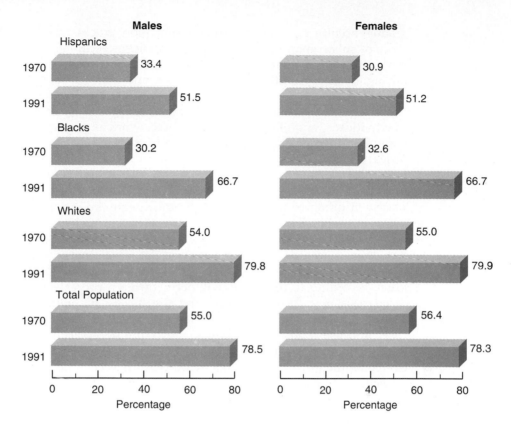

Males

Hispanics

1970 33.4

1991 51.5

Blacks

1970 30.2

1991 66.7

Whites

1970 54.0

1991 79.8

Total Population

1970 55.0

1991 78.5

0 20 40 60 80
Percentage

Females

1970 30.9

1991 51.2

1970 32.6

1991 66.7

1970 55.0

1991 79.9

1970 56.4

1991 78.3

0 20 40 60 80
Percentage

FIGURE 11.7

Hispanics, Blacks, Whites, and Total Population Aged 25 and over Who Completed Four Years of High School or More, by Percentages, 1970 and 1991

SOURCE: U.S. Bureau of the Census.

laissez faire attitude, allowing the passage of time for acculturation and economic improvement, or we can seek an interventionist means to resolve the problems. Through bilingual and other educational programs, job training programs, and business investment incentives for more job opportunities, we can improve the system to help the newcomers realize the American Dream that brought them here.

The Conflict View

Analysts of internal colonialism maintain that the continued residential segregation of Mexican Americans in ghetto areas of cities in five southwestern states is unlike the European immigrant pattern, in which the level of segregation declined with length of residence in the United States. Instead of a gradual acculturation or structural assimilation process, they see the persistence of subordination, with Mexican Americans confined to certain areas of rental properties controlled by absentee landlords and restricted to low-paying job opportunities, inferior schools, and many other forms of discrimination.

Economic exploitation is another dimension of conflict analysis. Mexicans, Puerto Ricans, and other Caribbean peoples work as migrant farm laborers in many parts under abysmal conditions for meager pay despite repeated exposés. City sweatshops—employing thousands of illegal aliens, refugees, and low-skilled legal immigrants—operate in clandestine settings, prospering from the toil of low-wage employees. The rise of an ethnic bourgeoise—the *padrino* in urban or farm settings, the token elite among the Chicano population, or the small middle class with other Hispanic and West Indian groups—only helps control the rest, say conflict theorists, and does not foretell an economic upgrading and assimilation of the remaining group members.

Resolution of the inferior status of millions of Hispanic and Haitian Americans, according to this view, will occur through protest movements, organized resistance to exploitation, and the flexing of political muscle. New citizens need to realize more fully their commonalities, take a lesson from the Irish, and use their ballot power to create the necessary changes to benefit themselves. If they effectively wield their political clout, they will begin to overcome the power differential existing in the social and economic spheres as well.

The Interactionist View

Anglo-Hispanic relations often are strained by inaccurate perceptions. Members of dominant groups tend to think of one Spanish-speaking public, when a variety exist, each preferring different foods, music, and recreation, and having different cultural attributes. Too many Anglos interpret Hispanic ethnic subcommunities, parallel social institutions, and limited command of English as being detrimental to the cohesiveness of American society, failing to realize that 83 percent are first-generation Americans repeating a resettlement pattern of earlier European immigrants. Extensive poverty among many Hispanics often generates the classic "blaming the victim" approach or culture-of-poverty thinking. Instead of confronting the problem of poor education and lack of job skills and job opportunities, some find fault with the group itself, reacting with avoidance, indifference, or paternalistic actions.

In our previous discussion about eye contact, physical proximity, the notions of hurrying, and revelance of time, we identified a few areas of potential cultural misunderstanding. Add to this Anglo impatience with language problems, black concern about economic competition, taxpayer resistance to increased welfare demands, labor union fears of wages undermined by cheap labor, and nativist alarm at the failure of the melting pot to "melt" the Hispanics, and you have further reasons for members of dominant groups to stereotype the Latinos as an increasing social problem. Because perceptions influence interaction patterns and social policy, the potential for tensions and conflict is strong. The antibilingual ordinance passed by Florida's Dade County voters in 1980 is but one illustration of people defining a situation and acting on that definition.

For Hispanics, clinging to one's culture and ethnic identity is a matter of pride and personal commitment to a rich heritage. Some find it their only solace against discrimination, and even those who achieve economic mobility retain a strong ethnic identification. Washed afresh with new waves of Hispanic immigrants, the ethnic communities retain an ethnic vitality, prompting even successful Hispanics to hold onto their ethnic traditions. Interactionists thus point to the resiliency of an ethnic self-definition, somewhat at odds with assimilationist views.

Retrospect

In many ways the Hispanic and West Indian immigrants have been repeating the patterns of earlier racial and ethnic groups. Coming in large numbers from impoverished lands, many have entered the lowest strata of society, clustered together in substandard housing units, and faced the problems of adjustment, deprivation, frustration, and pathology (sickness and crime). Marked as strangers by their language, customs, and physical appearance, they have difficulty being accepted and gaining economic security. Ironically, the Hispanic poor face the same problems and are condemned for them in the same way as earlier groups. They also are condemned for failing to overcome these problems immediately, even though other groups often took three generations to do so. Dominant-minority response patterns are thus quite similar to those of earlier immigrant peoples.

What is particularly significant for the Hispanic and West Indian immigrants in comparison to other groups is the changed structural conditions. The restrictive immigration laws in the 1920s drastically curtailed the great influx of southern, eastern, and central Europeans. This means that those immigrants already here did not receive continuous cultural reinforcement from new arrivals. Not only is there a sizable flow of new arrivals, but also rapid and inexpensive communications and transportation now encourage return trips to the not-so-far-away homeland. In addition, the earlier European immigrants encountered sometimes heavy-handed attempts at Americanization, whereas today's immigrants come at a time when pluralism and ethnic resurgence are common among members of the dominant group.

Another crucial change in structural conditions has taken place in technology and the job market. When the European poor came to America, they could find many unskilled and semiskilled jobs. There were many evils and abuses in industry, but an immigrant could secure a little piece of the American Dream through hard physical labor. The immigrant today enters a contracting labor market, not an expanding one, and so jobs are harder to find. Technology has eliminated a great many low-skill jobs and reduced the total number of blue-collar jobs, and the demand now is for skilled blue-collar and white-collar workers. The poor of the Western Hemisphere are not qualified for these positions; they find they cannot improve their lot through hard physical labor because this labor is no longer there to be found.

During the mass European migration, the fledgling labor unions struggled to improve, and eventually did improve, the economic situation of the immigrant workers. As the economy contracts, the government uses welfare as the answer to the economic problems of today's nonworking poor. In fact throughout the 1950s and 1960s the government encouraged individuals to apply for welfare by liberalizing eligibility requirements. With structural unemployment leaving no alternative, the system maneuvers many Hispanics and West Indians into dependence on welfare.

Highly visible because of their numbers, language, culture, and poverty, many find themselves the objects of resentment, hostility, and overt discrimination from the dominant society. The familiar pattern of blaming the victim results in negative stereotyping, social segregation, and all shades of prejudice and discrimination against the Hispanic or West Indian poor.

Not all are poor, of course. For those who are not, attaining economic security means a very different life experience. Other positive factors offer some promise of easing the transition to American life: bilingual education, increased public awareness, a greater tolerance for cultural pluralism, civic and governmental programs. Serious problems still remain for a disproportionate number of Hispanic and West Indian Americans, however, and it is too soon to tell whether the new legislation designed to control illegal aliens will have any impact on the Hispanic and West Indian poor.

Even if greater upward mobility occurs, this will not necessarily lead to assimilation. Many variables within both the dominant and minority societies are encouraging cultural and structural pluralism. The present-day public focus is more on eliminating the problems of poverty among culturally distinct groups than on eliminating the cultural distinctions. Just how successful these efforts will be has yet to be determined.

Review Questions

1. What are some of the cultural value orientations shared to some degree by most Hispanics?
2. What changes in American structural conditions make upward mobility difficult for many of the newcomers?
3. How diverse a group are Mexican Americans? What factors continue poverty status among so many of them?
4. What factors distinguish the Puerto Rican experience from that of other Hispanic groups?
5. How do Cubans differ in cultural values and economic mobility?
6. Who are some of the other Hispanic and Caribbean peoples migrating in significant numbers, and why are they doing so?

Suggested Readings _____

Acuña, Rodolf. *Occupied America,* 2d ed. New York: Harper & Row, 1980.

A comprehensive analysis of current Chicano problems and struggles, rooted in nineteenth-century military conquest, offering an internal colonialism approach.

Ashabranner, Brent. *The New Americans.* New York: Dodd, Mead, 1983.

Fine, sweeping study of the various Hispanic groups in the United States, with analytical data on each.

Chavez, Leo R. *Shadowed Lives: Undocumented Immigrants in American Society.* Fort Worth, TX: Harcourt Brace Jovanovich, 1992.

Profiles unskilled and skilled Mexican illegals residing in rural and urban America.

Cortés, Carlos E. (ed.). *Latinos in the United States.* New York: Arno Press, 1980.

A rich anthology of useful overviews and studies of all Latinos in Florida, Chicago, and New York City, including Dominicans and Haitians.

Fitzpatrick, Joseph P. *Puerto Rican Americans: The Meaning of Migration to the Mainland,* 2d ed. Englewood Cliffs, NJ: Prentice-Hall, 1987.

A detailed sociological portrait of Puerto Ricans, their cultural attributes, including religion and racial attitudes, and their assimilation problems.

Lewis, Oscar. *La Vida: A Puerto Rican Family in the Culture of Poverty—San Juan and New York.* New York: Random House, 1965.

Controversial yet classic case study of Puerto Rican families that argues the existence of a self-perpetuating poverty subculture.

Moore, Joan W., and Harry Pachon. *Hispanics in the United States.* Englewood Cliffs, NJ: Prentice-Hall, 1985.

A fine analysis of the values, socioeconomic characteristics, and acculturation patterns of the various Hispanic American groups.

Rodriguez, Clara E. *Puerto Ricans: Born in the U.S.A.* Boston: Unwin Hyman, 1989.

Detailed look at New York Puerto Ricans, particularly racial perceptions, education, and housing.

PART **IV**

OTHER MINORITIES

"I suffer not a woman to teach, nor to usurp authority over the man, but to be in silence."

— *I Timothy 2:12*

12

Chester Higgins, Jr./Photo Researchers

Religious Minorities

Any study of race and ethnicity must include religion as well. For some immigrant groups—German and Russian Jews or Irish and Italian Catholics, for instance—religion and ethnicity have been heavily intertwined, providing the focus for understanding both their group solidarity and initial societal hostility toward them. Sometimes the religious group itself is an ethnic group—the Amish, for example. Another aspect of intergroup relations is the unfortunate reality that religion can also generate ingroup—outgroup stereotyping, misunderstandings, and conflict, just as racial and ethnic groups sometimes do.

Religion, like race and ethnicity, often evokes an emotional response in people, sometimes more so. Many individuals find it difficult to be neutral about religion. For some it is impossible to accept the idea that religious beliefs other than their own are equally legitimate. Because religion may serve as the basis for accepting or rejecting mates, friends, neighbors, schools, and employees, it could have a polarizing effect. Religious differences not only differentiate persons but can be divisive as well, by emphasizing separateness or superiority, thereby defining others as inferior (heretics, infidels, heathens, and nonbelievers). Because religion does stir strong feelings, our previous considerations of how people respond to defined strangers become even more pertinent when we discuss religious minorities.

We are a more secular society today; religious differences no longer fan the flames of intense bigotry and acts of mob violence. We may not be torn apart like Northern Ireland or Bosnia, but to assume that religious harmony prevails throughout the land would be a mistake. Religious conflicts still occur, incorrect stereotypes still find acceptance, and religious prejudice still exists. Because of their beliefs, some religious minorities—such as the Amish and Rastafarians—encounter conflicts with the dominant society. Issues such as abortion, birth control, and school prayer continue to bring people of varying religious beliefs into conflict with one another as well. In this chapter we shall examine both past and present patterns of religious tolerance and conflict in the United States, specifically discussing some groups who have either experienced problems similar to those confronted by racial or ethnic groups discussed in previous chapters or who continue as viable religious subcultures in this pluralistic society. This emphasis means we shall not look at other religions that, even if larger, do not represent religioethnic configurations and minority group status.

SOCIOHISTORICAL PERSPECTIVE _____

Since the time of the Pilgrims, this nation has been the haven for many religious groups fleeing persecution and seeking religious freedom. Some instances of religious intolerance did occur during colonial times though, such as the expulsion of Anne Hutchinson and Roger Williams and their followers from Massachusetts and the denial of political office-holding to Catholics in Maryland. As the isolated settlements, many of a single religious persuasion, evolved into interactive colonies, Anglo-Saxon Protestantism dominated. Nevertheless, the Founding Fathers built into the Constitution two fundamental principles: separation of church and state, and freedom of religion. Those two hallmarks bestowed a unique legacy on American culture that continues to the present day. Unlike most nations, in which one or a few faiths dominate, the United States has an immense diversity of faiths. Over 1,500 religious groups exist, 200 of which are conventional Christian and Jewish denominations, 24 of which have a membership exceeding 1 million.[1]

What is notable about so many immigrant groups is the significance religion has played in their lives. The church, synagogue, or temple so often became the major social institution of their ethnic communities, functioning both as a spiritual bond reinforcing group identity and as the social, educational, even political base of their activities. Harvard University—founded in 1630—illustrates an early effort to educate clergy to minister to the spiritual needs of the people. Visits to various New England towns reveal a church prominently situated by the village green, in the center of the community, the place in which town meetings brought participatory democracy to reality. Similarly, in the remnants of white ethnic neighborhoods in Northern cities, in Midwestern farming communities, in the Southwestern states, and in specific places such as St. Augustine, Florida, or New Orleans, the still-standing religious edifices and recorded ethnic community histories and studies offer abundant testimony to the role religion played among first- and second-generation Americans.

The clergy have always provided important leadership among racial and ethnic groups. In addition to spiritual guidance, they often have provided the rallying force to enhance community cohesiveness and economic and social welfare, while advocating to the host society improved circumstances for their people. Priests, rabbis, and ministers frequently have been in the forefront of concerted efforts to ease immigrant transition to American life and their entry into the economic mainstream. Black ministers, such as Martin Luther King and Jesse Jackson, have consistently been in the vanguard for civil rights and equality. Religious leaders throughout American history have played an important role not only in shaping the values and moral behavior of their congregations but in influencing public policy, encouraging charitable activities, and implementing the spirit of the Constitution.

Unfortunately, not all religious leaders have been magnanimous in promoting equality, nor have all religions experienced tolerance in the American experience. Some—Catholics, Jews, and Mormons—have been victims of discrimination, persecution, and even violence. Others—Amish, Christian Scientists, Jehovah's Witnesses, and Rastafarians—have come into conflict with society over their religious beliefs. Even though the ideal culture stresses freedom of religion, in practice religious bigotry and intolerance have caused suffering and hardship to some religious minorities in the United States.

CATHOLIC AMERICANS

Catholicism did not gain easy acceptance in the United States. By the mid-seventeenth century, all the colonies had passed laws designed to thwart Catholic immigration, most of them denying Catholics citizenship, voting, and office-holding rights.[2] Until 1830 the nation remained almost exclusively a Protestant domain. For the next 30 years immigration had a profound political and social impact on the nation. Over a half-million immigrants in the 1830s, 1.7 million in the 1840s, and 2.6 million in the 1850s—the great bulk of them Roman Catholics, mostly Irish and German peasants—entered the country. A feeling of alarm spread among Protestant Americans, who believed that Catholics would subvert the nation.

Societal Hostility

Samuel F. B. Morse, inventor of the telegraph and son of a militant minister, railed against an alleged papist conspiracy to overwhelm the nation with Catholic immigrants and take control. He exhorted Americans not to be "deceived by Jesuit-controlled immigrants." Instead they should "fly to protect the vulnerable places of your Constitution and Laws. Place your guards; you will need them, and quickly too.—And first, shut your gates."[3]

Lurid, best-selling exposés of the Catholic Church appeared. Rebecca Reed fabricated a story about her life in a convent in Charlestown, Massachusetts, that resulted in the burning of that Ursuline Convent in 1834. Two years later the most infamous of these inflammatory works appeared: *Awful Disclosures of the Hotel Dieu Nunnery of Montreal* by Maria Monk. The author claimed to be an escaped nun who had been kept prisoner in the Montreal convent against her will and forced to have sexual relations with priests. Resisting nuns were killed, as were any babies born; all bodies were thrown into a lime pit. Even though Maria Monk was later discredited as a prostitute and fraud when investigations uncovered no evidence to support her charges, many believed her story. The monograph was frequently reprinted, selling hundreds of thousands of copies and spawning a sequel and many imitators.

Throughout the 1850s nativist hostility against Catholics intensified, with the Know-Nothing movement spearheading most of the agitation. Not unexpectedly, violence erupted. Mobs rioted, burning Catholic churches, schools, convents, and homes. One particularly effective diatribe against Catholics was Josiah Strong's *Our Country* (1855), which accused Catholic immigrants of immorality, crime, corruption, and socialism. Reprinted in numerous editions, it incited the public for decades. The Reverend Justin H. Fulton was also effective, his anti-Catholic books *Rome in America* (1887) and *Washington in the Lap of Rome* (1888) claiming that there was a Catholic threat to America's liberty through the school system and control of the government. Another Maria Monk type, Margaret Lisle Shepherd, published her autobiography, *My Life in a Convent* (1887), claiming to be an escaped nun who fled priests' carnal lust. Her story, although false, was widely believed and added to the anti-Catholic chorus.

In 1887 a short-lived but highly successful anti-Catholic organization, the American Protective Association (APA), emerged out of Iowa to become a national force of about 500,000 members.[4] Dedicated to keeping Catholics out of office, employing only Protestants, and being noncooperative with Catholics in any strikes, the APA struck a responsive chord with many working-class Americans believing Catholic immigrants were coming to take their jobs,

"The Attack on the Outer Ramparts—First the House of Refuge—then the Public Schools—then the Constitution." The ramparts guard the non-sectarian institutions seen under attack by the Roman Catholic Church, led by Irish priests (the Irish vote is represented by the flag: in *hoc signo vinces*). From the left, those guarding the ramparts and repulsing the priestly attack are *Puck,* the *New York Times,* the *New York Evening Post,* and the *New York Herald.* (Source: Joseph Keppler, Puck, April 22, 1885.) *(The Distorted Image/Courtesy Anti-Defamation League of B'Nai Brith)*

particularly after the panic of 1893 and the ensuing unemployment. Enjoying some success in the East and none in the South, the APA was most successful throughout the Midwest. Although its endorsed candidates gained control of city governments in Detroit, Kansas City, and Milwaukee, resulting in the firing of all Catholic officials in those cities, the APA sowed the seeds of its own destruction. Internecine fighting, charges of corruption, and embezzlement of funds, and a violent reputation combined to bring a rapid decline of the APA so that it had no power after 1896.[5]

Anti-Catholicism did not end, however. In 1911 General Nelson Miles, former Army Chief of Staff and Congressional Medal of Honor recipient, organized the Guardians of Liberty in upstate New York. Dedicated to keeping Catholics out of office because they would supposedly take their orders from Rome, this group never did have any real political clout. An anti-Catholic publication, *The Menace,* developed over 1.5 million readers, mostly rural. The Catholic Church lost its lawsuit to revoke *The Menace*'s mailing privileges on the grounds of obscenity because of its graphic depictions of the alleged immorality of the Catholic Church.[6] A total of 61 anti-Catholic periodicals appeared prior to World War I.[7]

The post–World War I period saw the resurrection of the Ku Klux Klan, dedicated to the theme of Catholicism and Judaism as alien to Americanism. As discussed more fully in Chapter 6, the KKK grew to a membership of 2 to 3 million members and was partly responsible for passage of the restrictive immigration laws of 1921 and 1924. Thereafter it declined in numbers and influence, its final hurrah a slanderous campaign in 1928 against Democratic presidential candidate, Al Smith, the Catholic governor of New York.

Values and Practices

Several factors help explain nativist hostility against American Catholics in past years. We must first remember that religion played a far greater role in people's lives in previous centuries, making religious differences of greater concern. Generations of Catholic–Protestant conflict in Europe had formed a legacy of latent antagonism among European Americans. American Protestantism had evolved along with the American culture, stressing individualism and self-reliance, whether in making one's fortune or gaining salvation through the teachings of the Bible. Several of the parallel social institutions of Catholics provided ammunition for Protestant attack and anxiety.

Religion

Because Catholics followed church dogma, or prescribed doctrine, operating their local churches as part of a vast bureaucracy with a hierarchy of authority reaching back to the pope in Rome as the head of the church, many Protestants feared this structure would undermine the American way of life. They envisioned millions of Catholic immigrants marching to the orders of a foreign potentate (the pope), as unthinking, indoctrinated, docile followers; if such people gained political office, some Protestants feared control of the country from Rome. The physical presence of priests and nuns, the building of churches, convents, and parochial schools—all virtually nonexistent in the United States before—served to confirm the worst Protestant fears.

Other Catholic practices puzzled and disturbed many Protestant Americans. They considered vows of celibacy among priests and nuns as unnatural, which led many Protestants to believe the lurid fabrications that were printed about the sexual practices within the religious orders and the priesthood. Mandatory attendance at the weekly repetition of the same mass ceremony, then spoken in Latin, seemed to them both un-American and repressive of individual thought. Use of a private confessional booth to tell one's sins to a priest, unlike the usual Protestant practice of silent confession during worship services, seemed bizarre to some. Although Catholics themselves understood and accepted the context of their own beliefs and practices, to Protestants these outgroup differences were not only strange but threatening.

Education

Perhaps more than anything else, Catholic education generated the most conflict between Catholics and Protestants. In public schools daily reading from the King James Bible was one of several factors prompting Catholics to establish parochial schools in order to provide religious training and moral guidance for their children. Efforts in the 1840s to obtain public funding for parochial schools, or substitution of the Catholic version of the Bible for Catholic students in public schools, generated fierce controversy in Boston, New York, Philadelphia, and Cincinnati.[8] The issue of public funding for parochial schools flared up again in the 1870s, but the opposition of President Grant and the Republican party negated any organized nativist opposition. Efforts in the 1880s in Massachusetts and several Midwestern states (Ohio, Illinois, and Wisconsin) to regulate parochial schools generated intense controversy.[9] Throughout this period Protestant periodicals argued that the public school system would end the "ignorance and superstition" of Catholic children, and so campaigned not only against public funding of parochial schools but for their elimination.[10]

The Present Scene

Today Roman Catholics in the United States number over 57 million, the largest single religious denomination in the country. Overt discrimination against them has ended, and except for recent Haitian and Hispanic Catholic immigrants, they are assimilated into the economic and political mainstream. They can be found in all occupations and in many leadership roles. John F. Kennedy became the first Catholic president in 1960, and in Congress Catholics rank first among the denominations of our national legislators.

Greater dialogue occurs between Protestant and Catholic religious leaders, an outgrowth of the ecumenical movement initiated by Pope John XXIII over two decades ago. An acute shortage of priests has obliged the laity to become more active: reading scripture, leading music, and distributing communion at services, and taking leadership positions in nearly every phase of the church's life: religious instruction, family life bureaus, and financial and administrative positions. With both men and women handling these church tasks, Catholics have in some ways become more like several Protestant denominations and thus less "different" to outsiders. Catholic social views tend to agree with those of conservative Protestants in regard to a variety of subjects, including pornography, abortion, birth control, and school prayer. Perhaps the best evidence of greater religious and ethnic tolerance, however, lies in the rise in Catholic–Protestant intermarriages. From about 18 percent in the 1920s, the Catholic intermarriage rate had increased to approximately 40 percent by 1990.[11]

Problem areas still remain. Public funding for parochial schools remains a controversial subject and has been consistently rejected by Congress. Surveys show as many as 85 percent of Catholic Americans reject church teaching on birth control, dividing about equally on the anti-abortion position of the church. A growing shortage of priests, partly due to the celibacy requirement, is another serious concern.

JEWISH AMERICANS

Jewish people are a unique minority because they are not a specific nationality, racial, ethnic, or even religious grouping. Although religion has been an important bond among Jews, it is not a cohesive force in that three separate branches of Judaism exist—Orthodox, Conservative, and Reform; many agnostics and atheists also identify themselves as Jews. Varying in physical appearance, native languages, and cultural attributes, Jewishness is that elusive quality Franklin Giddings called "consciousness of kind." Jews are people who think of themselves as such, with outgroup members treating them accordingly. In 1946 Jean-Paul Sartre wrote that a Jew is someone whom other people identify as a Jew. Among conservative factions within Judaism, however, Jewish identity is limited only to those who are born of a Jewish mother or who are converts.

Immigration Before 1880

The first group of Jewish immigrants—four men, six women, and 13 younger people—arrived in New Amsterdam in 1654 as refugees from the Portuguese takeover of Dutch-ruled Brazil. Benefiting from tolerant Dutch rule, Jews experienced open acceptance in this settlement. Later many Jewish refugees of Spanish and Portuguese origin, fleeing the Spanish Inquisition, came to the United States by way of Holland, the West Indies, or South America. By the end of the eighteenth century, about 2,000 to 3,000 Sephardic Jews were living in America.[12]

Most of our earlier comments about nativist hostility against Catholics apply equally well to Jewish immigrants. All the English colonies discouraged Jewish immigration, also passing statutes against their voting or holding office. When Jews were permitted to vote in New York in 1736, a group of residents claimed the election was fraudulent on that basis.[13] When the Know-Nothing movement reached its height in the 1850s, the Know-Nothings criticized and discriminated against "this peculiar race of people."[14] During the Civil War former Know-Nothing member Ulysses S. Grant, acting on unwarranted charges that Jews were profiteering through smuggling and cotton speculation, issued General Order Number 11, expelling all civilian Jews from his military jurisdiction.[15] On January 4, 1863, Lincoln revoked this order.

By the mid-nineteenth century the second wave of Jewish migration had begun. These Ashkenazic Jews came mostly from the German provinces; they were more prosperous and better educated than earlier German Jewish immigrants. This was the first mass Jewish immigration—groups of entire families from a single locality or community. From an 1840 Jewish population of 15,000 Jewish Americans increased to 50,000 in 1850, 150,000 in 1860, and 250,000 in 1880. By that time, Jewish American communities were almost exclusively German communities.

Newcomers and Tension

The third wave was the most significant—in numbers, cultural influence, work contributions, and dominant-group reaction. From 250,000 in 1880 the Jewish population rose to almost 3 million before generally restrictive immigration laws were enacted in the 1920s. The initial impetus for this massive migration was the pogrom that followed the assassination of Czar Alexander II (1881). Although no Jews were involved in the regicide, the czarist government used them as a scapegoat to divert people's attention from long-festering social, political, and economic grievances. This marked the beginning of a long series of pogroms, with many attacks, loss of lives, and extensive property damage in Jewish communities throughout the Russian Empire's Pale of Settlement. In addition to the need to escape government-incited violence, there were powerful economic incentives for emigration. Some people came to escape destitution. Others fled from economic instability that resulted from government efforts to industralize Russia.

Considerable cultural tensions developed among Jews from the different areas of Europe. Some Sephardic Jews, the first to be transplanted to America, considered themselves superior to German Jewish newcomers (Ashkenazic), who later looked with disdain on newcomers from eastern Europe. Although a few Jewish immigrants from central and eastern Europe had arrived as early as the eighteenth century, for some Jewish ethnics the distinctions based on place of origin and time of arrival in America persisted well into the mid-1940s, as this report indicates:

The earlier arrivals scarred the later ones as crude, superstitious, and economically indigent, and the latter despised the former as snobs and religious renegades. As recently as 1925, one student of immigrant groups asserted that "intermarriage between a Sephardic Jew and a Russian Jew, for instance, is as rare, if not rarer, than intermarriage between Jew and Gentile." Even within each of these divisions of Jews there was at first aversion to marriage with some of the subdivisions. Bavarian Jews hesitated to marry with those German Jews who came from the area near the Polish border, derisively labelled "Pollacks." The Russian Jew looked down on the Polish and Galician Jews and refused to marry them or permit his children to do so. Although these intra-Jewish barriers to marriage have largely disappeared in recent times, first generation Jewish parents may still go through the motions of embarrassment when their children marry the sons and daughters of a ridiculed sub-group.[16]

Thus ethnic prejudices as well as cultural and class differences led to strain between the "old" Jewish population and the "new" Jewish arrivals. Some German Jews, who had by this time supplanted the Sephardic Jews as an ethnic elite, were embarrassed by their lowly co-religionists with their strange appearance, Yiddish language, and orthodox religious practices. At first, many rejected the new arrivals, partly out of fear that growing anti-Semitic feeling in American society would place all Jews—old and new—into one negative category. Soon, however, the established community developed organizations that helped the newcomers adjust to their surroundings. Additionally, they made strenuous efforts to settle the newcomers in widely dispersed farm communities, away from the congested urban centers.[17]

Anti-Semitism

Anti-Jewish stereotyping spread in the arts and the media as it had for other immigrant groups, such as the Irish and Asians. On stage the Jew was sometimes depicted as either a scoundrel or a comic character. Newspapers and magazines at times ran cartoons and editorials that were clearly anti-Semitic in nature. One example was *Life* magazine, published in New York City, where the Jewish population rose from 4 percent in 1880 to 25 percent in 1910. The magazine called the city "Jew York" and attacked the ostensible Jewish clannishness, pushiness, and domination of the theater. In the early twentieth century about half of the actors, songwriters, publishers, and entrepreneurs in New York City were Jewish; this included those who worked in the flourishing Yiddish-language theater serving the immigrant community. *Life*'s editors launched a 10-year attack on the "Jewish Theatrical Trust," accusing it of poisoning American values, of lowering the moral tone by running lascivious plays for profit. The accusations were false or distorted. The Yiddish theater may have catered to a specific ethnic group and thus was "different," but the plays were not lewd or lascivious.

Two notorious incidents emphasize the heights anti-Semitic feelings reached in the late nineteenth and early twentieth centuries. In the first instance Joseph Seligman, an eminent banker and frequent guest of President

Grant at the White House (and who declined an offer to be Secretary of the Treasury), was denied accommodations in 1877 at a fashionable resort hotel in Saratoga Springs, New York. Although he and his family had stayed there several times before, the hotel's new policy of "not accepting Israelites" made headlines across the country. This incident brought latent anti-Jewish attitudes into the open, and many other establishments quickly followed suit.

The second incident concerned Leo Frank, the manager of an Atlanta pencil factory, who was hastily convicted on very flimsy evidence of murdering a young factory girl. Many felt that he was convicted because he was a Jew. His case in 1913 led directly to the formation of the B'nai B'rith's Anti-Defamation League. With prominent Georgia newspapers and clergymen calling for a new trial and many Jews financing his appeal, anti-Semitic feelings intensified in the state. When the governor commuted Frank's execution to life imprisonment, an act praised by the Georgia press, some of the dead girl's friends and neighbors abducted Frank from the state prison, transported him 175 miles to the girl's hometown, and lynched him.

It was more than a local episode. The nationwide press coverage of the incident included comments about racial nationalism and antagonism toward the "Parasite Race." Anti-Semitism of varying intensity has continued to the present day. It ebbed in the 1920s and flourished again during the Depression. The Silver Shirts, led by William Pelley, and the National Union for Social Justice, headed by the "radio priest," Father Charles Coughlin, were two of the most active movements against the Jews in the late 1930s. Anti-Semitic behavior has declined since World War II, in part because of revulsion against Nazi genocide and in part because pluralism has become more generally accepted. Incidents still occur at rare intervals, mostly acts of vandalism or desecration. Some analysts suggest that the roots of anti-Semitism can be found in the teachings of Christianity (now renounced in the Catholic Church by Vatican II), which had blamed the Jews for the death of Christ.[18] Latent anti-Semitism may manifest itself for many reasons, such as status or economic rivalries.

In recent years researchers have found mixed patterns regarding anti-Semitism. In 1987, for example, the American Jewish Committee (AJC) recorded more than 1000 anti-Semitic incidents in the United States.[19] Yet in 1992 the National Opinion Research Center, in an analytical study commissioned by the AJC, found a significant decline in anti-Semitic attitudes in comparison to previous national studies dating back to 1958.[20]

Upward Mobility

Like other "new" immigrants many of the East European Jews who came here were very poor. Most thus settled in great numbers in the large cities that were ports of entry (Boston, New York, and Philadelphia). A great many went to work in the garment industry, while others became street peddlers until they saved enough capital to open their own stores. Since two-thirds of the Jewish male immigrants were skilled workers, compared with an average of

---

BOX 12.1   THE ETHNIC EXPERIENCE

"One night someone broke my store window and took out some leather hats and shirts [1950]. They caught three boys and they called me up at home in the middle of the night and said we have to go right away to the store to fix the window and then go to the police station. So, naturally, it was a big shock for us and we went to the store.

"Then we went to the police station. We came there and the captain said, 'You have to press charges.' So we said, 'We don't want to press charges. If they're young boys, if it's the first or second time, give them a warning and let them go.' Then came a sergeant and he said that these boys already have been in many troubles, and they wouldn't let me not press charges. So I did.

"I had to go next day to court. There were the hats there and the shirts and so on. I went maybe four-five times and nothing happened. Once, one boy was missing. Next time the other boys were missing and so on. I went maybe six times more and I explained to the judge, 'Mister Judge, please, I gave all my answers what you need.' And I said to the Assistant District Attorney, 'Please, will you tell the judge that I am an only storekeeper. I am only one in the store and I have to close up always the store and so on.' And he told the story, what I said, to the judge.

"And you know what the judge answered me? 'You go back to your government, to your country where you came, if you don't like the laws of this country!'

"So I started to cry, because in front of these thieves, in front of the old people in the room, he said it to me. This I call really prejudice, very bad prejudice."

SOURCE: Czechoslovakian Jewish immigrant who came to the United States in 1948 at age 31. (He was the sole survivor of his family of the Holocaust.)

---

20 percent of the males from other immigrant groups, their absorption into the American economy was eased somewhat.[21] Many social scientists cite this immigrant group as one that climbed the socioeconomic ladder more quickly and more widely than most other groups, although prejudices have limited their ascent to middle-management positions.[22]

Several cultural factors have contributed to the success of some first- and many second-generation Jewish Americans. First, because of discrimination in Europe, they had been relegated to such self-sustaining occupations as merchant, scholar, and self-employed artisan. Thus they brought with them skills and knowledge useful in an industrial society, together with values that encouraged deferred gratification, seriousness of purpose, patience, and perseverance—precisely those virtues stressed by the Protestant Ethic of middle-class America. Second, during the period of great immigration, 1880 to 1920, most Jews came here along with members of their families; in many

| BOX 12.2 | THE ETHNIC EXPERIENCE |

"I heard a lot about the streets in America being paved with gold but I knew one thing, because I came in contact with GI's and I saw they came from different backgrounds in different parts of the country, and I knew one thing—that I was going to have to work in the United States. People didn't actually still say the streets were paved with gold, but this was still the belief in Europe because, you know, the dollar was the Almighty. In Europe you could buy five-six times with the dollar what you could buy in the United States. So this was why people still believed the streets were paved with gold. All what you needed was a shovel. But I knew. I was prepared. I never was disappointed in coming here to the United States.

"What is to me the American Dream? To some people maybe it's a bigger car or a bigger house. This is their dream. Take more vacations. Sure, we need vacations, but I think our way of life should be to practice just what we preach, just what we have in our Constitution. I mean, not to discriminate against people of all kinds, because this country—if it really is a melting pot—for this one reason, because it is so great this country, because from so many countries, the idea can be put together."

SOURCE: Polish Jewish immigrant who came to the United States in 1948 at age 35.

other ethnic groups males usually came first and then either returned to the old country or else sent for their families.[23] Jews had traditionally placed a heavy emphasis on family responsibility, and having the entire family unit together from the outset gave them greater emotional stability and an advantage in cooperative efforts to start a new life. Sometimes the immigrant experience produced emotional and psychological strain within families, however. Third was the Jewish people's traditional emphasis on learning—especially for boys. Even if the children were illiterate in the language of their country of origin, and this was less often true than with many other immigrant groups, they had learned Hebrew and, as a result, the discipline of study. By the time he was 13, a Jewish boy, if raised in a religious family, was prepared to read from the Torah for his bar mitzvah. Today, a large number of Jewish girls also participate in this ceremony (called bat mitzvah, for girls). Within the Jewish culture this positive orientation toward learning carried over to American public education and secular studies. While parents toiled in low-status factory jobs, they were encouraging their children to further their education and then enter the professions. The high percentage of Jewish youth attending public and private colleges in the first few decades of the twentieth century is all the more remarkable because of their limited residency in the United States and because most Americans placed less emphasis on a college education in those times.[24]

Gordon reports that by the 1940s the occupational distribution of Jews was comparable to that of members of high-status Protestant denominations.[25] Yet Jews have been significantly underrepresented in some industries, such as steel, oil, banking, and insurance. Not all experienced upward mobility. Thousands of Jewish poor, especially the aged, exist on a level far from the stereotyped portrait of the successful Jews.

Social Interaction

Social ostracism often accompanied the economic successes of the Jewish people. Higher economic status did not necessarily mean a comparable increase in social prestige. Even when Jews gained positions with higher levels of income, they still found themselves excluded from social and recreational clubs and were forced to establish parallel social and recreational organizations for themselves. They also encountered restrictions in housing; admissions quotas for colleges, universities, and professional schools; and other obstacles designed to keep them at a social, economic, and educational distance from white Protestants.

Although many Jewish middle-class families moved to the suburbs after World War II, in keeping with a trend in the larger society, many social scientists reported continuing social segregation in the 1950s and 1960s. Social distance is sometimes measured by the degree of primary relationships between Jews and Gentiles. In his Detroit study Gerhard Lenski found that the frequency of close associations between the two groups declined after adolescence, particularly at the time of choosing a mate.[26] In his study of Elmira, John P. Dean found that approximately 75 percent of his Jewish sample socialized occasionally with their closest non-Jewish friends, but few were regular participants in a mixed social clique.[27] Herbert J. Gans reported that the Jewish suburban housewives of Park Forest, outside of Chicago, participated in daytime social activities of the entire neighborhood, but that in the evening and on weekends their social relationships were confined to other Jews.[28] Albert Gordon suggested that this pattern of relative isolation in suburban evening or weekend social gatherings was fairly common and not necessarily a voluntary choice.[29] Milton Gordon, echoing the concept of the triple melting pot,[30] suggested that Catholics, Protestants, and Jews all tend to interact in meaningful primary relationships with members of their own religioethnic group.[31]

In the 1990s that observation seems less true. A major study commissioned by the Council of Jewish Federations (CJF) revealed that interfaith marriages among American Jews had increased from 9 percent in 1964 to 52 percent by 1990.[32] Although some experts argue that religious intermarriage does not reflect values emphasizing assimilation, others agree with Gordon that increased intermarriage is one of the final stages of assimilation.[33] At the very least, such a pattern reveals a significant increase in meaningful primary relationships between Gentiles and Jews.

A more significant finding from the CJF study was that only 28 percent of the children of mixed marriages are brought up as Jews, 31 percent are reared in no religion at all, and 41 percent are reared in another faith or in an amalgam of Judaism and other beliefs.[34] This gloomy finding, coupled with a low birthrate and immigration, has led Jewish traditionalists to be fearful about the future of American Judaism, with predictions of the Jewish American population dropping by over 1 million from its present 5.9 million.[35] Others lament that intermarriage will mean more divorces, alcoholism, and family violence than in past all-Jewish families.[36] Jewish sociologists and modernists are more optimistic, seeing the Jewish community in America as a cohesive and dynamic source of networks and resources maintained by the forces of social structure, thereby ensuring its continued vitality.[37]

Jewish Identity

Among the large numbers of Jewish immigrants in the late nineteenth and early twentieth centuries, the synagogue played a significant role in their community structure. At the same time, it had to compete with a variety of cultural, ideological, and self-help organizations supported by many Jews.

This interfaith marriage between a Filipino American and a Jewish American shows marital assimilation in racial, ethnic, and religious terms. A Council of Jewish Federations study revealed that by 1990 Jewish interfaith marriages had reached 52 percent, and the children in these marriages were not being raised in the Jewish faith. *(Joel Gordon)*

Classes offered by organizations such as the Educational Alliance on New York's Lower East Side provided opportunities for acculturation. Together the synagogues and organizations served as cohesive bonds, laying the foundation for community organization, social activities, and a feeling of belonging.[38]

As Jews became more highly educated and assimilated, the ethnicity that had closely secured European immigrants to their religious traditions lost its hold. New focal points of Jewish identity became building and supporting the nation of Israel, as well as politics and social concerns within the United States. Many Jewish Americans today see religion less as an inherited ethnic identity and more as a personal choice of belief and practice.[39] Jewish survey data show that only 20 percent of American Jews (half of them Orthodox) are seriously religious.[40] Affixed to their Jewishness in cultural terms but secular in their beliefs, such people are more likely to intermarry and assimilate. It is to them that rabbis and leaders in the Reform branch of Judaism have been reaching out in an effort to maintain the Jewish community. Yet rabbis and leaders in the more traditional Conservative and Orthodox branches view welcoming interfaith couples as diluting Judaism. This emotional issue continues as both groups struggle to ensure the survival of American Jewry and somehow maintain the integrity of Jewish thought, values, and institutions.

Recent Immigrants

Partly counterbalancing fears of a decline in the Jewish American population has been a renewed influx of immigrants and refugees in recent years. Since 1971 over 85,000 Israelis have migrated to the United States. In just three years, 1988 to 1990, approximately 109,000 Soviet Jewish refugees entered the country.[41] The most favored settlement areas have been the New York and Los Angeles metropolitan regions. Jewish Americans now number about 5.9 million.

THE MORMONS

The Church of Jesus Christ of Latter-Day Saints (LDS) offers a fascinating portrait of a religious group evolving from a despised and persecuted people to a highly successful and respected church. As we shall discuss, they are unique as a minority group because their principal migration was to leave the United States. Their resettlement in the Rocky Mountains in the 1840s gave them an enduring sense of territoriality and shared tradition.[42]

The Early Years

By his own account, at age 18 Joseph Smith received the first of several visitations from the angel Moroni, who guided him to a hidden stack of golden plates, each eight inches square.[43] Aided by two stones called the Urim and Thummin, Joseph Smith translated the hieroglyphics into the *Book of Mormon,* a massive and controversial work. Mormons believe it to be the true word of God, providing the foundation of their faith. Two years after translating the book in 1830, Joseph Smith—now 25 years old—founded the Mormon faith in the western New York State region in which he then lived. Within a year the church had over 1,000 members.

As the church continued to grow rapidly under the charismatic leadership of Joseph Smith, it attracted enemies. Fleeing harassment in New York and then Ohio, the Mormons resettled in Missouri, incurring further hostility because of their antislavery views, growing political power, and cooperative communities seen as threatening by their more individualistically oriented neighbors on the sparsely settled frontier.[44] Expelled by the governor in 1838, the Mormons moved to Illinois, where they would face their worst clashes. By now their encouragement of plural marriage, together with their growing numbers and strength, inflamed societal hostility into frequent acts of violence. When Joseph Smith and his brother, Hyrum, were murdered in 1844 by a mob storming the jail in which they had been incarcerated, further violence ensued. Raids, pitched battles, burned homes and temples, rape of Mormon women, even artillery pieces used by both sides brought Mormon existence to a crisis stage.

Facing extermination or forced assimilation, most of the Mormons—under the leadership of Brigham Young—migrated westward until they reached the

Hostility against the Mormons was quite severe from 1830 to 1847, prompting frequent acts of violence and murder. On October 30, 1838, two hundred militiamen—urged by Governor Lilburn Boggs of Missouri to exterminate or drive the Mormons from the state "for the public good"—attacked the Mormons at member Jacob Haun's flour mill. They left fifteen wounded and seventeen dead, including a nine-year-old boy deliberately shot through the head because one trooper feared that "nits will make lice." *(Culver Pictures, Inc.)*

Great Salt Lake Valley in 1847. Intergroup conflict had strengthened their group identity and cohesiveness, and now the Mormons experienced steady and rapid growth in the isolated Salt Lake region.[45] Part of this growth was due to the arrival throughout the nineteenth century of tens of thousands of converts from England and Scandinavia. The discovery of gold in California ended Mormon isolation, however, because they were located along the best route to the California gold fields.

Mormon scholars Bruce Campbell and Eugene Campbell suggest that Mormon theocratic political power apparently threatened federal control of the Utah territory and thus control of the route to California, generating several decades of government attempts to alter Mormon economic, political, and social institutions.[46] One instance was President Buchanan's sending troops to Utah in 1857 to force the replacement of Brigham Young as territorial governor with a non-Mormon. An actual short war followed in which over 100 people were killed, with the Mormons prevailing and Young remaining as governor.

Government efforts next shifted to an attack on polygyny, the Mormon practice of men having more than one wife. Although permitted by church doctrine, polygyny occurred among only 10 to 15 percent of the eligible males, two-thirds of whom had one additional wife.[47] Lurid newspaper stories about alleged Mormon depravity inflamed public opinion and created a stereotype of Mormon males as evil, seductive, promiscuous, sexually virile libertines. Non-Mormon opportunists produced such products as Brigham Young Tablets and Mormon Bishop Pills that were supposedly able to increase sexual desire or ability.[48] In 1862 Lincoln signed the Morill Act, forbidding bigamy in U.S. territories. Continually harassed by federal agents after the Civil War, the Mormons challenged the law as an infringement on their religious freedom. In 1878 the U.S. Supreme Court ruled in *Reynolds v. United States* that the law was constitutional.

Unable to gain access to church records to prove the multiple marriages, the government passed a new law in 1882 against anyone living in "lewd cohabitation," effectively sending hundreds of Mormon polygamists to jail. In 1887 the Edmunds-Tucker Act dissolved the Mormon Church as a legal entity and provided for the confiscation of church property. When this law was upheld by the Supreme Court in 1890 as constitutional also, church president Wilford Woodruff's Manifesto ended the open practice of plural marriage. President Benjamin Harrison then granted a pardon to all imprisoned polygamists. In 1896 Utah was permitted to become a state, beginning a new era of relations between Christians and Mormons.

Values and Practices

Following the behavioral code set by Joseph Smith, whom they believe was a prophet of God, Mormons do not smoke or drink any form of alcoholic beverages, coffee, tea, or carbonated beverages. Emphasis is on group rather than individual activities so that group identification is promoted. Especially encouraged are any of the performing arts, team sports, or organized recreational activities. Other aspects of the Mormon faith, as described below, are deeply embedded in their social institutions.

Family

Mormons place heavy emphasis on the family, both as the primary agent for socializing people into the Mormon belief system and as the basic social organization in the eternal Kingdom of God.[49] Anything undermining family growth or stability is discouraged; for example, premarital or extramarital sex, indecent language, immodest behavior, abortion, birth control, intermarriage, and divorce. Among active, observing Mormons these problems occur far less often than among those who are less religiously involved. Drugs and premarital sex are a problem among Mormon teenagers and young adults, although to a lesser degree than the national average, particularly among active Mormons.[50]

Unlike typical American families in which each person pursues individual interests and activities, Mormon families do many things together. Monday is set aside as home family night, and entire families attend other social and sporting events with the emphasis on the intermingling of different age groups. The extended-family-kinship network manifests itself in annual summer reunions and in the search for dead ancestors to secure for the ancestors a proxy baptism or sealing ceremony in a Mormon temple to allow them into God's presence in the Celestial World. Through the Mormon Genealogical Society more than 10 billion names have been preserved on microfilm—from vital statistics, census materials, church records, and other official records. This extensive collection is increased every year and is available free of charge to Mormons and non-Mormons alike for genealogical investigation.

Education

Following Joseph Smith's revelation in 1833 about intelligence being the glory of God, Mormons place great stress on education. Mormons founded both the University of Utah (the oldest university west of the Mississippi) and Brigham Young University (the nation's largest church-related university with almost 25,000 students enrolled). Utah leads the nation in literacy and in the percentage of enrolled college students and college graduates.[51]

Religion

A vigorous and systematic missionary program brings in about 80,000 converts annually.[52] About 50,000 young missionaries, aged 19 to 22, are in the field at any given time, fulfilling a cherished two-year assignment. Mormon world membership is nearly 9 million, more than the Episcopal and Presbyterian churches combined, two pillars of the American religious establishment. Their 4.5 million American membership makes the Mormons the sixth largest religious body in the United States.[53] Another significant factor in the spectacular growth of the Mormon Church is their practice of tithing, giving 10 percent of their gross income to the church. Income from tithing supports the missionary program and the operational costs of Brigham Young University, where tuition costs were only about $1,800 annually for church members in 1992. The spectacular growth in membership means that soon Americans will comprise the minority segment of this worldwide major faith.

Economics

Mormons take care of their own poor, without public welfare assistance. Each stake (a district comparable to a Catholic diocese) operates either a farm, ranch, orchard, cannery, or factory producing goods through donated labor. Through a national exchange program to 150 bishops' storehouses resembling small supermarkets, the Mormon poor receive their needed foodstuffs. Other items—clothing, toiletries, and household items—are also available there, provided through monthly cash donations of other Mormons.

The Mormon Church is possibly the richest church in the world, with daily revenues of about $12.8 million.[54] In addition to its income from tithing, it includes a wide variety of investments, totaling over $10 billion:

> The Mormon Church owns some of the choicest hotels and motels in the West. It owns department stores, insurance companies, radio and television stations, and a newspaper. It has vast real estate holdings, both in the United States and abroad. It owns skyscrapers in such diverse places as Salt Lake City and New York City.
>
> LDS also has a major interest in the United States beet sugar industry. It owns 700,000 acres of Florida ranchland, which means that the church is probably the largest landowner in the state. Additionally, LDS has 100,000 acres of ranchland in Canada and a large sugar plantation in Hawaii. It owns dozens of mills, factories, and stores and hundreds of farms. The church also has large holdings in a number of well-known corporations. And the list of assets could be extended.[55]

Current Problem Areas

Although the Mormons had incurred the wrath of many whites for their opposition to slavery in the 1840s, by the 1960s they were under attack for "racist" church doctrine. Blacks could become church members, but they could not join the priesthood. In June 1978 church president Spencer W. Kimball announced a divine revelation that blacks could be given the priesthood. Only two other revelations—Brigham Young's guidance to Utah and Wilford Woodruff's ending plural marriage—had been reported since Joseph Smith's death. Wide acceptance followed, usually with great relief, and the church adapted rather easily.

Charges of sexism have also been brought against the church. Church leaders believe the women's liberation movement and the Equal Rights Amendment (ERA) divert women from their primary role, thereby undermining family stability.[56] Higher education for women has always been encouraged, and women are not prohibited from working; they are not permitted, however, to be part of the church hierarchy. All church leaders are male, and some Mormon women have been excommunicated for publicly protesting this practice. Most Mormon women appear satisfied with their role, but some are obviously dissatisfied.

Some observers believe Mormon society has been turning inward since the 1960s, reversing an earlier pattern of both outreach and receptivity to external influence.[57] The more permissive attitudes toward abortion, divorce, gay rights, sexual permissiveness, and women's liberation all point, in the Mormon's view, to a disintegration of moral values, prompting a growing cultural insularity, a sharper boundary between Mormons and the rest of society. Today the Mormon church is widely seen as a conservative repository of old-fashioned values and an American success story.

THE AMISH

The Amish, direct descendants of the Swiss Anabaptists who believe only in adult baptism as practiced by the early Christians, also are a branch of the Mennonites. Their founder, a Mennonite bishop named Jakob Ammann, began a sectarian movement when a schism arose in 1693 over enforcement of the *Meidung*. Still practiced among the Amish today, the *Meidung,* or shunning, is a powerful mechanism of social control that enables them to maintain their way of life.

When a bishop, acting on the near-unanimous vote of the congregation, imposes the *Meidung* on an errant member, others, including family members, cannot look on, talk, or associate with that person without also being placed under the ban. Informal sanctions such as ridicule and group disapproval, followed by formal admonition by clergy if necessary, precede such an action. Seldom imposed but also not rare, the *Meidung* can be revoked if the transgressor admits the error and personally asks the congregation for forgiveness.[58]

Although some may have come earlier, the first documented arrival of the Amish in America is 1727, when a few families left Switzerland and settled in Pennsylvania.[59] Migration continued from this region and Germany from 1727 to 1780, with large numbers of Alsatian and Bavarian Amish migrating from 1815 to 1840, establishing communities in Ontario, Illinois, and Ohio.[60] With an intensive agricultural orientation, the Amish found the unlimited availability of land in the New World so attractive an inducement that they completely transplanted to America. Their subculture became extinct in Europe, the Amish remaining there being absorbed into the dominant society.

Values, Symbols, and Practices

Forming *gemeinschaft* communities—intimate, homogeneous, and characterized by strong religious tradition—the Amish have remained remarkably constant in a radically changing dominant society. Their communities are highly integrated because their social institutions—family, school, church, and economic endeavors—are complementary and consistent in values and expectations; young and old live similar lives. The entire group shares the same life-style and restrictions, accepting them as the will of God.

Pride is a major sin, so wearing jewelry or other efforts at promoting physical attraction are forbidden; boasting is rare, and seeking a leadership role is frowned on. No Amish seeks political office of any kind, many not even registering to vote. Here we must make a distinction between the more conservative Old Order Amish, who live mostly in Pennsylvania, and the somewhat less conservative communities in Midwestern states. The latter tend to vote Republican and adamantly oppose farm subsidies, believing they would undermine their self-help social system.

Clothing is an important symbol of group identity, maintaining separatism from outgroups and continuity within the community. In an unchanged 250-year tradition, the men wear low-crown, wide-brim hats; coats without collars, lapels, or pockets; trousers with suspenders but without cuffs or creases. Belts and gloves, even in cold weather, are not permitted. Women wear solid color, one-piece dresses, with long skirts and aprons, keeping their heads covered at all times, whether indoors or outdoors. Clothing thus expresses a common understanding and mutual affection among those sharing similar traditions and expectations.[61] Other aspects of appearance—beards but not mustaches for all married men and a special braided hairstyle for females—reinforce further this orientation.

Language serves as another symbolic attribute of the *unser Satt Leit* (our sort of people). Pennsylvania Dutch (the word *Dutch* derives from *Deutsch,* meaning "German") is a German dialect resembling Palatine German folk speech and is common to all Amish, regardless of where they live.[62] English is their second language, usually introduced to a child on entering school and learned without difficulty. High German is used exclusively for the preaching service and formal ceremonies; the family teaches High German to their children so all can understand it when it is used in sermons and hymns.[63]

Amish farmers use a team of horses instead of tractors and gain an additional benefit from the natural supply of fertilizer. Amish homes may be lacking in modern conveniences, but they are clean, solid, kept in good repair, and like the farms, well run:

> Newer Amish houses differ from the traditional variety in a number of ways. They tend to be smaller, and many do not have a "farmhouse" appearance at all. In fact, except for such items as no electrical wiring and the lack of curtains, they often look much like non-Amish houses. In the matter of modern appliances and equipment, the differences between "traditional" and "new" are even more significant.
>
> The Amish have never permitted their members to use electricity furnished by public power lines. The church has been unyielding on this point, and the prohibition has served to restrict the kinds of devices and appliances available to members. Over the years, however, the followers of Jacob Ammann have come up with some rather interesting alternatives: bottled gas, batteries, small gen-

Their Sunday worship service ended, these Amish folk socialize for a while before returning home. This picture offers a good illustration of their traditional clothing, the facial hair of the men, and the special braids of the women, all of which help maintain group identity and multigenerational continuity. *(David S. Strickler/Monkmeyer Press Photo Service)*

erators, air pressure, gasoline motors, hydraulic power. The net result has been a variety of modern devices that have become available to the Amish, not only in their homes, but in their barns, workshops, stores, and offices. . . .

Amish homes in the Lancaster area, furthermore, though surprisingly modern in certain respects, are without electricity. There are no light bulbs, illumination being provided by oil lamps or gas-pressured lanterns. And the list of prohibitions remains long: dishwashers, clothes dryers, microwaves, blenders, freezers, central heating, vacuum cleaners, air conditioning, power mowers, bicycles, toasters, hair dryers, radios, television—all are taboo.[64]

Some Amish congregations have accepted parts of modern life. The Beachy Amish, founded by Amish bishop Moses M. Beachy in 1927, permit ownership of automobiles and certain other modern conveniences, and the "New Amish" allow telephones, electricity, and tractors.[65]

The Amish consider adolescence the most dangerous period of an individual's life. Because of physical and emotional changes and peer group influence exceeding family control, adolescents strain for independence, to be

children no longer. As a result, the Amish community has somewhat institutionalized adolescent rebellion, allowing teenagers to make mistakes, test
the cultural boundaries, and date. However, exposure to high school world-
liness is forbidden, the teens receiving vocational training at home instead.
Because baptism does not occur until the late teens or early twenties, adults
are more tolerant of discreet adolescent other-worldly activities, which may
include going to the movies, having a photograph taken, owning a radio, and
occasionally wearing non-Amish clothes.[66] A small degree of youth problems—
drunkenness, disrespect, joyriding, and even buying a car—occasionally con-
front the Old Order Amish, but most young people return to Amish ways on
baptism and the assumption of adult responsibilities. About 20 percent of
Amish youth may leave, often joining a more liberal Mennonite group.[67]
However, only a very small percentage of the baptized Amish ever leave.[68]

If an individual wishes to remain part of the community, the Amish insist
on an endogamous marriage. The Amish do not practice birth control and so
have a high birthrate; they have grown from 59,304 in 1970 to over 100,000
today. Social class has no meaning to the Amish, and all share a strong sense
of social obligation to one another. This includes helping others when disaster
or tragedy strikes, and home care rather than institutionalization for the aged.

Conflicts with Society

The Amish oppose social security or any form of insurance, believing the
Christian brotherhood is responsible for its own people. Because they would
not accept social security payments, they refused to pay the mandatory self-
employment social security tax. In the years of conflict with the government
over this issue, the government confiscated some Amish farms and horses to
collect the owed taxes. Finally, Amish leaders went to Washington, astound-
ing the legislators by their request to be exempted from government benefits.
Consequently, a law was passed, exempting them from both payments and
benefits.

Compulsory school attendance until age 16 provided another arena of conflict for the Amish with society. Because the Amish refused to send their
children to high school, they were harassed and arrested by state officials. A
Wisconsin case ultimately reached the U.S. Supreme Court, resulting in a
unanimous ruling in favor of the Amish. For them eighth-grade education is
sufficient, with farm vocational training occurring thereafter.

An Indiana sect permits car ownership but forbids having photographs
taken, believing them to be graven images. When that state required photographs on driver licenses in 1976, the Amish requested an exemption. When
the state refused, the Amish were once again drawn into conflict with authority over their religious principles.

Tourism is an annoyance for the Amish, especially in Lancaster County,
Pennsylvania. Ignoring Amish religious beliefs against having their pictures
taken, camera-wielding tourists routinely do so. Sometimes when the Amish
have a church service in a home as is their custom, with their buggies parked

outside, tourists will pull up in cars, go up on the porch, look through the windows at them, and take their pictures.[69] Guided bus tours clog the narrow roads, block their vehicles, and park in front of their schools and farms. Motels, commercial "museums," and handicraft and souvenir outlets cover the region, none run by or approved of by the Amish.[70] The successful film *Witness*, made over the objections of the Amish as an invasion of their privacy, drew even more tourists. About 5 million tourists visit Lancaster County each year, 350 visitors for every Amish individual.[71]

Despite the problems, the Amish persist and survive. Non-Amish neighbors and leaders praise their integrity, work ethic, and neighborliness. Their birthrate, ingroup solidarity, and resistance to outside influences suggest they will continue as a persistent subculture for many more years.

THE RASTAFARIANS

Rastafarians provide a contemporary example of a misunderstood religious minority group that frequently experiences prejudice and harassment. They fulfill the characteristics of a minority group: unequal treatment, easily identifiable, self-conscious identity, real or assumed common ancestry, and endogamy.[72] The factors that direct attention to them are their skin color, distinctive hairstyling, and use of *ganja* (marijuana) for much the same purpose as the Navajo and Huichol Indians use peyote.

The Early Years

Marcus Garvey, Jamaican-born founder of the Back of Africa movement, was influential in Jamaica before leaving the island for the United States in 1916. On his departure he is supposed to have said, "Look to Africa, [where] a black king shall be crowned, for the day of deliverance is near."[73] When Ras Tafari was crowned as Emperor Haile Selassie in 1930, he added the titles "King of Kings" and "Lion of the Tribe of Judah," placing himself in the legendary line of King Solomon. The coronation of the young Ethiopian emperor reminded Garvey's followers of his words and seemed to fulfill the biblican prophecy of Revelation 5:2–5:

> And I saw a mighty angel, who announced in a loud voice, "Who is worthy to break the seals and open the scroll?" But there was no one in heaven or on earth or in the world below who could open the scroll or look inside it. Then one of the elders said to me, "Don't cry. Look! The Lion from Judah's tribe, the great descendant of David, has won the victory, and he can break the seven seals and open the scroll.

Finding other collaborating scriptural passages (Revelation 19:16, Psalm 68:4, and Daniel 7:9 describing the king's hair "like pure wool"), the Rastas believed themselves to be the black Israelites of the Diaspora. Four ministers—Leonard Howell, Joseph Hibbert, Archibald Dunkley, and Robert

Hinds—spread the message, attracting many followers. To black Jamaicans experiencing both economic frustration at the time of a worldwide depression and white colonial rule, the movement offered hope and the promise of a better day coming.

Three major themes dominated the early phase of the Rastafarian movement: the wickedness of whites, the superiority of blacks, and the eventual revenge of blacks against whites by means of enslavement.[74] Living at the bottom of the ladder in a highly stratified society, Jamaican blacks thus protested against white racism and economic exploitation through the Rastafarian movement. Since then most Rastafarians have taken a more conciliatory stance toward whites, no longer condemning them en masse.[75]

Believing the colonial social institutions enchained them, the Rastas flouted the laws, denying the jurisdiction of the rulers. Even working for taxpayers or social institutions implied recognition of the existing social structure, so the Rastas refused to do so. Instead, they eked out an existence off the land, living as squatters in temporary shacks. Because the Rastas were poor, these attitudes provided them with coping mechanisms while they awaited the end of their exile from Africa.

From Outcasts to Social Acceptance

The Rastas' rebelliousness, although passive, brought quick condemnation in the early years of the movement. Newspapers called them unpatriotic, despicable, and *ganja*-smoking criminals. Some schools refused to admit their children, while the government disrupted their meetings, arrested cult members, and raided and burned their homes.[76] Dominant-group persecution only served to further unify the Rastafarians. Finally, the Rastas invited the University of the West Indies (UWI) to conduct an impartial investigation of their movement. The UWI report did rehabilitate their public image, and a new period of reciprocal cooperation began between the Rastas and the dominant society. A high point was reached on April 21, 1966, when Haile Selassie visited Jamaica and some Rastas were invited to the residence of the Governor General for the first time to meet with the Emperor in private. Each year on that date Rastafarians in Jamaica and the United States celebrate the event.

In the past few decades Rastas have become more assimilated into the sociocultural milieu of the island society. Their expressive art forms have been featured in public exhibitions and at the annual National Festival; their imprint on Jamaican music, from ska to reggae, has been significant. Its appeal has widened to include many different groups among the American public as well as Jamaicans. As a socially recognized group, Rastafarians in Jamaica now attract members from the middle and upper classes as well.

Values, Symbols, and Practices

Although some Rastafarians do not wear long hair, most do so as a symbol of unity, power, freedom, defiance to outgroups, and in accordance with biblican custom.[77] Because they reject almost all chemically processed goods, Rastafarians do not use soap, shampoo, or combs. They are far from unsanitary, however, washing their hair and body in water and herbs very frequently. The hair grows long and is braided into dreadlocks.

Food is another symbol of religious identification. Rastafarians rarely eat meat, abhorring pork and preferring small fish and vegetables instead. They will not drink liquor, milk, or coffee, perferring instead herbal tea. No manufactured foods, salt, or processed shortening is used; natural foods and oil from dried coconut are the staples in *I-tal* food and cooking, the name signifying the Rastafarian diet.

Smoking *ganja* (marijuana) gave the Rastas *communitas,* a sense of cohesive unity.[78] By producing an altered state of consciousness, they could gain temporary escape from their lives of hardship. Gradually, smoking *ganja* became identified with seeking communion with the supernatural, experiencing the self as God.[79]

The Rastafarians' language also symbolizes their philosophy and perceptions of reality. A form of creole English, Rastafarian speech is almost devoid of subject–object opposition; *you* and *me* are almost never used, and *I and I* primary combination being used instead, even to outgroup members. Shedding the cognitive shell and asserting a new self-concept and world view that

Dreadlocks hair styling among Rastafarian men helps establish social distance, setting them apart from outgroup members while creating a recognizable ingroup bond. In contrast, their unique reggae music has attracted a large following among various age groups throughout most of American society. *(Peter Simon/Stock, Boston)*

they believe to be their natural, African state, Rastafarians use *I and I* to identify soulfully with others at a higher level than I–Thou or I–It relationships. An actual example from *The Rastafarian Voice* is, "Government claims it is interested in I and I planting the land. Yet when I and I plant food to feed I fellow African, I and I are harassed and driven off the land."[80]

Rastafarian Americans

Rastafarianism survives because of its adaptive capabilities. An existential interpretation of their doctrines has enabled the Rastas to adjust to industrialism and to American society without sacrificing their naturistic ethic. When increased numbers of Jamaicans migrated to the United States (346,000 since 1971), many Rastafarians were among them.

Mostly poor, unskilled workers, the Rastafarians tend to live in low-rent urban neighborhoods. Their cultural orientations isolate them from both white and black Americans, the social distance forging a small, cohesive subculture. Rastafarians frequently encounter problems with the police, their appearance and regular use of marijuana making them inviting targets. Their ingroup solidarity, adaptability, and social distance from the dominant society make the Rastafarians likely to remain a persistent subculture, much like the Gypsies.

THE SHAKERS

Even though the United Society of Believers in Christ's Second Appearing—or Shakers, as they are most commonly known—may now be disappearing, leaving behind no religious legacy, they have left their mark in other ways. With a 200-year history, they have been both the largest and longest-lasting communistic movement in the United States. At the peak of their membership in the mid-nineteenth century, they numbered at least 17,000 and possibly as high as 64,000.[81]

The Early Years

Ann Lee, an illiterate Englishwoman from a poor family, was the founder of the United Society. Born in Manchester in 1736, at age 22 she joined a radical religious sect whose worship services included both silent meditation and sudden bursts of shouting, singing, and agitated shakings of the body. Because leaders Jane and James Wardley were former Quakers, the group became known as "Shaking Quakers" or "Shakers." After four children died in early infancy, the last birth a most difficult one that seriously endangered her life, Ann Lee became convinced sexual desire and carnal pleasure violated God's will. Sex was the root of all evil—the reason Adam and Eve were driven from the Garden of Eden and the cause of problems in her own time.

Convincing her colleagues about the sins of the flesh through her charismatic powers, she began preaching against the established church for allowing marriage and sexual practice. When she was arrested for disturbing the peace and kept in solitary confinement for two weeks, her colleagues—already anticipating the imminent second coming of Christ—now saw Ann Lee as a female messiah because they believed in the male–female duality of God and all spiritual beings. Mother Ann Lee, as she was now called, was the female counterpart of a spirit earlier appearing in the person of Jesus.

A divine revelation led Ann Lee and eight followers to migrate to the New World in May 1774. By August 1774 they were in Niskayuna, an area just outside Albany, New York, where they built a settlement. Within a few years they began attracting many converts but at the same time gaining many enemies. Suspected in those revolutionary times of being British sympathizers and unpopular for their religious views, female leadership, and Lee's claim to being the female reincarnation of Christ, the Shakers experienced brutal abuse. They were imprisoned, fined, attacked by mobs, beaten, and clubbed. Ann Lee was stoned and badly mauled on several occasions, her brother once suffering a severe skull fracture from a rock.

From 1781 to 1783 Ann Lee and her disciples traveled throughout the Northeast, gaining many converts and establishing a base for several new Shaker communities. Within a year, though, Mother Ann was dead at age 48. Effective leadership and missionary activities enabled the Believers to expand over the next 75 years, with 19 communities developing in eight states.[82] Some of these communities also encountered mob violence and persecution, as well as the frontier perils of Indian attack, inadequate medical facilities, and battles against the elements. Nevertheless they grew and prospered despite their isolation—most communities being situated hundreds of miles apart from each other.

Values and Practices

With celibacy as a basic tenet of their faith, Shakers employed extensive sex segregation in their daily activities. Men and women had separate work areas, dined in silence at separate tables seating four to eight in a communal dining room, and avoided all physical contact with one another, including shaking hands. They had separate doorways in many of their buildings, wide hallways to prevent brushing against one another, and were not permitted to pass by one another on the stairs. Children—either those of converts or those adopted from orphanages—attended sex-segregated schools and grew up untouched by members of the opposite sex. Because they also thought the millennium was near, Shakers had no concern about the need to propagate.

Believing idleness, even in conversation, was a temptation for the devil to corrupt them, Shakers glorified work and spent most of their waking moments engaged in some form of manual labor. Their deep commitment to work resulted in top-quality products, whether in their buildings, distinctive furniture, or farm produce, earning them a reputation for selling choice quality goods. Their strict moral code and ordered existence, while unique to their life-style, followed a pattern of deliberately planned and coordinated activities found in typical utopian communes.[83]

The Shakers also believed in the ideal of common property practiced by the early Christians (Acts 4:32). Their common ownership of all property made everyone equal regardless of age, race, or gender, enabling them to fulfill the Christian virtues of humility and charity; no one was servant or master. In the eighteenth and nineteenth centuries, such pioneering of women's rights and racial equality (blacks and slaves were fully admitted as free and equal members) was a bold concept for the times.

Why would total sexual denial and extensive work schedules appeal to thousands of converts? We must first remember that in the eighteenth and nineteenth centuries divorce was rare and socially unacceptable; with sexual gratification considered a male prerogative, women seldom viewed marriage in sexual terms.[84] Unhappy couples had an alternative to their present state by joining the Shakers. Widows—having no means of support since both life insurance and jobs for women were rare—could gain both emotional and economic security in the Shaker community. Others—unable to function in a competitive society due to personality, limited ability, or life orientation—could find a peaceful haven with the Shakers.

Whatever the reason, Shaker life appealed to people from all walks of life—professionals, skilled and unskilled workers, merchants, artisans, and

The frenzied and animated exuberance of Shaker dancing served as an enjoyable group activity and emotional outlet from the hard work and personal restraint practiced all week. This wood engraving depicts one version of the circle dance, with numerous participants and ''wallflowers.'' Note the gender-segregated seating. *(Library of Congress)*

craftspeople; most were Protestant, some Jewish, generally from working-class backgrounds. Blacks and foreign-born also joined. Out of their com bined efforts came a number of significant inventions: the circular saw, screw propeller, clothespin, cut nail, brimstone match, flat broom, revolving oven, threshing machine, and various machines for printing labels, cutting leather, and making broom handles.[85] Their simple, straight, functional styling also has made an indelible mark on American furniture.

Shaker observance of the Sabbath was a joyous event, culminating in an emotional release through frenzied and animated dancing. Again the sexes never touched each other. One frequent version of dance was formation of two circles, one within the other, males forming one circle and females another. They would chant, sing, clap hands, grouping and regrouping in various patterns. Some dances actually were marches in rhythm, accompanied by varying body movements such as swinging arms. A more ecstatic dance included jerking one's head back and forth or side to side with limbs and trunk twitching in every direction.[86] Undoubtedly such participation was an effective outlet from the total restraint practiced all week long.

Decline and Virtual Disappearance

Several factors contributed to the decline of the United Society. Industrialization ushered in the factory system, undermining the Shaker economy whose handicraft system could not compete with less expensive, mass-produced products. Values about sex changed, with Americans developing more positive attitudes about sexual pleasure. Improvements in transportation (railroad and automobile) and communication (telegraph and telephone), together with national population growth and land development, reduced Shaker isolation and separatism. The emergence of governmental social welfare programs for the elderly, widowed, orphaned, or sick eliminated economic security as a motive for joining. As American society changed, the Shakers found it increasingly difficult to gain new converts and keep their younger members. As their membership aged, their dance rituals lost their vigor, replaced by more conservative songs and instrumental music, ending the exuberance of the sect.[87] By the turn of the century, most of the Shaker communities were in a state of precipitous decline, and by 1925 most had vanished.

Most of the Shaker buildings still stand, serving as museums or as facilities for schools, state institutions, religious orders, or private residencies. One Shaker community still exists at Sabbathday Lake, Maine. Less than a dozen, mostly elderly, members live there, benefiting from revenues generated through tourism. Although gaining a trickle of converts, even in the past few years, the community may not remain viable for much longer.

MUSLIM AMERICANS _____

Although many Westerners usually think of Islam as an Arab religion, most Muslims throughout the world are not Arabs. Indonesia contains the largest

Muslim population (about 180 million). Other countries with large Muslim populations include India (about 100 million), China (about 38 million), and the former Soviet Union (about 30 million). Throughout the many black African countries, Islam has millions of believers. Worldwide, Islam embraces over 950 million people, making it second only to Christianity in membership.

About 10 percent of the early Syrian immigrants were Muslims and Druze. After 1908 the Ottoman government began drafting Muslim Arabs into the Turkish army, and several thousand immigrated to the United States to escape military service.[88] In 1916 a large group of Muslim Arabs settled in Dearborn, Michigan, to work at the nearby Ford Motor Company plant. That legacy continues today, with Dearborn now boasting the largest Muslim community in the United States.[89]

Because their numbers were relatively few and because few Muslim women came to the United States before World War II, only four mosques were built up until that time. Without women, communities and institutions had little chance to develop.[90]

Since World War II, and especially after 1965, many Muslim immigrants from all parts of the world have come to the United States. Hundreds of mosques now pepper the American landscape, and construction of others is in the planning stage. Today Muslim Americans number over 2 million.[91]

Values and Practices

In Islamic belief Muhammad was the greatest prophet, completing a line of prophets from Adam through Moses to Jesus. Islam translates to "submission to one all-powerful God," and it incorporates many of the beliefs and practices of the Jewish and Christian faiths. Muslims subscribe to a rigorous Holy Law, or Shari'ah, based on teachings from the Quran (or Koran). They keep the Sabbath on Friday and do not eat pork or drink alcoholic beverages.

> The Shari'ah also requires all Muslims to fulfill the "five pillars of faith." The first pillar, the profession of faith, involves stating and believing the words "There is no God but the One God and Muhammed is His Messenger." The second pillar directs believers to bow in prayer toward the holy city of Mecca five times a day. According to the third, Muslims must give alms to the poor and needy. The fourth pillar requires fasting during the daylight hours throughout the holy month of Ramadan, the ninth month of the Muslim calendar, during which Muhammed received his first revelation from God. To fulfill the fifth pillar, Muslims must make a pilgrimage to Mecca at least once in their lifetime.[92]

To the Muslims, religious beliefs and the social mores of public conduct and private experience are all inseparable. Submission to the will of Allah means a prescribed code of conduct in every facet of life, including personal hygiene. Muslims, for example, eat their food only with the right hand and clean their body after defecating only with the left hand. Thus a reprehensible sight to them is witnessing Westerners using their left hands to place food in their mouths.

As non-Western peoples immigrate to the United States and organize their ethnic communities, construction of their religious edifices soon follows. This mosque in Manhattan at Third Avenue and 96th Street is one of the latest additions to over 2,000 temples and mosques now in the United States. *(John Sotomayor/New York Times Pictures)*

Conservative in their values and attitudes, Muslims also reject American preoccupation with materialism and their self-indulgent pleasures at the expense of obligations to family and community. Female immodesty, societal sexual permissiveness, and pornography, as well as high rates of alcohol and drug use, illegitimate births, abortions, and divorce all concern Muslims who are attempting to maintain the integrity of their way of life.

RELIGION AND AMERICAN SOCIETY ⸻⸻⸻⸻

Religion is a very important aspect of American culture. Public opinion polls have consistently found 94 to 96 percent of Americans saying they believe in God, and nearly 75 percent believing in a life after death. Such responses are from two to three times greater than in other Western nations.[93] Over 147 million Americans belong to a church or synagogue, about 60 percent of the population.[94] After a steady decline through the mid-1970s, the proportion of Americans attending weekly worship services and finding religion an increasing influence on their lives has been rising (see Figure 12.1). Although 43 percent attendance at weekly worship service may appear low, it is by far the

484

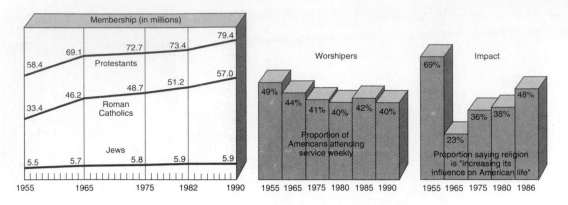

FIGURE 12.1
Vital Signs

SOURCE: Gallup Opinion Poll, "Religion in America," in *The Gallup Report,* U.S. Bureau of the Census.

highest of all developed countries; for example, only 15 percent of the British attend church weekly. Undoubtedly some Americans use religion for social rather than religious purposes, finding in their church a source a community and reaffirmation of American values of humanitarianism, work, individualism, and group conformity.

As we mentioned earlier, much religious diversity exists in the United States. The influx of Asian immigrants, for instance, has increased the number of followers of Eastern religions such as Buddhism or Hinduism to more than 1 million. Another 10 million practice disciplines derived from Hinduism, including Yoga and Transcendental Meditation.

Even Catholicism and Protestantism have great diversity within their churches; they are not the monolithic entities some assume them to be. The ethnic diversity of the Catholic Church—French, German, Hispanic, Irish, Italian, and Polish, to name but a few—results in varying forms of religious behavior among these subgroups.[95] The Irish, as the Italians and Poles have long recognized, dominate American Catholicism; at present Irish Americans represent 15 percent of the Catholic population yet comprise about half of the U.S. bishops. Protestants range from the more liberal Congregationalists and Episcopalians with their formal religious ceremonies, to the more conservative American Lutherans and American Baptists with their less elaborate worship services. The Amish and Shakers are but two of the many different Protestant faiths, as are such fundamentalists as the Missouri Synod Lutherans and Southern Baptists with their strict interpretations of the Bible.[96]

Civil Religion

Sociologist Robert Bellah has suggested that the United States has a "civil religion," a shared belief system incorporating all religious elements into a

| BOX 12.3 | **THE INTERNATIONAL SCENE** |

The French, who never really pictured their country as a land of immigrants, have in recent years reacted quite impassionately to the presence of 3.3 million North African Arab immigrants and their French-born children. Recruited in the 1970s to feed France's industrial expansion, these Muslim immigrants came from the former French territories of Algeria, Morocco, and Tunisia. They are known collectively as Maghrebins, from the Arabic word *maghreb,* meaning "the land where the sun sets."

A government study released in June 1991 showed that 71 percent of French citizens felt the country had too many Arabs, 45 percent said too many blacks, and 94 percent acknowledged that racism was widespread. Reflecting this antiforeign sentiment, Jean-Marie Le Pen, leader of the antiforeign National Front, garnered about 15 percent of the vote in the 1988 presidential election.

Those French who oppose the Maghrebins say their Islamic religion makes assimilation impossible. Their concept of French identity clearly leaves no room for the religiously different. They object to the annual month-long, dawn-to-dusk fast during the Moslem month of Ramadan, arguing that it disrupts work schedules. Another weak argument is the required annual ritual sacrifice of a lamb or ram by every family because it inconveniences neighboring apartment residents. Concerned about Islamic fundamentalism in Iran, Algeria, and elsewhere, the French worry about its impact on the Arabs in France. Experts say such fears are groundless, that perhaps only a thousand fundamentalists live in France, and that only 5 to 10 percent of the French Muslims go to services regularly, much like other French religionists.

Perhaps a reality check occurred when fears of French Muslim violence over French participation in the Gulf War never materialized. Like others of their social class, the French Muslims are more concerned about education, housing, and jobs than international politics.

sanctification and celebration of the American way of life.[97] Our Pledge of Allegiance identifies us as a nation "under God." All our coins and paper money declare, "In God We Trust," the back of our one-dollar bills also containing the now-obscure symbols of the Trinity (triangle) and the omniscience of God (the eye within the triangle). Congress begins each session with a prayer; presidents regularly schedule prayer breakfasts with government leaders and they mention God in almost all their state of the union and inaugural addresses. Religion is an important element in oaths of office, courtroom procedures, and most formal public occasions. Scouting emphasizes "God and Country" in the Scout Oath and in an award by that name. The list is virtually endless.

Current Controversies

The U.S. Supreme Court often has been involved in controversial decisions interpreting the First Amendment's stipulation about separation of church and state. In its efforts to maintain government neutrality in maximizing religious freedom, the court has sometimes outraged religious advocates of particular moral issues. Its most controversial decisions have been those banning prayer in public schools and involving abortion. Other decisions—upholding Amish exemption from compulsory education laws, permitting certain forms of federal assistance to parochial schools (lunches, books)—encourage certain religious activities while striving to maintain First Amendment principles.

School prayer and abortion continue as controversial issues. Proposed constitutional amendments have not gained sufficient support for passage, though religious groups persist in their efforts. Catholics, Mormons, Lutherans, Baptists, and other conservative sects and denominations have combined their efforts to overturn the abortion ruling through lobbying and support of sympathetic legislators. School prayer does not generate the same degree of emotion, but it too unites people of different faiths to effect a change. Opposing them are both strict constitutionalists and people of more liberal religious persuasions.

Creationists, those supporting a literal interpretation of the Bible, have been crusading in recent years for a "balanced treatment" about the origins of life. Objecting to both textbooks and curriculum on the subject of evolution, Christian fundamentalists insisted the book of Genesis be included as well. Arkansas, Louisiana, and Mississippi passed legislation requiring such an approach, and 18 other states were considering similar laws when a Federal District Court in early 1982 struck down the Arkansas law as a violation of the First Amendment. In 1984 Texas—the fourth-largest school textbook market in the country—removed the state requirement that all books specify evolution as only one of several explanations. Despite these setbacks, creationists continue their battle against the evolutionists.

SOCIOLOGICAL PERSPECTIVES _____

Each of our three theoretical frameworks provides a means of understanding the significance of religion in intergroup relations and within the activities of convergent and persistent subcultures as well. Though different in emphasis, these perspectives offer unifying themes to religious pluralism in the United States.

The Functionalist View

In *The Elementary Forms of Religious Life* (1912), Émile Durkheim identified religion as an integrative bond for society, a theme elaborated on by modern functionalists. Religion, they maintain, serves as a social "cement," uniting people with shared values and beliefs, bringing them together to celebrate harvests and life-cycle events. Religion gives meaning and purpose to one's life, offering individuals emotional and psychological support in both good and bad times. Religious teachings also help maintain social control, reinforcing important values and norms and providing moral standards.

Each of the groups discussed in this chapter—Catholics, Jews, Mormons, Amish, Rastafarians, Shakers, and Muslims—found their religious bonds to be a means of strengthening their resolve and identity in a pluralistic and sometimes harsh society. Catholic and Jewish immigrants usually lived in ethnic neighborhoods with their church or synagogue as the focal point of their community activities, easing their transition to the American life-style. Experiencing acts of hostility, Mormons, Rastafarians, and Shakers—often Catholics and Jews also—drew closer to other ingroup members and sustained hope through their faith. Because of their strong religious convictions, the Amish and Shakers remained constant in their ways despite a changing world all around them. Mormons, Muslims, and Rastafarians, in particular, function in the secular world but maintain their sense of identity and purpose through adherence to specific religious tenets.

As separatist minorities, the Amish and Shakers developed economic and social interaction patterns intensifying their values and beliefs. All aspects of their daily lives have functioned together in harmony, eliminating stress and conflict between religion and daily living. Amish institutionalization of adolescent rebelliousness and Shaker dancing exuberance both operate as safety releases for otherwise strict communes. The socialization efforts by Amish, Catholics, Jews, and Mormons of children and youth, though varying greatly in approach and intensity, serve to transmit and sustain over generations a continuing social system organized around specific religious beliefs and practices. Language, symbols, and rituals further instill a shared religious identity and social bond.

The Conflict View

Karl Marx and later conflict theorists thought religion a social control mechanism to protect the interests of those in power. The dominant religion of a society represents the ruling economic and political class, and it legitimizes the existing social structure, blunting people's frustration, anger, and pain with the promise of an afterlife reward. Religion can be a divisive factor, breeding dissension and violence, though conflict theorists suggest the real reasons behind such altercations are economic and political in nature. What appears to be religious bigotry or fanaticism is usually, say the conflict theorists, a struggle for power and control disguised as a religious matter. Even the participants may be unaware of the reality of the situation, caught up as they are in the religious justification given for the conflict.

Note how nativist alarm over mid-nineteenth-century Catholic immigrants centered on their perceived growing political strength; fears of papal rule of

America were very real then. Loss of political control still haunted Protestant Americans 30 years later. The American Protective Association even dedicated itself to keeping Catholics out of office! Problems arose for Rastafarians in Jamaica because they challenged the political status quo, and the Mormons in Illinois and Missouri made enemies because of their political strength in those states. Shakers, thought to be Tory sympathizers, incurred the wrath of their neighbors during the revolutionary period. The Amish, on the other hand, sought no political leadership or economic competition and so encountered little hostility for those reasons.

Economic competition did create religious antagonism against Catholics and Jews. The rebelliousness of striking Irish laborers against mine and factory owners sparked anti-Catholic reactions, as did the recessions in the 1870s and 1890s, causing workers to fear that Catholics would take away their jobs. Rapid upward mobility among Jewish Americans ignited fears of their dominance, resulting in unflattering Shylock stereotyping and exclusion from organizations and establishments of affluent Christians. Such actions support conflict theory argumentation that the roots of religious confrontation, whether peaceful or violent, actually lie in political and economic resource distributions.

The Interactionist View

Appearance is one key element in perceptions of those religiously different. Away from their worship services, most Americans offer few clues about their religious preference, but some do, however. When an outsider sees a physically distinct believer—a Hasidic Jew, a Hare Krishna follower, an Amish person, or a Rastafarian, for instance—those dissimilarities announce a social distance and tend to lessen chances of close interaction patterns. Those physical clues may even foster negative responses. Conversely, this outward appearance becomes a source of comfort and reinforced religious identity to a fellow believer. Wearing of religious symbols—perhaps ashes on one's forehead on Ash Wednesday or a Star of David on a necklace—also may induce positive or negative reactions.

Self-identity emerges out of the orderliness of day-by-day accomplishments of individuals interacting face to face, interpreting and reinterpreting their ways of doing things. These shared definitions become more solidified and the group members a more cohesive unit under insulated conditions. Amish and Shakers living in their separate communities, and the Mormons in the Utah Territory, succeeded in developing their own social systems whose totality encompassed all aspects of daily life, thereby reinforcing the precepts of their religious beliefs. Rastafarians, in rejecting the dominant economic system and language syntax, created their own symbolic world so differentiated from the dominant society that their everyday interrelationships with one another reinforced their group solidarity. Even Catholics and Jews, as well as the Mormons of modern times, benefit from such cooperative interpretation with one another because studies show each tends to interact in primary group relations outside religious settings with members of the same faith.[98] For members of all faiths, the religious bond serves both to unite and insulate, preserved and maintained through daily interactions with like-minded individuals.

Societal labeling of dissimilar religious minorities often results in negative attitudes and actions, with an avoidance response thereby promoting subcultural insularity. If Catholics are attacked as "docile and superstitious," Jews as "mercenary," Mormons as "chauvinistic," Amish as "backward," Rastafarians as "potheads," and Shakers as "weird," group members are more likely to turn inward for the sense of personal worth denied them in the outside world.

Retrospect

Founded on the principle of religious freedom, the United States became a place of refuge for people of many faiths. Yet religious tolerance has not always prevailed; some groups have been harassed, experiencing both verbal and physical abuse as they sought the right to follow their beliefs.

Throughout much of the nation's history, Catholics have been vilified and abused. Anti-Catholic actions include colonial statutes against political participation, vicious pamphlets and books, hostile political party platforms, Know-Nothing and Ku Klux Klan demonstrations and violence, American Protective Association activities. Proposed aid to parochial schools remains controversial, as do Catholic positions on abortion, birth control, and nuclear arms. Catholics today are the largest single religious denomination in the country.

Jewish Americans encountered many of the same problems as Catholics, often from the same nativist groups. Overt anti-Semitic stereotyping and actions continued well into the twentieth century. Jewish upward mobility occurred more quickly than for most other immigrants because more came as skilled workers with families intact, and their religious emphasis on learning encouraged secular education and entry into better-paying jobs. A high intermarriage rate, a cause for concern among many Jewish leaders, is seen by others as irrelevant to continued vitality in the Jewish community.

The Latter-Day Saints offer an example of a persecuted minority, expelled from several states, growing into a large, successful, and respectable church. Their emphasis on family and education earns them high praise, as do their economic investments and assistance to their poor. Although criticisms about plural marriages and racism have ended through changes in church doctrine, charges of sexism still remain, though most Mormon women appear satisfied in their role.

Both the Amish and Shakers are long-lasting examples of a persistent subculture. Whereas the Amish remain a vibrant and growing community, the Shakers appear to be disappearing after a 200-year existence. Rastafarians are becoming more numerous as Jamaican immigration increases, and they too are a separatist minority opposed to assimilation. Muslims are growing in numbers and many of their conservatives parallel those of the Catholic and Mormon faiths.

Today religion remains an important aspect of American culture, as indicated by public opinion polls and rising church attendance. A civil religion exists, as do controversies over abortion, school prayer, and teaching evolution theory.

Functionalists stress the integrative aspects of religion, while conflict theorists analyze the underpinnings of economic and political power struggles as the basis for religious conflict. Interactionists examine how social interpretations foster ingroup solidarity and outgroup acceptance or hostility.

Review Questions

1. Discuss how Catholic Americans of the past illustrated minority experiences comparable to those of many immigrant nationality groups.
2. Apply the concepts of prejudice, stereotyping, marginality, and xenophobia to the Jewish experience in America.
3. Discuss the similarity–attraction bond in the societal response to the Mormons.
4. How do the Amish illustrate a persistent subculture?
5. DIscuss the similarity–attraction bond and societal response to the Rastafarians.
6. What unique features about the Shakers led to their early popularity and present near-extinction?
7. What similarities and differences can be found between Muslims and other major American religions?
8. Discuss the role of religion in present-day American culture.
9. How do the three sociological perspectives help us to understand religion?

Suggested Readings

ANDERSON, CHARLES H. *White Protestant Americans: From National Origins to Religious Group.* Englewood Cliffs, NJ: Prentice-Hall, 1970.
A readable, comprehensive account of cultural dominance of Anglo-Americans and their role in interethnic relations.

BALTZELL, E. DIGBY. *The Protestant Establishment.* New York: Vintage Books, 1966.
A classic study of the history, power, and life-styles of the white, Anglo-Saxon elite in the United States.

BARRETT, LEONARD. *The Rastafarians: Sounds of Cultural Dissonance.* Boston: Beacon Press, 1977.
A highly readable study of Rastafarian history, ideology, and impact on society.

CURRAN, THOMAS J. *Xenophobia and Immigration, 1820–1930.* New York: Twayne Publishers, 1975.

A detailed historical account of nativist efforts and political actions against Catholics and Jews.

HERBERG, WILL. *Protestant–Catholic–Jew,* rev. ed. Garden City, NY: Anchor Books, 1960.

A somewhat controversial argument that a religious triple melting pot now forms group affiliation and identity.

HOSTETLER, JOHN A. *Amish Society,* 3d ed. Baltimore, MD: Johns Hopkins Press, 1980.

A classic and outstanding study of Amish society, with a thorough insider's view of their values and practices.

KEPHART, WILLIAM M. AND WILLIAM M. ZELLNER. *Extraordinary Groups: The Sociology of Unconventional Life-Styles,* 4th ed. New York: St. Martin's Press, 1991.

A fine sociological examination of the Amish, Mormons, and Shakers, as well as several other groups.

SILBERMAN, CHARLES E. *A Certain People: America's Jews and Their Lives Today,* New York: Summit Books, 1985.

An optimistic, comprehensive, and interesting book of today's Jewish American community, their assimilation, and the concerns about intermarriage and population decline.

STARK, RODNEY, AND WILLIAM S. BAINBRIDGE. *The Future of Religion.* Berkeley: University of California Press, 1985.

Provides comprehensive overview of various religious groups, from traditional denominations to cults.

The Bettmann Archive

13

Women in America

Sexism is an ideology, or set of generalized beliefs, that one sex is superior to the other. For centuries the presumption of male superiority led to patterns of prejudice and discrimination against women, and many of those patterns still remain. Only in the past 30 years has the problem of sexism become widely understood and a matter of public concern. Previously, women had been subordinate to men in virtually all societies throughout history, recorded comments reflecting this cultural bias.[1] Aristotle, for example, thought men active by nature and women passive, making women intellectually and morally inferior to men.[2] In 1879 Gustave LeBon, a founder of social psychology, made the following observation:

> In the most intelligent races, as among the Parisians, there are a large number of women whose brains are closer in size to those of gorillas than to the most developed male brains. This inferiority is so obvious that no one can contest it for a moment; only its degree is worth discussion. All psychologists who have studied the intelligence of women, as well as poets and novelists, recognize today that they represent the most inferior forms of human evolution and that they are closer to children and savages than to an adult, civilized man. They excel in fickleness, inconstancy, absence of thought and logic, and incapacity to reason. Without doubt there exist some distinguished women, very superior to an average man, but they are as exceptional as the birth of any monstrosity, as, for example, of a gorilla with two heads; consequently, we may neglect them entirely.[3]

More recently, Freudian psychologists have advanced notions of gender differences affecting behavior. Freud believed that the fact that males have a penis made them more aggressive, while "penis envy" made females feel shame and a sense of inferiority. Erik Erikson suggested that male genitalia influenced boys to be questing, aggressive, and outward thrusting, and female genitalia directed girls to be concerned about boundaries, limits, and "interiors." Today such notions have been refuted by cross-cultural studies demonstrating variances in sex role norms and behavior as developed through the socialization process and societal expectations of men and women.

Not everyone had been blind to the effects of male domination. In an appendix to his classic and influential analysis of black–white relations, *An American Dilemma,* Gunnar Myrdal noted a parallel to the position of women and blacks in American society.[4] In fact, he observed, the legal position of women and children defined as being under the control of the male head of the household had provided the basis for the legal position of black servants in the seventeenth century. Sociologist Helen Hacker in 1951 identified major areas of sexual discrimination in American society, describing women as marginal in a masculine society.[5] Not until the 1960s, however, did the feminist movement make any headway, partially launched by Betty Friedan's consciousness-raising book, *The Feminine Mystique.*

As public awareness of women as an oppressed group increased, the parallels of their status to that of racial and ethnic groups became more obvious. For example, the minority group characteristics we discussed in Chapter 1 apply to women, too.[6] Women are born into their gender identity and are easily identifiable by physical and cultural characteristics. In addition, women now recognize their commonality with one another as victims of sexism, an ideology, like that of racism, used to justify their unequal treatment.

A fifth characteristic, the minority-group practice of endogamy, may seem inappropriate, yet in marriage the domination–subordination lines are also manifest. Traditional marriage ceremonies provide for the male to cherish his wife while she promises to obey her husband. When the ceremony ends, they often are pronounced not "husband and wife," but "man and wife," grafting her identity and maiden name onto her relationship to her husband. Property laws, credit regulations, social security benefits, divorce laws, even telephone listings have long reinforced this less than equal status, although recent changes have occurred in some of these areas.

SOCIOHISTORICAL PERSPECTIVE _____

Early colonists in the New World, recreating in miniature the social systems of their homelands, continued male dominance patterns. In settlements and the advancing frontier, women were valuable "commodities," both for their skills and labor in the battle for survival and as sexual property in a region with a shortage of women. Although some instances of female independence in land ownership, inheritance, and voting rights did occur in those early years, for the most part women remained subordinate to men, with few individual rights except as appendages to their husbands. The U.S. Constitution did not give voting rights to women, and the courts, until many decades later, did not interpret its other provisions regarding full and equal participation as applicable to women either.[7]

As the nation grew and prospered, as the Industrial Revolution changed the very nature of American society, a dichotomy emerged regarding the role of women. Poor women, mostly from immigrant families, went to work in the factories at low-skilled jobs for lower wages than men.[8] Middle- and upper-class women, usually native-born, from families of prosperous merchants and industrialists, were elevated to a pedestal, as towers of moral strength, refinement, and soothing comfort to their world-weary males. Prevailing values in the nineteenth and early twentieth centuries held that the nature of women was to please and the nature of men was to achieve.[9]

Legal restrictions denied women any right to self-determination. They could not vote, own property in their own name, testify in court, make a legal contract, spend their own wages without their husband's permission, or even

| BOX 13.1 | **THE GENDER EXPERIENCE** |

"I long to hear that you have declared an independency—and by the way in the new Code of Laws which I suppose it will be necessary for you to make I desire you would Remember the Ladies, and be more generous and favourable to them than your ancestors. Do not put such unlimited power into the hands of the Husbands. Remember all men would be tyrants if they could. If particular care and attention is not paid to the Ladies we are determined to foment a Rebellion, and will not hold ourselves bound by any Laws in which we have no voice, or Representation.

"That your Sex are Naturally Tyrannical is a Truth so thoroughly established as to admit of no dispute, but such of you as wish to be happy willingly give up the harsh title of Master for the more tender and endearing one of Friend. Why then, not put it out of the power of the vicious and the Lawless to use us with cruelty and indignity with impunity. Men of Sense in all Ages abhor those customs which treat us only as the vassals of your Sex. Regard us then as Beings placed by Providence under your protection and in imitation of the Supreme Being make use of that power only for our happiness."

SOURCE: Letter from Abigail Adams to John Adams, March 31, 1776.

retain guardianship over their own children if their husband died or deserted them. Because men were supposedly active and women passive, only men were thought to enjoy sex; any woman who also enjoyed it was considered deviant and degenerate. A double standard in sexual conduct thus emerged. In a similar vein, female public speaking was a strong taboo because a passive, refined lady would not behave so crudely.

Did everyone think and act this way in the nineteenth century? Certainly not, but these were the prevailing norms. Still, the abolitionist movement attracted female activists to fight against the continuance or expansion of slavery. The New York State legislature in 1848 acted to protect the property rights of married women, and in 1869 Wyoming Territory gave women the right to vote, continuing that practice after becoming a state in 1890, the first state to do so.

Efforts to give all women the right to vote met with fierce resistance. As the suffragettes held rallies, protest marches, and demonstrations, they were ridiculed, insulted, and abused—slapped, tripped, pelted with overripe fruits and vegetables and burning cigar stubs. Chaining themselves to the posts, fences, and grillwork of public buildings, these early feminists were arrested and jailed. In 1913 in Washington, DC, federal troops were brought in to quell the unrest. In 1916 six months of picketing at the White House ended with mass arrests and imprisonment when the women refused to pay what they labeled "unjust" fines. Hostility against such challenges to the male estab-

This Currier & Ives print, inspired in 1869 by Wyoming Territory giving women the right to vote, illustrates the sexism of the times. ''Brass,'' or arrogance, was the label given feminists, suggested also by their signs, cigar smoking, and domineering. The woman seated is a showgirl, then someone of low repute. *(Culver Pictures, Inc.)*

lishment is indicated by this account of how the prison guards maltreated the demonstrators:

> I saw Miss Lincoln, a slight young girl, thrown to the floor. Mrs. Nolan, a delicate old lady of seventy-three, was mastered by two men. . . . Whittaker [the prison superintendent] in the center of the room directed the whole attack, inciting the guards to every brutality. Two men brought in Dorothy Day, twisting her arms above her head. Suddenly they lifted her and brought her body down twice over the back of an iron bench. . . . The bed broke Mrs. Nolan's fall, but Mrs. Cosu hit the wall. They had been there a few minutes when Mrs. Lewis, all doubled over like a sack of flour, was thrown in. Her head struck the iron bed and she fell to the floor senseless. As for Lucy Burns, they handcuffed her wrists and fastened the handcuffs over her head to the cell door.[10]

Finally in 1919 Congress passed the Nineteenth Amendment, giving women the right to vote. Ratified a year later it became the law of the land. Yet other feminist reforms did not follow. Women did not use their newly gained political power much, and a very few won elective office in proportion to their numbers. About 90 percent of the suffragettes ceased further activist measures as the feminist movement faded until it was resurrected some 40 years later. Antisuffrage groups remained active, though, successfully cam-

World War II created a manpower shortage in America's factories that was filled by women, who constituted 36 percent of the total labor force. This scene of a woman working an axle lathe for a manufacturer of wheels and axles for railroads typifies the demanding work ably performed by female workers in many different industries at that time. *(Library of Congress)*

paigning locally to prevent women from serving on juries, holding elected office, or getting jobs competitive with males.

Following passage of the Nineteenth Amendment, labor-force participation by women increased to about 25 percent, though job discrimination continued. Females rarely held decision-making positions and were the first fired during the Great Depression.[11] Society still frowned on the career woman, tolerating only women who were working for needed supplemental income. The approved female role was still as the good wife and mother, her prime responsibility being to the home.[12]

World War II changed all that—temporarily. Now women were needed in all work areas, contributing to the war effort while the men fought the enemy. The percentages of women working increased to 36 percent, with training programs and child-care centers often available to them. Both a postwar recession and GIs returning to their former jobs resulted in the firing of 2 million women within 15 months after the war ended. As child-care centers were dismantled, public propaganda led to women leaving their jobs and returning to their home responsibilities full time. Nevertheless, the proportion of women working gradually increased, exceeding 50 percent by the 1980s.

BOX 13.2   **THE INTERNATIONAL SCENE**

Until recently Japanese men and women had clearly defined roles: The man worked and the woman stayed home with the children. However, a battle of the sexes has been quietly escalating. National surveys reveal that most Japanese men look upon a decent family life as a part of adulthood and seek in a wife one who will be a good housekeeper. Women, on the other hand, are rebelling. Educated, employed, and independent-minded, many no longer feel compelled to be married by age 25.

A 1991 poll by the *Asahi Shimbun* found that the women thought that three of every five Japanese men were unreliable. Social indicators bear out the attitudinal surveys. The number of unmarried men and women over 30 has doubled since 1970. The birthrate has declined precipitously. As the population ages and the tax base shrinks, government bureaucrats worry about the future labor force and redirection of financial resources to support the retired population.

So concerned is the Japanese government that in Summer 1992 the Institute of Population Problems, a part of Tokyo's Health and Welfare Ministry, sent out questionnaires to 13,000 single Japanese citizens asking them their views on families and children. Survey results simply reinforced the opinion polls and marriage statistics. Japanese women are increasingly rejecting the traditional female role, and the men don't know how to behave around independent-minded women.

The 1960s was a decade of social activism inspired by many factors, including the Camelot promise of the Kennedy administration, with Kennedy being the nation's first president born in the twentieth century. Kennedy appointed a Presidential Commission on the Status of Women, which documented extensive sexual discrimination in the country. When Congress failed to act on the commission's recommendations, a number of feminist advocates formed the National Organization for Women (NOW) in 1966, and a new phase of the feminist movement began. Resisted at first by most other women's groups, the New Left, and even civil rights groups, the feminist movement eventually gained acceptance, succeeding in its efforts to end many forms of sex discrimination that were economic in nature.

THE REALITY OF SEXUAL DIFFERENCES _____

Men and women differ biologically, but do they differ in other ways too? Are women naturally more tender, loving, nurturing, and passive? Are men more aggressive, intelligent, and dominant? When Freud argued that biology was destiny, he was simply restating a prevailing belief that had existed for centuries. Abundant evidence almost everywhere demonstrated a lower status for women, suggesting their inferiority rested on biological differences. Yet how much of these "natural" differences actually results from sociocultural factors and how much is truly innate? We still do not know, because untangling the impact of cultural molding from inherent capabilities has been virtually impossible so far. Still we do have some clues from research investigations.

Biological Explanations

Aside from physical and reproductive differences, males and females are biologically distinct in other ways. Females tend to have a lower infant mortality rate, a higher tolerance for pain, and greater longevity. Their size and weight tend to give males greater physical strength. Scientists studying newborn infants, however, have not detected any significant differences in personality traits between the sexes.

In one longitudinal study tracking 275 children from birth through the first grade, researchers determined that sex hormones are not linked to male and female behavior patterns. Analyzing five sex hormones present at birth, they found little variation in type or amount between boys and girls. Stereotypical behavior in such areas as muscle strength, moods, aggression, intellectual ability, irritability, crying, and activity level could not be linked to sex hormones. A wide variation of behavior distributions existed among the children but not between genders.[13]

British geneticist Anne Moir, in her 1991 book *Brain Sex: The Real Difference Between Men & Women,* cites numerous studies showing gender-specific differences of the brain.[14] Such findings may not be "politically correct," she argues, but they are nonetheless factual. For example, men have fewer fibers connecting the verbal and emotional areas of the brain, making it more difficult for them to express emotions. However, males demonstrate a superior ability to understand abstract relationships, which may make them more naturally suited to disciplines such as mathematics and engineering.

Using biological differences as an argument for behavioral differences becomes weak when cross-cultural comparisons are made. Why, for example, are women often physical laborers in Russia, as well as about one-third of the engineers and three-fourths of the physicians? The answer lies in society's definitions of gender identity and of the appropriate behavioral roles within that identity.

Socialization and Sex Roles

Although gender identity is an ascribed status, one given at birth, society shapes that identity through socialization. In this process of learning traits and activities that are desirable and correct, individuals internalize approved sex role behavior as a real part of themselves. These cultural dictates of appropriate male–female conduct sometimes vary from one society to another, as anthropologist Margaret Mead found, for example, among three tribes in

New Guinea.[15] The Arapesh culture produced both men and women with decidedly feminine traits, whereas the Mundugamor produced both sexes with pronounced masculine traits. However, among the Tchambuli the usual sex-role behavior of western society was completely reversed. Mead's findings emphasized the influential role of culture and socialization in developing sexual differentiation.

In much of the world male dominance has both existed and been reinforced by the writings of male philosophers and religious leaders. Sexist ideology is promoted in the sacred books of the world's three major religions, evoking supernatural justification for male supremacy. Islam's Koran states, ''Men are superior to women on account of qualities in which God has given them pre-eminence.'' In the New Testament Saint Paul proclaims, ''Let the woman learn in silence with all subjection. But I suffer not a woman to teach, nor to usurp authority over the man, but to be in silence . . . she shall be saved in childbearing, if they continue in faith and charity and holiness with sobriety.'' Finally, the morning prayer of the Orthodox Jews includes the line, ''Blessed art Thou, oh Lord our God, King of the Universe, that I was not born a woman.''

Childhood Socialization

Influenced by such value pronouncements, but even more so by their own upbringing, parents convey their expectations to children in thousands of ways. Studies show mothers and fathers touch, handle, speak to, play with, and discipline children differently, depending on the child's sex. Children learn to play differently, girls more often in exclusive dyadic relationships and boys more likely in larger groups.[16] Boys usually grow up experiencing more expansive territory on their bikes or hikes, requiring numerous adaptive decisions, while girls generally experience a more structured, narrower world, limiting their opportunities to develop self-reliance. Children also learn from parental and other adult role models, assuming attitudes and evaluations of their gender.

The impact of parents, family, friends, school, and the media in shaping differences in gender behavior extends to personalities as well. Because of childhood experiences, boys tend to become more inquisitive, self-assured, and convinced they can control things whereas girls tend to become more passive, timid, and fearful of new situations. Although individuals vary in personality and temperament, this pattern emerges through the socialization process to match self-evaluations with the unequal rewards of the system, thereby completing the vicious circle of justification.[17]

On the basis of an 11-year longitudinal study of culturally influenced sex differences among boys and girls, psychologist Jeanne Bloch has identified seven areas where the two sexes vary:

1. *Aggression.* Boys tend to be more aggressive in various activities.
2. *Activity.* Boys tend to have more outdoor activities, to be more curious and explore unfamiliar worlds.

3. *Impulsiveness.* Boys tend to resist temptations less, which is partly indicated by their higher accident rate.

4. *Anxiety.* Girls tend to be more fearful and anxious, their greater compliance and obedience manifesting their anxiety.

5. *Importance of Social Relations.* Girls tend to have greater concern for the welfare of the group, to compromise more, and to understand better the feelings of others.

6. *Quality of Self-Concept.* Males tend to view themselves as more powerful and in control, seeing themselves as able to make things happen.

7. *Achievement-Related Activities.* Males tend to set higher goals and be more confident, blaming failure on external factors, whereas females blame themselves.[18]

Socialization is a lifelong process, and throughout one's childhood, adolescence, and adulthood a continuous array of experiences reinforces early influences. Toys, games, textbooks, teachers' attitudes and actions, and peer influence have all helped maintain sexual stereotypes. Most influential is the role of the media, particularly television commercials and programming. If we are to believe television, only males live life with gusto, buy cars, and have group fun, whereas women use the right shampoo to avoid the "frizzies," wear a seductive perfume, or get their floors to really shine.[19] A content analysis of the lyrics of many of today's hit songs and the images conveyed in many music videos reveals the continuance of sexual stereotyping.

Advertising

The impact of advertising in reinforcing traditional sex roles and stereotypes is very pervasive. Lucy Komisar argues that:

> Advertising is an insidious propaganda machine for a male supremacist society. . . . [It] legitimizes the idealized, stereotyped roles of woman as temptress, wife, mother, and sex object, and portrays women as less intelligent and more dependent than men. . . . It makes women feel unfeminine if they are not pretty enough and guilty if they do not spend most of their time in desperate attempts to imitate gourmet cooks and eighteenth century scullery maids. . . . It creates false, unreal images of women that reflect males' fantasies rather than flesh and blood human beings.[20]

Research on television advertising reveals: (1) males do most of the commercial voiceovers; (2) women tend to perform typical family activities, usually in the home, benefiting men, but men carry out a wide variety of activities; (3) women are younger than men; (4) fewer girls and women appear than boys and men.[21] Moreover, as Erving Goffman observed, subtle forms of sexism are common in print advertising as well:

> (1) Overwhelmingly, a woman is taller than a man only when the man is her social inferior; (2) a woman's hands are seen just barely touching, holding or caressing—never grasping, manipulating or shaping; (3) when a photograph of

men and women illustrates an instruction of some sort the man is always instructing the woman—even if the men and women are actually children (that is, a male child will be instructing a female child); (4) when an advertisement requires someone to sit or lie on a bed or a floor that someone is almost always a child or a woman, hardly ever a man; (5) when the head or eye of a man is averted it is only in relation to a social, political, or intellectual superior, but when the eye or head of a woman is averted it is always in relation to whatever man is pictured with her; (6) women are repeatedly shown mentally drifting from the scene while in close physical touch with a male, their faces lost and dreamy, "as though his aliveness to the surroundings and his readiness to cope were enough for both of them"; (7) concomitantly, women, much more than men, are pictured at the kind of psychological loss or remove from a social situation that leaves one unoriented for action (e.g., something terrible has happened and a woman is shown with her hands over her mouth and her eyes helpless with horror).[22]

Today's world is hardly static regarding sexual inequality, as women continue to make gains in all areas. Yet we remain in a transitional stage, and socialization inequities continue. One team of researchers pointed out that the computing culture puts out obstacles for little girls, even though computers will be the principal tools in 25 percent of all jobs in a few years.[23] The video arcade is a den of teenage male culture, they say, where the main role of girls is to admire the performance of their boyfriends, not to play themselves. Arcade games and home computer software transplant street-corner society to a TV monitor with games of destruction, sports, and tests of spatial skills—games designed by males for males—hardly the kind of world girls find enticing.

IMMIGRANT AND MINORITY WOMEN _____

Before we look at women in contemporary America in the next section, we first need to consider the impact of socialization and subcultural communities on the role of many women in American society. Almost all immigrants, past and present, have come from traditional societies with clearly defined sex-role models of behavior and responsibility. Those internalized self-concepts and expectations were not only part of everyday life in their homeland but also continuing norms within their ethnic communities after immigration. In those culturally insulated neighborhoods with their parallel social institutions, women seldom worked outside the home, performing instead their traditional responsibilities for their families within the home.

Vestiges of White Ethnic Orientations

In many northeastern U.S. cities, numerous elderly immigrant poor live on meager, fixed incomes, struggling to survive in decaying neighborhoods no longer cohesive or homogeneous. Most of these elderly are female, with a limited command of English, because their traditional role in an ethnic community did not necessitate English fluency and most arrived in the United States long before the advent of the feminist movement. Lacking job skills and much formal education, unfamiliar with the workings of a bureaucratic society or reluctant to seek public assistance, they cling to the remnants of their familiar world. For them, being a woman who is advanced in years and unprepared for independence, life presents daily challenges.

Often overlooked in any discussion of most aspects of ethnicity are second-generation adult Americans. Yet their primary socialization revolved around Old World value orientations and traditional sex-role models, shaping their perceptions of the world somewhat differently than that of children of native-born parents. Studies of working-class Americans, many of whom are second-generation Americans of central, southern, and eastern European heritage, reveal some of these continuing values and attitudes. In a typical working-class family, the woman does not work outside the home; she devotes her energies entirely to the family, while the male serves as breadwinner and supreme authority of the household.

The women's movement has brought problems to these families. Lillian Rubin's field research shows that many working-class women are frustrated and lonely, not experiencing in their lives the heralded liberation television portrays.[24] Males, providing their wives with all the attributes of a good life—home, car, necessities, and luxuries—are puzzled by their wives' unhappiness. Because their value orientations are sex-segregated, working-class husbands and wives may experience great difficulty communicating with each other.

One avenue of role expansion for workingmen's wives has been increased participation in the civic arena of service, politics, and social action. Sociologist Irene Dabrowski reports that their widespread neighborhood involvement stems from urban problems disrupting "Little Italys," "Polish Towns," and "South Sides," thereby "weakening family ties, eroding economic self-sufficiency, and even threatening the very existence of these largely white ethnic communities."[25] In a case study of Carondelet, an ethnic working-class neighborhood on the south side of St. Louis, Dabrowski found neighborhood women in three-fourths of all community organizations and half of all leadership positions, achieving moderate success in preserving the vitality and stability of their community.[26]

Today's Minority Women

Machismo, the pervasive value orientation of the male as provider and dominant force in the family, impacts heavily on the daily lives of lower-income Hispanic women. Problems arise among low-income Hispanic-Americans when only the female is able to find work or earns more than her spouse, creating family strain as internalized male self-image and role behavior—as culturally prescribed—are threatened by economic reality. Hispanic women who work or go to school must still completely fulfill their traditional home responsibilities, placing extensive demands on them to maintain both spheres of work adequately.

The status and roles of Asian American women vary with their place of birth and that of their husbands, as well as their educational levels. Generally, those foreign-born women maintain very traditional family and sex roles. The higher the education and the more Americanized the women are, the higher their status. Although more Asian women are combining career and family roles, Lucy Jen Huang reports that the Chinese wife tends to assume the role of "co-pilot and helper to her husband rather than be totally equalitarian in the relationship."[27] Akemi Kikumura and Henry H. L. Kitano suggest that the personal dissatisfaction among Japanese American women in their expected female roles may be a primary reason for their more rapid acculturation and greater outgroup marriage rate.[28]

The dichotomy among blacks, discussed in Chapter 10, relates directly to the status and role of the black female in American society. College-educated black females are more likely to benefit from the women's liberation movement in employment, income, and equalitarian marriages, although their higher ratio to black male college graduates can be a disadvantage in finding a spouse of the same race.[29] In contrast low-income black women do not identify with the women's movement because many of its demands seem irrelevant to their needs. Black feminist Bell Hooks observes:

> Today masses of black women in the U.S. refuse to acknowledge that they have much to gain by the feminist struggle. They fear feminism. They have stood in place so long that they are afraid to move. They fear change. They fear losing what little they have. They are afraid to openly confront white feminists with their racism or black males with their sexism, not to mention white males with their racism and sexism.[30]

Two basic themes emerge from a consideration of women in various racial and ethnic groups: cultural attributes and intensified subordinate status. Not only do immigrant groups recreate in miniature their old familiar worlds to obtain a secure place in an alien country, but also their evolving ethnic self-consciousness and community organization foster maintenance of accompanying male-dominance patterns as well. These traditional gender roles have either reflected sexism within the entire society or else resisted recent advances in sexual equality. Moreover, as both a woman and a minority group member, an individual is at a double disadvantage, simultaneously encountering prejudice and discrimination on two fronts—her sex and her race or ethnicity.

Special concerns of minority women include involuntary sterilization, monolingual education and services, high infant and maternal mortality rates, housing, psychological and employment testing, reduced enforcement of affirmative action, deportation of Hispanic mothers of American-born children, special-admission quality education programs, unemployment, welfare programs, and the family.[31] One black delegate to the National Women's Convention summed up the double disadvantages of minority women:

> Minority women share with all women the experience of sexism as a barrier to their full rights of citizenship. . . . But the institutionalized bias based on race, language, culture and/or ethnic origin in governance of territories or localities has led to the additional oppression and exclusion of minority women and to the conditions of poverty from which they disproportionally suffer.[32]

WOMEN IN CONTEMPORARY AMERICA _____

The justification for considering women as a minority group and for speaking of the existence of sexism becomes readily understandable through examination of leading social indicators. As we did for African and Hispanic Americans in earlier chapters, we shall now direct our attention to the comparative status of women in terms of education, employment, and income. Additionally, we shall look at sexual harassment, law, and politics to illustrate why the U.S. Commission on Civil Rights in 1976 concluded, "Discrimination against women exists in every facet of American society."[33]

Education

For many generations, education was sex-segregated. Males and females often attended different schools or were physically and academically separated in "co-educational" schools. For example, the still-standing Henry Street grammar school in New York's Lower East Side—a well-known white ethnic area for over a century—contains either the word "Boys" or "Girls" engraved over one of its two opposite-end entrances. Women were once taught only the social graces and given moral education. Teaching academic subjects to females was then considered a waste of time, one Harvard professor in 1911 even proclaiming that such an attempt would "weaken the intellect of the teacher."[34]

Even after females overcame these prejudices and took academic subjects alongside males, the educational system maintained sexism in both obvious and subtle ways. Teachers and counselors with traditional sex-role expectations fostered sex-linked aspirations and career choices. Children's books and textbooks reinforced sex stereotypes, with male characters heavily outnumbering females and portrayed as active and adventuresome in contrast to the more passive females. Stereotypical activities—boys creating or earning money and girls shopping, cooking, and sewing—existed in all texts, even in mathematics. Throughout all of them the exclusive use of male pronouns further biased children's education. Most of these stereotypical depictions have been eliminated through court challenges and pressures on publishers, but problems still remain.[35]

Although much has changed in the past 20 years, gender bias in the schools remains, according to a report issued in February 1992 by the American Association of University Women Educational Foundation.[36] Girls enter the first grade with the same or better skills and ambitions as boys, but classroom sexist

---

BOX 13.3	BARBAROUS RITUALS

Woman Is:
- kicking strongly in your mother's womb, upon which she is told, "It must be a boy, if it's so active!"
- being confined to the Doll Corner in nursery school when you are really fascinated by Tinker Toys.
- being labeled a tomboy when all you wanted to do was climb that tree to look out and see a distance.
- seeing grownups chuckle when you say you want to be an engineer or doctor when you grow up—and learning to say you want to be a mommy or nurse, instead.
- dreading summertime because more of your body with its imperfections will be seen—and judged.
- liking math or history and getting hints that boys are turned off by smart girls.
- discovering that what seems like everything worthwhile doing in life "isn't feminine," and learning to just delight in being feminine and "nice"—and feeling somehow guilty.
- swinging down the street feeling good and smiling at people and being hassled like a piece of meat in return.
- brooding about "how far" you should go with the guy you really like. Will he no longer respect you? Will you get—oh God—a "reputation"? Or, if not, are you a square? Being pissed off because you can't just do what you feel like doing.
- finding that the career you've chosen exacts more than just study or hard work—an emotional price of being made to feel "less a woman."
- being bugged by men in the office who assume that you're a virginal prude if you don't flirt, and that you're an easy mark if you are halfway relaxed and pleasant.
- wanting to go back to school, to read, to join something, do something. Why isn't home enough for you? What's wrong with you?
- feeling a need to say "thank you" when your guy actually fixes himself a meal now that you're dying with the 'flu.
- being widowed, or divorced, and trying to get a "good" job—at your age.
- getting older, getting lonelier, getting ready to die—and knowing it wouldn't have had to be this way after all.

SOURCE: From Robin Morgan, *Going Too Far: The Personal Chronicle of a Feminist* (New York: Vintage Books, 1978), 107–113.

---

conditioning results in lower self-confidence and aspirations by the time they graduate from high school. Two out of three of the nation's teachers may be women, but they tend to favor gender stereotypes, recalling more positively the assertive male students while liking least the assertive females. Teachers call on boys more often, give them more detailed criticism, and praise more

---

| BOX 13.4 | **THE INTERNATIONAL SCENE** |

One of Canada's best-known lobbying organizations for women's rights, the National Action Committee on the Status of Women, released a report in May 1992 on the high rates of sexual abuse and economic discrimination Canadian women suffer. Among the report's findings were the following:

- Women who worked full time earned only 67.6 percent of what men did in 1990.
- Women had taken off 5.2 days from work in 1990 for family responsibilities, compared to 1.9 in 1977. Men's time off remained virtually unchanged.
- Of single-parent families headed by women, 57 percent lived below the poverty line, a figure unchanged since 1974.
- About 75 percent of women lived out the last quarter of their lives in poverty.
- One in four women would be sexually assaulted at some point in their lives.
- In 1991, between 65 and 80 hours of paid work a week had been required to support a family compared to 45 hours in the 1970s.

---

the intellectual content of boys' work while more likely praising girls for their neatness. Teachers also allow boys to shout out answers and take risks, but they reprimand girls as rude for doing the same thing. In addition, few educators encourage girls to pursue careers in math and science.

As Table 13.1 shows, the median school years completed are very close between males and females when controlled for race. Although parity has been reached in the level of educational attainment, choice of college academic fields of study still reflects significant gender differentiation (see Table 13.2). Women are underrepresented in such male-dominated fields as computer and information services, engineering, and the physical sciences, but they are overrepresented in the traditional female career areas of education, nursing, and home economics. Advanced degrees conferred in medicine, dentistry, law, and engineering show a steady lessening of the sex-ratio imbalance, ranging now from 3 to 2 in law to over 6 to 1 in engineering (see Table 13.3).

Employment

Over 57 percent of all women work, up from almost 43 percent in 1970.[37] The greatest increase in working women has been among wives with school-aged children. By 1990 about 73 percent of mothers with children aged 6 to 13 were

TABLE 13.1

YEARS OF SCHOOL COMPLETED, BY SEX, RACE, AND SPANISH ORIGIN: 1991

Percent of Population Completing

Race and Sex	Population (1,000)	Elementary School			High School			College		Median School Years Completed
		0–4 Years	5–7 Years	8 Years	1–3 Years	4 Years	1–3 Years	4 Years or More		
White	136,299	2.0	3.4	4.5	10.2	39.1	18.6	22.2	12.8
Male	65,394	2.2	3.6	4.5	9.9	36.1	18.4	25.4	12.8
Female	70,905	1.8	3.3	4.5	10.5	41.8	18.8	19.3	12.7
Black	17,096	4.7	6.4	4.1	18.0	37.7	17.5	11.5	12.4
Male	7,626	6.5	6.3	4.3	16.3	38.3	17.0	11.4	12.4
Female	9,470	3.3	6.6	3.9	19.4	37.2	17.9	11.6	12.4
Spanish Origin	11,208	12.5	14.8	6.3	15.1	29.3	12.3	9.7	12.0
Male	5,509	12.9	14.8	6.1	14.7	28.5	13.0	10.0	12.1
Female	5,699	12.1	14.7	6.5	15.5	30.1	11.7	9.4	12.0
Total All Races	158,694	2.4	3.8	4.4	11.0	38.6	18.4	21.4	12.7

SOURCES: U.S. Bureau of the Census, *Current Population Reports*, U.S. Government Printing Office, Washington, DC, Series P-20, No. 462.

TABLE 13.2

FEMALE-EARNED BACHELOR'S DEGREES BY FIELD OF STUDY BY PERCENTAGES OF TOTAL

	1980	1989
Business and management	33.6	46.7
Communications	52.1	60.4
Computer and information sciences	30.4	30.7
Education	73.2	77.7
Engineering	9.3	13.6
Foreign languages	75.7	73.3
Health sciences	82.8	84.9
Home economics	95.1	90.6
Law	42.9	60.3
Life sciences	42.2	50.2
Math	42.1	46.0
Physical sciences	23.6	29.7
Psychology	63.3	70.8
Social sciences	43.6	44.4
Visual and performing arts	63.1	61.5

SOURCE: U.S. National Center for Education Statistics, *Digest of Education Statistics,* 1990.

TABLE 13.3

DEGREES CONFERRED IN SELECTED PROFESSIONS

Type of Degree	1960	1970	1980	1989
Medicine (M.D.)				
Men	6,645	7,615	11,416	10,326
Women	387	699	3,486	5,128
Dentistry (D.D.S., D.M.D.)				
Men	3,221	3,684	4,558	3,139
Women	26	34	700	1,108
Law (LL.B, J.D.)				
Men	9,010	14,115	24,893	21,048
Women	230	801	10,754	14,519
Engineering				
Men	45,453	63,227	80,001	76,627
Women	171	526	7,642	12,164

SOURCE: U.S. National Center for Education Statistics, *Digest of Education Statistics,* 1990.

TABLE 13.4

LABOR FORCE PARTICIPATION FOR WIVES, HUSBANDS PRESENT, BY AGE OF CHILDREN, 1975 AND 1990, BY PERCENTAGES

	Total		Black		White	
	1975	1990	1975	1990	1975	1990
No children under 18	43.8	50.5	54.1	65.6	43.6	57.0
With children under 18	44.9	65.8	58.4	75.4	43.6	65.2
Children under 6	36.7	59.7	54.9	71.5	34.7	57.5
Children 6 to 13	51.8	72.6	71.8	81.4	50.7	71.8
Children 14 to 17	53.5	74.4	52.3	73.2	53.4	74.5

SOURCE: U.S. Bureau of Labor Statistics, Bulletin 2340, U.S. Government Printing Office, Washington, DC, 1992.

TABLE 13.5

EMPLOYED PERSONS, SELECTED OCCUPATIONS, BY SEX AND PERCENTAGES, 1991

Female		Male	
Registered nurses	94.8	Architects	82.9
Elementary school teachers	85.9	Engineers	91.8
Bank tellers	90.3	Lawyers and judges	71.1
Bookkeepers	91.5	Dentists	89.9
Data entry keyers	86.0	Physicians	79.9
Dental hygienists	99.8	Science technicians	70.2
File clerks	80.9	Securities & financial services	71.1
Receptionists	97.1	Mail carriers, post office	72.2
Secretaries	99.0	Carpenters	98.7
Telephone operators	89.2	Automobile mechanics	99.2
Typists	95.1	Electrical & electronic repair	90.4
Waiters	81.6	Barbers	81.7
Nursing aides, orderlies	89.2	Telephone installers	93.5
Private household workers	96.0	Truck drivers	95.8

SOURCE: U.S. Bureau of Labor Statistics, Employment and Earnings, U.S. Government Printing Office, Washington, DC, January 1992.

working, up from 52 percent in 1975. Over 58 percent of all women with children under 6 were working, up from 37 percent in 1975.[38] In almost all categories the percentage of black working mothers was significantly higher (see Table 13.4).

One outcome of the feminist movement has been the entry of women into fields once exclusively a male occupational domain. This experienced helicopter pilot may be a woman, but she is part of only 3 percent of the female pilots and navigators. Many occupations remain heavily dominated by one gender. *(Bob Daemmrich/Stock, Boston)*

Despite the increase in the rate of female participation in the labor force and in females' proportional representation in previously male-dominated occupations, significant differences in male-female career categories remain. First, a female occupational ghetto exists, with many women in traditional low-paying, low-status jobs. Such "pink-color" jobs include bank tellers, bookkeepers, cashiers, health technicians, librarians, sales clerks, secretaries, and telephone operators. Over 60 percent of all working women are mired in low-paying clerical and sales jobs. Male-dominated occupations, on the other hand, tend to be the higher-paying, higher-status positions (see Table 13.5 and Figure 13.1).

Another problem is the **glass ceiling,** a real but unseen discriminatory policy among companies that limits the upward mobility of women into top management positions, high-profile transfers, or changes in key assignments. A 1991 Department of Labor report on the glass ceiling revealed that only 3 percent of top executive positions at the largest U.S. corporations are held by women, a figure that has not changed in over 10 years.[39] One means by which women have bucked this system of subtle discrimination is to start their own businesses. In 1990 3.1 million women did so, a 50 percent increase over 1980.[40]

Income

Ever since pay equity became a civil rights goal in the 1970s, minorities and women have made progress. In 1991 women earned 74 cents for every dollar earned by men, up from 59 cents in 1977.[41] Until 1989 women were narrowing the gap by making more money, but as the economy slumped thereafter, the gap narrowed further when men's average wages dropped.

Occupational distribution by gender into lower-paying and higher-paying fields of work partially explains the remaining income disparity. However, women still earn less than men in almost every field, including those dominated by females (see Table 13.6). A portion of this difference may be due to variations in qualifications, seniority, and number of hours worked, but even when these variables are controlled for, the disparity still exists. Catharine MacKinnon has observed:

> Controlling for differences in education, skills, and experience (factors which themselves could be created by discrimination), studies have found a remaining difference between men's and women's salaries of between 20 and 43 percent, a difference which can be explained only as discrimination.[42]

Generally, the median earnings across all educational categories of year-round, full-time workers are higher for males than for females, and for whites than for blacks. Black males earn slightly more than three-fourths of the income of white males with a comparable education, whereas black females earn almost the same as white females within similar educational attainment levels.[43] However, this apparent pay equity among black and white females often actually results from black women working longer hours and being in the labor force longer than white women.[44] This pay inequity suggests that sexual discrimination further compounds the problems of racial discrimination in the workplace.

When we consider the growing number of households headed by women (see Figure 13.3), this pattern takes on alarming significance. About 13 percent of all white families and about 46 percent of all black families are headed by women, whose greater probability of limited earning power has a negative impact on the family's economic health. Female-headed families are the fastest growing segment of the population living in poverty, prompting many to call this trend the *feminization of poverty*.[45] One out of three female-headed families now lives in poverty, having increased from 1.8 million families in 1969 to over 3.2 million in 1990.[46]

SEXUAL HARASSMENT _____

For years sexual harassment continued because it was kept secret and considered to be an individual, personal problem. Supposedly, a male, attracted

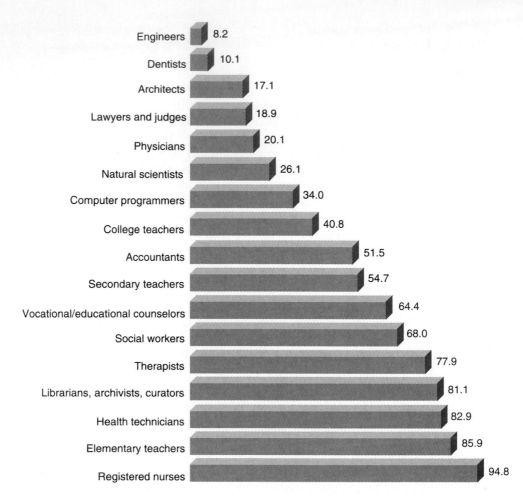

FIGURE 13.1
Female Professional and Technical Workers, by Percent, 1991
SOURCE: U.S. Bureau of Labor Statistics.

to a particular female, made sexual advances and received a positive, negative, or "maybe" response. Until 1976, women kept mostly silent, thinking the experience an individual encounter and not realizing it was part of a larger pattern connected to their subordination and vulnerability in the occupational structure.

Redbook magazine's 1976 survey of 9,000 women defined the extent of the problem, 90 percent reported having experienced sexual harassment at work. The women's movement brought heightened awareness of the group basis of this problem. Then the federal government's Merit System Protection Board, in a 1978–1980 study, reported a $189 million cost in hiring, training, absenteeism, and job-turnover expenses caused by harassment. When private industry costs are included, the figure probably runs into billions. The govern-

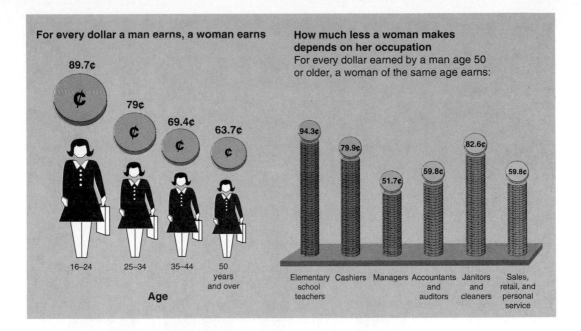

FIGURE 13.2
Comparative Earnings of Men and Women
SOURCE: U.S. Department of Labor.

TABLE 13.6	MEDIAN WEEKLY EARNINGS IN SELECTED OCCUPATIONS BY SEX IN 1990, EXCLUDING SELF-EMPLOYED		
Occupation	**Male**	**Female**	**Female Percentage of Male Earnings**
College Professors	$808	$620	77
Computer Programmers	$691	$573	83
Elementary Teachers	$575	$513	89
Financial Managers	$837	$558	67
Managers, Marketing and Public Relations	$902	$616	68
Nurses Aides, Orderlies	$284	$248	87
Personnel Managers	$881	$604	69
Registered Nurses	$616	$608	99
Sales	$505	$292	58
Secretaries, Typists	$387	$341	88
Waiters, Waitresses	$266	$194	73

SOURCE: U.S. Department of Labor, *Employment and Earnings,* January 1991.

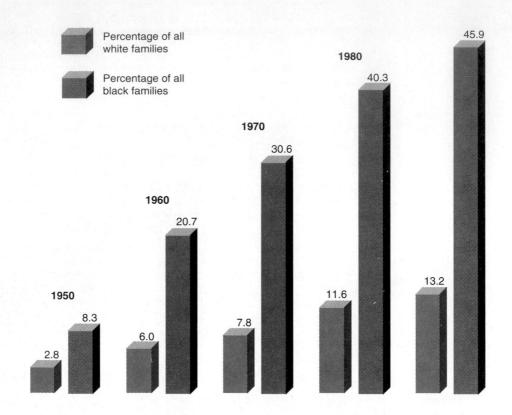

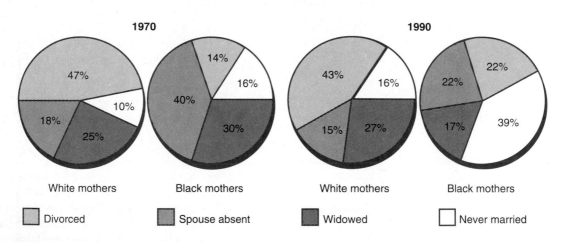

FIGURE 13.3
Households Headed by Women
SOURCE: U.S. Bureau of the Census.

ment survey also estimated that 1 percent, or about 9,000 female federal employees, had been victims of attempted rape by supervisors or coworkers.

In 1979, attorney and university professor Catharine A. MacKinnon wrote the first book on this subject, *Sexual Harassment of Working Women: A Case of Sex Discrimination.* She identified sexual harassment as either a single occurrence at work or a series of incidents, ranging along a continuum of varying intensity, including:

> verbal sexual suggestions or jokes, constant leering or ogling, brushing against your body "accidentally," a friendly pat, squeeze or pinch or arm against you, catching you alone for a quick kiss, the indecent proposition backed by the threat of losing your job, or forced sexual relations.[47]

Some men's assumption that their superior position at work also involves sexual privileges is rooted in centuries of male domination:

> Sexual harassment by a boss or supervisor harkens back, in a way, to the medieval practice of *droit du seigneur,* which gave the feudal lord the right to sleep the first night with the bride of any of his vassals. Although feudalism ended many centuries ago, some people still feel that to be a boss is to be at least semi-divinely ordained—to have certain inalienable rights. . . . The idea of using a paycheck as a license for sex seems ludicrous, if not sick, but it happens all the time. Men who would never think or at least never follow through on, the idea of pinching a woman's breast in a bus or on the street, feel free to subject their secretary to this humiliation as if it were a job-given right.[48]

Since 1980 the courts have generally used 31 pages of guidelines from the federal Equal Employment Opportunity Commission to protect employees from conduct considered illegal under Title VII of the Civil Rights Act of 1964. These guidelines define sexual harassment as:

> Unwelcome sexual advances, requests for sexual favors, and other verbal or physical conduct of a sexual nature . . . when submission is made a condition of employment, or rejection of the advance is used as the basis for future employment decision, or interfering with the individual's performance or creating an intimidating, hostile, or offensive working environment.

Other obnoxious and questionable behaviors, however, escape this definition. California's Fair Employment and Housing Department has established more down-to-earth guidelines: unsolicited written, verbal, or physical contacts; suggestive or obscene notes; continual leering; obscene gestures; display of obscene objects or pictures; blocking movements by physical touching; and forced involvement in obscene joking. Although these forms of sexual harassment are not specifically mentioned, recent court decisions in Florida and California declared them as such, thereby establishing judicial precedent for future cases.[49] For males uncertain about what constitutes acceptable behavior with females, a General Motors representative has suggested a good "rough measure" of sexual harassment: "Would you be embarrassed to have your remarks displayed in the newspaper or actions described to your family?"[50]

The Hill–Thomas Hearings

Televised hearings by the Senate Judiciary Committee in September 1991 on sexual harassment charges by Anita Hill against Supreme Court nominee Clarence Thomas stunned the nation. As people listened with rapt attention, three days of testimony enlightened the public about how lewd and crude remarks constitute sexual harassment. However, the charges were never resolved to anyone's satisfaction. Anita Hill became a folk hero, received numerous offers of speaking engagements, and was honored in 1992 by the American Bar Association. Clarence Thomas became a Supreme Court Justice, immediately making his presence felt in the writing of opinions.

Public opinion polls taken right after the confirmation hearings showed the public believing Thomas by a 3 to 1 margin. A year later a new poll showed a dramatic shift to an evenly divided public, and an increase from 8 to 39 percent in those who thought the committee treated Hill unfairly.[51] More significantly, Anita Hill's charges and the inept performance of the all-male Senate committee proved to be a political catalyst that caused more women than ever before to run for state and national offices in 1992. Membership in

The extraordinary televised hearing of Anita Hill testifying before the all-male Senate Judiciary Committee on charges of sexual harassment against U.S. Supreme Court nominee Clarence Thomas riveted the nation's attention. This hearing raised public consciousness and inspired many women to run for office. *(Rick Reinhard/Impact Visuals)*

and donations to women's political action committees increased, and complaints about sexual harassment jumped significantly.

The Tailhook Scandal

Ironically, another major sexual harassment incident occurred in September 1991.[52] The scene was the gathering of U.S Navy combat aviators at the annual convention of the Tailhook Association (named after the device that catches planes landing on aircraft carriers). Lining the third-floor corridor of the Las Vegas Hilton, 70 Naval officers under the influence of alcohol sexually molested 26 female officers and civilians attempting to pass by. The men shoved the women against their will down the gantlet between the men, all the while groping and grabbing their breasts, crotches, or buttocks, tearing at clothes and panties, drenching them with alcohol, kissing and biting them before they reached the other end of the corridor.

A formal complaint filed by one of the victims of this sexual assault, who was a helicopter pilot and admiral's aide, was at first ignored by her superiors. When the Naval Investigative Service did investigate a month later, the navy men closed ranks and an epidemic of amnesia swept through the ranks. The aide went public with her story in June 1992, and Congress and the Pentagon began investigating. Early fallout was the resignation of the Secretary of the Navy, the forced retirement of two admirals, the demotion of the officer who first ignored the complaint, and the disbanding of the Tailhook Association.

Sexual harassment has been an ongoing problem in all branches of the military for years, but the situation may be improving. Just as Anita Hill's testimony has galvanized public awareness of verbal sexual harassment, the Tailhook episode appears to have spurred the Pentagon into taking steps to change these conditions.

SEXISM AND THE LAW

Stereotyping females as passive and in need of protection became institutionalized in law. Many labor laws, originally intended to prevent the exploitation of women, became a means of restricting their job opportunities and income potential. A vast array of state laws assuming certain female inabilities ran counter to reality. As sociologist Rosalind J. Dworkin wryly commented:

> A mother can carry her 40-pound child, move furniture in her home, and finish her housekeeping chores late at night. But the same woman, working outside the home, legally could not carry more than 30 pounds of weight or work overtime in some states. . . . [T]hese protective laws . . . degrade women to a childlike status by assuming they are unable, or not wise enough, to protect themselves, individually or collectively, from exploitation.[53]

Although many of these laws are changing, compliance does not necessarily follow. Many women do not know their legal rights or find the difficulties involved in securing them to outweigh the rewards. Moreover, the courts are hardly free of sexism themselves. In 1983 New Jersey became the first state to complete a self-review of sexism in the state court system. Among other findings it discovered the following:

1. Women received lower personal injury settlements, especially if they were housewives, because juries failed to recognize the value of their work.
2. Judges failed to enforce the new law against wife beating and domestic violence.
3. Judges set child-support payments in divorce cases too low, with no strong enforceable sanctions against nonpayment by fathers.

Female attorneys also complained that 86 percent of their colleagues and 66 percent of the judges had made demeaning jokes or hostile remarks about their sex.[54] As New Jersey took steps to eliminate such practices, pressure from female lawyers elsewhere led other states to conduct similar self-reviews. In 1991 the California State Bar Association proposed a code for lawyers that bans words or conduct reflecting any bias in sex as well as race, religion, national origin, sexual orientation, age, disability, and socioeconomic status.

Because changing hundreds of state laws is a long, difficult process, Congress approved the Equal Rights Amendment (ERA) in 1972, intending it to extend full and equal legal rights to women. The proposed Amendment's wording was brief: "Equality of rights under the law shall not be denied or abridged by the United States or by any state on account of sex." Required to be ratified by three-fourths of the states, a total of 38, it gained approval by only 35. The failure of the ERA was caused by the opposition of numerous groups, including many women, labor leaders or activists, as well as conservatives, religious groups, and insurance companies.

WOMEN AND POLITICS

Earlier we noted that, once they secured voting rights, women did not use their political power to improve their lives or win their proportional share of elected office. For decades their representation in national, state, and local elected offices was highly disproportionate. In 1990, for example, only two of 100 U.S. senators were female; 27 of 435 congressional representatives; three of 50 governors; and 17 percent of all state legislators.[55] The elections in 1992, the overstated "Year of the Woman," did result in significant female representational gains: six female senators and 47 female congressional representatives are serving in the 103rd Congress. However, 22 of the 24 women elected to the House won open seats, thanks to retirements and the once-a-decade opportunity created by redistricting. These gains reduce somewhat the gender imbalance, but it remains a significant difference. Future elections will determine whether the watershed year of 1992 can be repeated in terms of further female gains in elected office.

In 1981, President Ronald Reagan appointed the first woman to the U.S. Supreme Court—Associate Justice Sandra Day O'Connor. Since her appointment many women have been appointed to federal, state, and county judicial positions, but she remained the only woman on the nation's highest court until 1993. *(Rick Eilking/Reuters/Bettmann)*

Besides the Anita Hill controversy galvanizing the female vote, other factors encouraged female victories at the polls. Widespread corruption in the political process reduced its appeal to men, much as the once-prestigious male occupational field of clerical work yielded to female entry.[56] A suburban majority and a baby-boomer majority existed for the first time in 1992, voting blocs that give big advantages to female candidates.[57]

What accounted for lack of female political involvement for so many years prior to 1992? The question has intrigued both sociologists and political scientists, and the emerging explanations are many and varied. Most political careers evolve out of training, experience, and leadership in law or business careers, areas in which women have participated only slightly. Males control the political parties, often resisting placement of women in organizational power positions or as viable candidates for "serious" offices.[58] Politics has been a male bastion for so many generations that male politicians tend to view the female politican as a stranger, one whose feminine values and way of life appear incompatible with the world of politics. Therefore, both men and women also prefer male leaders, placing more confidence in them. Women also do not form a voting bloc because they are not residentially segregated and they do not tend to vote along socioeconomic lines.

Even when women had entered political contests earlier, differential media coverage had a negative effect on their campaigns. In studying news coverage of male and female U.S. Senate candidates in 1982 to 1986, Kim Kahn and Edie Goldenberg found that female candidates received less coverage and that the coverage they did receive concentrated more on their visibility and less on their positions on issues. They concluded that such patterns served as a critical obstacle.[59] It would appear that 1992 marked the end of such a problem, as female candidates overcame the credibility gap about their viability as candidates. Their effectiveness as legislators will determine their "reelectability."

SOCIOLOGICAL ANALYSIS _____

Every society has had a gender-based division of labor, but this has not always meant sexual inequality. Why, then, has the male role been considered superior in many societies? Functionalists, conflict theorists, and interactionists differ in explaining both the reasons for male dominance and in advocating what steps should be taken.

The Functionalist View

In preindustrial societies, from which most immigrants to America have come, assigned work tasks by gender effectively created a smoothly functioning society. Such was also the case in early nineteenth-century America when distinct sex roles facilitated social stability, women and men understanding their place and function in the society. Sociologists Talcott Parsons and Robert Bales maintained that the efficient functioning of a society, indeed its very survival, depends on satisfying both instrumental and expressive needs.[60] Males have traditionally performed the instrumental tasks—goal-oriented activities necessary for family survival, such as earning a living or finding food to supplement the female agriculturalists and herbalists. Females have handled the expressive tasks—providing harmony, love, emotional support, and stability within the family. Today, many are questioning why these necessary tasks should be gender-linked and not shared or reversed if desired.

As mentioned earlier under biological explanations, the tendencies of males to be larger, stronger, and more aggressive may explain their emergence as dominant in the social order.[61] As male dominance continued over the generations, a sexist ideology evolved to justify the existing order as "natural," gender role and status becoming institutionalized through socialization and practice. As long as society remained relatively unchanged, sex-role differentiation did not emerge as a concern to most people or generate a female group consciousness and desire for change.

Social changes caused by the Industrial Revolution threw the gender-based social structure out of balance. Machines reduced the male advantage of greater strength for work tasks, and reductions in the infant mortality rate and family size, together with labor-saving home appliances, freed women from spending most of their adult lives and waking hours raising small children. Values, attitudes, and expectations about women's proper role did not change as rapidly as social and economic conditions. This cultural lag caused strain among individuals, families, and in society itself.

Among twentieth-century immigrants, both past and present, family and traditions have been two vital means of preserving identity and stability in a new country. Those with traditional sex-role value orientations experience problems adapting to a more egalitarian society. Working Hispanic women present a conflict to the machismo concept of the male as the sole provider. Social activities and dating practices among teenage girls challenge traditional homeland norms about adolescent male–female interaction. Higher education for women runs counter to traditional notions about its value for females who should just marry and bear children.

Achieving sexual equality, functionalists stress, requires a restoration of a balance between expectations and actual conditions. To some, changes have been too extensive and system harmony requires a return to the past, with clearly defined sex roles restoring a stable family life and an efficient division of labor. Most functionalists, however, call for redefined sex roles and adjustments in the family system and other social institutions to eliminate sexual discrimination. Changes in societal conditions and expectations require system adjustments if the dysfunctions are to be overcome.

The Conflict View

Male dominance and subordination of women and sexual inequality and discrimination are simply illustrations for conflict theorists of the universal human problems of exploitation and oppression. Substituting the words *men* and *women* for names of dominant and minority groups, or *gender* for *class*, enables us to incorporate women as a group in Marxian concepts of false consciousness, exploitation, awakened awareness, and organized challenges to the social order. In fact, Friedrich Engels observed that the first class oppression in history was of "the female sex by the male."[62]

When the economic contributions of the two sexes were fairly even, as in hunting and gathering societies, sexual equality existed to a high degree. Women in those societies gathered a good share of edible foods, but the men were not always successful in their hunting expeditions, thus making the gender-based activities of both important. Agrarian and pastoral societies drew on greater male strength for needed labors in plowing, irrigation, building, crafts, and military defense. Sexual inequality then became more marked as disparities in economic contributions, a pattern continuing into early industrial societies, with women working only in low-paying positions.[63]

In industrial societies female dependence on male breadwinners kept women in an inferior position, an unchallenged situation until increasing numbers of women entered the labor force. The demands of recent years for sexual equality correlates with women's growing economic contributions. In other words conflict theorists maintain that women's economic position determines the degree of equality in relations between men and women in society.[64] As they achieved greater economic independence, women developed a heightened awareness of a shared bond of exploitation, and the feminist movement gained momentum and many successes in eliminating sexist discrimination.

A society's cultural characteristics, which are the product of generations of thought and reinforced patterns of behavior, live on through the social institutions that perpetuate the sexist ideology that women are childlike, passive, and inferior. For centuries the social structure of most societies placed males in controlling positions of political, economic, and social power. The subordinate role of women in society and in the family clearly benefited men, giving them little incentive to change the sex-role patterns. A prevailing male value system placed men in a superior status by putting women in an inferior one, defining the female role as supportive to the more highly valued male activities. In classic Marxian theory, only the social action of the subordinate group in challenging this arrangement can effect a change.

Who benefits from sexual inequality? Males do, in terms of higher status, better jobs, higher pay, greater life satisfaction, and more leisure time at home while their wives fulfill domestic and child-care chores. Business and industry reap higher profits, possibly 23 percent of all corporate profits, by employing women at lower rates than men.[65] This oppression of women exacts some costs for both sexes as well: denial of full human development and full use of one's talents; loss to the society of much human creativity and leadership; and individual suffering in economic deprivation and emotional and psychological strain.

The Interactionist View

Through social interaction, as well as the internalization of others' expectations, the self emerges. From birth through adulthood, children go through a socialization process that shapes their sense of identity on the basis of cultural value orientations about sex roles. All the socialization agents—family, school, peers, church, media—promote sex-role identity and norms in various ways, including example and reinforcement. Social definitions of appropriate behavior, emotions, and goals for boys or girls become internalized as desirable attributes for acceptance and praise. Because these social definitions begin so early, are so pervasive, and are accepted by those so defined, they appear to be "natural," explaining how "Nature" or "God" intended us to be.

In this socially constructed reality of shared expectations about gender capabilities and proper behavior, people interact with one another on the basis of their cultural conditioning. Men do not, however, consciously and deliberately subjugate women, who passively submit to their masters. For the most part both sexes long interacted with one another in a taken-for-granted manner as to their "place" in the social structure. William I. Thomas's famous statement (1911) indicates both the consequences of social definitions, including sexism, as well as the "male reality" of his time: "If men define a situation as real, it is real in its consequences."

Technological changes have altered our social structure and life expectations. As a result traditional sex roles no longer find acceptance among many women. Yet a consensus does not exist about what it means to be male and female, a fact that creates an ambiguous situation. Sex roles may be blurring, but strongly held concepts of masculinity and femininity remain popular and influential. We live in a transitional period, when we are redefining sex roles while many aspects of traditional sex-role attitudes and practices continue. How long and difficult will this transitional period be? No one knows, although evidence from surveys on sex-role attitudes shows increased acceptance of women in nontraditional sex roles among both men and women.[66] As new patterns of male–female interaction become institutionalized in various social arenas, we may expect to find greater acceptance of sexual equality.

Because the socialization process is so critical, interactionists stress the need to change its content and approach. Thus parents can be made more aware of existing sexual biases in behavioral expectations of their children, encouraging them to develop fully all aspects of their personalities. Through education and the media, a more enlightened approach, eliminating sexual stereotypes, and providing varied role models of either gender, could do much to promote change and sexual equality. The media and the academic world could also do much to resocialize women to overcome their past conditioning and to resocialize all adults to a more egalitarian value system. This perspective holds that ideas tend to have a life of their own and, by concentrating on how we interpret the world, we can create a new social reality.

Retrospect

American society has only recently recognized sexism as a social problem although it has existed for centuries. Minority-group characteristics—ascribed status, physical and cultural visibility, unequal treatment, and shared-group awareness—apply to women just as they do to various racial and ethnic groups. The practice of endogamy does not apply, but in marriage the dominant–subordinate roles are often quite obvious.

Throughout much of American history, male dominance patterns prevailed. Women lacked voting, contract, and property rights and were even denied the right to enjoy sex without being thought deviant. After a long struggle women gained the right to vote nationally in 1919 but did not harness any political power to effect change or elect many women to office. During World War II many women worked, but peacetime brought an emphasis on the home as a "woman's proper place." In the 1960s the feminist movement began anew, fostering social awareness and still unfolding social change.

Despite some biological differences between the sexes in size, strength, and longevity, socialization is what shapes gender identity and sex-role behavior. Entrenched value orientations result in a conditioning process producing differential behavior patterns and life goals. The resultant sexual inequality is evident throughout society and doubly so among minority women. In education, employment, income, legal status, and political power, women's status has improved but still remains far removed from parity with men.

Functionalists contend that gender-based division of labor was an efficient means to a smoothly functioning society in the past, but they argue that technology has since thrown the social system out of balance, requiring some form of adjustment. Conflict theorists stress the oppression of women as economically based and beneficial to male status and power. Interactionists focus on the social interpretation of reality through socialization and interaction patterns, suggesting that changing the content of the socialization process will eliminate sexual inequality.

Review Questions

1. How can we consider women as a minority group?
2. What are some examples of past male discrimination against women?
3. Discuss the biological and sociological explanations of sex-role behavior.
4. What are some examples of problems of sexism among first- and second-generation Americans?
5. What examples of sexual discrimination can we find in education, work, income, and law?
6. How do the three major sociological perspectives explain sexism?

Suggested Readings

ANDERSON, MARGARET. *Thinking About Women: Sociological Perspective on Sex and Gender,* 2d ed. New York: Macmillan, 1988.

  A thorough examination of major issues of race, class, and gender as applied to major feminist and sociological theories.

FREEMAN, JO (ED.). *Women: A Feminist Perspective,* 2d ed. Palo Alto, CA: Mayfield, 1979.

  A fine collection of feminist writings about women and their encounters with male-dominated society.

FRIEDAN, BETTY. *The Feminine Mystique.* New York: Norton, 1963.

  A classic and still pertinent work criticizing myths about female passivity and fulfillment only as wife and mother.

GIELE, JANET ZOLLINGER. *Women and the Future: Changing Sex Roles in Modern America.* New York: Free Press, 1978.

  A very fine coverage of sex-role images and changes in major social institutions, with discussion of future possibilities.

HESS, BETH B., AND MYRA MARX FERREE (EDS.). *Analyzing Gender: A Handbook of Social Science Research.* Newbury Park, CA: Sage, 1987.

  This anthology covers feminist concerns regarding mass media, family roles, female sexuality, and health issues.

KANTER, ROSABETH MOSS. *Men and Women of the Corporation.* New York: Basic Books, 1977.

  A well-written account of subtle and overt forms of sexual discrimination and gender career choices in corporations.

MACKINNON, CATHARINE A. *Sexual Harassment of Working Women: A Case of Sex Discrimination.* New Haven, CT: Yale University Press, 1979.

  An excellent legal and sociological analysis of actual instances of sexual harassment in the work place.

MEAD, MARGARET. *Sex and Temperament in Three Primitive Societies.* New York: Morrow, 1963.
 A classic demonstration of the different effects of socialization on male–female attitudes and behavior in three New Guinea tribes.

MORGAN, ROBIN (ED.). *Sisterhood is Powerful.* New York: Random House, 1970.
 Still the most comprehensive collection of writings from the women's liberation movement covering virtually all aspects of life.

TAVRIS, CAROL, AND CAROLE WADE. *The Longest War: Sex Differences in Perspective,* 2d ed. New York: Harcourt Brace Jovanovich, 1984.
 An excellent overview of the societal implications from male–female perspectives.

PART **V**

PRESENT AND FUTURE STATUS OF MINORITY GROUPS

"By the middle of the twenty-first century, today's minorities will comprise nearly one-half of all Americans."

— *William P. O'Hare*

14

Rick Eilking/Reuters/Bettmann

The American Mosaic

As a nation of immigrants, the United States has had many different groups of strangers arrive and interact with its people. The strangers have perceived a different world that the native population took for granted, and their reactions have ranged from wonder to bewilderment to dismay, from fulfilled expectations to culture shock. Because their language, appearance, and culture background often made them conspicuous, the newcomers were categorically identified and judged as a group rather than individually. Native-born Americans sometimes welcomed these strangers, sometimes were impatient, and sometimes were intolerant; they helped or exploited or ignored the newcomers.

Throughout the nation's history, then, varied patterns of majority–minority relations have existed. Ethnocentric values have prompted the natural development of ingroup loyalty and outgroup hostility among both indigenous and migrant groups. Competition for scarce resources, colonialism, and political dominance by the Anglo-Saxon core groups also provided a basis for conflict. However, the resulting prejudicial attitudes and discriminatory actions varied greatly in intensity. Additionally both attitudes and social and economic conditions in this country have changed over the years, and this has affected the newcomers' experience.

Not all groups have come for the same reasons, and they have not come from the same backgrounds. Because of variations in social class, education, and occupational skills, not all immigrants have begun at the bottom of the socioeconomic ladder. Some have come as sojourners, intending to stay only long enough to earn enough money for a better life back in their homeland. Some have come with the desire to be American citizens in every sense of the word; others have insisted on retaining their own culture.

American attitudes toward the newcomers also have varied. Dominant attitudes, as well as sociological analyses, have tended to focus on either assimilation or pluralism as the preferred minority adaptation. Which process the public considers more acceptable will greatly influence dominant–minority relations. For example, if assimilation is held to be the "proper" goal, then evidence of pluralism will probably be a target for negative reaction. In recent years many people, but not all, have been more receptive to pluralism, and government policies and actions have reflected this orientation. Also, there has been increased suburban ethnicity from Asian, Hispanic, and other middle-class immigrants. Manifestations of the social processes of pluralism suggest that although minority groups may still encounter problems of adjustment and acceptance, these are not compounded by overt pressures for Americanization to the same extent as in the past.

How important is ethnicity today? Are immigration and assimilation concerns justified? What is the future of ethnicity in the United States? In this chapter we shall attempt to answer those questions, as we examine theories of ethnic consciousness and behavior, ethnic stratification in today's society, and the issues of bilingual education, legal and illegal immigration, and political correctness in a multicultural society.

ETHNIC CONSCIOUSNESS _____

Sociologists have long been interested in the attitudinal and behavioral patterns that emerge when people migrate into a society with a different culture. For example, what factors encourage or discourage ethnic self-awareness or maintenance of one's culture? If succeeding generations supposedly identify less with their country of origin, how do we explain the resurgence of ethnicity among white ethnics in recent years? Are there ethnic differentials in social mobility, social change, and behavior patterns even among third-generation Americans? Sociologists have frequently raised these questions, and a number of sociological theories have been offered in an effort to synthesize the diversity of ethnic experience.

Country of Origin as a Factor

Mary Sengstock believes that focusing on the relationship between the migrant and the country of origin will lead to a better understanding of the degree of assimilation.[1] She contends that the assumption that a migrant group is affected primarily by factors in the receiving country is wrong. This may have been more true of those groups that came here prior to World War I, when transportation and communication were limited. Furthermore, immigration restrictions in the 1920s sharply curtailed the number of new immigrants, and the assimilation process was less impeded when newcomers were not arriving to reinforce the language and customs of the old country. In today's world, however, an immigrant group can maintain contact with the country of origin not only through airmail letters but also, more importantly, through long-distance telephone calls, rapid transportation, and the continued arrival of newcomers. The Mexican and Puerto Rican communities benefit from geographical proximity, and the homeland can exert more influence over its emigrants than in years past. Where there is greater social contact, cultural transmission also is greater.

The degree of stability or social change in the homeland will have a profound effect on the migrant community's sociocultural patterns and life-style:

> Where the country of origin has experienced a relatively stable or gradually changing culture, the effect on the immigrant community will most likely be to encourage retention of the ethnic culture. This is much the same case as has occurred with Puerto Ricans and Mexican-Americans.

Some societies, however, have experienced drastic changes in recent years. When groups of immigrants from such areas experience constant immigration and other types of contact with the mother country, one might expect such contact to produce profound effects on the immigrant community as well.[2]

Sengstock uses a study of Chaldean immigrants from Iraq who settled in Detroit both before and after World War II to illustrate her position. Iraq is now an independent nation–state, not a colonial land of different tribes all under the control of another nation. It is struggling to replace centuries-old tribal rivalries with the unity of nationalism. The changes have reached the Detroit community through visitors and immigrants:

> Recent immigrants are less likely to exhibit the traditional family orientation of their predecessors. They are more likely to exhibit the bureaucratic, urban, secular characteristics of the modern nation-state Iraq now is. They are also more likely to identify themselves as Iraqis or Arabs than were the early immigrants. . . . It seems likely that the "modern" pattern will eventually be the established pattern in the Detroit community, since the older immigrants remain the sole repository for the village tradition, and most of them are well advanced in age.[3]

As the Chaldeans illustrate, it appears that recent immigrants who have more education and more experience with urban settings and bureaucracies will be more likely to interact with others. Thus willingness to extend one's social contacts to members of other groups could, suggests Sengstock, produce a more assimilable group.

The social structure of an immigrant group's country of origin, then, may help to explain both nationalistic sentiment and social interaction with others in the adopted country.

The Three-Generation Hypothesis

Historian Marcus Hansen conceptualized a normal pattern of ethnic revival in what he called the "Law of the Return of the Third Generation."[4] The third generation, more secure in its socioeconomic status and American identity, becomes interested in the ethnic heritage that the second generation neglected in its efforts to overcome discrimination and marginality. Simply stated, "What the child wishes to forget, the grandchild wishes to remember." Hansen, who based his conclusions mainly on Midwestern Swedish Americans, reaffirmed his position several years later:

> Whenever any immigrant group reaches the third-generation stage in its development a spontaneous and almost irresistible impulse arises which forces the thoughts of many people of different professions, different positions in life and different points of view to interest themselves in that one factor which they have in common: heritage—the heritage of blood.[5]

What Hansen has suggested here is a pattern in the fall and rise of ethnic identity in succeeding generations of Americans. His hypothesis generated extensive discussion in the academic community, resulting in studies and commentaries that both supported and criticized his views.

In a study of Irish and Italian Catholics in Providence, Rhode Island, John Goering had mixed results.[6] He found that ethnic consciousness was steadily declining in succeeding generations in some respects but emerging in a negative sense in other respects as a backlash to the black civil rights movement and the hippie phenomenon of the 1960s. He concluded that this ethnic revival was "less as a source of cultural or religious refreshment than as the basis for organizing the skepticism associated with discontent and racial confrontation."[7] Another interesting observation by Goering was that the ideology of the first- and second-generation Irish and Italian Americans living in the ethnic ghetto is more "American" and tolerant of American society than that of the third generation living outside the ghetto:

> Ethnicity is not clearly perceived in the ghetto. The boundaries of the ghetto became the boundaries of the real world. The awareness of ethnicity, and its divisiveness, comes with the "children of the uprooted." All forms of ethnic consciousness are not associated with the ethnic ghetto.[8]

These comments follow Hansen's law in that they assume that the second generation perceives its ethnicity as a disadvantage in being accepted in American society. However, Goering perceived growing ethnic awareness among third-generation members not as a progression but as a regression to the "seclusiveness of ethnicity in resentment against unattained promises."[9]

Neil Sandburg's study, cited in the section on Polish Americans, found that subjects in the Los Angeles area tended to be less ethnic over several generations.[10] In a similar study of Italian Americans in two suburbs of Providence, Rhode Island, John P. Roche also found increased assimilation over several generations and lower levels of attitudinal ethnicity.[11] Other writers have suggested that events in one's homeland or the situation of one's fellow ethnics in other parts of the world may heighten ethnic awareness.[12]

Perhaps one of the most comprehensive rebuttals of the three-generation hypothesis was that of Harold Abramson, who argued that the many dimensions of ethnic diversity preclude any macrosocial theory about ethnic consciousness.[13] In addition to differences in time period, which may have influenced the experience, adjustment, and intergenerational conflict or consensus of ethnic groups, there is also a diversity within the groups themselves. Possibly only the better educated among each ethnic group, being in wider contact with the outside world and more ambivalent about their identity, experience an ethnic resurgence, while the majority have quietly progressed in some steady fashion. The enormous variability of the American social structure also affects what will happen to the grandchildren of all ethnic groups:

> Here I am talking about the diversity of region, of social stratification, of urban and rural settlement. In other words, the immigrants of Old and New and continuing migrations, the blacks of the North and of the South, the native American Indians, all experience *their* encounters with America under vastly

different conditions. The French-Canadians in depressed mill towns of New England, the Hungarians and Czechs in company coal towns of Pennsylvania, and the Chicanos in migrant labor fields of California, do not experience the social mobility or social change of the Irish in Boston politics, the Jews in the garment industry of New York, or the Japanese in the professions of Hawaii. Not only are there traditional cultural factors to explain these phenomena, but there are structural reasons of settlement, region, and the local composition of the ethnic mosaic as well.[14]

Additionally the responses of different traditional cultures to the forces of society vary. For example, the Irish and Italians have different levels of attachment to Catholicism. Persisting diversity makes it difficult to describe the American experience in any generalized manner.

THE CHANGING FACE OF ETHNICITY _____

In the past 30 years, we have seen social scientists shift from an emphasis on a resurgence of ethnicity to a suggestion that, at least for those of European ancestry, ethnicity was in its twilight stage. Obviously for those relatively new groups of immigrants, ethnicity is a very real component of their everyday lives and will remain so for some time, much as it once was for first- and second-generation European Americans. But what of the "white ethnics"? For them ethnicity has evolved into a very different form.

The White Ethnic Revival

In the late 1960s and 1970s some observers noted an increased ethnic consciousness among urban Catholic groups, whom they categorized as "white ethnics." Some, such as John Goering, saw this as a backlash to the efforts of blacks, hippies, and liberals.[15] Others, such as Andrew Greeley, saw it as an affirmation of Hansen's law.[16] Greeley suggested that the final stage of assimilation included the new generation's interest in its heritage. It had nothing to do with the militant black and Indian social movements because that was an earlier stage in the assimilation process. Greeley attributed the white ethnic revival to the last phase, when Hansen's law becomes operative. The third generation has a strong interest in the cultural and artistic background of their ethnic tradition. They take trips to the old country out of curiosity and occasional "amused compassion." Greeley saw this increased ethnic awareness as a deliberate, self-conscious effort among young ethnics.[17]

Michael Novak interpreted the ethnic revival not as a part of the assimilation process but as evidence of "unmeltable ethnics," or pluralism.[18] He noted that many working-class ethnics resented the limitations the Protestant Establishment imposed upon their realization of the American Dream. Just as they were beginning to improve their socioeconomic status and education levels without government assistance, politicians created protected minority categories that not only excluded them but allowed those categories to leap-frog past them before they themselves had fully mainstreamed. The white ethnic visibility, said Novak, was thus a militant assertiveness of perceived injustice.

Soon other voices challenged the suggestion of an ethnic resurgence. Herbert Gans, for example, argued that we were witnessing a temporary phenomenon brought on by upward mobility and the assimilation process. Rather than a resurgence, what was happening was the entry of many ethnics into the arts, academia, and politics.

> One reason is the decline of Irish and WASP control of American politics, and the political mobility of Italian-Americans, Polish-Americans, and others into important local and national positions. This political mobility has been developing for a long time and has more to do with the fact that many members of these ethnic groups have achieved middle class status, and thus economic power and political power, than with a new ethnic consciousness. . . .
>
> Second, and far more important, the urban and suburban white working class has also achieved more political power in the last few years, and since many of the members of that class are Catholic ethnics, their new influence has been falsely ascribed to a newly emerging ethnic pride. What has actually happened is that for the first time in a long time, the white working class has become politically visible, but their demands have been labeled as ethnic rather than working class.[19]

By the 1960s Jewish and Catholic intellectuals now associated with universities began to focus greater attention on previously unrepresented ethnics in scholarly and theoretical discussions.[20] Ethnic writers thereby popularized the concept of an ethnic resurgence while others such as Gunnar Myrdal contended no such thing was occurring.[21] From a more distant perspective, we now recognize that the so-called revival actually was a passing stage.

Ethnicity as a Social Process

Ethnicity is a creation of an American pluralist society. Usually culture shock and an emerging self-consciousness lead immigrant groups to think of themselves in terms of an ethnic identity and to become part of an ethnic community for the social and emotional support they need to begin a new life in their adopted country. That community is revitalized with a continued influx of new arrivals.

Some sociologists have argued that ethnicity should be regarded not as an ascribed attribute with only the two discrete categories of assimilation and pluralism, but as a continuous variable. In a review of the recent literature, William L. Yancey, Eugene P. Ericksen, and Richard N. Juliani conclude that ethnic behavior is conditioned by occupation, residence, and institutional affiliation—the structural situations in which groups have found themselves.[22] The old immigrants, migrating before the Industrial Revolution, had a more dispersed residential pattern than did the new immigrants, who were

German

Highest densities: Wisconsin 54%, South Dakota 51%, North Dakota 51%, Nebraska 50%, Iowa 50%, Minnesota 46%, Kansas 39%, Indiana 38%, Ohio 38%.

Scottish

Highest densities: North Carolina 8%, Texas 8%, Maine 6%, Vermont 5%, Utah 5%, New Hampshire 5%, Florida 5%, Pennsylvania 4%, California 4%.

English

States with the highest densities of English: Utah 44%, Maine 30%, Idaho 29%, Vermont 26%, New Hampshire 24%, Wyoming 22%, Oregon 20%, Delaware 18%.

Italian

Highest densities: Rhode Island 20%, Connecticut 19%, New Jersey 19%, New York 16%, Massachusetts 14%, Alabama 13%, New Mexico 11%.

Go west, go east

At first they came to New England, the Carolinas and what are now the mid-Atlantic states. Then they crossed the Appalachians and headed west. Now, the destination for many immigrants is California, and most are reaching it by going east or north—from Asia or Latin America. In 1991, 40 percent of new immigrants settled in California, almost four times more than came to New York, which until 1976 was the first choice of new arrivals.

These maps show the biggest concentrations of ethnic groups—500,000 or more in a state—as identified in the 1990 census. California is the top choice for immigrants from China, El Salvador, Guatemala, Hong Kong, India, Iran, Korea, Mexico, the Philippines, and Vietnam. New York has the most from Bangladesh, Colombia, the Dominican Republic, Ecuador, Guyana, Jamaica, Pakistan, and the former Soviet Union.

Captions below the maps show where specific ethnic groups make up the biggest shares of a state's population, such as South Dakota with its large percentage of people of German descent.

☐ States in color are those with at least 500,000 persons of the indicated ethnic groups in the latest census

French

Highest densities: Vermont 24%, New Hampshire 19%, Massachusetts 18%, Rhode Island 13%, Louisiana 13%, Connecticut 8%, Michigan 7%.

Dutch

Highest densities: Iowa 6%, Michigan 6%, South Dakota 5%, Oklahoma 5%, Oregon 4%, Kansas 4%, Idaho 4%, Indiana 4%, Montana 3%, Arkansas 3%.

African American

Highest densities: Mississippi 36%, Louisiana 31%, South Carolina 30%, Georgia 27%, Alabama 26%, Maryland 25%, North Carolina 22%.

Mexican

Highest densities: Texas 23%, New Mexico 22%, California 20%, Arizona 17%, Colorado 8%, Illinois 5%, Wyoming 4%, Kansas 3%.

Irish

Highest densities: Massachusetts 26%, Rhode Island 21%, New Hampshire 21%, Delaware 21%, Oklahoma 20%, Missouri 20%, Arkansas 20%, West Virginia 19%.

Polish

Highest densities: Wisconsin 10%, Michigan 10%, Connecticut 10%, Illinois 8%, New Jersey 8%, Pennsylvania 7%, New York 7%.

FIGURE 14.1
Where We Settled

SOURCE: Basic data from U.S. Bureau of the Census.

bunched together because of concentrated large-scale urban employment and the need for low-cost housing near the place of employment. Similarly when immigrants arrived, they were drawn to the areas of economic expansion, and the migration chains—the subsequent arrival of relatives and friends— continued the concentrated settlement pattern (Figure 14.1).

> The Germans and Irish, who were earlier immigrants, concentrated in the older cities such as Philadelphia and St. Louis. By contrast, the new immigrants from Poland, Italy and Russia concentrated in Buffalo, Cleveland, Detroit and Mil-waukee, as well as in some of the older cities with expanding opportunities. Different migration patterns occurred for immigrants with and without skills. . . . Rewards for skilled occupations were greater, and the skilled immi-grant went to the cities where there were opportunities to practice his trade. Less highly skilled workers went to the cities with expanding opportunities. Thus, the Italian concentration in construction and the Polish in steel were related to the expansion of these industries as these groups arrived. The Jewish concentration in the garment industry may have been a function of their previ-ous experience as tailors, but it is also dependent upon the emergence of the mass production of clothing in the late nineteenth century.[23]

Like Gans, these authors conclude that group consciousness is generated and becomes crystallized within the work relationships, common residential areas, interests, and life-styles of working-class conditions. Moreover, normal communication and participation in ethnic organizations on a cosmopolitan level can reinforce ethnic identity even among residentially dispersed groups.[24]

Stanley Lieberson and Mary C. Waters examined the location of ethnic and racial groups in the United States on the basis of the 1980 census and patterns of internal migration in 1975–1980. They found that the longer a group had been in the United States, the less geographically concentrated it was. This was hardly a surprising finding, but their analysis of internal migration pat-terns revealed that ethnicity still affected the changing spatial patterns:

> We have concluded that although current patterns of internal migration are tending to reduce some of the distinctive geographic concentrations in the na-tion, this will still not fully eliminate distinctive ethnic concentrations. This is because groups differ in their propensity to leave and in their propensity to enter each area in a way that reflects the existing ethnic compositions of the areas. Thus, even with the massive level of internal migration in the United States, there is no evidence that the ethnic linkage to region is disappearing.[25]

Lieberson and Waters observe that a numerically small group that is highly concentrated in a small number of localities possesses greater political and social influence than if it were more uniformly dispersed. Thus the linkage between demographic size and location will influence visibility, occupational patterns, interaction patterns, intermarriage, and assimilation.

Stanford M. Lyman and William A. Douglass believe that social process offers a more dynamic conception of race and ethnicity, but they suggest that such processes are not necessarily unidirectional or evolutionary, leading to acculturation and assimilation.[26] Instead, there are several different possible strategies as contending ethnic groups attempt to adjust to one another.

> A minority might attempt to: (1) become fully incorporated into the larger society; (2) participate actively in the public life of the larger society while retaining significant aspects of its own cultural identity; (3) emphasize ethnic identity in the creation of new social positions and pattern activities not formerly found within the society; (4) retain confederational ties with the larger society at the same time that it secures territorial and communal control for itself; (5) secede from the larger society and form a new state or enter into the plural structure of another state; (6) establish its own hegemony over the society in which it lives.[27]

Not all of these strategies have been used in the United States, but any or all of them may lead to problems and disruption in a pluralistic society. Each of these strategies, it should be added, is in dialectical relationship with patterns in the larger society; a minority's "choice" is heavily dependent on these prevailing patterns. (See Box 14.1 for a summary of various explanations for ethnic consciousness.)

Symbolic Ethnicity

Among first-generation Americans, ethnicity is an everyday reality that is taken for granted. For most immigrants living in an ethnic community, the shared communal interactions make one's ethnic identity a major factor in daily life. Not yet structurally assimilated, they find their ethnicity to be the link to virtually everything they say or do, what they join, or whom they befriend or marry.

What happens to the ethnicity of subsequent generations depends on the immediate environment. As Richard D. Alba reaffirmed in a 1990 study in Albany, New York, the presence of ethnic neighborhoods or organizations in the vicinity helps sustain a strong sense of ethnic identity.[28] For most whites of European origin, living away from visible ethnic links and being now part of the societal mainstream, their ethnic identity is of less importance than their occupational and social identity. Ethnicity now rests on acknowledgment of one's ancestry through attachment to a few ethnic symbols not pertinent to everyday life.[29]

Alba speaks of a twilight stage of ethnicity among white ethnics. High intermarriage rates have not only lessened the intergenerational transmission of distinctive cultural traits but have also diversified the ethnic ancestry of third- and fourth-generation European Americans. A coalesced new ethnic group, European Americans, has emerged. Its ethnicity is muted and symbolic, a personal and voluntary identity that finds expression in such activities as:

> Church and synagogue attendance, marching in a St. Patrick's or Columbus Day parade, voting for a political candidate of a similar ethnicity, or supporting a

---

| BOX 14.1 | REASONS FOR ETHNIC CONSCIOUSNESS |

Country of Origin

1. Psychological nearness through rapid communications and transportation.
2. Geographical proximity.
3. Degree of stability or social change in the homeland.
4. Social contact with recent immigrants.

Three-Generation Hypothesis

1. Second generation emphasizes American ways and neglects own heritage.
2. Third generation rediscovers ethnic identity.

Other Explanations

1. Religion replaces national origin as basis of identity.
2. Ethnicity less perceived in ethnic community than in real world.
3. Outside events may heighten ethnic awareness.
4. Only better educated of a group become ethnically self-conscious.
5. Variations in time, social structure, and within ethnic groups encourage different types of responses.

The Changing Face of Ethnicity

1. White ethnic revival a backlash or affirmation of Hansen's law.
2. Resiliency of ethnic identity even through acculturation.
3. Increased visibility and attention, not an ethnic revival.
4. Ethnicity a social process affected by and affecting residence.
5. Symbolic ethnicity now the most common form among European Americans.

---

political cause associated with the country of origin, such as the emigration of Russian Jews to Israel or the reunification of Ireland.[30]

Although socially assimilated and integrated into a middle-class society, third- and fourth-generation European Americans maintain this quiet link with their origins. As Herbert Gans suggests, it can find form in small details, such as objects in the home with an ethnic meaning, occasional participation in ritual, or a fondness for ethnic cuisine.[31] One can remain interested in the immigrant experience, participate in ethnic political and social activities, or even visit the homelands of one's ancestors. All these private, leisure-time activities help preserve one's ethnicity in symbolic ways, giving a special sense of self in the homogenized cultural world of white America.

Black Americans express symbolic ethnicity through such elements as musical styles; fashion and dress styles (Afros, braids, dreadlocks, tribal symbols

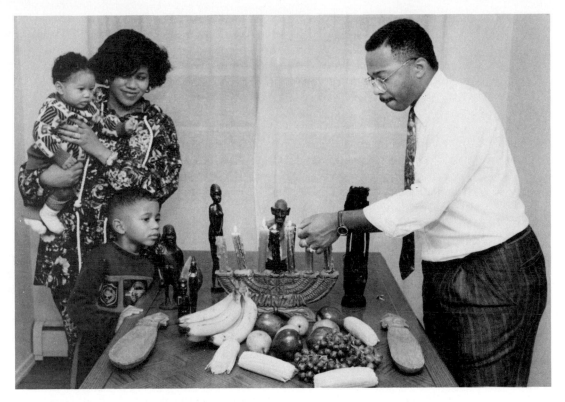

For most native-born Americans, symbolic ethnicity in occasional private activities is common. This African American family, whose native-born roots pre-date the Civil War, prepare for Kwanzaa, a traditional African harvest celebration. *(Kathy McLaughlin/The Image Works)*

cut into the hair, bandanna headbands, Kufi hats, harem pants, African beads); cuisine (soul food); and festivals (such as Kwanzaa, an African harvest celebration). Sometimes called **cultural nationalism,** a movement toward black solidarity through encouragement of African culture and values, these activities resemble other ethnic group descendents' proudly recalling their heritage.

ETHNIC STRATIFICATION

Some groups, such as the blacks, Hispanics, and American Indians, have received much attention; those findings are reported in the chapters in this book dealing with each specific group. For other ethnic groups the data are limited, both in frequency of reporting and in recording generational change. Much of the information from the Census Bureau is limited to the foreign-born, thereby restricting available information on second- and third-generation

Americans, except in the regional studies done by social scientists. Also, the Department of Labor's measurement of occupational position and shift does not specifically measure ethnic movement except by race and for Hispanics. Moreover, many of the more recent Third World immigrants have yet to be included in the data that are reported.

Achievement and Mobility

In a composite study of almost 18,000 respondents, Andrew M. Greeley reported some surprising findings in his comparisons of non-Spanish-speaking white ethnics.[32] In terms of occupational stratification and occupational mobility, Jews, Episcopalians, and Presbyterians were the most successful of all religious groups. In terms of educational stratification, the same three groups rank first, second, and third, respectively, but in terms of educational mobility the most successful are Jews, Catholics, and Presbyterians, in that order. For average income, Jews, Catholics, and Episcopalians are in the first three positions, and the standard deviation is far greater among Episcopalians and Presbyterians than in other groups, indicating a much wider range in income levels.

When Greeley refined the data to control for both religion and nationality, the rank order in terms of family income was Jews, Irish Catholics, Italian Catholics, German Catholics, Polish Catholics, Episcopalians, Presbyterians, Slavic Catholics, British Protestants, French Catholics, Methodists, German Protestants, Lutherans, Scandinavian Protestants, "American" Protestants, Irish Protestants, and Baptists. When only northern metropolitan regions are considered, the Catholic groups do even better. This ranking contrasts with the prevailing stereotype of wealthy WASPs and working-class Catholic ethnic groups. According to this study, the Jewish and Catholic ethnic groups have surpassed the older Protestant ethnic groups in terms of average family income.

One stratification expert, David Featherman, pointed to several misleading interpretations by Greeley.[33] Most importantly he stresses that Greeley uses family income as a measure of economic achievement and ambition. There is a difference in occupational achievement between income from the full-time employment of the household head only and income from the simultaneous employment of several family members, even if some of them work only part time. Larger immigrant families have more potential earners. Higher income from overtime employment taken out of economic necessity or from blue-collar union power does not necessarily imply occupational achievement either. Moreover, says Featherman, the data actually show that "few substantive educational and occupational differences remain among white, non-Spanish groups once the disadvantages and advantages of social backgrounds are controlled."[34] Featherman disputes Greeley's interpretation that Catholics have "made it big" economically; instead, he sees them from the same data as being very close to the national average. Both men agree that many white ethnic groups and denominations have been generally integrated into the American economy.

Each racial and ethnic group is represented at all levels of income, and so one must also be careful in discussing the average incomes Greeley reports. Also, because that study did not include Asians, Indians, Hispanics, and blacks, it does not give a complete picture of ethnic stratification. Increasing intermarriage by national origin, religion, and race, in declining order of frequency, further complicates the measurement of ethnic occupational distribution.

Stanley Lieberson and Donna K. Carter used the rates of inclusion in *Who's Who* between 1924 and 1974 as a measure of assimilation and achievement of blacks and five white ethnic groups.[35] Since 1944 Jews have moved significantly ahead of the English, who are closely followed by the Scandinavians. Italians and Slavs have also significantly increased their representation, and all five groups are becoming similar. Blacks rank lowest, sharply different from the whites, but have been moving upward since 1944.

Another study by Richard D. Alba and Gwen Moore revealed greater ethnic heterogeneity among the American elite in major economic, political, and social institutions.[36] White Anglo-Saxon Protestants were overrepresented in most sectors of the elite, dramatically so in business and Congress, where they were also numerically dominant (see Table 14.1). Constituting only 22.9

TABLE 14.1	**ETHNIC REPRESENTATION IN THE ELITE, BY PERCENTAGES[a]**					
	WASPs	Other Protestants	Irish Catholics	Other Catholics	Jews	Minorities
Overall elite	43.0	19.5	8.5	8.7	11.3	3.9
Business	57.3	22.1	5.3	6.1	6.9	0.0
Labor	23.9	15.2	37.0	13.0	4.3	2.2
Political parties	44.0	18.0	14.0	4.0	8.0	4.0
Voluntary organizations	32.7	13.5	1.9	7.7	17.3	19.2
Mass media	37.1	11.3	4.8	9.7	25.8	0.0
Congress	53.4	19.0	6.9	8.6	3.4	3.4
Political appointees	39.4	28.8	1.5	13.6	10.6	3.0
Civil servants	35.8	22.6	9.4	9.4	15.1	3.8
National population						
Men born before 1932	22.9	22.5	4.2	17.2	2.9	14.4
College-educated men born before 1932	31.0	19.8	6.0	15.5	8.9	5.2

[a] Americans who are not white or Protestant tend to be underrepresented in positions of decision-making authority. Although the situation is improving, the disparity still remains.

SOURCE: From Richard D. Alba and Gwen Moore, "Ethnicity in the American Elite," *American Sociological Review,* vol. 47 (June 1982), p. 377. Reprinted by permission of the American Sociological Association and the authors.

percent of all men born before 1932 and 31 percent of the college educated, they comprise 43 percent of the elite group. Jewish representation among the elite places them second, at or above their population proportion in all elite sectors, particularly the mass media. Irish Catholics also were at or above their population proportion in most sectors, particularly as labor and political party leaders. Other underrepresented Catholics include groups of European ancestry and protected minority groups. Ethnicity remains an important factor for entry into the elite, although not an exclusionary one.

The extent to which other countries begin, continue, or cease to send large numbers of immigrants will partially determine the cultural impact of these immigrants on American society. Moreover, as different parts of the world become primary sending areas, the interests of the newly naturalized citizens, and in turn American foreign policy, become increasingly involved in developments in those parts of the world. Table 14.2 shows the leading suppliers of immigrants since 1820, and Table 14.3 shows the changes in immigration patterns since the immigration law changed. Table 14.2 shows the past dominance of countries from Europe and the Western Hemisphere in total numbers. Table 14.3 shows the impact of the current immigration law, with significant shifts in country representation among the leaders. Many immigrants still come from European countries, but there has been a decided increase in the number of immigrants from Asia. As the chain-migration process occurs among these immigrants, it is reasonable to assume that there will continue to be large numbers of them among the strangers coming to these shores.

CURRENT ETHNIC ISSUES

Two highly controversial issues punctuate race and ethnic relations in the United States: immigration and bilingual education. Although the latter is a fairly new issue, arguments against both are repetitions of those hotly debated issues in the late nineteenth and early twentieth centuries. Nativist fears of being overrun by too many "non-American types" and of their cultural pluralism undermining societal cohesion are quite similar to concerns raised by past generations. A third hot issue is "political correctness." Unlike the other two, this issue is relatively new and embraces women's and homosexual rights as well.

Immigration Fears

About 7.3 million legal immigrants (including illegal aliens granted amnesty) came to the United States between 1981 and 1990, exceeding the number from every other decade in the nation's history except 1901–1910 when 8.8 million arrived. Legislation in 1990 setting a 700,000 immigrant ceiling for 1992–1994 and 675,000 thereafter could result in over 12 million immigrants in this decade, since spouses, children, and parents are exempt from the numeric limitation.

| TABLE 14.2 | **LEADING SUPPLIERS OF EMIGRANTS TO THE UNITED STATES: 1820–1991** |

1. Germany	7,094,352
2. Italy	5,403,424
3. United Kingdom	5,135,918
4. Mexico	4,836,652
5. Ireland	4,729,741
6. Austria/Hungary[a]	4,347,237
7. Canada	4,315,516
8. Soviet Union	3,475,263
9. Caribbean	2,841,768
10. Sweden	1,285,717
11. Philippines	1,095,403
12. China	938,371
13. Norway	801,778
14. France	791,565
15. Greece	706,833

[a] Data for Austria/Hungary were not reported until 1861. Austria and Hungary have been reported separately since 1905. From 1938 to 1945 Austria is included in figures for Germany.

SOURCE: U.S. Immigration and Naturalization Service, Annual Report, U.S. Government Printing Office, Washington, DC. *Statistical Yearbook 1991,* Table 2.

| TABLE 14.3 | **MAJOR SOURCES OF NEWCOMERS TO THE UNITED STATES** |

1965		1991	
1. Canada	38,327	1. Mexico	946,167
2. Mexico	37,969	2. Philippines	63,596
3. United Kingdom	27,358	3. Soviet Union	56,980
4. Germany	24,045	4. Vietnam	55,307
5. Cuba	19,760	5. Haiti	47,527
6. Colombia	10,885	6. El Salvador	47,351
7. Italy	10,821	7. India	45,064
8. Dominican Republic	9,504	8. Dominican Republic	41,405
9. Poland	8,465	9. China, Mainland	33,025
10. Argentina	6,124	10. Korea	26,518
11. Ireland	5,463	11. Guatemala	25,527
12. Ecuador	4,392	12. Jamaica	23,828
13. China and Taiwan	4,057	13. Pakistan	20,355
14. France	4,039	14. Colombia	19,702
15. Haiti	3,609	15. Iran	19,569

SOURCE: U.S. Immigration and Naturalization Service, Annual Report (Washington, D.C.: U.S. Government Printing Office, 1991, Table C, pg. 20.

For some people, such large numbers are cause for concern about the country's ability to absorb so many immigrants. Echoing xenophobic fears of earlier generations, they worry that Americans will "lose control" of their country to foreigners. In actuality the impact of 7.3 million foreigners on a 1990 U.S. population exceeding 248 million is less than that of 8.8 million on a 1910 U.S. population of 92 million. The 1980s immigration rate (annual immigration totals divided by the annual U.S. population total) was 2.7 percent compared to a 10.4 percent rate in 1901–1910.[37] Furthermore, with just 8.6 percent of the total U.S. population foreign-born in 1990, their proportion is one of the smallest since 1850, when the federal government began keeping such statistics.

Besides numbers, nativist fears also focus on the changing racial composition of the nation. The 1990 census revealed that since 1980, the nonwhite, nonblack category of "Other Races" increased 63 percent to 19 million. ("Other Races" includes Native Americans, Eskimos, Aleuts, Asians, and Pacific Islanders.) In the same period the white population grew 9.8 percent to 188.4 million and the black population 6.0 percent to 26.5 million.[38] Much of this population growth is from immigration, but another key variable is the higher birth rate among immigrant families.

Because the white percentage of the population dropped from 83 to 80 percent between 1980 and 1990, some "experts" have predicted that whites will be a minority in the United States by the latter half of the next century. Such thoughts feed the fears of nativists and cause resentment, hostility, and even ethnoviolence. This assumption that people of color will be in the majority may eventually become true. However, the future may bring a massive influx of East Europeans, changes in immigration law, a declining birth rate among subsequent generations of immigrant families, and other changes in migration patterns, each of which could alter the present trend.

A 1992 *Business Week*/Harris Poll revealed that most Americans are apprehensive about the current influx of immigrants, with 68 percent of all respondents saying today's immigration is bad for the country.[39] The public worries that immigrants take away jobs, drive down wages, and use too many government services. Although 73 percent of blacks compared to 49 percent of nonblacks believe businesses would rather hire immigrants, the blacks expressed more positive feelings about immigrants than did nonblacks. For example, 47 percent of blacks compared to 62 percent nonblacks wanted fewer immigrants to come; 60 percent of blacks compared to 49 percent of nonblacks thought immigrants bring needed skills to this country; 77 percent of blacks compared to 49 percent of nonblacks favor bilingual education.

How real are nativist fears? Data from the 1980s show that the economic benefits to the nation far outstrip the costs.[40] An unprecedented 1.5 million college-educated immigrants joined the work force, many helping our high-tech industries to remain competitive. Some 11 million working immigrants earned over $240 billion a year, paying more than $90 billion in taxes, far more than the estimated $5 billion immigrants received in welfare. Immigrants helped revitalize cities and older suburbs by opening businesses, buying

This cartoon, remarkably similar to those preceding immigration legislation in the 1920s, appeared first in the *Miami Herald* in 1984 and was reprinted in both *Time* and *Newsweek,* giving it a widespread national audience. It effectively captures nativist fears of the country being inundated with a tidal wave of aliens, a response pattern displayed earlier against the Irish and then the southern and eastern Europeans. *(UPI/Bettmann Newsphotos)*

homes, paying taxes, and shopping locally. Jefferson Boulevard in south Dallas, for example, changed from a dying inner-city business district filled with vacant stores to a thriving area of 800 businesses there and on neighboring streets, three-fourths of them owned by Hispanic Americans. More than 80 Korean American merchants invigorated Broad Avenue, the main thoroughfare in the older suburb of Palisades Park, New Jersey, just west of New York City. Without the immigrants, these and other areas would have suffered a shrinking tax base. Further evidence is that the nation's 10 largest cities grew by 4.7 percent in the 1980s; without the immigrants these cities would have endured a 7 percent population decline.

Illegal Aliens

Despite stricter laws imposing severe sanctions on employers who hire undocumented aliens, a constant inflow of illegals slip across U.S. borders.

Over 300,000 people each year become naturalized U.S. citizens. Of the 15 countries with the most immigrants since 1970, Asian countries have higher naturalization rates than elsewhere. Vietnam leads with 83 percent, then China and the Philippines at 64 percent each; Korea, 59 percent; India, 52 percent. *(Ulrike Welsch/Photo Researchers, Inc.)*

Agents from the Immigration and Naturalization Service apprehend more than 1 million illegal aliens each year, but an estimated 200,000 successfully elude detection. These illegals are often unskilled, poorly educated individuals who take low-paying jobs in the service sector or else work as laborers in agriculture and construction.

About 93 percent of all illegal aliens are Mexican, and a brief examination of the push–pull factors quickly explains the continuing flow. More than half of Mexico's labor force is unemployed or underemployed. A high birthrate is rapidly increasing that country's present 90 million population, straining the economy still further. Job opportunities are the obvious pull factor, and the nearness of the border with its 1,950-mile length makes slipping across relatively easy.

Other major sources of illegal aliens are El Salvador, Guatemala, Honduras, Dominican Republic, Colombia, and Jamaica. Poor living standards, a depressed economy, and often, guerilla warfare in their homeland drives these people to seek a better life in the United States by any means.

Bilingual Education

Offering **bilingual education**—teaching subjects in both English and the student's native language—can be a transition program (gradually phasing in English completely over several years) or a maintenance program (continual native-language teaching to sustain one's heritage). For many Americans who assumed that English-speaking schools provided the heat for the melting pot, the popularity of bilingual education—particularly maintenance programs—became a sore point. Some saw such efforts as counterproductive because they would reduce assimilation and cohesiveness in American society, while simultaneously isolating ethnic groups from one another. Advocates of bilingual programs emphasize that they are developing *bi*lingualism—fluency in both English and one's native tongue—and that many youngsters are illiterate in both when they begin school.

Public funding for bilingual education began in 1968 when Congress passed the Bilingual Education Act, designed for low-income families only. Two years later the Department of Health, Education, and Welfare specified that school districts with any national origin group of more than 5 percent had a legal obligation to provide bilingual programs for low-income families. In 1974 two laws significantly expanded bilingual programs. The Bilingual Act eliminated the low-income requirement and urged that children receive a variety of courses that provided appreciation of their cultural heritage. The Equal Opportunity Act included failure to take "appropriate action" to overcome language barriers that impeded equal participation in school as an illegal form of denying equal educational opportunity. Teaching English as a Second Language (ESL) programs have since expanded to function in about 125 languages, including 20 Native American languages. With 5 million immigrant children expected to enter the public schools in the 1990s, schools—especially urban ones—will be struggling for funds, space, and qualified teachers for their various bilingual programs.[41]

Difficulty with the English language while they were students often is cited by older naturalized American citizens as one of their most difficult times of adjustment and gaining acceptance. Bilingual proponents argue that their program eases that adjustment and accelerates the learning process. Carmel Sandoval of the National Education Association, which strongly supports bilingual education, maintains the program not only "helps the kids who don't speak English—but it even reduces their astronomical dropout rates."[42]

Opponents find the programs too costly, frequently staffed by paraprofessionals who themselves are not very fluent in English, or simply subsidizing political activities of vocal minority groups. Furthermore, they complain that the "transitional" bilingual programs are not transitional and that students remain in such classes for many years, thereby learning little English. When a 1985 Massachusetts Board of Education report confirmed this point, that substantial numbers of its Hispanic students remained in bilingual classes for six or more years, critics became more vocal.[43] That same year a policy change

Bilingual education functions in about 125 languages, twenty of them Native American. Controversy over its cost, effectiveness, and alleged "ethnic tribalism" continues to provoke many Americans. Recent studies show that immersion programs have success rates comparable to bilingual programs. *(Van Bucher/Photo Researchers, Inc.)*

allowed up to 25 percent of federal funds to be used for English immersion programs instead, in which students are taught in English with their native language used only as a backup support system. Then a 1988 law specified that unless stringent guidelines were met no student could be in a federally funded transitional bilingual program for more than three years.

How effective is bilingual education in helping children learn English? Early studies reported positive outcomes in bilingual programs, but educational researchers criticized them as methodologically flawed.[44] More recent studies have reported conflicting findings, thereby keeping the issue controversial. Two 1987 General Accounting Office reports[45] and a 1991 longitudinal study under the sponsorship of the U.S. Department of Education[46] all concluded that bilingual education was successful in aiding limited-English-proficient students to achieve academic success. However, the Education Department's report also found bilingual and immersion programs to be comparable in their success rates. Students in total immersion, short-term, and long-term bilingual programs learned English at about the same rate in all three groups, and they also improved their verbal and math skills as fast or faster than did other students in the general population.

The English-Only Movement

Opponents of bilingual education argue that the program encourages "ethnic tribalism," fostering separation instead of a cohesive society. Indeed, in recent years Hispanic leaders from such groups as the National Council of La Raza and the League of United Latin American Citizens (LULAC), in promoting "language rights," have insisted that the Hispanic language and culture be maintained at public expense, both in the schools and in the workplace. The oldest Hispanic civil rights group still in existence, LULAC was founded in 1929. Ironically, this organization began as an assimilationist organization, accepting only U.S. citizens as members, conducting official proceedings in English, and officially declaring as one of its goals "to foster the acquisition and facile use of the official language of our country."[47]

With more than 300,000 Hispanic immigrants a year pouring into Florida and the American Southwest, the extensive use of Spanish has alarmed some nativists who have spearheaded efforts to make English the official language for all public business. The largest national lobbying group, U.S. English, was co-founded by Japanese immigrant S. I. Hayakawa, a former U.S. senator from California and former president and linguistics professor at San Francisco State University. By 1989 it claimed 350,000 members, and its success prompted attacks on it as being anti-immigrant, racist, divisive, and dangerous.[48] The group's goals are to eliminate or reduce bilingual education, to abolish multilingual ballots, to prevent state or local expenditures on translating road signs and government documents, and translating to assist non-English-speaking patients at public hospitals.

By 1990 17 states had passed English-only legislation. Thirteen other states rejected similar proposals. New Mexico's legislation went beyond rejecting the proposal; in 1989 it approved "English Plus," stating, "Proficiency in more than one language is to the economic and cultural benefit of our State and Nation." Then in 1990 a federal judge struck down Arizona's official English law, declaring that the state constitutional amendment violated First Amendment rights. Advocates of language pluralism expect the judicial ruling to serve as the precedent for other state challenges.

Although proponents of English legislation claim that such action is necessary to preserve a common language and provide a necessary bridge across a widening language barrier within the country, numerous polls and studies demonstrate that the action is unnecessary. Echoing similar newspaper polls in California, Colorado, and elsewhere, a 1990 *Houston Chronicle* poll showed 87 percent of Hispanics believed it was their "duty to learn English" as quickly as possible. A 1985 Rand Corporation study, for example, revealed that 98 percent of Latino parents in Miami, compared to 94 percent of Anglo parents, felt it was essential for their children to become competent in English. A 1984 survey conducted by the National Opinion Research Center showed that 81 percent of Hispanics believe that speaking and understanding English is a "very important" obligation of citizenship. Only 2 percent thought it was not an obligation.[49]

Speaking against the English-only movement, the American Jewish Committee stated:

> It is not necessary to make English the official language of the United States. . . . English is the principle language used in the United States. Virtually all government agencies conduct their business in English and virtually all public documents are written in English. It is de facto the official language of the U.S. The use of additional languages to meet the needs of language minorities does not pose a threat to America's true common heritage and common bond—the quest for freedom and opportunity.[50]

Today's nativist fears about language should remind us of Washington's and Franklin's similar eighteenth-century concerns that were given in Chapter 5. The reality is that immigrants hold on to their language for a while, but both economic pressures to move up and acculturation push Hispanic Americans to learn English. More important, studies consistently show that Hispanics not only want to learn English but that they do learn it. The continuing immigration of Hispanic people gives the false impression that Hispanic Americans are not learning it; those who are so visible are the newcomers beginning the acculturation process.

Multiculturalism

In its early phase, during the 1970s, *multiculturalism* meant the inclusion of material in the school curriculum that related the contributions of non-European peoples to the nation's history. Next followed efforts to change all areas of the curriculum in schools and colleges to reflect the diversity of American society and to develop in individuals an awareness and appreciation for the impact of non-European civilizations on American culture. The intent of this movement was to promote an expanded American identity, one that recognized previously excluded groups as an integral component of the whole, both in heritage and in actuality.

In recent years some multiculturalists have moved away from an assimilationist or integrative approach, rejecting a common bond of identity among the distinct minority groups. The new multiculturalists advocate "minority nationalism" and "separatist pluralism," in which they seek not a collective American national identity but specific, separate group identities.[51]

To create a positive group identity, the multiculturists not only advocate teaching and maintaining their own cultural customs, history, values, and festivals. They also refuse to acknowledge the dominant culture's customs, history, values, and festivals. Two examples are Native American objections to Columbus Day parades and Afrocentrists who downgrade Western culture, arguing that it was merely a derivative of Afro-Egyptian culture. Another striking example is the argument that only those with power can be racist. This view, typified at Oberlin College, holds that because whites have power they are intrinsically racist whereas people of color lack power and so cannot be racist.[52] Opponents counter that racism can and does exist within any group, regardless of how much power that group has.

BOX 14.2   **THE INTERNATIONAL SCENE**

For many generations the French saw themselves as a seamless population bloc, whose culture directly descended from the tribes of ancient Gaul. Those who lived in the provinces—Alsatians, Bretons, Catalans, Provencals, and Savoyards, for example—were trained in the schools to become "French." Physically punished if they spoke their provincial dialects during recess, all were homogenized into the dominant culture, with the brightest students finishing their education in Paris.

The millions of Italian, Polish, and Spanish immigrants who entered France, despite their common Catholic faith and European heritage, did not mainstream easily. At the turn of the century in southern France, for instance, a massacre of Italians occurred. Just before World War II, the French government imposed a ban against the establishment of any organizations by foreigners; it remained in effect until 1981. Assimilation, or Franco-conformity, was the allowable choice, not pluralism.

By 1991, France had 4 million registered immigrants and perhaps half a million *clandestines* (illegal aliens), most coming from Muslim North Africa. Many French became concerned that their nation was losing its cultural identity because of the large influx of immigrants whose appearance, language, religion, and values were so different.

Echoing former Prime Minister Michel Rocard's call for a new recognition of French diversity and by implication encouraging a multiculturalist viewpoint, President François Mitterrand observed, "We are French. Our ancestors are the Gauls, and we are also a little Roman, a little German, a little Jewish, a little Italian, a small bit Spanish, more and more Portuguese, who knows, maybe Polish, too. And I wonder whether we aren't already a bit Arab."

Another battleground for multiculturalists became courses in Western civilization. Some institutions, such as Providence College in Rhode Island, expanded such course requirements and made them interdisciplinary; other institutions, such as Stanford University, questioned their inclusion at all. At many institutions the proposals for curriculum change ranged from mandatory inclusion of non-Western and women's studies courses as part of degree requirements to the exclusion of any Western history or culture courses.

Political Correctness

As various groups pursued the liberation of the American mind from its narrow perspective, advocates also looked beyond curricular change. By 1990 various streams of liberation—including those of peoples of color, feminism, gay rights, and the movement for the interests of the handicapped—became a coalition movement that became known as **political correctness.**

Advocates sought to create on college campuses a tolerant atmosphere for all peoples. Required courses on racism, sexism, and ethnic diversity were only one approach. Through the advocates' lobbying efforts, numerous universities established "forbidden speech" and inappropriate behavior codes designed to protect groups from abuse and exclusion. Some speech codes focused on abusive or offensive language, including racial and sexual epithets. Other universities were more sweeping in their restrictions, such as the University of Connecticut at Storrs, which also outlawed "inappropriately directed laughter." On several campuses disciplinary action against some students and faculty for racist or sexist remarks did occur.

Critics emerged, charging that the advocates of "politically correct" were themselves ethnocentric and intolerant of opinions differing from theirs. They argued that Western civilization, in its cosmopolitan nature and absorption of aspects of other cultures, was more tolerant and inclusive than the divisive and exclusive positions of the multiculturalists.[53]

Opponents also complained that the course substitutions were watering down the curriculum. They argued that politically correct educators were depriving students of the opportunity to grapple with civilization's greatest thinkers by substituting, in the name of multiculturalism, the works of inferior females and minority writers for those of "dead white males." Allan Bloom's *The Closing of the American Mind,* Roger Kimball's *Tenured Radicals,* Charles Sykes' *The Hollow Men,* and *Illiberal Education: The Politics of Race and Sex on Campus* by Dinesh D'Souza attacked what they saw as the suppression of intellectual freedom on the nation's campuses.[54] Advocates of cultural diversity countered that the traditionalists and neoconservatives were disguising the defense of intellectual rigor and the preeminence of the great books merely to preserve their own cultural and political supremacy.

"Political correctness" became a controversial term with praiseworthy or derogatory connotations, depending on one's perspective. The hottest area of debate focused on the campus speech codes which, opponents maintained, violated First Amendment rights of free speech. The issue raised is similar to that in Chapter 3 on the concept of justice. At what point do efforts to secure justice for one group (in this case eliminating biased expression) infringe on the rights of others?

In June 1992 the U.S. Supreme Court answered the question in a decision that First Amendment experts say sweeps away all the speech codes at public institutions. The case of *R.A.V. vs. City of St. Paul* concerned a hate crime involving a teenage skinhead who burned a cross on the lawn of the only black family in a working-class neighborhood. Unanimously, the court overturned that city's ordinance banning behavior that "arouses anger, alarm or resentment in others on the basis of race, color, creed, religion or gender." In the majority opinion, Justice Antonin Scalia made clear that regulation of expression (speech) that is based on hostility or favoritism to particular messages is unconstitutional. Because most college speech codes rest on a similar laundry list of offense categories, they are presumably in trouble. Colleges will probably return to general student conduct codes instead of specific ones dealing with speech.

The assertiveness of various liberation groups, such as these senior citizen gay activists, coalesced by 1990 into a movement known as political correctness. It seeks to create a tolerant atmosphere for all minority groups, but critics charge these advocates are themselves intolerant or others' views. *(Beryl Goldberg/Monkmeyer Press Photo Service)*

ETHNIC DIVERSITY IN THE FUTURE

In December 1992 the Census Bureau, in assuming continuation of present demographic trends, reported a dramatic change in the composition of American society by the mid-twenty-first century. These estimates include an average of 680,000 immigrants and 200,000 illegal aliens entering the country each year for the next six decades. Fertility rates, which had been at 1.8 children per mother in the late 1980s had risen to 2.1. Showing no sign of dropping, that rate was used in the population projections (see Figure 14.2).

However, the Census Bureau reports the cumulative effects of immigration will be more important than births to people already living in the United States. By the mid-twenty-first century, it said, 21 percent of the population, an estimated 82 million, will be either people who arrived after 1991 or children of those immigrants.

The rapid growth of the Hispanic population, says the Census Bureau, will enable the Hispanics of all races to surpass the black population in 2013, when there will be 42.1 million Hispanics and 42 million blacks. By 2050 Hispanics will number 81 million, or 21 percent of the total population. Blacks will then be 62 million, or 16 percent.

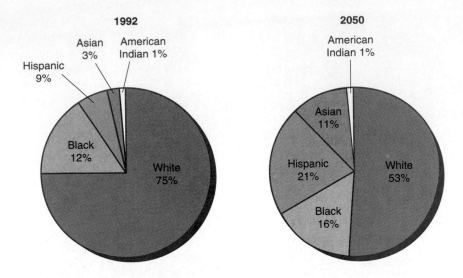

FIGURE 14.2
America's Growing Diversity

SOURCE: U.S. Bureau of the Census projections.

The nation's Asian population will grow to 41 million, or 11 percent, by 2050. Native Americans will increase to 5 million by then, remaining at 1 percent of the total. Non-Hispanic whites will peak at 208 million around 2030, then fall to 202 million, or 53 percent, by 2050.

What will these dramatic changes mean? Will a xenophobic reaction to these trends change our immigration policies? Will we accept ourselves as a truly pluralist nation? Will we be a socially integrated or a divided society? What will future generations consider a minority? In a crowd, in the workplace, it will be hard to tell the difference. What kind of a society will we be? The future is unknown to us, but here are a few possibilities:

1. Economic growth is a critical factor in curbing ethnic antagonism and absorbing more minority people into the mainstream of American life. Yet our nation's cities, home to many diverse minority peoples, are unable to provide the necessary economic opportunities. Recent urban boycotts, firebombings, riots, and other forms of violence are often symptoms of the frustration and anger vented by or against Asians, blacks, and Hispanics because of economic deprivation.

It would appear that a concentrated national effort aimed at sustained economic growth, full employment, and urban revitalization would do much to reduce many of the tensions and problems of dominant–minority relations. When economic security for all U.S. residents replaces chronic unemployment, underemployment, dependency, hopelessness, frustration, and despair, then we will have eliminated one of the major causes of negative judgments and treatments of various racial and ethnic groups.

2. Many social scientists feel that more and more Americans are becoming aware of the pluralistic reality of American society and that often their own "hangups" cause them to be prejudiced. If this awareness becomes more widespread and can be translated into action, this may be the beginning of a truly integrated society.

3. It may be argued that heightened racial and ethnic self-awareness will ultimately lead to greater societal cohesion, not to divisiveness. The predominance of an Anglo-conformity assimilationist viewpoint worked to the disadvantage of those who were considered "different" or "unassimilable." An awareness of diversity and an insistence on acceptance of one's own particular racial and ethnic identity will, it is hoped, lead people to allow others that same prerogative. In time greater tolerance for other groups might even lead to an appreciation of their differences.

4. Racism, which is relatively new in human history but as old as American history, is another critical factor in dominant–minority relations. America is no longer as racist a society as it once was, but many problems remain. People of color still experience discrimination, ethnoviolence, and exclusion. Economic security, as discussed, would seem to be a key means of overcoming much of the existing racial bias, as exemplified by the past and present experiences of the Chinese and Japanese. We could express the very same thoughts about sexism and sex discrimination as well; both retreat in the face of heightened awareness and economic independence among American women.

5. Finally, young people seem to have an increasing tendency to relate to people as individuals rather than on the basis of race, religion, nationality, or even social class, although they remain interested in those factors. The degree to which that attitude spreads among others and is retained by the young people as they grow older will greatly determine what American society will become.

Economic growth, increased awareness of pluralism, and a greater tendency to relate to individuals as individuals may allow the strangers in our midst to be perceived more favorably than their predecessors were. When the predominant attitude toward strangers becomes one of acceptance rather than suspicion, and when the newcomers are perceived as equals and sources of cultural enrichment rather than as inferiors and threats to the status quo, then race and ethnic relations will be more positive. Whether this ideal can ever become reality is the challenge before us.

Review Questions

1. What are some of the explanations for ethnic consciousness? Which seems most plausible? Why?
2. What does ethnic stratification suggest about upward mobility in the United States?

3. What do current immigration patterns indicate to us? Is immigration a problem for native-born Americans?
4. What are the pros and cons of bilingual education?
5. What are the varying viewpoints about multiculturalism and political correctness?
6. What is the future of ethnicity in the United States?

Suggested Readings _____

ALLEN, JAMES P., AND EUGENE J. TURNER. *We the People: An Atlas of America's Ethnic Diversity.* New York: Macmillan, 1988.
     An effective atlas with 110 maps showing the migration and population distribution of 67 ethnic groups.

GORDON, MILTON. M. *Assimilation in American Life.* New York: Oxford University Press, 1964.
     A highly influential and still pertinent book offering an analysis of the role of race and ethnicity in American life and the different forms assimilation takes.

MINDEL, CHARLES H., AND ROBERT W. HABENSTEIN (EDS.). *Ethnic Families in America: Patterns and Variations,* 3d ed. New York: Elsevier, 1988.
     An excellent portrait of 15 racial and ethnic groups, their family characteristics, and the impact of the women's movement on ethnic family life.

NEWMAN, WILLIAM M. *American Pluralism.* New York: Harper & Row, 1973.
     An argument for a social pluralism theory and analysis of the consequences of discrimination and conflict.

NOVAK, MICHAEL. *The Rise of the Unmeltable Ethnics.* New York: Macmillan, 1971.
     A provocative and influential book examining assimilation problems of white ethnics and their reactions to efforts on behalf of today's identified minorities.

SOWELL, THOMAS. *Ethnic America: A History.* New York: Basic Books, 1981.
     A fine comparative analysis of major racial and ethnic groups in the United States, with discussion of reasons for their varying success in American society.

THERNSTROM, STEPHAN (ED.). *Harvard Encyclopedia of American Ethnic Groups.* Cambridge, MA: Harvard University Press, 1980.
     An outstanding, comprehensive reference source for information about hundreds of U.S. racial and ethnic groups.

Glossary

Abstract Typification The generalization of people or things into broad categories.

Acceptance A minority response to prejudice and discrimination; based on powerlessness, fear for personal safety, or economic security, or fatalism.

Accommodation A tendency to accept the situation as it exists, without seeking to change it or make others conform; pluralism.

Acculturation The process by which a group changes its distinctive cultural traits to conform with those of the host society.

Achieved Status One's socially defined position in a society based on individual accomplishments or failings.

Action-Oriented Level of Prejudice A positive or negative predisposition to engage in discriminatory behavior toward members of a particular group.

Afrocentrism A viewpoint emphasizing African culture and its influence on Western civilization and American black behavior.

Amalgamation The biological and cultural blending of two or more groups of people into a distinct new type; the melting pot theory.

Americanization The effort to have ethnic groups quickly give up their cultural traits and adopt those of the dominant American group.

Anglo-conformity A behavioral adherence to the established white Anglo-Saxon Protestant prototype; what many ethnocentric Americans mean by assimilation.

Annihilation The extermination of a specific group of people.

Ascribed Status One's socially defined, unchangeable position in a society based on such arbitrary factors as age, sex, race, or family background.

Assimilation The process by which members of racial or ethnic minorities are able to function within a society without indicating any marked cultural, social, or personal differences from the people of the majority group.

Authoritarian Personality A set of distinct personality traits, including conformity, insecurity, and intolerance, said to be common among many prejudiced people.

Avoidance A minority-group response to prejudice and discrimination by migrating or withdrawing to escape further problems; a majority-group attempt to minimize contact with specific minority groups through social or spatial segregation.

Bilingual Education Teaching subjects in both English and one's native language to develop fluency in both.

Bipolarization Two opposite trends occurring simultaneously.

Categoric Knowing A stereotype of others based merely on information obtained visually and perhaps verbally.

Chain Migration A sequential flow of immigrants to a locality previously settled by friends, relatives, or other compatriots.

Cognitive Level of Prejudice The beliefs and perceptions about other racial or ethnic groups.

Conflict Theory A sociological perspective emphasizing conflict as an important influence and permanent feature of life.

Convergent Subculture A subgroup gradually becoming completely integrated into the dominant culture.

Cultural Assimilation Changing cultural patterns of behavior to those of the host society; acculturation.

Cultural Determinism A theory that a group's culture explains its position in society and its achievements or lack of them.

Cultural Differentiation Those differences between cultures making one group distinguishable from another.

Cultural Diffusion The spread of ideas, inventions, and practices from one culture to another.

Cultural Drift A gradual change in the values, attitudes, customs, and beliefs of the members of a society.

Cultural Nationalism A movement toward black solidarity through encouragement of African culture and values.

Cultural Pluralism Two or more culturally distinct groups coexisting in relative harmony.

Cultural Relativism The perception and judging of another culture or subculture from the perspective of the other culture rather than that of one's own culture.

Cultural Transmission The passing on of a society's culture from one generation to another.

Culture The values, attitudes, customs, beliefs, and habits shared by members of a society.

Culture of Poverty A controversial viewpoint arguing the disorganization and pathology of lower-class culture is self-perpetuating through cultural transmission.

Culture Shock Feelings of disorientation, anxiety, and a sense of being threatened when unpreparedly brought into contact with another culture.

Cumulative Causation Gunnar Myrdal's term for the vicious-circle process in which prejudice and discrimination each mutually "causes" the other, thereby continuing and intensifying the cycle.

De Facto Discrimination Unequal and differential treatment of a group or groups that is entrenched in social customs and institutions.

Defiance A peaceful or violent action to challenge openly what a group considers a discriminatory practice.

De Jure Discrimination Unequal and differential treatment of a group or groups that is established by law.

Deviance Characteristics or behavior violating social norms and thereby negatively valued by many people in that society.

Differentiation The social theory that societies tend to treat their members differently because of race, religion, age, sex, or other factors.

Discrimination Differential and unequal treatment of other groups of people, usually along racial, religious, or ethnic lines.

Displaced Aggression Hostility directed against a powerless group rather than against the more powerful cause of the feelings of hostility.

Dominant Group Any culturally or physically distinctive social grouping possessing economic, political and social power, and discriminating against a subordinate minority group.

Dysfunction A disruption of the equilibrium in a social system or of the functioning of some unit within the system.

Economic Determinism A theory that a society's economic base establishes its culture and general characteristics.

Emotional Level of Prejudice The feelings aroused in a group by another racial or ethnic group.

Endogamy The tendency for people to marry only within their own social group.

Ethclass A social group classification based on a combination of race, religion, social class, and regional residence.

Ethnic Antagonism Various forms of intergroup hostility, including ideologies, beliefs, behavior, and institutionalized practices.

Ethnic Behavior A concept that members of different ethnic groups behave differently in similar situations.

Ethnic Consciousness A self-awareness of ethnic identity; the deliberate maintenance of one's culture in another cultural environment.

Ethnic Group A group of people who share a common religion, nationality, culture, and/or language.

Ethnicity A cultural concept in which a large number of people who share learned or acquired traits and close social interaction regard themselves and are regarded by others as a single group on that basis.

Ethnocentrism A tendency to judge other cultures or subcultures by the standards of one's own culture.

Ethnogenesis A process in which immigrants hold onto some homeland values, adapt others, and adopt some values of the host country.

Ethnography The study of the way of life of a people.

Ethnophaulism A derogatory word or expression used to describe or refer to a racial or ethnic group.

Ethnoviolence Behavior ranging from verbal harassment and threats to murder against people targeted solely because of their race, religion, ethnicity, or sexual orientation.

Eurocentrism A viewpoint emphasizing Western civilization, history, literature, and other humanities.

Exogamy The tendency for people to marry outside their own social group.

Exploitation The selfish utilization of the labor of others for profit at their expense.

Expulsion The forced removal of a group of people from an area.

False Consciousness Holding attitudes not accurately reflecting the objective facts of the situation.

Fatalism A belief that events are determined by fate and thus beyond human control.

First-Generation American Someone born in another country who migrated to the United States.

Folkways Norms that a society considers useful but not essential; their violation evokes only a mild negative response.

Frustration A behavioral response when expectations remain unsatisfied; sometimes linked to scapegoating.

Functional Theory A sociological perspective emphasizing societal order and stability, with harmonious interdependent parts.

Gemeinschaft A small, tradition-dominated community characterized by intimate primary relationships and strong feelings of group loyalty.

Glass Ceiling A real but unseen discriminatory policy that limits female upward mobility into top management positions.

Group A collectivity of people closely interacting with one another on the basis of shared expectations about behavior.

Hansen's Law A theory that what the child of an immigrant wishes to forget, the grandchild wishes to remember; also called the three-generation hypothesis.

Hegemony Leadership or predominant influence exercised by one group over others, whether on a racial, religious, cultural, or linguistic basis.

Historicity Historical actuality or authenticity; past experiences.

Ideology A generalized set of beliefs that explains and justifies the interests of those who hold them.

Ingroup The group to which an individual belongs and feels loyalty.

Institution Patterns of behavior organized to meet a basic need of a society, such as family, education, religion, economics, or politics.

Institutionalized Discrimination Differential and unequal treatment of a group or groups that deeply pervades social customs and institutions and usually is subtle and informal.

Interactionist Theory A sociological perspective emphasizing the shared interpretations and interaction patterns in everyday life.

Intergenerational Mobility The change in social status within a family from one generation to the next.

Internal Colonialism A concept explaining the experiences of blacks, Chicanos, and Native Americans in terms of economic exploitation and rigid stratification.

Invasion–Succession The ecological process in which one group displaces another group in a residential area or business activity.

Jigsaw Method A teaching technique to promote cooperation and better intergroup understanding.

Jim Crow Laws Southern state segregation laws, passed in the 1890s and early twentieth century, which covered use of all public facilities, including schools, restaurants, transportation, waiting rooms, rest rooms, drinking fountains, and parks.

Kye A rotating credit fund enabling Korean Americans to start or expand their businesses.

Linguistic Relativity The recognition that different languages dissect and present reality differently.

Machismo Value orientation defining masculinity in varying terms of virility, honor, and provision for one's family.

Marginality The situation of individuals who are the product of one culture but are attempting to live within another, and therefore are not fully a part of either one.

Marianismo Value orientation accepting male dominance and emphasis on family responsibilities.

Marital Assimilation A pattern of intermarriage of minority-group members with dominant-group members.

Melting Pot Theory An idealistic idea that many diverse peoples would blend both biologically and culturally, forming a distinct new breed—the American; amalgamation.

Middleman Minority A minority group occupying an intermediate occupational position in trade or commerce between the top and bottom strata.

Minority Group A culturally and physically distinctive group receiving unequal treatment, an ascribed status, a sense of shared identity, and practicing endogamy.

Mores Norms that society considers essential; their violation evokes a strong negative response.

Multiculturalism Ranges from efforts for an all-inclusive curriculum to an emphasis on separatist pluralism.

Nativist One who advocates a policy of protecting the interests of native inhabitants against those of immigrants.

Negative Self-image The result of social conditioning or differential treatment or both, causing people or groups to believe themselves inferior.

"New" Immigrants A term used by the Dillingham Commission (1907–1911) to identify immigrants from southern, central, and eastern Europe.

Norms The internalized rules of conduct that embody the fundamental expectations of society.

Objectivity Disciplining oneself to examine and interpret reality with the least possible amount of personal bias and distortion.

Occupational Mobility Ability to change one's job position in terms of status and economic reward.

"Old" Immigrants A term used by the Dillingham Commission (1907–1911) to identify immigrants from northern and western Europe.

Outgroup Any group to which an individual does not belong or feel loyalty.

Paralinguistic Signals Use of sounds, but not words, which convey distinct meanings.

Parallel Social Institutions A subcultural replication of institutions of the larger society, such as churches, schools, organizations.

Paternalism A condescending treatment of adults, managing and regulating their affairs as a father would handle his children's affairs.

Persistent Subculture A subgroup adhering to its own way of life and resisting absorption into the dominant culture.

Personality An individual's typical patterns of thought, feeling, and action.

Pluralism A state in which minorities can maintain their distinctive subcultures and simultaneously interact with relative equality in the larger society.

Political Correctness Movement to create tolerant atmosphere for all peoples, including ban on abusive or offensive language. Critics use the term to attack its First Amendment infringements.

Power Differential The uneven distribution of power, whether economic, political, or social.

Power Theory A concept that the relative power of the indigenous and migrant groups determines the outcome of their interaction.

Prejudice A system of negative beliefs, feelings, and action-orientations regarding a certain group or groups of people.

Primary Group A small number of people who interact with one another in close, personal, and meaningful relationships.

Push-Pull Factors The forces that encourage migration from one country to another.

Race A categorization in which a large number of people sharing visible physical characteristics regard themselves or are regarded by others as a single group on that basis.

Racial Stratification Differences in socioeconomic status within a society that is structured according to race.

Racism False linkage of biology and sociocultural behavior to assert the superiority of one race.

Random Sample A scientific selection of people from a larger population in which everyone has an equal chance to be chosen.

Reciprocal Typifications People's categorizations of one another based on their share experiences.

Redlining Unwillingness of some banks to make loans in lower-income minority neighborhoods.

Reference Group A group to which people may or may not belong but to which they refer when evaluating themselves and their behavior.

Relative Deprivation A lack of resources, or rewards, in one's standard of living in comparison with others in the society.

Reputational Method A technique for measuring social class by questioning people of others' social standing.

Reverse Discrimination An action to overcome discrimination against one group resulting in discrimination against another group.

Role Behavior determined by the status the individual occupies.

Scapegoating Placing blame on others for something that is not their fault.

Second-Generation American A child born in the United States of immigrant parents; can also refers to a child born elsewhere but raised from a young age in the United States by immigrant parents.

Secondary Group A collectivity of people who interact on an impersonal or limited emotional basis for some practical or specific purpose.

Selective Perception A tendency to see or accept only that information agreeing with one's value orientations or consistent with one's attitudes about other groups.

Self-fulfilling Prophecy A prediction that so influences behavior that the consequence is a realization of the prediction.

Self-justification A defense mechanism whereby people denigrate another person or group to justify maltreatment of them.

Separatist Pluralism Effort to seek specific, separate group identity rather that a collective American national identity.

Sexism Institutionalized prejudice and discrimination based on gender.

Situational Ethnicity Ethnic consciousness generated by residence, special events, work relationships, or working-class life-style.

Social Change Any alteration, whether gradual or swift in the patterns of social behavior or the social structure.

Social Class A categorization designating people's places in the stratification hierarchy on the basis of similarities in income, property, power, status, and life-style.

Social Conditioning A socialization process through which people are molded to fit into the social system.

Social Construction of Reality The process by which definitions of reality are socially created, objectified, internalized, and then taken for granted.

Social Discrimination Exclusion of outgroup members members from close relationships with ingroup members.

Social Distance The degree of closeness or remoteness one desires in interaction with members of a particular group.

Social Hierarchy The stratified levels of status within a group or society.

Social Identity Theory Holds that ingroup members enhance their self-image by considering their group better than others.

Social Interaction The reciprocal process by which people act and react toward one another.

Social Mobility The change from one status to another in a stratified society.

Social Norms Generally shared rules or expectations of what is and is not proper behavior.

Social Organization Any grouping formed to provide a means of social interaction among individuals.

Social Segregation A situation in which participation in social, fraternal, service, and other types of activities is confined to members of the ingroup.

Social Stratification The hierarchy within a society based on the unequal distribution of resources, power, or prestige.

Social Structure The organized patterns of behavior in a social system governing people's interrelationships.

Socialization The process of social interaction by which people acquire personality and learn the culture or subculture of their group.

Society A group of individuals who share a common culture and territory.

Socioeconomic Status (SES) A social prestige ranking as determined by numerous factors, including occupation, income, educational background, and place of residence.

Spatial Segregation The physical separation of a minority group from the rest of society, such as in housing or education.

Split Labor Market A concept explaining ethnic antagonism on the basis of conflict between higher-paid and lower-paid labor.

Status A socially defined position in society.

Stereotype An oversimplified generalization attributing certain traits or characteristics to any person in a group without regard to individual differences.

Structural Assimilation The large-scale entrance of minority-group members into primary–group relationships with the host society in its social organizations and institutions.

Structural Conditions Those large-scale factors affecting society, such as industrialization, economic vitality, and stratification.

Structural Differentiation Status distinctions for different racial and ethnic groups entrenched within the social system.

Structural Discrimination Differential treatment of groups of people that is entrenched in the institutions of a society.

Structural Pluralism Coexistence of racial and ethnic groups in separate subsocieties also divided along social class and regional boundaries.

Subculture A group that shares in the overall culture of a society while retaining its own distinctive traditions and life-style.

Subjectivity Observing the world from one's own viewpoint, as shaped by cultural input, personal opinion, emotions, and experiences.

Subordinate Less powerful than another group that possesses political, economic, or technological advantages.

Superordinate Possessing superior power, whether political, economic, or technological.

Symbol Anything that can be understood to signify something else, such as a word or gesture that symbolizes an attitude or feeling.

Symbolic Ethnicity Identifying with one's heritage through ethnic foods, holidays, and political and social activities.

Symbolic Interaction The use of symbols, such as signs, gestures, and language, through which people interact with one another.

Third-Generation American Someone born in the United States whose grandparents migrated to the United States.

Three-Generation Hypothesis *See* Hansen's Law.

Thomas Theorem An observation that if people define situations as real, then they are real in their consequences.

Triple Melting Pot Theory The concept that intermarriage is occurring among various nationalities within the three major religious groupings.

Value Judgment A personal or subjective opinion based on the values of the observer.

Value Neutrality An ideal state, never fully possible, in which the observer eliminates all personal bias in order to be completely objective.

Notes

Chapter 1

1. Aristotle, *The Rhetoric*, Appleton, New York, 1932.
2. See, for example, Theodore Newcomb, "The Acquaintance Process: Looking Mainly Backward," *Journal of Personality and Social Psychology* 36 (1978), 1075–1083.
3. Donn Byrne et al., "The Ubiquitous Relationship: Attitude Similarity and Attraction. A Cross-Cultural Study," *Human Relations* 24 (1971), 201–207.
4. Emory S. Bogardus, "Comparing Racial Distances in Ethiopia, South Africa, and the United States," *Sociology and Social Research* 52 (1968), 149–156.
5. See Tom W. Smith and Glenn R. Dempsey, "The Polls: Ethnic Social Distance and Prejudice," *Public Opinion Quarterly* 47 (1983), 584–600.
6. James Dyer, Arnold Vedlitz, and Stephen Worchel, "Social Distance among Racial and Ethnic Groups in Texas: Some Demographic Correlates," *Social Science Quarterly* 70 (1989), 607–616.
7. Anthony Walsh, "Becoming an American and Liking It as Functions of Social Distance and Severity of Initiation," *Sociological Inquiry* 60 (1990), 177–189.
8. Lyn H. Lofland, *A World of Strangers*, Basic Books, New York, 1973, p. 16.
9. Georg Simmel, "The Stranger," in *The Sociology of Georg Simmel*, ed. Kurt H. Wolff, Free Press, New York, 1950.
10. Alfred Schutz, "The Stranger," *American Sociological Review* 69 (May 1944), 449–507.
11. William Graham Sumner, *Folkways*, Ginn, Boston, 1906, p. 13.
12. See Henri Taifel, *Human Groups and Social Categories*, Cambridge University Press, Cambridge, U.K., 1981.
13. See Marc J. Schwartz, "Negative Ethnocentrism," *Journal of Conflict Resolution* 5 (March 1961), 75–81.
14. Robin M. Williams, Jr., *Strangers Next Door*, Prentice-Hall, Englewood Cliffs, NJ, 1964, p. 23.
15. Robert A. Levine and Donald T. Campbell, *Ethnocentrism: Theories of Conflict, Ethnic Attitudes, and Group Behavior*, Wiley, New York, 1972, pp. 68, 202.
16. Kenneth E. Boulding, *Conflict and Defense: A General Theory*, Harper, New York, 1962, pp. 162–163; Lewis A. Coser, *Sociological Theory: A Book of Readings*, Macmillan, New York, 1957, pp. 87–110; P. C. Rosenblatt, "Origins and Effects of Group Ethnocentrism and Nationalism," *Journal of Conflict Resolution* 8 (1964), 131–146; M. Sherif and C. W. Sherif, *Groups in Harmony and Tension*, Harper, New York, 1953, p. 196.
17. Brewton Berry, *Race and Ethnic Relations*, 3d ed., Houghton Mifflin, Boston, 1965, p. 55.
18. Morton Klass and Hal Hellman, *The Kinds of Mankind*, Lippincott, New York, 1971, p. 61.
19. Molefi Kete Asante, *The Afrocentric Idea*, Temple University Press, Philadelphia, 1987.
20. Martin E. Spencer, "Multiculturalism, 'Political Correctness,' and the Politics of Identity," thematic paper presented at the annual meeting of the Eastern Sociological Society, Arlington, VA, April 5, 1992.
21. Immanuel Velikovsky, *Oedipus and Akhnaton*, Doubleday, New York, 1960, p. 96.
22. See Albert Szymanski, "Racial Discrimination and White Gain," *American Sociological Review* 41 (1976), 403–414; Sidney M. Willhelm, "Can Marxism Explain America's Racism?" *Social Problems* 28 (1980), 98–112.
23. Erving Goffman, *The Presentation of Self in Everyday Life*, Doubleday, Garden City, NY, 1959.
24. Peter L. Berger and Thomas Luckmann, *The Social Construction of Reality*, Doubleday, Garden City, NY, 1963.

25. Donald Young, *American Minority Peoples*, Harper, New York, 1932, p. viii.

26. Louis Wirth, "The Problem of Minority Groups," in *The Science of Man in the World Crisis*, ed. Ralph Linton, Columbia University Press, New York, 1945.

27. Richard Schermerhorn, *Comparative Ethnic Relations*, Random House, New York, 1970, p. 8.

28. Tamotsu Shibutani and Kian M. Kwan, *Ethnic Stratification*, Macmillan, New York, 1965.

29. Schermerhorn, *Comparative Ethnic Relations*, p. 12.

30. Charles Wagley and Marvin Harris, *Minorities in the New World*, Columbia University Press, New York, 1964.

31. See Ashley Montagu, *Man's Most Dangerous Myth: The Fallacy of Race*, 5th ed., Oxford University Press, New York, 1974.

32. See Maria P. P. Root (ed.), *Racially Mixed People in America*, Sage, Newbury Park, CA, 1992. See also J. C. Brigham and L. W. Biesbrecht, "All in the Family: Racial Attitudes," *Journal of Communication* 26 (1976), 69–74.

33. Brewton Berry and Henry L. Tischler, *Race and Ethnic Relations*, 4th ed., Houghton Mifflin, Boston, 1978, pp. 30–32.

34. Milton Gordon, *Assimilation in American Life*, Oxford University Press, New York, 1964, p. 27; Shibutani and Kwan, *Ethnic Stratification*, p. 47; Jerry D. Rose, *Peoples: The Ethnic Dimension in Human Relations*, Rand McNally, Chicago, 1976, pp. 8–12.

Chapter 2

1. Louis Schneider and Charles Bonjean (eds.), *The Idea of Culture in the Social Sciences*, Cambridge University Press, Cambridge, U.K., 1973.

2. The importance of symbols to social interaction has drawn much attention in sociology. See Benjamin L. Whorf, *Language, Thought and Reality*, Wiley, New York, 1956; Gertrude Jaeger and Philip Selznick, "A Normative Theory of Culture," *American Sociological Review* 29 (October 1964), 653–659; Herbert Blumer, *Symbolic Interaction: Perspective and Method*, Prentice-Hall, Englewood Cliffs, NJ, 1969.

3. Harry C. Bredemeier and Richard M. Stephenson, *The Analysis of Social Systems*, Holt, Rinehart, and Winston, New York, 1962, p. 3.

4. Bear climbing a tree as seen from other side. Giraffe going by a second-story window. Hot dog on a hamburger roll. Aerial view of two Mexicans in a canoe.

5. This connection between Lippmann's comments, the Droodles, and human response to definitions of stimuli was originally made by Harry C. Bredemeier and Richard M. Stephenson, *The Analysis of Social Systems*, pp. 2–3.

6. Edward O. Wilson, *Sociobiology*, The Belknap Press of Harvard University Press, Cambridge, MA, 1975, p. 550.

7. Desmond Morris, *Manwatching: A Field Guide to Human Behavior*, Abrams, New York, 1977.

8. William I. Thomas, "The Relation of Research to the Social Process," in *Essays on Research in the Social Sciences*, The Brookings Institution, Washington, DC, 1931, p. 189.

9. See the discussion on p. 104.

10. Gregory Razran, "Ethnic Dislike and Stereotypes: A Laboratory Study," *Journal of Abnormal and Social Psychology* 45 (1950), 7–27.

11. Copyright © 1949 by Richard Rodgers and Oscar Hammerstein II. Copyright renewed. Williamson Music, Inc., owner of publication and allied rights for the Western Hemisphere and Japan. International copyright secured. All rights reserved. Used by permission.

12. John Gillis, *The Ways of Men*, Appleton-Century-Crofts, New York, 1948, p. 556.

13. For a case study of England from 1000 to 1899, see Margaret T. Hodgen, *Change and History*, Wenner-Gren Foundation for Anthropological Research, New York, 1952.

14. Stanley Lieberson, "A Societal Theory of Race and Ethnic Relations," *American Sociological Review* 26 (December 1961), 902–910.

15. See Andrew M. Greeley, *The American Catholic: A Social Portrait*, Basic Books, New York, 1977, Chapter 1; also Richard D. Alba, *Italian Americans: Into the Twilight of Ethnicity*, Prentice-Hall, Englewood Cliffs, NJ, 1985, pp. 9–12.

16. Mary C. Sengstock, "Social Change in the Country of Origin as a Factor in Immigrant Conceptions of Nationality," *Ethnicity* 4 (March 1977), 54–69.

17. W. Lloyd Warner and Paul S. Lunt, *The Social Life of a Modern Community*, Yankee City Series, Vol. 1, Yale University Press, New Haven, CT, 1941.

18. W. Lloyd Warner and Leo Srole, *The Social System of American Ethnic Groups*, Yankee City Series, Vol. 3, Yale University Press, New Haven, CT, 1945.

19. Alan C. Kerckhoff, *Socialization and Social Class*, Prentice-Hall, Englewood Cliffs, NJ, 1972, pp. 126–128.

20. John C. Leggett, "Working Class Consciousness in an Industrial Community," unpublished Ph.D. thesis, University of Michigan, 1962, reported in Bruno Bettelheim and Morris Janowitz, *Social Change and Prejudice*, Free Press, New York, 1964, p. 33.

21. Richard Centers, *The Psychology of Social Classes: A Study of Class Consciousness*, Princeton University Press, Princeton, NJ, 1949; Oscar Glantz, "Class Consciousness and Political Solidarity," *American Sociological Review* 23 (August 1958), 375–382; Robert W. Hodge and Donald J. Treiman, "Class Iden-

tification in the U.S.," *American Journal of Sociology* 73 (March 1968), 535–547; Werner S. Landecker, "Class Crystallization and Class Consciousness," *American Sociological Review* 28 (April 1963), 219–229; Robert T. Morris and Raymond J. Murphy, "A Paradigm for the Study of Class Consciousness," *Sociology and Social Research* 50 (April 1966), 298–313.

22. Colin Greer (ed.), *Divided Society*, Basic Books, New York, 1974, p. 34.

23. Milton M. Gordon, *Assimilation in American Life*, Oxford University Press, New York, 1964.

24. William M. Newman, *American Pluralism*, Harper & Row, New York, 1973, p. 84.

25. Gordon, *Assimilation in American Life*, p. 47.

26. See August B. Hollingshead, "Trends in Social Stratification: A Case Study," *American Sociological Review* 17 (December 1952), 685–686; Raymond Mack (ed.), *Race, Class and Power*, 2d ed., Van Nostrand Reinhold, New York, 1963; John Leggett, *Class, Race and Labor*, Oxford University Press, New York, 1968.

27. Thomas M. Pettigrew, "The Changing but Not Declining Significance of Race," *Michigan Law Review* 77 (January–March 1979), pp. 917–924; Charles V. Willie, "The Inclining Significance of Race," *Society* 15 (July/August 1978), pp. 10–15.

28. E. Franklin Frazier, *The Negro Family in Chicago*, University of Chicago Press, Chicago, 1932; see also *The Negro Family in the United States*, rev. ed., University of Chicago Press, Chicago, 1966.

29. Daniel P. Moynihan, *The Negro Family: The Case for National Action*, U.S. Department of Labor, Washington, D.C., 1965.

30. Ibid., p. 5.

31. Ibid., p. 6.

32. Ibid., pp. 30, 47.

33. Moynihan, "Families Falling Apart," *Society* (July/August 1990), pp. 21–22.

34. Originally in Daniel Patrick Moynihan, "A Family Policy for the Nation," *America* 113 (September 18, 1965), pp. 280–283. See also Moynihan, "Families Falling Apart," p. 21; David Gergen, "A Few Candles in the Darkness," *U.S. News & World Report* (May 25, 1992), p. 44.

35. Bill Moyers, "The Vanishing Family: Crisis in Black America," CBS Special Report, Columbia Broadcasting System, 1986; for an analysis of both Moynihan's report and Moyers' documentary, see Patricia Hill Collins, "A Comparison of Two Works on Black Family Life," *Signs* 14 (1989), 875–884.

36. Oscar Lewis, *La Vida*, Vintage, New York, 1966, pp. xlii–lii.

37. Ibid., p. xlv.

38. Edward C. Banfield, *The Unheavenly City: The Nature and Future of Our Urban Crisis*, Little, Brown, Boston, 1970, pp. 210–211.

39. Joe R. Feagin, "Poverty: We Still Believe that God Helps Those Who Help Themselves," *Psychology Today* 6 (November 1972), 101–110, 129; "Black and White: A Newsweek Poll," *Newsweek*, March 7, 1988, p. 23.

40. Michael Harrington, *The Other America: Poverty in the United States*, Penguin, Baltimore, MD, 1963, p. 21.

41. William Ryan, *Blaming the Victim*, rev. ed., Vintage, New York, 1976.

42. Charles A. Valentine, *Culture and Poverty*, University of Chicago Press, Chicago, 1968, p. 129.

43. Lola M. Irelan, Oliver C. Moles, and Robert M. O'Shea, "Ethnicity, Poverty, and Selected Attitudes: A Test of the 'Culture of Poverty' Hypothesis," *Social Forces* 47 (1969), 405–413.

44. Eliot Liebow, *Tally's Corner: A Study of Negro Streetcorner Men*, Little, Brown, Boston, 1967, pp. 222–223. See also Ulf Hannerz, *Soulside: Inquiries into Ghetto Culture and Community*, Columbia University Press, New York, 1969.

45. See Alan S. Berger and William Simon, "Black Families and the Moynihan Report: A Research Evaluation," *Social Problems* 22 (1974), 145–161; Barbara E. Coward et. al., "The Culture of Poverty Debate: Some Additional Data," *Social Problems* 21 (1974), 621–634.

46. James E. Blackwell, *The Black Community: Diversity and Unity*, Dodd, Mead, New York, 1975.

47. Charles V. Willie, *A New Look at Black Families*, 2d ed., General Hall, New York, 1981; R. Hill, *The Strengths of Black Families*, Emerson Hall Publishers, New York, 1972; Andrew Billingsley, *Black Families in White America*, Prentice-Hall, Englewood Cliffs, NJ, 1968.

48. Hyman Rodman, "The Lower Class Value Stretch," *Social Forces* 42 (1963), 205–215.

49. L. Richard Della Fave, "The Culture of Poverty Revisited: A Strategy for Research," *Social Problems* 21 (1974), 609–621.

50. Robert E. Park, *Race and Culture*, Free Press, Glencoe, IL, 1949, p. 150.

51. Seymour M. Lipset, "Changing Social Status and Prejudice: The Race Theories of a Pioneering American Sociologist," *Commentary* 9 (May 1950), 479.

52. Stanford M. Lyman, *The Black American in Sociological Thought: A Failure of Perspective*, Putnam, New York, 1972, pp. 49–50.

53. Warner and Srole, *The Social System of American Ethnic Groups*, pp. 285–286.

54. See Fred B. Silberstein and Melvin Seeman, "Social Mobility and Prejudice," *American Journal of Sociology* 60 (November 1959), 258–264; Joseph Greenblum and Leonard J. Pearlin, "Vertical Mobility and Prejudice: A Socio-Psychological Analysis," in *Class, Status and Power*, ed. Richard Bendix and S. M. Lipset, Free Press, Glencoe, IL, 1953, pp. 483–491.

55. Bettelheim and Janowitz, *Social Change and Prejudice,* pp. 29–34.

56. Donald L. Noel, "A Theory of the Origin of Ethnic Stratification," *Social Problems* 16 (Fall 1968), 157–172.

57. Lewis A. Coser, "Conflict: Social Aspects," in *International Encyclopedia of the Social Sciences,* ed. David Sills, Macmillan, New York, 1968, pp. 234–235.

58. Ralf Dahrendorf, *Class and Class Conflict in Industrial Society,* Stanford University Press, Stanford, CA, 1959, pp. 215–218.

59. Max Weber, "Class, Status, Party," 1922, in *From Max Weber,* trans. and ed. Hans Gerth and C. Wright Mills, Oxford University Press, New York, 1946, pp. 193–194.

60. See Hubert M. Blalock, Jr., *Toward a Theory of Minority-Group Relations,* Wiley, New York, 1967, pp. 199–203.

61. James M. O'Kane, "Ethnic Mobility and the Lower-Income Negro: A Socio-Historical Perspective," *Social Problems* 16 (1969), 309–311; see also Leonard Reissman and Michael N. Halstead, "The Subject Is Class," *Sociology and Social Research* 54 (1970), 301–304.

62. Ibid., pp. 303–311.

63. See Robert Blauner, "Internal Colonialism and Ghetto Revolt," *Social Problems* 16 (1969), 397; Stuart L. Hills, "Negroes and Immigrants in America," *Sociological Focus,* 3 (Summer 1970), 85–96; Nathan Glazer, "Blacks and Ethnic Groups," *Social Problems* 18 (1971), 444–461.

64. Newman, *American Pluralism,* p. 53.

65. Barbara Solomon, *Ancestors and Immigrants,* University of Chicago Press, Chicago, 1956, pp. 59–61.

66. John Higham, *Strangers in the Land,* Rutgers University Press, New Brunswick, NJ, 1955, p. 247.

67. George R. Stewart, *American Ways of Life,* Doubleday, Garden City, NY, 1954, pp. 23, 28.

68. Gordon, *Assimilation in American Life,* pp. 70–71.

69. Ibid., p. 81.

70. See Gerhard Lenski, *The Religious Factor,* Doubleday, Garden City, NY, 1961, pp. 326–330; Will Herberg, *Protestant–Catholic–Jew,* Doubleday, Garden City, NY, 1955; William M. Dobriner, *Class in Suburbia,* Prentice-Hall, Englewood Cliffs, NJ, 1963; Bennett M. Berger, *Working Class Suburbs,* 2d ed., University of California Press, Berkeley, CA, 1960.

71. Louis Wirth, "The Problem of Minority Groups," in *The Science of Man in the World Crisis,* ed. Ralph Linton, Columbia University Press, New York, 1945.

72. Solomon, *Ancestors and Immigrants,* pp. 59–81.

73. Newman, *American Pluralism,* p. 63.

74. J. Hector St. John de Crèvecoeur, *Letters from an American Farmer,* Albert and Charles Boni, New York, 1925, pp. 54–55. Reprinted from the original edition, London, 1782.

75. Frederick Jackson Turner, *The Frontier in American History,* Henry Holt, New York, 1920, p. 351.

76. Israel Zangwill, *The Melting-Pot: Drama in Four Acts,* Macmillan, New York, 1921, p. 33.

77. Actually, any student of western civilizations would point out that centuries of invasions, conquests, boundary changes, and so on had often resulted in cross-breeding and that truly distinct or pure ethnic types were virtually nonexistent long before the eighteenth century.

78. Gordon, *Assimilation in American Life,* pp. 109–110.

79. Ruby Jo Reeves Kennedy, "Single or Triple Melting Pot? Intermarriage Trends in New Haven, 1870–1940," *American Journal of Sociology* 49 (January 1944), 331–339; see also her follow-up study in *American Journal of Sociology* 58 (July 1952), 52–59.

80. See Will Herberg, *Protestant–Catholic–Jew,* Doubleday, Garden City, NY, 1955.

81. Henry Pratt Fairchild, *Immigration,* Macmillan, New York, 1925, p. 396 ff.

82. Herberg, *Protestant–Catholic–Jew,* pp. 33–34.

83. Newman, *American Pluralism,* p. 67.

84. Horace M. Kallen, "Democracy *Versus* the Melting Pot," *The Nation,* Feb. 18, 1915, pp. 190–194; Feb. 25, 1915, pp. 217–220.

85. Gordon, *Assimilation in American Life,* p. 135.

Chapter 3

1. See Hortense Powdermaker, *Probing Our Prejudices,* Harper, New York, 1941, p. 1.

2. Louis Wirth, "Race and Public Policy, *The Scientific Monthly* 58 (1944), 303.

3. Ralph L. Rosnow, "Poultry and Prejudice," *Psychology Today* (March 1972), 53.

4. Reported by Daniel Wilner, Rosabelle Price Walkley, and Stuart W. Cook, "Residential Proximity and Intergroup Relations in Public Housing Projects," *Journal of Social Issues* 8, No. 1 (1952), 45. See also James W. Vander Zanden, *American Minority Relations,* 3d ed., Ronald Press, New York, 1972, p. 21.

5. Bernard M. Kramer, "Dimensions of Prejudice," *Journal of Psychology* 27 (April 1949), 389–451.

6. L. Perry Curtis, Jr., *Apes and Angels: The Irishman in Victorian Caricature,* Smithsonian Press, Washington, DC, 1971.

7. Eliot Aronson, *The Social Animal,* 2d ed., Freeman, San Francisco, 1984, p. 174.

8. David Katz and Kenneth Braly, "Racial Stereotypes of One Hundred College Students," *Journal of Abnormal and Social Psychology* 28 (October–December 1933), 280–290; G. M. Gilbert, "Stereotype Persistence and Change Among College Students," *Jour-*

nal of Abnormal and Social Psychology 46 (1951), 245–254; Marvin Karlins, Thomas L. Coffman, and Gary Walters, "On the Fading of Social Stereotypes: Studies in Three Generations of College Students," *Journal of Personality and Social Psychology* 13 (1969), 1–16.

9. See, for example, Leonard Gordon, "College Student Stereotypes of Blacks and Jews on Two Campuses: Four Studies Spanning 50 Years," *Sociology and Social Research* 70 (April 1986), 200–201.

10. Howard J. Ehrlich, *The Social Psychology of Prejudice*, Wiley, New York, 1973, p. 22.

11. Erdman Palmore, "Ethnophaulisms and Ethnocentrism," *American Journal of Sociology* 67 (January 1962), 442–445.

12. Irving Lewis Allen, *Unkind Words: Ethnic Labeling from Redskin to Wasp*, Bergin & Garvey, New York, 1990, p. 3.

13. See Jeffrey H. Goldstein, "Theoretical Notes on Humor," *Journal of Communication* 26 (1976), 102–112.

14. Jeffrey H. Goldstein, *Social Psychology*, Academic Press, New York, 1980, p. 368.

15. U.S. Commission on Civil Rights, *Window Dressing on the Set: Women and Minorities in Television*, U.S. Government Printing Office, Washington, DC, 1977; *Window Dressing on the Set: An Update*, 1979.

16. George Gerbner, quoted in "Life According to TV," *Newsweek*, December 6, 1982, pp. 136 ff.

17. Ibid.

18. See "Minorities and the Media," *Electronic Media*, July 8, 1991, pp. 29–36.

19. Sheryl Graves, "How to Encourage Positive Racial Attitudes," paper presented at the biennial meeting of the Society for Research in Child Development, 1975, Denver, CO.

20. For an overview of research on this program, see Stuart H. Surlin, "Five Years of 'All in the Family': A Summary of Empirical Research Generated by the Program," *Mass Comm Review* 3 (1976). See also J. C. Brigham and L. W. Biesbrecht, "All in the Family: Racial Attitudes," *Journal of Communication* 26 (1976), 69–74.

21. Neil Vidmar and Milton Rokeach, "Archie Bunker's Bigotry," *Journal of Communication* 24 (1974), 36–47.

22. S. Robert Lichter and Linda S. Lichter, "Television's Impact on Ethnic and Racial Images," American Jewish Committee, New York, 1988.

23. Herbert Blumer, "Race Prejudice as a Sense of Group Position," *Pacific Sociological Review* 1 (1958), 3–7.

24. William M. Newman, *American Pluralism*, Harper & Row, New York, 1973, p. 197.

25. See Marvin B. Scott and Stanford M. Lyman, "Accounts," *American Sociological Review* 33 (February 1968), 40–62.

26. Philip Mason, *Patterns of Dominance*, Oxford University Press, New York, 1970, p. 7. Also, Philip Mason,

Race Relations, Oxford University Press, New York, 1970, pp. 17–29.

27. T. W. Adorno, Else Frankel-Brunswik, Daniel J. Levinson, and R. Nevitt Sanford, *The Authoritarian Personality*, Harper & Row, New York, 1950.

28. H. H. Hyman and P. B. Sheatsley, "The Authoritarian Personality: A Methodological Critique," in *Studies in the Scope and Method of "The Authoritarian Personality,"* ed. R. Christie and M. Jahoda, Free Press, Glencoe, IL, 1954.

29. Solomon E. Asch, *Social Psychology*, Prentice-Hall, Englewood Cliffs, NJ, 1952, p. 545.

30. E. A. Shils, "Authoritarianism: Right and Left," in *Studies in the Scope and Method of "The Authoritarian Personality."*

31. D. Stewart and T. Hoult, "A Social-Psychological Theory of 'The Authoritarian Personality.' " *American Journal of Sociology* 65 (1959), 274.

32. H. C. Kelman and Janet Barclay, "The F Scale as a Measure of Breadth of Perspective," *Journal of Abnormal and Social Psychology* 67 (1963), 608–615.

33. For an excellent summary of authoritarian studies and literature, see John P. Kirscht and Ronald C. Dillehay, *Dimensions of Authoritarianism: A Review of Research and Theory*, University of Kentucky Press, Lexington, 1967.

34. George E. Simpson and J. Milton Yinger, *Racial and Cultural Minorities: An Analysis of Prejudice and Discrimination*, Harper & Row, New York, 1953, p. 91.

35. Ibid., pp. 62–79.

36. H. J. Ehrlich, *The Social Psychology of Prejudice*, Wiley, New York, 1974; G. Sherwood, "Self-Serving Biases in Person Perception," *Psychological Bulletin* 90 (1981), 445–459; T. A. Wills, "Downward Comparison Principles in Social Psychology," *Psychological Bulletin* 90 (1981), 245–271.

37. Jennifer Crocker and Ian Schwartz, "Prejudice and Ingroup Favoritism in a Minimal Intergroup Situation: Effects of Self-Esteem," *Personality and Social Psychology Bulletin* Vol. 11, No. 4 (December 1985), 379–386.

38. John Dollard, Leonard W. Doob, Neal E. Miller, O. H. Mowrer, and Robert P. Sears, *Frustration and Aggression*, Yale University Press, New Haven, CT, 1939; A. F. Henry and J. F. Short, Jr., *Suicide and Homicide*, Free Press, New York, 1954; Neal Miller and Richard Bugelski, "Minor Studies in Aggression: The Influence of Frustration Imposed by the Ingroup on Attitudes Expressed Toward Outgroups," *Journal of Psychology* 25 (1948), 437–442; Stuart Palmer, *The Psychology of Murder*, T. Y. Crowell, New York, 1960; Brenden C. Rule and Elizabeth Percival, "The Effects of Frustration and Attack on Physical Aggression," *Journal of Experimental Research on Personality* 5 (1971), 111–188.

39. Leviticus 16:5–22.

40. Gordon W. Allport, "The ABC's of Scapegoating," 5th rev. ed., Anti-Defamation League pamphlet, New York.

41. Carl I. Hovland and Robert R. Sears, "Minor Studies of Aggression: Correlation of Lynchings with Economic Indices," *Journal of Psychology* 9 (Winter 1940), 301–310.

42. Miller and Bugelski, "Minor Studies of Aggression," pp. 437–442.

43. Donald Weatherley, "Anti-Semitism and the Expression of Fantasy Aggression," *Journal of Abnormal and Social Psychology* 62 (1961), 454–457.

44. See Leonard Berkowitz, "Whatever Happened to the Frustration-Aggression Hypothesis?" *American Behavioral Scientist* 21 (1978), 691–708; L. Berkowitz, *Aggression: A Social Psychological Analysis,* McGraw-Hill, New York, 1962.

45. D. Zillman, *Hostility and Aggression,* Lawrence Erlbaum, Hillsdale, NJ, 1979; R. A. Baron, *Human Aggression,* Plenum Press, New York, 1977; N. Pastore, "The Role of Arbitrariness in the Frustration-Aggression Hypothesis," *Journal of Abnormal and Social Psychology* 47 (1952), 728–731.

46. A. H. Buss, "Instrumentality of Aggression, Feedback, and Frustration as Determinants of Physical Aggression," *Journal of Personality and Social Psychology* 3 (1966), 153–162.

47. J. R. Averill, "Studies on Anger and Aggression: Implications for Theories of Emotion," *American Psychologist* 38 (1983), 1145–1160.

48. Talcott Parsons, "Certain Primary Sources and Patterns of Aggression in the Social Structure of the Western World," *Essays in Sociological Theory,* Free Press, New York, 1964, pp. 298–322.

49. For an excellent review of Parsonian theory in this area, see Stanford M. Lyman, *The Black American in Sociological Thought: A Failure of Perspective,* Putnam, New York, 1972, pp. 145–169.

50. John Dollard, "Hostility and Fear in Social Life," *Social Forces* 17 (1938), 15–26.

51. Muzafer Sherif, O. J. Harvey, B. Jack White, William Hood, and Carolyn Sherif, *Intergroup Conflict and Cooperation: The Robbers Cave Experiment,* University of Oklahoma Institute of Intergroup Relations, Norman, OK, 1961. See also M. Sherif, "Experiments in Group Conflict," *Scientific American* 195 (1956), 54–58.

52. Donald Young, *Research Memorandum on Minority Peoples in the Depression,* Social Science Research Council, New York, 1937, pp. 133–141.

53. Andrew Greeley and Paul Sheatsley, "The Acceptance of Desegregation Continues to Advance," *Scientific American* 210 (1971), 13–19; T. F. Pettigrew, "Three Issues in Ethnicity: Boundaries, Deprivations, and Perceptions," in M. Yinger and S. J.

Cutler (eds.), *Major Social Issues: A Multidisciplinary View,* Free Press, New York, 1978; R. D. Vanneman and T. F. Pettigrew, "Race and Relative Deprivation in the United States," *Race* 13 (1972), 461–486.

54. See Harry H. L. Kitano, "Passive Discrimination in the Normal Person," *Journal of Social Psychology* 70 (1966), 23–31.

55. Thomas Pettigrew, "Regional Differences in Anti-Negro Prejudice," *Journal of Abnormal and Social Psychology* 59 (1959), 28–36.

56. Jeanne Watson, "Some Social and Psychological Situations Related to Change in Attitude," *Human Relations* 3 (1950), 15–56.

57. John Dollard, *Caste and Class in a Southern Town,* 3d ed., Doubleday Anchor Books, Garden City, NY, 1957.

58. See Gordon W. Allport, *The Nature of Prejudice,* Addison-Wesley, Reading, MA, 1954, p. 251 ff.; Robin M. Williams, Jr., *Strangers Next Door,* Prentice-Hall, Englewood Cliffs, NJ, 1964, p. 150 ff.; James W. Vander Zanden, *American Minority Relations,* 3d ed., Ronald Press, New York, 1972, pp. 460–469.

59. Brewton Berry and Henry L. Tischler, *Race and Ethnic Relations,* 4th ed., Houghton Mifflin, Boston, 1978, p. 250. See also David G. Myers, *Social Psychology,* 2nd ed., McGraw-Hill, New York, 1987, pp. 55–56.

60. Elliot Aronson and Neal Osherow, "Cooperation, Prosocial Behavior, and Academic Performance: Experiments in the Desegregated Classroom," *Applied Social Psychology Annual* 1 (1980), 163–196.

61. Gertrude J. Selznick and Stephen Steinberg, *The Tenacity of Prejudice,* Harper & Row, New York, 1969.

62. For evidence of both findings, see Robin M. Williams, Jr., *The Reduction of Intergroup Tensions,* Social Science Research Council, Washington, DC, 1947, p. 27 ff.; Gordon W. Allport, *The Nature of Prejudice,* p. 483 ff.

63. Charles H. Stember, *Education and Attitude Change,* Institute of Human Relations Press, New York, 1961.

64. Blumer, "Race Prejudice as a Sense of Group Position," pp. 3–7.

65. Allport, *The Nature of Prejudice.*

66. John Weiss, "The State of Intergroup Relations," presentation at Second National Consultation on Ethnic America, Fordham University, June 23, 1988.

67. Williams, *Strangers Next Door,* pp. 124–125.

68. Robert K. Merton, "Discrimination and the American Creed," in *Discrimination and National Welfare,* ed. Robert M. MacIver, Harper, New York, 1949, pp. 99–126.

69. Hubert M. Blalock, Jr., *Toward a Theory of Minority Group Relationships,* Capricorn Books, New York, 1970, pp. 204–207. For insight into the origin of this argument, see Stanford M. Lyman, "Cherished Values and Civil Rights," *The Crisis* 71 (December 1964), 645–654, 695.

70. William M. Newman, *American Pluralism*, Harper & Row, New York, 1973, p. 231.
71. John Rawls, *A Theory of Justice*, The Belknap Press of Harvard University, Cambridge, MA, 1971.
72. Joseph Tussman and Jacobus tenBroek, "The Equal Protection of the Laws," *California Law Review* 37 (September 1949), 341–381.
73. Ibid., p. 380.
74. Ibid., p. 381.
75. John Gpuhl and Susan Welch, "The Impact of the Bakke Decision on Black and Hispanic Enrollment in Medical and Law Schools," *Social Science Quarterly* 71 (1990), 458–473.

Chapter 4

1. See Robin M. Williams, Jr., "The Reduction of Intergroup Tensions," *Social Science Research Council Bulletin* 57 (1947), 61; William J. Wilson, *Power, Racism, and Privilege*, Free Press, New York, 1973, pp. 47–68.
2. President's Commission on Law Enforcement and Administration of Justice, *Task Force Report: The Courts*, U.S. Government Printing Office, Washington, DC, 1967; Lee Silverstein, *Defense of the Poor in Criminal Cases in American State Courts*, I, American Bar Association, New York, 1965; Caleb Foote, "The Bail System and Equal Justice," *Federal Probation* 23 (September 1959), 45–47; Rita M. James, "Status and Competence of Jurors," *American Journal of Sociology* 64 (May 1959), 565–566.
3. Clifford R. Shaw and Henry D. McKay, *Juvenile Delinquency and Urban Areas*, University of Chicago Press, Chicago, 1942.
4. John P. Clark and Eugene P. Wenninger, "Socioeconomic Class and Area as Correlates of Illegal Behavior Among Juveniles," *American Sociological Review* 27 (December 1962), 826–843; Karl Schnessler, "Components of Variation in City Crime Rates," *Social Problems* 9 (1962), 314–323.
5. Albert K. Cohen, *Delinquent Boys*, Free Press, Glencoe, IL, 1955.
6. For a study of Chinese gangs, see Stanford M. Lyman, "Red Guard on Grant Avenue: The Rise of Youthful Rebellion in Chinatown," *The Asian in North America*, A-B-C Clio Press, Santa Barbara, CA, 1977, pp. 177–200. The classic study on Italian gangs is William F. Whyte, *Street Corner Society*, University of Chicago Press, Chicago, 1943.
7. Jackson Toby, "Hoodlum or Business Man: An American Dilemma," in *The Jews*, ed. Marshall Sklare, Free Press, Glencoe, IL, 1958, pp. 544–549.
8. Kurt Lewin, *Resolving Social Conflicts*, Harper & Row, New York, 1948, pp. 186–200.
9. Gordon W. Allport, *The Nature of Prejudice*, 1954, Addison-Wesley, Reading, MA, pp. 152–153.
10. Gunnar Myrdal, *An American Dilemma*, McGraw-Hill, New York, 1964, pp. 25–28; originally published by Harper, 1944.
11. Gordon W. Allport, "The Role of Expectancy," in *Tensions That Cause Wars*, ed. H. Cantril, University of Illinois Press, Urbana, 1950, chap. 2.
12. Allport, *The Nature of Prejudice*, p. 160.
13. Robert K. Merton, *Social Theory and Social Structure*, Free Press, Glencoe, IL, 1957, pp. 290–291.
14. Robert E. Park, "Human Migration and the Marginal Man," *American Journal of Sociology* 33 (May 1928), 891; see also Everett V. Stonequist, *The Marginal Man*, Scribner, New York, 1937.
15. George E. Simpson and J. Milton Yinger, *Racial and Cultural Minorities: An Analysis of Prejudice and Discrimination*, 4th ed., Harper & Row, New York, 1972, p. 186.
16. Milton M. Goldberg, "A Qualification of the Marginal Man Theory," *American Sociological Review* 6 (February 1941), 52–58.
17. Hubert M. Blalock, Jr., *Toward a Theory of Minority Group Relations*, Wiley, New York, 1967, pp. 79–84.
18. Edna Bonacich, "A Theory of Middleman Minorities," *American Sociological Review* 38 (1973), 583–594.
19. Edna Bonacich and John Modell, *The Economic Basis of Ethnic Solidarity*, University of California Press, Berkeley, CA, 1980, p. 30.
20. See Gideon Sjoberg, "The Preindustrial City," *American Journal of Sociology* 60 (March 1955), 438–445; Claude S. Fischer, *The Urban Experience*, 2d ed., Harcourt Brace Jovanovich, New York, 1984, p. 13; Lyn H. Lofland, *A World of Strangers*, Basic Books, New York, 1973, p. 50.
21. See Noel P. Gist and Sylvia F. Fava, *Urban Society*, 6th ed., Thomas Y. Crowell, New York, 1974, p. 204.
22. See Allport, *The Nature of Prejudice*, pp. 53–54.
23. Deuteronomy 2:32–35; 3:1, 3–4, 6–7.
24. Arnold J. Toynbee, *A Study of History*, Oxford University Press, London, 1934, p. 465.
25. G. P. Murdock, *Our Primitive Contemporaries*, Macmillan, New York, 1934, pp. 16–18.
26. See I. D. MacCrone, *Race Attitudes in South Africa*, Oxford University Press, London, 1937, pp. 89–136.
27. Donald Pierson, *Negroes in Brazil*, University of Chicago Press, Chicago, 1942, p. 6.
28. For recent discussions on black lynchings, see *Social Forces* 67 (March 1989), 605–633.
29. See Gunnar Myrdal, *An American Dilemma*, Harper & Row, New York, 1944, pp. 566, 1350.
30. Stanley Lieberson, "A Societal Theory of Race and Ethnic Relations," *American Sociological Review* 26 (December 1961), 902–910.
31. William J. Wilson, *Power, Racism, and Privilege*, Free Press, New York, 1973, pp. 47–65.
32. Robert Blauner, "Internal Colonialism and Ghetto Revolt," *Social Problems* 16 (Spring 1969), 393–406.

33. Ibid., p. 397.
34. Edna Bonacich, "A Theory of Ethnic Antagonism: The Split Labor Market," *American Sociological Review* 37 (1972), 547–559.
35. Ibid., p. 554.
36. Ibid., p. 550.
37. See Alexander Saxton, *The Indispensable Enemy: Labor and the Anti-Chinese Movement in California*, University of California Press, Berkeley, CA, 1971.
38. Mike Hilton, "The Split Labor Market and Chinese Immigration, 1848–1882," presented at the 72d annual meeting of the American Sociological Association, 1977.
39. Ibid., pp. 4–5.

Chapter 5

1. Nathan Glazer and Daniel P. Moynihan, *Beyond the Melting Pot,* 2d ed., M.I.T. Press, Cambridge, MA, 1970, p. 1.
2. Maldwyn Allen Jones, *American Immigration,* University of Chicago Press, Chicago, 1960, p. 40.
3. Quoted in *American Observer* 50 (November 29, 1971), 4.
4. Quotations and commentary taken from John C. Miller, *Crisis in Freedom,* Little, Brown, Boston, 1951, pp. 41–42.
5. W. S. Shaw to Abigail Adams, Cambridge, MA, May 20, 1798, *Adams Papers,* Vol. 8, No. 48, Massachusetts Historical Society.
6. R. Ernst, "The Living Conditions of the Immigrant," in *The Urbanization of America,* ed. A. M. Wakestein, Houghton Mifflin, Boston, 1949, p. 266.
7. Carleton Beals, *Brass Knuckle Crusade,* Hastings House, New York, 1960, p. 5.
8. Ibid.
9. Ray Allen Billington, *The Protestant Crusade, 1800–1860,* Macmillan, New York, 1938, p. 388.
10. John Higham, *Strangers in the Land,* Atheneum, New York, 1973, p. 7.
11. Harriet Martineau, *Society in America,* 1837, quoted in *American Observer* 50 (November 29, 1971), 4.
12. *The Journals and Miscellaneous Notebooks of Ralph Waldo Emerson,* eds. Ralph H. Orth and Alfred K. Ferguson, The Belknap Press of Harvard University Press, Cambridge, MA, 1971, IX, 299–300.
13. William Bradford, *Of Plymouth Plantation,* ed. Harvey Wish, Capricorn Books, New York, 1962, p. 29.
14. Ibid., p. 33.
15. Ibid., pp. 16–17, 184.
16. Rowland Berthoff, *British Immigrants in Industrial America, 1790–1950,* Harvard University Press, Cambridge, MA, 1953, pp. 30–56.
17. Ibid., pp. 125–131.
18. Ilja M. Dijour, "A Seminar on the Integration of Immigrants," 1960, p. 6, quoted in Wilbur S. Shepperson, *Emigration and Disenchantment: Portraits of Englishmen Repatriated from the United States,* University of Oklahoma Press, Norman, 1965, p. 182.
19. Wilbur S. Shepperson, *Emigration and Disenchantment: Portraits of Englishmen Repatriated from the United States,* University of Oklahoma Press, Norman, 1965, pp. 16–17, 184.
20. A Report of the Commissioner of Immigration upon the Causes Which Incite Immigration to the U.S., 52nd Congress, 1st session (1891–1892), *House Executive Document 235,* Part I, pp. 260, 282.
21. Berthoff, *British Immigrants in Industrial America, 1790–1950,* pp. 103–104.
22. U.S. Immigration and Naturalization Service, *1990 Statistical Yearbook,* Washington, DC, 1991, Table 2, p. 50.
23. Ibid.
24. Hans Koningsberger, *Holland and the United States,* Netherlands Information Service, New York 1968, p. 20.
25. Arthur Henry Hirsch, *The Huguenots of Colonial South Carolina,* Shoe String Press, Hamden, CT, 1962, p. 95.
26. Miller, *Crisis in Freedom,* pp. 13, 42–43.
27. T. Lynn Smith and Vernon J. Parenton, "Acculturation Among the Louisiana French," *American Journal of Sociology* 44 (November 1938), 357.
28. Vernon J. Parenton, "Socio-Psychological Integration in a Rural French-Speaking Section of Louisiana," *The Southwestern Social Science Quarterly* 30 (December 1949), 195.
29. Carl A. Brasseaux, "Four Hundred Years of Acadian Life in North America," *Journal of Popular Culture* 23 (Summer 1989), p. 13.
30. Ibid., p. 17.
31. Cecyle Trepanier, "The Cajunization of French Louisiana: Forging a Regional Identity," *The Geographical Journal* 157 (July 1991), 161–171.
32. U.S. Bureau of the Census, Ethnic and Hispanic Branch, 1990 Census Special Tabulations, 1990 CPH-L-89.
33. Marcus L. Hansen and J. B. Prebner, *The Mingling of the Canadian and American Peoples,* Yale University Press, New Haven, CT, 1940, pp. 123–168.
34. Albert B. Faust, *The German Element in the United States,* Arno Press, New York, 1969, I, 66–72.
35. Quoted in W. C. Smith, *Americans in the Making,* Appleton-Century, New York, 1939, p. 394.
36. Maurice R. Davie, *World Immigration,* Macmillan, New York, 1936, p. 36.
37. Brewton Berry and Henry I. Tischler, *Race and Ethnic Relations,* 4th ed., Houghton Mifflin, Boston, 1979, p. 186.

38. Maldwyn Allen Jones, *American Immigration*, University of Chicago Press, Chicago, 1960, pp. 45–46.

39. Maldwyn Allen Jones, "Scotch-Irish," in Stephan Thernstrom, Ann Orlov, and Oscar Handlin (eds.), *Harvard Encyclopedia of American Ethnic Groups*, The Belknap Press, Cambridge, MA, 1980, pp. 899–900.

40. Quoted in James M. Smith, *Freedom's Fetters*, Cornell University Press, Ithaca, NY, 1956, p. 25.

41. Charles F. Marden and Gladys Meyer, *Minorities in American Society*, 5th ed., Van Nostrand Reinhold, New York, 1978, p. 77.

42. Edward Everett, "Letters on Irish Emigration," in *Historical Aspects of the Immigration Problem, Select Documents*, ed. Edith Abbott, University of Chicago Press, Chicago, 1926, pp. 462–463.

43. Peter I. Rose, *They and We*, 2d ed., Random House, New York, 1974, p. 39.

44. For information about middleman minorities, see Hubert M. Blalock, Jr., *Toward a Theory of Minority Group Relations*, Wiley, New York, 1967, pp. 79–84; Edna Bonacich, "A Theory of Middleman Minorities," *American Sociological Review* 38 (October 1973), 583–594.

45. Oscar Handlin, *Boston's Immigrants*, rev. ed., Harvard University Press, Cambridge, MA, 1959, p. 176.

46. Ellen Horgan Biddle, "The American Catholic Irish Family," in Charles H. Mindel and Robert W. Habenstein (eds.), *Ethnic Families in America: Patterns and Variations*, 2d ed., Elsevier, New York, 1981, p. 96.

47. Alfred J. Kutzik, "American Social Provision for the Aged: An Historical Perspective," in Donald E. Gelfand and Alfred J. Kutzik (eds.), *Ethnicity and Aging: Theory, Research, and Policy*, Springer, New York, 1979, pp. 32–65.

48. Arnold Shrier, *Ireland and the American Emigration, 1850–1900*, University of Minnesota Press, Minneapolis, 1958, p. 34.

49. Carl Wittke, *The Irish in America*, Russell and Russell, New York, 1970, pp. 191–192.

50. Robert Kelley, *The Cultural Pattern in American Politics: The First Century*, Knopf, New York, 1979, pp. 195, 237.

51. Joel T. Headley, *The Great Riots of New York, 1712–1873*, Bobbs-Merrill, Indianapolis, 1970; James McCague, *The Second Rebellion*, Dial Press, New York, 1968.

52. Joseph P. O'Grady, *How the Irish Became Americans*, Twayne, New York, 1973; Edgar Litt, *Beyond Pluralism: Ethnic Politics in America*, Scott, Foresman, Glencoe, IL, 1970, chap. 8.

53. Richard Krickus, *Pursuing the American Dream: White Ethnics and the New Populism*, Indiana University Press, Bloomington, 1976, chap. 4; D. W. Brogan, *Politics in America*, Harper, New York, 1954.

54. Judith Waldrop, "Irish Eyes on America," *American Demographics*, March 1989, p. 6.

55. "Irish Americans: The Second Coming," *The Economist*, July 27, 1991, p. 26.

56. Rose, *They and We*, p. 68.

57. Ole E. Rolvaag, *Giants in the Earth*, Copyright, 1927, by Harper & Brothers, p. 425.

58. Peter Kivisto, *Immigrant Socialists in the United States*, Fairleigh Dickinson University Press, Madison, NJ, 1984, pp. 72–74.

59. Peter Kivisto, "Form and Content of Immigrant Socialist Ideology: The Case of the Finnish-American Left," *Siirtolaisuus* 3 (1983), 12–13.

60. Peter Kivisto, "The Decline of the Finnish American Left, 1925–1945," *International Migration Review* 17 (1983), 65–94.

61. Paul C. Nyholm, *The Americanization of the Danish Lutheran Churches in America*, Augsburg Publishing House, Minneapolis, 1963, pp. 249–291.

62. Merle Curti, *The Making of an American Community: A Case Study of Democracy in a Frontier County*, Stanford University Press, Stanford, CA, 1959, pp. 84, 96, 101, 104, 112.

63. Carl Chrislock, *Ethnicity Challenged: The Upper Midwest Norwegian American Experience in World War*, Northfield, MN, 1981, pp. 40, 44.

64. Kendric C. Babcock, *The Scandinavian Element in the United States*, 1914, reprint ed., Arno Press and The New York Times, New York, 1969, pp. 15–16.

65. James G. Leyburn, *The Scotch-Irish: A Social History*, University of North Carolina Press, Chapel Hill, 1962, chap. 16.

66. Ibid.

67. J. Hector St. John de Crèvecoeur, *Letters from an American Farmer*, Albert and Charles Boni, New York, 1925, pp. 54–55. Reprinted from the original edition, London, 1782.

Chapter 6

1. "From Farm to Factory: Immigrant Adjustment to American Industry," *Spectrum* 1 (May 1975), 1.

2. Milton M. Gordon, *Assimilation in American Life*, Oxford University Press, New York, 1964, p. 136.

3. Madison Grant, *The Passing of the Great Race*, 1916; reprint edition, Arno Press and *The New York Times*, 1970, p. 91.

4. Gordon, *Assimilation in American Life*, p. 97.

5. Ronald M. Pavalko, "Racism and the New Immigration: Toward A Reinterpretation of the Experiences of White Ethnics in American Society," *Sociology and Social Research* 65 (1981), 56–77.

6. Isaac A. Hourwich, *Immigrants and Labor,* B. W. Huebach, Inc., New York, 1922; quoted in Pavalko, "Racism and the New Immigration," p. 8.
7. Pavalko, p. 2.
8. Ibid., p. 24.
9. See the discussion on pp. 102–103; see also Gordon, *Assimilation in American Life,* pp. 137–138.
10. Ellwood P. Cubberly, *Changing Conceptions of Education,* Houghton Mifflin, Boston, 1909, pp. 15–16.
11. John Higham, *Strangers in the Land: Patterns of American Nativism, 1860–1925,* Rutgers University Press, New Brunswick, NJ, 1955, pp. 137–138.
12. *Public Opinion* I (1886), 82–86.
13. *The Age of Steel,* quoted in *Public Opinion* I (1886), 355.
14. Henry Pratt Fairchild, *The Melting Pot Mistake,* Little, Brown, Boston, 1926, quoted in *American Observer* 50 (November 29, 1971), 5.
15. Victor R. Greene, *The Slavic Community on Strike,* University of Notre Dame Press, South Bend, IN, 1968, pp. 40–41.
16. Ibid., pp. 49–50.
17. See Charles B. Nam, "Nationality Groups and Social Stratification in America," *Social Forces* 37, (1959), 328–333.
18. Vincent N. Parrillo, *Strangers to These Shores,* 3rd ed., Macmillan, New York, 1990, p. 178.
19. Henryk Sienkiewicz, *Portrait of America, Letters of Henryk Sienkiewicz,* ed. and trans. Charles Morley, Columbia University Press, New York, 1959, pp. 272–273.
20. Ibid., p. 279.
21. William I. Thomas and Florian Znaniecki, *The Polish Peasant in Europe and America,* 5 vols., B. G. Badger, Boston, 1918–1920.
22. "Immigrants and Religion: The Persistence of Ethnic Diversity," *Spectrum* 1 (September 1975), 2.
23. Helena Znaniecki Lopata, *Polish Americans: Status Competition in an Ethnic Community,* Prentice-Hall, Englewood Cliffs, NJ, 1976, p. 92.
24. Ibid., p. 145.
25. Beverly Duncan and Otis Dudley Duncan, "Minorities and the Process of Stratification," *American Sociological Review* 33 (June 1968), 356–364; Stanley Lieberson, *Ethnic Patterns in American Cities,* Free Press, New York, 1963, p. 189.
26. Lopata, *Polish Americans,* p. 95.
27. Neil C. Sandberg, *Ethnic Identity and Assimilation: The Polish-American Community,* Praeger, New York, 1974.
28. See the discussion on pp. 44–45.
29. Lopata, *Polish Americans,* p. 148.
30. "Polish Americans: No Jokes, Less Solidarity," *The Economist,* October 5, 1991, p. 33.
31. U.S. Immigration and Naturalization Service, *1990 Statistical Yearbook,* Table 18, p. 84.
32. Emil Lengyel, *Americans from Hungary,* Lippincott, New York, 1948, p. 128.
33. New York *Tribune,* September 11–12, 1897, pp. 1, 3.
34. Irving Lewis Allen, *Unkind Words,* New York, Bergin & Garvey, 1990, pp. 31, 62.
35. John Körösföy (ed.), *Hungarians in America,* Szabadság, Cleveland, 1941, pp. 15–28.
36. Ian Hancock, "Gypsies," in Stephen Thernstrom ed., *Harvard Encyclopedia of American Ethnic Groups,* Harvard University Press, Cambridge, MA, 1980, p. 441.
37. Werner Cohn, "Some Comparison Between Gypsy (North American Rom) and American English Kinship Terms," *American Anthropologist* 71 (June 1969), 477–478.
38. Glen W. Davidson, " 'Gypsies': People with a Hidden History," in *The Rediscovery of Ethnicity,* ed. Sallie TeSelle, Harper & Row, New York, 1973, p. 84.
39. Allan Pinkerton, *The Gypsies and the Detectives,* G. W. Carleton & Company, New York, 1879, pp. 68–69.
40. Rena C. Gropper, *Gypsies in the City,* Darwin, Princeton, NJ, 1975, pp. 60–66.
41. Gulbun Coker, "Romany Rye in Philadelphia: A Sequel," *Southwestern Journal of Anthropology* 22 (1966), 85–100.
42. Jean-Paul Clebert, *The Gypsies,* Vista, London, 1963, p. 96.
43. Jan Yoors, *The Gypsies,* Simon & Schuster, New York, 1967, p. 7.
44. Anne Sutherland, *Gypsies: The Hidden Americans,* Free Press, New York, 1975, p. 232.
45. Gropper, *Gypsies in the City,* p. 162.
46. Sutherland, *Gypsies: The Hidden Americans,* p. 248.
47. Carol Miller, "American Rom and the Ideology of Defilement," in Farnham Rehfisch, ed., *Gypsies, Tinkers, and Other Travelers,* Academic Press, New York, 1975, p. 41.
48. Ronald Lee, *Goddam Gypsy: An Autobiographical Novel,* Tundra, Montreal, 1971, pp. 29–30.
49. Sutherland, *Gypsies: The Hidden Americans,* p. 264.
50. Gropper, *Gypsies in the City,* pp. 92–93.
51. Miller, "American Rom and the Ideology of Defilement," pp. 45–46.
52. Hancock, "Gypsies," p. 444.
53. Peter Maas, *King of the Gypsies,* Viking, New York, 1975, pp. 29–31.
54. Carol Silverman, "Everyday Drama: Impression Management of Urban Gypsies," in Matt T. Salo, ed., *Urban Anthropology, Special Issue* 11 (Fall–Winter 1982), 382.
55. Ibid., p. 29.
56. Sutherland, Gypsies: *The Hidden Americans,* p. 98.
57. Hancock, "Gypsies," p. 441.
58. Based on data from Mark Wischnitzer, *Visas to Freedom,* prepared by Hebrew Immigration Assistance

Society, World Publishing Company, Cleveland, 1956; U.S. Immigration and Naturalization Service, *Annual Report:* U.S. Government Printing Office, Washington, DC, 1981, Table 13, p. 63.

59. Wasyl Halich, *Ukrainians in the United States,* University of Chicago Press, Chicago, 1937; reprint edition by Arno Press and *The New York Times,* 1970, pp. 28–29.

60. Jerome Davis, *The Russians and Ruthenians in America,* Doran, New York, 1992; reprint edition by Arno Press and *The New York Times,* 1970, p. 104.

61. Jerome Davis, *The Russian Immigrant,* Macmillan, New York, 1922; reprint edition by Arno Press and *The New York Times,* 1970, p. 98.

62. Edward T. Devine, "Family and Social Work," in Jerome Davis, *The Russians and Ruthenians in America,* p. 32.

63. Davis, *The Russian Immigrant,* pp. 173–174.

64. John Higham, *Strangers in the Land: Patterns of American Nativism, 1860–1925,* Rutgers University Press, New Brunswick, NJ, 1955, pp. 230–231; see also Frederick R. Barkley, "Jailing Radicals in Detroit," *Nation* 110 (1920), 136.

65. U.S. Immigration and Naturalization Service, *1990 Statistical Yearbook,* U.S. Government Printing Office, Washington, DC, 1991, Table 27, p. 103.

66. Susan Katz, "Nurturing Holy Traditions," *Insight* (January 11, 1988), 15.

67. *The Letters of Sacco and Vanzetti,* ed. Marion D. Frankfurter and Gardner Jackson, Viking, New York, 1928, p. 377.

68. Higham reports, for example, that under the heading "Italians" in the 1902 *New York Tribune Index,* 55 of the 74 entries were clear accounts of crime and violence (*Strangers in the Land,* p. 363).

69. For an excellent insight into the Italian community of Chicago's West Side, see Gerald D. Suttles, *The Social Order of the Slum,* University of Chicago Press, Chicago, 1968.

70. See Rudolph Vecoli, *The Peoples of New Jersey,* Van Nostrand, Princeton, NJ, 1965, pp. 221–236.

71. Herbert J. Gans, *The Urban Villagers,* Free Press, New York, 1962, pp. 204–205.

72. William Foote Whyte, *Street Corner Society,* University of Chicago Press, Chicago, 1943, p. 274.

73. Richard D. Alba, "The Twilight of Ethnicity Among Americans of European Ancestry: the Case of the Italians," *Ethnic and Racial Studies* 8 (January 1985), 141.

74. Richard D. Alba, *Italian Americans: Into the Twilight of Ethnicity,* Prentice-Hall, Englewood Cliffs, NJ, 1985, p. 159.

75. Leonard Dinnerstein and David M. Reimers, *Ethnic Americans,* Harper & Row, New York, 1975, p. 43.

76. In 1972 a Boston city survey, the Omnibus Survey, revealed that its sizable Greek immigrant population had a zero unemployment rate, no one on welfare, and a median income $4,000 above the Boston average.

77. Theodore Saloutos, *The Greeks in the United States,* Harvard University Press, Cambridge, MA, 1964, pp. 78–79.

78. Henry Pratt Fairchild, *Greek Immigration,* Yale University Press, New Haven, CT, 1911, pp. 239, 241–242.

79. Gerald A. Estep, "Portuguese Assimilation in Hawaii and California," *Sociology and Social Research* 26 (September 1941), 64.

80. Donald R. Taft, *Two Portuguese Communities in New England,* reprint edition, Arno Press, New York, 1969, p. 79.

81. Ibid., p. 348.

82. See Louis Adamic, *A Nation of Nations,* Harper, New York, 1945, pp. 287–288.

83. Marjorie Housepian, *The Unremembered Genocide,* "A Commentary Report," American Jewish Committee, New York, 1965, p. 31.

84. Frank A. Stone, *Armenian Studies for Secondary Students,* Parousia Press, Storrs, CT, 1975, p. 8.

85. Emory S. Bogardus, "Comparing Racial Distance in Ethiopia, South Africa, and the United States," *Sociology and Social Research* 52 (1968), 149–156.

86. Gary A. Kulhanjian, *The Historical and Sociological Aspects of Armenian Immigration to the United States, 1890 to 1930,* R. and E. Research Associates, San Francisco, 1975, p. 25.

87. Ibid., p. 29.

88. "Armenians in California," *The Economist* January 19, 1991, p. 28.

Chapter 7

1. See Lee E. Huddleston, *Origins of the American Indians: European Concepts, 1492–1729,* University of Texas Press, Austin, 1967.

2. U.S. Bureau of the Census, *1990 Census Profile,* No. 2, U.S. Government Printing Office, Washington, DC, June 1991, p. 6.

3. John Boyd Thacher (ed.), *Christopher Columbus,* Vol. 1, AMS Press, Inc., New York, 1967, I, 533.

4. Michel de Montaigne, "Of Cannibals," bk I., ch. 31, in *The Complete Works of Montaigne,* translated by Donald M. Frame, Stanford University Press, Stanford, CA, 1957, pp. 150–159.

5. See Lewis Hanke, *The First Social Experiments in America: A Study in the Development of Spanish Indian Policy in the Sixteenth Century,* Peter Smith, Gloucester, MA, 1964.

6. Douglas Edward Leach, *Flintlock and Tomahawk, New England in King Philip's War,* Norton, New York, 1958, pp. 20–22.

7. George Catlin, *Letters and Notes of the Manners, Customs and Conditions of the North American Indians* (London, 1841), Dover, New York, 1973, I, pp. 102–103.

8. Bruce E. Johansen, *Forgotten Founders: How the American Indian Helped Shape Democracy*, Gambit, New York, 1982. See also Jack Weatherford, *Indian Givers: How the Indians of the Americas Transformed the World*, Crown Publishers, New York, 1988.

9. Wilcomb E. Washburn, *The Indian in America*, Harper & Row, New York, 1975, p. 32.

10. Ibid., pp. 39–40.

11. See D'Arcy McNickle, *They Came Here First: The Epic of the American Indian*, J. B. Lippincott, Philadelphia, 1949, p. 128.

12. Anthony F. C. Wallace, *The Death and Rebirth of the Seneca*, Knopf, New York, 1970, p. 28; John Axtell, "The Scholastic Philosophy of the Wilderness," *William and Mary Quarterly* 29 (1972), 359.

13. Albert Britt, *Indian Chiefs*, Books for Libraries Press, Freeport, NY, 1969, p. 8.

14. Ibid., p. 26.

15. See Keith H. Basso, " 'To Give Up on Words': Silence in Western Apache Culture," *Southwestern Journal of Anthropology* 26 (1970), 213–230.

16. Alice Marriott and Carol K. Rachlin, *American Epic: The Story of the American Indian*, Mentor, New York, 1969, p. 114.

17. Edward H. Spicer, "American Indians," in *Harvard Encyclopedia of American Ethnic Groups*, eds. Stephen Thernstrom, Ann Orlov, and Oscar Handlin, The Belknap Press, Cambridge, MA, 1980, pp. 85–86.

18. Alvin M. Josephy, Jr., *The Indian Heritage of America*, Knopf, New York, 1968, p. 324.

19. Dale Van Every, *Disinherited: The Lost Birthright of the American Indian*, Discus Avon Books, New York, 1966, p. 163.

20. James Mooney, *Myths of the Cherokee*, 19th Annual Report, Bureau of American Ethnology, Washington, DC, 1900, p. 130.

21. James D. Richardson, *Messages and Papers of the President*, Washington, DC, 1897, III, p. 497.

22. From *Man's Rise to Civilization as Shown by the Indians of North America from Primeval Times to the Coming of the Industrial State* by Peter Farb, p. 310. Copyright © 1968 by Peter Farb. Reprinted by permission of the publishers of E. P. Dutton.

23. Ibid., p. 309.

24. Ibid.

25. Elizabeth S. Grobsmith and Beth R. Ritter, "The Ponca Tribe: The Process of Restoration of a Federally Terminated Tribe," *Human Organization* 51 (Spring 1992), 2.

26. See Theodore Stern, *The Klamath Tribe*, University of Washington Press, Seattle, 1966.

27. Alvin M. Josephy, Jr., *The Indian Heritage of America*, Knopf, New York, 1968, p. 354.

28. Randy Fitzgerald, "Comeback in Indian Country," *Reader's Digest*, October 1989, p. 33.

29. Ibid.

30. Daniel Cohen, "Tribal Enterprise," *The Atlantic Monthly*, October 1989, p. 32.

31. Kate Ballen, "Maine Indians as B-School Study," *Fortune*, April 22, 1991, p. 16.

32. For an excellent depiction of the harshness of reservation life, see Murray Wax, *Indian-Americans: Unity and Diversity*, Prentice-Hall, Englewood Cliffs, NJ, 1971, pp. 65–87.

33. "This Land Is Their Land," *Time*, January 14, 1991, p. 18.

34. Robert W. Blum, Brian Harmon, Linda Harris, Lois Bergelsen, and Michael D. Resnick, "American Indian–Alaska Native Youth Health," *JAMA, The Journal of the American Medical Association* 267 (March 25, 1992), 1637.

35. Indian Health Service, *Trends in Indian Health, 1990*. U.S. Department of Health and Human Services, Rockville, MD, 1990.

36. Spero M. Manson, Janette Beals, Rhonda Wiegman Dick, and Christine Duclos, "Risk Factors for Suicide Among Indian Adolescents at a Boarding School," *Public Health Reports* 104 (1989) 609–614.

37. Blum, et al., "American Indian–Alaska Native Youth Health," p. 1642.

38. Steven Paul Schinke et al., "Preventing Substance Abuse with American Indian Youth," *Social Casework* 66 (April 1985), 213–219.

39. Philip A. May, "Contemporary Crimes and the American Indian: A Survey and Analysis of the Literature," *Plains Anthropologist* 27 (Fall 1982), 225–238.

40. Carol Chiago Lujan, "Alcohol-Related Deaths of American Indians," *JAMA, The Journal of the American Medical Association* 267 (March 11, 1992), 1384.

41. Edwin Lemert, "Drinking Among American Indians," in *Alcoholism, Science and Society Revisited*, Edith Lisansky Gomberg, Helene Raskin White, and John A. Carpenter (eds.), University of Michigan Press, Ann Arbor, 1982, pp. 80–95.

42. Blum, et al., "American Indian–Alaska Native Youth Health, p. 1643.

43. Michael P. Nofz, "Alcohol Abuse and Culturally Marginal American Indians," *Social Casework: The Journal of Contemporary Social Work* (February 1988), 67–73.

44. Laurence A. French and Jim Hornbuckle, "Alcoholism among Native Americans: An Analysis," *Social Work* 25 (July 1980), 279.

45. 1969 Report of U.S. Senate Committee on Labor and Public Welfare, Special Subcommittee on In-

dian Education, quoted in Josephy, *Red Power*, pp. 156–157.

46. American Indian Policy Review Commission, "Report on Indian Education," Washington, DC, 1976, p. 253.

47. Ibid., p. 245.

48. Ibid., p. 123.

49. American Indian Policy Review Commission, "Report on Urban and Rural Non-Reservation Indians," Washington, DC, 1976, p. 25.

50. Indian Health Service, *Trends in Indian Health, 1990*; Gerard E. Gipp, "Promoting Cultural Relevance in American Indian Education," *Education Digest*, November 1991, p. 58.

51. Lee Little Soldier, "The Education of Native American Students," *Equity & Excellence* Summer 1990, p. 66.

52. Bobby Wright and William G. Tierney, "American Indians in Higher Education," *Change*, March–April 1991, p. 17.

53. Sar A. Levitan, William B. Johnston, and Robert Taggart, *Minorities in the United States: Problems, Progress and Prospects*, Public Affairs Press, Washington, DC, 1975, p. 84.

54. Thomas M. Becker, Charles Wiggins, Corinne Peek, Charles R. Key, and Jonathan M. Samet, "Mortality from Infectious Diseases among New Mexico's American Indians, Hispanic Whites, and Other Whites, 1958–1987," *The American Journal of Public Health* 80 (March 1990), 320–323.

55. Task Force on Indian Economic Development, *Report of the Task Force on Indian Economic Development*, U.S. Government Printing Office, Washington, DC, 1986, p. 17.

56. Dean Foust, "Uncle Sam Can't Keep Track of His Trillions," *Business Week*, September 2, 1991, p. 72.

57. Steve Huntley et al., "America's Indians: 'Beggars in Our Own Land'," *U.S. News & World Report*, May 23, 1983, p. 72.

58. "The Landless Landed," *The Economist*, June 8, 1991, p. 32.

59. Scott Kerr, "The New Indian Wars," *The Progressive*, April 1990, p. 22.

60. Ibid.

61. Paul Schneider and Dan Lamont, "Other People's Trash: A Last-Ditch Effort to Keep Corporate Garbage Off the Reservation," *Audubon* 93 (July–August 1991), 115.

62. Mary Hager, "Dances With Garbage," *Newsweek*, April 19, 1991, p. 36.

63. Schneider and Lamont, "Other People's Trash," pp. 108–119.

64. John E. Milich, "Contaminant Cove," *The Progressive*, January 1989, p. 23.

65. Aric Press, et al., "The Indian Water Wars," *Newsweek*, June 13, 1983, pp. 80–81.

66. Thomas R. McGuire, "Federal Indian Policy: A Framework for Evaluation," *Human Organization* 49 (1990), 214.

67. Press, "The Indian Water Wars, p. 80.

68. Marjorie Charlier, "Settling Water Rights Is a Drain on Treasury," *The Wall Street Journal*, June 5, 1992, p. B1.

69. Josephy, *Red Power*, p. 4.

70. Quoted in Morris Freedman and Carolyn Banks (eds.), *American Mix*, Lippincott, Philadelphia, 1972, pp. 46–47.

71. See Dee Brown, *Bury My Heart at Wounded Knee*, Holt, New York, 1970.

72. "Wounded Knee: The Media Coup d'Etat," *Nation*, 216 (June 25, 1973), 807.

73. "Sioux Chiefs Urged to Reject U.S. Offer," *The New York Times*, September 2, 1979, p. 22.

74. "Tribe Files Suit for $11 Billion Over Black Hills," *The New York Times*, July 19, 1980, p. 5.

75. "Appeals Court Rejects Suit by Indians Over Black Hills," *The New York Times*, June 3, 1981, p. 18.

76. Susan Dillingham, "Indian High Finance," *Insight* (January 12, 1987), 46.

77. "Dances with Lawyers," *The Economist*, August 10, 1991, p. A18.

78. Dean Kuipers, "Return of the Native," *Omni* 103 (September 1990), 22.

79. Alvin M. Josephy, Jr., "The American Indian and the Bureau of Indian Affairs," Special Report to the President, Feb. 11, 1969, Sec. V.

80. Daniel Cohen, "Tribal Enterprise," pp. 35–36.

81. American Indian Policy Review Commission, "Report on Trust Responsibilities and Federal–Indian Relations, Including Treaty Review," Washington, DC, 1976, pp. 3–6.

82. Randy Fitzgerald, "Comeback in Indian Country," p. 36.

83. Daniel Cohen, "Tribal Enterprise," p. 36.

84. Nancy Gibbs, "This Land Is Their Land," *Time*, January 14, 1991, p. 18.

85. Bureau of the Census, *Summary Population and Housing Characteristics: United States*, U.S. Government Printing Office, Washington, DC, March 1992, Table 9, p. 402.

86. "Census Reveals Changes as It Paints a Picture of Metropolitan America," *The New York Times*, August 1, 1992, p. L8.

87. Douglas Martin, "Indians Seek a New Life in New York City," *The New York Times*, March 22, 1987, p. 17.

88. C. Matthew Snipp and Gary D. Sandefur, "Earnings of American Indians and Alaskan Natives: The Effects of Residence and Migration," *Social Forces* 66 (June 1988), 994–1008.

89. John A. Price, "The Migration and Adaptation of American Indians to Los Angeles," *Human Organization* 27 (Summer 1968), 168–175.

90. Theodore D. Graves, "The Personal Adjustment of Navaho Indian Migrants to Denver, Colorado," *American Anthropologist* 72 (1970), 35–54.

91. Bruce A. Chadwick and Joseph H. Strauss, "The Assimilation of American Indians into Urban Society: The Seattle Case," *Human Organization* 34 (Winter 1975), 359–369. See also Joan Ablon, "Relocated American Indians in the San Francisco Bay Area: Social Interaction and Indian Identity," *Human Organization* 23 (Winter 1964), 296–304.

92. John A. Price, "North American Indian Families," in *Ethnic Families in America*, eds. Charles H. Mindel and Robert W. Haberstein, Elsevier, New York, 1976, p. 266.

93. See Howard M. Bahr, "An End to Visibility," in *Native Americans Today*, pp. 404–407. One significant exception is Edmund Wilson, *Apologies to the Iroquois*, Farrar, Straus and Cudahy, New York, 1960. This book includes Joseph Mitchell's study, "The Mohawks in High Steel."

94. Joseph, *The Indian Heritage of America*, p. 32.

95. Ibid.

96. Ibid., p. 34.

Chapter 8

1. U.S. Bureau of the Census, *1990 Census Profile: Race and Hispanic Origin*, U.S. Government Printing Office, Washington, DC, June 1991, p. 1.

2. Susumu Awonohara, "Spicier Melting Pot," *Far Eastern Economic Review* 150 (November 22, 1990), 30; Kathy Bodovitz and Brad Edmondson, "Asian America," *American Demographics* 13 (July 1991), S16–17.

3. Edwin P. Hoyt, *Asians in the West*, Nelson, New York, 1974, p. 123.

4. See, for example, Melford Weiss, "The Research Experience in a Chinese American Community," *Journal of Social Issues* 33 (1977), 120–132; Bernard Wong, "Social Stratification, Adaptive Strategies and the Chinese Community of New York," *Urban Life* 5 (1976), 33–52.

5. Ellie McGrath, "Confucian Work Ethic," *Time* (March 28, 1983), 52.

6. "China," *Encyclopedia Britannica*, 7th ed., 1842, Vol. 6.

7. Otis Gibson, *The Chinese in America*, Hitchcock and Walden, Cincinnati, 1877, pp. 51–52.

8. Ibid.

9. Alexander Saxton, *The Indispensable Enemy: Labor and the Anti-Chinese Movement in California*, University of California Press, Berkeley, 1971, p. 63.

10. Ibid.

11. Mike Hilton, "The Split Labor Market and Chinese Immigration, 1848–1882," presented to the 72d annual meeting of the American Sociological Association, 1977, p. 7.

12. Ibid., p. 5.

13. Hinton Helper, *The Land of Gold: Reality Versus Fiction*, Baltimore, 1855, pp. 94–96, quoted in Saxton, *The Indispensable Enemy*, p. 19.

14. "The Growth of the U.S. Through Emigration—The Chinese," *The New York Times*, Sept. 3, 1865.

15. *The New York Times*, June 7, 1868.

16. Senator James G. Blaine, *Congressional Record* (February 14, 1879), p. 1301.

17. U.S. Immigration and Naturalization Service, *Annual Report*, U.S. Government Printing Office, Washington, DC, 1926, pp. 170–181.

18. Ibid.

19. American Federation of Labor, Proceedings, 1893, p. 73.

20. D. Y. Yuan, "New York Chinatown," in *Minority Problems*, eds. Arnold M. Rose and Caroline B. Rose, Harper & Row, New York, 1965, pp. 277–284.

21. Albert W. Palmer, *Orientals in American Life*, Friendship Press, New York, 1934, pp. 1–2, 7.

22. Stanford M. Lyman, "Conflict and the Web of Group Affiliation in San Francisco's Chinatown, 1850–1910," *Pacific Historical Review* 43 (November 1974), 473–499. This work is based on Georg Simmel's two theoretical essays, "Conflict" and "The Web of Group Affiliation."

23. Ibid., 494–499.

24. S. W. Kung, *Chinese in American Life*, University of Washington Press, Seattle, 1962, p. 89.

25. Stanford M. Lyman, "Marriage and the Family Among Chinese Immigrants to America," *Phylon* 29 (Winter 1968), 324.

26. Ibid., pp. 322–323.

27. U.S. Immigration and Naturalization Service, *1990 Statistical Yearbook*, U.S. Government Printing Office, Washington, DC, Table 12, pp. 71–73.

28. Lyman, "Marriage and the Family Among Chinese Immigrants to America," p. 327.

29. Ibid., p. 330.

30. Ibid., p. 328.

31. *Congressional Record*, October 21, 1943, p. 8626.

32. "Our Big Cities Go Ethnic," *U.S. News & World Report*, March 21, 1983, p. 50.

33. U.S. Bureau of the Census, *1980 Census of the Population: National Origin and Language*, Vol. 2, U.S. Government Printing Office, Washington, DC, 1984, Table 99.

34. U.S. Public Health Service, Centers for Disease Control, *Public Health Reports*, November–December 1989, p. 652.

35. U.S. Bureau of the Census, *1990 Census*, Summary Tape 3A.

36. Lucy Jen Huang, "The Chinese American Family," in *Ethnic Families in America*, eds. Charles H.

Mindel and Robert W. Habenstein, Elsevier, New York, 1976, p. 144.

37. Stanford M. Lyman, "Generation & Character: The Case of the Japanese-Americans," in *East Across the Pacific: Historical and Sociological Studies of Japanese Immigration and Assimilation*, eds. Hilary Conroy and T. Scott Miyakawa. Reprinted by permission of American Bibliographical Center–Clio Press, Inc., Santa Barbara, CA, © 1972, p. 279. Also in S. Lyman, *The Asian in North America*, Clio Press, Santa Barbara, CA, 1977, pp. 151–176.

38. Morton Grodzins, *Americans Betrayed*, University of Chicago Press, Chicago, 1949.

39. Lyman, "Generation & Character: The Case of the Japanese-Americans," pp. 279–280. Reprinted by permission of ABC–Clio, Inc., Santa Barbara, CA, © 1972.

40. Eugene V. Rostow, "Our Worst Wartime Mistake," *Harper's Magazine*, 191 (September 1945), 193–201.

41. See Michi Weglyn, *Years of Infamy: The Untold Story of America's Concentration Camps*, Morrow, New York, 1976.

42. Esther B. Rhoads, "My Experience with the Wartime Relocation of Japanese," in *East Across the Pacific: Historical and Sociological Studies of Japanese Immigration and Assimilation*, eds. Hilary Conroy and T. Scott Miyakawa, pp. 131–132. Reprinted by permission of ABC–Clio, Inc., Santa Barbara, CA, © 1972.

43. Ted Nakashima, "Concentration Camp, U.S. Style," *The New Republic*, June 15, 1942, 822–823.

44. Justice Robert H. Jackson, dissenting opinion, *Korematsu v. United States of America*, Vol. 65, Supreme Court Reporter, 1944, pp. 206–208.

45. Bill Hosokawa, *Nisei: The Quiet Americans*, William Morrow, New York, 1969, pp. 439–446.

46. John Leo, "An Apology to Japanese Americans," *Time*, May 2, 1988, p. 70.

47. Harry H. L. Kitano, *Japanese Americans: The Evolution of a Subculture*, 2d ed., Prentice-Hall, Englewood Cliffs, NJ, 1976, p. 132.

48. See Kitano, *Japanese Americans*, pp. 23–24, 107–108.

49. "The Glass Ceiling," *The Economist* 311 (June 3, 1989), 24.

50. Harry H. L. Kitano, *Japanese Americans*, p. 127. See also John Connor, *Tradition and Change in Three Generations of Japanese Americans*, Nelson-Hall, Chicago, 1977.

51. U.S. Bureau of the Census, Ethnic and Hispanic Branch, 1990 Census Special Tabulations.

52. See Susumu Awanohara, "Scapegoats No More," *Far Eastern Economic Review*, November 22, 1990, p. 16.

53. Harry H. L. Kitano and Roger Daniels, *Asian Americans: Emerging Minorities*, Prentice-Hall, Englewood Cliffs, NJ, 1988. See also Darrel Montero,

Japanese Americans: Changing Patterns of Ethnic Affiliation, Westview, Boulder, CO, 1980.

54. U.S Immigration and Naturalization Service, *1990 Statistical Yearbook*, Table 2, p. 50.

55. Jeremy Schlosberg, "Turning Japanese," *American Demographics*, May 1990, p. 48.

56. *Morrison et al. v. California* (1934), No. 487, Vol. 291, United States Supreme Court Reports, U.S. Government Printing Office, Washington, DC, 1934, pp. 85–86.

57. Davis McEntire, *The Labor Force in California: A Study of Characteristics and Trends in Labor Force, Employment and Occupations in California, 1900–1950*, University of California Press, Berkeley, 1952, p. 62.

58. Carey McWilliams, *Brothers Under the Skin*, Little, Brown, Boston, 1951, p. 239.

59. Sylvain Lazarus, San Francisco Municipal Court, January 1936, quoted in Manuel Braken, *I Have Lived with the American People*, Caxton, Caldwell, CA, 1948, pp. 136–138.

60. Letter from Sylvester Saturday, in *Time* 27 (May 11, 1936), 4.

61. Letter from Ernest D. Ilustre, in *Time* 27 (April 27, 1936), 3.

62. McWilliams, *Brothers Under the Skin*, p. 244.

63. Bernicio T. Catapusan, "Filipino Intermarriage Problems in the United States," *Sociology and Social Research* 22 (1938), 265–272.

64. For an excellent sociological study of Filipinos in dance halls, see Paul G. Cressey, *The Taxi-Dance Hall*, University of Chicago Press, Chicago, 1932, pp. 145–176.

65. R. T. Feria, "War and the Status of the Filipino Immigrants," *Sociology and Social Research* 31 (1946), 50.

66. Victor Nee and Jimy Sanders, "The Road to Parity: Determinants of the Socioeconomic Achievements of Asian Americans, *Ethnic and Racial Studies* 8 (January 1985), 75–93.

67. "The Glass Ceiling," pp. 24–26.

68. H. Brett Melendy, "Filipinos," in *Harvard Encyclopedia of American Ethnic Groups*, eds. Stephen Thernstrom, Ann Orlov, Oscar Handlin, Harvard University Press, Cambridge, MA, 1980, 354–362.

69. Harold H. Sunoo and Sonia S. Sunoo, "The Heritage of the First Korean Women Immigrants in the United States: 1903–1924," *Korean Christian Journal* 2 (Spring 1977), 144.

70. Ibid., p. 146.

71. Ibid., pp. 144, 165.

72. Bernice H. Kim, "The Koreans in Hawaii," *Social Science* 9 (1934), 409.

73. Lee Houchins and Chang-su Houchins, "The Korean Experience in America, 1903–1924," *Pacific Historical Review* 43 (November 1974), 560.

74. Eui Hang Shin and Hyung Park, "An Analysis of Causes of Schisms in Ethnic Churches: The Case of Korean-American Churches," *Sociological Analysis* 49 (1988), 234–235.

75. Ill Soo Kim, *New Urban Immigrants: The Korean Community in New York*, Princeton University Press, Princeton, NJ, 1981, p. 198.

76. Marian Dearman, "Structure and Function of Religion in the Los Angeles Korean Community: Some Aspects," in *Koreans in Los Angeles: Prospects and Promises*, eds. E. Y. Yu, E. H. Phillips, and E. S. Yang, Koryo Research Institute, Los Angeles, 1982, p. 175.

77. Ill Soo Kim, "Organizational Patterns of Korean-American Methodist Churches: Denominationalism and Personal Community," in *Rethinking Methodist History*, R. E. Richey and K. E. Rowe (eds.), Kingswood Books, Nashville, 1985, p. 234.

78. Hei Chu Kim, Won Moo Hurh, and Kwang Chung Kim, "Ethnic Roles of the Korean Church in the Chicago Area," paper presented at the annual meeting of the Korean Christian Scholars Association, 1979.

79. Shin and Park, "An Analysis of Causes of Schisms in Ethnic Churches: The Case of Korean-American Churches," pp. 234–248.

80. Susumu Awonahara, "All in the Family," *Far Eastern Economic Review* 151 (March 14, 1991), 36.

81. Pauline Yoshihashi and Sarah Lubman, "American Dreams," *The Wall Street Journal*, June 16, 1992, p. A1.

82. Awonahara, "All in the Family," pp. 36–37.

83. Eva Pomice, "The Ties That Bind—and Enrich," *U.S. News & World Report* (April 25, 1988), 42–46.

84. Kwang C. Kim, "Intra- and Inter-Ethnic Group Conflicts: The Case of Korean Small Business in the United States," presented to the 11th annual meeting of the Korean Christian Scholars, 1977, p. 23.

85. See Edna Bonacich, "A Theory of Middleman Minorities," *American Sociological Review* 38 (1973), 583–594.

86. *A Study of Selected Socioeconomic Characteristics of Ethnic Minorities Based on the 1990 Census. Vol. 2: Asian Americans*, Washington, DC, U.S. Government Printing Office, 1993, pp. 105, 134, 142.

87. Emory S. Bogardus, "Comparing Racial Distance in Ethiopia, South Africa, and the United States," *Sociology and Social Research* 52 (1968), 149–156.

88. Won Moo Hurh, "Comparative Study of Korean Immigrants in the United States: A Typology," *Korean Christian Journal* 2 (Spring 1977), 68.

89. "Future of Refugees: The Furor and the Facts," *U.S. News and World Report*, May 19, 1975, 16.

90. Paul D. Starr and Alden E. Roberts, "Community Structure and Vietnamese Refugee Adaptation: The Significance of Context," *International Migration Review* 16 (1982), 595–608.

91. The author acknowledges a substantial debt and gratitude to Walter H. Slote, Ph.D., and Stephen Young, J. D., for sharing their expertise about the Vietnamese and Vietnamericans.

92. Walter H. Slote, "Adaption of Recent Vietnamese Immigres to the American Experience: A Psycho-Cultural Approach," paper presented at the 29th annual meeting of the Association for Asian Studies, March 1977, p. 9.

93. Ibid., p. 11.

94. Han T. Doan, "Vietnamericans: Bending Low or Breaking in the Acculturation Process?" presented to the 72d annual meeting of the American Sociological Association, 1977, pp. 14–15.

95. Ibid., p. 12.

96. Ibid.

97. Peter I. Rose, "Southeast Asia to America," *Catholic Mind* (March–April 1984), 11–25.

98. See Walter H. Slote, "Psychodynamic Structures in Vietnamese Personality," *Transcultural Research in Mental Health* 2 (1972).

99. Doan, "Vietnamericans: Bending Low or Breaking in the Acculturation Process?", pp. 9–11, 15.

100. Starr and Roberts "Community Structure and Vietnamese Refugee Adaptation," pp. 595–608.

101. Bayard Webster, "Studies Report Refugees Plagued by Persistent Stress," *The New York Times*, September 11, 1979, p. C1.

102. Kathleen Day and David Holley, "Vietnamese Create Their Own Saigon," *Los Angeles Times*, September 30, 1984, p. 1.

103. David DeVoss, "A Long Way From Home," *Los Angeles Times*, January 5, 1986, p. 1.

104. Jon K. Matsuoka, "Differential Acculturation Among Vietnamese Refugees," *Social Work* 35 (July 1990), 341–345.

105. Betty Rairdan and Zana Roe Higgs, "When Your Patient Is a Hmong Refugee," *American Journal of Nursing* 92 (March 1992), 52–55.

106. U.S. Bureau of the Census, Pres Release CB91–215, June 12, 1991, Table 5A, p. 10.

107. See, for example, Tou-Fou Vang, "The Hmong of Laos," in *Bridging Cultures: Southeast Asian Refugees in America*, Asian American Community Mental Health Training Center, Los Angeles, 1981.

108. Kathleen McInnis, "Ethnic-Sensitive Work with Hmong Refugee Children," *Child Welfare* 70 (September–October 1990), 577.

109. Ibid., p. 576.

110. U.S. Commission on Civil Rights, *Recent Activities Against Citizens and Residents of Asian Descent*, U.S.

Government Printing Office, Washington, DC, 1986.

111. Joe Feagin, *Racial and Ethnic Relations*, 3d ed., Prentice-Hall, Englewood Cliffs, NJ, 1989, pp. 14–15.

112. Harry H. L. Kitano and Roger Daniels, *Asian Americans: Emerging Minorities*, Prentice-Hall, Englewood Cliffs, NJ, 1988, pp. 188–190.

113. Pauline Yoshihashi and Sarah Lubman, "American Dreams," p. A6.

114. John D. Kasarda, "Why Asians Can Prosper Where Blacks Fail," *Wall Street Journal*, May 28, 1992, p. A18.

115. Louis Winnick, "America's 'Model Minority'," *Commentary* 90 (August 1990), 23.

116. See Howard G. Chua-Eoan, "Strangers in Paradise," *Time*, April 9, 1990, pp. 32–35.

117. See Daniel Goleman, "Probing School Success of Asian Americans," *The New York Times*, September 11, 1990, p. C1.

Chapter 9

1. U.S. Immigration and Naturalization Service, *1990 Statistical Yearbook*, U.S. Government Printing Office, Washington, DC, December 1991, Table 2, p. 50.

2. U.S. Bureau of the Census, Ethnic and Hispanic Branch, 1990 Census Special Tabulations, 1990 CPH–1–90, p. 1.

3. U.S. Immigration and Naturalization Service, *1990 Statistical Yearbook*, Table 40, p. 124.

4. Emory S. Bogardus, "Comparing Racial Distance in Ethiopia, South Africa, and the United States," *Sociology and Social Research* 52 (1968), 149–156; Won Moo Hurh, "Comparative Study of Korean Immigrants in the United States," *Korean Christian Journal* 2 (Spring 1977), 60–99.

5. Gurdial Singh, "East Indians in the United States," *Sociology and Social Research* 30 (1946), 210–211.

6. Joan M. Jensen, "Apartheid: Pacific Coast Style," *Pacific Historical Review* 38 (1969), 335–340.

7. Gary R. Hess, "The Forgotten Asian Americans: The East Indian Community in the United States," *Pacific Historical Review* 43 (1974), 580.

8. Singh, "East Indians in the United States," pp. 210–211.

9. "Hindu Invasion," *Collier's* 45 (March 26, 1910), 15.

10. Hess, "The Forgotten Asian Americans: The East Indian Community in the United States," pp. 583–584.

11. Juan L. Gonzales, Jr., "Asian Indian Immigration Patterns: The Origins of the Sikh Community in California," *International Migration Review* 20 (Spring 1986), 46.

12. Hess, "The Forgotten Asian Americans: The First East Indian Community in the United States," 590.

13. *Ibid.*, p. 593.

14. *Ibid.*, pp. 593–594.

15. U.S. Immigration and Naturalization Service, *1990 Statistical Yearbook*, Table 2, p. 50.

16. U.S. Bureau of the Census, Press Release CB91–215, June 12, 1991, Table 1, p. 3.

17. Susumu Awanohara, "Political Indian Summer," *Far Eastern Economic Review* 151 (May 23, 1991), 35.

18. William Claiborne, "Mother India's Children—Born to Lose," *Washington Post News Service*, February 6, 1983.

19. George Becker, "Asian Spice in the Melting Pot," *New York Sunday News Magazine*, November 28, 1976, pp. 7–21.

20. Susumu Awanohara, "Political Indian Summer," p. 35.

21. Louis Winnick, "America's 'Model Minority'," *Commentary* 90 (August 1990), 27–28.

22. Rosalind J. Dworkin, "Differential Processes in Acculturation: The Case of the Asiatic Indians," Educational Resources Information Center (ERIC) ED 178–430, 1980.

23. U.S. Bureau of the Census, Press Release CB91–215, June 12, 1991, Table 5B, p. 12.

24. Isabel Wilkerson, "Among Arabs in U.S., New Dreams," *The New York Times*, March 13, 1988, p. L 10.

25. John Zogby, *Arab America Today*, Arab American Institute, Washington, DC, 1990, pp. 1–3.

26. Edward T. Hall, *The Hidden Dimension*, Doubleday, Garden City, NY, 1966, pp. 144–153.

27. *Ibid.*, p. 149.

28. Ayad Al-Qazzaz, *Transactional Links Between the Arab Community in the U.S. and the Arab World*, California Central Press, Sacramento, 1979, p. 33.

29. *Ibid.*, p. 34.

30. John Zogby, *Arab America Today*, pp. 1–2.

31. Vincent N. Parrillo, "Arab American Immigrant Communities: Diversity and Parallel," paper presented at annual meeting of Eastern Sociological Society, Baltimore, MD, March 1983; Vincent N. Parrillo, "Arab American Residential Segregation: Differences in Patterns," paper presented at annual meeting of Eastern Sociological Society, Boston, March 1984.

32. See Carol Agocs, "Ethnic Settlement in a Metropolitan Area: A Typology of Communities," *Ethnicity* 8 (1981), 127–148; B. Aswad, *Arabic Speaking Communities in American Cities*, Center for Migration Studies, New York, 1974.

33. Philip M. Kayal and Joseph M. Kayal, *The Syrian–Lebanese in America*, Twayne, New York, 1975, pp. 50, 61.

34. Alixa Naff, *The Arab Americans*, Chelsea House, New York, 1988, pp. 59, 72.

35. Cyril Anid, *I Grew with Them*, Paulist Press, Jounieh, Lebanon, 1967, p. 18.

36. Morris Berger, "America's Syrian Community," *Commentary* 25, No. 4 (1958), 316.

37. Ibid., p. 111.

38. Kayal and Kayal, *The Syrian–Lebanese in America*, p. 108.

39. Ibid., pp. 197–200.

40. Milton M. Gordon, *Assimilation in American Life*, Oxford University Press, New York, 1964.

41. Isabel Wilkerson, "Among Arabs in U.S., New Dreams," *The New York Times*, March 13, 1988, p. 10.

42. Ibid.

43. Philip Harsham, "Arabs in America: The Transplanted Ones," *Aramco World Magazine* 26, No. 2 (1975), 6.

44. Maboud Ansari, *Iranian Immigrants in the United States: A Case Study of Dual Marginality*, Associated Faculty Press, New York, 1988, pp. 65–67.

45. Ibid., p. 73.

46. Ibid., pp. 46–62.

47. U.S. Immigration and Naturalization Service, *1990 Statistical Yearbook*, Table 2, p. 50.

48. Ibid., Table 16, p. 79.

49. U.S. Bureau of the Census, Press Release 1990 CPH–L–90, p. 1.

50. Ansari, *Iranian Immigrants in the United States*, p. 106.

51. Ebrahim Biparva, "Immigration: Bloodless Revolution," paper presented at annual meeting of Eastern Sociological Society, Arlington, VA, April 5, 1992.

52. Mary C. Sengstock, "Social Change in the Country of Origin as a Factor in Immigrant Conceptions of Nationality," *Ethnicity* 4 (March 1977), 54–69.

53. Ibid., p. 61.

54. U.S. Bureau of the Census, 1990 Census Special Tabulations, 1990 CPH–L–90, p. 1, and 1990 CPH–L–89, p. 1.

55. U.S. Immigration and Naturalization Service, *1990 Statistical Report*, Table 3, p. 52.

56. Lewis V. Thomas and Richard N. Krye, *The United States and Turkey and Iran*, Harvard, Cambridge, MA, 1952, pp. 139–140.

57. Bogardus, "Comparing Racial Distance in Ethiopia, South Africa, and the United States," p. 152.

58. U.S. Bureau of the Census, 1990 Census Special Tabulations, 1990 CPH–L–90, p. 1.

59. U.S. Immigration and Naturalization Service, *1990 Statistical Report*, Table 3, p. 52.

60. Ibid., Table 20, p. 87.

61. Ibid., Table 18, p. 84.

Chapter 10

1. Ira De Augustine Reid, *The Negro Immigrant, 1939*, reprint ed., Arno Press and *The New York Times*, New York, 1969, p. 32.

2. See James O. Buswell, III, *Slavery, Segregation and Scripture*, Eerdmans, Grand Rapids, MI, 1964; George D. Kelsey, *Racism and the Christian Understanding of Man*, Scribner's, New York, 1965; W. E. B. DuBois, *The World and Africa*, International Publishers, New York, 1965; Keith Irvine, *The Rise of the Colored Races*, Norton, New York, 1970.

3. Irvine, *The Rise of the Colored Races*, p. 13.

4. DuBois, *The World and Africa*, pp. 19–20.

5. See the discussion on pp. 68–70.

6. See the discussion on pp. 99–101.

7. See the discussion on pp. 30–36.

8. Pitirim A. Sorokin, *Contemporary Sociological Theories*, Harper, New York, 1928, pp. 291–301.

9. The following three sections are partly drawn from Brewton Berry and Henry L. Tischler, *Race and Ethnic Relations*, 4th ed., Houghton Mifflin, Boston, 1979, pp. 48–52.

10. See Kenneth Pearson, "On Our Present Knowledge of the Relationship of Mind and Body," *Annals of Eugenics* 1 (1925–1926), 382–406; Otto Klineberg, *Race Differences*, Harper & Row, New York, 1935, pp. 84, 86.

11. Stanford M. Lyman, *Chinese Americans*, Prentice-Hall, Englewood Cliffs, NJ, 1974.

12. Berry and Tischler, *Race and Ethnic Relations*, p. 51.

13. Basil Davidson, *African Kingdoms*, Time-Life, New York, 1966, pp. 21–22.

14. See the discussion on pp. 36–38.

15. See Thomas Sowell, "New Light on Black I.Q." *The New York Times Magazine*, March 27, 1977, p. 57.

16. Audrey Shuey, *The Testing of Negro Intelligence*, J. P. Bell, Lynchburg, VA, 1958, p. 318.

17. Arthur R. Jensen, "How Much Can We Boost I.Q. and Scholastic Achievement?" *Harvard Educational Review* 39 (1969), 1–123. In December 1979, Jensen reexamined this issue, claiming that assumptions about biased tests are inaccurate, since mean differences remain despite attempts to raise black test scores; see Arthur R. Jensen, *Bias in Mental Testing*, Free Press, New York, 1980.

18. Sowell, "New Light on Black I.Q.," p. 57 ff.

19. Ossie Davis, "The English Language Is My Enemy," *IRCD Bulletin* 5 (Summer 1969), 13.

20. See C. Vann Woodward, *The Strange Career of Jim Crow*, 2d ed., Oxford University Press, New York, 1966.

21. Gunnar Myrdal, *An American Dilemma*, McGraw-Hill, New York, 1964.

22. Ibid., pp. 25–38.

23. Dewey H. Palmer, "Moving North: Migration of Negroes During World War I," *Phylon,* 27 (Spring 1967), 52–62.

24. *The New York Times,* March 9, 1925, p. 16.

25. W. E. B. DuBois, *Dusk of Dawn,* Harcourt, Brace, New York, 1940, p. 264.

26. The Supreme Court specifically cited Kenneth B. Clark's study on negative self-image among black school children. For detailed information on the social scientists' role in the decision, see Kenneth B. Clark, *Prejudice and Your Child,* 2d ed., Beacon Press, Boston, 1963.

27. Jerome H. Skolnick, *The Politics of Protest: Violent Aspects of Protest and Confrontation,* National Commission on the Causes and Prevention of Violence, Washington, DC, 1969, pp. 101–102.

28. U.S. Bureau of the Census, *Statistical Abstract of the United States, 1992,* U.S. Government Printing Office, Washington, DC, 1992, Table 432, p. 267.

29. See Alphonso Pinkney, *Black Americans,* Prentice-Hall, Englewood Cliffs, NJ, 1969.

30. Lewis M. Killian, *The Impossible Revolution, Phase II,* Random House, New York, 1975, p. 70.

31. Charles Silberman, *Crises in Black and White,* Random House, New York, 1964, p. 8.

32. See Robin M. Williams, Jr., "Social Change and Social Conflict: Race Relations in the United States, 1944–1964," *Sociological Inquiry* 35 (Winter 1965), 20–24. Also, Stanley Lieberson and Arnold R. Silverman, "The Precipitants and Underlying Conditions of Race Riots," *American Sociological Review* 30 (1965), 887–898.

33. From the Report of the National Advisory Commission on Civil Disorders, U.S. Government Printing Office, Washington, DC, 1968.

34. "Major U.S. Racial Disturbances Since 1965," *Facts on File* 52 (May 7, 1992), 328.

35. *Ibid.*

36. See Brian Duffy, "Days of Rage," *U.S. News & World Report,* May 11, 1992, pp. 21–26.

37. Pauline Yoshihashi and Sarah Lubman, "American Dreams," *Wall Street Journal,* June 19, 1992, p. 1.

38. Robert L. Boyd, "Black and Asian Self-Employment in Large Metropolitan Areas: A Comparative Analysis," *Social Problems* 37 (May 1990), 268.

39. *Ibid.,* p. 269.

40. See Brian Duffy, "Days of Rage."

41. Findings reported by Lyle Jones at annual meetings of American Psychological Association, Anaheim, California, August 1983.

42. See Felicity Barringer, "White–Black Disparity in Income Narrowed in 80's, Census Shows," *The New York Times,* July 24, 1991, pp. 1, 16.

43. Diane Pierce, *The Feminization of Poverty: Women, Work, and Welfare,* University of Chicago Press, Chicago, 1978.

44. U.S. Bureau of the Census, *Statistical Abstract of the United States, 1992,* Table 719, p. 457.

45. David Whitman and Jeannye Thornton, "A Nation Apart," *U.S. News & World Report,* March 17, 1986, p 18,

46. U.S. Bureau of the Census, *Statistical Abstract of the United States: 1992,* Table 1224, p. 716.

47. Paul Glastris, "A Housing Program That Really Works," *U.S. News & World Report,* February 27, 1989, pp. 26–27.

48. John Schwartz, "The Return of 'Redlining'!" *Newsweek,* May 16, 1988, p. 44.

49. William P. O'Hare and Margaret L. Usdansky, "What the 1990 Census Tells Us About Segregation in 25 Large Metros," *Population Today,* Population Reference Bureau, 20 (September 1992), 6.

50. William J. Wilson, *The Declining Significance of Race,* University of Chicago Press, Chicago, 1978.

51. Thomas Sowell, *Ethnic America,* Basic Books, New York, 1981.

52. Carl Gershman, "A Matter of Class," *The New York Times Magazine,* October 5, 1980, pp. 24 ff.

53. Charles V. Willie, *Caste and Class Controversy,* General Hall, New York, 1979.

54. Kenneth B. Clark, "The Role of Race," *The New York Times Magazine,* October 5, 1980, pp. 25 ff.

55. William J. Wilson, *The Truly Disadvantaged: The Inner City, the Underclass, and Public Policy,* University of Chicago Press, Chicago, 1987.

56. *Ibid.,* p. 58.

57. Gary Orfield, "Ghettoization and Its Alternatives," in ed. Paul E. Peterson, *The New Urban Reality,* The Brookings Institution, Washington, DC, 1988, p. 103.

58. For a comparative analysis of native-born and foreign-born blacks, see Ira De Augustine Reid, *The Negro Immigrant,* 1939, reprint ed., Arno Press and The New York Times, New York, 1969.

59. Muruku Waiguchu, "Relations Between African and Afro-American Students in the United States," paper presented at the 7th annual meeting of the African Heritage Studies Association, 1978.

60. *Ibid.,* pp. 5, 16.

61. Lyn H. Lofland, *A World of Strangers,* Basic Books, New York, 1973.

62. Robert Blauner, "Internal Colonialism and Ghetto Revolt," *Social Problems* 16 (1969), 393–408.

Chapter 11

1. U.S. Bureau of the Census, *Statistical Abstract of the United States, 1991,* U.S. Government Printing Office, Washington, DC, 1992, Table 1359, p. 820.

2. U.S. Immigration and Naturalization Service, *1990 Statistical Yearbook,* U.S. Government Printing Office, Washington, DC, 1991, Table 58, p. 167.

3. Ronald Hilton, *The Latin Americans: Their Heritage and their Destiny,* Lippincott, New York, 1973, pp. 40–41.
4. Celia S. Heller, *Mexican-American Youth: Forgotten Youth at the Crossroads,* Random House, New York, 1966; William Madsen, *The Mexican-Americans of South Texas,* Holt, New York, 1964, pp. 15–17.
5. Joseph P. Fitzpatrick, *Puerto Rican Americans,* 2d ed., Prentice-Hall, Englewood Cliffs, NJ, 1987, p. 100.
6. U.S. Bureau of the Census, Special Release, 1990 CPH–L–93, pp. 1–14.
7. Clara Rodriguez, *The Ethnic Queue in the U.S.: The Case of the Puerto Ricans,* R & E Research Associates, San Francisco, 1974, p. 92.
8. Fitzpatrick, *Puerto Rican Americans,* pp. 105–106.
9. For some excellent cross-cultural analyses of attitudes regarding distance between people, see Edward Hall, *The Hidden Dimension,* Doubleday, Garden City, NY, 1966; E. Hall, *Silent Language,* Doubleday, Garden City, NY, 1959.
10. U.S. Bureau of Census, *Current Population Reports,* Series P-25, No. 995, 1991.
11. U.S. Bureau of the Census, Special Release CB91-215, June 12, 1991, p. 3.
12. "Portrait of a Nation in Numbers: Findings of the 1990 U.S. Census," *Facts on File,* June 25, 1992, p. 469.
13. U.S. Bureau of the Census, "1990 Census Profile: Race and Hispanic Origin," No. 2, June 1991, p. 5.
14. See, for example, "English as the Official Language," American Jewish Committee, June 29, 1987, pp. 3–4.
15. Joan W. Moore, *Mexican Americans,* Prentice-Hall, Englewood Cliffs, NJ, 1970, p. 100.
16. Ed Ludwig and James Santibanex (eds.), *The Chicanos,* Penguin, Baltimore, 1971, pp. 2–3.
17. Moore, *Mexican Americans,* p. 43.
18. Ibid.
19. Carey McWilliams, *North from Mexico,* Greenwood Press, New York, 1968, pp. 247–250.
20. Christopher Jaeger, *Minority and Low Income High Schools: Evidence of Educational Inequality in Metro Los Angeles,* Metropolitan Opportunity Project, Chicago, 1987.
21. Florence Kluckhohn and Fred L. Strodtbeck, *Variations in Value Orientations,* Row, Peterson, Evanston, IL, 1961.
22. See Moore, *Mexican Americans,* pp. 129–130.
23. Leo Grebler, Joan Moore, and Ralph Guzman, *The Mexican American People,* Free Press, New York, 1970, pp. 423–439.
24. See the discussion on pp. 45–50.
25. See, for example, Moore, *Mexican Americans,* pp. 44–45.
26. U.S. Immigration and Naturalization Service, *1990 Statistical Yearbook,* Table 12, p. 72.
27. Ibid., Table 16, p. 79.
28. U.S. Bureau of the Census, Ethnic and Hispanic Branch, 1990 Special Census Tabulations, 1990 CPH–L–91.
29. U.S. Bureau of the Census, "The Hispanic Population in the United States: March 1988," *Current Population Reports* Series P–60, No. 438, U.S. Government Printing Office, Washington, DC, 1989.
30. See Ernest L. Chavez, Ruth Edwards, and S. R. Oetting, "Mexican American and White American School Dropouts' Drug Use, Health Status, and Involvement in Violence," *Public Health Reports,* November–December 1989, pp. 594–604.
31. U.S. Immigration and Naturalization Service, *1990 Statistical Yearbook,* p. 163.
32. Rodriguez, *The Ethnic Queue in the U.S.: The Case of the Puerto Ricans,* pp. 83–85.
33. Ibid., p. 83.
34. Fitzpatrick, *Puerto Rican Americans,* pp. 106–107.
35. U.S. Bureau of the Census, *Statistical Abstract of the United States: 1991,* U.S. Government Printing Office, Washington, DC, 1991, Table 1421, p. 821.
36. Cary Davis, Carl Haub, and JoAnne Willette, "U.S. Hispanics: Changing the Face of America," *Population Bulletin,* Vol. 38, No. 3, Population Reference Bureau, Washington, DC, 1983, pp. 23–24.
37. U.S. Bureau of the Census, 1990 Census Special Tabulations, CPH–L–91.
38. Extrapolated from U.S. Bureau of the Census, *Statistical Abstract of the United States: 1991,* Table 1421, p. 821, and Census Special Tabulations, 1990, CPH–L–91, p. 1.
39. Rita M. Maldonado, "Why Puerto Ricans Migrated to the United States in 1947–73," *Monthly Labor Review,* U.S. Department of Labor, Bureau of Labor Statistics, September 1976, p. 14.
40. Fitzpatrick, *Puerto Rican Americans,* p. 70.
41. The example is from Fitzpatrick, p. 70.
42. Ibid., p. 74.
43. See Oscar Handlin, *The Uprooted,* Little, Brown, Boston, 1951, p. 135.
44. Nathan Glazer and Daniel P. Moynihan, *Beyond the Melting Pot,* 2d ed., MIT, Cambridge, MA, 1970, pp. 103–104.
45. For a more detailed discussion of the role of religion among Puerto Ricans, see Fitzpatrick, *Puerto Rican Americans,* pp. 115–129; also Rodriguez, *The Ethnic Queue in the U.S.: The Case of the Puerto Ricans,* pp. 95–99.
46. Fitzpatrick, *Puerto Rican Americans,* p. 130.
47. Ibid., p. 136.
48. Ibid.
49. U.S. Bureau of the Census, 1990 Census Special Tabulations, 1990 CPH–L–91.

50. Clara Rodriguez, "Assimilation in the Puerto Rican Communities of the U.S.: A New Focus," presented to the 72d annual meeting of the American Sociological Association, 1977, p. 8.

51. Teri Agins, "Latin Oases: To Hispanics in the U.S., A Bodega, or Grocery, Is a Vital Part of Life," *Wall Street Journal*, March 15, 1985, p. 1.

52. Carol J. Kaufman and Sigfredo A. Hernandez, "The Role of the Bodega in a U.S. Puerto Rican Community," *Journal of Retailing* 67 (Winter 1991), 378.

53. Fitzpatrick, *Puerto Rican Americans*, pp. 53–58.

54. U.S. Bureau of the Census, "The Hispanic Population in the United States: March 1988," p. 1.

55. See John D. Kasarda, "Jobs, Migration, and Emerging Urban Mismatches," pp. 148–198, in Michael G. H. McGeary and Laurence E. Lynn, Jr. (eds.), *Urban Change and Poverty*, National Academy Press, Washington, DC, 1988.

56. U.S. Bureau of the Census, *Statistical Abstract of the United States: 1991*, Tables 43 and 45, pp. 38, 40.

57. Nicholas Lehman, "The Other Underclass," *Atlantic Monthly*, December 1991, p. 102.

58. U.S. Bureau of the Census, *Statistical Abstract of the United States: 1991*, Table 45, p. 40.

59. U.S. Bureau of the Census, "The Hispanic Population in the United States," pp. 1–4.

60. Robert Aponte, "Urban Hispanic Poverty: Disaggregations and Explanations," *Social Problems* 38 (November 1991), 516–528.

61. Douglas Gurak and Luis Falcon, quoted in Nicholas Lehman, "The Other Underclass," p. 107.

62. Dennis M. Roth, "Hispanics in the U.S. Labor Force: A Brief Review," in Congressional Research Service, *The Hispanic Population of the United States: An Overview*, U.S. Government Printing Office, Washington, DC, 1983, Tables 5 and 6.

63. U.S. Bureau of the Census, 1990 Census Special Tabulations, 1990 CPH–L–91 and 1990 CPH–L–90.

64. Tom Alexander, "Those Amazing Cuban Emigres," *Fortune Magazine* 74 (October 1966), 144–146.

65. David Brock, "Exiles Flourish in Freedom of Miami's Melting Pot," *Insight*, February 29, 1988, pp. 13–19.

66. U.S. Bureau of the Census, 1990 Census Special Tabulations, 1990 CPH–L–91.

67. Richard Severo, "Spanish Influx Felt in Washington Heights," *The New York Times*, August 12, 1976, p. 33. © 1976 by The New York Times Company. Reprinted by permission.

68. Rolando A. Alum and Felipe P. Manteiga, "Cuban and American Values: A Synoptic Comparison," *Mosaic* 3 (1977), 11–12.

69. U.S. Immigration and Naturalization Service, *1990 Statistical Yearbook*, Table 2, pp. 49–50.

70. Ibid., p 91.

71. Patricia Ruggles, Donald Manson, John Trutko, and Kathleen M. Thomas, "Refugees and Displaced Persons of the Central American Region," Urban Institute, Washington, DC, 1985; Patricia Ruggles, Michael Fix, and Kathleen M. Thomas, "Profile of the Central American Population in the United States," Urban Institute, Washington, DC, 1985.

72. U.S. Bureau of the Census, 1990 Census Special Tabulations, 1990 CPH–L–91.

73. Nicholas Lehman, "The Other Underclass," p. 101.

74. See Nora Hamilton and Norma Stoltz Chinchilla, "Central American Migration: A Framework for Analysis," *Latin American Research Review* 26 (Winter 1991), 75–110.

75. U.S. Immigration and Naturalization Service, *1990 Statistical Yearbook*, Table 3, p. 53.

76. Ibid., Table G, p. 101.

77. Ibid., Table 30, p. 105.

78. Jeffrey Schmalz, "Nicaraguans Crowd the Miami Welcome Mat," *The New York Times*, November 20, 1988, p. 1.

79. U.S. Bureau of the Census, 1990 Census Special Tabulations, 1990 CPH–L–91.

80. Immigration and Naturalization Service, *1990 Statistical Yearbook*, Table 2, p. 50.

81. U.S. Bureau of the Census, 1990 Census Special Tabulations, 1990 CPH–L–89 and 1990 CPH–L–90.

82. U.S. Bureau of the Census, 1990 Census Special Tabulations, 1990 CPH–L–91.

83. U.S. Immigration and Naturalization Service, *1990 Statistical Yearbook*, Table 2, pp. 49–50.

84. C. R. Foster, "Creole in Conflict," *Migration Today* 8 (1990), 5–13.

85. E. Bourguignon, "Belief and Behavior in Haitian Folk Healing," in P. Pedersen, N. Sartorius, and A. Marsella (eds.), *Mental Health Services: The Cross-Cultural Context*, Sage, Beverly Hills, CA, 1984.

86. Alex Stepick and Carol Dutton Stepick, "People in the Shadows: Survey Research Among Haitians in Miami," *Human Organization* 49 (Spring 1990), 64–77.

87. U.S. Bureau of the Census, 1990 Census Special Tabulations, 1990 CPH–L–91.

88. U.S. Bureau of the Census, 1990 Census Special Tabulations, 1990 CPH–L–89.

89. M. G. Smith, *The Plural Society in the British West Indies*, University of California Press, Berkeley, CA, 1965, pp. 163–164.

90. Benjamin B. Ringer, *"We the People" and Others*, Tavistock, New York, 1983, p. 19.

91. Smith, *The Plural Society*.

92. Joan W. Moore, "American Minorities and 'New Nation' Perspectives," in F. James Davis (ed.), *Understanding Minority-Dominant Relations*, AMH Corporation, Arlington Heights, IL, 1979, pp. 40–53.

Chapter 12

1. "Many Seek Faith Along Other Paths," *U.S. News & World Report,* April 4, 1983, pp. 42–43; Constant Jacquet (ed.), *Yearbook of American and Canadian Churches 1983,* Abingdon Press, Nashville, TN, 1983, pp. 225–231.

2. Thomas J. Curran, *Xenophobia and Immigration, 1820–1930,* Twayne Publishers, Boston, 1975, pp. 12–13.

3. Samuel F. B. Morse, *Imminent Dangers to the Free Institutions of the United States through Foreign Immigration and the Present State of the Naturalization Laws: A Series of Numbers Originally Published in the New York Journal of Commerce Revised and Corrected with Additions,* New York, 1835.

4. Curran, *Xenophobia and Immigration, 1820–1930,* pp. 99–108.

5. Ibid., p. 107.

6. Ibid., p. 130.

7. Ibid., p. 131.

8. Ibid., pp. 32–35.

9. John Higham, *Strangers in the Land,* Atheneum, New York, 1973, p. 59.

10. Curran, *Xenophobia and Immigration, 1820–1930,* p. 78.

11. See Fran Schumer, "Star-Crossed," *New York,* August 2, 1990, p. 34.

12. Nathan Glazer, *American Judaism,* 2d ed., University of Chicago Press, Chicago, 1972, p. 14.

13. Curran, *Xenophobia and Immigration, 1820–1930,* p. 13.

14. Ibid., p. 76.

15. Ibid., pp. 76–77.

16. Milton L. Barron, "The Incidence of Jewish Intermarriage in Europe and America," *American Sociological Review* 1 (February 1946), 11.

17. See Joseph Brandes, *Immigrants to Freedom,* University of Pennsylvania Press, Philadelphia, 1971; Fred Rosenbaum, *Free to Choose: The Making of a Jewish Community in the American West,* The Judah I. Magnes Memorial Museum, Berkeley, CA, 1976.

18. See Jules Isaac, *The Teaching of Contempt: Christian Roots of Anti-Semitism,* Harcourt, Brace & World, New York, 1964; Malcolm Hay, *Europe and the Jews,* Beacon Press, Boston, 1960.

19. Reported in Joan C. Weiss, "Prejudice, Conflict, and Ethnoviolence: A National Dilemma," *USA Today,* May 1989, p. 28.

20. "Increase in Racial Tolerance Found," *Facts on File* 52 (January 16, 1992), 26.

21. Leonard Dinnerstein and David M. Reimers, *Ethnic Americans,* Harper & Row, New York, 1975, p. 44.

22. See Bernard C. Rosen, "Evaluation of Occupations: A Reflection of Jewish and Italian Mobility Differences," *American Sociological Review* 22 (1957), 546–553; Herbert J. Gans, "American Jewry: Present and Future," *Commentary,* May–June 1956, pp. 422, 430, 555, 563.

23. "Distribution of Immigrants," *Senate Documents,* 20 (61st Congress, 3rd Session), 47 ff.

24. Dinnerstein and Reimers, *Ethnic Americans,* p. 53: "By 1915 Jews comprised 85 percent of the student body at New York's free but renowned City College, one-fifth of those attending New York University and one-sixth of the students at Columbia."

25. Gordon, *Assimilation in American Life,* p. 185.

26. Gerhard Lenski, *The Religious Factor,* Doubleday, New York, 1961, pp. 33–34.

27. John P. Dean, "Patterns of Socialization and Association Between Jews and Non-Jews," *Jewish Social Studies* 17 (July 1955), 252–254.

28. Herbert J. Gans, "The Origin and Growth of a Jewish Community in the Suburbs: A Study of the Jews of Park Forest," in *The Jews: Social Patterns of an American Group,* ed. Marshall Sklare, Free Press, Glencoe, IL, 1958, p. 227.

29. Albert I. Gordon, *Jews in Suburbia,* Beacon Press, Boston, 1956.

30. See the discussion on p. 59.

31. Milton M. Gordon, *Assimilation in American Life,* pp. 173–224.

32. Two informative articles on Jewish assimilation are Seymour Martin Lipset, "A Unique People in an Exceptional Country," *Society* 28 (November–December 1990), 4–13; Shmuel A. Eisenstadt, "The Jewish Experience with Pluralism," *Society* 28 (1990), 21–25.

33. See Chaim I. Waxman, "Whither American Jewry?" *Society* 28 (1990), 34–41.

34. See Peter Steinfels, "Debating Intermarriage and Jewish Survival," *The New York Times,* October 18, 1992, p. 1, 40.

35. Edward Norden, "Counting the Jews," *Society* 28 (1990), 43.

36. Sylvia Barack Fishman, "The Changing American Jewish Family," *USA Today,* May 1991, p. 56.

37. See Chaim I. Waxman, "Whither American Jewry?" pp. 40–41.

38. See Hutchins Hapgood, *The Spirit of the Ghetto,* Belknap Press, Cambridge, MA, 1967.

39. Peter Steinfels, "Debating Intermarriage, and Jewish Survival," p. 40.

40. Kenneth L. Woodward, "The Intermarrying Kind," *Newsweek,* July 22, 1991, p. 49.

41. U.S. Immigration and Naturalization Service, *1990 Statistical Yearbook,* U.S. Government Printing Office, Washington, DC, Table 2, p. 48, and Table 27, p. 103.

42. Dean L. May, "Mormons," in Stephan Thernstrom (ed.), *Harvard Encyclopedia of American Ethnic Groups,* Harvard University Press, Cambridge, MA, 1980, pp. 720–721.

43. Joseph Smith, *Pearl of Great Price,* The Church of Jesus Christ of Latter-Day Saints, Salt Lake City, Utah, 1974, pp. 50–51.

44. See Marvin S. Hill, "The Rise of the Mormon Kingdom of God," in Richard Poll (ed.), *Utah's History*, Brigham Young University Press, Provo, UT, 1978.

45. Val Dan MacMurray and Perry H. Cunningham, "Mormons and Gentiles: A Study in Conflict and Persistence," in Donald E. Gefland and Russell D. Lee (eds.), *Ethnic Conflicts and Power: A Cross-National Perspective*, John Wiley, New York, 1973, pp. 205–218.

46. Bruce L. Campbell and Eugene E. Campbell, "The Mormon Family," in Charles H. Mindel and Robert W. Habenstein (eds.), *Ethnic Families in America*, 2d ed., Elsevier, New York, 1981, p. 389.

47. Stanley Ivins, "Notes on Mormon Polygamy," *Western Humanities Review*, 10 (1956), 233.

48. Lester E. Bush, "Mormon Elder's Wafers: Images of Mormon Virility in Patent Medicine Ads," *Dialogue: A Journal of Mormon Thought* 10 (1976), 89–93.

49. Campbell and Campbell, "The Mormon Family," p. 390.

50. John F. Galliher and Linda Basilick, "Utah's Liberal Drug Laws: Structural Foundations and Triggering Events," *Social Problems* 26 (1979), 284–297; Harold T. Christensen, "Some Next Steps in Mormon Family Research," in Phillip R. Kunz (ed.), *The Mormon Family*, Brigham Young University Press, Provo, UT, 1977, p. 413.

51. William J. Whalen, *The Latter-Day Saints in the Modern-Day World*, Day, New York, 1964, p. 17.

52. William M. Kephart, *Extraordinary Groups: An Examination of Unconventional Life-Styles*, 4th ed., St. Martin's Press, New York, 1991, p. 253.

53. U.S. Bureau of the Census, *Statistical Abstract of the United States*, 1992, Table No. 77, p. 59.

54. Jeffrey L. Shelor, "Latter-Day Struggles," *U.S. News & World Report*, September 28, 1992, pp. 73–78. See also Marilyn Warenski, *Patriarchs and Politics*, McGraw-Hill, New York, 1978, p. 82; Rodney Clapp, "Fighting Mormonism in Utah," *Christianity Today* July 16, 1982, p. 30; John Heinerman and Anson Shupe, *The Mormon Corporate Empire*, Beacon Press, Boston, 1985, pp. 109–116.

55. Kephart, *Extraordinary Groups*, p. 260.

56. May, "Mormons," p. 729.

57. Ibid., p. 731.

58. John A. Hostetler, *Amish Society*, 3d ed., Johns Hopkins Press, Baltimore, MD, 1980, pp. 62–65.

59. Ibid., p. 38.

60. Ibid., p. 40.

61. Ibid., p. 138.

62. Ibid., pp. 139–144.

63. Ibid.

64. Kephart, *Extraordinary Groups*, pp. 16–17.

65. Hostetler, *Amish Society*, pp. 276–277.

66. Gertrude Enders Huntington, "The Amish Family," in Mindel and Habenstein, *Ethnic Families in America*, p. 314.

67. Kephart, *Extraordinary Groups*, p. 38.

68. Ibid., p. 42.

69. Leon Daniel, "Amish Try to Hold Reins on Their Plain Way of Life," *United Press International*, August 12, 1983.

70. Kephart, *Extraordinary Groups*, pp. 37–38.

71. Donald Kraybill, *The Riddle of Amish Culture*, Johns Hopkins University Press, Baltimore, MD, 1989, p. 228.

72. Charles Wagley and Marvin Harris, *Minorities in the New World*, Columbia University Press, New York, 1958, p. 10.

73. M. G. Smith, R. Augier, and R. M. Nettleford, *The Rastafari Movement in Kingston, Jamaica*, Institute of Social and Economic Research, Kingston, Jamaica, 1960, p. 5.

74. George E. Simpson, "Political Cultism in West Kingston, Jamaica," *Social and Economic Studies* 4 (1955), 133–149.

75. Barry Chevannes, "Dread: The Rastafarians of Jamaica—A Review," *Caribbean Quarterly* 24 (1976), 61–69.

76. Neville G. Callam, "Invitation to Docility: Defusing the Rastafarian Challenge," *Caribbean Journal of Religion Studies* 3 (1980), 39.

77. Leonard Barrett, *The Rastafarians: Sounds of Cultural Dissonance*, Beacon Press, Boston, 1977, p. 138.

78. See Victor Turner, *The Ritual Process*, Cornell University Press, Ithaca, NY, 1969, p. 128.

79. Callam, "Invitation to Docility," p. 33.

80. *The Rastafarian Voice*, July 1975, quoted in Barrett, *The Rastafarians*, p. 144.

81. Kephart, *Extraordinary Groups*, p. 208.

82. See Marguerite Fellows Melcher, *The Shaker Adventure*, Western Reserve Press, Cleveland, 1968; Edward Andrews, *The People Called Shakers*, Oxford University Press, New York, 1953.

83. Rosabeth Moss Kanter, *Commitment and Community: Communes and Utopias in Sociological Perspective*, Harvard University Press, Cambridge, MA, 1973, p. 39.

84. Kephart, *Extraordinary Groups*, p. 205.

85. See Andrews, *The People Called Shakers*; Melcher, *The Shaker Adventure*; Henri Desroche, *The American Shakers: From Neo-Christianity to Presocialism*, University of Massachusetts Press, Amherst, MA, 1971.

86. Desroche, *American Shakers*, pp. 118–119.

87. Ibid., pp. 116–117.

88. Alixa Naff, *The Arab Americans*, Chelsea House, New York, 1988, p. 33.

89. Ibid., p. 45.

90. Ibid., p. 73.

91. John Zogby, *Arab America Today*, Arab American Institute, Washington, DC, 1990, p. 40.

92. Alixa Naff, *The Arab Americans*, p. 21.

93. See Andrew M. Greeley, *Religious Change in America*, Harvard University Press, Cambridge, MA, 1989.

94. U.S. Bureau of the Census, *Statistical Abstract of the United States: 1992,* Table 77, p. 58.

95. Harold J. Abramson, *Ethnic Diversity in Catholic America,* John Wiley, New York: 1973; Elmer Spreitzer and Eldon E. Snyder, "Patterns of Variation Within and Between Ethnoreligious Groupings," *Ethnicity* 2 (1975), 124–133.

96. Charles Y. Glock and Rodney Stark, "Is There an American Protestantism?" *Trans-action,* 3 (November–December 1965), 8–13, 48–49.

97. Robert Bellah, "Civil Religion in America," *Daedalus* 96 (1967), 1–21.

98. Lenski, *The Religious Factor;* Dean, "Patterns of Socialization and Association Between Jews and Non-Jews."

Chapter 13

1. Marvin Harris, "Why Men Dominate Women," *The New York Times Magazine,* November 13, 1977, p. 46.

2. See Vern L. Bullough, *The Subordinate Sex: A History of Attitudes Toward Women,* Penguin Books, New York, 1974.

3. Gustav LeBon, *Révue d'Anthropologie* (1879), pp. 60–61, quoted in Stephan Jay Gould, *The Mismeasure of Man,* W. W. Norton, New York, 1981, pp. 104–105.

4. Gunnar Myrdal, *An American Dilemma: The Negro Problem and Modern Democracy,* Harper, New York, 1944, pp. 1073–1078.

5. Helen M. Hacker, "Women as a Minority Group," *Social Forces* 30 (1951), 60–69.

6. Charles Wagley and Marvin Harris, *Minorities in the New World,* Columbia University Press, New York, 1958, p. 10.

7. Mary P. Ryan, *Womanhood in America: From Colonial Times to the Present,* 2d ed., New Viewpoints, Franklin Watts, New York, 1979.

8. See Edith Abbott, *Women in Industry: A Study in American Economic History,* 1919, quoted in Ryan, *Womanhood in America,* p. 54.

9. Ibid., p. 56.

10. Joyce Cowley, *Pioneers of Women's Liberation,* Merit, New York, 1969, p. 13.

11. William H. Chafe, *The American Woman: Her Changing Social, Economic, and Political Role,* Oxford University Press, New York, 1972.

12. Jo Freeman, *The Politics of Women's Liberation,* David McKay, New York, 1975, pp. 19–25.

13. "Sex Differences," *Society* 21 (September–October 1984), 4.

14. Anne Moir, *Brain Sex: The Real Difference Between Men & Women,* Carol Publishing Group, New York, 1991.

15. Margaret Mead, *Sex and Temperament,* William Morrow, New York, 1935, 1950, 1963.

16. Donna Eder and M. T. Hallinan, "The Meek Shall Not Inherit the Earth: Self-Evaluation and the Legitimacy of Stratification," *American Sociological Review* 45 (1978), 247.

17. Richard Della Fave, "Sex Differences in Children's Friendships," *American Sociological Review* 43 (1980), 955–970.

18. Featured in "The Pinks and the Blues," *Nova,* Public Broadcasting System, 1982.

19. See Gaye Tuchman, Arlene K. Daniels, and James Benet (eds.), *Hearth and Home: Images of Women in the Mass Media,* Oxford University Press, New York, 1978; see also discussion in Chapter 3.

20. Lucy Komisar, "The Image of Women in Advertising," in *Woman in Sexist Society: Studies in Power and Powerlessness,* (eds.) Vivian Gornick and Barbara K. Moran, Basic Books, New York, 1971, pp. 204, 211–212.

21. See Tuchman, Daniels, and Benet, *Hearth and Home: Images of Women in the Mass Media;* Matilda Butler and William Paisley, *Women and the Mass Media,* Human Sciences Press, New York, 1980, pp. 103–114.

22. Erving Goffman, *Gender Advertisements,* Harper/Colophon, New York, 1979, p. viii.

23. Sara Kiesler, Lee Sprovel, and Jacquelynne S. Eicles, "Second-Class Citizens?" *Psychology Today* 17 (March 1983), 40–48.

24. Lillian B. Rubin, *Worlds of Pain: Life in the Working-Class Family,* Basic Books, New York, 1976.

25. Irene Dabrowski, "Working-Class Women and Civic Action: A Case Study of an Innovative Community Role," *Policy Studies Journal* 2 (1983), 427–435.

26. Ibid.

27. Lucy Jen Huang, "The Chinese American Family," in Charles H. Mindel and Robert W. Habenstein (eds.), *Ethnic Families in America,* 2d ed., Elsevier, New York, 1981, p. 124.

28. Akemi Kikumura and Harry H. L. Kitano, "The Japanese American Family," in Mindel and Habenstein (eds.), *Ethnic Families in America,* pp. 54–56.

29. Robert Staples, *The World of Black Singles: Changing Patterns of Male/Female Relations,* Greenwood Press, Westport, CT, 1981.

30. Bell Hooks, *Ain't I a Woman: Black Women and Feminism,* South End Press, Boston, 1981, p. 195.

31. Janus Adams, "The Power Hook-up," *Essence,* 8 (1978), 80–81, 114–129.

32. Ibid., p. 125.

33. U.S. Commission on Civil Rights, *A Guide to Federal Laws and Regulations Prohibiting Sex Discrimination,* U.S. Government Printing Office, Washington, DC, 1976, p. 1.

34. C. P. Gilman, *Women and Education* (1911), in N. Reeves, *Womankind: Beyond the Stereotypes,* Aldine-Atherton, Chicago, 1971, p. 301.

35. Carol A. Whitehurst, *Women in America: The Oppressed Majority,* Goodyear, Santa Monica, CA, 1977.

36. Barbara Kantrowitz, "Sexism in the Schoolhouse," *Newsweek,* February 24, 1992, p. 62.

37. U.S. Bureau of the Census, *Statistical Abstract of the United States: 1992,* U.S. Government Printing Office, Washington, DC, 1992, Table 608, p. 381.

38. Ibid., Table 644, p. 391.

39. See Amy Saltzman, "Trouble at the Top," *U.S. News & World Report,* June 17, 1991, pp. 40–48.

40. Ibid., p. 44.

41. U.S. Bureau of the Census, *Current Population Reports,* Series P–60, No. 170.

42. Catharine A. MacKinnon, *Sexual Harassment of Working Women: A Case of Sex Discrimination,* Yale University Press, New Haven, CT, 1979.

43. U.S. Bureau of the Census, "The Black Population in the United States: March 1990 and 1989," *Current Population Reports,* Series P–20, No. 448, pp. 11–13.

44. Reynolds Farley and Walter Allen, *The Color Line and the Quality of Life in America,* Russell Sage Foundation, New York, 1987, pp. 320–325.

45. See Diana Pierce, *The Feminization of Poverty: Women, Work, and Welfare,* University of Chicago Press, Chicago, 1978.

46. "Portrait of a Nation in Numbers: Findings of the 1990 U.S. Census," *Facts on File,* June 25, 1992, p. 470.

47. P. D. Horn and J. C. Horn, *Sex in the Office: Power and Passion in the Workplace,* Addison-Wesley, Reading, MA, 1982, p. 70.

48. Ibid., p. 64.

49. See Ted Gest and Amy Saltzman, "Harassment: Men on Trial," *U.S. News & World Report,* October 21, 1991, pp. 38–40.

50. MacKinnon, *Sexual Harassment of Working Women,* p. 2.

51. Gloria Borger and Ted Gest, "The Untold Story," *U.S. News & World Report,* October 12, 1992, pp. 28–37.

52. See Eloise Salholz, "Deepening Shame," *Newsweek,* August 10, 1992, pp. 30–36; "Tailhook: Scandal Time," *Newsweek,* July 6, 1992, pp. 40–41; Peter Cary and Bruce B. Auster, "What's Wrong with the Navy?" *U.S. News & World Report,* July 13, 1992, pp. 22–29.

53. Rosalind J. Dworkin, "A Woman's Report," *The Minority Report,* 2d ed., Holt, Rinehart and Winston, New York, 1982, p. 384.

54. *The New York Times,* November 27, 1983, p. E7.

55. *Statistical Abstract of the United States,* 1991, Table 449, p. 267.

56. Barbara Ehrenreich, "Why Women Are Finally Winning," *Time,* June 22, 1992, p. 82.

57. Celinda Lake, "Women Won on the Merits," *The New York Times,* November 8, 1992, p. L22.

58. See Marianne Githens and Jewel L. Prestage, *A Portrait of Marginality: The Political Behavior of the American Women,* David McKay, New York, 1977.

59. Kim Fridkin Kahn and Edie N. Goldenberg, "Women Candidates in the News: An Examination of Gender Differences in U.S. Senate Campaign Coverage," *Public Opinion Quarterly* 55 (Summer 1991), 180–199.

60. Talcott Parsons and Robert Bales, *Family, Socialization, and Interaction Process,* Free Press, Glencoe, IL, 1955.

61. See Susan Brownmiller, *Against Our Will: Men, Women, and Rape,* Simon and Schuster, New York, 1975.

62. Friedrich Engels, *The Origin of the Family, Private Property, and the State,* International Publishers, New York, 1942.

63. See Alice Schlegel (ed.), *Sexual Stratification: A Cross-Cultural View,* Columbia University Press, New York, 1977.

64. Michael Gordon, *The American Family: Past, Present, and Future,* Random House, New York, 1978, p. 199.

65. Jan M. Newton, "The Political Economy of Women's Oppression," in Jean Ramage LePaluoto (ed.), *Women on the Move: A Feminist Perspective,* University of Oregon Press, Eugene, OR, 1973, p. 121.

66. P. B. Walters, "Trends in U.S. Men's and Women's Sex Role Attitudes: 1972–78," *American Sociological Review* 46 (1981), 453–460.

Chapter 14

1. Mary C. Sengstock, "Social Change in the Country of Origin as a Factor in Immigrant Conceptions of Nationality," *Ethnicity* 4 (March 1977), 54–69.

2. Ibid., pp. 56–57.

3. Ibid., pp. 61, 64.

4. Marcus L. Hansen, "The Third Generation in America," *Commentary* 14, No. 5 (November 1952), 492–500.

5. Marcus L. Hansen, "The Third Generation," in Oscar Handlin (ed.), *Children of the Uprooted,* Harper & Row, New York, 1966, pp. 255–271.

6. John M. Goering, "The Emergence of Ethnic Interests: A Case of Serendipity," *Social Forces* 49 (March 1971), 379–384.

7. Ibid., p. 383.

8. Ibid., pp. 381–382.

9. Ibid., p. 382.

10. Neil C. Sandberg, *Ethnic Identity and Assimilation: The Polish-American Community,* Praeger, New York, 1974.

11. John P. Roche, "Suburban Ethnicity: Ethnic Attitudes and Behavior Among Italian Americans in Two Suburban Communities," *Social Science Quarterly* 63 (1982), 145–153.

12. See, for example, Richard O'Connor, *The German Americans*, Little, Brown, Boston, 1968; or Bernard Wasserstein, "Jewish Identification Among Students at Oxford," *Jewish Journal of Sociology* 13 (December 1971), 131–151.

13. Harold J. Abramson, "The Religioethnic Factor and the American Experience: Another Look at the Three-Generation Hypothesis," *Ethnicity* 2 (1975), 163–177.

14. Ibid., p. 173.

15. John M. Goering, "The Emergence of Ethnic Interests," pp. 379–384.

16. Andrew M. Greeley, *Why Can't They Be Like Us?*, Dutton, New York, 1971, pp. 148–152.

17. Ibid., p. 152.

18. Michael Novak, *The Rise of the Unmeltable Ethnics*, Macmillan, New York, 1971.

19. Herbert Gans, p. xi of Foreword in Sandberg, *Ethnic Identity and Assimilation*.

20. See, for example, Stephen Steinberg, *The Ethnic Myth: Race, Ethnicity, and Class in America*, Beacon Press, Boston, 1981.

21. Gunnar Myrdal, "The Case Against Romantic Ethnicity," *Center Magazine* 7 (July–August 1974), pp. 26–30.

22. William L. Yancey, Eugene P. Ericksen, and Richard N. Juliani, "Emergent Ethnicity: A Review and Reformulation," *American Sociological Review* 41 (June 1976), 391–403.

23. Ibid., p. 393.

24. See also Amitai Etzioni, "The Ghetto: A Reevaluation," *Social Forces* 39 (1959), 255–262.

25. Stanley Lieberson and Mary C. Waters, "The Location of Ethnic and Racial Groups in the United States," *Sociological Forum* 2 (Fall 1987), 780–810.

26. Stanford M. Lyman and William A. Douglass, "Ethnicity: Strategies of Collective and Individual Impression Management," *Social Research* 40 (Summer 1973), 344–365.

27. Ibid., p. 345.

28. Richard D. Alba, *Ethnic Identity: The Transformation of White America*, Yale University Press, New Haven, CT, 1990.

29. Richard D. Alba, *Italian Americans: Into the Twilight of Ethnicity*, Prentice–Hall, Englewood Cliffs, NJ, 1985, pp. 159–175.

30. Yancey et al., "Emergent Ethnicity," p. 399.

31. Herbert J. Gans, "Symbolic Ethnicity: The Future of Ethnic Groups and Cultures in America," *Ethnic and Racial Studies* 2 (January 1979), 1–20.

32. Andrew M. Greeley, *Ethnicity, Denomination, and Inequality*, Sage Research Papers in the Social Sciences, Vol. 4, series 90–109 (Studies in Religion and Ethnicity), Sage Publications, Beverly Hills, CA, 1976.

33. David L. Featherman in a review of Greeley's book in *Sociological Analysis* 38 (Summer 1977), 176–179.

34. Ibid., p. 178.

35. Stanley Lieberson and Donna K. Carter, "Making It in America: Differences between Eminent Blacks and White Ethnic Groups," *American Sociological Review* 44 (June 1979), 347–366.

36. Richard D. Alba and Gwen Moore, "Ethnicity in the American Elite," *American Sociological Review* 47 (1982), 373–383.

37. U.S. Bureau of the Census, *Statistical Abstract of the United States: 1992*, U.S. Government Printing Office, Washington, DC, 1992, Table 5, p. 10.

38. U.S. Census Bureau, *1990 Census Special Tabulations*, CB 91–215, June 1991, Table 1, p. 3.

39. Michael J. Mandel and Christopher Farrell, "The Immigrants," *Business Week*, July 13, 1992, pp. 114–122.

40. Ibid.

41. Connie Leslie, "Classrooms of Babel: A Record Number of Immigrant Children Pose New Problems for Schools," *Newsweek*, February 11, 1991, pp. 56–57.

42. "Teaching in English-Plus," *Newsweek*, February 7, 1977, p. 65.

43. Abigail M. Thernstrom, "Bilingual Miseducation," *Commentary*, February 1990, pp. 44–48.

44. See, for example, ed. Gary Imhoff, *Learning in Two Languages*, Transaction, New Brunswick, NJ, 1990.

45. U.S. General Accounting Office, *Bilingual Education: Information on Limited English Proficient Students* (GAO/HRD–87–85BR, Washington, DC, 1987; see also U.S. General Accounting Office, *Bilingual Education: A New Look at the Research Evidence* (GAO/PEMD–87–12BR), Washington, DC, 1987.

46. J. D. Ramirez, S. D. Yuen, and D. R. Ramsey, *Final Report: Longitudinal Study of Structured English Immersion Strategy, Early-Exit and Late-Exit Transitional Bilingual Education Programs for Language-Minority Children*, Aguirre International, San Mateo, CA, 1991.

47. Linda Chavez, "Hispanics vs. Their Leaders," *Commentary*, October 1991, pp. 47–49.

48. Mark R. Halton, "Legislating Assimilation: The English-Only Movement," *The Christian Century*, November 29, 1989, pp. 1119–1121.

49. Reported in "English as the Official Language," official policy statement of the American Jewish Committee, June 29, 1987, pp. 3–4.

50. Ibid., p. 5.

51. Martin E. Spencer, "Multiculturalism, Political Correctness and the Politics of Identity," thematic paper presented at the annual meeting of the Eastern Sociological Society, Arlington, VA, April 5, 1992.

52. Jacob Weisbergm, ''Thin Skins,'' *The New Republic*, February 18, 1991, p. 23.

53. See Stephen Goode, ''All Opinions Welcome— Except the Wrong Ones,'' *Insight*, April 22, 1991, pp. 8–17; John Leo, ''The Academy's New Ayatollahs,'' *U.S. News & World Report*, December 10, 1990, p. 22; John Leo, ''Our Misguided Speech Police,'' *U.S. News & World Report*, April 8, 1991, p. 25.

54. Allan Bloom, *The Closing of the American Mind*, Simon and Schuster, New York, 1987; Roger Kimball, *Tenured Radicals*, Harper & Row, New York, 1990; Charles Sykes, *The Hollow Men*, Regaery Gateway, Lanham, MD, 1990; Dinesh D'Souza, *Illiberal Education: The Politics of Race and Sex on Campus*, Free Press, New York, 1991.

Appendix I

STEREOTYPES IN THREE GENERATIONS OF PRINCETON UNDERGRADUATES

Trait	Checking Trait (%)			Trait	Checking Trait (%)		
	1933	1951	1967		1933	1951	1967
Americans				**English**			
Industrious	48	30	23	Sportsmanlike	53	21	22
Intelligent	47	32	20	Intelligent	46	29	23
Materialistic	33	37	67	Conventional	34	25	19
Ambitious	33	21	42	Tradition	31	42	21
Progressive	27	5	17	loving			
Pleasure loving	26	27	28	Conservative	30	22	53
Alert	23	7	7	Reserved	29	39	40
Efficient	21	9	15	Sophisticated	27	37	47
Aggressive	20	8	15	Courteous	21	17	17
Straightforward	19	—	9	Honest	20	11	17
Practical	19	—	12	Industrious	18	—	17
Sportsmanlike	19	—	9	Extremely	18	—	7
Individualistic[a]	—	26	15	nationalistic			
Conventional[b]	—	—	17	Humorless	17	—	11
Scientifically minded[b]	—	—	15	Practical[b]	—	8	25
Ostentatious[b]	—	—	15				
Chinese				**Germans**			
Superstitious	34	18	8	Scientifically minded	78	62	47
Sly	29	4	6	Industrious	65	50	59
Conservative	29	14	15	Stolid	44	10	9
Tradition loving	26	26	32	Intelligent	32	32	19
Loyal to family ties	22	35	50	Methodical	31	20	21
Industrious	18	18	23	Extremely			
Meditative	19	—	21	nationalistic	24	50	43
Reserved	17	18	15	Progressive	16	3	13
Very religious	15	—	6	Efficient	16	—	46
Ignorant	15	—	7	Jovial	15	—	5
Deceitful	14	—	5	Musical	13	—	4
Quiet	13	19	23	Persistent	11	—	4
Courteous[b]	—	—	20	Practical	11	—	9
Extremely nationalistic[b]	—	—	19	Aggressive[a]	—	27	30
Humorless[b]	—	—	17	Arrogant[a]	—	23	18
Artistic[b]	—	—	15	Ambitious[b]	—	—	15

STEREOTYPES IN THREE GENERATIONS OF PRINCETON UNDERGRADUATES
(*Continued*)

Trait	Checking Trait (%)			Trait	Checking Trait (%)		
	1933	1951	1967		1933	1951	1967
Irish				**Japanese**			
Pugnacious	45	24	13	Intelligent	45	11	20
Quick tempered	39	35	43	Industrious	43	12	57
Witty	38	16	7	Progressive	24	2	17
Honest	32	11	17	Shrewd	22	13	7
Very religious	29	30	27	Sly	20	21	3
Industrious	21	8	8	Quiet	19	—	14
Extremely nationalistic	21	20	41	Imitative	17	24	22
Superstitious	18	—	11	Alert	16	—	11
Quarrelsome	14	—	5	Suave	16	—	0
Imaginative	13	—	3	Neat	16	—	7
Aggressive	13	—	5	Treacherous	13	17	1
Stubborn	13	—	23	Aggressive	13	—	19
Tradition loving[b]	—	—	25	Extremely			
Loyal to family ties[b]	—	—	23	nationalistic[a]	—	18	21
Argumentative[b]	—	—	20	Ambitious[b]	—	—	33
Boastful[b]	—	—	17	Efficient[b]	—	—	27
				Loyal to family ties[b]	—	—	23
				Courteous[b]	—	—	22
Italians							
Artistic	53	28	30	**Jews**			
Impulsive	44	19	28				
Passionate	37	25	44	Shrewd	79	47	30
Quick tempered	35	15	28	Mercenary	49	28	15
Musical	32	22	9	Industrious	48	29	33
Imaginative	30	20	7	Grasping	34	17	17
Very religious	21	33	25	Intelligent	29	37	37
Talkative	21	23	23	Ambitious	21	28	48
Revengeful	17	—	0	Sly	20	14	7
Physically dirty	13	—	4	Loyal to family ties	15	19	19
Lazy	12	—	0	Persistent	13	—	9
Unreliable	11	—	3	Talkative	13	—	3
Pleasure loving[a]	—	28	33	Aggressive	12	—	23
Loyal to family ties[b]	—	—	26	Very religious	12	—	7
Sensual[b]	—	—	23	Materialistic[b]	—	—	46
Argumentative[b]	—	—	19	Practical	—	—	19

STEREOTYPES IN THREE GENERATIONS OF PRINCETON UNDERGRADUATES
(*Continued*)

Trait	Checking Trait (%)			Trait	Checking Trait (%)		
	1933	1951	1967		1933	1951	1967
Negroes[c]				**Turks**			
Superstitious	84	41	13	Cruel	47	12	9
Lazy	75	31	26	Very religious	26	6	7
Happy-go-lucky	38	17	27	Treacherous	21	3	13
Ignorant	38	24	11	Sensual	20	4	9
Musical	26	33	47	Ignorant	15	7	13
Ostentatious	26	11	25	Physically dirty	15	7	14
Very religious	24	17	8	Deceitful	13	—	7
Stupid	22	10	4	Sly	12	7	7
Physically dirty	17	—	3	Quarrelsome	12	—	9
Naive	14	—	4	Revengeful	12	—	6
Slovenly	13	—	5	Conservative	12	—	11
Unreliable	12	—	6	Superstitious	11	—	5
Pleasure loving[a]	—	19	26	Aggressive[b]	—	—	17
Sensitive[b]	—	—	17	Quick tempered[b]	—	—	13
Gregarious[b]	—	—	17	Impulsive[b]	—	—	12
Talkative[b]	—	—	14	Conventional[b]	—	—	10
Imitative[b]	—	—	13	Pleasure loving[b]	—	—	11
				Slovenly[b]	—	—	10

[a]Indicates the additional traits reported by Gilbert (1951).
[b]Indicates the new traits needed in 1967 to account for the 10 most frequently selected traits today.
[c]The title "Negroes" is the word employed in the study.

SOURCE: Marvin Karlins, Thomas L. Coffman, and Gary Walters, "On the Fading of Social Stereotypes: Studies in Three Generations of College Students," *Journal of Personality and Social Psychology* 13 (1969): Table 1, pp. 4–5. Reprinted by permission.

Appendix II

IMMIGRATION BY COUNTRY: FOR DECADES 1820–1991[a]

Countries	1820	1821 –1830	1831 –1840	1841 –1850	1851 –1860	1861 –1870	1871 –1880
All Countries	**8,385**	**143,439**	**599,125**	**1,713,251**	**2,598,214**	**2,314,824**	**2,812,191**
Europe	7,690	98,797	495,681	1,597,442	2,452,577	2,065,141	2,271,925
Austria-Hungary[b,e]	—	—	—	—	—	7,800	72,969
Belgium	1	27	22	5,074	4,738	6,734	7,221
Denmark	20	169	1,063	539	3,749	17,094	31,771
France	371	8,497	45,575	77,262	76,358	35,986	72,206
Germany[b,e]	968	6,761	152,454	434,626	951,667	787,468	718,182
Great Britain:							
England	1,782	14,055	7,611	32,092	247,125	222,277	437,706
Scotland	268	2,912	2,667	3,712	38,331	38,769	87,564
Wales	—	170	185	1,261	6,319	4,313	6,631
Not specified[c]	360	7,942	65,347	229,979	132,199	341,537	16,142
Greece	—	20	49	16	31	72	210
Ireland	3,614	50,724	207,381	780,719	914,119	435,778	436,871
Italy	30	409	2,253	1,870	9,231	11,725	55,759
Netherlands	49	1,078	1,412	8,251	10,789	9,102	16,541
Norway	3	91	1,201	13,903	20,931	71,631	95,323
Sweden[d]						37,667	115,922
Poland[e]	5	16	369	105	1,164	2,027	12,970
Portugal	35	145	829	550	1,055	2,658	14,082
Romania[l]	—	—	—	—	—	—	11
Spain	139	2,477	2,125	2,209	9,298	6,697	5,266
Switzerland	31	3,226	4,821	4,644	25,011	23,286	28,293
U.S.S.R.[e,f]	14	75	277	551	457	2,512	39,284
Other Europe	—	3	40	79	5	8	1,001
Asia	6	30	55	141	41,538	64,759	124,160
China	1	2	8	35	41,397	64,301	123,201
India	1	8	39	36	43	69	163
Japan[g]	—	—	—	—	—	186	149
Turkey	1	20	7	59	83	131	404
Other Asia	3	—	1	11	15	72	243
Western Hemisphere	387	11,564	33,424	62,469	74,720	166,607	404,044
Canada & Newfoundland[h]	209	2,277	13,624	41,723	59,309	153,878	383,640
Mexico	1	4,817	6,599	3,271	3,078	2,191	5,162
West Indies	164	3,834	12,301	13,528	10,660	9,046	13,957
Central America	2	105	44	368	449	95	157
South America	11	531	856	3,579	1,224	1,397	1,128

IMMIGRATION BY COUNTRY: FOR DECADES 1820–1991 *(Continued)*

Countries	1881 –1890	1891 –1900	1901 –1910	1911 –1920	1921 –1930	1931 –1940	1941 –1950
All Countries	**5,246,613**	**3,687,564**	**8,795,386**	**5,735,811**	**4,107,209**	**528,431**	**1,035,039**
Europe	4,735,484	3,555,352	8,056,040	4,321,887	2,463,194	347,552	621,124
Albania[k]	—	—	—	—	—	2,040	85
Austria	353,719	529,707	2,145,266	453,649	32,868	3,563	24,860
Hungary[b,e]				442,693	30,680	7,861	3,469
Belgium	20,177	18,167	41,635	33,746	15,846	4,817	12,189
Bulgaria[j]	—	160	39,280	22,533	2,945	938	375
Czechoslovakia[k]	—	—	—	3,426	102,194	14,393	8,347
Denmark	88,132	50,231	65,285	41,983	32,430	2,559	5,393
Estonia	—	—	—	—	—	506	212
Finland[k]	—	—	—	756	16,691	2,146	2,503
France	50,464	30,770	73,379	61,897	49,610	12,623	38,809
Germany[b,e]	1,452,970	505,152	341,498	143,945	412,202	114,058	226,578
Great Britain:							
England	644,680	216,726	388,017	249,944	157,420	21,756	112,252
Scotland	149,869	44,188	120,469	78,357	159,731	6,887	16,131
Wales	12,640	10,557	17,464	13,107	13,012	735	3,209
Not specified[c]	168	67	—	—	—	—	—
Greece	2,308	15,979	167,519	184,201	51,084	9,119	8,973
Ireland	655,482	388,416	339,065	146,181	220,591	13,167	26,967
Italy	307,309	651,893	2,045,877	1,109,524	455,315	68,028	57,661
Latvia[k]	—	—	—	—	—	1,192	361
Lithuania[k]	—	—	—	—	—	2,201	683
Luxembourg[o]	—	—	—	—	—	565	820
Netherlands	53,701	26,758	48,262	43,718	26,948	7,150	14,860
Norway[d]	176,586	95,015	190,505	66,395	68,531	4,740	10,100
Poland[e]	51,806	96,720	—	4,813	227,734	17,026	7,571
Portugal	16,978	27,508	69,149	89,732	29,994	3,329	7,423
Romania[l]	6,348	12,750	53,008	13,311	67,646	3,871	1,076
Spain	4,419	8,731	27,935	68,611	28,958	3,258	2,898
Sweden[d]	391,776	226,266	249,534	95,074	97,249	3,960	10,665
Switzerland	81,988	31,179	34,922	23,091	29,676	5,512	10,547
U.S.S.R.[e,f]	213,282	505,290	1,597,306	921,201	61,742	1,356	548
Yugoslavia[j]	—	—	—	1,888	49,064	5,835	1,576
Other Europe	682	122	665	8,111	22,983	2,361	3,983
Asia	69,942	74,862	323,543	247,236	112,059	16,081	32,360
China	61,711	14,799	20,605	21,278	29,907	4,928	16,709
India	269	68	4,713	2,082	1,886	496	1,761
Japan[g]	2,270	25,942	129,797	83,837	33,462	1,948	1,555
Turkey	3,782	30,425	157,369	134,066	33,824	1,065	798
Other Asia	1,910	3,628	11,059	5,973	12,980	7,644	11,537
Western Hemisphere	426,967	38,972	361,888	1,143,671	1,516,716	160,037	354,804
Canada & Newfoundland[h]	393,304	3,311	179,226	742,185	924,515	108,527	171,718
Mexico[i]	1,913	971	49,642	219,004	459,287	22,319	60,589
West Indies	29,042	33,066	107,548	123,424	74,899	15,502	49,725
Central America	404	549	8,192	17,159	15,769	5,861	21,665
South America	2,304	1,075	17,280	41,899	42,215	7,803	21,831
Other America[m]	—	—	—	—	31	25	29,276

See notes and source at end of table.

IMMIGRATION BY COUNTRY: FOR DECADES 1820–1991 *(Continued)*

Countries	1951 –1960	1961 –1970	1971 –1980	1981 –1990	1991	Total 1820 –1991
All Countries	2,515,479	3,321,677	4,493,314	7,338,062	1,827,167	58,821,181
Europe	1,325,640	1,123,363	800,368	761,550	146,671	37,247,731
Austria[b,e]	67,106	20,621	9,478	18,340	3,511	1,832,457
Hungary[b,e]	36,637	5,401	6,550	6,545	944	1,668,704
Belgium	18,575	9,192	5,329	7,066	701	211,257
Bulgaria[j]	104	619	785	2,342	623	71,107
Czechoslovakia[k]	918	3,273	6,023	7,227	625	146,426
Denmark	10,984	9,201	2,609	5,370	629	371,041
Finland[k]	4,925	4,192	2,868	3,265	369	37,715
France	51,121	45,237	25,069	32,353	3,978	791,565
Germany[b,e]	477,765	190,796	43,986	91,961	10,887	7,094,352
Greece	47,608	85,969	92,369	38,377	2,929	706,833
Ireland	57,332	37,461	44,731	31,969	4,608	4,729,741
Italy	185,491	214,111	129,368	67,254	30,316	5,403,424
Netherlands	52,277	30,606	10,492	12,238	1,303	375,535
Norway[d]	22,935	15,484	3,941	4,164	554	801,778
Poland[e]	9,985	53,539	37,234	83,252	17,106	623,442
Portugal	19,588	76,065	101,710	40,431	4,576	505,837
Romania[l]	1,039	2,531	12,393	30,857	6,786	211,627
Spain	7,894	44,659	39,141	20,433	2,663	287,811
Sweden[d]	21,697	17,116	6,531	11,018	1,242	1,285,717
Switzerland	17,675	18,453	8,255	8,849	1,003	360,442
U.S.S.R.[e,f]	584	2,336	38,961	57,677	31,557	3,475,263
United Kingdom	204,468	214,518	155,572	159,173	16,768	5,135,918
Yugoslavia	8,225	20,381	30,540	18,762	2,802	139,073
Other Europe	16,350	11,604	9,287	8,234	1,183	183,157
Asia	150,106	427,771	1,507,178	2,738,157	342,157	6,361,337
Cambodia	11	85	7,648	111,971	3,251	122,966
China[q]	9,657	34,764	124,326	346,747	23,995	938,371
India	1,973	27,189	164,134	250,786	42,707	498,423
Iran	3,388	10,339	45,136	116,172	9,927	186,778
Israel	25,476	29,602	37,713	44,273	5,116	142,656
Japan[g]	46,250	39,988	49,775	47,085	5,600	467,844
Korea	7,635	37,654	243,299	333,746	25,430	667,678
Laos	14	213	22,092	145,714	9,950	169,028
Philippines[p]	27,318	113,086	319,039	548,764	68,750	1,095,403
Taiwan[q]	—	—	—	118,105	13,274	131,379
Turkey	3,519	10,142	13,399	23,233	3,466	415,793
Vietnam	366	4,932	225,642	280,782	14,847	473,124
Western Hemisphere	996,944	1,716,374	1,982,529	3,615,225	1,297,580	14,365,128
Canada and Newfoundland[h]	377,952	413,310	249,560	156,938	19,931	4,315,516
Mexico[i]	299,811	453,937	640,294	1,655,843	947,923	4,836,652
Caribbean	123,091	470,213	741,126	872,051	138,591	2,841,768
Central America	44,751	101,330	134,640	468,088	110,820	930,448
South America	91,628	257,954	295,741	461,847	80,308	11,330,611

See notes and source at end of table.

IMMIGRATION BY COUNTRY: FOR DECADES 1820–1991 *(Continued)*

Countries	1820	1821 –1830	1831 –1840	1841 –1850	1851 –1860	1861 –1870	1871 –1880
Africa	1	16	54	55	210	312	358
Australia & New Zealand	—	—	—	—	—	36	9,886
Pacific Islands (U.S. Adm.)	—	—	—	—	—	—	1,028
Not Specified	301	33,032	69,911	53,144	29,169	17,969	790

Countries	1881 –1890	1891 –1900	1901 –1910	1911 –1920	1921 –1930	1931 –1940	1941 –1950
Africa	857	350	7,368	8,443	6,286	1,750	7,367
Australia & New Zealand	7,017	2,740	11,975	12,348	8,299	2,231	13,805
Pacific Islands (U.S. Adm.)	5,557	1,225	1,049	1,079	427	780	5,437
Not Specified[n]	789	14,063	33,523	1,147	228	—	142

Countries	1951 –1960	1961 –1970	1971 –1980	1981 –1990	1991	Total Years: 1820–1991
Africa	14,092	28,954	80,779	176,893	33,542	367,687
Australia and New Zealand	11,506	19,562	23,788	20,529	2,471	143,722
Oceania	12,976	5,560	17,454	24,676	4,590	67,961
Not Specified[n]	12,491	93	12	1,032	156	304,816

[a]From 1820–1867 figures represent alien passengers arrived; from 1868–1891 and 1895–1897, immigrant aliens arrived; from 1892–1894 and 1898 to the present time, immigrant aliens admitted. Data for years prior to 1906 relates to country whence alien came; thereafter, to country of last permanent residence. Because of changes in boundaries and changes in lists of countries, data for certain countries is not comparable throughout.
Since July 1, 1868, the data are for fiscal years ending June 30. Prior to fiscal year 1869, the periods covered are as follows: from 1820–1831 and 1843–1849, the years ended on September 30 — 1843 covers 9 months; and from 1832–1842 and 1850–1867, the years ended on December 31 — 1832 and 1850 cover 15 months. For 1868 the period ended on June 30 and covers 6 months.
[b]Data for Austria-Hungary was not reported until 1861. Austria and Hungary have been recorded separately since 1905. From 1938–1945, Austria is included in Germany.
[c]Great Britain not specified. From 1901–1951, included in other Europe.
[d]From 1820–1868, the figures for Norway and Sweden are combined.
[e]Poland recorded as a separate country from 1820–1898 and since 1920. From 1899–1919 Poland is included with Austria-Hungary, Germany, and Russia.
[f]From 1931–1963 the U.S.S.R. is broken down into European U.S.S.R. and Asian U.S.S.R. Since 1964 total U.S.S.R. has been reported in Europe.
[g]No record of immigration from Japan until 1861.
[h]Prior to 1920 Canada and Newfoundland are recorded as British North America. From 1820–1898 the figures include all British North American possessions.
[i]No record of immigration from Mexico from 1886–1893.
[j]Bulgaria, Serbia, and Montenegro were first reported in 1899. Bulgaria has been reported separately since 1920; also in 1920 a separate enumeration was made for the Kingdom of Serbs, Croats, and Slovenes. Since 1922 the Serbs, Croat, and Slovene Kingdom has been recorded as Yugoslavia.

ᵏCountries added to the list since the beginning of World War I are included with the countries to which they belonged. Figures available since 1920 for Czechoslovakia and Finland and, since 1924, for Albania, Estonia, Latvia, and Lithuania.
ˡNo record of immigration from Romania until 1880.
ᵐIncluded with countries not specified to 1925.
ⁿThe figure 33,523 in column headed 1901–1910 includes 32,897 persons returning in 1906 to their homes in the United States.
ᵒFigures for Luxembourg are available since 1925.
ᵖBeginning with the year 1952, Asia includes the Philippines. From 1934–1951 the Philippines are included in the Pacific Islands. Prior to 1934 the Philippines are recorded in separate tables as insular travel.
ᑫBeginning with the year 1957, China includes Taiwan; after 1982 Mainland China and Taiwan are separate.

SOURCE: U.S. Immigration and Naturalization Service, Annual Report, U.S. Government Printing Office, Washington, DC, 1991, Tables 2 and 3.

Index